THE AMERICAN IDENTITY

SEVEN ISSUES

THE

American

IDENTITY

SEVEN ISSUES

A COLLEGE READER

Sam S. Baskett
Theodore B. Strandness
MICHIGAN STATE UNIVERSITY

D. C. HEATH AND COMPANY

BOSTON

Preface

The editors' aim in *The American Identity* is to provide a body of readings suitable for use in either the college composition course or courses in American Civilization. More specifically, as its title indicates, the book deals with the broad issue of the national identity. What, it asks, distinguishes the American? The question has been repeatedly raised in the course of this nation's emergence, and it has been repeatedly — and variously — answered. The chorus of defining voices — rural and urban, casual and insistent, educated and illiterate, conservative and radical, religious and secular, foreign and native — has persisted for three hundred years.

The American Identity is intended to set the student in search of some answers, to make him curious about what he as an American really is — what he believes in and why, what he lives for, where he comes from, where he is headed. The book's various sections focus on such presumably abiding national characteristics as the American's love of money, his unusual respect for women, his hankering for the practical, his suspicion of authority, his fondness for machinery, his commitment to equality. The writings within each section are arranged to show emerging patterns and establish historical perspective.

While it treats its various subjects with some fulness, *The American Identity* does not aim to be comprehensive. It strives not so much to cover as to introduce the issues with which it deals, and to do so in a way which will stimulate thought and encourage further study. Selections included to provide historical perspective are generally not extensive, but they are sufficient to show the student that there *is* a perspective in which the matters in question may profitably be viewed. The inevitable problem of space has meant that not all authors and selections appear which the editors would have liked to include; at the same time, most of the major names in the American canon are here along with a considerable number of significant essays, poems, short stories, and other works from the broad range of American writing.

The plan of *The American Identity* makes it ideally suited to the composition classroom. It supplies an essential that is too often lacking, namely an effectively coherent body of significant material with which the student may engage over an extended period of time. Each of the sections is a unit in itself and the instructor may use as many or as few as he chooses. Taken in combination, however, the sections provide a growing frame of reference — so necessary for significant development in both reading and writing — each gaining increased significance through its close relationship to the others. Moreover, by the time the student has worked substantially in *The American*

Identity he will have done considerably more than improve his language skills; he will have significantly increased his understanding of what it means to be a member of American society. While this might suggest chauvinism, anyone who looks into the following pages will quickly discover that the aim of the editors is not so much patriotic zeal as the not too incompatible one of intelligent national awareness.

Because *The American Identity* is concerned with both ideas and the manner of their expression, selections have been chosen for their language, form, and style, as well as for the light they throw on particular issues. They have also been chosen with an eye to balance and variety among genre and rhetorical types, so that the teacher who wishes to emphasize methods of development and literary types will easily find it possible to do so. Most particularly, however, the selections have been chosen because they deal with issues that remain urgently alive. In short, the editors have sought to provide a collection of American writings which in arrangement, subject matter, and quality of expression will both challenge the student and engage his interest. The comments which precede each of the selections are intended to channel this interest toward discussion and writing by the student as a natural outgrowth of his reading and thinking. An extension of these comments in the form of a booklet of Suggestions for Teachers is available on request to the publisher.

We are grateful for the help in this book's preparation which we have received from many colleagues at Michigan State University, and we extend special thanks to members of the library staff for their willingness to obtain and frequently reproduce necessary materials. For valuable criticism of the book in early manuscript we are indebted to Professor Robert E. Streeter of the University of Chicago. To editor Allen K. Workman of D. C. Heath and Company we owe the most; his patience and perspicuity have been unfailing.

S. S. B.

T. B. S.

Contents

THE PURSUIT OF THE DOLLAR

The Protestant Ethic

Nineteenth-Century Individualism

The Reign of the Bitch-Goddess

The Emergence of a New Ethic

The Mythological Base

THE SENSE OF NATIONALITY

Patriotism of the Early Republic

In Civil Strife

To Save the World for Democracy: Retrospect

Search for National Meaning

New Sovereignties

TOWN AND COUNTRY

Country

Town

City

MEN AND MACHINES

A New Turn to Human Affairs

The March of the Machines

Life in the Machine Age

What Hath Man Wrought?

Analytic Contents

I. LITERARY TYPES

Fictional Episode

Poetry—chronologically by poet's birth date

II. EXPOSITION: MEANS AND MODES

Definition

Analysis

Cause and Effect

Comparison and Contrast

Analogy

Example and Illustration

Argument and Persuasion

Characterization

Description

Personal Narrative

Personal Correspondence

Interrogation

Report

Public Address

THE AMERICAN IDENTITY

SEVEN ISSUES

As Others See Us

As Others See Us

America has, from its very beginning, been the subject of lively comment by foreign observers. Much of what they have had to say has been critical. A common complaint has been, for example, that of Müller-Freienfels, a German traveler in the twenties: "The people impress one as having been standardized. All these clean-shaven men . . . seem to have been produced somewhere in a Ford factory. . . . In no other country are the individuals reduced to such a dead-level as in the United States. . . ." Much of the comment, on the other hand, has been hopeful and enthusiastic — such as Bishop Berkeley's notion that the New World would produce "time's noblest offspring."

"What then is the American, this new man?" So asked a Frenchman, Crèvecoeur, almost two centuries ago, and people all over the world are still asking. Okinawans, living in their American-occupied island, would like to know. Hitler guessed wrong. Russians see the answer as through a Marxian glass, darkly. The British are still working to correct ideas which date from a time when Americans were "colonials." Frenchmen, seeing a combined image of conformity, Coca Cola, and juke boxes, express contempt for American ways and fear for their growing influence on Gallic mores. South Americans look toward the Colossus of the North, wanting help and dubious of accepting it.

While observers from abroad do not always agree on what the American identity is, they do agree that there *is* such an identity, a common set of peculiar national characteristics. Frequently these characteristics concern matters of which we remain unaware because we take them so entirely for granted — the American attitude toward women, say, or government, or schools. If we will make a conscious attempt to "see ourselves as others see us," we can perhaps begin to discover what we are.

What then is the American, this new man?

This New Man
MICHEL DE CRÈVECOEUR

Michel Guillaume Jean de Crèvecoeur (1735–1813), born in Normandy, came to Canada in 1754 to serve under Montcalm. When Quebec fell to the British in 1759 he made his way to New York and, after ten years of traveling about, became a farmer in Orange County. Uprooted by the

American Revolution—from which he unsuccessfully tried to remain aloof
—he returned to France. After publishing *Letters from an American Farmer* (twelve essays about America) in 1782 and 1783, he came back
to New York as French Consul. There he found his wife dead, his farm
burned, and his family scattered. In 1790 he went back to France, where
he remained for the rest of his life.

The selection here printed from Letter III is perhaps the best known
of many attempts to answer the question, "What is an American?"
Crèvecoeur's answer is both general and specific: he touches on a number
of the characteristics that during the past two hundred years have come
to be considered "American" and then embodies them in "an epitome."
It should be noted that in comparing Americans with Europeans Crèvecoeur evaluates as well as defines. Also, as in all the Letters, Crèvecoeur
tends to romanticize the simple agrarian life.

". . . What a change . . . !"

He is an American, who, leaving behind him all his ancient prejudices and
manners, receives new ones from the new mode of life he has embraced, the
new government he obeys, and the new rank he holds. He becomes an
American by being received in the broad lap of our great *Alma Mater*.

Here individuals of all nations are melted into a new race of men, whose
labors and posterity will one day cause great changes in the world. Americans
are the western pilgrims, who are carrying along with them that great mass of
arts, sciences, vigour, and industry, which began long since in the east; they
will finish the great circle. The Americans were once scattered all over
Europe; here they are incorporated into one of the finest systems of population
which has ever appeared, and which will hereafter become distinct by the
power of the different climates they inhabit. The American ought, therefore,
to love this country much better than that wherein either he or his forefathers
were born. Here the rewards of his industry follow with equal steps the
progress of his labour, his labour is founded on the basis of nature, *self-interest*;
can it want a stronger allurement? Wives and children, who before in vain
demanded of him a morsel of bread, now, fat and frolicsome, gladly help their
father to clear those fields whence exuberant crops are to arise to feed and to
clothe them all; without any part being claimed, either by a despotic prince,
a rich abbot, or a mighty lord. Here religion demands but little of him; a
small voluntary salary to the minister, and gratitude to God; can he refuse
these? The American is a new man, who acts upon new principles; he must
therefore entertain new ideas, and form new opinions. From involuntary
idleness, servile dependence, penury, and useless labor, he has passed to toils
of a very different nature, rewarded by ample subsistence.—This is an
American. . . .

An European, when he first arrives, seems limited in his intentions, as
well as in his views; but he very suddenly alters his scale; two hundred miles
formerly appeared a very great distance; it is now but a trifle; he no sooner
breathes our air than he forms schemes, and embarks in designs he never
would have thought of in his own country. There the plenitude of society

confines many useful ideas, and often extinguishes the most laudable schemes which here ripen into maturity. Thus Europeans become Americans.

But how is this accomplished in that crowd of low, indigent people, who flock here every year from all parts of Europe? I will tell you; they no sooner arrive than they immediately feel the good effects of that plenty of provisions we possess: they fare on our best food, and they are kindly entertained; their talents, character, and peculiar industry are immediately enquired into; they find countrymen everywhere disseminated, let them come from whatever part of Europe.

Let me select one as an epitome of the rest; he is hired, he goes to work, and works moderately; instead of being employed by a haughty person, he finds himself with his equal, placed at the substantial table of the farmer, or else at an inferior one as good; his wages are high, his bed is not like that bed of sorrow on which he used to lie: if he behaves with propriety, and is faithful, he is caressed, and becomes, as it were, a member of the family. He begins to feel the effects of a sort of resurrection; hitherto he had not lived, but simply vegetated; he now feels himself a man, because he is treated as such; the laws of his own country had overlooked him in his insignificancy; the laws of this cover him with their mantle. Judge what an alteration there must arise in the mind and thoughts of this man; he begins to forget his former servitude and dependence; his heart involuntarily swells and glows; this first swell inspires him with those new thoughts which constitute an American. What love can he entertain for a country where his existence was a burden to him! if he is a generous good man, the love of this new adoptive parent, will sink deep into his heart. He looks around, and sees many a prosperous person, who but a few years before was as poor as himself. This encourages him much; he begins to form some little scheme, the first, alas, he ever formed in his life. If he is wise, he thus spends two or three years, in which time he acquires knowledge, the use of tools, the modes of working the lands, felling trees, etc. This prepares the foundation of a good name, the most useful acquisition he can make. He is encouraged; he has gained friends; he is advised and directed; he feels bold; he purchases some land; he gives all the money he has brought over, as well as what he has earned, and trusts to the God of harvests for the discharge of the rest. His good name procures him credit; he is now possessed of the deed, conveying to him and his posterity the fee simple, and absolute property of two hundred acres of land, situated on such a river. What an epoch in this man's life! He is become a freeholder, from perhaps a German boor — he is now an American, a Pennsylvanian. He is naturalized; his name is enrolled with those of the other citizens of the province. Instead of being a vagrant, he has a place of residence; he is called the inhabitant of such a county, or of such a district, and for the first time in his life counts for something; for hitherto he had been a cypher. I only repeat what I have heard many say, and no wonder their hearts should glow, and be agitated with a multitude of feelings, not easy to describe. From nothing to start into being; from a servant to the rank of a master; from being the slave of some despotic prince, to become a free man, invested with lands, to which every municipal blessing is annexed! What a change indeed! It is in consequence of that change, that he becomes an American.

[1782]

The Spirit of the Place   D. H. LAWRENCE

D. H. Lawrence (1885–1930), English poet, essayist, playwright, and novelist, had a miner for a father and a teacher for a mother. He himself trained to be a teacher but became instead one of the more important British writers of the twentieth century. His interest in the United States brought him to Taos, New Mexico, in the early 1920's. Returned to Europe, he died at the age of forty-four from the tuberculosis with which he had lived during most of his life. "The Spirit of the Place" is from his free-wheeling *Studies in Classic American Literature* (1923).

In the first sentence of this essay Lawrence names the American artist as his topic, though he is actually writing about Americans in general. Employing a highly individual style, Lawrence indicates some of the conflicts that he sees at the basis of American life — conflicts which he believes led to the settlement of the new continent. Although he refuses to accept our cherished cliché that America is "the land of the free," Lawrence is hardly "anti-American." Rather, he asserts in a series of challengingly paradoxical statements that being an American is a highly complicated affair.

". . . Henceforth be mastered. . . ."

Let us look at [the] American artist. . . . How did he ever get to America, to start with? Why isn't he a European still, like his father before him?

Now listen to me, don't listen to him. He'll tell you the lie you expect. Which is partly your fault for expecting it.

He didn't come in search of freedom of worship. England had more freedom of worship in the year 1700 than America had. Won by Englishmen who wanted freedom, and so stopped at home and fought for it. And got it. Freedom of worship? Read the history of New England during the first century of its existence.

Freedom anyhow? The land of the free! This the land of the free! Why, if I say anything that displeases them, the free mob will lynch me, and that's my freedom. Free? Why I have never been in any country where the individual has such an abject fear of his fellow countrymen. Because, as I say, they are free to lynch him the moment he shows he is not one of them.

No, no, if you're so fond of the truth about Queen Victoria, try a little about yourself.

Those Pilgrim Fathers and their successors never came here for freedom of worship. What did they set up when they got here? Freedom, would you call it?

They didn't come for freedom. Or if they did, they sadly went back on themselves.

All right then, what did they come for? For lots of reasons. Perhaps least of all in search of freedom of any sort: positive freedom, that is.

They came largely to get *away* — that most simple of motives. To get away. Away from what? In the long run, away from themselves. Away from everything. That's why most people have come to America, and still do come. To get away from everything they are and have been.

"Henceforth be masterless."

Which is all very well, but it isn't freedom. Rather the reverse. A hopeless sort of constraint. It is never freedom till you find something you really *positively want to be*. And people in America have always been shouting about the things they are *not*. Unless of course they are millionaires, made or in the making.

And after all there is a positive side to the movement. All that vast flood of human life that has flowed over the Atlantic in ships from Europe to America has not flowed over simply on a tide of revulsion from Europe and from the confinements of the European ways of life. This revulsion was, and still is, I believe, the prime motive in emigration. But there was some cause, even for the revulsion.

It seems as if at times man had a frenzy for getting away from any control of any sort. In Europe the old Christianity was the real master. The Church and the true aristocracy bore the responsibility for the working out of the Christian ideals: a little irregularly, maybe, but responsible nevertheless.

Mastery, kingship, fatherhood had their power destroyed at the time of the Renaissance.

And it was precisely at this moment that the great drift over the Atlantic started. What were men drifting away from? The old authority of Europe? Were they breaking the bonds of authority, and escaping to a new more absolute unrestrainedness? Maybe. But there was more to it.

Liberty is all very well, but men cannot live without masters. There is always a master. And men either live in glad obedience to the master they believe in, or they live in a frictional opposition to the master they wish to undermine. In America this frictional opposition has been the vital factor. It has given the Yankee his kick. Only the continual influx of more servile Europeans has provided America with an obedient labouring class. The true obedience never outlasting the first generation.

But there sits the old master, over in Europe. Like a parent. Somewhere deep in every American heart lies a rebellion against the old parenthood of Europe. Yet no American feels he has completely escaped its mastery. Hence the slow, smouldering patience of American opposition. The slow, smouldering, corrosive obedience to the old master Europe, the unwilling subject, the unremitting opposition.

Whatever else you are, be masterless.

"Ca Ca Caliban
Get a new master, be a new man."

Escaped slaves, we might say, people the republics of Liberia or Haiti. Liberia enough! Are we to look at America in the same way? A vast republic of escaped slaves. When you consider the hordes from eastern Europe, you might well say it: a vast republic of escaped slaves. But one dare not say this of the Pilgrim Fathers, and the great old body of idealist Americans, the modern Americans tortured with thought. A vast republic of escaped slaves. Look out, America! And a minority of earnest, self-tortured people.

The masterless.

"Ca Ca Caliban
Get a new master, be a new man."

What did the Pilgrim Fathers come for, then, when they came so grue-somely over the black sea? Oh, it was in a black spirit. A black revulsion from Europe, from the old authority of Europe, from kings and bishops and popes. And more. When you look into it, more. They were black, masterful men, they wanted something else. No kings, no bishops maybe. Even no God Almighty. But also, no more of this new "humanity" which followed the Renaissance. None of this new liberty which was to be so pretty in Europe. Something grimmer, by no means free-and-easy.

America has never been easy, and is not easy to-day. Americans have always been a certain tension. Their liberty is a thing of sheer will, sheer tension: a liberty of THOU SHALT NOT. And it has been so from the first. The land of THOU SHALT NOT. Only the first commandment is: THOU SHALT NOT PRESUME TO BE A MASTER. Hence democracy.

"We are the masterless." That is what the American Eagle shrieks. It's a Hen-Eagle.

The Spaniards refused the post-Renaissance liberty of Europe. And the Spaniards filled most of America. The Yankees, too, refused, refused the post-Renaissance humanism of Europe. First and foremost, they hated masters. But under that, they hated the flowing ease of humour in Europe. At the bottom of the American soul was always a dark suspense, at the bottom of the Spanish-American soul the same. And this dark suspense hated and hates the old European spontaneity, watches it collapse with satisfaction.

Every continent has its own great spirit of place. Every people is polarized in some particular locality, which is home, the homeland. Different places on the face of the earth have different vital effluence, different vibration, different chemical exhalation, different polarity with different stars: call it what you like. But the spirit of place is a great reality. The Nile valley produced not only the corn, but the terrific religions of Egypt. China pro-duces the Chinese, and will go on doing so. The Chinese in San Francisco will in time cease to be Chinese, for America is a great melting pot.

There was a tremendous polarity in Italy, in the city of Rome. And this seems to have died. For even places die. The Island of Great Britain had a wonderful terrestrial magnetism or polarity of its own, which made the British people. For the moment, this polarity seems to be breaking. Can England die? And what if England dies?

Men are less free than they imagine; ah, far less free. The freest are perhaps least free.

Men are free when they are in a living homeland, not when they are straying and breaking away. Men are free when they are obeying some deep, inward voice of religious belief. Obeying from within. Men are free when they belong to a living, organic, *believing* community, active in fulfilling some unfulfilled, perhaps unrealized purpose. Not when they are escaping to some wild west. The most unfree souls go west, and shout of freedom. Men are freest when they are most unconscious of freedom. The shout is a rattling of chains, always was.

Men are not free when they are doing just what they like. The moment you can do just what you like, there is nothing you care about doing. Men are only free when they are doing what the deepest self likes.

And there is getting down to the deepest self! It takes some diving.

Because the deepest self is way down, and the conscious self is an obstinate monkey. But of one thing we may be sure. If one wants to be free, one has to give up the illusion of doing what one likes, and seek what IT wishes done.

But before you can do what IT likes, you must first break the spell of the old mastery, the old IT.

Perhaps at the Renaissance, when kingship and fatherhood fell, Europe drifted into a very dangerous half-truth: of liberty and equality. Perhaps the men who went to America felt this, and so repudiated the old world altogether. Went one better than Europe. Liberty in America has meant so far the breaking away from *all* dominion. The true liberty will only begin when Americans discover IT, and proceed possibly to fulfill IT. IT being the deepest *whole* self of man, the self in its wholeness, not idealistic halfness.

That's why the Pilgrim Fathers came to America, then; and that's why we come. Driven by IT. We cannot see that invisible winds carry us, as they carry swarms of locusts, that invisible magnetism brings us as it brings the migrating birds to their unforeknown goal. But it is so. We are not the marvellous choosers and deciders we think we are. IT chooses for us, and decides for us. Unless of course we are just escaped slaves, vulgarly cocksure of our ready-made destiny. But if we are living people, in touch with the source, IT drives us and decides us. We are free only so long as we obey. When we run counter, and think we will do as we like, we just flee around like Orestes pursued by the Eumenides.

And still, when the great day begins, when Americans have at last discovered America and their own wholeness, still there will be the vast number of escaped slaves to reckon with, those who have no cocksure, ready-made destinies.

Which will win in America, the escaped slaves, or the new whole men?

The real American day hasn't begun yet. Or at least, not yet sunrise. So far it has been the false dawn. That is, in the progressive American consciousness there has been the one dominant desire, to do away with the old thing. Do away with masters, exalt the will of the people. The will of the people being nothing but a figment, the exalting doesn't count for much. So, in the name of the will of the people, get rid of masters. When you have got rid of masters, you are left with this mere phrase of the will of the people. Then you pause and bethink yourself, and try to recover your own wholeness.

So much for the conscious American motive, and for democracy over here.

Democracy in America is just the tool with which the old mastery of Europe, the European spirit, is undermined. Europe destroyed, potentially, American democracy will evaporate. America will begin.

American consciousness has so far been a false dawn. The negative ideal of democracy. But underneath, and contrary to this open ideal, the first hints and revelations of IT. IT, the American whole soul.

You have got to pull the democratic and idealistic clothes off American utterance, and see what you can of the dusky body of IT underneath.

"Henceforth be masterless."

Henceforth be mastered.

[1923]

American Public Schools   DENIS W. BROGAN

Denis W. Brogan (1900–   ) was born in Scotland and educated in France, England, and America. From 1925 to 1927 he was at Harvard, where he earned an M.A. in American history, a subject on which he has lectured at several British universities. Since 1939 he has been a professor of political science at the University of Cambridge. The following essay is from *The American Character* (1944).

Brogan's writings on American life are characterized by friendly understanding and critical insight. In the present selection, for example, he finds good qualities in American schools, but he also finds much to criticize, either directly or by implication. Brogan's style is so easy and apparently unargumentative that one must read carefully to determine the extent to which he actually favors what he calls "Americanism." Because his organization is casual, careful reading is likewise required to connect the last several paragraphs to the line of thought Brogan has been developing. The careful reader will also make allowances for possible changes in American schools during the two decades since *The American Character* was written.

"*. . . The social and political role of American education cannot be understood if it is thought of as being primarily a means of formal instruction. . . .*"

The word "school" in America covers every type of educational institution. Being "at school" may mean being at a kindergarten or at Harvard. School, too, has kept much of its Greek meaning. It is a system of organization and training for leisure as well as work. And it has become more and more adjusted to its environment, undertaking to do more than it can (which is very American) and doing much more than it seems to do (which is also very American).

The social and political role of American education cannot be understood if it is thought of as being primarily a means of formal instruction. If it is so thought of, it will be overrated and underrated. It will be overrated because the figures of two million college students, of seven million high school students, will dazzle the visitor used to seeing opportunities for higher education doled out (except in Soviet Russia) on a combined class-and-intellectual basis. It will be underrated if, at any stage below the highest (that is, below the great universities), the academic standards are compared with those of a good English, French, or pre-Hitler German school. If these millions of boys and girls are to be judged by their academic accomplishments, they will be judged harshly. But they are not to be so judged, for their schools are doing far more than instruct them: they are letting them instruct each other in how to live in America.

Of those millions, a large section will be the children of immigrants to whom English is still largely a foreign tongue. Of these millions, a very large portion will be the children of migrants from different parts of the United States. Others will be the children of rural-bred parents, forced to adjust themselves to the new urban world. They have to learn a common language, common habits, common tolerances, a common political and national faith. And they do. It is this aim and this success that justifies the lavish buildings of the local high school; not merely the classrooms and the laboratories, but the gymnasium, the field-house where basketball can be played in comfort in the depth of the bitter winter, the swimming pools in which the summer heat can be endured.

It is true that the teachers are relatively badly paid and have an inferior social as well as economic standing, insecure tenure and politics making their condition worse. More money spent on men might get better results than more money spent on buildings. But it is easier to get the materials for buildings than the materials for teachers. As long as American society remains individualistic, competitive, confident that the answers to the present are in the future, not in the past, it is going to take more than money to seduce the right men and women in adequate numbers away from the life of action. And, a point too seldom remembered, the necessity for providing teachers for the two million college students hampers recruiting for high schools. In many cases, the colleges are doing what is really high school work and it matters comparatively little where the good teachers are, as long as they are teaching.

The political function of the schools is to teach Americanism, meaning not merely political and patriotic dogma, but the habits necessary to American life. This justifies the most extravagant items in the curriculum. Since the ability to play bridge is one of the marks of Americanism in a suburb, it is reasonable that there should be bridge clubs in schools. The main political achievement of the high schools and grammar schools is to bring together the young of all classes and all origins, to provide, artificially, the common background that in an old, rural society is provided by tradition, by the necessary collaboration of village life. The elementary schools — the "grade" schools — do this, too, but as far as an American town is broken up into racial blocs, the Ethan Allen Public School may have mainly Polish pupils, the Zachary Chandler mainly Welsh. Only in the Warren G. Harding High School is a big enough common pool formed in which Americans can be made.

Some of that Americanization is, of course, done deliberately and formally. Mr. Carlton Hayes pointed out long ago that the ritual of flag worship and oath-taking in an American school is a religious observance. Little boys and girls, in a school from which religion in the old sense is barred, solemnly rising each morning and reciting together the "American's Creed" are performing a religious exercise as truly as if they began the day with "I believe in God the Father Almighty" or asserted that "There Is No God but God."

And that these daily rituals are religious has been at last affirmed by the Supreme Court in a series of cases in which the children of a fanatical sect, Jehovah's Witnesses, had been excluded from schools for refusing to give to the flag honors that, so their parents had taught them, were due to God alone. In 1940, all the Court except Chief Justice Stone held that flag worship was among the things that were Caesar's. Since that year, however, they have decided by a majority that the religious rights of the children were being infringed. What is significant in the case is not the Court's reversal of itself but the reality of the issue presented to it. For to the Court, and to the overwhelming majority of the American people, the objections of the Witnesses were as unintelligible as the objections of the Christians to making a formal sacrifice to the Divine Emperor were to Trajan and Pliny. The school board of Minersville, Pennsylvania, was faced with a real problem when it was asked to admit that children refusing to take part in the most sacred rite of the day should be allowed to associate with the believing children of the formally unestablished national church of the United States. So, too, was the State of Oregon when it found Catholic and Lutheran children refusing to go to the schools it provided. But in both cases the Supreme Court held, finally, that compulsory Americanism was not Americanism at all, that coerced belief was not what the American people needed to stay united. This was not Germany or Russia but the country of Jefferson and Justice Holmes.

The flag worship of the American school and the American nation was brought home to the British public in an episode that, if funny, was also very revealing. For the London makers of ladies' underwear who adorned their garments with American flags were innocent of any insulting or even frivolous intention. At the same time, a revue chorus in London was attired in Union Jack handkerchiefs and nothing else — to the public indifference. But the flag, in America, is more than a mere symbol among many others. It is the regimental color of a regiment in which all Americans are enrolled. Its thirteen stripes and forty-eight stars are symbols far better understood than the complicated heraldry of crosses of Saint George, Saint Andrew, and Saint Patrick imposed on each other in a way that only experts understand. It was Lincoln's task to see that the number of stars in the flag was not diminished by eleven during his term of office. It was the discovery that the flag still flew over Fort McHenry, despite the British fleet, that moved Francis Scott Key to write:

Oh, say, can you see by the dawn's early light,
What so proudly we hailed at the twilight's last gleaming;
Whose broad stripes and bright stars, thro' the perilous fight,
O'er the ramparts we watched were so gallantly streaming?

What he wrote in 1814, tens of millions of Americans have since sung or tried to sing. And when Barbara Frietchie in Whittier's poem told-off Stonewall Jackson with:

"Shoot if you must this old gray head,
But spare your country's flag," she said,

she was speaking for all Americans for whom the Stars and Stripes was still their country's flag as it had been, till recently, that of General Jackson.

Thus Americanization by ritual is an important and necessary part of the function of the American school. And because it is best carried out in schools, it matters little that the high school curriculum has been so widened that it no longer means a great deal that this boy or that girl has graduated from it — if we are looking for proof of academic achievement. But graduation from high school is reasonable proof that a great deal has been learned about American ways of life, that lessons in practical politics, in organization, in social ease have been learned that could not have been learned in factory or office.

And if the high school seems to devote too much time and money to social life, penalizing the poor boy or girl more than a theoretically less democratic educational system might do, it is thus early impressing an awkward truth on the boy or girl who is both mediocre and poor. It also penalizes the really able boy or girl who is not kept in good enough intellectual training. And if the main business of the school is, in fact, the Americanization of the children of newcomers, the parents of "old American stock" have a good reason (to add to less good ones) for not sending their children to learn what they know already, at the cost of diminishing their chance of learning what they do not know. If English is native to your children and to their home, it is not merely undemocratic to object to having their progress held up and their accent debased by the tone of a high school largely immigrant in composition.

For the task of an American school in many regions is to teach the American language, to enable it to compete with Spanish, with French, with Yiddish, with Polish, with German, with Swedish. Another task is to give, through the language and the literature of the language, a common vocabulary and a common fund of allusion, fable, and sentiment. With a fluid population this has not been easy. And the countless teachers who have labored, pedantically, formally, with complete and erroneous conviction that there were correct standards, have been heroes as important in the mass as was William McGuffey whose *Eclectic Readers* sold over one hundred and twenty million copies and helped to make the Union. The teachers were heroes because, although English won against all its rivals, it was itself going through important changes, in vocabulary, in grammar, in sound, becoming the new tongue we are beginning to call American. The teachers who stuck by the rules, who worshipped at the New England shrines in Concord, were bound to lose, but their struggle was not pure waste. For the common tongue, hammered out by millions of immigrants, by millions of migrants, would have been poor in vocabulary and structure but for the people Mr. Mencken calls the dominies and who call themselves schoolmen. The creation of general literacy and a common written and spoken tongue, intelligible everywhere except possibly in the deep South, is an achievement as remarkable as the creation of Mandarin Chinese or Low Latin or Hellenistic Greek, and this tongue is certain to be the new *lingua franca* of the world.

The making of American has been mixed-up in English minds with the making of American slang. Slang, as we should know, is one of the great sources of language. French is improved Latin slang. And slang has contributed a good deal to American. It is a generation since Mr. Dooley said that when his countrymen had finished with the English language it would look as if it had been run over by a musical comedy. Since then it has been run over by *Hellzappopin*. But it is possible, indeed very easy, to overestimate the role of slang. It is more and more the creation of professional artists, "makers." The Hollywood prose masters provide a current and often short-lived jargon; the boys and girls, men and women, who wish to be on the beam or in the groove, may murmur with admiration, "I wish I had said that." And Whistler's classical answer to Wilde is certainly appropriate: "You will, Oscar — you will!" But not for long. Some slang will enter the language; some words will lose their meanings or acquire new ones; syntax will be loosened up. But formal speech as taught in schools will still be very important. The high school English teacher, for all her pedantry, is as much a maker of the American language as Messrs. Runyon and O'Hara. Two streams of language may run roughly parallel, but in time they will merge; they will provide America with many interesting variations, do for American what its dual Germanic and Latin character does for English. That time has not yet come, but it is on the way. And the future character of this truly national tongue is foreshadowed in the drawing by Mr. Peter Arno in which an indignant citizen tells another: "I consider your conduct unethical and lousy."

Most American parents do not want, or are not able, to send their children to anything but public high schools, and the life in such a school is a training in life for America. It may be and often is a training in life *against* Europe. For Europe is the background from which many of the children are reacting and from which they must be delivered if they are to be Americanized. For nearly all immigrants, America is promotion, and this promotion is more clearly felt by their children. The old people may hanker after the old country, but the children — whatever sentimental feelings for their ancestral homes they may have, especially when provoked — are, above all else, anxious to be Americans.

Necessarily something is lost here. The least-common-denominator Americanism of the schools is not a complete substitute for a native culture. What the first-generation American children learn to despise may include elements in their moral diet that are not replaced. A new American whose pride in that promotion involves mere contempt for the habits, what Americans call the "folkways" or "mores," of his parents is not necessarily a good American.

So attempts are made to instill pride in the ancestral cultures of the European lands from which the immigrants come. The University of Pittsburgh, located in one of the main melting pots of America, has a set of rooms illustrating the culture of various European countries. In the case of the Greeks, the room may instill adequate pride; in the case of the Scots (if any such need is felt) a shrine of Robert Burns may serve. But, for many of the peasant immigrants, the old country is backward though beloved, while for their children it is merely backward.

Americanization comes not from preservation of Slovak or Italian peasant culture, but from speedy assimilation to "American" culture. And that assimilation may take the form of distinction in anything that the American world obviously values. In the narrow sense of culture, there may even be a temptation to go for those courses that have no immigrant stigma on them. Thus I have been told by an eminent Scandinavian-American that it is difficult to get good students of Scandinavian literature and language at the University of Minnesota, although most of the students have fairly recent Scandinavian connections. They will study French but not Swedish, for "French is not a servant's language." Latin, emblem of functionless "culture," plays something of the same role; it is a symbol of liberation.

Study is not the only way up to Americanization, to acceptation. Sport is another — and one that does the job more dramatically for the newcomers gifted with what it takes to excel in competitive contests, with what is needed to win personal and community and institutional glory.

When Fanny Ellsler, the ballet dancer, came to Boston, her performance was solemnly inspected from the highest motives by Emerson and Margaret Fuller. "The dance began; both sat serenely silent; at last Emerson spoke. 'Margaret,' he said, 'this is poetry.' 'No, Waldo,' replied Margaret; 'it is not poetry, it is religion.'" And the great football games of today are religious ceremonies in this sense. It is significant that the graduating classes in Muncie High School a generation ago took such mottoes as "Deo duce" and today take mottoes stressing the "Bearcat Spirit," the "Bearcats" being the school basketball team. But a Greek would know where he was at a basketball game uniting boys and girls, parents and civic leaders, in a common passion for competitive achievement. It may be hard on the academic work of the school. It may even slightly annoy a schoolboy, who like Mr. Burton Rascoe combines excellence in gymnastic and music (as the Greeks put it), to find that his views on literature are less interesting to the other sex than his prowess at football. But sport, school sport, college sport, does unite the parents, the children, and the community. And sport is rigorously democratic. The sons of Czechs and Poles can score there, can break through the barriers that stand in the way of the children of "Bohunks" and "Polacks." And although Harvard may secretly rejoice when it can put a winning team on to Soldiers' Field whose names suggest the *Mayflower,* it would rather put on a team that can beat Yale, even though it is not a "Yankee" team, than go down to defeat with the descendants of generations of Brahmins. And in the Middle West, sport is a real means of promotion. The Ohio high school that produced the great Negro runner, Jesse Owens, was prouder of him than if he had made Phi Beta Kappa at Ohio State; and Hitler would have made a less serious mistake if he had snubbed a great American scholar whose race he didn't like than he did by sulking at the Olympic Games when the Herrenvolk were beaten by a Negro. It is a frontier tradition; Lincoln's great strength gave him a prestige that helped him as a lawyer and politician. The great athlete performing for the glory of the school, college, state or nation, is a less egoistic figure than the great scholar pursuing his own studies with an undemocratic concentration. And the Negroes, whose greatest hero is Joe Louis, not Paul Robeson, are not substantially wrong so far. In American society as it is, a Negro heavy-weight champion, like a Negro tap-dancer, is a better adjusted figure than a great Negro artist — or America is a less maladjusted society for them. Of course, this will not and should not last. The Irish were rising when their great hero became Governor Al Smith, rather than a successor of John L. Sullivan, the "Boston strong boy." But to get assent to a Negro's *right* to be heavy-weight champion is something — as those will agree who remember the frenzied search round 1910 for a "white hope" to save the heavy-weight championship from the indignity of being held by Jack Johnson. Great Indian athletes like Jim Thorpe, great Negro football heroes like Paul Robeson in his earlier days, the polyglot teams put on the field by the great Swedish coach Knut Rockne for the "Irish" of Notre Dame — these become "All American" figures in a wider and deeper sense than that in which the Yale of Walter Camp understood the term.

The cheer leaders, the new "jongleurs de Notre Dame," the "majorettes," shapely young women more or less involved with musical instruments, the massed cheering sections of the students, the massed yelling sections of the alumni — these are the equivalent of the crowds at the great Hellenic festivals in which barbarians were not allowed to compete. The Rose Bowl, the Cotton Bowl, the other intersectional games — these are instruments of national unity, and the provision of such instruments is no mean duty of colleges and universities. It is a religious exercise of a kind a Greek would have understood, however remote it may be from the university as understood by Abelard or Saint Thomas Aquinas or John Harvard.

The university, as these men understood it, exists all the same and exists to play a great national part, for the level of academic learning in America is perhaps the only branch of American life where the promise of rapid progress upward has been consistently kept. It is not as easy to define the nature of that progress as it is to affirm its existence.

Things have changed a great deal since the ideal of American college education was "Mark Hopkins at one end of a log and a student at the other." Then the college existed to provide a common background for lawyers and doctors and divines; it was small and select, not select in a social or financial sense, but select in that only those who accepted the old intellectual order of things were catered for. It was a decisive moment when President Eliot of Harvard (which had long ceased to concentrate on providing for a "learned ministry") introduced the elective system. The college abandoned any idea of imposing a hierarchy of subjects. The student could select what he wanted from the menu provided; *à la carte* had succeeded *table d'hôte*. But in newer, less secure, less rich institutions than Harvard, the change went farther than that, for not only was the student free to choose from what was offered — he was entitled to complain if the college did not offer what he wanted to learn, or even what he wanted to learn in the sense that it was all he could hope to learn. As more and more students came to college with varying school preparation, as life grew more complex and the techniques of life and business more impressive in their results, the unity of college life disappeared. Boys and girls were no longer taken in hand by a successor of Mark Hopkins and given a few general ethical and philosophical ideas suitable to a world still pretty much agreed on fundamentals. They were visitors to an institution that seemed to have more in common with the Mark Hopkins Hotel in San Francisco than with the Williams College of a century ago; and from the glass-walled bar, "The Top of the Mark," they could see the modern world, the bridges and skyscrapers of San Francisco, and across the Bay the lights of Berkeley where the University of California provides for all tastes, from addicts of the Greek theater to the most modern biological and physical techniques.

In this necessary adaptation of the old university ideal to the modern American world, much was lost, or not provided; there was not as yet a common standard of reference for educated men; a mass of information was stored and techniques were imparted in institutes physically associated for historical reasons. But of course, the universities and colleges like the high schools, served other than merely academic ends. *Our Town* illustrates high school mating which would have taken place anyway. *The Miracle of Morgan's Creek* shows a suitor taking cookery so as to be close to his beloved during her high school career, but he was bound to be close to her anyway. But the college movie, play (*The Poor Nut*) and novel rightly illustrates the more important phenomenon of exogamous marriage, of the bringing together boys and girls who otherwise would not meet at all.

And the very success of the school system in Americanizing the American young may result in the killing of natural curiosity. For example, the cult of the Constitution leads to the exclusive identification of a political concept like "liberty" with the American constitutional system. This being so, a Latin-American "republic" with a paper constitution like the American is regarded as "free" while Canada is not. For Canada is part of an "empire" with a monarch at the head of it. Some two-thirds of the American people, accordingly, think that Canada pays taxes to Britain; even in the states bordering on the Dominion, about half the Americans think this! In the same way, the word "republic" has an almost magical significance for the Americans. Plutarch, as Mr. Wells once suggested, had a good deal to do with this; but, whatever the origins of the belief, it is now part of the American credo that only citizens of a republic can be free. And no matter what romantic interest Americans may display in the human side of monarchy, it should never be forgotten that, politically, they regard it as a childish institution. Mark Twain, a very pro-English American, refused for that very reason to write one of his amusing, critical travel books about England. But he did write two books about England, all the same: *The Prince and the Pauper* and *A Connecticut Yankee at the Court of King Arthur*. How deeply anti-monarchical, anti-clerical, anti-traditional, those books are!

And in *Huckleberry Finn*, the traditional American view of royalty as

expensive foolishness is admirably set forth in Huck's remark to Nigger Jim:
"Sometimes I wish we could hear of a country that's out of kings."

A great many Americans still think like Huck Finn. And it must be
remembered that for Americans the great event of their own and of world
history was the destruction of the royal power of George III and the establishment of a Constitution guaranteeing to each State "a republican form of
government." It is in that light that the modern world is seen by nearly all
Americans.

[1944]

The Boundless Empire   ROBERT JUNGK

Robert Jungk (1914–   ) was a nineteen-year-old Jewish student in
Berlin when Adolph Hitler came to power. Arrested for anti-Nazi activities, he was later released and went to Paris to study at the Sorbonne.
Returning to his under-cover work in Germany, he was again forced to
flee. First in Czechoslovakia, then in France, and finally in Switzerland,
he continued his efforts against the Third Reich. After the war he became
an American correspondent for some Swiss newspapers, travelling about
the country to gain the impressions presented in *Tomorrow Is Already
Here* (1954), from which the following essay is taken.

Largely unconcerned with "the façade" of American life, Jungk is
frankly critical in his description of what he believes to be the current
national ethos. Looking beyond political and social developments, he
bases his criticism on emerging patterns of belief. Ironically, he sees a
growing pessimism as the most hopeful aspect of contemporary America.

". . . The stake is the throne of God. . . ."

When Christopher Columbus undertook to seek the shortest sea route to
India for his Queen, he knew so little about the region for which he was
embarking that he accidentally found a "New World." The x-millionth
visitor who travels to America today in the wake of the great seafarer tends
to take with him rather too much than too little information concerning his
destination. For nearly every one of us has felt the influence of Americanism
in some form or other before ever setting foot on American soil. For us all, in
the course of recent years, Uncle Sam has been transformed from a distant
relative into a near neighbor, an almost daily visitor with whose home, customs
and habits we believe ourselves to be better acquainted through an abundance
of magazines, books, pictures and films, than many a country geographically
nearer at hand.

Even so, Columbus's lot may well fall to the best-informed modern traveler. He comes to an utterly different country from what he had supposed. Behind the picture of the new world familiar from a distance he discovers another, highly singular one, which appears to him strange and dangerous.

Only under protest does the visitor gradually admit to his mind impressions which run counter to his expectations. At first he wishes to dispose of them as exceptions, set them aside as transitory phenomena. But slowly it dawns upon him that the sum of all these "appearances" may represent a new and singular reality, an entirely different America still in the process of taking shape.

Certainly the outward signs do not reveal much of this other America. They are fair and freshly cleaned. The Statue of Liberty stands welcoming at the entrance to New York harbor with a promise of tolerance and humanity. The skyscrapers beckon in rows of gleaming windows and duly radiate optimism. Nowhere are the symbols of a freedom-loving democracy, proud of its origins, hidden or impugned. On the contrary: precisely because from year to year they are losing their real influence and strength, they are given a more conspicuous place in the show windows. But in fact, "the log-cabin President," "the rugged individualist," "the self-made man who worked his way from rags to riches" — have scarcely more connection with the actual present of the United States than cathedrals, castles, cancan and folk music have with the postwar realities of Europe. They have become museum pieces, attractions for tourists and grateful topics for speakers at a loss for ideas on patriotic occasions.

For the United States, too, despite outward appearances, has changed profoundly in the past two decades — at least as profoundly as the European countries convulsed by inner and outer upheaval. Something is breaking through the façade of the new world which I should like to refer to as the *newest world:* an America no longer in agreement with the guiding principles of its previous history and presenting, ever more plainly, features of a totalitarian nature.

In order to come in contact with this newest world one must leave the urban centers and ride out into the suburbs where the working world overlaps the living world, and individual human existence increasingly fits itself into the uniform of standardization. The centers of these groups are no longer the church, the school or the town hall, but the centers of production and consumption, the factory and the "supermarket."

But the newest world is seen most clearly after one has bidden farewell to the metropolitan civilization of the East and Middle West and turned to the once rural or entirely unsettled area of the South, Southwest and West; for that is where the evidences of the other America have been multiplying since the beginning of the Second World War with the rapidity of a gold-mining town.

Here are the great armament factories with their brand-new mass migrations, the metallic shimmer of oil refineries and mechanized network of chemical industries. Here, above all, are the military reserves, the laboratory towns, the testing grounds. Not only geographically are they segregated: politically, too, they lead a life apart. The rights of freedom have been largely suspended in them, and experiments are attempted with every form of administration from open dictatorship through enlightened absolutism to outright socialism.

One who has had contact with these forthright manifestations of the newest world will recognize them also where they have not yet emerged with such distinctness. For all that is uniform, standardized, inhuman in its exclusive striving toward efficiency, is still today so interwoven with the democratic, Christian and humanitarian pattern of the "good old days" that it is not immediately discernible.

There is a reason for this. Whereas in other countries totalitarianism erupted with revolutionary violence and then set to work immediately to wipe out the traces of a freedom-loving past, the process in the United States is taking an evolutionary form. Therefore we find an interplay of the old and the new, of the remains of freedom and the beginnings of slavery, which indicate that the final decision has yet to be reached. Even those few who are deliberately working toward a new tyranny opposed to the American tradition are clever enough to make use of this phraseology of freedom.

For this trend in the United States there are, of course, various illuminating and relevant political explanations. But such an approach is not within the scope of the present book. Here an attempt will be made to portray and explain the disquieting development in another way. For it arises, in my view, from a process reaching far beyond the internal or external political orientations of the moment.

Looked at historically, the tendency away from freedom seems to spring from the same source which yesterday and the day before watered the tree of American liberty; that is, the constant striving to open up new domains, the constant pressure toward new boundaries. The frontier, which in the course of a century and a half was pushed from the Atlantic to the Pacific, has deeply influenced America's thinking, her spiritual climate, and, not least, her domestic economy during the nineteenth century. It symbolized the country's unconfined spirit of progress, it was the cause of the perpetual stresses due to the finding of new riches. At the frontier there were no rules, none of the impediments of civilization. It was the paradise of the pioneer, the land of "unlimited possibilities," in which every man of sufficient strength and spirit could stake out a claim upon the future.

But by about 1890 the pioneers had conquered and occupied the entire territory of their own nation. The dynamic energy of the frontiersman had to seek new goals which could lie only beyond the sea or in the great tracts of land to the north or south.

It might at that time have been possible for the pressure toward new frontiers to have transformed itself into "pure imperialism." But the voices which prophesied an imperial destiny for the United States and tried to point the way to adventures in colonial conquest gained little hearing. After the short and not very popular war with Spain the adolescent power preferred to turn to other than territorial conquest. It sought, under the guidance of science and technology, for frontiers not to be found on maps: frontiers open to anyone who attacked them with energy and dared to cross them.

While other powers quarreled over provinces, islands, tracts of wilderness, thereby ruining each other, America went to work to develop her factories and laboratories. The new pioneers were enterprising financiers, scientists and engineers. These fertile minds did not need to be persuaded. If they were not already in the country they came willingly to the United States, attracted by the vast resources and potentialities for development which they found nowhere else in the world.

Thus the United States in the course of half a century developed into the foremost scientific and technical power. Her new frontiers lay and still lie mainly in her own laboratories and workshops. The apparent broadening of territorial boundaries in the last few years through the establishment of a world-wide net of military bases is indubitably defensive in scope. This wide-spread defense belt is intended primarily to serve a vastly more far-reaching and ambitious strategy, daily and hourly being carried on in the experimental centers of the homeland.

For the Americans today are concerned with bigger things than land ownership. They are fundamentally more ambitious than even their sharpest adversaries believe. Their efforts do not aspire to the mastery of continents, still less to that of the entire globe, but to higher things far than these. America is striving to win power over the sum total of things, complete and absolute mastery of nature in all its aspects.

This bid for power is not directed against any nation, class or race. It assails no particular way of government but the ways of creation, which have scarcely fluctuated within the memory of man. Clouds and wind, plant and beast, the boundless heavens themselves are to be subjugated. The stake is higher than dictators' seats and presidential chairs. The stake is the throne of God. To occupy God's place, to repeat his deeds, to re-create and organize a man-made cosmos according to man-made laws of reason, foresight and efficiency: that is America's ultimate objective. Toward this her chief efforts are directed.

This is a revolution as convinced of its successful outcome as any other revolutionary movement. It is furthered by statesmen, applauded by the masses, encouraged by the police. For it promises all riches, it proposes to take nothing from anyone. It destroys whatever is primitive, whatever grows in disordered profusion or evolves through patient mutation. What it cannot observe and measure it subdues indirectly to its power. It says the unsayable. It knows no awe.

The slaves employed by the Grasp of Omnipotence are not foreign nations but the elements themselves. Each year, it has been calculated, this army of "slave energies" increases by millions of "horsepower" and "heat units." Nothing is left untouched, nothing unexplored. Even the inmost core of heaven and of matter must be utilized — the sources of life and of the soul. There is no pause for death, no respect for time. Present, past, future are jugglers' balls to be tossed about. How tame an amateur was Prometheus compared with his distant American disciples!

It was long assumed that this reaching for omnipotence could remain without influence upon America's religious, moral and political character. But as elsewhere, and in some respects more strikingly, with the rise of the applied sciences and technology, the pillars of democracy, Christianity and personal ethics in the United States have begun to totter. Where formerly

belief and conscience were the sole criterion, the names of the new judges are
purpose and *results*. To these the only valid question is: "What is it good
for?" All and everything, the smallest and the largest, must now be submitted to the test of utility.

Even man, the actual inventor and director of this purpose-bound world,
has in the end been unable to keep himself free of the new bondage. Because
of the happiness it promises, the American pays the highest possible price for
this grasp at omnipotence — his freedom as a God-made person. His individual impotence is the price of a share in the omnipotence. The frontier of
our time imposes on those who seek it a condition unknown to the pioneers
who preceded them: subordination to collective effort and discipline.

In those days, each man could set out on his own, with company of his
choosing, his firearms, a team of horses or oxen and a covered wagon full of
provisions, into the unknown distance which promised wealth. The still un-
exploited soil was waiting for him, harvests and money rewarded his efforts
with tangible satisfactions.

How different are the new pioneers! Their laboratories, workshops, testing grounds are not their own. They themselves are conceivable only as the
vanguard of a gigantic industrial army. Behind the construction and launching of each rocket, each splitting of an atom, each chemical experiment, each
working of an electronic brain, stands a highly developed technical apparatus,
an enormous sum of sacrifices in time, strength, money and individual liberty.
Only in his financial, organizational and personal relationship to the hierarchy
of the joint enterprise is the pioneer of today conceivable.

It naturally follows that the new pioneer himself is subject to the application of the same methods he applies to the conquest of nature. He, too, is
scientifically observed, tested for his capacities, made use of down to his smallest ability and, like any other tool, discarded as soon as he ceases to fulfill the
required purpose. The "free will" must in this connection be flatly classed
as an unstable element and ruled out — man, the uncertain factor, must be
replaced by as reliable a type as possible. As in every revolution, the rebels,
the Prometheans, the discontented must disappear. The reliable, tractable,
average man becomes the new ideal pioneer.

Thus in the United States there is now in formation a world such as
there has never been before. It is a man-designed, pre-arranged, highly controlled and continually "improved" creation. It has its own kind of beauty
and terror. For although the human creators have taken pains to ban fate,
chance, catastrophe, misfortune and death from their creation, the banished
ones return all the more insistently: errors of calculation by the statistical
planners, failures of technical equipment, accidents and explosions bring an
accumulation of disaster.

Even the old dark myths of the veiled picture whose draperies no one
may lift, of ghosts, demons, regions of witchery, even of hell itself, take on
fresh valuations in this so precisely calculated, so rationally founded world.
For the average man moves about in this test-tube world, this secondary
nature, quite as uncertainly as did his forebears in primitive nature, because
only the specialists — and often not even they — understand the things and
powers they have brought into being.

This newest world is no far Utopia, no fable of the year 1984 or of a still more distant century. We are not, as in the novels of Wells, Huxley and Orwell, safely separated by the broad moat of time from that overcoming, ravenous future. The new, the different and the frightening is already among us. And so — as history shows — has it ever been. The morrow is already present in today, but harmlessly masked still, hidden and disguised behind the familiar. The future is no fantasy cleanly distinguished from actual life: the future has already begun. But it still can, if recognized in time, be changed.

In this newest world, infused by the future, the distinction between day and night, between light and darkness, has lost its validity. The act of the first biblical day of creation is annulled by this latest resurrection of Prometheus. That the modern process of production shall not suffer interruption the artificial suns of electrical projectors burn from sundown to sunrise. In nearly all the big cities of America may be found emporiums and drugstores which announce "We never close." It will be only a short step to the moment when the "northern lights effect" already being developed in a California laboratory will tear the nightdress from heaven forever.

And so it goes with each single act of creation described in holy writ. Man produces artificial matter, he builds his own heavenly bodies and prepares to release them into the firmament. He creates new species of plants and animals, he places his own mechanical beings, robots fitted with superhuman perception, in the world.

There is just one thing he cannot do. It is not given him to cry, in the words of the Bible, "And behold! It was very good." He may never relax his hands in his lap and say that his creation is completed. Restlessness and discontent remain with him. "For behind each door we open lies a passage with many other doors which again we must unlock, only to find, behind each, others to still others," a chemical research worker — one of the creators of artificial worlds — once remarked to me.

It seems as though the import of all this creation were no more than further creation. Production calls for ever more production, each discovery for further discoveries to serve as a protection against the consequences of the preceding one. Man no longer finds leisure in which to enjoy the world. He consumes himself in fear and worry about it. No sense of joy and no hosanna accompany the new act of creation.

This dissatisfaction with the man-made newest world, often so strongly felt in the United States as to find vent in fearful and destructive imaginings, seems to me one of the most hopeful signs for her future. Pessimism about civilization is no longer the fashionable pose of a small circle of artists and intellectuals, but the general expression of a deep and critical concern.

To be sure, such doubt still exists side by side in the same breast with the old spirit of boundless, wanton activity, of daring much and hoping all. But the shriller the *happiness* propaganda becomes, the more self-satisfied the smile of satisfaction over the "highest standard of living in the world," the more disturbing grow the doubts.

There are many who seek relief in "amusement," in sexuality, alcohol or neurosis — the so-called escapists. There are others who resign themselves, and some few who battle consciously against the trend forward into totalitarian, technicalized mass existence. Attempts are being made to humanize labor, to fit the machine to human psychology, to decentralize the swollen conglomerations.

But at present all this has a quality of play-acting or of deliberate cult. The great spiritual change, which would have to express itself in the recognition once again of human limits and the rediscovery of moderation, is not yet apparent. Help for this lies neither in messianic preaching nor in impatience. The transformation can indeed come only from bitter experience. Only when the convulsive grasp at omnipotence finally relaxes, when the *hubris* dissolves and gives place to humility — only then will America be recovered by Him Whom it has discarded, by God.

[1954]

The Number One Question   NORMAN COUSINS

Norman Cousins (1912–   ) was born in Union, New Jersey. After graduating from Columbia University in 1933, he went to work for the New York *Evening Post*, then for *Current History*, and, in 1940, for the *Saturday Review*, where his editorials soon became a respected feature. One of them, "Modern Man Is Obsolete," written at the time the atom bomb was dropped on Hiroshima, was expanded into what is probably his best known book. Cousins has traveled to many parts of the world and wrote "The Number One Question" as the result of a trip taken for the American government to India, Pakistan, and Ceylon in 1951.

Cousins' experience with foreign audiences concerning "the number one question" led him to present his information in the form of a debate. There was some danger in doing so because debates-in-print have a way of seeming both artificial and melodramatic. Cousins effectively avoids such a result by careful characterization of his opponent, himself, and the occasion, by skillful organization, by a conclusion that does not claim too much, and by what appears to be fair reporting.

"... each time I had spoken, without exception, the issue of race prejudice in the United States came up. ..."

At a Junior College in Lahore, the university city of Pakistan, I ran into trouble. In the question period following my talk a student of perhaps nineteen or twenty demanded the floor, then leveled a long and accusing finger at me.

"You have come to the wrong place if you expect us to believe your propaganda about America," he said in a tense and angry voice. "We know

Reprinted by permission of *The Saturday Review* and the author.

the truth about America, and we students protest your use of the platform of this college to try to pass off dishonest and untruthful stories about the United States. Since you have already spoken, it is too late to do anything about it. We can, however, enter a protest with the principal of the school for having invited you to speak. And we can demand that a representative or a supporter of the Soviet Union be permitted to come here and talk to us about conditions in that country."

As the student spoke the head of the college, seated at my right, was visibly disturbed. He got up and walked to the front of the platform, interrupted the student, then began to apologize to me publicly for what he described as an "unfortunate outburst."

"I ask that the speaker ignore this demonstration of bad manners," the principal said. "Here in Pakistan we give honor and not insults to our guests. I am sure I speak for the large majority of the students here in admonishing our ill-tempered and ill-mannered member."

It appeared from the general applause at this point that most of the students agreed with the principal. I regretted, however, that he had disciplined the student openly. Actually, the student was not to blame. I had set the stage for his protest by expressing the hope that everyone would feel completely free to take issue with anything I said during my talk. My purpose in coming to Pakistan was to have the fullest possible exchange of views. Accordingly, I assured the principal that I didn't feel that what the student said reflected in any way upon the hospitality of the college, and that I was anxious to have the student enlarge on his remarks. What, in particular, did he object to in my talk as being propaganda?

The student seemed reluctant to get to his feet, and I asked the principal to assure him that it was entirely in order for him to continue to speak as openly as he did a moment ago. The principal seemed a little dubious at first about my request, then instructed the student to comply with the wishes of the speaker.

"I am sorry if what I said was regarded as an insult," the student began, "and I am sorry if I seemed angry. But you can understand how disturbing it is to hear things that we believe to be false and how unfair it is not to be able to hear at first hand about the Soviet Union if we are officially assembled to hear about the United States.

"You have asked me what it is in particular I disliked about your talk. Much of what you said about the United States was very general. You tried to give us confidence in America's intentions in the world. Frankly, I believe you to be an apologist for the American people at a time when America is committing great crimes in the world. If you really wanted to be honest with us" — and here his voice took on the same tenseness and harshness it had when he had spoken the first time — "you would have admitted all the ugly things you do to people in America who do not happen to have a fair white skin."

At this point there were staccato shouts of approval and a short burst of applause. This emboldened the student, and he raised his voice.

"In America there are twenty million people who are called citizens but who are not citizens at all. They have been condemned as inferior beings and they are not allowed to participate in what you call your democracy. They do not enjoy the same protection under the laws you give to white people. If a colored person commits a crime, however minor that crime may be, he is apt to be seized by crowds. Your lynchings are the purest form of mob justice in the world.

"If a colored person becomes ill does he have available to him the same hospital and medical facilities as does the white? If he wants to travel somewhere is it not true that he is compelled to sit in a specially designated section, so that he will not contaminate the pure white travelers? Can the colored person sit down at the same school desk, at the same dining table, or register at the same hotel? Why do you insult the intelligence of the world by calling yourself a democracy when twenty million of your people are forced because of the accident of skin coloration to live in slums and eat inferior food and go to inferior schools and work at inferior jobs? Is this what you mean when you say that in a democracy the individual must be given every opportunity to develop himself and to fulfill his highest potential? Those are just words. Stupid, dishonest words, and you do no credit to yourself when you say them."

The principal stood up and once again started to reprimand the student when I asked that he be allowed to complete his statement.

"I am grateful to you for your courtesy," the student said, "but I want you to know how I feel. Everyone of us sitting here feels the same way about your wicked and cruel race prejudice in the United States" — loud applause from the audience — "and every time we read about a lynching or about that very distinguished American, Ralph Bunche, not accepting a high position in the American State Department because he would have to live in Washington, where he would have to stay out of the best hotels and restaurants and accept the status of an inferior person in the very capital of the country he was called upon to serve — when we read about this, we shake our heads, sadly, then we shake our fists, because what you do is not only an insult to a great human being like Mr. Bunche, but a direct insult to all people in the world who do not happen to have white skins like yourself.

"Often we read about members of our Government and their families who have gone to the United States on official business and how they are openly insulted in the streets by ignorant and evil Americans and how they are turned away from hotels or deprived of seats in public transportation carriers or made to feel inferior. The chairman speaks of hospitality. You are entitled to it. But no country in the world offends the others with its lack of hospitality as does America. We are fully aware of the embarrassment felt by our people when they visit your so-called great democracy.

"Well, we will tell you one thing. We are not inferior. There is the entire Moslem world that is involved in this. And there are the peoples of India and China and Indonesia and Japan and South America. One day you are going to discover that you and your stupid prejudices are alone in the world and that the overwhelming majority of the world's peoples have decided that they have put up long enough with your fancy talk of superiority and your fancy airs and your evil discriminations."

The atmosphere in the small auditorium seemed supercharged. Under the whiplash of the student's emotional outburst the audience was being transformed into an angry entity. He had touched off something powerful and harsh in the group, producing a mass countenance of vengeful bitterness. The principal saw it and moved quickly to head it off.

"A question period is for questions," he said strongly. "If you have a question, ask it, but no speeches."

"I intended what I said to be a question," the student said. "Does the speaker deny that race discrimination and prejudice exist in the United States, and if so, how does he reconcile it with his general statements about democracy in America?"

The student sat down and smiled triumphantly in response to the murmuring approval of his fellows. Though the majority of the students may not have agreed with the tone and temper of his remarks, they seemed to be generally sympathetic to his basic argument. This did not surprise me. By the time I came to Lahore I had spoken perhaps fifty times at various public meetings in the Far East. And each time I had spoken, without exception, the issue of race prejudice in the United States came up. Out of the countless hundreds of questions that were asked me everywhere this was by all odds the one asked most frequently. Indeed, you could almost count on it to lead off any general question period, no matter what the particular subject matter of the talk happened to be. If I spoke about education in the United States or about journalism or about books or about American foreign policy, the first question was apt to be about lynchings or segregation. Nor did the auspices under which I spoke make much difference. Whether it was a gathering of conservative businessmen at a Rotary session in Bombay, or a small meeting of Government officials in New Delhi, or a conference of editors, writers, and publishers in Calcutta, or a teachers' college for women, or a convention of theologians, the question unfailingly came up. Generally, of course, it would be asked with far more tact and moderation than had just been shown by the young Lahore student, but it was just as deep and insistent.

Before leaving the United States I had been warned that this was something I could expect to encounter almost everywhere I went, but not until I had to contend with it day after day was I able to comprehend how strong and basic it is in the thinking of the Eastern people. I had thought from what I had read that our identification with the British in Asia or our own Far Eastern foreign policy would be the chief targets of criticism. These were of concern, certainly, but they were small matters compared to the criticism against us on color grounds. You were conscious of it in almost everything that happened. Day after day the local newspapers would play it up prominently on the front pages. Frequently the news would be distorted or exaggerated, and sometimes news items ostensibly having nothing to do with the problem of the Negro in America would carry some strained reference to it. The question would come up in polite and sometimes not-so-polite conversation. People seemed to have all the details about the exclusion of a colored applicant from a Southern university the day before, or the complete account of what happened when Indian or Pakistan individuals appearing in American public thoroughfares in their own national dress were insulted or accosted as freaks or dangerous foreigners. Not infrequently these critics claimed a great deal more information about the color problem than actually existed.

I was astounded at the weird misconceptions of the nature and extent of the color problem in America. It was not unusual to find well-educated persons thinking in terms of the problem as it existed perhaps fifty years ago, making generalizations about the whole of the United States that were only true regionally.

It should be obvious, of course, that color is the biggest telling point in Communist propaganda against America. The revolution in Asia today takes different forms in different places, compounded generally of the struggle for freedom from outside domination, of the longing for basic justice and opportunity, of the so-far losing fight against disease and enfeeblement. But through it all runs something constant and powerful. It is the quest for self-respect, a revolution of pride. It is the deep determination to end the Age of Indignity. This is a mighty and growing natural force which the Communists are putting to their own use. Forget everything else the Communists are doing or saying about us in their propaganda. Forget for the moment about the charges of atomic diplomacy, war-mongering, aggression, and all the other stereotyped nonsense. All this is easily enough answered. The one argument we have yet to meet effectively is the one that touches Asian peoples where they are most sensitive and where they have a personal sense of involvement. Color.

I should have been very much surprised, for example, if there was no direct connection between the patent pro-Soviet feeling of the Lahore student and his mountainous resentment against America on color grounds. One might suppose that the natural antagonism between Communism and the deeply felt religion of the Moslems would act as a bar to Communist propaganda activity. Yet in Pakistan I found a surprising disposition in some quarters to accept at face value many of the rosy interpretations of life and politics in the Soviet Union, with a corresponding tendency to believe the worst about America. Behind these attitudes was usually the conviction that the Soviet was the champion of equality while the United States was the global headquarters of race prejudice.

What do we say when we are confronted with these attitudes and arguments? In my own case, during the early part of my trip I think I made a serious mistake in attempting an answer. I think I was overly circumspect, overly cautious and diplomatic, overly concerned about stepping on sensitive toes. After a while, however, I realized I would have to be completely direct and blunt, almost to the point of seeming militant. By the time I got to Lahore I was pretty well tuned up for the challenge.

I began in my reply by saying that, certainly, race prejudice exists in the United States and is a serious problem there. Having said that, it was important to make a distinction between the problem as it actually existed and the problem as presented by Soviet propaganda and as generally reported in the press, not excluding the influential *Times* of Pakistan. The condition of the American Negro was bad enough, but it did not even remotely resemble the deliberate exaggerations and distortions that were concocted for propaganda purposes and that were, unfortunately, so widely accepted.

Yes, race prejudice existed, I said, but did the students suppose that nothing was being done about it? Did they suppose that the overwhelming majority of the American people were not aware of the problem and were doing nothing about it? Did they know anything about the work of such organizations as the National Association for the Advancement of Colored People under Walter White, a Negro himself and one of the most respected and influential American citizens? Were they familiar with the reports of the NAACP, which made it clear that greater progress had been made in the past fifteen years than in the previous fifty? Were they aware of inspiring advances which indicated that America was well on its way towards eliminating the evil of segregation? A slow but steady integration was taking place — without widespread violence. Educational opportunities were increasingly in evidence. Many states had prescribed penalties against job discrimination on racial grounds. The hideous denial of the ballot box to colored American citizens was being abolished. In town after town throughout the South Negroes were being elected and appointed to public office. Old taboos against Negroes in professional sports were practically extinct. The nation's finest prize-fighters were Negroes. In baseball the man who was probably the most popular player in the game today was a Negro. In literature, science, philosophy, religion, music, the dance, Negroes were making outstanding contributions and enjoyed the esteem of their fellow-Americans.

Now this progress wasn't fast enough or deep enough — admittedly — and it could never be fast enough to suit many millions of Americans who were aware of the challenge and who had been working for many years to meet it and who would not be content until it was completely solved. But the important thing was that they *were* at work on it, that historic progress was being made. The important thing, too, was that the Government itself was not a party to the crime or the party behind the crime, as happened in Germany with respect to race and religious prejudice under Nazism. Indeed, the executive branch of the American Government had been in the role of prodder to get action by Congress and the States in removing racial barriers.

But the problem of prejudice, I went on, was not a uniquely American problem. It was a human problem. It existed inside people. It was the problem of inferiority and superiority. It was that corrupting and corroding experience that took place inside a person when he arrogated to himself certain privileges which he denied to others on the basis of what he liked to think were nature's own laws. I was deeply disheartened, for example, by the prejudice and discrimination I had seen on the Indian subcontinent. In the leading hotels of Bombay, owned and operated by Indians, was posted the sign, "South Africans Not Admitted." Among Indians themselves, I frequently found discrimination according to color and caste as severe as any I had observed in the United States. National laws had been passed against the inequities of Untouchability, yet many of the evils persisted. What was worse, many of the Untouchables were willing parties to the social contract of prejudice. In Pakistan, and I hoped that those present would correct me if I was wrong, I had found evidence of religious intolerance and prejudice. This was nothing official, so far as either state or theology was concerned, but it was there just the same. There was an unfortunate attitude of superiority of religion that inevitably made for prejudice. So far as minorities were concerned, there was a distinct prejudice against Sikhs.

I brought this up not by way of admonition, nor even by way of using the glass-house theory to obtain immunity from criticism. I brought this up only by way of indicating that the problem of prejudice knew no national boundaries. To a large extent it was a common problem. Perhaps all peoples working together inside the United Nations might be able to contribute to the self-understanding that would have to go into the making of any basic attack on the problem of prejudice — racial, social, religious, economic, political. Perhaps such a common effort might be more constructive than the destructive and often ill-informed criticism that served only to enlarge misunderstanding and therefore prejudice.

This was my attempt at an answer which would be neither apologetic nor self-righteous. I was gratified by the response of the students, especially when it led to a friendly post-lecture discussion with the student who had asked the question in the first place. He said he was satisfied with the answer but felt that we were at fault for not making our story known all over the world.

There was certainly no argument about that.

[1951]

The Frontier Impulse

In 1536, after eight years spent wandering through the Middle, South, and Far West, the Spanish explorer Cabeza de Vaca wrote: "We ever held it certain that going toward the sunset we would find what we desired." They never did find what they desired, but the hope they expressed would not die. As Henry David Thoreau observed more than three hundred years later, the myth of Eldorado gave form and meaning to countless American lives.

The opening pieces in this section set the frontier myth. Captain John Smith promises a new life and Vachel Lindsay and James Fenimore Cooper raise this promise to legendary status. It is possible for man to be reborn, they seem to say; it is possible for him to be an Adam in the New World. But is it? Cooper sadly faces the inevitability of the demise of "nature's nobleman," and Miller sees the myth begin to disappear in the light of reality.

More hopefully, Thoreau and Whitman assert that the frontier can be mental and spiritual as well as geographical and cultural: Eldorado is in the mind. Both are concerned with the metaphysical basis of man's restlessness; both seek the significance of his westering search.

If the frontier can be an optimistic dream in fancy, it can also be a harsh reality in fact, a reality of man's desperate struggle with a new and inhospitable country. What is the human product of such an environment? Is man on the frontier degraded or ennobled by his surroundings? Some of the many views in this matter are presented in the selections by Timothy Dwight, Timothy Flint and Clarence King.

Today the frontier is gone, says historian Walter Prescott Webb; and John Steinbeck and Wayne Kernodle sadly agree. What now? Heinz Haber's space frontier? If so, the words of Marlowe's Tamburlaine continue to speak across the centuries:

> Nature that fram'd us of four elements,
> Warring within our breasts for regiment,
> Doth teach us all to have aspiring minds.
> Our souls, whose faculties can comprehend
> The wondrous architecture of the world
> And measure every wand'ring planet's course,
> Still climbing after knowledge infinite
> And always moving as the restless spheres,
> Wills us to wear ourselves, and never rest. . . .

The aspiring spirit of Renaissance man which we see in Captain John Smith today finds expression at Cape Canaveral.

The Myth

A Call for Americans   JOHN SMITH

One of the first "Americans," Captain John Smith (1579–1631) sailed
to Virginia in 1606. Here at Jamestown occurred his famous Pocahontas
adventure which has given him a permanent place in American legend.
Smith's later expeditions to the area he named New England provided
him with the information he needed to write *A Description of New
England* (1616), from which "A Call for Americans" is taken. Though
the Massachusetts Puritans found the maps of this book helpful, they
rather bluntly declined Smith's offer to lead the group to New England.
Smith does include some specific facts about life in the New World
in this passage, but his main argument is emotional as he emphasizes the
fascination of a new life on a new continent — the dream which for later
Americans was to have such a persistent appeal. In effect, like later
writers, he provides a "myth" to justify leaving home. At the same time
that he argues for emigration, however, he manages to remain a patriotic
Englishman. Smith belittled his writing ability, referring to his "rude,
military hand"; nevertheless his style often reflects the Elizabethan's love
of classical allusion, antithesis and balance.

". . . Then, who would live at home idly . . . ?"

Who can desire more content, that hath small meanes; or but only his merit
to advance his fortune, than to tread and plant that ground hee hath purchased
by the hazard of his life? If he have but the taste of virtue and magnanimitie,
what to such a minde can bee more pleasant than planting and building a
foundation for his Posteritie, gotte from the rude earth, by Gods Blessing and
his owne industrie, without prejudice to any? If hee have any graine of faith
or zeale in Religion, what can hee doe lesse hurtfull to any: or more agreeable
to God than to seeke to convert those poore Salvages to know Christ, and
humanitie, whose labors with discretion will triple requite thy charge and
paines? What so truely suites with honour and honestie, as the discovering
things unknowne? erecting Townes, peopling Countries, informing the ignorant, reforming things unjust, teaching virtue; and gaine to our Native mother-
countrie a kingdom to attend her: find imployment for those that are idle,
because they know not what to doe: so farre from wronging any, as to cause
Posteritie to remember thee; and remembering thee, ever honour that remembrance with praise?
Consider: What were the beginnings and endings of the Monarkies of

the *Chaldeans,* the *Syrians,* the *Grecians,* and *Romanes,* but this one rule: What was it they would not doe for the good of the commonwealth or their Mother-citie? For example: *Rome,* What made her such a Monarchesse, but onely the adventures of her youth, not in riots at home, but in dangers abroade? and the justice and judgement out of their experience when they grewe aged. What their ruine and hurt but this: The excesse of idlenesse, the fondnesse of Parents, the want of experience in Magistrates, the admiration of their unde-served honours, the contempt of true merit, their unjust jealousies, their poli-ticke incredulities, their hypocriticall seeming goodnesse, and their deeds of secret lewdnesse? finally, in fine, growing onely formall temporists, all that their predecessors got in many years, they lost in a few daies. Those by their pain and vertues became Lords of the world; they by their ease and vices be-came slaves to their servants. This is the difference betwixt the use of Armes in the field and on the monuments of stones, the golden age and the leaden age, prosperitie and miserie, justice and corruption, substance and shadowes, words and deeds, experience and imagination, making Commonwealths and marring Commonwealths, the fruits of vertue and the conclusions of vice.

Then, who would live at home idly (or thinke in himselfe any worth to live) onely to eate, drink, and sleepe, and so die? Or by consuming that care-lesly [which] his friends got worthily? Or by using that miserably, that main-tained vertue honestly? Or for being descended nobly, pine with the vaine vaunt of great kindred, in penurie? Or (to maintaine a silly shewe of bravery) toyle out thy heart, soule, and time, basely; by shifts, tricks, cards, and dice? Or by relating newes of others' actions, sharke here or there for a dinner or supper; deceive thy friends by faire promises and dissimulation, in borrowing where thou never intendest to pay; offend the lawes, surfeit with excesse, burden thy Country, abuse thy selfe, despaire in want, and then couzen thy kindred, yea even thine owne brother, and wish thy parents death (I will not say damnation) to have their estates? though thou seest what honours and rewards the world hath yet for them [who] will seeke them and worthily deserve them. . . .

And lest any should think the toile might be insupportable, though these things may be had by labour and diligence, I assure my selfe there are [those] who delight extreamly in vaine pleasure, that take much more paines in *England* to enjoy it than I should doe heere [in *New England*] to gaine wealth sufficient; and yet I thinke they should not have halfe such sweet content, for our pleasure here is still gaines: in *England* charges and losse. Heer nature and liberty affords us that freely which in *England* we want or it costeth us dearely. What pleasure can be more than (being tired with any occasion a-shore, in planting Vines, Fruits, or Hearbs, in contriving their owne Grounds, to the pleasure of their owne mindes, their Fields, Gardens, Orchards, Buildings, Ships, and other works, &c.) to recreate themselves before their owne doores, in their owne boates upon the Sea, where man, woman and childe, with a small hooke and line, by angling, may take diverse sorts of excellent fish at their pleasures? And is it not pretty sport to pull up two pence, six pence, and twelve pence as fast as you can haule and veare a line? He is a very bad fisher [that] cannot kill in one day with his hooke and line, one, two, or three hundred Cods: which dressed and dried, if they be sould there for ten shillings the hundred, though in England they will give more than twentie, may not both the servant, the master, and marchant be well content with this gaine? If a man worke but three days in seaven, he may get more than hee can spend, unlesse he will be excessive. Now that Carpenter, Mason, Gardiner, Taylor, Smith, Sailer, Forgers, or what other, may they not make this a pretty recreation though they fish but an houre in a day, to take more than they eate in a weeke? or if they will not eate it, because there is so much better choice, yet sell it, or [ex]change it with the fisher men or marchants for any thing they want. And what sport doth yeeld a more pleasing content and lesse hurt or charge than angling with a hooke, and crossing the sweet ayre from Ile to Ile over the silent streames of a calme Sea? Wherein the most curious may find pleasure, profit, and content.

Thus, though all men be not fishers, yet all men, whatsoever, may in other matters doe as well. For necessity doth in these cases so rule a Commonwealth, and each in their severall functions, as their labors in their qualities may be as profitable, because there is a necessary mutuall use of all.

For Gentlemen, what exercise should more delight them than ranging dayly those unknowne parts, using fowling and fishing, for hunting and hawking? and yet you shall see the wilde-haukes give you some pleasure, in seeing them stoope (six or seaven after one another) an houre or two together, at the skuls of fish in the faire harbours, as those a-shore at a foule; and never trouble nor torment yourselves with watching, mewing, feeding, and attending them: nor kill horse and man with running and crying, *See you not a hawk?* For hunting also: the woods, lakes, and rivers affoord not onely chase sufficient for any that delights in that kind of toyle or pleasure; but such beasts to hunt, that besides the delicacy of their bodies for food, their skins are so rich as may well recompence thy dayly labour with a Captain's pay.

For labourers, if those that sowe hemp, rape, turnups, carrats, cabidge, and such like give 20, 30, 40, 50 shillings yearely for an acre of ground, and meat, drinke and wages to use it, and yet grow rich; when better, at least as good ground, may be had and cost nothing but labour, it seems strange to me any such should there grow poore.

My purpose is not to perswade children from their parents; men from their wives; nor servants from their masters: onely such as with free consent may be spared: But that each parish or village, in Citie or Countrey, that will but apparell their fatherlesse children, of thirteen or fourteen years of age, or young married people that have small wealth to live on; heere by their labour may live exceeding well: provided alwaies that first there bee a sufficient power to command them, houses to receive them, meanes to defend them, and meet provisions for them; for any place may be overlain: and it is most necessarie to have a fortresse (ere this grow to practice) and sufficient masters (as Carpenters, Masons, Fishers, Fowlers, Gardiners, Husbandmen, Sawyers, Smiths, Spinsters, Taylors, Weavers, and such like) to take ten, twelve, or twentie, or as ther is occasion, for Apprentises. The Masters by this may quicklie growe rich; these may learne their trades themselves to doe the like, to a generall and an incredible benefit for King and Countrey, Master and Servant.

[1616]

Over the Appalachian Barricade   VACHEL LINDSAY

When he was twenty-six Vachel Lindsay (1879–1931) set out on a vagabond tour through the American West, reciting his poems for food and lodging and distributing his *Rhymes To Be Traded for Bread* (1912). Throughout the remainder of his life he continued in the role of the troubadour, wanderer, evangelist of culture. Such well-known poems as "The Congo" and "General William Booth Enters Heaven" caused him to be known as "the jazz Blake, St. Francis of Assisi playing the saxophone at the Fireman's Ball." At his best Lindsay strikes a conventional-unconventional note that is still exciting to the American ear — particularly when his poems are chanted, as their author intended them to be. "Over the Appalachian Barricade" is Part I of "In Praise of Johnny Appleseed" (1921).

The romantic appeal of pioneer life is epitomized in Lindsay's free-verse characterization of John Chapman, who became the legendary Johnny Appleseed. With a sequence of images to give structure to his poem, Lindsay illustrates the transforming effect of "crossing the Appalachians." The transformed Chapman is hardly a realistic frontiersman, for Lindsay is attempting to portray something more than the exploits of an eccentric pioneer.

> "*...The glory of the nations ...*
> *Crossed the Appalachians. ...*"

In the days of President Washington,	*To be read like old leaves*
The glory of the nations,	*on the elm tree of Time.*
Dust and ashes,	*Sifting soft winds with*
Snow and sleet,	*sentence and rhyme.*
And hay and oats and wheat,	5
Blew west,	
Crossed the Appalachians,	
Found the glades of rotting leaves, the soft deer-pastures,	
The farms of the far-off future	
In the forest.	10
Colts jumped the fence,	
Snorting, ramping, snapping, sniffing,	
With gastronomic calculations,	
Crossed the Appalachians,	
The east walls of our citadel	15
And turned to gold-horned unicorns,	
Feasting in the dim, volunteer farms of the forest.	
Stripedest, kickingest kittens escaped,	
Caterwauling "Yankee Doodle Dandy,"	

Renounced their poor relations,   20
Crossed the Appalachians,
And turned to tiny tigers
In the humorous forest.
Chickens escaped
From farmyard congregations,   25
Crossed the Appalachians,
And turned to amber trumpets
On the ramparts of our Hoosiers' nest and citadel,
Millennial heralds
Of the foggy mazy forest.   30
Pigs broke loose, scrambled west,
Scorned their loathsome stations,
Crossed the Appalachians,
Turned to roaming, foaming wild boars
Of the forest.   35
The smallest, blindest puppies toddled west
While their eyes were coming open,
And, with misty observations,
Crossed the Appalachians,
Barked, barked, barked   40
At the glow-worms and the marsh lights and the lightning-bugs
And turned to ravening wolves
Of the forest.
Crazy parrots and canaries flew west,
Drunk on May-time revelations,   45
Crossed the Appalachians,
And turned to delirious, flower-dressed fairies
Of the lazy forest.
Haughtiest swans and peacocks swept west,
And, despite soft derivations,   50
Crossed the Appalachians,
And turned to blazing warrior souls
Of the forest,
Singing the ways
Of the Ancient of Days.   55
And the "Old Continentals
In their ragged regimentals,"
With bard's imaginations,
Crossed the Appalachians.
And   60
A boy
Blew west,
And with prayers and incantations,
And with "Yankee Doodle Dandy,"
Crossed the Appalachians,   65
And was "young John Chapman,"
Then

"Johnny Appleseed, Johnny Appleseed,"
Chief of the fastnesses, dappled and vast,
In a pack on his back,   70
In a deer-hide sack,
The beautiful orchards of the past,
The ghosts of all the forests and the groves —
In that pack on his back
In that talisman sack,   75
Tomorrow's peaches, pears, and cherries,
Tomorrow's grapes and red raspberries,
Seeds and tree-souls, precious things,
Feathered with miscroscopic wings,
All the outdoors and the child heart knows,   80
And the apple, green, red, and white,
Sun of his day and his night —
The apple allied to the thorn,
Child of the rose.
Porches untrod of forest houses   85
All before him, all day long,
"Yankee Doodle" his marching song;
And the evening breeze
Joined his psalms of praise
As he sang the ways   90
Of the Ancient of Days.
Leaving behind august Virginia,
Proud Massachusetts, and proud Maine,
Planting the trees that would march and train
On, in his name to the great Pacific,   95
Like Birnam wood to Dunsinane,
Johnny Appleseed swept on,
Every shackle gone,
Loving every sloshy brake,
Loving every skunk and snake,   100
Loving every leathery weed,
Johnny Appleseed, Johnny Appleseed,
Master and ruler of the unicorn-ramping forest,
The tiger-mewing forest,
The rooster-trumpeting, boar-foaming, wolf-ravening forest, 105
The spirit-haunted forest, fair-enchanted,
Stupendous and endless,
Searching its perilous ways
In the name of the Ancient of Days.

                                                          [1921]

The Life and Death of Leatherstocking   JAMES FENIMORE COOPER

James Fenimore Cooper (1789–1851) grew up in the then wilderness of
Otsego Lake, New York, becoming familiar with the places and persons
that later figured so largely in his novels. These novels, incidentally, he
began writing when, in 1819, reading an English work aloud to his wife,
he remarked, "I could write you a better book myself." During the remaining half of his life Cooper steadily turned out the books which make
him the first major American fiction writer. The following sequence,
taken from four novels in the Leatherstocking Series (Cooper's most
substantial achievement), describes some characteristic actions and attitudes of the hero — variously named Leatherstocking, Deerslayer, Hawk-
eye, Pathfinder, and Natty Bumppo.

Despite some obvious weaknesses, the characterization of Leather-
stocking is impressive. In *The Deerslayer* (1841) he is in his early
twenties, as yet unformed but already more than life size, contrasting
sharply with his companion, the "real" frontiersman. In his later career
of some sixty years we see him as a kind of "American Adam" moving
symbolically from Lake Otsego to the Western plains. In the preface to
The Pathfinder (1840) Cooper writes of "the wonderful means by which
Providence is clearing the way for the advancement of civilization across
the whole American continent." Leatherstocking is memorable as the
representative of the advance wave of the western impulse. But the noble
son of nature cannot survive the second wave: the hunter-pathfinder is
inevitably succeeded by the settler-plowman. Although Cooper's stilted
diction and conventional characters are often distracting, his work has an
imaginative power that makes these flaws seem relatively minor.

". . . The figure was colossal. . . ."

[THE YOUNG DEERSLAYER]

Deerslayer, as Hurry called his companion, was a very different person in
appearance, as well as in character. In stature he stood about six feet in his
moccasins, but his frame was comparatively light and slender, showing
muscles, however, that promised unusual agility, if not unusual strength.
His face would have had little to recommend it except youth, were it not for
an expression that seldom failed to win upon those who had leisure to examine
it, and to yield to the feeling of confidence it created. This expression was
simply that of guileless truth, sustained by an earnestness of purpose, and a
sincerity of feeling, that rendered it remarkable. At times this air of integrity
seemed to be so simple as to awaken the suspicion of a want of the usual
means to discriminate between artifice and truth; but few came in serious
contact with the man, without losing this distrust in respect for his opinions
and motives.

Both these frontiermen were still young, Hurry having reached the age
of six or eight and twenty, while Deerslayer was several years his junior.
Their attire needs no particular description, though it may be well to add that

it was composed in no small degree of dressed deer-skins, and had the usual signs of belonging to those who pass their time between the skirts of civilized society and the boundless forests. There was, notwithstanding, some attention to smartness and the picturesque in the arrangements of Deerslayer's dress, more particularly in the part connected with his arms and accoutrements. His rifle was in perfect condition, the handle of his hunting-knife was neatly carved, his powder-horn was ornamented with suitable devices lightly cut into the material, and his shot-pouch was decorated with wampum. On the other hand, Hurry Harry, either from constitutional recklessness, or from a secret consciousness how little his appearance required artificial aids, wore everything in a careless, slovenly manner, as if he felt a noble scorn for the trifling accessories of dress and ornaments. Perhaps the peculiar effect of his fine form and great stature was increased rather than lessened, by this un-studied and disdainful air of indifference.

"Come, Deerslayer, fall to, and prove that you have a Delaware stomach, as you say you have had a Delaware edication," cried Hurry, setting the example by opening his mouth to receive a slice of cold venison steak that would have made an entire meal for a European peasant; "fall to, lad, and prove your manhood on this poor devil of a doe with your teeth, as you've already done with your rifle."

"Nay, nay, Hurry, there's little manhood in killing a doe, and that too out of season; though there might be some in bringing down a painter or a catamount," returned the other, disposing himself to comply. "The Delawares have given me my name, not so much on account of a bold heart, as on account of a quick eye, and an actyve foot. There may not be any cowardyce in over-coming a deer, but sartain it is, there 's no great valor." . . .

"The Delawares themselves are no heroes," muttered Hurry through his teeth, the mouth being too full to permit it to be fairly opened, "or they would never have allowed them loping vagabonds, the Mingos, to make them women."

"That matter is not rightly understood — has never been rightly explained," said Deerslayer earnestly, for he was as zealous a friend as his companion was dangerous as an enemy; "the Mengwe fill the woods with their lies, and mis-construct words and treaties. I have now lived ten years with the Delawares, and know them to be as manful as any other nation, when the proper time to strike comes."

"Harkee, Master Deerslayer, since we are on the subject we may as well open our minds to each other in a man-to-man way; answer me one question; you have had so much luck among the game as to have gotten a title, it would seem, but did you ever hit anything human or intelligible: did you ever pull trigger on an inimy that was capable of pulling one upon you?"

This question produced a singular collision between mortification and correct feeling, in the bosom of the youth, that was easily to be traced in the workings of his ingenuous countenance. The struggle was short, however; uprightness of heart soon getting the better of false pride and frontier boast-fulness.

"To own the truth, I never did," answered Deerslayer; "seeing that a fitting occasion never offered. The Delawares have been peaceable since my sojourn with 'em, and I hold it to be onlawful to take the life of man, except in open and generous warfare."

"What! did you never find a fellow thieving among your traps and skins, and do the law on him with your own hands, by way of saving the magistrates trouble in the settlements, and the rogue himself the cost of the suit?"

"I am no trapper, Hurry," returned the young man proudly: "I live by the rifle, a we'pon at which I will not turn my back on any man of my years, atween the Hudson and the St. Lawrence. I never offer a skin that has not a hole in its head besides them which natur' made to see with or to breathe through."

[*The Deerslayer* 1841]

[THE PATHFINDER: A SORT OF ADAM]

Few knew the Pathfinder intimately without secretly coming to believe him to be one of extraordinary qualities. Ever the same, simple-minded, faithful, utterly without fear, and yet prudent, foremost in all warrantable enterprises, or what the opinion of the day considered as such, and never engaged in anything to call a blush to his cheek, or censure on his acts; it was not possible to live much with this being, who, in his peculiar way, was a sort of type of what Adam might have been supposed to be before the fall, though certainly not without sin, and not feel a respect and admiration for him, that had no reference to his position in life. It was remarked that no officer passed him without saluting him as if he had been his equal; no common man, without addressing him with the confidence and freedom of a comrade. The most surprising peculiarity about the man himself, was the entire indifference with which he regarded all distinctions that did not depend on personal merit. He was respectful to his superiors from habit, but had often been known to correct their mistakes and to reprove their vices, with a fearlessness that proved how essentially he regarded the more material points, and with a natural discrimination that appeared to set education at defiance. In short, a disbeliever in the ability of man to distinguish between good and evil without the aid of instruction, would have been staggered by the character of this extraordinary inhabitant of the frontier. His feelings appeared to possess the freshness and nature of the forest in which he passed so much of his time, and no casuist could have made clearer decisions in matters relating to right and wrong; yet he was not without his prejudices, which, though few, and colored by the character and usages of the individual, were deep-rooted, and had almost got to form a part of his nature. But the most striking feature about the moral organization of Pathfinder, was his beautiful and unerring sense of justice. This noble trait (and without it no man can be truly great; with it, no man other than respectable) probably had its unseen influence on all who associated with him; for the common and unprincipled brawler of the camp had been known to return from an expedition made in his company, rebuked by his sentiments, softened by his language, and improved by his example. As might have been expected, with so elevated a quality, his fidelity was like the immovable rock. Treachery in him was classed among the things that are impossible, and as he seldom retired before his enemies, so was he never known, under any circumstances that admitted of an alternative, to abandon a friend. The affinities of such a character were, as a matter of course, those of like for like. His associates and intimates, though more or less determined by chance, were generally of the highest order, as to moral propensities; for he appeared to possess a species of instinctive discrimination that led him insensibly to himself, most probably, to cling closest to those whose characters would best reward his friendship. In short, it was said of the Pathfinder, by one accustomed to study his fellows, that he was a fair example of what a just-minded and pure man might be, while untempted by unruly or ambitious desires, and let to follow the bias of his feelings, amid the solitary grandeur and ennobling influences of a sublime nature; neither led aside by the inducements which influence all to do evil amid the incentives of civilization, nor forgetful of the Almighty Being, whose spirit pervades the wilderness as well as the towns.

[*The Pathfinder*   1840]

[CIVILIZATION'S MARCH]

[The "pigeon-roosts" of the South had broken up, and "a flock that the eye cannot see the end of" passes northward over the frontier village.]

If the heavens were alive with pigeons, the whole village seemed equally in motion, with men, women, and children. Every species of fire-arms, from the French ducking-gun with a barrel near six feet in length, to the common horseman's pistol, was to be seen in the hands of the men and boys; while bows and arrows, some made of the simple stick of a walnut sapling, and others in a rude imitation of the ancient cross-bows, were carried by many of the latter.

The houses and the signs of life apparent in the village, drove the alarmed birds from the direct line of their flight towards the mountains, along the sides and near the bases of which they were glancing in dense masses, equally wonderful by the rapidity of their motion, and their incredible numbers.

We have already said, that across the inclined plane which fell from the steep ascent of the mountain to the banks of the Susquehanna, ran the highway, on either side of which a clearing of many acres had been made at a very early day. Over those clearings, and up the eastern mountain, and along the dangerous path that was cut into its side, the different individuals posted themselves, and in a few moments the attack commenced.

Among the sportsmen was the tall, gaunt form of Leather-stocking walking over the field, with his rifle hanging on his arm, his dogs at his heels; the latter now scenting the dead or wounded birds, that were beginning to tumble from the flocks and then crouching under the legs of their master, as if they participated in his feelings at this wasteful and unsportsmanlike execution.

The reports of the fire-arms became rapid, whole volleys rising from the plain, as flocks of more than ordinary numbers darted over the opening, shadowing the field like a cloud; and then the light smoke of a single piece would issue from among the leafless bushes on the mountain, as death was hurled on the retreat of the affrighted birds, who were rising from a volley, in a vain effort to escape. Arrows, and missiles of every kind were in the midst of the flocks; and so numerous were the birds, and so low did they take their flight, that even long poles, in the hands of those on the sides of the mountain, were used to strike them to the earth. . . .

So prodigious was the number of the birds, that the scattering fire of the guns, with the hurling of missiles, and the cries of the boys, had no other effect than to break off small flocks from the immense masses that continued to dart along the valley, as if the whole of the feathered tribe were pouring through that one pass. None pretended to collect the game, which lay scattered over the fields in such profusion as to cover the very ground with the fluttering victims.

Leather-stocking was a silent, but uneasy spectator of all these proceedings, but was able to keep his sentiments to himself until he saw the introduction of the swivel into the sports.

"This comes of settling a country!" he said; "here have I known the pigeons to fly for forty long years, and, till you made your clearings, there was nobody to skear or to hurt them. I loved to see them come in the woods, for they were company to a body; hurting nothing; being, as it was, as harmless as a garter-snake. But now it gives me sore thoughts when I hear the frighty things whizzing through the air, for I know it's only a motion to bring out all the brats in the village. Well! the Lord won't see the waste of his creatures for nothing, and right will be done to the pigeons, as well as others, by and by. There's Mr. Oliver, as bad as the rest of them, firing into the flocks, as if he was shooting down nothing but Mingo warriors."

Among the sportsmen was Billy Kirby, who, armed with an old musket, was loading, and without even looking into the air, was firing and shouting as his victims fell even on his own person. He heard the speech of Natty, and took upon himself to reply —

"What! old Leather-stocking," he cried, "grumbling at the loss of a few pigeons! If you had to sow your wheat twice, and three times, as I have done, you wouldn't be so massyfully feeling toward the divils. — Hurrah, boys! scatter the feathers! This is better than shooting at a turkey's head and neck, old fellow."

"It's better for you, maybe, Billy Kirby," replied the indignant old hunter, "and all them that don't know how to put a ball down a rifle barrel, or how to bring it up again with a true aim; but it's wicked to be shooting into flocks in this wasty manner; and none do it, who know how to knock over a single bird. If a body has a craving for pigeon's flesh, why, it's made the same as all other creatures, for man's eating; but not to kill twenty and eat one. When I want such a thing I go into the woods till I find one to my liking, and then I shoot him off the branches, without touching the feather of another, though there might be a hundred on the same tree. You couldn't do such a thing, Billy Kirby — you couldn't do it, if you tried."

"What's that, old corn-stalk! you sapless stub!" cried the wood-chopper. "You have grown wordy, since the affair of the turkey; but if you are for a single shot, here goes at that bird which comes on by himself."

The fire from the distant part of the field had driven a single pigeon below the flock to which it belonged, and, frightened with the constant reports of the muskets, it was approaching the spot where the disputants stood, darting first to one side, and then to the other, cutting the air with the swiftness of lightning and making a noise with its wings, not unlike the rushing of a bullet. Unfortunately for the wood-chopper, notwithstanding his vaunt, he did not see this bird until it was too late to fire as it approached, and he pulled his trigger at the unlucky moment when it was darting immediately over his head. The bird continued its course with the usual velocity.

Natty lowered the rifle from his arm when the challenge was made, and waiting for a moment, until the terrified victim had got in a line with his eye, and had dropped near the bank of the lake, he raised it again with uncommon rapidity, and fired. It might have been chance, or it might have been skill, that produced the result; it was probably a union of both; but the pigeon whirled over in the air, and fell into the lake, with a broken wing. At the sound of his rifle, both his dogs started from his feet, and in a few minutes the "slut" brought out the bird still alive.

The wonderful exploit of Leather-stocking was noised through the field with great rapidity, and the sportsmen gathered in, to learn the truth of the report.

"What!" said young Edwards, "have you really killed a pigeon on the wing, Natty, with a single ball?"

"Haven't I killed loons before now, lad, that dive at the flash?" returned the hunter. "It's much better to kill only such as you want, without wasting your powder and lead, than to be firing into God's creatures in this wicked manner. But I came out for a bird, and you know the reason why I like small game, Mr. Oliver, and now I have got one I will go home, for I don't relish to see these wasty ways that you are all practysing, as if the least thing wasn't made for use, and not to destroy."

"Thou sayest well, Leather-stocking," cried Marmaduke, "and I begin to think it time to put an end to this work of destruction."

"Put an ind, Judge, to your clearings. An't the woods His work as well as the pigeons? Use, but don't waste. Wasn't the woods made for the beasts and birds to harbor in? and when man wanted their flesh, their skins, or their feathers, there's the place to seek them. But I'll go to the hut with my own game, for I wouldn't touch one of the harmless things that cover the ground here, looking up with their eyes on me, as if they only wanted tongues to say their thoughts."

With this sentiment in his mouth, Leather-stocking threw his rifle over his arm, and followed by his dogs stepped across the clearing with great caution, taking care not to tread on one of the wounded birds in his path. He soon entered the bushes on the margin of the lake, and was hid from view. . . .

[Natty Bumppo is accused of killing a buck, and when a constable appears at his cabin with a search warrant, he refuses him admittance. The sheriff then gets together a group and returns to the cabin to discover "only its smouldering ruins."]

The party gradually drew together about the heap of ashes and ends of smoking logs, while a dim flame in the centre of the ruin, which still found fuel to feed its lingering life, threw its pale light, flickering with the passing currents of the air, around the circle, now showing a face with eyes fixed in astonishment, and then glancing to another countenance, leaving the former shaded in the obscurity of night. Not a voice was raised in inquiry, nor an exclamation made in astonishment. The transition from excitement to disappointment was too powerful in its effects for speech: and even Richard lost the use of an organ that was seldom known to fail him.

The whole group were yet in the fulness of their surprise, when a tall form stalked from the gloom into the circle, treading down the hot ashes and dying embers with callous feet, and, standing over the light, lifted his cap, and exposed the bare head and weather-beaten features of the Leather-stocking. For a moment he gazed at the dusky figures who surrounded him, more in sorrow than in anger, before he spoke.

"What would ye with an old and helpless man?" he said. "You've driven God's creaters from the wilderness, where his providence had put them for his own pleasure, and you've brought in the troubles and diviltries of the law, where no man was ever known to disturb another. You have driven me, that have lived forty long years of my allotted time in this very spot, from my home and the shelter of my head, least you should put your wicked feet and wasty ways in my cabin. You've driven me to burn these logs, under which I've eaten and drunk, the first of Heaven's gifts, and the other of the pure springs, for the half of a hundred years, and to mourn the ashes under my feet, as a man would weep and mourn for the children of his body. You've rankled the heart of an old man, that has never harmed you or yourn, with bitter feelings towards his kind, at a time when his thoughts should be on a better world; and you've driven him to wish that the beasts of the forest, who never feast on the blood of their own families, was his kindred and race: and now, when he has come to see the last brand of his hut, before it is melted into ashes, you follow him up, at midnight, like hungry hounds on the track of a worn-out and dying deer! What more would ye have? for I am here — one to many. I come to mourn, not to fight; and, if it is God's pleasure, work your will on me."

When the old man ended, he stood, with the light glimmering around his thinly-covered head, looking earnestly at the group, which receded from the pile, with an involuntary movement, without the reach of the quivering rays, leaving a free passage for his retreat into the bushes, where pursuit, in the dark, would have been fruitless. Natty seemed not to regard this advantage, but stood facing each individual in the circle, in succession, as if to see who would be the first to arrest him. After a pause of a few moments, Richard begun to rally his confused faculties, and advancing, apologized for his duty, and made him his prisoner. The party now collected, and, preceded by the Sheriff, with Natty in their centre, they took their way towards the village.

During the walk, divers questions were put to the prisoner concerning his reasons for burning the hut, and whither Mohegan had retreated; but to all of them he observed a profound silence, until, fatigued with their previous duties, and the lateness of the hour, the Sheriff and his followers reached the village, and dispersed to their several places of rest, after turning the key of a gaol on the aged and apparently friendless Leather-stocking.

[*The Pioneers*   1823]

[BEYOND THE BIG RIVER]

[*The Prairie* (1827) completes the story of Leatherstocking. In its first chapter Cooper describes the meeting on the western prairies of the almost ninety-year-old Bumppo and an emigrant wagon train. Already driven from the forests, Natty now sees the unwelcome entry of civilization onto the "hungry prairies" beyond the Mississippi. The year is 1804, "the first year of our possession" of the Louisiana Territory.]

The harvest of the first year of our possession had long been passed, and the fading foliage of a few scattered trees was already beginning to exhibit the hues and tints of Autumn, when a train of wagons issued from the bed of a dry rivulet, to pursue its course across the undulating surface, of what, in the language of the country of which we write, is called a "rolling prairie." The vehicles, loaded with household goods and implements of husbandry, the few straggling sheep and cattle that were herded in the rear, and the rugged appearance and careless mien of the sturdy men who loitered at the sides of the lingering teams, united to announce a band of emigrants seeking for the Eldorado of the West. Contrary to the usual practice of the men of their caste, this party had left the fertile bottoms of the low country, and had found its way, by means only known to such adventurers, across glen and torrent, over deep morasses and arid wastes, to a point far beyond the usual limits of civilized habitations. In their front were stretched those broad plains, which extend, with so little diversity of character, to the bases of the Rocky Mountains; and many long and dreary miles in their rear, foamed the swift and turbid waters of La Platte.

The appearance of such a train in that bleak and solitary place was rendered the more remarkable by the fact, that the surrounding country offered so little that was tempting to the cupidity of speculation, and, if possible, still less that was flattering to the hopes of an ordinary settler of new lands.

The meagre herbage of the prairie promised nothing in favor of a hard and unyielding soil, over which the wheels of the vehicles rattled as lightly as if they travelled on a beaten road; neither wagons nor beasts making any deeper impression than to mark that bruised and withered grass, which the cattle plucked from time to time, and as often rejected, as food too sour for even hunger to render palatable.

Whatever might be the final destination of these adventurers, or the secret causes of their apparent security in so remote and unprotected a situation, there was no visible sign of uneasiness, uncertainty, or alarm, among them. Including both sexes, and every age, the number of the party exceeded twenty.

At some little distance in front of the whole, marched the individual, who, by his position and air, appeared to be the leader of the band. He was a tall, sun-burnt man, past the middle age, of a dull countenance and listless manner. His frame appeared loose and flexible; but it was vast, and in reality of prodigious power. It was only at moments, however, as some slight impediment opposed itself to his loitering progress, that his person, which, in its ordinary gait seemed so lounging and nerveless, displayed any of those energies which lay latent in his system, like the slumbering and unwieldy, but terrible, strength of the elephant. The inferior lineaments of his countenance were coarse, extended, and vacant; while the superior, or those nobler parts which are thought to affect the intellectual being, were low, receding, and mean. . . .

Perhaps there was little in this train, or in the appearance of its proprietors, that is not daily to be encountered on the highways of this changeable and moving country. But the solitary and peculiar scenery, in which it was so unexpectedly exhibited, gave to the party a marked character of wildness and adventure.

In the little valleys, which, in the regular formation of the land, occurred at every mile of their progress, the view was bounded on two of the sides by the gradual and low elevations which give name to the description of prairie we have mentioned; while on the others, the meagre prospect ran off in long, narrow, barren perspectives, but slightly relieved by a pitiful show of coarse, though somewhat luxuriant vegetation. From the summits of the swells, the eye became fatigued with the sameness and chilling dreariness of the landscape. The earth was not unlike the ocean, when its restless waters are heaving heavily, after the agitation and fury of the tempest have begun to lessen. There was the same waving and regular surface, the same absence of foreign objects, and the same boundless extent to the view. Indeed so very striking was the resemblance between the water and the land, that, however much the geologist might sneer at so simple a theory, it would have been difficult for a poet not to have felt, that the formation of the one had been produced by the subsiding dominion of the other. Here and there a tall tree rose out of the bottoms, stretching its naked branches abroad, like some solitary vessel; and, to strengthen the delusion, far in the distance appeared two or three rounded thickets, looming in the misty horizon like islands resting on the waters. It is unnecessary to warn the practised reader, that the sameness of the surface, and the low stands of the spectators, exaggerated the distances; but, as swell appeared after swell, and island succeeded island, there was a disheartening assurance that long and seemingly interminable tracts of territory must be passed, before the wishes of the humblest agriculturist could be realized.

Still, the leader of the emigrants steadily pursued his way, with no other guide than the sun, turning his back resolutely on the abodes of civilization, and plunging at each step more deeply, if not irretrievably into the haunts of the barbarous and savage occupants of the country. As the day drew nigher to a close, however, his mind, which was, perhaps, incapable of maturing any connected system of forethought, beyond that which related to the interests of the present moment, became, in some slight degree troubled with the care of providing for the wants of the hours of darkness.

On reaching the crest of a swell that was a little higher than the usual elevations, he lingered a minute, and cast a half curious eye, on either hand, in quest of those well known signs which might indicate a place where the three grand requisites of water, fuel, and fodder, were to be obtained in conjunction.

It would seem that his search was fruitless; for after a few moments of indolent and listless examination, he suffered his huge frame to descend the gentle declivity, in the same sluggish manner that an over fatted beast would have yielded to the downward pressure.

His example was silently followed by those who succeeded him, though not until the young men had manifested much more of interest, if not of concern, in the brief inquiry, which each in his turn made on gaining the same look-out. It was now evident, by the tardy movements both of beasts and men, that the time of necessary rest was not far distant. The matted grass of the lower land presented obstacles which fatigue began to render formidable, and the whip was becoming necessary to urge the lingering teams to their labor. At this moment, when, with the exception of the principal individual, a general lassitude was getting the mastery of the travellers, and every eye was cast, by a sort of common impulse, wistfully forward, the whole party was brought to a halt, by a spectacle as sudden as it was unexpected.

The sun had fallen below the crest of the nearest wave of the prairie, leaving the usual rich and glowing train on its track. In the centre of this flood of fiery light a human form appeared, drawn against the gilded background as distinctly, and seemingly as palpable, as though it would come within the grasp of any extended hand. The figure was colossal; the attitude musing and melancholy; and the situation directly in the route of the travellers. But imbedded, as it was, in its setting of garish light, it was impossible to distinguish its just proportions or true character.

The effect of such a spectacle was instantaneous and powerful. The man in front of the emigrants came to a stand, and remained gazing at the mysterious object with a dull interest, that soon quickened into superstitious awe. His sons, so soon as the first emotions of surprise had a little abated, drew slowly around him, and as they who governed the teams gradually followed their example, the whole party was soon condensed in one silent and wondering group. . . .

In the meantime the hues of the heavens had often changed. In place of the brightness which had dazzled the eye, a grey and more sober light had succeeded, and as the setting lost its brilliancy, the proportions of the fanciful form became less exaggerated, and finally distinct. Ashamed to hesitate, now that the truth was no longer doubtful, the leader of the party resumed his journey, using the precaution, as he ascended the slight acclivity, to release his own rifle from the strap, and to cast it into a situation more convenient for sudden use.

There was little apparent necessity, however, for such watchfulness. From the moment when it had thus unaccountably appeared, as it were, between the heavens and the earth, the stranger's figure had neither moved nor given the smallest evidence of hostility. Had he harbored any such evil intention, the individual who now came plainly into view seemed but little qualified to execute them.

A frame that had endured the hardships of more than eighty seasons was not qualified to awaken apprehension in the breast of one as powerful as the emigrant. Notwithstanding his years, and his look of emaciation, if not of suffering, there was that about this solitary being, however, which said that time, and not disease, had laid his hand heavily on him. His form had withered, but it was not wasted. The sinews and muscles, which had once denoted great strength, though shrunken, were still visible; and his whole figure had attained an appearance of induration, which, if it were not for

the well known frailty of humanity, would have seemed to bid defiance to
the further approaches of decay. His dress was chiefly of skins, worn with the
hair to the weather; a pouch and horn were suspended from his shoulders;
and he leaned on a rifle of uncommon length, but which, like its owner,
exhibited the wear of long and hard service.

As the party drew nigher to this solitary being, and came within a distance
to be heard, a low growl issued from the grass at his feet, and then a tall,
gaunt, toothless hound arose lazily from his lair, and shaking himself, made
some show of resisting the nearer approach of the travellers.

"Down, Hector, down," said his master, in a voice that was a little tremulous and hollow with age. "What have ye to do, pup, with men who journey
on their lawful callings?"

"Stranger, if you are much acquainted in this country," said the leader of
the emigrants, "can you tell a traveller where he may find necessaries for the
night?"

"Is the land filled on the other side of the Big River?" demanded the old
man solemnly, and without appearing to hearken to the other's question; "or
why do I see a sight I had never thought to behold again?"

"Why, there is country left, it is true, for such as have money, and ar' not
particular in the choice," returned the emigrant; "but to my taste, it is getting
crowdy. What may a man call the distance from this place to the nighest
point on the main river?"

"A hunted deer could not cool his sides in the Mississippi, without travelling a weary five hundred miles."

"And what may you name the district hereaway?"

"By what name," returned the old man, pointing significantly upwards,
"would you call the spot where you see yonder cloud?"

The emigrant looked at the other like one who did not comprehend his
meaning, and who half suspected he was trifled with; but he contented himself by saying —

"You ar' but a new inhabitant, like myself, I reckon, stranger, otherwise
you would not be backward in helping a traveller to some advice; words cost
but little, and sometimes lead to friendships."

"Advice is not a gift, but a debt that the old owe to the young. What
would you wish to know?"

"Where I may 'camp for the night. I'm no great difficulty maker as to bed
and board; but all old journeyers like myself know the virtue of sweet water,
and a good browse for the cattle."

"Come, then, with me, and you shall be master of both; and little more
is it that I can offer on this hungry prairie."

As the old man was speaking, he raised his heavy rifle to his shoulder with
a facility a little remarkable for his years and appearance, and without further
words led the way over the acclivity to the adjacent bottom.

[*The Prairie*   1827]

[At the end of *The Prairie* the dying Leatherstocking is placed "so as to
let the light of the setting sun fall full upon the solemn features." He requests

that his remains not be sent back to the place of his forbears: "Let me sleep where I have lived — beyond the din of the settlements." He dies with his gaze "fastened on the clouds which hung around the western horizon, reflecting the bright colors, giving form and loveliness to the glorious tints of an American sunset."]

Exodus for Oregon   JOAQUIN MILLER

Joaquin Miller (1839–1914) was born in Indiana "in a covered wagon, pointed west." By 1852 the family was in Oregon. In 1855 Miller ran away to mine gold in California and ended up as a cook in a roadhouse. Two years later he had married a squaw and was living with the Modoc Indians. He was still not twenty years old. Back in Oregon again, he attended college, was admitted to the bar, taught school, started a pony express, bought a newspaper, and remarried. 1871 found him in England, where he published his *Songs of the Sierras* to wide acclaim. Though most of Miller's work is now forgotten, he is remembered as a spectacular personality who gave heroic celebration to the great American West.

Miller once said "To me a poem must be a picture"; and "Exodus for Oregon" is probably more notable for its pictures than for such qualities as narrative strength, imaginative insight or the metrical felicity of its Spenserian stanzas.

> *". . . a tale it was of lands of gold*
> *That lay below the sun. . . ."*

A tale half told and hardly understood;
The talk of bearded men that chanced to meet,
That lean'd on long quaint rifles in the wood,
That look'd in fellow faces, spoke discreet
And low, as half in doubt and in defeat   5
Of hope; a tale it was of lands of gold
That lay below the sun. Wild-wing'd and fleet
It spread among the swift Missouri's bold
Unbridled men, and reach'd to where Ohio roll'd.

Then long chain'd lines of yoked and patient steers;   10
Then long white trains that pointed to the west,
Beyond the savage west; the hopes and fears
Of blunt, untutor'd men, who hardly guess'd
Their course; the brave and silent women, dress'd
In homely spun attire, the boys in bands,   15

The cheery babes that laugh'd at all, and bless'd
The doubting hearts, with laughing lifted hands! . . .
What exodus for far untraversed lands!

The Plains! The shouting drivers at the wheel;
The crash of leather whips; the crush and roll   20
Of wheels; the groan of yokes and grinding steel
And iron chain, and lo! at last the whole
Vast line, that reach'd as if to touch the goal,
Began to stretch and stream away and wind
Toward the west as if with one control;   25
Then hope loom'd fair, and home lay far behind;
Before, the boundless plain, and fiercest of their kind.

At first the way lay green and fresh as seas,
And far away as any reach of wave;
The sunny streams went by in belt of trees;   30
And here and there the tassel'd tawny brave
Swept by on horse, look'd back, stretch'd forth and gave
A yell of warn, and then did wheel and rein
Awhile, and point away, dark-brow'd and grave,
Into the far and dim and distant plain   35
With signs and prophecies, and then plunged on again.

Some hills at last began to lift and break;
Some streams began to fail of wood and tide,
The somber plain began betime to take
A hue of weary brown, and wild and wide   40
It stretch'd its naked breast on every side.
A babe was heard at last to cry for bread
Amid the deserts; cattle low'd and died,
And dying men went by with broken tread,
And left a long black serpent line of wreck and dead.   45

Strange hunger'd birds, black-wing'd and still as death,
And crown'd of red with hookèd beaks, blew low
And close about, till we could touch their breath —
Strange unnamed birds, that seem'd to come and go
In circles now, and now direct and slow,   50
Continual, yet never touch the earth;
Slim foxes slid and shuttled to and fro
At times across the dusty weary dearth
Of life, look'd back, then sank like crickets in a hearth.

Then dust arose, a long dim line like smoke   55
From out of riven earth. The wheels went groaning by,
Ten thousand feet in harness and in yoke,
They tore the ways of ashen alkali,

And desert winds blew sudden, swift and dry.
The dust! it sat upon and fill'd the train!   60
It seem'd to fret and fill the very sky.
Lo! dust upon the beasts, the tent, the plain,
And dust, alas! on breasts that rose not up again.

They sat in desolation and in dust
By dried-up desert streams; the mother's hands   65
Hid all her bended face; the cattle thrust
Their tongues and faintly call'd across the lands.
The babes, that knew not what this way through sands
Could mean, did ask if it would end today . . .
The panting wolves slid by, red-eyed, in bands   70
To pools beyond. The men look'd far away,
And, silent, saw that all a boundless desert lay.

They rose by night; they struggled on and on
As thin and still as ghosts; then here and there
Beside the dusty way before the dawn,   75
Men silent laid them down in their despair,
And died. But woman! Woman, frail as fair
May man have strength to give to you your due;
You falter'd not, nor murmured anywhere,
You held your babes, held to your course, and you   80
Bore on through burning hell your double burdens through.

Men stood at last, the decimated few,
Above a land of running streams, and they?
They push'd aside their boughs, and peering through
Beheld afar the cool, refreshing bay;   85
Then some did curse, and some bend hands to pray;
But some look'd back upon the desert, wide
And desolate with death, then all the day
They mourned. But one, with nothing left beside
His dog to love, crept down among the ferns and died.   90

[1873]

The Metaphysic

Walking   HENRY DAVID THOREAU

Henry David Thoreau (1817–1862) liked to say that he had "travelled a good deal in Concord" — his home town. He had gone to its school, and to it he returned to teach after graduating from Harvard in 1837. In 1841 he gave up teaching and went to live with the Emersons, serving as general handy-man and, more importantly, as the older man's disciple. It was on Emerson's land that he built his Walden cabin. (See p. 229.) The character of Thoreau that appears in "Walking" is perhaps the one that is remembered best, that of the poet-naturalist, although his importance as the social reformer in "Civil Disobedience" is not to be overlooked.

Thoreau's love of walking, preferably toward the West, he sees as corresponding to a deep metaphysical urge, an urge that is at once racial and individual, physical and spiritual. Man's magnetic needle points West, but for Thoreau the West is a symbol for meanings in several dimensions, dimensions which are brought together by the metaphor of the sun in the final paragraphs. Thoreau's style, noted for its purity, is a fitting instrument for the man who described himself as "a mystic, a transcendentalist, and a natural philosopher."

". . . So we saunter toward the Holy Land. . . ."

What is it that makes it so hard sometimes to determine whither we will walk? I believe that there is a subtle magnetism in Nature, which, if we unconsciously yield to it, will direct us aright. It is not indifferent to us which way we walk. There is a right way; but we are very liable from heedlessness and stupidity to take the wrong one. We would fain take that walk, never yet taken by us through this actual world, which is perfectly symbolical of the path which we love to travel in the interior and ideal world; and sometimes, no doubt, we find it difficult to choose our direction, because it does not yet exist distinctly in our idea.

When I go out of the house for a walk, uncertain as yet whither I will bend my steps, and submit myself to my instinct to decide for me, I find, strange and whimsical as it may seem, that I finally and inevitably settle southwest, toward some particular wood or meadow or deserted pasture or hill in that direction. My needle is slow to settle, — varies a few degrees, and does not always point due southwest, it is true, and it has good authority for this variation, but it always settles between west and south-southwest. The future lies that way to me, and the earth seems more unexhausted and richer on that side. The outline which would bound my walks would be, not a circle, but a parabola, or rather like one of those cometary orbits which have been thought to be non-returning curves, in this case opening westward, in which my house occupies the place of the sun. I turn round and round irresolute sometimes for a quarter of an hour, until I decide, for a thousandth time, that I will walk into the southwest or west. Eastward I go only by force; but westward I go free. Thither no business leads me. It is hard for me to believe that I shall find fair landscapes or sufficient wildness and freedom behind the eastern horizon. I am not excited by the prospect of a walk thither; but I believe that the forest which I see in the western horizon stretches uninterruptedly toward the setting sun, and there are no towns nor cities in it of enough consequence to disturb me. Let me live where I will, on this side is the city, on that the wilderness, and ever I am leaving the city more and more, and withdrawing into the wilderness. I should not lay so much stress on this fact, if I did not believe that something like this is the prevailing tendency of my countrymen. I must walk toward Oregon, and not toward Europe. And that way the nation is moving, and I may say that mankind progress from east to west. Within a few years we have witnessed the phenomenon of a south-eastward migration, in the settlement of Australia; but this affects us as a retrograde movement, and, judging from the moral and physical character of the first generation of Australians, has not yet proved a successful experiment. The eastern Tartars think that there is nothing west beyond Thibet. "The world ends there," say they; "beyond there is nothing but a shoreless sea." It is unmitigated East where they live.

We go eastward to realize history and study the works of art and literature, retracing the steps of the race; we go westward as into the future, with a spirit of enterprise and adventure. The Atlantic is a Lethean stream, in our passage over which we have had an opportunity to forget the Old World and its institutions. If we do not succeed this time, there is perhaps one more chance for the race left before it arrives on the banks of the Styx; and that is in the Lethe of the Pacific, which is three times as wide.

I know not how significant it is, or how far it is an evidence of singularity, that an individual should thus consent in his pettiest walk with the general movement of the race; but I know that something akin to the migratory instinct in birds and quadrupeds, — which, in some instances, is known to have affected the squirrel tribe, impelling them to a general and mysterious movement, in which they were seen, say some, crossing the broadest rivers, each on its particular chip, with its tail raised for a sail, and bridging narrower streams with their dead, — that something like the *furor* which affects the domestic cattle in the spring, and which is referred to a worm in their tails, — affects both nations and individuals, either perennially or from time to time. Not a flock of wild geese cackles over our town, but it to some extent unsettles the value of real estate here, and, if I were a broker, I should probably take that disturbance into account.

> "Than longen folk to gon on pilgrimages,
> And palmeres for to seken strange strondes."

Every sunset which I witness inspires me with the desire to go to a West as distant and as fair as that into which the sun goes down. He appears to migrate westward daily, and tempt us to follow him. He is the great Western Pioneer whom the nations follow. We dream all night of those mountain-ridges in the horizon, though they may be of vapor only, which were last gilded by his rays. The island of Atlantis, and the islands and gardens of the Hesperides, a sort of terrestrial paradise, appear to have been the Great West of the ancients, enveloped in mystery and poetry. Who has not seen in imagination, when looking into the sunset sky, the gardens of the Hesperides, and the foundation of all those fables?

Columbus felt the westward tendency more strongly than any before. He obeyed it, and found a New World for Castile and Leon. The herd of men in those days scented fresh pastures from afar.

> "And now the sun had stretched out all the hills,
> And now was dropped into the western bay;
> At last *he* rose, and twitched his mantle blue;
> To-morrow to fresh woods and pastures new."

Where on the globe can there be found an area of equal extent with that occupied by the bulk of our States, so fertile and so rich and varied in its productions, and at the same time so habitable by the European, as this is? Michaux, who knew but part of them, says that "the species of large trees are much more numerous in North America than in Europe; in the United States there are more than one hundred and forty species that exceed thirty feet in height; in France there are but thirty that attain this size." Later botanists more than confirm his observations. Humboldt came to America to realize his youthful dreams of a tropical vegetation, and he beheld it in its greatest perfection in the primitive forests of the Amazon, the most gigantic wilderness on the earth, which he has so eloquently described. The geographer Guyot, himself a European, goes farther, — farther than I am ready to follow him; yet not when he says: "As the plant is made for the animal, as the vegetable world is made for the animal world, America is made for the man of the Old World. . . . The man of the Old World sets out upon his way. Leaving the highlands of Asia, he descends from station to station towards Europe. Each of his steps is marked by a new civilization superior to the preceding, by a greater power of development. Arrived at the Atlantic, he pauses on the shore of this unknown ocean, the bounds of which he knows not, and turns upon his footprints for an instant." When he has exhausted the rich soil of Europe, and reinvigorated himself, "then recommences his adventurous career westward as in the earliest ages." So far Guyot.

From this western impulse coming in contact with the barrier of the Atlantic sprang the commerce and enterprise of modern times. The younger Michaux, in his "Travels West of the Alleghanies in 1802," says that the common inquiry in the newly settled West was, " 'From what part of the world have you come?' As if these vast and fertile regions would naturally be the place of meeting and common country of all the inhabitants of the globe."

To use an obsolete Latin word, I might say, *Ex Oriente lux; ex Occidente* FRUX. From the East light; from the West fruit.

Sir Francis Head, an English traveler and a Governor-General of Canada, tells us that "in both the northern and southern hemispheres of the New World, Nature has not only outlined her works on a larger scale, but has painted the whole picture with brighter and more costly colors than she used in delineating and in beautifying the Old World. . . . The heavens of America appear infinitely higher, the sky is bluer, the air is fresher, the cold is intenser, the moon looks larger, the stars are brighter, the thunder is louder, the lightning is vivider, the wind is stronger, the rain is heavier, the mountains are higher, the rivers longer, the forests bigger, the plains broader." This statement will do at least to set against Buffon's account of this part of the world and its productions.

Linnæus said long ago, "Nescio quæ facies *læta, glabra* plantis Americanis: I know not what there is of joyous and smooth in the aspect of American plants"; and I think that in this country there are no, or at most very few, *Africanæ bestiæ*, African beasts, as the Romans called them, and that in this respect also it is peculiarly fitted for the habitation of man. We are told that within three miles of the center of the East-Indian city of Singapore, some of the inhabitants are annually carried off by tigers; but the traveler can lie down in the woods at night almost anywhere in North America without fear of wild beasts.

These are encouraging testimonies. If the moon looks larger here than in Europe, probably the sun looks larger also. If the heavens of America appear infinitely higher, and the stars brighter, I trust that these facts are symbolical of the height to which the philosophy and poetry and religion of her inhabitants may one day soar. At length, perchance, the immaterial heaven will appear as much higher to the American mind, and the intimations that star it as much brighter. For I believe that climate does thus react on man, — as there is something in the mountain-air that feeds the spirit and inspires. Will not man grow to greater perfection intellectually as well as physically under these influences? Or is it unimportant how many foggy days there are in his life? I trust that we shall be more imaginative, that our thoughts will be clearer, fresher, and more ethereal, as our sky, — our understanding more comprehensive and broader, like our plains, — our intellect generally on a grander scale, like our thunder and lightning, our rivers and mountains and forests, — and our hearts shall even correspond in breadth and depth and grandeur to our inland seas. Perchance there will appear to the traveler something, he knows not what, of *læta* and *glabra,* of joyous and serene, in our very faces. Else to what end does the world go on, and why was America discovered?

To Americans I hardly need to say, —

"Westward the star of empire takes its way."

As a true patriot, I should be ashamed to think that Adam in paradise was more favorably situated on the whole than the backwoodsman in this country.

Our sympathies in Massachusetts are not confined to New England; though we may be estranged from the South, we sympathize with the West. There is the home of the younger sons, as among the Scandinavians they took to the sea for their inheritance. It is too late to be studying Hebrew; it is more important to understand even the slang of to-day.

Some months ago I went to see a panorama of the Rhine. It was like a dream of the Middle Ages. I floated down its historic stream in something more than imagination, under bridges built by the Romans, and repaired by later heroes, past cities and castles whose very names were music to my ears, and each of which was the subject of a legend. There were Ehrenbreitstein and Rolandseck and Coblentz, which I knew only in history. They were ruins that interested me chiefly. There seemed to come up from its waters and its vine-clad hills and valleys a hushed music as of Crusaders departing for the Holy Land. I floated along under the spell of enchantment, as if I had been transported to an heroic age, and breathed an atmosphere of chivalry.

Soon after, I went to see a panorama of the Mississippi, and as I worked my way up the river in the light of to-day, and saw the steamboats wooding up, counted the rising cities, gazed on the fresh ruins of Nauvoo, beheld the Indians moving west across the stream, and, as before I had looked up the Moselle, now looked up the Ohio and the Missouri and heard the legends of Dubuque and of Wenona's Cliff — still thinking more of the future than of the past or present, — I saw that this was a Rhine stream of a different kind; that the foundations of castles were yet to be laid, and the famous bridges were yet to be thrown over the river; and I felt that *this was the heroic age itself,* though we know it not, for the hero is commonly the simplest and obscurest of men.

The West of which I speak is but another name for the Wild; and what I have been preparing to say is, that in Wildness is the preservation of the World. Every tree sends its fibers forth in search of the Wild. The cities import it at any price. Men plough and sail for it. From the forest and wilderness come the tonics and barks which brace mankind. Our ancestors were savages. The story of Romulus and Remus being suckled by a wolf is not a meaningless fable. The founders of every state which has risen to eminence have drawn their nourishment and vigor from a similar wild source. It was because the children of the Empire were not suckled by the wolf that they were conquered and displaced by the children of the northern forests who were.

I believe in the forest, and in the meadow, and in the night in which the corn grows. We require an infusion of hemlock-spruce or arbor-vitæ in our tea. There is a difference between eating and drinking for strength and from mere gluttony. The Hottentots eagerly devour the marrow of the koodoo and other antelopes raw, as a matter of course. Some of our Northern Indians eat raw the marrow of the Arctic reindeer, as well as the various other parts, including the summits of the antlers, as long as they are soft. And herein, perchance, they have stolen a march on the cooks of Paris. They get what usually goes to feed the fire. This is probably better than stall-fed beef and slaughter-house pork to make a man of. Give me a wildness whose glance no civilization can endure, — as if we lived on the marrow of koodoos devoured raw.

There are some intervals which border the strain of the wood-thrush, to which I would migrate, — wild lands where no settler has squatted; to which, methinks, I am already acclimated.

The African hunter Cummings tells us that the skin of the eland, as well as that of most other antelopes just killed, emits the most delicious perfume of trees and grass. I would have every man so much like a wild antelope, so much a part and parcel of Nature, that his very person should thus sweetly advertise our senses of his presence, and remind us of those parts of Nature which he most haunts. I feel no disposition to be satirical, when the trapper's coat emits the odor of musquash even; it is a sweeter scent to me than that which commonly exhales from the merchant's or the scholar's garments. When I go into their wardrobes and handle their vestments, I am reminded of no grassy plains and flowery meads which they have frequented, but of dusty merchants' exchanges and libraries rather.

A tanned skin is something more than respectable, and perhaps olive is a fitter color than white for a man, — a denizen of the woods. "The pale white man!" I do not wonder that the African pitied him. Darwin the naturalist says, "A white man bathing by the side of a Tahitian was like a plant bleached by the gardener's art, compared with a fine, dark green one, growing vigorously in the open fields."

Ben Jonson exclaims, —

"How near to good is what is fair!"

So I would say, —

How near to good is what is *wild!*

Life consists with wildness. The most alive is the wildest. Not yet subdued to man, its presence refreshes him. One who pressed forward incessantly and never rested from his labors, who grew fast and made infinite demands on life, would always find himself in a new country or wilderness, and surrounded by the raw material of life. He would be climbing over the prostrate stems of primitive forest-trees. . . .

We hug the earth, — how rarely we mount! Methinks we might elevate ourselves a little more. We might climb a tree, at least. I found my account in climbing a tree once. It was a tall white-pine, on the top of a hill; and though I got well pitched, I was well paid for it, for I discovered new mountains in the horizon which I had never seen before, — so much more of the earth and the heavens. I might have walked about the foot of the tree for three-score years and ten, and yet I certainly should never have seen them. But, above all, I discovered around me, — it was near the end of June, — on the ends of the topmost branches only, a few minute and delicate red cone-like blossoms, the fertile flower of the white pine looking heavenward. I carried straightway to the village the topmost spire, and showed it to stranger jurymen who walked the streets, — for it was court-week, — and the farmers and lumber-dealers and wood-choppers and hunters, and not one had ever seen the like before, but they wondered as at a star dropped down. Tell of ancient architects finishing their works on the tops of columns as perfectly as on the lower and more visible parts! Nature has from the first expanded the minute blossoms of the forest only toward the heavens, above men's heads and unobserved by them. We see only the flowers that are under our feet in the meadows. The pines have developed their delicate blossoms on the highest twigs of the wood every summer for ages, as well over the heads of Nature's red children as of her white ones: yet scarcely a farmer or hunter in the land has ever seen them.

Above all, we cannot afford not to live in the present. He is blessed over all mortals who loses no moment of the passing life in remembering the past. Unless our philosophy hears the cock crow in every barn-yard within our horizon, it is belated. That sound commonly reminds us that we are growing rusty and antique in our employments and habits of thought. His philosophy comes down to a more recent time than ours. There is something suggested by it that is a newer testament, — the gospel according to this moment. He has not fallen astern; he has got up early and kept up early, and to be where he is is to be in season, in the foremost rank of time. It is an expression of the health and soundness of Nature, a brag for all the world, — healthiness as of a spring burst forth, a new fountain of the Muses, to celebrate this last instant of time. Where he lives no fugitive slave laws are passed. Who has not betrayed his master many times since last he heard that note?

The merit of this bird's strain is in its freedom from all plaintiveness. The singer can easily move us to tears or to laughter, but where is he who can excite in us a pure morning joy? When, in doleful dumps, breaking the awful stillness of our wooden sidewalk on a Sunday, or perchance, a watcher in the house of mourning, I hear a cockerel crow far or near, I think to myself, "There is one of us well, at any rate," — and with a sudden gush return to my senses.

We had a remarkable sunset one day last November. I was walking in a meadow, the source of a small brook, when the sun at last, just before setting, after a cold gray day, reached a clear stratum in the horizon, and the softest, brightest morning sunlight fell on the dry grass and on the stems of the trees in the opposite horizon and on the leaves of the shrub-oaks on the hillside, while our shadows stretched long over the meadow eastward, as if we were the only motes in its beams. It was such a light as we could not have imagined a moment before, and the air also was so warm and serene that nothing was wanting to make a paradise of that meadow. When we reflected that this was not a solitary phenomenon, never to happen again, but that it would happen forever and ever an infinite number of evenings, and cheer and reassure the latest child that walked there, it was more glorious still.

The sun sets on some retired meadow, where no house is visible, with all the glory and splendor that it lavishes on cities, and perchance as it has never set before, — where there is but a solitary marsh-hawk to have his wings gilded by it, or only a musquash looks out from his cabin, and there is some little black-veined brook in the midst of the marsh, just beginning to meander, winding slowly round a decaying stump. We walked in so pure and bright a light, gilding the withered grass and leaves, so softly and serenely bright, I thought I had never bathed in such a golden flood, without a ripple or a murmur to it. The west side of every wood and rising ground gleamed like the boundary of Elysium, and the sun on our backs seemed like a gentle herdsman driving us home at evening.

So we saunter toward the Holy Land, till one day the sun shall shine more brightly than ever he has done, shall perchance shine into our minds and hearts, and light up our whole lives with a great awakening light, as warm and serene and golden as on a bankside in autumn.

[1862]

Passage to India   WALT WHITMAN

Like Thoreau, Walt Whitman (1819–1892) travelled much in a narrow compass, though he did witness more of American life and participated more extensively in it than did the New Englander. Born on Long Island, Whitman also lived in Brooklyn, Washington, and Camden, New Jersey. His most important journey was his trip to New Orleans, where he lived for three months in 1848; and this experience of the South, the Mississippi Valley and the Great Lakes area strongly influenced his poetry. At eleven Whitman went to work, first as an office boy and then as a printer's devil. Later he became a school teacher, newspaper editor, and part-time politician. When "Passage to India" was published in 1871 Whitman had been known for fifteen years as the author of *Leaves of Grass*. In the five years previous to the writing of this poem, the transatlantic cable had been laid, the Suez Canal had been opened, and the transcontinental railroad had been completed. Thus Whitman's own intense, broad, and variegated experience together with the events of the age had prepared the way for this ambitious poem.

In "Passage to India" Whitman chants grandly of the individual who is aware of being part of a process larger than himself. The poem, despite its romantic exuberance, is carefully organized. It draws from the history of the "feverish children" of Adam in their westward climb to the pinnacle of nineteenth century material achievement and calls for a different kind of passage in the future, a passage for which the centuries-long western march had been but a preparation and a symbol. Something of Whitman's larger intention in the poem is indicated in his own comment: "I meant, while in a sort continuing the theme of my first chants, to shift the slides, and exhibit the problem and paradox of the same ardent and fully appointed personality entering the sphere of the resistless gravitation of spiritual law, and with cheerful face estimating death, not at all as the cessation, but as somehow what I feel it must be, the entrance upon far the greatest part of existence, and something that life is at least as much for, as it is for itself. . . . The physical and the sensuous, in themselves or in their immediate continuations, retain holds upon me which I think are never entirely releas'd; and these holds I have not only not denied, but hardly wish'd to weaken."

". . . are they not all the seas of God? . . ."

1

Singing my days,
Singing the great achievements of the present,
Singing the strong light works of engineers,
Our modern wonders, (the antique ponderous Seven outvied,)
In the Old World the east the Suez canal,   5
The New by its mighty railroad spann'd,
The seas inlaid with eloquent gentle wires;
Yet first to sound, and ever sound, the cry with thee O soul,
The Past! the Past! the Past!

The Past — the dark unfathom'd retrospect!   10
The teeming gulf — the sleepers and the shadows!
The past — the infinite greatness of the past!
For what is the present after all but a growth out of the past?
(As a projectile form'd, impell'd, passing a certain line, still keeps on,
So the present, utterly form'd, impell'd by the past.)   15

2

Passage O soul to India!
Eclaircise the myths Asiatic, the primitive fables.

Not you alone proud truths of the world,
Nor you alone ye facts of modern science,
But myths and fables of eld, Asia's, Africa's fables,   20
The far-darting beams of the spirit, the unloos'd dreams,
The deep diving bibles and legends,
The daring plots of the poets, the elder religions;
O you temples fairer than lilies pour'd over by the rising sun!
O you fables spurning the known, eluding the hold of the known, mount-
        ing to heaven!   25
You lofty and dazzling towers, pinnacled, red as roses, burnish'd with gold!
Towers of fables immortal fashion'd from mortal dreams!
You too I welcome and fully the same as the rest!
You too with joy I sing.

Passage to India!   30
Lo, soul, seest thou not God's purpose from the first?
The earth to be spann'd, connected by network,
The races, neighbors, to marry and be given in marriage,
The oceans to be cross'd, the distant brought near,
The lands to be welded together.   35

A worship new I sing,
You captains, voyagers, explorers, yours,
You engineers, you architects, machinists, yours,

You, not for trade or transportation only,
But in God's name, and for thy sake O soul.   40

3

Passage to India!
Lo soul for thee of tableaus twain,
I see in one the Suez canal initiated, open'd,
I see the procession of steamships, the Empress Eugenie's leading the van,
I mark from on deck the strange landscape, the pure sky, the level sand in
    the distance,   45
I pass swiftly the picturesque groups, the workmen gather'd,
The gigantic dredging machines.

In one again, different, (yet thine, all thine, O soul, the same,)
I see over my own continent the Pacific railroad surmounting every barrier,
I see continual trains of cars winding along the Platte carrying freight and
    passengers,   50
I hear the locomotives rushing and roaring, and the shrill steam-whistle,
I hear the echoes reverberate through the grandest scenery in the world,
I cross the Laramie plains, I note the rocks in grotesque shapes, the buttes,
I see the plentiful larkspur and wild onions, the barren, colorless sage-
    deserts,
I see in glimpses afar or towering immediately above me the great moun-
    tains, I see the Wind river and the Wahsatch mountains,   55
I see the Monument mountain and the Eagle's Nest, I pass the Promon-
    tory, I ascend the Nevadas,
I scan the noble Elk mountain and wind around its base,
I see the Humboldt range, I thread the valley and cross the river,
I see the clear waters of lake Tahoe, I see forests of majestic pines,
Or crossing the great desert, the alkaline plains, I behold enchanting
    mirages of waters and meadows,   60
Marking through these and after all, in duplicate slender lines,
Bridging the three or four thousand miles of land travel,
Tying the Eastern to the Western sea,
The road between Europe and Asia.

(Ah Genoese thy dream! thy dream!   65
Centuries after thou art laid in thy grave,
The shore thou foundest verifies thy dream.)

4

Passage to India!
Struggles of many a captain, tales of many a sailor dead,
Over my mood stealing and spreading they come,   70
Like clouds and cloudlets in the unreach'd sky.

Along all history, down the slopes,
As a rivulet running, sinking now, and now again to the surface rising,

A ceaseless thought, a varied train — lo, soul, to thee, thy sight, they rise,
The plans, the voyages again, the expeditions;   75
Again Vasco da Gama sails forth,
Again the knowledge gain'd, the mariner's compass,
Lands found and nations born, thou born America,
For purpose vast, man's long probation fill'd,
Thou rondure of the world at last accomplish'd.   80

5

O vast Rondure, swimming in space,
Cover'd all over with visible power and beauty,
Alternate light and day and the teeming spiritual darkness,
Unspeakable high processions of sun and moon and countless stars above,
Below, the manifold grass and waters, animals, mountains, trees,   85
With inscrutable purpose, some hidden prophetic intention,
Now first it seems my thought begins to span thee.

Down from the gardens of Asia descending radiating,
Adam and Eve appear, then their myriad progeny after them,
Wandering, yearning, curious, with restless explorations,   90
With questionings, baffled, formless, feverish, with never-happy hearts,
With that sad incessant refrain, *Wherefore unsatisfied soul?* and *Whither*
        O mocking life?

Ah who shall soothe these feverish children?
Who justify these restless explorations?
Who speak the secret of impassive earth?   95
Who bind it to us? what is this separate Nature so unnatural?
What is this earth to our affections? (unloving earth, without a throb to
        answer ours,
Cold earth, the place of graves.)

Yet soul be sure the first intent remains, and shall be carried out,
Perhaps even now the time has arrived.   100

After the seas are all cross'd, (as they seem already cross'd,)
After the great captains and engineers have accomplish'd their work,
After the noble inventors, after the scientists, the chemist, the geologist,
        ethnologist,
Finally shall come the poet worthy that name,
The true son of God shall come singing his songs.   105

Then not your deeds only O voyagers, O scientists and inventors, shall be
        justified,
All these hearts as of fretted children shall be sooth'd,
All affection shall be fully responded to, the secret shall be told,
All these separations and gaps shall be taken up and hook'd and link'd
        together,

The whole earth, this cold, impassive, voiceless earth, shall be completely
     justified,   110
Trinitas divine shall be gloriously accomplish'd and compacted by the true
     son of God, the poet,
(He shall indeed pass the straits and conquer the mountains,
He shall double the cape of Good Hope to some purpose,)
Nature and Man shall be disjoin'd and diffused no more,
The true son of God shall absolutely fuse them.   115

6

Year at whose wide-flung door I sing!
Year of the purpose accomplish'd!
Year of the marriage of continents, climates and oceans!
(No mere doge of Venice now wedding the Adriatic,)
I see O year in you the vast terraqueous globe given and giving all,   120
Europe to Asia, Africa join'd, and they to the New World,
The lands, geographies, dancing before you, holding a festival garland,
As brides and bridegrooms hand in hand.

Passage to India!
Cooling airs from Caucasus far, soothing cradle of man,   125
The river Euphrates flowing, the past lit up again.

Lo soul, the retrospect brought forward,
The old, most populous, wealthiest of earth's lands,
The streams of the Indus and the Ganges and their many affluents,
(I my shores of America walking to-day behold, resuming all,)   130
The tale of Alexander on his warlike marches suddenly dying,
On one side China and on the other side Persia and Arabia,
To the south the great seas and the bay of Bengal,
The flowing literatures, tremendous epics, religions, castes,
Old occult Brahma interminably far back, the tender and junior Buddha,   135
Central and southern empires and all their belongings, possessors,
The wars of Tamerlane, the reign of Aurungzebe,
The traders, rulers, explorers, Moslems, Venetians, Byzantium, the Arabs,
     Portuguese,
The first travelers famous yet, Marco Polo, Batouta the Moor,
Doubts to be solv'd, the map incognita, blanks to be fill'd,   140
The foot of man unstay'd, the hands never at rest,
Thyself O soul that will not brook a challenge.

The mediæval navigators rise before me,
The world of 1492, with its awaken'd enterprise,
Something swelling in humanity now like the sap of the earth in spring,   145
The sunset splendor of chivalry declining.

And who art thou sad shade?
Gigantic, visionary, thyself a visionary,

With majestic limbs and pious beaming eyes,
Spreading around with every look of thine a golden world,   150
Enhuing it with gorgeous hues.

As the chief histrion,
Down to the footlights walks in some great scena,
Dominating the rest I see the Admiral himself,
(History's type of courage, action, faith,)   155
Behold him sail from Palos leading his little fleet,
His voyage behold, his return, his great fame,
His misfortunes, calumniators, behold him a prisoner, chain'd,
Behold his dejection, poverty, death.

(Curious in time I stand, noting the efforts of heroes,   160
Is the deferment long? bitter the slander, poverty, death?
Lies the seed unreck'd for centuries in the ground? lo, to God's due occa-
        sion,
Uprising in the night, it sprouts, blooms,
And fills the earth with use and beauty.)

7

Passage indeed O soul to primal thought,   165
Not lands and seas alone, thy own clear freshness,
The young maturity of brood and bloom,
To realms of budding bibles.

O soul, repressless, I with thee and thou with me,
Thy circumnavigation of the world begin,   170
Of man, the voyage of his mind's return,
To reason's early paradise,
Back, back to wisdom's birth, to innocent intuitions,
Again with fair creation.

8

O we can wait no longer,   175
We too take ship O soul,
Joyous we too launch out on trackless seas,
Fearless for unknown shores on waves of ecstasy to sail,
Amid the wafting winds, (thou pressing me to thee, I thee to me, O soul,)
Caroling free, singing our song of God,   180
Chanting our chant of pleasant exploration.

With laugh and many a kiss,
(Let others deprecate, let others weep for sin, remorse, humiliation,)
O soul thou pleasest me, I thee.

Ah more than any priest O soul we too believe in God,   185
But with the mystery of God we dare not dally.

O soul thou pleasest me, I thee,
Sailing these seas or on the hills, or waking in the night,
Thoughts, silent thoughts, of Time and Space and Death, like waters
    flowing,
Bear me indeed as through the regions infinite,   190
Whose air I breathe, whose ripples hear, lave me all over,
Bathe me O God in thee, mounting to thee,
I and my soul to range in range of thee.

O Thou transcendent,
Nameless, the fibre and the breath,   195
Light of the light, shedding forth universes, thou centre of them,
Thou mightier centre of the true, the good, the loving,
Thou moral, spiritual fountain — affection's source — thou reservoir,
(O pensive soul of me — O thirst unsatisfied — waitest not there?
Waitest not haply for us somewhere there the Comrade perfect?)   200
Thou pulse — thou motive of the stars, suns, systems,
That, circling, move in order, safe, harmonious,
Athwart the shapeless vastnesses of space,
How should I think, how breathe a single breath, how speak, if, out of
    myself,
I could not launch, to those, superior universes?   205

Swiftly I shrivel at the thought of God,
At Nature and its wonders, Time and Space and Death,
But that I, turning, call to thee O soul, thou actual Me, .
And lo, thou gently masterest the orbs,
Thou matest Time, smilest content at Death,   210
And fillest, swellest full the vastness of Space.

Greater than stars or suns,
Bounding O soul thou journeyest forth;
What love than thine and ours could wider amplify?
What aspirations, wishes, outvie thine and ours O soul?   215
What dreams of the ideal? what plans of purity, perfection, strength,
What cheerful willingness for others' sake to give up all?
For others' sake to suffer all?

Reckoning ahead O soul, when thou, the time achiev'd,
The seas all cross'd, weather'd the capes, the voyage done,   220
Surrounded, copest, frontest God, yieldest, the aim attain'd,
As filled with friendship, love complete, the Elder Brother found,
The Younger melts in fondness in his arms.

9

Passage to more than India!
Are thy wings plumed indeed for such far flights?   225
O soul, voyagest thou indeed on voyages like those?

Disportest thou on waters such as those?
Soundest below the Sanscrit and the Vedas?
Then have thy bent unleash'd.

Passage to you, your shores, ye aged fierce enigmas!   230
Passage to you, to mastership of you, ye strangling problems!
You, strew'd with the wrecks of skeletons, that, living, never reach'd you.

Passage to more than India!
O secret of the earth and sky!
Of you O waters of the sea! O winding creeks and rivers!   235
Of you O woods and fields! of you strong mountains of my land!
Of you O prairies! of you gray rocks!
O morning red! O clouds! O rains and snows!
O day and night, passage to you!

O sun and moon and all you stars! Sirius and Jupiter!   240
Passage to you!

Passage, immediate passage! the blood burns in my veins!
Away O soul! hoist instantly the anchor!
Cut the hawsers — haul out — shake out every sail!
Have we not stood here like trees in the ground long enough?   245
Have we not grovel'd here long enough, eating and drinking like mere
        brutes?
Have we not darken'd and dazed ourselves with books long enough?

Sail forth — steer for the deep waters only,
Reckless O soul, exploring, I with thee, and thou with me,
For we are bound where mariner has not yet dared to go,   250
And we will risk the ship, ourselves and all.

O my brave soul!
O farther farther sail!
O daring joy, but safe! are they not all the seas of God?
O farther, farther, farther sail!   255

[1871]

The Human Product

The Character of Pioneers   TIMOTHY DWIGHT

Timothy Dwight (1752–1817) was the grandson of Jonathan Edwards (see p. 130) and a leading Calvinist in his own right. As a young man teaching at Yale, he brought on a nervous breakdown by overwork. To recover his health, he took to extensive hiking and horse-back riding, activities which furnished material for his *Travels in New England and New York* (1821–22). Despite the narrowness of his social and religious views, Dwight was a great teacher and educational leader. A lifelong Federalist in his politics (see Griswold's comment, p. 226), he was thoroughly opposed to the Jeffersonianism of the American frontier.

These remarks selected from Dwight's *Travels* express his dark view of natural man. This view is underlined by the reasons which he gives for emigration and by the manner in which he writes of those reasons.

"... These men cannot live in regular society. They are too idle, too talkative, too passionate, too prodigal, and too shiftless ..."

Vermont has been settled entirely from the other States of New-England. The inhabitants have, of course, the New-England character, with no other difference beside what is accidental. In the formation of Colonies, those who are first inclined to emigrate are usually such as have met with difficulties at home. These are commonly joined by persons, who, having large families and small farms, are induced for the sake of settling their children comfortably to seek for new and cheaper lands. To both are always added the discontented, the enterprizing, the ambitious, and the covetous. Many of the first and some of all these classes are found in every new American country, within ten years after its settlement has commenced. From this period kindred, friendship, and former neighborhood prompt others to follow them. Others still are allured by the prospect of gain, presented in every new country to the sagacious from the purchase and sale of lands: while not a small number are influenced by the brilliant stories, which everywhere are told concerning most tracts during the early progress of their settlement.

A considerable part of all those who *begin* the cultivation of the wilderness may be denominated *foresters*, or *Pioneers*. The business of these persons is no other than to cut down trees, build log-houses, lay open forested grounds to cultivation, and prepare the way for those who come after them. These men cannot live in regular society. They are too idle, too talkative, too passionate, too prodigal, and too shiftless to acquire either property or character.

They are impatient of the restraints of law, religion, and morality; grumble about the taxes by which Rulers, Ministers, and Schoolmasters are supported; and complain incessantly, as well as bitterly, of the extortions of mechanics, farmers, merchants, and physicians to whom they are always indebted. At the same time they are usually possessed, in their own view, of uncommon wisdom; understand medical science, politics, and religion better than those who have studied them through life; and, although they manage their own concerns worse than any other men, feel perfectly satisfied that they could manage those of the nation far better than the agents to whom they are committed by the public. After displaying their own talents and worth, after censuring the weakness and wickedness of their superiours, after exposing the injustice of the community in neglecting to invest persons of such merit with public offices in many an eloquent harangue, uttered by many a kitchen fire, in every blacksmith's shop, and in every corner of the streets, and finding all their efforts vain, they become at length discouraged and under pressure of poverty, the fear of a gaol, and the consciousness of public contempt, leave their native places and betake themselves to the wilderness.

Here they are obliged either to work or to starve. They accordingly cut down some trees and girdle others; they furnish themselves with an ill-built log-house and a worse barn; and reduce a part of the forest into fields, half-enclosed and half-cultivated. The forests furnish browse; and their fields yield a stinted herbage. On this scanty provision they feed a few cattle: and with these and the penurious products of their labour, eked out by hunting and fishing, they keep their families alive.

A farm, thus far cleared, promises immediate subsistence to a better husbandman. A log-house, thus built, presents, when repaired with moderate exertions, a shelter for his family. Such a husbandman is therefore induced by these little advantages, where the soil and situation please him, to purchase such a farm, when he would not plant himself in an absolute wilderness. The proprietor is always ready to sell: for he loves this irregular, adventurous, half-working, and half-lounging life; and hates the sober industry and prudent economy by which his bush pasture might be changed into a farm, and himself raised to thrift and independence. The bargain is soon made. The forester, receiving more money for his improvements than he ever before possessed and a price for the soil somewhat enhanced by surrounding settlements, willingly quits his house to build another like it, and his farm to girdle trees, hunt, and saunter in another place. His wife accompanies him only from a sense of duty or necessity, and secretly pines for the quiet, orderly, friendly society to which she originally bade a reluctant farewell. Her husband, in the meantime, becomes less and less a civilized man; and almost every thing in the family which is amiable and meritorious is usually the result of her principles, care, and influence.

The second proprietor is commonly a *farmer,* and with an industry and spirit, deserving no small commendation, changes the desert into a fruitful field.

This change is accomplished much more rapidly in some places than in others, as various causes, often accidental, operate. In some instances a settlement is begun by farmers and assumes the aspect of regular society from its commencement. This, to some extent, is always the fact: and the greater number of the first planters are, probably, of this description: but some of them also are foresters, and sometimes a majority.

You must have remarked a very sensible difference in the character of different towns through which I have passed. This diversity is in no small degree derived from the original character of the planters in the different cases.

The class of men who have been the principal subject of these remarks have already straggled onward from New-England, as well as from other parts of the Union, to Louisiana. In a political view their emigration is of very serious utility to the ancient settlements. All countries contain restless inhabitants, men impatient of labour; men who will contract debts without intending to pay them, who had rather talk than work, whose vanity persuades them that they are wise and prevents them from knowing that they are fools, who are delighted with innovation, who think places of power and profit due to their peculiar merits, who feel that every change from good order and established society will be beneficial to themselves, who have nothing to lose and therefore expect to be gainers by every scramble, and who, of course, spend life in disturbing others with the hope of gaining something for themselves. Under despotic governments they are awed into quiet; but in every free community they create, to a greater or less extent, continual turmoil, and have often overturned the peace, liberty, and happiness of their fellow-citizens. In the Roman Commonwealth, as before in the Republics of Greece, they were emptied out as soldiers upon the surrounding countries, and left the sober inhabitants in comparative quiet at home. It is true, they often threw these States into confusion and sometimes overturned the government. But if they had not been thus thrown off from the body politic, its life would have been of a momentary duration. As things actually were, they finally ruined all these States. For some of them had, as some of them always will have, sufficient talents to do mischief, at times, very extensive. The Gracchi, Clodius, Marius, and Mark Antony were men of this character. Of this character is every demagogue, whatever may be his circumstances. Power and profit are the only ultimate objects which every such man, with a direction as steady as that of the needle to the pole, pursues with a greediness unlimited and inextinguishable.

Formerly the energetic government established in New-England, together with the prevailing high sense of religion and morals and the continually pressing danger from the French and the savages, compelled the inhabitants into habits of regularity and good order, not surpassed perhaps in the world. But since the American Revolution, our situation has become less favourable to the existence, as well as to the efficacy, of these great means of internal peace. The former exact and decisive energy of the government has been obviously weakened. From our ancient dangers we have been delivered, and the deliverance was a distinguished blessing: but the sense of danger regularly brings with it a strong conviction that safety cannot be preserved without exact order and a ready submission to lawful authority.

The institutions and the habits of New-England, more I suspect than those of any other country, have prevented or kept down this noxious disposition, but they cannot entirely prevent either its existence or its effects. In mercy, therefore, to the sober, industrious, and well-disposed inhabitants, Providence has opened in the vast Western wilderness a retreat sufficiently alluring to draw them away from the land of their nativity. We have many troubles even now: but we should have many more if this body of foresters had remained at home.

[1821]

The Backwoodsman   TIMOTHY FLINT

Timothy Flint (1780–1840) was a Massachusetts missionary whose description of his travels in *Recollections of the Last Ten Years* (1826) gives a first-hand view of life in the early American West. "The Backwoodsman" is taken from this book.

Flint wished, he said, "to vindicate a class of people who have been grossly misrepresented, and misunderstood,—the western backwoodsman." In this passage he proceeds skillfully, using devices designed to be convincing without being belligerently argumentative. His gentleness, indirection, and agreeableness help disguise the fact that he has made some sweeping affirmations.

"*. . . The backwoodsman of the west . . . is generally an amiable and virtuous man. . . .*"

The people in the Atlantic states have not yet recovered from the horror, inspired by the term "backwoodsman." This prejudice is particularly strong in New England, and is more or less felt from Maine to Georgia. When I first visited this country, I had my full share, and my family by far too much for their comfort. In approaching the country, I heard a thousand stories of gougings, and robberies, and shooting down with the rifle. I have travelled in these regions thousands of miles under all circumstances of exposure and danger. I have travelled alone, or in company only with such as needed protection, instead of being able to impart it; and this too, in many instances, where I was not known as a minister, or where such knowledge would have had no influence in protecting me. I never have carried the slightest weapon of defense. I scarcely remember to have experienced any thing that resembled insult, or to have felt myself in danger from the people. I have often seen men that had lost an eye. Instances of murder, numerous and horrible in their circumstances, have occurred in my vicinity. But they were such lawless rencounters, as terminate in murder every where, and in which the drunkenness, brutality, and violence were mutual. They were catastrophes, in which quiet and sober men would be in no danger of being involved.

When we look round these immense regions, and consider that I have been in settlements three hundred miles from any court of justice, when we look at the position of the men, and the state of things, the wonder is, that so few outrages and murders occur. The gentlemen of the towns, even here, speak often with a certain contempt and horror of the backwoodsmen. I have read, and not without feelings of pain, the bitter representations of the learned and virtuous Dr. Dwight, in speaking of them. He represents these vast regions, as a grand reservoir for the scum of the Atlantic states. He characterizes in the mass the emigrants from New England, as discontented coblers, too proud, too much in debt, too unprincipled, too much puffed up with self-conceit, too strongly impressed that their fancied talents could not find scope in their own country, to stay there. It is true there are worthless people here, and the most so, it must be confessed, are from New England. It is true there are gamblers, and gougers, and outlaws; but there are fewer of them, than from the nature of things, and the character of the age and the world, we ought to expect. But it is unworthy of the excellent man in question so to designate this people in the mass.

The backwoodsman of the west, as I have seen him, is generally an amiable and virtuous man. His general motive for coming here is to be a freeholder, to have plenty of rich land, and to be able to settle his children about him. It is a most virtuous motive. And notwithstanding all that Dr. Dwight and Talleyrand have said to the contrary, I fully believe, that nine in ten of the emigrants have come here with no other motive.

You find, in truth, that he has vices and barbarisms, peculiar to his situation. His manners are rough. He wears, it may be, a long beard. He has a great quantity of bear or deer skins wrought into his household establishment, his furniture, and dress. He carries a knife, or a dirk in his bosom, and when in the woods has a rifle on his back, and a pack of dogs at his heels. An Atlantic stranger, transferred directly from one of our cities to his door, would recoil from a rencounter with him. But remember, that his rifle and his dogs are among his chief means of support and profit. Remember, that all his first days here were passed in dread of the savages. Remember, that he still encounters them, still meets bears and panthers.

Enter his door, and tell him you are benighted, and wish the shelter of his cabin for the night. The welcome is indeed seemingly ungracious: "I reckon you can stay," or "I suppose we must let you stay." But this apparent ungraciousness is the harbinger of every kindness that he can bestow, and every comfort that his cabin can afford. Good coffee, corn bread and butter, venison, pork, wild and tame fowls are set before you. His wife, timid, silent, reserved, but constantly attentive to your comfort, does not sit at the table with you, but like the wives of the patriarchs, stands and attends on you. You are shown to the best bed which the house can offer. When this kind of hospitality has been afforded you as long as you choose to stay, and when you depart, and speak about your bill, you are most commonly told with some slight mark of resentment, that they do not keep tavern. Even the flaxen-headed urchins will turn away from your money.

In all my extensive intercourse with these people, I do not recollect but one instance of positive rudeness and inhospitality. It was on the waters of the Cuivre of the upper Mississippi; and from a man to whom I had presented bibles, who had received the hospitalities of my house, who had invited me into his settlement to preach. I turned away indignantly from a cold and reluctant reception here, made my way from the house of this man, — who was a German and comparatively rich, — through deep and dark forests, and amidst the concerts of wolves howling on the neighbouring hills. Providentially, about midnight, I heard the barking of dogs at a distance, made my way to the cabin of a very poor man, who arose at midnight, took me in, provided supper, and gave me a most cordial reception.

With this single exception, I have found the backwoodsmen to be such as I have described; a hardy, adventurous, hospitable, rough, but sincere and upright race of people. I have received so many kindnesses from them, that it becomes me always to preserve a grateful and affectionate remembrance of them. If we were to try them by the standard of New England customs and opinions, that is to say, the customs of a people under entirely different circumstances, there would be many things in the picture, that would strike us offensively. They care little about ministers, and think less about paying them. They are averse to all, even the most necessary restraints. They are destitute of the forms and observances of society and religion; but they are sincere and kind without professions, and have a coarse, but substantial morality, which is often rendered more striking by the immediate contrast of the graceful bows, civility, and professions of their French Catholic neighbours, who have the observances of society and the forms of worship, with often but a scanty modicum of the blunt truth and uprightness of their unpolished neighbours.

[1826]

The Newtys of Pike   CLARENCE KING

Clarence King (1842–1901) was a graduate of the Sheffield Scientific School at Yale who in 1863 got a job with the California State Geological Survey. On the basis of this experience he persuaded Congress in 1867 to authorize the ambitious Survey of the Fortieth Parallel with himself in charge. By the time he was thirty he was an acknowledged leader in American geology. An inspired raconteur and conversationalist, King was a blend of scientific and literary interests, of the frontier and eastern culture, of speculative miner and disinterested geologist. Author of numerous specialized reports, his *Mountaineering in the Sierra Nevada* (1872), from which "the Newtys of Pike" is taken, was a great popular success. In *At Home and Abroad* (1860) Bayard Taylor wrote as follows about the Pikes, a western species whom we meet in this account by King: "A Pike in the California dialect, is a native of Missouri, Arkansas, Northern Texas, or Southern Illinois. The first emigrants that came over the plains were from a Pike County, Missouri. . . . [The Pike] is the Anglo-Saxon relapsed into semi-barbarism. He is long, lathy, and sallow; he expectorates vehemently; he takes naturally to whiskey; he has the 'shakes' his life long at home, though he generally manages to get rid of them in California; he has little respect for the rights of others; he distrusts men in 'store clothes,' but venerates the memory of Andrew Jackson."

Although there are various clues in "The Newtys of Pike" that King is a man of science, the author's literary interests predominate, showing particularly in the devices designed to bring out the humor of his subject. There is some uncertainty of tone in the sketch, perhaps because in King's attitude toward the Newtys there is also some uncertainty.

". . . It was one of those histories common enough through this wide West, yet never failing to startle me with its horrible lesson of social disintegration, of human retrograde. . . ."

Our return from Mount Tyndall to such civilization as flourishes around the Kaweah outposts was signalized by us chiefly as to our *cuisine,* which offered now such bounties as the potato, and once a salad, in which some middle-aged lettuce became the vehicle for a hollow mockery of dressing. Two or three days, during which we dined at brief intervals, served to completely rest us, and put in excellent trim for further campaigning all except Professor Brewer, upon whom a constant toothache wore painfully, — my bullet-mould failing even upon the third trial to extract the unruly member.

It was determined we should ride together to Visalia, seventy miles away, and, the more we went, the impatienter became my friend, till we agreed to push ahead through day and night, and reached the village at about sunrise in a state of reeling sleepiness quite indescribably funny.

At evening, when it became time to start back for our mountain camp, my friend at last yielded consent to my project of climbing the Kern Sierras to attempt Mount Whitney; so I parted from him, and, remaining at Visalia, outfitted myself with a pack-horse, two mounted men, and provisions enough for a two weeks' trip.

I purposely avoid telling by what route I entered the Sierras, because there lingers in my breast a desire to see once more that lovely region, and failing, as I do, to confide in the people, I fear lest, if the camp I am going to describe should be recognized, I might, upon revisiting the scene, suffer harm, or even come to an untimely end. I refrain, then, from telling by what road I found myself entering the region of the pines one lovely twilight evening, two days after leaving Visalia. Pines, growing closer and closer, from sentinels gathered to groups, then stately groves, and at last, as the evening wore on, assembled in regular forest, through whose open tops the stars shone cheerfully.

I came upon an open meadow, hearing in front the rush of a large brook, and directly reached two camp-fires, where were a number of persons. My two hirelings caught and unloaded the pack-horse, and set about their duties, looking to supper and the animals, while I prospected the two camps. That just below me, on the same side of the brook, I found to be the bivouac of a company of hunters, who, in the ten minutes of my call, made free with me, hospitably offering a jug of whiskey, and then went on in their old eternal way of making bear-stories out of whole cloth.

I left them with a belief that my protoplasm and theirs must be different, in spite of Mr. Huxley, and passed across the brook to the other camp. Under noble groups of pines smouldered a generous heap of coals, the ruins of a mighty log. A little way from this lay a confused pile of bedclothes, partly old and half-bald buffalo-robes, but, in the main, thick strata of what is known to irony as comforters, upon which, outstretched in wretched awkwardness of position, was a family, all with their feet to the fire, looking as if they had been blown over in one direction, or knocked down by a single bombshell. On the extremities of this common bed, with the air of having gotten as far from each other as possible, the mother and father of the Pike family reclined; between them were two small children — a girl and boy — and a huge girl, who, next the old man, lay flat upon her back, her mind absorbed in the simple amusement of waving one foot (a cowhide eleven) slowly across the fire, squinting, with half-shut eye, first at the vast shoe and thence at the fire, alternately hiding bright places and darting the foot quickly in the direction of any new display of heightening flame. The mother was a bony sister, in the yellow, shrunken, of sharp visage, in which were prominent two cold eyes and a positively poisonous mouth; her hair, the color of faded hay, tangled in a jungle around her head. She rocked jerkily to and fro, removing at intervals a clay pipe from her mouth in order to pucker her thin lips up to one side, and spit with precision upon a certain spot in the fire, which she seemed resolved to prevent from attaining beyond a certain faint glow.

I have rarely felt more in difficulty for an overture to conversation, and was long before venturing to propose, "You seem to have a pleasant camp-spot here." The old woman sharply, and in almost a tone of affront, answered, "They's wus, and then again they's better."

"Does well for our hogs," inserted the old man. "We've a band of pork that make out to find feed."

"Oh! how many have you?" I asked.

"Nigh three thousand."

"Won't you set?" asked Madame; then, turning, "You, Susan, can't you try for to set up, and not spread so? Hain't you no manners, say?"

At this the massive girl got herself somewhat together, and made room for me, which I declined, however.

"Prospectin'?" inquired Madame.

"I say huntin'," suggested the man.

"Maybe he's a cattle-feller," interrupted the little girl.

"Goin' somewhere, ain't yer?" was Susan's guess.

I gave brief account of myself, evidently satisfying the social requirements of all but the old woman, who at once classified me as not up to her standard. Susan saw this, so did her father, and it became evident to me in ten minutes' conversation that they two were always at one, and made it their business to be in antagonism to the mother. They were then allies of mine from nature, and I felt at once at home. I saw too that Susan, having slid back to her horizontal position when I declined to share her rightful ground, was watching with subtle solicitude that fated spot in the fire, opposing sympathy and squints accurately aligned by her shoe to the dull spot in the embers, which slowly went out into blackness before the well-directed fire of her mother's saliva.

The shouts which I heard proceeding from the direction of my camp were easily translatable into summons for supper. Mr. Newty invited me to return later and be sociable, which I promised to do, and, going to my camp, supped quickly and left the men with orders about picketing the animals for the night, then, strolling slowly down to the camp of my friends, seated myself upon a log by the side of the old gentleman. Feeling that this somewhat formal attitude unfitted me for partaking to the fullest degree the social ease around me, and knowing that my buckskin trousers were impervious to dirt, I slid down in a reclined posture with my feet to the fire, in absolute parallelism with the rest of the family.

The old woman was in the exciting dénouement of a coon-story, directed to her little boy, who sat clinging to her skirt and looking in her face with absorbed curiosity. "And when Johnnie fired," she said, "the coon fell and busted open." The little boy had misplaced his sympathies with the raccoon, and having inquired plaintively, "Did it hurt him?" was promptly snubbed with the reply, "Of course it hurt him. What do you suppose coons is made for?" Then turning to me she put what was plainly enough with her a test-question: "I allow you have killed your coon in your day?" I saw at once that I must forever sink beneath the horizon of her standards, but, failing in real experience or accurate knowledge concerning the coon, knew no subterfuges would work with her. Instinct had taught her that I had never killed a coon, and she had asked me thus ostentatiously to place me at once and forever before the family in my true light. "No, ma'am," I said; "now you speak of it, I realize that I never have killed a coon." This was something of a staggerer to Susan and her father, yet as the mother's pleasurable dissatisfaction with me displayed itself by more and more accurate salivary shots at the fire, they rose to the occasion, and began to palliate my past. "Maybe," ventured Mr. Newty, "that they don't have coon round the city of York"; and I felt that I needed no self-defence when Susan firmly and defiantly suggested to her mother that perhaps I was in better business.

Driven in upon herself for some time, the old woman smoked in silence, until Susan, seeing that her mother gradually quenched a larger and larger circle upon the fire, got up and stretched herself, and giving the coals a vigorous poke swept out of sight the quenched spot, thus readily obliterating the results of her mother's precise and prolonged expectoration; then flinging a few dry boughs upon the fire illumined the family with the ruddy blaze, and sat down again, leaning upon her father's knee with a faint light of triumph in her eye.

I ventured a few platitudes concerning pigs, not penetrating the depths of that branch of rural science enough to betray my ignorance. Such sentiments as "A little piece of bacon well broiled for breakfast is very good," and "Nothing better than cold ham for lunch," were received by Susan and her father in the spirit I meant, — of entire good-will toward pork generally. I now look back in amusement at having fallen into this weakness, for the Mosaic view of pork has been mine from infancy, and campaigning upon government rations has, in truth, no tendency to dim this ancient faith.

By half past nine the gates of conversation were fairly open, and our part of the circle enjoyed itself socially, — taciturnity and clouds of Virginia plug

reigning supreme upon the other. The two little children crept under comforters somewhere near the middle of the bed, and subsided pleasantly to
sleep. The old man at last stretched sleepily, finally yawning out, "Susan,
I do believe I am too tired out to go and see if them corral bars are down.
I guess you'll have to go. I reckon there ain't no bears round to-night." Susan
rose to her feet, stretched herself with her back to the fire, and I realized for
the first time her amusing proportions. In the region of six feet, tall, square-
shouldered, of firm iron back and heavy mould of limb, she yet possessed that
suppleness which enabled her as she rose to throw herself into nearly all the
attitudes of the Niobe children. As her yawn deepened, she waved nearly
down to the ground, and then, rising upon tiptoe, stretched up her clinched
fists to heaven with a groan of pleasure. Turning to me, she asked, "How
would you like to see the hogs?" The old man added, as an extra encouragement, "Pootiest band of hogs in Tulare County! There's littler of the real
sissor-bill nor Mexican racer stock than any band I have ever seen in the
State. I driv the original outfit from Pike County to Oregon in '51 and '52."
By this time I was actually interested in them, and joining Susan we passed
out into the forest.

The full moon, now high in the heavens, looked down over the whole
landscape of clustered forest and open meadow with tranquil silvery light.
It whitened measurably the fine spiry tips of the trees, fell luminous upon
broad bosses of granite which here and there rose through the soil, and
glanced in trembling reflections from the rushing surface of the brook. Far
in the distance moonlit peaks towered in solemn rank against the sky.

We walked silently on four or five minutes through the woods, coming at
last upon a fence which margined a wide circular opening in the wood. The
bars, as her father had feared, were down. We stepped over them, quietly
entered the enclosure, put them up behind us, and proceeded to the middle,
threading our way among sleeping swine to where a lonely tree rose to the
height of about two hundred feet. Against this we placed our backs, and
Susan waved her hand in pride over the two acres of tranquil pork. The eye,
after accustoming itself to the darkness, took cognizance of a certain ridgyness
of surface which came to be recognized as the objects of Susan's pride.

Quite a pretty effect was caused by the shadow of the forest, which, cast
obliquely downward by the moon, divided the corral into halves of light and
shade.

The air was filled with heavy breathing, interrupted by here and there a
snore, and at times by crescendos of tumult, caused by forty or fifty pigs doing
battle for some favorite bed-place.

I was informed that Susan did not wish me to judge of them by dark, but
to see them again in the full light of day. She knew each individual pig by
its physiognomy, having, as she said, "growed with 'em."

As we strolled back toward the bars a dusky form disputed our way, — two
small, sharp eyes and a wild crest of bristles were visible in the obscure light.
"That's Old Arkansas," said Susan; "he's eight year old come next June, and
I never could get him to like me." I felt for my pistol, but Susan struck a
vigorous attitude, ejaculating, "S-S-oway, Arkansas!" She made a dash in his
direction; a wild scuffle ensued, in which I heard the dull thud of Susan's

shoe, accompanied by, "Take that, dog-on-you!" a cloud of dust, one shrill squeal, and Arkansas retreated into the darkness at a business-like trot.

When quite near the bars the mighty girl launched herself into the air, alighting with her stomach across the topmost rail, where she hung a brief moment, made a violent muscular contraction, and alighted upon the ground outside, communicating to it a tremor quite perceptible from where I stood. I climbed over after her, and we sauntered under the trees back to camp.

The family had disappeared; a few dry boughs, however, thrown upon the coals, blazed up, and revealed their forms in the corrugated topography of the bed.

I bade Susan good night, and before I could turn my back she kicked her number-eleven shoes into the air, and with masterly rapidity turned in, as Minerva is said to have done, in full panoply.

I fled precipitately to my camp, and sought my blankets, lying awake in a kind of half-revery, in which Susan and Arkansas, the old woman and her coons, were the prominent figures. Later I fell asleep, and lay motionless until the distant roar of swine awoke me before sunrise next morning.

Seated upon my blankets, I beheld Susan's mother drag forth the two children, one after another, by the napes of their necks, and, shaking the sleep out of them, propel them spitefully toward the brook; then taking her pipe from her mouth she bent low over the sleeping form of her huge daughter, and in a high, shrill, nasal key, screeched in her ear, "Yew Suse!"

No sign of life on the part of the daughter.

"Susan, *are* you a-going to get up?"

Slight muscular contraction of the lower limbs.

"Will you hear me, *Susan?*"

"Marm," whispered the girl, in low, sleepy tones.

"Get up and let the *hogs* out!"

The idea had at length thrilled into Susan's brain, and with a violent suddenness she sat bolt upright, brushing her green-colored hair out of her eyes, and rubbing those valuable but bleared organs with the ponderous knuckles of her forefingers.

By this time I started for the brook for my morning toilet, and the girl and I met upon opposite banks, stooping to wash our faces in the same pool. As I opened my dressing-case her lower jaw fell, revealing a row of ivory teeth rounded out by two well-developed "wisdoms," which had all that dazzling grin one sees in the show-windows of certain dental practitioners. It required but a moment to gather up a quart or so of water in her broad palms, and rub it vigorously into a small circle upon the middle of her face, the moisture working outward to a certain high-water mark, which, along her chin and cheeks, defined the limits of former ablution; then, baring her large red arms to the elbow, she washed her hands, and stood resting them upon her hips, dripping freely, and watching me with intense curiosity.

When I reached the towel process, she herself twisted her body after the manner of the Belvedere torso, bent low her head, gathered up the back breadths of her petticoat, and wiped her face vigorously upon it, which had the effect of tracing concentric streaks irregularly over her countenance.

I parted my hair by the aid of a small dressing-glass, which so fired Susan that she crossed the stream with a mighty jump, and stood in ecstasy by my side. She borrowed the glass, and then my comb, rewashed her face, and fell to work diligently upon her hair.

All this did not so limit my perception as to prevent my watching the general demeanor of the family. The old man lay back at his ease, puffing a cloud of smoke; his wife, also emitting volumes of the vapor of "navy plug," squatted by the camp-fire, frying certain lumps of pork, and communicating an occasional spiral jerk to the coffee-pot, with the purpose, apparently, of stirring the grounds. The two children had gotten upon the back of a contemplative ass, who stood by the upper side of the bed quietly munching the corner of a comforter.

My friend was in no haste. She squandered much time upon the arrangement of her towy hair, and there was something like a blush of conscious satisfaction when she handed me back my looking-glass and remarked ironically, "O no, I guess not, — no, sir."

I begged her to accept the comb and glass, which she did with maidenly joy.

This unusual toilet had stimulated with self-respect Susan's every fibre, and as she sprung back across the brook and approached her mother's camp-fire, I could not fail to admire the magnificent turn of her shoulders and the powerful, queenly poise of her head. Her full, grand form and heavy strength reminded me of the statues of Ceres, yet there was withal a very unpleasant suggestion of fighting trim, a sort of prize-ring manner of swinging the arms, and hitching of the shoulders. She suddenly spied the children upon the jackass, and with one wide sweep of her right arm projected them over the creature's head, and planted her left eleven firmly in the ribs of the donkey, who beat a precipitate retreat in the direction of the hog-pens, leaving her executing a *pas seul*, — a kind of slow, stately jig, something between the minuet and the *juba*, accompanying herself by a low-hummed air and a vigorous beating of time upon her slightly lifted knee.

It required my Pike County friends but ten minutes to swallow their pork and begin the labors of the day.

The mountaineers' camp was not yet astir. These children of the forest were well chained in slumber; for, unless there is some special programme for the day, it requires the leverage of a high sun to arouse their faculties, dormant enough by nature, and soothed into deepest quiet by whiskey. About eight o'clock they breakfasted, and by nine had engaged my innocent camp-men in a game of social poker.

I visited my horses, and had them picketed in the best possible feed, and congratulated myself that they were recruiting finely for the difficult ride before me.

Susan, after a second appeal from her mother, ran over to the corral and let out the family capital, who streamed with exultant grunt through the forest, darkening the fair green meadow gardens, and happily passing out of sight.

When I had breakfasted I joined Mr. Newty in his trip to the corral, where we stood together for hours, during which I had mastered the story of his years since, in 1850, he left his old home in Pike of Missouri.

It was one of those histories common enough through this wide West, yet never failing to startle me with its horrible lesson of social disintegration, of human retrograde.

That brave spirit of Westward Ho! which has been the pillar of fire and cloud leading on the weary march of progress over stretches of desert, lining the way with graves of strong men; of new-born lives; of sad, patient mothers, whose pathetic longing for the new home died with them; of the thousand old and young whose last agony came to them as they marched with eyes strained on after the sunken sun, and whose shallow barrows scarcely lift over the drifting dust of the desert; that restless spirit which has dared to uproot the old and plant the new, kindling the grand energy of California, laying foundations for a State to be, that is admirable, is poetic, is to fill an immortal page in the story of America; but when, instead of urging on to wresting from new lands something better than old can give, it degenerates into mere weak-minded restlessness, killing the power of growth, the ideal of home, the faculty of repose, it results in that race of perpetual emigrants who roam as dreary waifs over the West, losing possessions, love of life, love of God, slowly dragging from valley to valley till they fall by the wayside, happy if some chance stranger performs for them the last rites, — often less fortunate, as blanched bones and fluttering rags upon too many hillsides plainly tell.

The Newtys were of this dreary brotherhood. In 1850, with a small family of that authentic strain of high-bred swine for which Pike County is widely known, as Mr. Newty avers, they bade Missouri and their snug farm good by, and, having packed their household goods into a wagon drawn by two spotted oxen, set out with the baby Susan for Oregon, where they came after a year's march, tired, and cursed with a permanent discontent. There they had taken up a rancho, a quarter-section of public domain, which at the end of two years was "improved" to the extent of the "neatest little worm fence this side of Pike," a barn, and a smoke-house. "In another year," said my friend, "I'd have dug for a house, but we tuck ager and the second baby died." One day there came a man who "let on that he knowed" land in California much fairer and more worthy tillage than Oregon's best, so the poor Newtys harnessed up the wagon and turned their backs upon a home nearly ready for comfortable life, and swept south with pigs and plunder. Through all the years this story had repeated itself, new homes gotten to the edge of completion, more babies born, more graves made, more pigs, who replenished as only the Pike County variety may, till it seemed to me the mere multiplication of them must reach a sufficient dead weight to anchor the family; but this was dispelled when Newty remarked: "These yer hogs is awkward about moving, and I've pretty much made my mind to put 'em all into bacon this fall, and sell out and start for Montana."

Poor fellow! at Montana he will probably find a man from Texas who in half an hour will persuade him that happiness lies there. . . .

[As I rode away] the picture of this family stood before me in all its deformity of outline, all its poverty of detail, all its darkness of future, and I believe I thought of it too gravely to enjoy as I might the subtle light of comedy which plays about these hard, repulsive figures.

In conversation I had caught the clew of a better past. Newty's father was a New-Englander, and he spoke of him as a man of intelligence and, as I should judge, of some education. Mrs. Newty's father had been an Arkansas judge, not perhaps the most enlightened of men, but still very far in advance of herself. The conspicuous retrograde seemed to me an example of the most hopeless phase of human life. If, as I suppose, we may all sooner or later give in our adhesion to the Darwinian view of development, does not the same law which permits such splendid scope for the better open up to us also possible gulfs of degradation, and are not these chronic emigrants whose broken-down wagons and weary faces greet you along the dusty highways of the far West melancholy examples of beings who have forever lost the conservatism of home and the power of improvement?

[1872]

The Backward View

The Leader of the People   JOHN STEINBECK

John Steinbeck (1902–   ) is known for such novels as *Tortilla Flat*
(1935), *In Dubious Battle* (1936), and *The Grapes of Wrath* (1939),
a powerful story of the westward journey of dispossessed "Okies" who
become California migrant workers. (See p. 415.) Born in Salinas,
Steinbeck has rarely lived outside California, the locale of most of his
fiction, including the following story. *Cannery Row* (1945) and *East
of Eden* (1952) are later novels which also have California settings and
themes.

"The Leader of the People" may be seen either as Jody's, Carl's, or
the grandfather's story. In the course of it, each is "initiated," each learns
something about life that he hadn't known before, and, in different ways
and to different degrees, the knowledge of each is related to his individual
experience of being an American. Steinbeck is often accused of sentimentality in portraying the common folk, but it is doubtful that this charge
could be made to stand against "The Leader of the People." Careful
characterization, narrative interest, significant theme, illuminating use of
symbols, accurate reflection of common speech are some of the qualities
which contribute to the effectiveness of the story.

". . . 'Westering isn't a hunger any more. It's all done.' . . ."

On Saturday afternoon Billy Buck, the ranch-hand, raked together the last of
the old year's haystack and pitched small forkfuls over the wire fence to a few
mildly interested cattle. High in the air small clouds like puffs of cannon
smoke were driven eastward by the March wind. The wind could be heard
whishing in the brush on the ridge crests, but no breath of it penetrated down
into the ranch-cup.

The little boy, Jody, emerged from the house eating a thick piece of
buttered bread. He saw Billy working on the last of the haystack. Jody
tramped down scuffing his shoes in a way he had been told was destructive
to good shoe-leather. A flock of white pigeons flew out of the black cypress
tree as Jody passed, and circled the tree and landed again. A half-grown
tortoise-shell cat leaped from the bunkhouse porch, galloped on stiff legs across
the road, whirled and galloped back again. Jody picked up a stone to help

the game along, but he was too late, for the cat was under the porch before the stone could be discharged. He threw the stone into the cypress tree and started the white pigeons on another whirling flight.

Arriving at the used-up haystack, the boy leaned against the barbed wire fence. "Will that be all of it, do you think?" he asked.

The middle-aged ranch-hand stopped his careful raking and stuck his fork into the ground. He took off his black hat and smoothed down his hair. "Nothing left of it that isn't soggy from ground moisture," he said. He replaced his hat and rubbed his dry leathery hands together.

"Ought to be plenty mice," Jody suggested.

"Lousy with them," said Billy. "Just crawling with mice."

"Well, maybe, when you get all through, I could call the dogs and hunt the mice."

"Sure, I guess you could," said Billy Buck. He lifted a forkful of the damp ground-hay and threw it into the air. Instantly three mice leaped out and burrowed frantically under the hay again.

Jody sighed with satisfaction. Those plump, sleek, arrogant mice were doomed. For eight months they had lived and multiplied in the haystack. They had been immune from cats, from traps, from poison and from Jody. They had grown smug in their security, overbearing and fat. Now the time of disaster had come; they would not survive another day.

Billy looked up at the top of the hills that surrounded the ranch. "Maybe you better ask your father before you do it," he suggested.

"Well, where is he? I'll ask him now."

"He rode' up to the ridge ranch after dinner. He'll be back pretty soon."

Jody slumped against the fence post. "I don't think he'd care."

As Billy went back to his work he said ominously, "You'd better ask him anyway. You know how he is."

Jody did know. His father, Carl Tiflin, insisted upon giving permission for anything that was done on the ranch, whether it was important or not. Jody sagged farther against the post until he was sitting on the ground. He looked up at the little puffs of wind-driven cloud. "Is it like to rain, Billy?"

"It might. The wind's good for it, but not strong enough."

"Well, I hope it don't rain until after I kill those damn mice." He looked over his shoulder to see whether Billy had noticed the mature profanity. Billy worked on without comment.

Jody turned back and looked at the side-hill where the road from the outside world came down. The hill was washed with lean March sunshine. Silver thistles, blue lupins and a few poppies bloomed among the sage bushes. Halfway up the hill Jody could see Doubletree Mutt, the black dog, digging in a squirrel hole. He paddled for a while and then paused to kick bursts of dirt out between his hind legs, and he dug with an earnestness which belied the knowledge he must have had that no dog had ever caught a squirrel by digging in a hole.

Suddenly, while Jody watched, the black dog stiffened, and backed out of the hole and looked up the hill toward the cleft in the ridge where the road came through. Jody looked up too. For a moment Carl Tiflin on horseback stood out against the pale sky and then he moved down the road toward the house. He carried something white in his hand.

The boy started to his feet. "He's got a letter," Jody cried. He trotted away toward the ranch house, for the letter would probably be read aloud and he wanted to be there. He reached the house before his father did, and ran in. He heard Carl dismount from his creaking saddle and slap the horse on the side to send it to the barn where Billy would unsaddle it and turn it out.

Jody ran into the kitchen. "We got a letter!" he cried.

His mother looked up from a pan of beans. "Who has?"

"Father has. I saw it in his hand."

Carl strode into the kitchen then, and Jody's mother asked, "Who's the letter from, Carl?"

He frowned quickly. "How did you know there was a letter?"

She nodded her head in the boy's direction. "Big-Britches Jody told me." Jody was embarrassed.

His father looked down at him contemptuously. "He *is* getting to be a Big-Britches," Carl said. "He's minding everybody's business but his own. Got his big nose into everything."

Mrs. Tiflin relented a little. "Well, he hasn't enough to keep him busy. Who's the letter from?"

Carl still frowned on Jody. "I'll keep him busy if he isn't careful." He held out a sealed letter. "I guess it's from your father."

Mrs. Tiflin took a hairpin from her head and slit open the flap. Her lips pursed judiciously. Jody saw her eyes snap back and forth over the lines. "He says," she translated, "he says he's going to drive out Saturday to stay for a little while. Why, this is Saturday. The letter must have been delayed." She looked at the postmark. "This was mailed day before yesterday. It should have been here yesterday." She looked up questioningly at her husband, and then her face darkened angrily. "Now what have you got that look on you for? He doesn't come often."

Carl turned his eyes away from her anger. He could be stern with her most of the time, but when occasionally her temper arose, he could not combat it.

"What's the matter with you?" she demanded again.

In his explanation there was a tone of apology Jody himself might have used. "It's just that he talks," Carl said lamely. "Just talks."

"Well, what of it? You talk yourself."

"Sure I do. But your father only talks about one thing."

"Indians!" Jody broke in excitedly. "Indians and crossing the plains!"

Carl turned fiercely on him. "You get out, Mr. Big-Britches! Go on, now! Get out!"

Jody went miserably out the back door and closed the screen with elaborate quietness. Under the kitchen window his shamed, downcast eyes fell upon a curiously shaped stone, a stone of such fascination that he squatted down and picked it up and turned it over in his hands.

The voices came clearly to him through the open kitchen window. "Jody's damn well right," he heard his father say. "Just Indians and crossing the plains. I've heard that story about how the horses got driven off about a thousand times. He just goes on and on, and he never changes a word in the things he tells."

When Mrs. Tiflin answered her tone was so changed that Jody, outside the window, looked up from his study of the stone. Her voice had become soft and explanatory. Jody knew how her face would have changed to match the tone. She said quietly, "Look at it this way, Carl. That was the big thing in my father's life. He led a wagon train clear across the plains to the coast, and when it was finished, his life was done. It was a big thing to do, but it didn't last long enough. Look!" she continued, "it's as though he was born to do that, and after he finished it, there wasn't anything more for him to do but think about it and talk about it. If there'd been any farther west to go, he'd have gone. He's told me so himself. But at last there was the ocean. He lives right by the ocean where he had to stop."

She had caught Carl, caught him and entangled him in her soft tone.

"I've seen him," he agreed quietly. "He goes down and stares off west over the ocean." His voice sharpened a little. "And then he goes up to the Horseshoe Club in Pacific Grove, and he tells people how the Indians drove off the horses."

She tried to catch him again. "Well, it's everything to him. You might be patient with him and pretend to listen."

Carl turned impatiently away. "Well, if it gets too bad, I can always go down to the bunkhouse and sit with Billy," he said irritably. He walked through the house and slammed the front door after him.

Jody ran to his chores. He dumped the grain to the chickens without chasing any of them. He gathered the eggs from the nests. He trotted into the house with the wood and interlaced it so carefully in the wood-box that two armloads seemed to fill it to overflowing.

His mother had finished the beans by now. She stirred up the fire and brushed off the stove-top with a turkey wing. Jody peered cautiously at her to see whether any rancor toward him remained. "Is he coming today?" Jody asked.

"That's what his letter said."

"Maybe I better walk up the road to meet him."

Mrs. Tiflin clanged the stove-lid shut. "That would be nice," she said. "He'd probably like to be met."

"I guess I'll just do it then."

Outside, Jody whistled shrilly to the dogs. "Come on up the hill," he commanded. The two dogs waved their tails and ran ahead. Along the roadside the sage had tender new tips. Jody tore off some pieces and rubbed them on his hands until the air was filled with the sharp wild smell. With a rush the dogs leaped from the road and yapped into the brush after a rabbit. That was the last Jody saw of them, for when they failed to catch the rabbit, they went back home.

Jody plodded on up the hill toward the ridge top. When he reached the little cleft where the road came through, the afternoon wind struck him and blew up his hair and ruffled his shirt. He looked down on the little hills and

ridges below and then out at the huge green Salinas Valley. He could see
the white town of Salinas far out in the flat and the flash of its windows
under the waning sun. Directly below him, in an oak tree, a crow congress
had convened. The tree was black with crows all cawing at once.

Then Jody's eyes followed the wagon road down from the ridge where he
stood, and lost it behind a hill, and picked it up again on the other side. On
that distant stretch he saw a cart slowly pulled by a bay horse. It disappeared
behind the hill. Jody sat down on the ground and watched the place where
the cart would reappear again. The wind sang on the hilltops and the puff-
ball clouds hurried eastward.

Then the cart came into sight and stopped. A man dressed in black dis-
mounted from the seat and walked to the horse's head. Although it was so far
away, Jody knew he had unhooked the checkrein, for the horse's head dropped
forward. The horse moved on, and the man walked slowly up the hill beside
it. Jody gave a glad cry and ran down the road toward them. The squirrels
bumped along off the road, and a road-runner flirted its tail and raced over
the edge of the hill and sailed out like a glider.

Jody tried to leap into the middle of his shadow at every step. A stone
rolled under his foot and he went down. Around a little bend he raced, and
there, a short distance ahead, were his grandfather and the cart. The boy
dropped from his unseemly running and approached at a dignified walk.

The horse plodded stumble-footedly up the hill and the old man walked
beside it. In the lowering sun their giant shadows flickered darkly behind
them. The grandfather was dressed in a black broadcloth suit and he wore
kid congress gaiters and a black tie on a short, hard collar. He carried his
black slouch hat in his hand. His white beard was cropped close and his
white eyebrows overhung his eyes like moustaches. The blue eyes were
sternly merry. About the whole face and figure there was a granite dignity,
so that every motion seemed an impossible thing. Once at rest, it seemed the
old man would be stone, would never move again. His steps were slow and
certain. Once made, no step could ever be retraced; once headed in a direction, the path would never bend nor the pace increase nor slow.

When Jody appeared around the bend, Grandfather waved his hat slowly
in welcome, and he called, "Why, Jody! Come down to meet me, have you?"

Jody sidled near and turned and matched his step to the old man's step
and stiffened his body and dragged his heels a little. "Yes, sir," he said. "We
got your letter only today."

"Should have been here yesterday," said Grandfather. "It certainly should.
How are all the folks?"

"They're fine, sir." He hesitated and then suggested shyly, "Would you
like to come on a mouse hunt tomorrow, sir?"

"Mouse hunt, Jody?" Grandfather chuckled. "Have the people of this
generation come down to hunting mice? They aren't very strong, the new
people, but I hardly thought mice would be game for them."

"No, sir. It's just play. The haystack's gone. I'm going to drive out the
mice to the dogs. And you can watch, or even beat the hay a little."

The stern, merry eyes turned down on him. "I see. You don't eat them,
then. You haven't come to that yet."

Jody exclaimed, "The dogs eat them, sir. It wouldn't be much like hunt-ing Indians, I guess."

"No, not much — but then later, when the troops were hunting Indians and shooting children and burning teepees, it wasn't much different from your mouse hunt."

They topped the rise and started down into the ranch-cup, and they lost the sun from their shoulders. "You've grown," Grandfather said. "Nearly an inch, I should say."

"More," Jody boasted. "Where they mark me on the door, I'm up more than an inch since Thanksgiving even."

Grandfather's rich throaty voice said, "Maybe you're getting too much water and turning to pith and stalk. Wait until you head out, and then we'll see."

Jody looked quickly into the old man's face to see whether his feelings should be hurt, but there was no will to injure, no punishing nor putting-in-your-place light in the keen blue eyes. "We might kill a pig," Jody suggested.

"Oh, no! I couldn't let you do that. You're just humoring me. It isn't the time and you know it."

"You know Riley, the big boar, sir?"

"Yes. I remember Riley well."

"Well, Riley ate a hole into that same haystack, and it fell down on him and smothered him."

"Pigs do that when they can," said Grandfather.

"Riley was a nice pig, for a boar, sir. I rode him sometimes, and he didn't mind."

A door slammed at the house below them, and they saw Jody's mother standing on the porch waving her apron in welcome. And they saw Carl Tiflin walking up from the barn to be at the house for the arrival.

The sun had disappeared from the hills by now. The blue smoke from the house chimney hung in flat layers in the purpling ranch-cup. The puff-ball clouds, dropped by the falling wind, hung listlessly in the sky.

Billy Buck came out of the bunkhouse and flung a wash basin of soapy water on the ground. He had been shaving in mid-week, for Billy held Grandfather in reverence, and Grandfather said that Billy was one of the few men of the new generation who had not gone soft. Although Billy was in middle age, Grandfather considered him a boy. Now Billy was hurrying toward the house too.

When Jody and Grandfather arrived, the three were waiting for them in front of the yard gate.

Carl said, "Hello, sir. We've been looking for you."

Mrs. Tiflin kissed Grandfather on the side of his beard, and stood still while his big hand patted her shoulder. Billy shook hands solemnly, grin-ning under his straw mustache. "I'll put up your horse," said Billy, and he led the rig away.

Grandfather watched him go, and then, turning back to the group, he said as he had said a hundred times before, "There's a good boy. I knew his father, old Mule-tail Buck. I never knew why they called him Mule-tail except he packed mules."

Mrs. Tiflin turned and led the way into the house. "How long are you going to stay, Father? Your letter didn't say."

"Well, I don't know. I thought I'd stay about two weeks. But I never stay as long as I think I'm going to."

In a short while they were sitting at the white oilcloth table eating their supper. The lamp with the tin reflector hung over the table. Outside the dining-room windows the big moths battered softly against the glass.

Grandfather cut his steak into tiny pieces and chewed slowly. "I'm hungry," he said. "Driving out here got my appetite up. It's like when we were crossing. We all got so hungry every night we could hardly wait to let the meat get done. I could eat about five pounds of buffalo meat every night."

"It's moving around does it," said Billy. "My father was a government packer. I helped him when I was a kid. Just the two of us could about clean up a deer's ham."

"I knew your father, Billy," said Grandfather. "A fine man he was. They called him Mule-tail Buck. I don't know why except he packed mules."

"That was it," Billy agreed. "He packed mules."

Grandfather put down his knife and fork and looked around the table. "I remember one time we ran out of meat —" His voice dropped to a curious low sing-song, dropped into a tonal groove the story had worn for itself. "There was no buffalo, no antelope, not even rabbits. The hunters couldn't even shoot a coyote. That was the time for the leader to be on the watch. I was the leader, and I kept my eyes open. Know why? Well, just the minute the people began to get hungry they'd start slaughtering the team oxen. Do you believe that? I've heard of parties that just ate up their draft cattle. Started from the middle and worked toward the ends. Finally they'd eat the lead pair, and then the wheelers. The leader of a party had to keep them from doing that."

In some manner a big moth got into the room and circled the hanging kerosene lamp. Billy got up and tried to clap it between his hands. Carl struck with a cupped palm and caught the moth and broke it. He walked to the window and dropped it out.

"As I was saying," Grandfather began again, but Carl interrupted him. "You'd better eat some more meat. All the rest of us are ready for our pudding."

Jody saw a flash of anger in his mother's eyes. Grandfather picked up his knife and fork. "I'm pretty hungry, all right," he said. "I'll tell you about that later."

When supper was over, when the family and Billy Buck sat in front of the fireplace in the other room, Jody anxiously watched Grandfather. He saw the signs he knew. The bearded head leaned forward; the eyes lost their sternness and looked wonderingly into the fire; the big lean fingers laced themselves on the black knees. "I wonder," he began, "I just wonder whether I ever told you how those thieving Piutes drove off thirty-five of our horses."

"I think you did," Carl interrupted. "Wasn't it just before you went up into the Tahoe country?"

Grandfather turned quickly toward his son-in-law. "That's right. I guess I must have told you that story."

"Lots of times," Carl said cruelly, and he avoided his wife's eyes. But he felt the angry eyes on him, and he said, " 'Course I'd like to hear it again."

Grandfather looked back at the fire. His fingers unlaced and laced again. Jody knew how he felt, how his insides were collapsed and empty. Hadn't Jody been called a Big-Britches that very afternoon? He arose to heroism and opened himself to the term Big-Britches again. "Tell about Indians," he said softly.

Grandfather's eyes grew stern again. "Boys always want to hear about Indians. It was a job for men, but boys want to hear about it. Well, let's see. Did I ever tell you how I wanted each wagon to carry a long iron plate?"

Everyone but Jody remained silent. Jody said, "No. You didn't."

"Well, when the Indians attacked, we always put the wagons in a circle and fought from between the wheels. I thought that if every wagon carried a long plate with rifle holes, the men could stand the plates on the outside of the wheels when the wagons were in the circle and they would be protected. It would save lives and that would make up for the extra weight of the iron. But of course the party wouldn't do it. No party had done it before and they couldn't see why they should go to the expense. They lived to regret it, too."

Jody looked at his mother, and knew from her expression that she was not listening at all. Carl picked at a callus on his thumb and Billy Buck watched a spider crawling up the wall.

Grandfather's tone dropped into its narrative groove again. Jody knew in advance exactly what words would fall. The story droned on, speeded up for the attack, grew sad over the wounds, struck a dirge at the burials on the great plains. Jody sat quietly watching Grandfather. The stern blue eyes were detached. He looked as though he were not very interested in the story himself.

When it was finished, when the pause had been politely respected as the frontier of the story, Billy Buck stood up and stretched and hitched his trousers. "I guess I'll turn in," he said. Then he faced Grandfather. "I've got an old powder horn and a cap and ball pistol down to the bunkhouse. Did I ever show them to you?"

Grandfather nodded slowly. "Yes, I think you did, Billy. Reminds me of a pistol I had when I was leading the people across." Billy stood politely until the little story was done, and then he said, "Good night," and went out of the house.

Carl Tiflin tried to turn the conversation then. "How's the country between here and Monterey? I've heard it's pretty dry."

"It is dry," said Grandfather. "There's not a drop of water in the Laguna Seca. But it's a long pull from '87. The whole country was powder then, and in '61 I believe all the coyotes starved to death. We had fifteen inches of rain this year."

"Yes, but it all came too early. We could do with some now." Carl's eye fell on Jody. "Hadn't you better be getting to bed?"

Jody stood up obediently. "Can I kill the mice in the old haystack, sir?"

"Mice? Oh! Sure, kill them all off. Billy said there isn't any good hay left."

Jody exchanged a secret and satisfying look with Grandfather. "I'll kill every one tomorrow," he promised.

Jody lay in his bed and thought of the impossible world of Indians and buffaloes, a world that had ceased to be forever. He wished he could have been living in the heroic time, but he knew he was not of heroic timber. No one living now, save possibly Billy Buck, was worthy to do the things that had been done. A race of giants had lived then, fearless men, men of a staunchness unknown in this day. Jody thought of the wide plains and of the wagons moving across like centipedes. He thought of Grandfather on a huge white horse, marshaling the people. Across his mind marched the great phantoms, and they marched off the earth and they were gone.

He came back to the ranch for a moment, then. He heard the dull rushing sound that space and silence make. He heard one of the dogs, out in the dog-house, scratching a flea and bumping his elbow against the floor with every stroke. Then the wind arose again and the black cypress groaned and Jody went to sleep.

He was up half an hour before the triangle sounded for breakfast. His mother was rattling the stove to make the flames roar when Jody went through the kitchen. "You're up early," she said. "Where are you going?"

"Out to get a good stick. We're going to kill the mice today."

"Who is 'we'?"

"Why, Grandfather and I."

"So you've got him in it. You always like to have someone in with you in case there's blame to share."

"I'll be right back," said Jody. "I just want to have a good stick ready for after breakfast."

He closed the screen door after him and went out into the cool blue morning. The birds were noisy in the dawn and the ranch cats came down from the hill like blunt snakes. They had been hunting gophers in the dark, and although the four cats were full of gopher meat, they sat in a semi-circle at the back door and mewed piteously for milk. Doubletree Mutt and Smasher moved sniffing along the edge of the brush, performing the duty with rigid ceremony, but when Jody whistled, their heads jerked up and their tails waved. They plunged down to him, wriggling their skins and yawning. Jody patted their heads seriously, and moved on to the weathered scrap pile. He selected an old broom handle and a short piece of inch-square scrap wood. From his pocket he took a shoelace and tied the ends of the sticks loosely together to make a flail. He whistled his new weapon through the air and struck the ground experimentally, while the dogs leaped aside and whined with apprehension.

Jody turned and started down past the house toward the old haystack ground to look over the field of slaughter, but Billy Buck, sitting patiently on the back steps, called to him, "You better come back. It's only a couple of minutes till breakfast."

Jody changed his course and moved toward the house. He leaned his flail against the steps. "That's to drive the mice out," he said. "I'll bet they're fat. I'll bet they don't know what's going to happen to them today."

"No, nor you either," Billy remarked philosophically, "nor me, nor any-one."

Jody was staggered by this thought. He knew it was true. His imagina-tion twitched away from the mouse hunt. Then his mother came out on the back porch and struck the triangle, and all thoughts fell in a heap.

Grandfather hadn't appeared at the table when they sat down. Billy nodded at his empty chair. "He's all right? He isn't sick?"

"He takes a long time to dress," said Mrs. Tiflin. "He combs his whiskers and rubs up his shoes and brushes his clothes."

Carl scattered sugar on his mush. "A man that's led a wagon train across the plains has got to be pretty careful how he dresses."

Mrs. Tiflin turned on him. "Don't do that, Carl! Please don't!" There was more of threat than of request in her tone. And the threat irritated Carl.

"Well, how many times do I have to listen to the story of the iron plates, and the thirty-five horses? That time's done. Why can't he forget it, now it's done?" He grew angrier while he talked, and his voice rose. "Why does he have to tell them over and over? He came across the plains. All right! Now it's finished. Nobody wants to hear about it over and over."

The door into the kitchen closed softly. The four at the table sat frozen. Carl laid his mush spoon on the table and touched his chin with his fingers.

Then the kitchen door opened and Grandfather walked in. His mouth smiled tightly and his eyes were squinted. "Good morning," he said, and he sat down and looked at his mush dish.

Carl could not leave it there. "Did — did you hear what I said?"

Grandfather jerked a little nod.

"I don't know what got into me, sir. I didn't mean it. I was just being funny."

Jody glanced in shame at his mother, and he saw that she was looking at Carl, and that she wasn't breathing. It was an awful thing that he was doing. He was tearing himself to pieces to talk like that. It was a terrible thing to him to retract a word, but to retract it in shame was infinitely worse.

Grandfather looked sidewise. "I'm trying to get right side up," he said gently. "I'm not being mad. I don't mind what you said, but it might be true, and I would mind that."

"It isn't true," said Carl. "I'm not feeling well this morning. I'm sorry I said it."

"Don't be sorry, Carl. An old man doesn't see things sometimes. Maybe you're right. The crossing is finished. Maybe it should be forgotten, now it's done."

Carl got up from the table. "I've had enough to eat. I'm going to work. Take your time, Billy!" He walked quickly out of the dining-room. Billy gulped the rest of his food and followed soon after. But Jody could not leave his chair.

"Won't you tell any more stories?" Jody asked.

"Why, sure I'll tell them, but only when — I'm sure people want to hear them."

"I like to hear them, sir."

"Oh! Of course you do, but you're a little boy. It was a job for men, but only little boys like to hear about it."

Jody got up from his place. "I'll wait outside for you, sir. I've got a good stick for those mice."

He waited by the gate until the old man came out on the porch. "Let's go down and kill the mice now," Jody called.

"I think I'll just sit in the sun, Jody. You go kill the mice."

"You can use my stick if you like."

"No, I'll just sit here a while."

Jody turned disconsolately away, and walked down toward the old hay-stack. He tried to whip up his enthusiasm with thoughts of the fat juicy mice. He beat the ground with his flail. The dogs coaxed and whined about him, but he could not go. Back at the house he could see Grandfather sitting on the porch, looking small and thin and black.

Jody gave up and went to sit on the steps at the old man's feet.

"Back already? Did you kill the mice?"

"No, sir. I'll kill them some other day."

The morning flies buzzed close to the ground and the ants dashed about in front of the steps. The heavy smell of sage slipped down the hill. The porch boards grew warm in the sunshine.

Jody hardly knew when Grandfather started to talk. "I shouldn't stay here, feeling the way I do." He examined his strong old hands. "I feel as though the crossing wasn't worth doing." His eyes moved up the side-hill and stopped on a motionless hawk perched on a dead limb. "I tell those old stories, but they're not what I want to tell. I only know how I want people to feel when I tell them.

"It wasn't Indians that were important, nor adventures, nor even getting out here. It was a whole bunch of people made into one big crawling beast. And I was the head. It was westering and westering. Every man wanted something for himself, but the big beast that was all of them wanted only westering. I was the leader, but if I hadn't been there, someone else would have been the head. The thing had to have a head.

"Under the little bushes the shadows were black at white noonday. When we saw the mountains at last, we cried — all of us. But it wasn't getting here that mattered, it was movement and westering.

"We carried life out here and set it down the way those ants carry eggs. And I was the leader. The westering was as big as God, and the slow steps that made the movement piled up and piled up until the continent was crossed.

"Then we came down to the sea, and it was done." He stopped and wiped his eyes until the rims were red. "That's what I should be telling instead of stories."

When Jody spoke, Grandfather started and looked down at him. "Maybe I could lead the people some day," Jody said.

The old man smiled. "There's no place to go. There's the ocean to stop you. There's a line of old men along the shore hating the ocean because it stopped them."

"In boats I might, sir."

"No place to go, Jody. Every place is taken. But that's not the worst—no, not the worst. Westering has died out of the people. Westering isn't a hunger any more. It's all done. Your father is right. It is finished." He laced his fingers on his knee and looked at them.

Jody felt very sad. "If you'd like a glass of lemonade I could make it for you."

Grandfather was about to refuse, and then he saw Jody's face. "That would be nice," he said. "Yes, it would be nice to drink a lemonade."

Jody ran into the kitchen where his mother was wiping the last of the breakfast dishes. "Can I have a lemon to make a lemonade for Grandfather?"

His mother mimicked—"And another lemon to make a lemonade for you."

"No, ma'am. I don't want one."

"Jody! You're sick!" Then she stopped suddenly. "Take a lemon out of the cooler," she said softly. "Here, I'll reach the squeezer down to you."

[1938]

Last of the Rugged Individualists   WAYNE KERNODLE

Wayne Kernodle, an anthropologist who teaches at William and Mary College, is the editor of two recent books describing contemporary American life.

Ironically, the backwoodsmen described in the following article have maintained their frontier qualities by remaining in one place. The unity of this anecdotal sketch—which has some of the qualities of the short story and some of the informal essay—derives from the consistency of the author's serious-humorous attitude toward his subject. Although Kernodle is an anthropologist, his interest in the "last of the rugged individualists" is not altogether scientific.

"... 'progress' is on its way to Pin Hook Gap. ..."

That fierce individualist, the Southern mountaineer, has long been one of America's favorite characters. He has given us a whole series of folk heroes, from Andrew Jackson and Davy Crockett to Li'l Abner. His songs have become a national fad. He has inspired a considerable literature, ranging from serious fiction to the hillbilly cartoon.

And now he is about to vanish, without hope of rescue. Even if there were any practical way to save him, he wouldn't stand for it. In his aggressive—some say arrogant—tradition of independence, he would rather go under than

Reprinted by permission of the author.

stand beholden to any rescuer. I know, because some of the last of these rugged individualists are my friends.

As the new highways push into dozens of once-hidden coves, they are destroying that isolation which, over the course of the generations, molded the character of the Southern highlander. It is a character which the rest of the country comprehended only dimly. He was ridiculed for his insularity, and capriciously celebrated for qualities which he probably never had and doesn't have now. What he is really like is well exemplified, I think, by the McCalls of Pin Hook Gap.

Perhaps it is best not to locate the place too precisely, because there is more than one Pin Hook Gap and more McCalls than the particular family I know. It is enough to say that it lies in the westernmost end of North Carolina, close to the high, craggy spine of the Appalachians that shuts the mountain country off from the coastal East. The Plott Balsams are here and Pisgah National Forest and the Blue Ridge Mountains and the Blacks. The Cherokee Indian Reservation is not far to the west. The mountains are high — the highest east of the Mississippi — but they are not peaks but domes, "balds," flat at the top and bare, or wooded with a kind of low, torn pine. Many have barely been explored, but they have names: Yellow Face, Dirty Britches, Inkem-Binkem. If you walk northwest of these ridges you come into a good thirty miles of nearly impassable balsam slicks and rhododendron thickets, briars, and dog hobble.

It is dense country. It is also beautiful country, with perhaps the most glorious displays of floral vegetation of any part of the United States — dogwood and azalea and laurel and rhododendron, and about them cool pine forest and a tumble of waterfalls. This is also the land of the black bear and of the deer which once provided a main source of food for the Cherokee nation. There are frequent reports of panthers and wildcats, though few of these are actually seen these days.

Pin Hook Gap is, roughly, in between the cities of Asheville, North Carolina, and Knoxville, Tennessee. The needs of the cities have brought roads to connect them, and Pin Hook Gap has felt the glory and the sorrow of being on the route of march. But the cities have not been corrupters directly or intentionally. The boondocks themselves have conceived their own transfiguration.

The total population of Pin Hook is five McCalls plus an assortment of bears, panthers, rattlesnakes, and wild pigs.

Young John McCall, who is seventy-three years old, and his brother Charlie, who is seventy, live in a tight little cabin nestled into a cove under Devil's Courthouse. One brother and his wife live about two hundred yards away, and another brother lives by himself in a shack about a half-mile back in the thicket. Neither Young John nor Charlie has married, and only two of the McCalls have ever been more than fifty miles from Pin Hook during their entire lives. That time was almost forty years ago, when Charlie went into the Army and stayed at training camp for about three weeks before coming back home for good.

A friend of mine, Al Moore, who lives part-time in Brevard, knew a cousin of the McCalls. Through him Al got directions to Pin Hook and the proper passwords that would get us in to John and Charlie's place. It took the two of us and Al's sister, Martha Kate, the better part of the morning, in a jeep, to make it to the top of Pin Hook Ridge. Then we started to drop off into the cove at a remarkably steep angle.

Here, following instructions, we started blowing the jeep horn every minute. When we finally came in sight of the cabin, we stopped and sat on the horn until a figure appeared on the porch. Then we just sat there. It must have been thirty minutes before anything happened. The man on the porch stood in the doorway, leaning on a rifle, and we sat there in the jeep — waiting.

Then I got the feeling that someone was close to the jeep and looked around. There stood Charlie McCall. He had made no sound coming and had given no indication that he was there. Al Moore — who has hiked almost every inch of the territory in this section from Rough Butt Bald to Tennessee Bald and then some — introduced us. We nodded and followed Charlie up to the cabin. From the yard we howdy-ed Young John, but I haven't shaken hands with him to this day.

The beginning was mighty slow. Neither of the McCalls was inclined to start any conversation. They answered questions with the fewest words possible. At first some of the words were unintelligible to me, but Al and Martha Kate seemed to understand them well enough.

Everything about the place expressed the independent way of life. Their father had built the cabin when he first came to Pin Hook. The furniture was all fashioned by hand from cherry and walnut. It had the simple, true lines of great workmanship and was both comfortable and as sturdy as the rocks which surrounded the cove. All of their belongings had been made with tools they had hammered out themselves. The long rifle which stood across the entrance to the house had a barrel made by Charlie McCall.

Both men were tall — more than six feet — and thin, but they were not skinny. Their blue eyes were clear and sharp and their hearing was acute. They were confident men but not arrogant, cunning but not slick. They manifested a serenity unmatched by anything I have seen in the urban world. We talked about their life, which included some mining for precious stones, mica, and minerals.

With some prompting, Charlie told us about a long and ferocious struggle with a panther the winter before.

"This painter used that aire place up thar," he said, pointing out a promontory which jutted out from the balsam thickets about two thousand feet above the cabin. "He was driv by hungry and cold — hit ud been asnowin' fur a week a more. One night we heerd bangin' on the roof. We'suns tuk the rifles and got outside. He come aflyin' off the roof at us. We shot at him and he tuk off. But he come back later and was tearin' and clawin' at the windows and doors and all over the top of the house. Finally he tore a hole in the roof and come pilin' in. We fit him with arn bars and sticks and finally driv him outa the front door. John hit him in the hint leg and he'uns scremt and wailed like a dyin' hog. We haint saw him since. He had tore up the place baddest."

In the summer the McCalls raise a plot of corn and some other vegetables, and kill a hog or two. The hogs are put into a barrel of salt brine to keep from "spiling." In late August and early September, when the berries are plentiful, they pick for days at a time and can them for winter, using an old wood-burning stove and hand-fashioned pots for the cooking. During the long winter months they work at their mining, at making the various articles necessary to keep life and limb together. What they do and how they do it is entirely up to them. They are independent, but will share a real offer of friendship. Their wishes are simple but include the great wish not to be "a-dickertated to" — by men or panthers.

When we arrived, the McCalls were just getting ready to go do some mining, and seemed itchy to get on with it. By this time it had started to rain a bit. We noticed that they were going bareheaded and with only rough denim jackets on their backs. Martha Kate ran back to the jeep and got a couple of plastic tablecloths and held them out to the McCalls. Then for a moment we were sorry, because we feared they were insulted. After a few moments John McCall took one of the tablecloths and put it over his shoulders. Charlie turned and went into the cabin. A few minutes later he returned, and into Martha Kate's hand he placed a beautiful clear ruby. She could not refuse this gesture and still maintain his friendship, so she merely let it lie in her open palm as Charlie pulled the old plastic cloth over his shoulders and he and John McCall walked off toward the hills beyond their rough-hewn homestead. Al, Martha Kate, and I went to the jeep and began our trip back to the way of life that might some day swallow up the McCalls and the painter — if he's still alive.

For "progress" is on its way to Pin Hook Gap. Thirty miles away from the McCall cabin you come out onto a good dirt road and to a little community in the valley. The people at the country store were talking about the engineers who had been making surveys for paving the road and connecting it with the Blue Ridge Parkway at Wagon Road Gap and thence to Routes 19 and 23. This will connect with Highway 441, which is known as the "Over the Smokies Highway," the most scenic route between Brevard, Waynesville, Newfound Gap, Gatlinburg, and Knoxville.

They were excited about the future and the new life it meant for them. And if you know something about the stringencies of their life, you can't blame them for looking forward to more money and the chance to buy the city things that ease the hardships. I just hope the engineers leave enough balsam, "rhododaniel," white spruce, and briar thickets between the road and the McCalls to drown out the whir of those great instruments of change, the automobiles, as they wind around Pin Hook on their way to the scenic beauties which await them at the parking lots of Tennessee Bald.

It is evident that this way of life is already doomed. Twenty-one years ago, when I made my first intimate contact with the people of this region, the individualistic spirit was the first thing you noticed about the people you met. They were not special people like the McCalls that you had to go out of your way to find. They were most everybody who lived there and they simply did what was to them right and natural.

It was on my first visit in 1938 that I met Turkey Plott and Sary Ellison. I was not a complete stranger to the hill country, but my previous visits had been confined to the protected atmosphere of a church-sponsored summer assembly for young people. This time I was more on my own, and I looked forward to the exploration of the vast and exciting depths of the Great Smoky Mountains, the Balsams Range, and Pisgah National Forest. My plan was to make contact with a man named Otie Moorefield, who had been described to me as knowing more about the deep woods in this area than any man alive. From him I hoped to get instructions on trails to take — or with luck even get him to take a hiking trip with me.

My search for Moorefield led indirectly to several people who later became intimate friends. For an hour after arriving, a total stranger in this small mountain community some forty miles from Asheville, I had sought my guide in vain. Two gaunt men had ignored my questions completely, and another had "never heerd of him." Finally I got a lead from a one-eyed, gimpy-legged fellow.

"I haint saw him all day," he said, "but he mought be at Turkey Plott's."

This turned out to be the hamlet's only café, across the street and down the block. Moorefield was not there, so I decided to eat something since I had had a long, cold trip from Asheville. Here in two surprising episodes, I discovered the individualism which then characterized this community — but does not now.

Sary Ellison, the daughter of Long Butt Ellison, worked as a waitress for Turkey Plott in a defiant and condescending fashion. The place was not awfully clean, and a fairly rough-looking crowd was in the place. When I ordered a hot roast-beef sandwich, milk, and coffee, Sary took the order and went about getting it together rather pokily. Turkey made some remark about "was she gonna take all day." Sary squared off and blared out in front of everybody present:

"Who do you think you air — Hitler or somebody?"

She then threw a dishrag in my plate of food, took off her apron, wrapped it around Turkey's neck, and said, "If'n you'uns want hit on the table so fast — git it thar yourself." And stalked out.

Everybody in the café but Turkey guffawed. Turkey brought me some more food. One of the men said to him:

"Ain't nobody gonna boss Sary around."

Turkey nodded. I gathered that everybody, including Turkey, knew that Sary would be back in a day or two, but that she wouldn't stay long if anybody started acting like "Hitler." Turkey didn't seem to be particularly mad at her, either. As a matter of fact, he said he "guessed he'd a done the same thing if he'd been her." And it wasn't five minutes before he demonstrated that he would.

The grease on my hot roast-beef sandwich was just starting to congeal when two unshaven giants lurched into the café and plopped down on the counter stools beside me. They smelled of tobacco juice and corn whiskey.

Both men were visibly mad and it wasn't just the whiskey, though this had reduced their caution somewhat. Frank Gash, the biggest one, pounded his meat-axe fist on the counter so hard my glass of milk jumped and skidded off onto the floor. For some crazy reason it didn't break, but landed right side up and sat there sloshing up and down. Gash bellowed, "Whar's Turkey Plott? I'm agonna kill 'im."

Turkey had gone back into the kitchen to get an order, but he heard Gash. He came charging out between the swinging doors that separated the two rooms so fast he nearly tore them off the hinges. Plott was probably the biggest and strongest man in western North Carolina at that time.

"Who's agonna kill Turkey?" he shouted.

Without waiting for an answer, he grabbed the two men by their coat collars and banged their heads together with such force you could hear the bones crack. Then he dragged them over the counter one at a time, lifting them above his head, and threw them through the front glass window.

When the glass stopped breaking, there ensued a most remarkable and wonderful quiet. Everybody went back to eating, and Turkey went back to the kitchen. Gash and his friend were picked up by the sheriff and put in jail. When they had recovered and been released, they stopped by to apologize to Turkey for the trouble they had caused. I never did find out what had set them off in the first place, because nobody ever talked about it after that.

This kind of immediate, vigorous expression was typical and is explained in part by the special cultural environment in which such people lived.

The western North Carolina folk like Turkey, Sary, Frank Gash, and their kind were largely of Anglo-Saxon descent. As pioneers, their ancestors had pushed into these wilderness areas, staked out their claims, and settled in for good. Until 1920, and almost until after World War II, the strain was only slightly adulterated by the various migrations. Protected in their isolation by the mountains and by their own reluctance to mingle with strangers, these mountaineers escaped much of the change which was occurring elsewhere. Because economic opportunities were not abundant, education and "refinement" were neglected.

The result was a strange mixture of the proud and the shy, the ignorant and the astute, the wise and the uneducated. In a real sense they lived apart from the main stream of American culture and thus developed ways of doing things that emphasized the importance of self-reliance and responsibility for one's own fate. This difference has been widely misunderstood, since the peculiar or sensational aspects of these people have been focused upon in such ways as to make them appear either stupid or comical, or both.

But many thoughtful people in this region, who have themselves shared this history, are watching the present changes with regret. The great levelers which have invaded their hinterland are radio, television, movies, industry, labor unions, paved roads, parkways, and tourists. What these things have done to Turkey Plott and Sary Ellison illustrates in miniature what is happening to the customs, attitudes, and ambitions of the whole region.

While Turkey, Sary, and the other inhabitants were going their usual way, the community was being surveyed by outsiders who wanted to locate a textile mill there. They needed a wide expanse of land, pure water, and a supply of moderately cheap labor. They found the land and water in abundance at the foot of the hill about three miles from town. The first investment to build the mill amounted to more than three million dollars; later this was doubled for additions. New roads were built, workmen were brought in from the outside, and all the skilled labor in the community was put on the job.

Executives and their families moved in, together with a myriad of white-collar workers and personnel experts to train the mountaineers who wanted to work in the mill.

At first this increased Turkey's business, and he added some booths "for ladies and gentlemen." He also hired two new waitresses. But a new, modern restaurant opened up near him and attracted most of the new people who wanted hygiene, soft music, tablecloths, and more courteous service. Turkey finally gave up. He sold his café, lock, stock, and swinging doors, and went to work as a construction foreman at the mill.

Sary married a young insurance salesman who later became president of a thriving firm in town. She and her husband live in a modern, ranch-style house in one of the new developments on the north side. She is president of the parent-teachers association and a charter member of the garden club. Her husband was voted "young man of the year" twice in a row and is now raising funds for a new community center, which is supposed to cut down on juvenile delinquency and rowdyism in town.

Turkey found it rough going for a while at the mill. He was a good foreman but was almost fired several times for being too demanding and for losing his temper. But he got hold of himself in time and calmed down to make a good, steady worker. For years he has been the chief of new construction and is known to be back of several plans to build better houses for the mill workers, athletic fields, and other recreational facilities. About the only time I see the fire in his eyes these days is when some die-hard native or stranger makes a crack about how the mill has taken over and ruined the place. But he talks hard now instead of hitting hard.

In varying ways such urban influences have begun to standardize the life of all mountaineers. Working hours, types of work, wages, clothes, speech, and manners that once were highly individualized are — in some places gradually, in others suddenly — becoming formalized.

There was, for example, Warrior Hull. He was a strong-minded man and able to back up what he said. You didn't have to wait a week to get his opinion, either. Warrior lived by himself in a rough-hewn cabin just outside a small mountain community near Pisgah Forest. He was an artisan in the old sense, and by experience an expert machinist. He put these talents to work at a small tannery in town, where he developed the reputation of being able to fix anything.

In time the tannery was bought by outside interests in the East, and a representative of the company made a visit to survey the investment and make suggestions for improvement. At one point he came upon Warrior working on a piece of equipment. After a while he said, "Look here, you — you can work more efficiently if you'll get organized better." No comment from Hull. The boss shouted:

"You listen to me! I mean business — I want this done differently."

Hull turned slowly, picked up a monkey wrench, and said:

"You git yore damn ass outa here and stop a-dickertatin' to me — I'll bust yore head with this here monkey wranch."

The gentleman withdrew and Hull went back to work.

There are bigger plants in Hull's town now. The population has doubled, from 3,500 to 7,000 or more, and two big mills dominate the community. Warrior Hull's type does not work for either one of them, so far as I can tell. The current residents of the town are a different breed entirely. Thirty years ago there were many Warrior Hulls, and today there are none, except those who have escaped further into the hills.

Warrior Hull is dead now. The shack he lived in, where I spent many a cold winter night sleeping in front of his open fireplace, was knocked down by a bulldozer. Over the top of Hull's way of life runs a new superhighway.

At the same time that Warrior Hull was resisting change to the end, however, there were others in the region who welcomed "progress" and allied themselves with it. Though raised in the pioneering traditions, they joined hands with those who offered new opportunities. Some of them had gone into the Army during World War I and returned home with new notions about how to improve their own lot and that of their town.

Calvern Jones was one of the men who helped bring "progress." As a boy he was just as towheaded, barefooted, and snaggled-toothed as any of the kids of his age. He hauled many a fruit jar of moonshine whiskey from his father's cabin to the town residents in his home-fashioned, two-wheeled cart. His regular missions were widely known and folks would often taunt him as he pulled his cart along the back streets. "What you got there, Cal — some fancy groceries?" Cal would stiffen, ball up his fists, and yell:

"None of yore God damn business — you yeller self-made son of a bitch."

The first world war did a lot for Cal. It got him out of the bootleg business and into the grocery store. His experience in the Army — the new ideas he picked up and the extra schooling he took — provided him with a new weave in his personality. Mr. Calvern Jones opened up a nice grocery store all his own and began to spout salesmanship and progress, along with the doctors, the lawyers, and the newspapermen.

And they finally got progress in the shape of two big mills which now threaten to choke out Calvern Jones and pollute the clear waters of the rivers with their dyes. A recent editorial in the town's weekly newspaper commented on poor business conditions. At present there is only one grocery store in the main business section and that is an A & P supermarket. There was a Dixie store and, of course, Calvern Jones' store. The Dixie was bought out by the A & P, and Jones was forced out because his building was condemned. Several relatively new buildings are still unrented and most of the clothing stores have gone broke. Only the eating places and the filling stations prosper.

This has happened at a time when the people of the community have much more money than they ever had before. Jones blames the two mills which progress brought. Nearly everybody works for one of the mills and makes good money. But with the new wide superhighways to Asheville and Hendersonville, people flock to the city to spend their wages. So it's good-by Jones' store, farewell to rat cheese, the cracker box, fresh country butter, and a ten-cent poke of cressy salad.

This orientation toward the city and the urban way of life seems to have become the dominant urge of the present population. It extends into their social, economic, religious, and recreational activities, and into customs, mannerisms, speech, and styles of dress.

The informal way of life has given way to formal organization. The social and civic activities are carried on by Rotary, Kiwanis, and Lions clubs which promote civic improvement — such as bigger and better highways into the towns and larger attractions for tourists.

Recreational activities of the old type like berry picking, mountain fox hunting, and folk dancing have also been disappearing under the onslaught of spectator sports. High-school football games on lighted fields, "huddle queen" contests, and folk festivals with imported rock-and-roll guitar players have crowded out many of the old-time street dances, informal hoedowns, and singing conventions which once were the major recreational outlets. Now kids sport Elvis Presley haircuts, talk hop slang, and dress "sharp." Their mothers belong to women's clubs.

The physical face of the communities in this region is changing, too. The kind of cabin Warrior Hull built has been replaced by rows of little white houses from Asheville to Toxaway. There is a developing sameness about everything, including the manicured camping sites for tourists, with neat piles of wood cut to the proper length for the outdoor grills. A few pure specimens like the McCalls remain. In another generation their type will disappear forever. Such men already are strangers in their own land.

[1960]

Empire Builders   ARCHIBALD MACLEISH

Archibald MacLeish (1892–) was born in Illinois and graduated from Yale in 1915. After serving in France during the first World War he got an LL.B. from Harvard and practiced law. Within a few years, however, he abandoned this profession for poetry and moved to France, where he lived until 1928. Later, besides being a prolific poet, he became an assistant editor of *Fortune*, Librarian of Congress and Harvard professor. *Conquistador*, an impressive and ambitious poem dealing with the Spanish conquest of Mexico, received a Pulitzer Prize in 1932. "Empire Builders" is a part of *Frescoes for Mr. Rockefeller's City*, which represents the considerable part of MacLeish's poetry speaking a strong concern for social issues. For a vivid first-hand account of the Lewis and Clark expedition, see Bernard De Voto's edition of their journals.

"Empire Builders" makes use of several contrasts — of speakers, of times, of pictures, of characters, of audiences, of tones — in communicating what MacLeish sees as the betrayal of American promises. It is interesting to read "Empire Builders" with MacLeish's lines from "Ars Poetica" in mind: "A poem should not mean/ But be."

> "... Men have forgotten how full clear and deep
> The Yellowstone moved on the gravel. ..."

[*The Museum Attendant:*]
This is *The Making of America In Five Panels:*

This is Mister Harriman making America:
Mister-Harriman-is-buying-the-Union-Pacific-at-Seventy:
The Santa Fe is shining on his hair:

This is Commodore Vanderbilt making America: 5
Mister-Vanderbilt-is-eliminating-the-short-interest-in-Hudson:
Observe the carving on the rocking chair:

This is J. P. Morgan making America:
(The Tennessee Coal is behind to the left of the Steel Company:)
Those in mauve are braces he is wearing: 10

This is Mister Mellon making America:
Mister-Mellon-is-represented-as-a-symbolical-figure-in-aluminum-
Strewing-bank-stocks-on-a-burnished-stair:

This is the Bruce is the Barton making America:
Mister-Barton-is-selling-us-Doctor's-Deliciousest-Dentifrice: 15
This is he in beige with the canary:

You have just beheld the makers making America:
This is *The Making of America In Five Panels:*
America lies to the West-South-West of the Switch-Tower:

There is nothing to see of America but land: 20

[*The Original Document under the Panel paint:*]
"To Thos. Jefferson Esq. his obd't serv't
M. Lewis: captain: detached:
                            Sir:

Having in mind your repeated commands in this matter:
And the worst half of it done and the streams mapped:

And we here on the back of this beach beholding the   25
Other ocean — two years gone and the cold

Breaking with rain for the third spring since St. Louis:
The crows at the fish bones on the frozen dunes:

The first cranes going over from south north:
And the river down by a mark of the pole since the morning: 30

And time near to return: and a ship (Spanish)
Lying in for the salmon: and fearing chance or the

Droughts or the Sioux should deprive you of these discoveries —
Therefore we send by sea in this writing:

                                   Above the
Platte there were long plains and a clay country: 35
Rim of the sky far off: grass under it:

Dung for the cook fires by the sulphur licks:
After that there were low hills and the sycamores:

And we poled up by the Great Bend in the skiffs:
The honey bees left us after the Osage River: 40

The wind was west in the evenings and no dew and the
Morning Star larger and whiter than usual —

The winter rattling in the brittle haws:
The second year there was sage and the quail calling:

All that valley is good land by the river: 45
Three thousand miles and the clay cliffs and

Rue and beargrass by the water banks
And many birds and the brant going over and tracks of

Bear elk wolves martin: the buffalo
Numberless so that the cloud of their dust covers them: 50

The antelope fording the fall creeks and the mountains and
Grazing lands and the meadow lands and the ground

Sweet and open and well-drained:
                               We advise you to
Settle troops at the forks and to issue licenses:

Many men will have living on these lands: 55
There is wealth in the earth for them all and the wood standing

And wild birds on the water where they sleep:
There is stone in the hills for the towns of a great people. . . ."

You have just beheld the Makers making America

They screwed her scrawny and gaunt with their seven-year panics: 60
They bought her back on their mortgages old-whore-cheap:
They fattened their bonds at her breasts till the thin blood ran from them:

Men have forgotten how full clear and deep
The Yellowstone moved on the gravel and grass grew
When the land lay waiting for her westward people!   65

[1933]

Ended: the 400 Year Boom   WALTER PRESCOTT WEBB

Walter Prescott Webb (1888–   ) grew up on the West Texas frontier.
"It was there," he says, "that I touched the hem of the garment of the
frontier, received my earliest impressions of the struggle of a people with
a new and arid country." He was educated at the University of Texas
where — except for an occasional year abroad — he has been a professor
of history since 1918.

The following essay is a lucid overview of the effect of the "Great
Frontier" on the "Metropolis" during the past four centuries. It sum-
marizes many of the specific comments about the frontier made by the
other writers in this section. Webb describes the economic, political, and
social impact of the Great Frontier and in the process defines what he
terms *modernity*. The concluding paragraphs point to the problem of a
time when "the house is full."

*". . . Western civilization today stands facing a closed frontier . . . a
unique situation in modern times. . . ."*

I

Since America led the way in evolving the frontier process, and leads the
world in the study of that process, we have no choice but to examine the
American experience and to note briefly how scholars came to attend it as a
field of study. American historians assume that the frontier process began
with the English settlement at Jamestown in 1607, and the year 1890 is
usually taken to mark the date when there was no more frontier available,
when the new land was no longer new. There may be some quibbling about
the dates, but they do bracket the three centuries of American frontier experience and experimentation.

From Walter Prescott Webb, "Ended: 400 Year Boom, Reflections on the Age of
the Frontier," *Harper's Magazine*, Vol. CCIII (October, 1951), 26–33. Reprinted by
permission of the author. For an extended treatment of the thesis set forth in this article,
see Walter Prescott Webb, *The Great Frontier*, Houghton Mifflin and Company, Boston.

It was the magnitude and the unbroken continuity of the experience that gave the frontier major importance in American life. It made no difference what other tasks the Americans had on their hands at a given time, there was the additional, ever-present one of moving into and settling new country. They did it while they fought for independence, before and after; they did it while they hammered out the principles of a democratic government shaped to the needs of frontiersmen; and they did not cease doing it in the period of civil strife. They never reached the limits of the vacancy they owned before they acquired another vacancy, by purchase, by treaty, by conquest, and in every case the frontiersmen infiltrated the country before the nation acquired it. Like locusts they swarmed, always to the west, and only the Pacific Ocean stopped them. Here in this movement beat the deep overtone of a nation's destiny, and to it all kept step unconsciously.

To say that the people were unconscious of the force that moved them, and of the medium in which they moved, is to state a fact which is easy to prove but hard to explain. It may be said that they were emotionally aware of the frontier long before they were intellectually cognizant of it. People could not have as their main task for three centuries working with raw land without getting its dirt under their nails and deep into their skins. The effects were everywhere, in democratic government, in boisterous politics, in exploitative agriculture, in mobility of population, in disregard for conventions, in rude manners, and in unbridled optimism. Though these effects were present everywhere they were not understood anywhere by the people who felt and reflected them. The frontier still lacked its philosopher, the thinker who could view the whole dramatic experience and tell what was its meaning. This philosopher arrived three years after the experience ended and told the American people that from the beginning the American frontier had been the dominant force, the determining factor, in their history thus far.

This hypothesis was presented to the American Historical Association in a paper entitled "The Significance of the Frontier in American History." The date was 1893 and the author was a young and then little-known historian. That paper made Frederick Jackson Turner a scholar with honor in his own country; it altered the whole course of American historical scholarship, and it is recognized as the most influential single piece of historical writing ever done in the United States. The key to his thesis is found in this sentence: "The existence of an area of free land, its continuous recession, and the advance of American settlement westward, explain American development." The general acceptance of this frontier hypothesis, and the fame of its author, came about because the people in America were emotionally prepared to understand this rationalization and explanation of their own long experience. Turner's pupils — many of whom became disciples — flocked to the diggings and have worked out in every cove and valley the rich vein which he uncovered, but not one of them, not even the master himself, took the next step to point out or at least to emphasize that the American frontier was but a small fragment of the Great Frontier. On that Great Frontier was also an area of free land; it was in continuous recession; and the advance of European settlement into it should explain the development of Western civilization in modern times just as the American advance explains American development.

II

What happened in America was but a detail in a much greater phenomenon, the interaction between European civilization and the vast raw lands into which it moved. An effort will be made here to portray the whole frontier, to suggest how it affected the life and institutions of Western civilization throughout the modern period; and as a basis for this exposition four propositions are submitted for consideration:

(1) Europe had a frontier more than a century before the United States was settled.

(2) Europe's frontier was much greater than that of the United States, or of any other one nation; it was the greatest of all time.

(3) The frontier of Europe was almost, if not quite, as important in determining the life and institutions of modern Europe as the frontier of America was in shaping the course of American history. Without the frontier modern Europe would have been so different from what it became that it could hardly be considered modern at all. This is almost equivalent to saying that the frontier made Europe modern.

(4) The close of the Great Frontier may mark the end of an epoch in Western civilization just as the close of the American frontier is often said to have marked the end of the first phase of American history. If the close of the Great Frontier does mark the end of an age, the modern age, then the institutions designed to function in a society dominated largely by frontier forces will find themselves under severe strain.

If we conceive of Western Europe as a unified, densely populated region with a common culture and civilization — which it has long had basically — and if we see the frontier also as a unit, a vast and vacant land without culture, we are in position to view the interaction between the two as a simple but gigantic operation extending over more than four centuries, a process that may appear to be the drama of modern civilization.

To emphasize the unity of western Europe, and at the same time set it off in sharp contrast to its opposite, the frontier, we may call it the Metropolis. Metropolis is a good name, implying what Europe really was, a cultural center holding within it everything pertaining to Western civilization. Prior to 1500 the Metropolis comprised all the "known" world save Asia, which was but vaguely known. Its area was approximately 3,750,000 square miles, and its population is estimated to have been about 100 million people.

There is no need to elaborate the conditions under which these people lived, but it should be remembered that by modern standards the society was a static one with well-defined classes. The population pressed hard on the means of subsistence. There was not much food, practically no money, and very little freedom. What is more important, there was practically no means of escape for those people living in this closed world. The idea of progress had not been born. Heaven alone, which could be reached only through the portals of death, offered any hope to the masses of the Metropolis.

Then came the miracle that was to change everything, the emancipator bearing rich gifts of land and more land, of gold and silver, of new foods for every empty belly and new clothing stuffs for every half-naked back. Europe, the Metropolis, knocked on the door of the Great Frontier, and when the door was opened it was seen to be golden, for within there was undreamed-of treasure, enough to make the whole Metropolis rich. The long quest of a half-starved people had at last been rewarded with success beyond comprehension.

Columbus has been accepted as the symbol, as the key that unlocked the golden door to a new world, but we know that he was only one of a group of curious investigators, Portuguese, Spanish, English, Dutch, and Scandinavian, men of the Metropolis and not of one country. Within a brief period, as history is told, Columbus and his prying associates pulled back the curtains of ignorance and revealed to the Metropolis three new continents, a large part of a fourth, and thousands of islands in oceans hitherto hardly known. They brought all of these — continents, oceans, and islands — and deposited them as a free gift at the feet of the impoverished Metropolis.

The Metropolis had a new piece of property and the frontier had a new owner. The Metropolitans were naturally curious about their property, and quite naturally began to ask questions about it. How big is it? Who lives on it? What is its inherent worth? What can I get out of it? They learned that the frontier had an area five or six times that of Europe; that it was practically vacant, occupied by a few primitive inhabitants whose rights need not be respected; that its inherent worth could only be guessed at. As to what can I get out of it?, the answer came in time clear and strong: You can get everything you want from gold and silver to furs and foods, and in any quantity you want, provided only that you are willing to venture and work! And more faintly came the small voice, hardly audible: Something all of you can get as a by-product is some measure of freedom.

The Metropolitans decided to accept the gifts. Instantly the divisions in Europe were projected into the frontier as each little European power that could man a ship seized a section of the frontier bigger than itself and tried to fight all the others off. Each nation wanted it all. The result was a series of wars lasting from 1689 to 1763 and from these wars England, France, and Spain emerged as chief owners of the frontier world. Their success was more apparent than real, for a spirit of freedom had been nurtured in the distant lands, and in less than fifty years England had lost her chief prize while Spain and France had lost practically everything.

But their loss, like their previous gain, was more apparent than real. True, by 1820 the Metropolis had lost title to most of the new land, but it had not lost something more precious than title — namely, the beneficent effects that the frontier exerted on the older countries. The political separation of most of North and South America relieved the Metropolis of responsibility and onerous obligations, but it did not cut off the abundance of profits. Europe continued to share in the riches and the opportunity that the opening of the golden door had made visible.

III

What was the essential character of the frontier? Was the direct force it exerted spiritual, intellectual, or was it material? The frontier was basically a vast body of wealth without proprietors. It was an empty land more than five times the size of western Europe, a land whose resources had not been exploited. Its first impact was mainly economic. Bathed in and invigorated by a flood of wealth, the Metropolis began to seethe with economic excitement.

With all the ships coming and going, the wharves of Europe were piled high with strange goods, the tables were set with exotic foods of delightful flavors, and new-minted coins of gold and silver rattled in the coffers of the market place. The boom began when Columbus returned from his first voyage, and it continued at an ever-accelerating pace until the frontier that fed it was no more. Assuming that the frontier closed about 1890, it may be said that the boom lasted approximately four hundred years. It lasted so long that it came to be considered the normal state, a fallacious assumption for any boom. It is conceivable that this boom has given the peculiar character to modern history, to what we call Western civilization.

Assuming that there was such a boom and that it lasted four hundred years, it follows that a set of institutions, economic, political, and social, would in that time evolve to meet the needs of the world in boom. Insofar as they were designed to meet peculiar conditions, these institutions would be specialized boomward. It is accepted that a set of institutions has developed since 1500, and we speak of them as modern to distinguish them from medieval institutions. Therefore we may well inquire whether our modern institutions — economic, political, and social, constituting the superstructure of Western civilization — are founded on boom conditions.

The factors involved, though of gigantic magnitude, are simple in nature and in their relation one to another. They are the old familiar ones of population, land, and capital. With the opening of the Great Frontier, land and capital rose out of all proportion to population, of those to share it, and therefore conditions were highly favorable to general prosperity and a boom. What we are really concerned with is an *excess* of land and an *excess* of capital for division among a relatively *fixed* number of people. The population did increase, but not until the nineteenth century did the extra population compare with the extra land and capital that had been long available.

For example, in 1500 the Metropolis had a population of 100 million people crowded into an area of 3,750,000 square miles. The population density for the entire Metropolis was 26.7 persons per square mile. For each person there was available about twenty-four acres, a ratio that changed little from 1300 to 1650. The opening of the frontier upset the whole situation by destroying the balance that had been struck between land and man. A land excess of nearly 20 million square miles became available to the same number of people, reducing population density to less than five, increasing the average area per individual to 148 acres instead of 24.

Capital may be considered in two forms, as gold and silver and as capital goods or commodities. The Metropolis was short of both forms of wealth throughout the medieval period, and the dearth of coin prior to the discoveries was most critical. It has been estimated that the total amount of gold and silver in Europe in 1492 was less than 200 million dollars, less than two dollars per person. Certainly there was not enough to serve the needs of exchange, which was carried on by barter, or to give rise to erudite theories of money economy. Then very suddenly the whole money situation changed.

By 1500 the Spaniards had cracked the treasure houses of the Great

Frontier and set a stream of gold and silver flowing into the Metropolis, a stream that continued without abatement for 150 years, and that still continues. This flood of precious metals changed all the relations existing between man and money, between gold and a bushel of wheat or a *fanega* of barley. That changed relationship wrought the price revolution because temporarily — so fast did the metals come — there was more money than things, and so prices rose to the modern level. This new money was a powerful stimulus to the quest for more, and set the whole Metropolis into the frenzy of daring and adventure which gave character to the modern age.

Since our concern here is with the excess of wealth over population, we may examine with interest the rise in the quantity of gold and silver. Taking the 200 million dollars of 1492 as a base, we find that by 1600 the amount had increased eightfold, by 1700 it had risen nearly twentyfold, by 1800 it stood at thirty-sevenfold, and by 1900 at a hundred-and-fourfold over what was on hand when the frontier was opened. Obviously this increase of precious metals was out of all proportion to the increase in population. If we grant that an excess of money makes a boom, then here in this new treasure was the stuff a boom needed. It is safe to say that out of each $100 worth of precious metals produced in the world since 1493, not less than $85 have been supplied by the frontier countries and not more than $15 by the Metropolis, including Asia. The bearing of these facts on the rise of a money economy, of modern capitalism, is something for the economists to think about.

The spectacular influx of precious metals should not obscure the fact that they constituted but the initial wave of wealth rolling into the Metropolis from the Great Frontier. Wave followed wave in endless succession in the form of material things, and each deposit left the Metropolis richer than before. Unfortunately the quantity of material goods cannot be measured, but we know it was enormous. South America sent coffee, Africa, cocoa, and the West Indies sent sugar to sweeten them. Strange and flavorsome fruits came from the tropics. From primeval forests came ship timbers, pitch, and tar with which to build the fleets for merchants and warriors. North America sent furs for the rich and cotton for the poor so that all could have more than one garment. The potato, adapted to the Metropolis, became second to bread as the staff of life. The New World gave Indian corn or maize, and the rich lands on which to grow it, and in time hides and beef came from the plains and pampas of two continents. Everywhere in Europe from the royal palace to the humble cottage men smoked American tobacco and under its soothing influence dreamed of far countries, wealth, and adventure. Scientists brought home strange plants and herbs and made plant experiment stations in scores of European gardens. In South America they found the bark of a tree from which quinine was derived to cure malaria and another plant which they sent to the East Indies to establish the rubber industry. No, it is not possible to measure the amount of goods flowing into Europe, but it can be said that the Great Frontier hung for centuries like the horn of plenty over the Metropolis and emptied out on it an avalanche of wealth.

At this point let us turn to the growth of population, the number of people who in a rough sense shared the excess of land and of precious metals. As stated above the population in 1500 stood at about 100 million, and it did not increase appreciably before 1650. All the people of European origin, whether in the Metropolis or in the Great Frontier, had a little more than doubled by 1800. Not until the nineteenth century was the increase rapid. By 1850 the increase was more than threefold, by 1900 more than fivefold, but in 1940 population had increased eightfold over that of 1500. The significant fact is that between 1500 and 1850 the quantity of both land and capital stood high out of all proportion to the quantity of population. Equally significant, and somewhat disturbing, is the fact that the excess of land incident to opening the frontier disappeared in the world census of 1930. By 1940 the enlarged Western world was more crowded than the small world of Europe was in 1500. It was the observation of this fact which led Dean Inge to remark in 1938 that "the house is full." Much earlier William Graham Sumner commented on the man-land ratio: "It is this ratio of population to land which determines what are the possibilities of human development or the limits of what man can attain in civilization and comfort." To put the matter in another way, if the boom rested on a four-century excess of land over population, the land base of the boom disappeared in 1930. . . .

IV

If the opening of the Great Frontier did precipitate a boom in Western civilization, the effects on human ideas and institutions must have been profound and far-reaching. In general such a boom would hasten the passing away of the ideas and institutions of a static culture and the sure appearance of others adapted to a dynamic and prospering society. There is no doubt that medieval society was breaking up at the time of the discoveries, that men's minds had been sharpened by their intellectual exercises, and that their spirits had been stirred by doubt. The thinkers were restless and inquiring, but what they lacked was room in which to try out their innovations, and a fresh and uncluttered soil in which some of their new ideas could take hold and grow. Their desires had to be matched with opportunity before they could realize on their aspirations, however laudable. The frontier offered them the room and the opportunity. It did not necessarily originate ideas, but it acted as a relentless sifter, letting some pass and rejecting others. Those that the frontier favored prospered, and finally matured into institutions; those it did not favor became recessive, dormant, and many institutions based on these ideas withered away. Feudal tenure, serfdom, barter, primogeniture, and the notion that the world was a no-good place in which to live are examples of things untenable in the presence of the frontier.

Since we are dealing with the modern age, it would be very helpful if we could discover what it emphasized most. Where was the chief accent of modernity? What has been its focus? *Who* has held the spotlight on the stage of history since 1500? There can be little doubt, though there may be enough to start an argument, that the answer to all these questions is: the Individual. It is he who has been emphasized, accented; it is on him that the spotlight has focused; it is his importance that has been magnified. He is — or was — the common denominator of modern times, and an examination of any strictly modern institution such as democracy or capitalism will reveal an individual at the core, trying to rule himself in one case and make some money in the other. Not God nor the devil nor the state, but the ordinary man has been the favorite child of modern history.

Did the Great Frontier, which was his contemporary, have any part in giving the individual his main chance, the triple opportunity of ruling himself, enriching himself, and saving his own soul on his own hook? These three freedoms were institutionalized in Protestantism, capitalism, and democracy — whose basic assumption is that they exist for the individual, and that the individual must be free in order to make them work. The desire for freedom men surely have always had, but in the old Metropolis conditions prevailed which made freedom impossible. Everywhere in Europe the individual was surrounded by institutions which, whether by design or not, kept him unfree. He was walled in by man-made regulations which controlled him from baptism to extreme unction.

Then the golden door of the Great Frontier opened, and a way of escape lay before him. He moved out from the Metropolis to land on a distant shore, in America, Australia, South Africa. Here in the wild and empty land there was not a single institution; man had left them, albeit temporarily, far behind. Regardless of what befell him later, for an instant he was free of all the restrictions that society had put upon him. In short, he had escaped his human masters only to find himself in the presence of another, a less picayunish one.

The character of the new master, before whom he stood stripped of his institutions, was so in contrast with that of the old one as to defy comparison. Man stood naked in the presence of nature. On this subject, Alexander von Humboldt said, "In the Old World, nations and the distinction of their civilization form the principal point in the picture; in the New World, man and his production almost disappear amidst the stupendous display of wild and gigantic nature." The outstanding qualities of wild and gigantic nature are its impersonality and impassiveness. Nature broods over man, casts its mysterious spells, but it never intervenes for or against him. It gives no orders, issues no proclamations, has no prisons, no privileges; it knows nothing of vengeance or mercy. Before nature all men are free and equal.

The important point is that the abstract man we have been following did not have to *win* his freedom. It was imposed upon him and he could not escape it. Being caught in the trap of freedom, his task was to adjust himself to it and to devise procedures which would be more convenient for living in such a state. His first task was to govern himself, for self-government is what freedom imposes.

Of course there was not just one man on the frontier. In a short time the woods were full of them, all trained in the same school. As the years went by, they formed the habits of freedom, cherished it; and when a distant government tried to take from them that to which they had grown accustomed, they resisted, and their resistance was called the American Revolution. The American frontiersmen did not fight England to gain freedom, but to preserve it and have it officially recognized by the Metropolis. "Your nation," wrote Herman Melville, "enjoyed no little independence before your declaration declared it." Whence came this independence? Not from parliaments or kings or legislative assemblies, but from the conditions, the room, the space, and the natural wealth amidst which they lived. "The land was ours," writes Robert Frost, "before we were the land's."

The other institution that magnified the importance of the individual was capitalism, an economic system under which each person undertakes to enrich himself by his own effort. It is only in the presence of great abundance that such a free-for-all system of wealth-getting can long operate. There must be present enough wealth to go around to make such an economy practicable. We have seen that the tapping of the frontier furnished just this condition, a superabundance of land, of gold and silver, and of commodities which made the principle of *laissez faire* tenable. In the frontier the embryonic capitalists of the sixteenth and seventeenth centuries hit a magnificent windfall which set them up in business by demonstrating that the game of wealth-getting was both interesting and profitable. For four hundred years, to paraphrase Bernard DeVoto, "men stumbled over fortunes looking for cows." Free homesteads in Kansas, free gold claims in California, and free grass on the Great Plains are examples of windfalls coming at the tag end of the frontier period, windfalls which come no more. In the larger sense the Great Frontier was a windfall for Europe.

There is an unpleasant logic inherent in the frontier boom hypothesis of modern history. We come to it with the reluctance that men always have when they come to the end of a boom. They look back on the grand opportunities they had, they remember the excitement and adventure of it, they tot up their accounts and hope for another chance. Western civilization today stands facing a closed frontier, and in this sense it faces a unique situation in modern times.

If we grant the boom, we must concede that the institutions we have, such as democracy and capitalism, were boom-born; we must also admit that the individual, this cherished darling of modern history, attained his glory in an abnormal period when there was enough room to give him freedom and enough wealth to give him independence. The future of the individual, of democracy and capitalism, and of many other modern institutions is deeply involved in this logic, and the lights are burning late in the capitals of the Western world where grave men are trying to determine what that future will be.

Meantime less thoughtful people speak of new frontiers, though nothing comparable to the Great Frontier has yet been found. The business man sees a business frontier in the customers he has not yet reached; the missionary sees a religious frontier among the souls he has not yet saved; the social worker sees a human frontier among the suffering people whose woes he has not yet alleviated; the educator of a sort sees the ignorance he is trying to dispel as a frontier to be taken; and the scientists permit us to believe that they are uncovering the real thing in a scientific frontier. But as yet no Columbus has come in from these voyages and announced: "Gentlemen, there is your frontier!" The best they do is to say that it is out beyond, that if you work hard enough and have faith enough, and put in a little money, you will surely find it. If you watch these peddlers of substitute frontiers, you will find that nearly every one wants you to buy something, give something, or believe in something. They want you to be a frontier for them. Unlike Columbus, they bring no continents and no oceans, no gold or silver or grass or forest to you.

I should like to make it clear that mankind is really searching for a new frontier which we once had and did not prize, and the longer we had it, the less we valued it; but now that we have lost it, we have a great pain in the heart, and we are always trying to get it back again. It seems to me that historians and all thoughtful persons are bound by their obligation to say that there is no new frontier in sight comparable in magnitude or importance to the one that is lost. They should point out the diversity and heterogeneity, not to say the absurdity, of so-called new frontiers. They are all fallacies, these new frontiers, and they are pernicious in proportion to their plausibility and respectability. The scientists themselves should join in disabusing the public as to what science can be expected to do. It can do much, but, to paraphrase Isaiah Bowman, it is not likely soon to find a new world or make the one we have much bigger than it is. If the frontier is gone, we should have the courage and honesty to recognize the fact, cease to cry for what we have lost, and devote our energy to finding the solutions to the problems now facing a frontierless society. And when the age we now call modern is modern no longer, and requires a new name, we may appropriately call it the Age of the Frontier, and leave it to its place in history.

[1951]

The Space Frontier

Frontiers

HEINZ HABER

Heinz Haber (1913–), author of a number of works on the space frontier, was born in Mannheim, Germany, and attended the University of Berlin, receiving the Ph.D. in physics (1939) and in astronomy (1944). He came to the United States in 1947 and now resides in California.

Haber sees the conquest of space as inevitable, considering the nature of man. He seems to suggest that the same qualities which caused men to cross the Atlantic and plunge into the wilderness will cause them to project themselves into space. He notes, without being specific, that there are "many human problems" involved in such a conquest.

". . . Only the vertical frontier is left. . . ."

The earth, our home planet, is explored. Since the explorer has made the airplane his chief tool, the last blank spaces on the world's map have melted away swiftly. Today comfortable air liners cross continents and oceans in regularly scheduled flights, and indifferent passengers ride safely over forbidding territory where courageous explorers perished of hunger, thirst, cold or exhaustion only a few decades ago.

From his conquered home planet man now looks expectantly toward the stars. Other, strangely alien worlds lure a new Columbus. Man would not be true to himself were he deaf to their call. The moon and the neighboring planets, Venus and Mars, irresistibly challenge his fancy with the same old spell that the seven seas once cast over their explorers. . . .

No technical difficulty and no economic reason will be potent enough to stop man from attempting to reach out into space. Exploring and expanding are man's second nature. The keen urge to expand is shared by man with all living beings. Plants and animals continuously attack virgin or abandoned spaces. Life stubbornly continues the struggle to extend its basis. It expands with staggering numbers of seeds at a terrible expense, wasting potential life indifferently. At the same time the many coexistent species maintain a well-balanced check on one another. Were it not for fierce competition between the many species, a few kinds would soon dominate the world.

But life spreads out not only from one generation to the next. The whole

From *Man in Space,* copyright 1953 by Heinz Haber. Used by special permission of the Bobbs-Merrill Company, Inc.

history of life through the paleological ages is a story of conquering expansion. The sea, the dry land and finally the air ocean became populated by an ever-increasing number of living species. As the result of the long, slow processes of evolution, plants and animals that were fit to survive in all terrestrial habitats emerged. It took many trials and failures of which we will never know. But the conquest by expansion went on. Today there is hardly a cubic inch of water, soil or air devoid of some form of life.

Man inherited the urge to expand from his mammalian ancestors. As a nomad he emerged in the dawn of intelligence. He immediately applied his superior power of reasoning to the task of expansion and survival in hostile territory. Prehistoric man had already conquered the planet — almost from pole to pole — before distinct centers of culture were developed. The mark of primitive man has been found on every continent and on all larger islands. Of course we reckon the history of the conquest of the world in terms of civilization. Civilized man conquered the planet all over again. His creative mind was directed toward the invention of new and better means of conveyance. The railroad, the automobile and finally the airplane accelerated the conquest of the earth to an explosive rate. If the history of exploration and settlement since the age of Columbus were condensed to a single second, the paths followed by civilized man would seem to flash around the globe like the cracks instantly produced in a crystal ball hit with a hammer. The swiftly progressing areas of expansion and civilization collided opposite to Europe, on the other side of the world. There the frontier ended, and with it man's immediate opportunity to fulfill his keen drive to expand.

Recently the historian Walter Prescott Webb analyzed the import of the lost frontier in this fashion:

> Western civilization today stands facing a closed frontier, and in this sense it faces a unique situation in modern times. . . . Free homesteads in Kansas, free gold claims in California, and free grass on the Great Plains are examples of windfalls . . . which come no more. . . . Meantime less thoughtful people speak of new frontiers, though nothing comparable to the Great Frontier has yet been found. The business man sees a business frontier in the customers he has not yet reached; the missionary sees a religious frontier among the souls he has not yet saved; the social worker sees a human frontier among the suffering people whose woes he has not yet alleviated; the educator of a sort sees the ignorance he is trying to dispel as a frontier to be taken; and the scientists permit us to believe that they are uncovering the real thing in a scientific frontier. But as yet no Columbus has come in from these voyages and announced: "Gentlemen, there is your frontier!"

The Great Frontier was essentially two-dimensional. Its unit was the square mile. This is because our habitat is essentially two-dimensional. In this respect our language is consistently erratic: a Texan speaks of the "wide-open spaces" when he refers to the vast flat plains of his home state. But even Texas is largely two-dimensional, if we disregard the curvature of the earth. Owing to the size of the world, however, we are not aware of traveling through all three dimensions of space when we move about on the face of the earth. It appears to man as though only a flat expanse were to his purpose. And that flat expanse has been conquered and thoroughly fenced in. Only the vertical frontier is left to his insatiable craving for exploring and expanding.

Because the frontier on earth is lost, alien worlds in the skies cast a powerful spell on modern man. No doubt this is the reason behind the fast-rising popularity of science-fiction literature. All too willingly the reader permits himself to be deluded by the thought of many worlds which might be substituted for the lost frontier on earth. The supply of science-fiction books and magazines has risen to fantastic proportions during the last ten years. Recently Hollywood has invaded the field. One particular motion picture carries to a conclusion the theme of the lost and the new frontiers. The earth is destroyed in a catastrophe of cosmic dimensions. The end of the world is brought about by the invasion of two planets which drift from outer space into the planetary system. The larger of the two annihilates the earth in a cataclysmic collision. Yet the smaller one — a second earth in size and equipment — is left circling the sun. A group of people escapes to the new earth in a scientifically designed ark.

The appeal of this plot is overwhelming. The old world has been joyfully discarded like a worn-out phonograph record, since everybody is tired of the old tune anyway. The pioneers land safely on the new world, stepping out of the rocketship into the sunny, virgin, seemingly endless expanse of a newly won frontier. Theirs is a wonderful and joyous future indeed.

Most planet stories and space operas are, of course, cheap entertainment. They simply project shallow human plots into planetary and galactic dimensions. The pulp magazines of science fiction have managed to render the term "space" almost unusable for the science of today.

But speculation as to the potentialities of science is too provocative not to have stimulated greater literary minds. H. G. Wells and Aldous Huxley have written ambitious and satirical pieces in this field. They were able to strike a happy balance between human dignity and scientific arrogance, and their novels offer much food for thought. Fiction sometimes has also an awe-inspiring way of becoming fact; in 1914 H. G. Wells described an atomic war in his science-fiction classic *The World Set Free*. The book is well worth a rereading now that Hiroshima is an event of the past. Yet, what the atom was in 1914 the rocket missile is today. It is not surprising that rockets, missiles and the conquest of space are beginning to compete closely with atomic energy for the attention of that part of the public which is interested in scientific progress. . . .

Like the initiators of the global age who left their coastal waters and ventured on the high seas in quest of new continents, we are preparing to launch our first frail craft into the vast ocean of space. Twenty years ago nobody expected that the tools of space flight would be developed so fast. Rocket engineers can be trusted to attack with equal determination and success the remaining obstacles that still block the road to space. However, each scientific problem, if solved successfully, begets new ones that are usually far more complex and involved. Rocket engineers have led us to the threshold of space, and we have reached the point where we face the most important and critical problem of space flight — man himself.

The human problem of space flight has many facets. There is the medical aspect, the problem of survival in the utter void beyond the limits of atmosphere. How will man fare in his ship or in the artificial satellite? Can he ever travel through the endless expanses of space that stretch between the earth, the moon and the planets? How will man's earth-conditioned frame and mind respond to the alien environment he will encounter? Then there is the question whether space flight can be considered a fruitful and advantageous enterprise. Will it be a mere adventure that could result in disastrous disappointment? Or can we indulge in the hope that the conquest of space will bring us a new frontier? Can the feat of Columbus be repeated on a planetary scale? What, in all, will the age of space be like? All these are questions that need to be answered, although we cannot expect clear-cut answers at this time. . . .

Whatever the final outcome, the conquest of space will most probably be attempted and accomplished as the result of a fundamental compulsion existing in man for exploration, progress and conquering expansion. Now, in the middle of this century, we find ourselves at the gates of space. It has become our task to analyze the many human problems that this revolutionary view implies.

[1953]

A Projection   REED WHITTEMORE

Reed Whittemore (1919–   ) is a poet and essayist who in 1954 was awarded the Harriet Monroe Prize by *Poetry* magazine.

Whittemore ironically casts considerable doubt on the satisfactions to be found on the new "vertical" frontier. His choice of words, symbols, and images suggests that he is poking fun at the whole concept. Actually, however, as he makes explicit in the last lines, he is raising questions more fundamental than those about man's explorations in space.

> *". . . Think of them out there,*
> *An ocean of space before them. . . ."*

I wish they would hurry up their trip to Mars,
Those rocket gentlemen.
We have been waiting too long; the fictions of little men
And canals,

And of planting and raising flags and opening markets   5
For beads, cheap watches, perfume and plastic jewelry —
All these begin to be tedious; what we need now
Is the real thing, a thoroughly bang-up voyage
Of discovery.

Led by Admiral Byrd   10
In the *Nina, Pinta* and *Santa Maria*
With a crew of one hundred experts
In physics, geology, war and creative writing,
The expedition should sail with a five-year supply of
Pemmican, Jello, Moxie,   15
Warm woolen socks and jars of Gramma's preserves.

Think of them out there,
An ocean of space before them, using no compass,
Guiding themselves by speculative equations,
Looking,   20
Looking into the night and thinking now
There are no days, no seasons, time
Is only on watches,
                       and landing on Venus
Through some slight error,
Bearing   25

Proclamations of friendship,
Declarations of interstellar faith,
Acknowledgements of American supremacy,
And advertising matter.

I wonder,   30
Out in the pitch of space, having worlds enough,
If the walled-up, balled-up self could from its alley
Sally.
I wish they would make provisions for this,
Those rocket gentlemen.   35

                                                        [1955]

The Puritan Inheritance

Pilgrim Passage   BENÉT
The Experience   TAYLOR
Huswifery   TAYLOR
Personal Narrative   EDWARDS
Sinners in the Hands of an Angry God   EDWARDS

The Religion of the Enlightenment

A Deist's Profession of Faith   PAINE
On the Religion of Nature   FRENEAU

Nineteenth-Century Affirmation

Thanatopsis   BRYANT
To a Waterfowl   BRYANT
The Moral Argument against Calvinism   CHANNING
Nature   EMERSON
Eight Poems   DICKINSON
Frontier Revival   CARTWRIGHT

The Skeptical Vein

Young Goodman Brown   HAWTHORNE
A Fundamentalist Examined   DARROW & BRYAN
The Hollow Men   ELIOT
#5   FERLINGHETTI
The Theology of Jonathan Edwards   MCGINLEY

Some Modern Credos

Credo   ROBINSON
Is Life Worth Living?   JAMES
New Thoughts Can Remake You   PEALE
i thank You God   CUMMINGS
West-running Brook   FROST
The Strong Are Saying Nothing   FROST
Of Modern Poetry   STEVENS
The Lost Dimension in Religion   TILLICH

Men's Ways with God

John Milton, the great Puritan poet of England, declared his intention to "justify the ways of God to men." *Paradise Lost* was the result, a poem which justified God by showing the sinfulness of man. As the *New England Primer* put it, "In Adam's fall / We sinnèd all." New England and Old England differed on some important matters, such as who on this earth should rule whom, but there was general agreement concerning the nature of man. He was corrupt.

In later periods God's ways with men came to seem less clear; today it is mainly concerning men's ways with God that we are able to agree. And American concepts of the Deity are various. The stern and awful God of the Puritans became, after a century or so, the remote and reasonable God of the American Enlightenment — for some of the more highly educated. A greater number of Americans, particularly those on the frontier, worshipped the God of salvation. This split between those who emphasized reason in religion and those who emphasized piety continues to the present time, although in differing manifestations. The changing ways of men with God are most strikingly seen when we compare the God of service in today's metropolitan YMCA, or the cozy Deity whom a Hollywood movie-queen termed "a livin' Doll," with their colonial Predecessor who wrathfully presided over a "bottomless gulf" of fire, hardly restrained from dropping man therein, as if he were "a spider or some loathsome insect."

Beginning in the nineteenth century a note of agnostic skepticism was sounded in some American writing about God. In a poem entitled "Thought," Walt Whitman, pondering whether "souls" are "destroyed," raised the question which was to be the subject of agonized contemplation for many: "Is only matter triumphant?" Robert Ingersoll, known as the great agnostic in the 1880's and 1890's, was celebrated and reviled for his lectures criticizing the Bible. This clash between skepticism and fundamentalism came into dramatic focus in the examination of William Jennings Bryan by Clarence Darrow at the Scopes "monkey trial" in 1925. The more searching contemporary writers on this topic, however, have abandoned both the skeptical and fundamentalist positions. And so Paul Tillich, prominent among the existentialist theologians, urges modern man to ask anew the religious question and in seeking answers to regain "the lost dimension" in religion.

The Puritan Inheritance

Pilgrim Passage　　　　　　　　　　STEPHEN VINCENT BENÉT

Stephen Vincent Benét (1898–1943) had already published his first book of poems when he enrolled at Yale in 1915. After earning an M.A. in 1920 he received a fellowship which enabled him to study at the Sorbonne and continue his writing. Unlike many American expatriates in the years after World War I, he did not go abroad in a spirit of revolt against American life; he did so simply to make his limited funds go as far as possible. His affection for things American is shown, for example, in his *John Brown's Body* (also written abroad), a Civil War epic which won him the Pulitzer Prize for poetry in 1929. Another such epic narrative was *Western Star,* a celebration of America's way west on which he was working at the outbreak of World War II. He put it aside to work for the Writer's War Board, and the completed portion was published posthumously in 1943.

The passage from *Western Star* here reprinted is a fair sample of Benét's work. Not a great poet, he yet wrote much that is a pleasure to read, particularly in the narrative vein and on native American subjects. He is notably successful in adapting his verse to the rhythms of normal speech. Since Benét is often called a romantic, it is interesting to compare what he has to say of the Puritans with that which appears in William Bradford's first-hand account, *Of Plimoth Plantation* (1620–47), and in the seventeenth-century poems of Edward Taylor which follow "Pilgrim Passage."

"*. . . Have you heard the news of Virginia? . . .*"

　　　　　　　　　　　　Oh, spread the news,
The news of golden Virginia across the sea,
And let it sink in the hearts of the strange, plain men
Already at odds with government and church,
The men who read their Bibles late in the night,
Dissenter and nonconformist and Puritan,
Let it go to Scrooby and stop at the pesthouse there,
Let it go to the little meeting at Austerfield.
(We must worship God as we choose. We must worship God
Though King and law and bishop stand in the way.)
It is far, in the North, and they will not touch us here,

Yet I hear they mean to harry the sheep of God
And His elect must be steadfast. I hear a sound
Like the first, faint roll of thunder, but it is far.
It is very far away.
Have you heard the news of Virginia?

                                   Friend, I have heard
The burning news of the elections of God,
The comfortable word, the clear promise sealed,
My heart is shaken with grace to my heart's root.
I have prayed and wrestled and drunk at the living fount
And God walks with me, guiding me with his hand.
What matters your little news and your tinsel world? . . .

                                        Take a pen
And dot the map of some Middle-Western State
Until you strike upon any one-street town,
Just big enough to have a name of its own,
West Center or Pottersburg or Little Prairie
(Three blocks of street and a post office — then the fields,
And the local stops for water there, once a day,
But the main-line buses never heard of the place.)
It isn't exact but it gives you an idea,
For Scrooby was a halt on the Great North Road
(And how many post offices are there, let's say, in Kansas
How many one-street towns?)
A pinpoint place where a handful of farmers met
With William Brewster, the educated postmaster,
To listen to Pastor Robinson preach the Word,
The new pure Word that the bishops did not know.
(And how many little churches and congregations
Will you find all over this country? How many small
Minority sects that argue and pass away?)
But, this year,
The small band made its decision. They had been jeered at,
By their country neighbors in the country way,
— "Puritan, 'ee? I'll give 'ee Puritan!" —
Suspected of this and that, their leaders fined
For nonconformance. Now they would flee away.

They tried to do so in secret — smuggle themselves
And their few goods out of England — and were caught,
Jailed a space for breaking the customs-laws
And then released. It wasn't harsh, for the time,
But to them it was persecution with fire and sword
And deepened their resolve. The next time went better.
One group was caught and questioned, released again,
But, at last, the whole band was safely across the Channel,
Soberly walking the streets of Amsterdam

And leaving some puzzled customs-officials behind
And a magistrate or two, who dimly remembered
A group of country bumpkins, given to praying,
Who'd been arrested on a technical charge
And then set free for lack of a clear-cut rule.
— The sort of case that bothers a magistrate,
Though part of the day's work —
                                        Except for that,
Their passing leaves no ripple behind in England. . . .

O God, the refuge of our fears,
Our buckler and our stay,
Within whose sight the rolling years
Are but a single day,
Behold us now, like Israel's band,
Cast forth upon the wave,
And may Thy strong and aweful hand
Be still outstretched to save!

It was over now, the living in the Dutch town,
The hard fare, the great labor, the quiet years,
The uneasy security, the exiled days,
The slow, difficult change from the life of husbandmen
To the trade-life, the town-life, the life of money and cloth.
They had seen themselves grow older and some grow broken,
And still with no sure future.
They had seen their children stunted by poverty
Beginning to change, to forget, as children will,
"Dirk Jans thinks it little sin to play at ball
And Annetje Pieters wears ruffles of Mechlin lace.
Aye, father, I know. Aye, mother, I am obedient.
But I thought no harm of talking to Captain Kieft
And the boys all say 'Donder und blitzen!' 'Tis just a saying.
And, mother, if Hendrik asks me, what may I say?"
— There never were children who did not say some such words —
But these were folk who believed in one thing so passionately
They would die ere they saw it broken.
                                        And they saw,
The leaders, no swift, spectacular martyrdom
(That they could have borne) but a long, grey wearing out
Under the endless trickle of alien years
These things — and the ending of the Dutch truce with Spain . . .
Thousands more coming, the slaughter in the night,
And what they saw, they saw
With the humble, stupendous arrogance of men
Who are quite sure God is with them.
Now, for God and land, they were going across the seas.

Methinks I hear a direful sound,
Proclaiming from the sky
That those whom Adam's chains have bound
Eternally must die.
Yet, to my soul, the voice is sweet
And gracious as the dew.
For God must winnow men like wheat
That He may save a few.

And yet — they had lived in Leyden eleven years,
There was street and house and habit that they must leave,
All the bonds of familiar custom — and more than these,
The friends, the flesh of their flesh,
Knitted to them by bone and sinew, knitted to them
By the burning peace of shared Sabbaths and quiet prayers.
For it was the boldest and strongest who were to go,
Not all, and Pastor Robinson was to stay,
The man who had been their pillar of fire and cloud,
Gentle, tolerant, steadfast, the dear saint
Who spread his wings above them and gave them rest.
There were good men who went but none who were quite John Robinson
And they were to miss him sorely.
                                   Now, at Delft Haven,
The two bands parted with fervency and tears.
They might meet again, they might never meet again,
And the large-eyed, solemn children prayed with their elders,
On the *Speedwell's* rocking deck
And Pastor Robinson blessed them from the shore.
Then the ropes were cast off, and suddenly
There was clear water between the ship and the land,
For the tide would not wait and that was the last leave-taking
For many, on bark or land.
And William Bradford remembers and sets it down,
Years later, the tears and the passionate embraces,
The night of little sleep before the sailing,
The kneeling crowd on the shore,
And the last, hard wrench when they knew the thing begun.
A man, writing down, years later, but remembering
With the very blood of his heart.
"But they knew they were pilgrims and looked not much on these things,
They lifted their eyes to the heavens, their dearest country,
And quieted their spirits."
                          And it was so.

With Gideon's sword and David's harp,
We march across the main
And though the blast blow keen and sharp,

Our God shall yet sustain,
To work His burning judgments still,
His mercies to adore
And build the Zion of His will
Where none hath stood before. . . .

She was a sturdy ship, with her double-decks,
High-sterned, slow-sailing, chunky, hard to wear out,
Long in the wine-trade, smelling of it still,
And known for that as a "sweet" ship, meaning a healthy one.
They steered her hundred and eighty tons with a whipstaff.
And she'd trudged the seas for years,
Slow, roomy, durable, smelling of salt and wine,
— A housewife of a ship, not a gallant lady,
Who would groan at storms but get through them and get home,
Like a housewife plodding, market-basket in hand —
The *Mayflower* — a common name for ships —
With Christopher Jones of Harwich for her master.
— And what he thought of the voyage, heaven knows,
His business being to sail the ship across,
Land his queer passengers somewhere and return home,
But that was his last voyage, though he knew it not,
For he died ten months after getting back to England,
Neither Puritan nor rogue, but the mere seaman
Who had done his seaman's task and gotten his death
And brought his ship home to sail under other captains.
For that is the chance of the sea.
                                    And the trudging housewife
Went on with her work, and plodded from port to port
Till she met the end of every laboring ship,
Though we do not know what it was.
                                    We only know
They appraised her, later — at least we think it was she —
And valued her at a hundred and sixty pounds,
Including fifteen pounds for a suit of worn sails.

Now she meets Atlantic, and labors in the grey seas.

And, for those aboard,
We think of them all of one stamp, which they were not.
There were a hundred and one of them all told
But only thirty-five from the Leyden church.
The rest were drawn from London and Southampton
And drawn sometimes, as needs must, from the sort of folk
Willing to stake their lives and seven years
Against a possible future and free land.
They did their best at the choosing, no doubt of that.
They chose Miles Standish, the little chimney soon fired,

Who was to be their buckler in the wilderness;
They picked up young John Alden at the last moment,
For he was a cooper and a hopeful youth;
But there were a number, neither saints nor Puritans,
Who grumbled even while they were still on board
At being ruled by the small band of Zion's men
And swore they would have their liberties, once ashore,
For the patent held for Virginia but not New England.
And, hearing them, Zion's leaders thought it well
To draw a compact, binding their own together
In a lawful government for the town to be,
— And that was to be a cornerstone, in time,
Of something they never visioned from first to last.
But they did not know it then. How could they know it?
They were taking emergency measures in an emergency;
They were founding Zion, not the United States.
— And the seed is sown, and it grows in the deep earth,
And from it comes what the sower never dreamed.

Let us count them now, the beginnings of New England.
There were thirty-eight grown men,
From Brewster and Carver, both of them in their fifties,
To young John Alden and the other bachelors,
Eighteen married women, three of them with child,
Twenty boys, eleven girls
(And seven of these were parish waifs from London
Or seem to have been and no one knows why they came,
But five of the seven died ere they were grown),
Nine servants, five men hired for various tasks,
Including two sailors who would stay but a year,
A spaniel dog and a great mastiff bitch.
And that is the roll. You could write the whole roll down
On a single sheet of paper, yes, even the dogs.
— And, when you have written them down, you write New England.

So think of them through the sixty-five long days
Of tempest and fair weather, of calm and storm,
They were not yet Pilgrim Fathers in steeple-hats,
Each with an iron jaw and a musketoon,
They were not Pilgrim Mothers, sure of their fame.
They were men and women and children, cramped in a ship,
Bound for an unknown land and wondering.
The godly prayed, the ungodly spat overside,
The sailors jeered now and then at the pious speeches,
The Billington boys behaved like limbs of Satan,
And the three pregnant women walked the decks
Or lay in their cabins, wondering at night
What hour their pains would strike and what would be born.

In fact, there were human beings aboard the *Mayflower*,
Not merely ancestors.
                              And yet there is
An unforced, almost childish sweetness about the whole
— The sweetness they could muster with their rigor,
The honey of the iron, the naïve
Devoted, confident wonder that made them pilgrims.
Were they sick? They staggered up to the decks and the air
And so felt better. Did the tempest break
And the ship's planks strain and leak? They braced the main beam
With an iron jackscrew they'd brought, and all was well.
They might long for the bliss of God and groan at His judgments,
But they brought with them butter and pease and beer
And the scurvy did not strike and the voyage was healthy.
Only one boy died, a servant of Doctor Fuller's,
While the crew lost four or five, and one most profane,
So God must be with them — God must be with them here,
On the sea as on the land, ever-present God,
With His great right hand outstretched like the Winter cloud.
And Elizabeth Hopkins labored and bore her child,
(*The cries in the narrow cabin, the women waiting*)
And they named the son Oceanus and rejoiced
For that was surely a sign of God's mercies, too,
A fine, strong boy and the mother alive and well.
And Susanna White and Mary Allerton
Knew their time was still to come,
And wondered, seeing the child, when it would be.

And so, at last, on the nineteenth of November,
On a clear, crisp morning, at daybreak,
With a slice of old moon still bright in the dawn-sky,
They saw the long dim outline of Cape Cod. . . .

                                                      [1943]

The Experience   EDWARD TAYLOR

Edward Taylor (c. 1645–1729) wrote some of the best religious poetry
of his time and certainly the best poetry of any kind in colonial America.
Born in England, he came to Massachusetts in 1668, graduated from
Harvard three years later, and served the frontier community of Westfield
as physician and minister for the remainder of his life. Taylor's poems

remained unknown in manuscript in the Yale library until their discovery in the 1930's. A collection was first published in 1939.

Like the English "metaphysical" poets whom he so much resembles, Taylor relies heavily on metaphor, employs rough metre, deals in hyperbole and sharp contrast, uses puns and other forms of word play. His use of the familiar and commonplace to symbolize high spiritual state — in the manner of the Puritan preacher — gives his poems a uniquely Puritan-American tone. Both "The Experience" and "Huswifery" are tightly constructed poems unified by consistent imagery. Both deal with the major subject of Puritan concern, namely man's relation to God. As a good Puritan, Taylor believed that man was corrupt; he also believed — and was doctrinally correct in believing — in the possibility of man's relation to God being a rapturous one.

". . . Oh! that my Heart thy Golden Harp might bee. . . ."

Oh! that I alwayes breath'd in such an aire,
　　As I suckt in, feeding on Sweet Content!
Disht up unto my Soul ev'n in that pray're
　　Pour'de out to God over last Sacrament.
　　What Beam of Light wrapt up my Sight to finde   5
　　Me neerer God than ere Came in my minde?

Most Strange it was! But yet more Strange that shine
　　Which fill'd my Soul then to the brim to spy
My nature with thy Nature all Divine
　　Together joynd in Him that's Thou, and I.   10
　　Flesh of my Flesh, Bone of my Bone: there's run
　　Thy Godhead, and my Manhood in thy Son.

Oh! that that Flame which thou didst on me Cast
　　Might me enflame, and Lighten e'ry where.
Then Heaven to me would be less at last   15
　　So much of heaven I should have while here.
　　Oh! Sweet though Short! I'le not forget the same.
　　My neerness, Lord, to thee did me Enflame.

I'le Claim my Right: Give place, ye Angells Bright.
　　Ye further from the Godhead stande than I.   20
My Nature is your Lord; and doth Unite
　　Better than Yours unto the Deity.
　　Gods Throne is first and mine is next; to you
　　Onely the place of Waiting-men is due.

Oh! that my Heart thy Golden Harp might bee   25
　　Well tun'd by Glorious Grace, that e'ry string
Screw'd to the highest pitch, might unto thee

All Praises wrapt in sweetest Musick bring.
I praise thee, Lord, and better praise thee would
If what I had, my heart might ever hold.   30

[1682/3]

Huswifery   EDWARD TAYLOR

"*. . . I am Cloathed in Holy robes for glory. . . .*"

Make me, O Lord, thy Spin[n]ing Wheele compleat;
    Thy Holy Worde my Distaff make for mee.
Make mine Affections thy Swift Flyers neate,
    And make my Soule thy holy Spoole to bee.
    My Conversation make to be thy Reele,   5
    And reele the yarn thereon spun of thy Wheele.

Make me thy Loome then, knit therein this Twine:
    And make thy Holy Spirit, Lord, winde quills:
Then weave the Web thyselfe. The yarn is fine.
    Thine Ordinances make my Fulling Mills.   10
    Then dy the same in Heavenly Colours Choice,
    All pinkt with Varnish't Flowers of Paradise.

Then cloath therewith mine Understanding, Will,
    Affections, Judgment, Conscience, Memory;
My Words and Actions, that their shine may fill   15
    My wayes with glory and thee glorify.
    Then mine apparell shall display before yee
    That I am Cloathd in Holy robes for glory.

[c. 1685]

Personal Narrative   JONATHAN EDWARDS

If Edward Taylor best expressed the Puritan's spiritual experience in
poetry, its best expression in prose was the *Personal Narrative* (written
around 1740) of Jonathan Edwards (1703–58), last of the great voices
of New England Calvinism. Graduated from Yale at seventeen, he continued on for two years in the study of theology. By 1729 he occupied

the Congregational pulpit at Northampton, Massachusetts, from which he preached sermons, such as *Sinners in the Hands of an Angry God* (1741), which powerfully contributed to the religious revival known as the Great Awakening. Edwards' most notable book is *Freedom of the Will* (1754), wherein he asserts God's absolute sovereignty as against "the Arminian notion of Liberty of Will."

Two major Puritan doctrines are illustrated in these selections from *Personal Narrative* and *Sinners in the Hands of an Angry God:* the absolute sovereignty of God and the equally absolute depravity of man. These doctrines were closely connected, but as here set forth it is the contrast between their effects which appears most striking — religious ecstasy on the one hand, terror on the other. The experience of supernatural grace makes all the difference. Edwards' stated aim in *Sinners* is to "awaken unconverted persons," and the means he employs to do so are awful indeed. (They are awful, that is, if we will think of an audience which literally cried out in despair; the near present-day equivalent would be a speaker's threatening his audience with atomic holocaust.) The standard devices of topic development are here, but back of them all is the appeal to fear expressed through terrible images.

". . . The appearance of everything was altered. . . ."

I had a variety of concerns and exercises about my soul from my childhood; but I had two more remarkable seasons of awakening, before I met with that change by which I was brought to those new dispositions, and that new sense of things, that I have since had. The first time was when I was a boy, some years before I went to college, at a time of remarkable awakening in my father's congregation. I was then very much affected for many months, and concerned about the things of religion, and my soul's salvation; and was abundant in religious duties. I used to pray five times a day in secret, and to spend much time in religious talk with other boys; and used to meet with them to pray together. I experienced I know not what kind of delight in religion. My mind was much engaged in it, and had much self-righteous pleasure; and it was my delight to abound in religious duties. I with some of my schoolmates joined together, and built a booth in a swamp, in a very retired spot, for a place of prayer. And besides, I had particular secret places of my own in the woods, where I used to retire by myself; and was from time to time much affected. My affections seemed to be lively and easily moved, and I seemed to be in my element, when engaged in religious duties. And I am ready to think, many are deceived with such affections, and such a kind of delight as I then had in religion, and mistake it for grace. . . .

From my childhood up, my mind had been full of objections against the doctrine of God's sovereignty, in choosing whom he would to eternal life, and rejecting whom he pleased; leaving them eternally to perish, and be everlastingly tormented in hell. It used to appear like a horrible doctrine to me. But I remember the time very well, when I seemed to be convinced, and fully satisfied, as to this sovereignty of God, and his justice in thus eternally disposing of men, according to his sovereign pleasure. But never could give an account, how, or by what means, I was thus convinced, not in the least imagining at the time, nor a long time after, that there was any extraordinary influence of God's Spirit in it; but only that now I saw further, and my reason apprehended the justice and reasonableness of it. However, my mind rested in it; and it put an end to all those cavils and objections. And there has been a wonderful alteration in my mind, with respect to the doctrine of God's sovereignty, from that day to this; so that I scarce ever have found so much as the rising of an objection against it, in the most absolute sense, in God shewing mercy to whom he will shew mercy, and hardening whom he will. God's absolute sovereignty and justice, with respect to salvation and damnation, is what my mind seems to rest assured of, as much as of any thing that I see with my eyes; at least it is so at times. But I have often, since that first conviction, had quite another kind of sense of God's sovereignty than I had then. I have often since had not only a conviction, but a delightful conviction. The doctrine has very often appeared exceedingly pleasant, bright, and sweet. Absolute sovereignty is what I love to ascribe to God. But my first conviction was not so.

The first instance that I remember of that sort of inward, sweet delight in God and divine things that I have lived much in since, was on reading those words, 1 Tim. i. 17. Now unto the King eternal, immortal, invisible, the only wise God, be honour and glory for ever and ever, Amen. As I read the words, there came into my soul, and was as it were diffused through it, a sense of the glory of the Divine Being; a new sense, quite different from any thing I ever experienced before. Never any words of Scripture seemed to me as these words did. I thought with myself, how excellent a Being that was, and how happy I should be, if I might enjoy that God, and be rapt up to him in heaven, and be as it were swallowed up in him for ever! I kept saying, and as it were singing, over these words of scripture to myself; and went to pray to God that I might enjoy him, and prayed in a manner quite different from what I used to do; with a new sort of affection. But it never came into my thought, that there was any thing spiritual, or of a saving nature in this. . . .

After this my sense of divine things gradually increased, and became more and more lively, and had more of that inward sweetness. The appearance of every thing was altered; there seemed to be, as it were, a calm, sweet, cast, or appearance of divine glory, in almost every thing. God's excellency, his wisdom, his purity and love, seemed to appear in every thing; in the sun, moon, and stars; in the clouds and blue sky; in the grass, flowers, trees; in the water and all nature; which used greatly to fix my mind. I often used to sit and view the moon for continuance; and in the day, spent much time in viewing the clouds and sky, to behold the sweet glory of God in these things; in the meantime, singing forth, with a low voice, my contemplations of the Creator and Redeemer. And scarce any thing, among all the works of nature, was so sweet to me as thunder and lightning; formerly, nothing had been so terrible to me. Before, I used to be uncommonly terrified with thunder, and to be struck with terror when I saw a thunder-storm rising; but now, on the contrary, it rejoiced me. I felt God, if I may so speak, at the first appearance of a thunder-storm; and used to take the opportunity, at such times, to fix myself in order to view the clouds, and see the lightnings play, and hear the majestic and awful voice of God's thunder, which oftentimes was exceedingly entertaining, leading me to sweet contemplations of my great and glorious God. While thus engaged, it always seemed natural to me to sing, or chant forth my meditations; or, to speak my thoughts in soliloquies with a singing voice. . . .

I remember the thoughts I used then to have of holiness; and said sometimes to myself, "I do certainly know that I love holiness, such as the gospel prescribes." It appeared to me, that there was nothing in it but what was ravishingly lovely; the highest beauty and amiableness — a divine beauty; far purer than any thing here upon earth; and that every thing else was like mire and defilement, in comparison of it.

Holiness, as I then wrote down some of my contemplations on it, appeared to me to be of a sweet, pleasant, charming, serene, calm nature; which brought an inexpressible purity, brightness, peacefulness and ravishment to the soul. In other words, that it made the soul like a field or garden of God, with all manner of pleasant flowers; enjoying a sweet calm, and the gently vivifying beams of the sun. The soul of a true Christian, as I then wrote my meditations, appeared like such a little white flower as we see in the spring of the year; low and humble on the ground, opening its bosom to receive the pleasant beams of the sun's glory; rejoicing as it were in a calm rapture; diffusing around a sweet fragrancy; standing peacefully and lovingly, in the midst of other flowers round about; all in like manner opening their bosoms, to drink in the light of the sun. There was no part of creature holiness, that I had so great a sense of its loveliness, as humility, brokenness of heart and poverty of spirit; and there was nothing that I so earnestly longed for. My heart panted after this, to lie low before God, as in the dust; that I might be nothing, and that God, might be ALL, that I might become as a little child.

While at New York, I was sometimes much affected with reflections on my past life, considering how late it was before I began to be truly religious; and how wickedly I had lived till then; and once so as to weep abundantly, and for a considerable time together. . . .

I have sometimes had a sense of the excellent fulness of Christ, and his meetness and suitableness as a Saviour; whereby he has appeared to me, far above all, the chief of ten thousands. His blood and atonement have appeared sweet, and his righteousness sweet; which was always accompanied with ardency of spirit; and inward strugglings and breathings, and groanings that cannot be uttered, to be emptied of myself, and swallowed up in Christ.

Once, as I rode out into the woods for my health, in 1737, having alighted from my horse in a retired place, as my manner commonly has been, to walk for divine contemplation and prayer, I had a view that for me was extraordinary, of the glory of the Son of God, as Mediator between God and man, and his wonderful, great, full, pure and sweet grace and love, and meek and gentle condescension. This grace that appeared so calm and sweet, appeared also great above the heavens. The person of Christ appeared ineffably excellent with an excellency great enough to swallow up all thought and conception — which continued as near as I can judge, about an hour; which kept me the greater part of the time in a flood of tears, and weeping aloud. I felt an ardency of soul to be, what I know not otherwise how to express, emptied and annihilated; to lie in the dust, and to be full of Christ alone; to love him with a holy and pure love; to trust in him; to live upon him; to serve and follow him; and to be perfectly sanctified and made pure, with a divine and heavenly purity. I have, several other times, had views very much of the same nature, and which have had the same effects. . . .

Though it seems to me, that, in some respects, I was a far better Christian, for two or three years after my first conversion, than I am now; and lived in a more constant delight and pleasure; yet, of late years, I have had a more full and constant sense of the absolute sovereignty of God, and a delight in that sovereignty; and have had more of a sense of the glory of Christ, as a Mediator revealed in the gospel. On one Saturday night, in particular, I had such a discovery of the excellency of the gospel above all other doctrines, that I could not but say to myself, "This is my chosen light, my chosen doctrine;" and of Christ, "This is my chosen Prophet." It appeared sweet, beyond all expression, to follow Christ, and to be taught, and enlightened, and instructed by him; to learn of him, and live to him. Another Saturday night, (January, 1739) I had such a sense, how sweet and blessed a thing it was to walk in the way of duty; to do that which was right and meet to be done, and agreeable to the holy mind of God; that it caused me to break forth into a kind of loud weeping, which held me some time, so that I was forced to shut myself up, and fasten the doors. I could not but, as it were, cry out, "How happy are they which do that which is right in the sight of God! They are blessed indeed, they are the happy ones!" I had, at the same time, a very affecting sense, how meet and suitable it was that God should govern the world, and order all things according to his own pleasure; and I rejoiced in it, that God reigned, and that his will was done.

[1740]

Sinners in the Hands of an Angry God   JONATHAN EDWARDS

". . . The bow of God's wrath is bent. . . ."

Natural men are held in the hand of God, over the pit of hell; they have deserved the fiery pit, and are already sentenced to it; and God is dreadfully provoked, his anger is as great towards them as to those that are actually suffering the executions of the fierceness of his wrath in hell, and they have done nothing in the least to appease or abate that anger, neither is God in the least bound by any promise to hold them up one moment; the devil is waiting for them, hell is gaping for them, the flames gather and flash about them, and would fain lay hold on them, and swallow them up. . . .

The use of this awful subject may be for awakening unconverted persons in this congregation. This that you have heard is the case of every one of you that are out of Christ. — That world of misery, that lake of burning brimstone, is extended abroad under you. There is the dreadful pit of the glowing flames of the wrath of God; there is hell's wide gaping mouth open; and you have nothing to stand upon, nor any thing to take hold of; there is nothing between you and hell but the air; it is only the power and mere pleasure of God that holds you up.

You probably are not sensible of this; you find you are kept out of hell, but do not see the hand of God in it; but look at other things, as the good state of your bodily constitution, your care of your own life, and the means you use for your own preservation. But indeed these things are nothing; if God should withdraw his hand, they would avail no more to keep you from falling, than the thin air to hold up a person that is suspended in it.

Your wickedness makes you as it were heavy as lead, and to tend downwards with great weight and pressure towards hell; and if God should let you go, you would immediately sink and swiftly descend and plunge into the bottomless gulf, and your healthy constitution, and your own care and prudence, and best contrivance, and all your righteousness, would have no more influence to uphold you and keep you out of hell, than a spider's web would have to stop a fallen rock. Were it not for the sovereign pleasure of God, the earth would not bear you one moment; for you are a burden to it; the creation groans with you; the creature is made subject to the bondage of your corruption, not willingly; the sun does not willingly shine upon you to give you light to serve sin and Satan; the earth does not willingly yield her increase to satisfy your lusts; nor is it willingly a stage for your wickedness to be acted upon; the air does not willingly serve you for breath to maintain the flame of life in your vitals, while you spend your life in the service of God's enemies. God's creatures are good, and were made for men to serve God with, and do not willingly subserve to any other purpose, and groan when they are abused to purposes so directly contrary to their nature and end. And the world would spew you out, were it not for the sovereign hand of him who hath subjected it in hope. There are black clouds of God's wrath now hanging directly over your heads, full of the dreadful storm, and big with thunder; and were it not for the restraining hand of God, it would immediately burst forth upon you. The sovereign pleasure of God, for the present, stays his rough wind; otherwise it would come with fury, and your destruction would come like a whirlwind, and you would be like the chaff of the summer threshing floor. . . .

The bow of God's wrath is bent, and the arrow made ready on the string, and justice bends the arrow at your heart, and strains the bow, and it is nothing but the mere pleasure of God, and that of an angry God, without any promise or obligation at all, that keeps the arrow one moment from being made drunk with your blood. Thus all you that never passed under a great change of heart, by the mighty power of the Spirit of God upon your souls; all you that were never born again, and made new creatures, and raised from being dead in sin, to a state of new, and before altogether unexperienced light and life, are in the hands of an angry God. However you may have reformed your life in many things and may have had religious affections, and may keep up a form of religion in your families and closets, and in the house of God, it is nothing but his mere pleasure that keeps you from being this moment swallowed up in everlasting destruction. However unconvinced you may now be of the truth of what you hear, by and by you will be fully convinced of it. Those that are gone from being in the like circumstances with you, see that it was so with them; for destruction came suddenly upon most of them; when they expected nothing of it, and while they were saying, Peace and safety: now they see, that those things on which they depended for peace and safety, were nothing but thin air and empty shadows.

The God that holds you over the pit of hell, much as one holds a spider, or some loathsome insect over the fire, abhors you, and is dreadfully provoked: his wrath towards you burns like fire; he looks upon you as worthy of nothing else, but to be cast into the fire; he is of purer eyes than to bear to have you in his sight; you are ten thousand times more abominable in his eyes, than the most hateful venomous serpent is in ours. You have offended him infinitely more than ever a stubborn rebel did his prince; and yet it is nothing but his hand that holds you from falling into the fire every moment. It is to be ascribed to nothing else, that you did not go to hell the last night; that you was suffered to awake again in this world, after you closed your eyes to sleep. And there is no other reason to be given, why you have not dropped into hell since you arose in the morning, but that God's hand has held you up. There is no other reason to be given why you have not gone to hell, since you have sat here in the house of God, provoking his pure eyes by your sinful wicked manner of attending his solemn worship. Yea, there is nothing else that is to be given as a reason why you do not this very moment drop down into hell.

O sinner! Consider the fearful danger you are in: it is a great furnace of wrath, a wide and bottomless pit, full of the fire of wrath, that you are held over in the hand of that God, whose wrath is provoked and incensed as much against you, as against many of the damned in hell. You hang by a slender thread, with the flames of divine wrath flashing about it, and ready every moment to singe it, and burn it asunder; and you have no interest in any Mediator, and nothing to lay hold of to save yourself, nothing to keep off the flames of wrath, nothing of your own, nothing that you ever have done, nothing that you can do, to induce God to spare you one moment. . . .

Consider this, you that are here present, that yet remain in an unregenerate state. That God will execute the fierceness of his anger, implies, that he will inflict wrath without any pity. When God beholds the ineffable extremity of your case, and sees your torment to be so vastly disproportioned to your strength, and sees how your poor soul is crushed, and sinks down, as it were, into an infinite gloom; he will have no compassion upon you, he will not forbear the executions of his wrath, or in the least lighten his hand; there shall be no moderation or mercy, nor will God then at all stay his rough wind; he will have no regard to your welfare, nor be at all careful lest you should suffer too much in any other sense, than only that you shall *not suffer beyond what strict justice requires*. Nothing shall be withheld, because it is so hard for you to bear. Ezek. viii. 18. "Therefore will I also deal in fury: mine eye shall not spare, neither will I have pity; and though they cry in mine ears with a loud voice, yet I will not hear them." Now God stands ready to pity you; this is a day of mercy; you may cry now with some encouragement of obtaining mercy. But when once the day of mercy is past, your most lamentable and dolorous cries and shrieks will be in vain; you will be wholly lost and thrown away of God, as to any regard to your welfare. God will have no other use to put you to, but to suffer misery; you shall be continued in being to no other end; for you will be a vessel of wrath fitted to destruction; and there will be no other use of this vessel, but to be filled full of wrath. God will be so far from pitying you when you cry to him, that it is said he will only "laugh and mock," Prov. i. 25, 26, &c. . . .

How awful are those words, Isa. lxiii. 3, which are the words of the great God. "I will tread them in mine anger, and will trample them in my fury, and their blood shall be sprinkled upon my garments, and I will stain all my raiment." It is perhaps impossible to conceive of words that carry in them greater manifestations of these three things, *viz.* contempt, and hatred, and fierceness of indignation. If you cry to God to pity you, he will be so far from pitying you in your doleful case, or showing you the least regard or favour, that instead of that, he will only tread you under foot. And though he will know that you cannot bear the weight of omnipotence treading upon you, yet he will not regard that, but he will crush you under his feet without mercy; he will crush out your blood, and make it fly, and it shall be sprinkled on his garments, so as to stain all his raiment. He will not only hate you, but he will have you, in the utmost contempt: no place shall be thought fit for you, but under his feet to be trodden down as the mire of the streets. . . .

Therefore, let every one that is out of Christ, now awake and fly from the wrath to come. The wrath of Almighty God is now undoubtedly hanging over a great part of this congregation: Let every one fly out of Sodom: "Haste and escape for your lives, look not behind you, escape to the mountain, lest you be consumed."

[1741]

The Religion of the Enlightenment

A *Deist's Profession of Faith*   THOMAS PAINE

Thomas Paine (1737–1809), born in England, finished with school at age thirteen and then pursued a variety of occupations, from school teacher to exciseman. Encouraged by Franklin to come to America, he arrived in Philadelphia in 1774 and two years later wrote the tremendously effective *Common Sense,* a pamphlet arguing for immediate independence of the American colonies in their struggle with England. When war came he supported it in a series of papers called *The American Crisis* (1776–1783). Similarly, when revolution came to France — where he had gone to live in 1789 — he defended that cause in *The Rights of Man* (1791–1792). While in France he also wrote *The Age of Reason,* from which the present selection is taken. He wrote it, he said, because "the people of France were running headlong into Atheism, and I had the work translated and published in their own language to stop them in that career, and fix them in the first article . . . of every man's Creed who has any Creed at all, 'I believe in God.'"

In giving his "thoughts upon religion," Paine espouses the tenets of deism, a set of beliefs popular among leaders of the Age of Enlightenment. (Jefferson and Franklin were deists.) Clearly he was no atheist, but the reasons for his persistent reputation as one are not hard to understand: his ideas were radically different from those who held to traditional beliefs, particularly the Calvinists; he expressed himself in an unequivocal and even belligerent fashion; and the popular appeal of his brisk and easy pamphleteering style made him a persuasive, and therefore a dangerous, voice.

". . . My own mind is my own church. . . ."

It has been my intention, for several years past, to publish my thoughts upon religion; I am well aware of the difficulties that attend the subject, and from that consideration, had reserved it to a more advanced period of life. I intended it to be the last offering I should make to my fellow citizens of all nations, and that at a time when the purity of the motive that induced me to it could not admit of a question, even by those who might disapprove the work.

The circumstance that has now taken place in France, of the total abolition of the whole national order of priesthood, and of everything appertaining to compulsive systems of religion, and compulsive articles of faith, has not only precipitated my intention, but rendered a work of this kind exceedingly necessary, lest, in the general wreck of superstition, of false systems of government, and false theology, we lose sight of morality, of humanity, and of the theology that is true.

As several of my colleagues, and others of my fellow-citizens of France, have given me the example of making their voluntary and individual profession of faith, I also will make mine; and I do this with all that sincerity and frankness with which the mind of man communicates with itself.

I believe in one God, and no more; and I hope for happiness beyond this life.

I believe in the equality of man, and I believe that religious duties consist in doing justice, loving mercy, and endeavoring to make our fellow-creatures happy.

But, lest it should be supposed that I believe many other things in addition to these, I shall, in the progress of this work, declare the things I do not believe, and my reasons for not believing them.

I do not believe in the creed professed by the Jewish church, by the Roman church, by the Greek church, by the Turkish church, by the Protestant church, nor by any church that I know of. My own mind is my own church.

All national institutions of churches, whether Jewish, Christian, or Turkish, appear to me no other than human inventions set up to terrify and enslave mankind, and monopolize power and profit.

I do not mean by this declaration to condemn those who believe otherwise; they have the same right to their belief as I have to mine. But it is necessary to the happiness of man, that he be mentally faithful to himself. Infidelity does not consist in believing, or in disbelieving; it consists in professing to believe what he does not believe.

It is impossible to calculate the moral mischief, if I may so express it, that mental lying has produced in society. When a man has so far corrupted and prostituted the chastity of his mind, as to subscribe his professional belief to things he does not believe, he has prepared himself for the commission of every other crime. He takes up the trade of a priest for the sake of gain, and in order to qualify himself for that trade, he begins with a perjury. Can we conceive anything more destructive to morality than this?

Soon after I had published the pamphlet Common Sense, in America, I saw the exceeding probability that a revolution in the system of government would be followed by a revolution in the system of religion. The adulterous connection of church and state, wherever it had taken place, whether Jewish, Christian, or Turkish, had so effectually prohibited, by pains and penalties, every discussion upon established creeds, and upon first principles of religion, that until the system of government should be changed, those subjects could not be brought fairly and openly before the world; but that whenever this should be done, a revolution in the system of religion would follow. Human inventions and priest-craft would be detected; and man would return to the pure, unmixed, and unadulterated belief of one God, and no more. . . .

*   *   *

But some perhaps will say — Are we to have no word of God — no revelation? I answer yes. There is a Word of God, there is a revelation.

THE WORD OF GOD IS THE CREATION WE BEHOLD: And it is in this word, which no human invention can counterfeit or alter, that God speaketh universally to man.

Human language is local and changeable, and is therefore incapable of being used as the means of unchangeable and universal information. The idea that God sent Jesus Christ to publish, as they say the glad tidings to all nations, from one end of the earth unto the other, is consistent only with the ignorance of those who know nothing of the extent of the world, and who believed, as those world-saviours believed, and continued to believe for several centuries, (and that in contradiction to the discoveries of philosophers and the experience of navigators), that the earth was flat like a trencher; and that a man might walk to the end of it.

But how was Jesus Christ to make anything known to all nations? He could speak but one language, which was Hebrew; and there are in the world several hundred languages. Scarcely any two nations speak the same language, or understand each other; and as to translations, every man who knows anything of languages, knows that it is impossible to translate from one language into another, not only without losing a great part of the original, but frequently of mistaking the sense; and besides all this, the art of printing was wholly unknown at the time Christ lived.

It is always necessary that the means that are to accomplish any end be equal to the accomplishment of that end, or the end cannot be accomplished. It is in this that the difference between finite and infinite power and wisdom discovers itself. Man frequently fails in accomplishing his end, from a natural inability of the power to the purpose; and frequently from the want of wisdom to apply power properly. But it is impossible for infinite power and wisdom to fail as man faileth. The means it useth are always equal to the end: but human language, more especially as there is not an universal language, is incapable of being used as an universal means of unchangeable and uniform information; and therefore it is not the means that God useth in manifesting himself universally to man.

It is only in the Creation that all our ideas and conceptions of a *word of God* can unite. The Creation speaketh an universal language, independently of human speech or human language, multiplied and various as they be. It is an ever existing original, which every man can read. It cannot be forged; it cannot be counterfeited; it cannot be lost; it cannot be altered; it cannot be suppressed. It does not depend upon the will of man whether it shall be published or not; it publishes itself from one end of the earth to the other. It preaches to all nations and to all worlds; and this word of God reveals to man all that is necessary for man to know of God.

Do we want to contemplate his power? We see it in the immensity of the creation. Do we want to contemplate his wisdom? We see it in the unchangeable order by which the incomprehensible Whole is governed. Do we want to contemplate his munificence? We see it in the abundance with which he fills the earth. Do we want to contemplate his mercy? We see it in his not withholding that abundance even from the unthankful. In fine, do we want to know what God is? Search not the book called the scripture, which any human hand might make, but the scripture called the Creation.

[1794]

On the Religion of Nature   PHILIP FRENEAU

Philip Freneau (1752–1832) was one of the first Americans to write poetry of a high order. Like Paine, he was much engaged in political controversy; like him, he was consistently a radical; and like him, he was a deist. Unlike Paine, his writing interests were often specifically literary, as in such poems as "The Indian Burying Ground," "The Wild Honey Suckle," and "To a Caty-did." His deistic "On the Religion of Nature" was published in 1815. For another note on Freneau, see page 288.

In this poem Freneau exhibits an appreciation of the harmonious order of nature, a standard deistic concept. His romantic attitude toward nature as well as his belief in human nature are in contrast to earlier views, as he pointedly indicates in the last two stanzas. The images of the poem, the abstract language, the metrical pattern, all contribute to a tone of balance and order well suited to the deistical message.

> "... Religion, such as nature taught,
>   With all divine perfection suits. ..."

The power that gives with liberal hand
    The blessings man enjoys, while here,
And scatters through a smiling land
    The abundant products of the year;
        That power of nature, ever bless'd,   5
        Bestow'd religion with the rest.

Born with ourselves, her early sway
    Inclines the tender mind to take
The path of right, fair virtue's way
    Its own felicity to make.   10
        This universally extends
        And leads to no mysterious ends.

Religion, such as nature taught,
    With all divine perfection suits;
Had all mankind this system sought   15
    Sophists would cease their vain disputes,
        And from this source would nations know
        All that can make their heaven below.

This deals not curses on mankind,
    Or dooms them to perpetual grief,   20
If from its aid no joys they find,
    It damns them not for unbelief;
        Upon a more exalted plan
        Creatress nature dealt with man —

Joy to the day, when all agree   25
  On such grand systems to proceed,
From fraud, design, and error free,
  And which to truth and goodness lead:
    Then persecution will retreat
    And man's religion be complete.   30

                                                              [1815]

Nineteenth-Century Affirmation

Thanatopsis   WILLIAM CULLEN BRYANT

William Cullen Bryant (1794–1878) was America's first poet to gain admiring recognition both at home and abroad. First trained to be a lawyer, he entered newspaper work and enjoyed a long and successful career as a New York editor. While still a young man he wrote many of his most famous poems, such as the two here printed. Both were written in 1815, though the present version of "Thanatopsis" (which means "view of death") is a revision that appeared in 1821.

Growing up in Massachusetts, Bryant adopted the Calvinist theology because, as he wrote later, "I heard nothing else taught from the pulpit, and supposed it to be the accepted belief of the religious world." These two poems show that Bryant early abandoned the religious system in which he had been raised, for neither accords with Calvinist principles: "Thanatopsis" is more stoical than anything else and "To a Waterfowl" finds evidence in nature of watchful and protective divine power. Although written in the same year and similar in certain respects (e.g., religious theme, interest in nature, amorphous images), the two poems are yet interestingly different in both content and form.

". . . All that breathe / Will share thy destiny. . . ."

> To him who in the love of Nature holds
> Communion with her visible forms, she speaks
> A various language; for his gayer hours
> She has a voice of gladness, and a smile
> And eloquence of beauty, and she glides   5
> Into his darker musings, with a mild
> And healing sympathy, that steals away
> Their sharpness, ere he is aware. When thoughts
> Of the last bitter hour come like a blight
> Over thy spirit, and sad images   10
> Of the stern agony, and shroud, and pall,
> And breathless darkness, and the narrow house,
> Make thee to shudder, and grow sick at heart; —
> Go forth, under the open sky, and list
> To Nature's teachings, while from all around —   15
> Earth and her waters, and the depths of air —
> Comes a still voice —
>   Yet a few days, and thee

The all-beholding sun shall see no more
In all his course; nor yet in the cold ground,
Where thy pale form was laid, with many tears,   20
Nor in the embrace of ocean, shall exist
Thy image. Earth, that nourished thee, shall claim
Thy growth, to be resolved to earth again,
And, lost each human trace, surrendering up
Thine individual being, shalt thou go   25
To mix for ever with the elements,
To be a brother to the insensible rock
And to the sluggish clod, which the rude swain
Turns with his share, and treads upon. The oak
Shall send his roots abroad, and pierce thy mould.   30

      Yet not to thine eternal resting-place
Shalt thou retire alone, nor couldst thou wish
Couch more magnificent. Thou shalt lie down
With patriarchs of the infant world — with kings,
The powerful of the earth — the wise, the good,   35
Fair forms, and hoary seers of ages past,
All in one mighty sepulchre. The hills
Rock-ribbed and ancient as the sun, — the vales
Stretching in pensive quietness between;
The venerable woods — rivers that move   40
In majesty, and the complaining brooks
That make the meadows green; and, poured round all,
Old Ocean's gray and melancholy waste, —
Are but the solemn decorations all
Of the great tomb of man. The golden sun,   45
The planets, all the infinite host of heaven,
Are shining on the sad abodes of death,
Through the still lapse of ages. All that tread
The globe are but a handful to the tribes
That slumber in its bosom. — Take the wings   50
Of morning, pierce the Barcan wilderness,
Or lose thyself in the continuous woods
Where rolls the Oregon, and hears no sound,
Save his own dashings — yet the dead are there:
And millions in those solitudes, since first   55
The flight of years began, have laid them down
In their last sleep — the dead reign there alone.
So shalt thou rest, and what if thou withdraw
In silence from the living, and no friend
Take note of thy departure? All that breathe   60
Will share thy destiny. The gay will laugh
When thou art gone, the solemn brood of care
Plod on, and each one as before will chase
His favorite phantom; yet all these shall leave

Their mirth and their employments, and shall come   65
And make their bed with thee. As the long train
Of ages glide away, the sons of men,
The youth in life's green spring, and he who goes
In the full strength of years, matron and maid,
The speechless babe, and the gray-headed man —   70
Shall one by one be gathered to thy side
By those, who in their turn shall follow them.

    So live that when thy summons comes to join
The innumerable caravan, which moves
To that mysterious realm, where each shall take   75
His chamber in the silent halls of death,
Thou go not, like the quarry-slave at night,
Scourged to his dungeon, but, sustained and soothed
By an unfaltering trust, approach thy grave,
Like one who wraps the drapery of his couch   80
About him, and lies down to pleasant dreams.

                                             [1821]

To a Waterfowl   WILLIAM CULLEN BRYANT

" . . . He . . ./ Will lead my steps aright. . . ."

       Whither, 'midst falling dew,
While glow the heavens with the last steps of day,
Far, through their rosy depths, dost thou pursue
      Thy solitary way?

       Vainly the fowler's eye   5
Might mark thy distant flight, to do thee wrong,
As, darkly painted on the crimson sky,
      Thy figure floats along.

       Seek'st thou the plashy brink
Of weedy lake, or marge of river wide,   10
Or where the rocking billows rise and sink
      On the chafed ocean side?

       There is a Power, whose care
Teaches thy way along that pathless coast, —
The desert and illimitable air,   15
      Lone wandering, but not lost.

> All day thy wings have fann'd,
> At that far height, the cold thin atmosphere;
> Yet stoop not, weary, to the welcome land,
>   Though the dark night is near.   20

> And soon that toil shall end,
> Soon shalt thou find a summer home, and rest,
> And scream among thy fellows; reeds shall bend,
>   Soon, o'er thy sheltered nest.

> Thou'rt gone, the abyss of heaven   25
> Hath swallowed up thy form, yet, on my heart
> Deeply hath sunk the lesson thou hast given,
>   And shall not soon depart.

> He, who, from zone to zone,
> Guides through the boundless sky thy certain flight,   30
> In the long way that I must trace alone,
>   Will lead my steps aright.

>   [1815]

The Moral Argument against Calvinism WILLIAM ELLERY CHANNING

William Ellery Channing (1780–1842) was born in Rhode Island, studied at Harvard, and in 1803 became pastor of a Congregational church in Boston. Breaking with orthodox Calvinism, he became a leading exponent of Unitarianism, a doctrine noted for its optimistic rationalism as much as for its emphasis on God as one rather than three persons (Trinitarianism).

In the present selection from an essay written for a periodical, Channing builds up his argument with such devices as citation of scripture, "plain sense," and analogy. The tone is one of moderation (he agrees at some points with his opposition) and firmness. The force of his arguments, the dignity of his style, the clarity of his expression, show why he was considered among the ablest writers of his generation.

". . . how mournfully the human mind may misrepresent the Deity. . . ."

The principal argument against Calvinism, in the General View of Christian Doctrines, is the *moral argument,* or that which is drawn from the inconsistency of the system with the Divine perfection. It is plain that a doctrine which contradicts our best ideas of goodness and justice, cannot come from the true and just God, or be a true representation of his character. This moral argument has always been powerful to the pulling down of the strongholds of Calvinism. Even in the dark period, when this system was shaped and finished at Geneva, its advocates often writhed under the weight of it; and we cannot but deem it a mark of the progress of society, that Calvinists are more and more troubled with the palpable repugnance of their doctrines to God's nature, and accordingly labour to soften and explain them, until in many cases the name only is retained. If the stern reformer of Geneva could lift up his head, and hear the mitigated tone in which some of his professed followers dispense his fearful doctrines, we fear, that he could not lie down in peace, until he had poured out his displeasure on their cowardice and degeneracy. He would tell them with a frown, that *moderate Calvinism* was a solecism, a contradiction in terms, and would bid them in scorn to join their real friend, Arminius. Such is the power of public opinion and of an improved state of society on creeds, that naked, undisguised Calvinism is not very fond of showing itself, and many, of consequence, know imperfectly what it means. What, then, is the system against which the View of Christian Doctrines is directed?

Calvinism teaches, that in consequence of Adam's sin in eating the forbidden fruit, God brings into life all his posterity with a nature wholly corrupt, so that they are utterly indisposed, disabled, and made opposite to all that is spiritually good, and wholly inclined to all evil, and that continually. It teaches, that all mankind, having fallen in Adam, are under God's wrath and curse, and so made liable to all miseries in this life, to death itself, and to the pains of hell forever. It teaches, that from this ruined race God out of his mere good pleasure has elected a certain number to be saved by Christ, not induced to this choice by any foresight of their faith or good works, but wholly by his free grace and love; and that having thus predestinated them to eternal life, he renews and sanctifies them by his almighty and special agency, and brings them into a state of grace, from which they cannot fall and perish. It teaches, that the rest of mankind he is pleased to pass over, and to ordain them to dishonour and wrath for their sins, to the honour of his justice and power; in other words, he leaves the rest to the corruption in which they were born, withholds the grace which is necessary to their recovery, and condemns them to "most grievous torments in soul and body without intermission in hell fire forever." Such is Calvinism, as gathered from the most authentic records of the doctrine. Whoever will consult the famous Assembly's Catechisms and Confession, will see the peculiarities of the system in all their length and breadth of deformity. A man of plain sense, whose spirit has not been broken to this creed by education or terror, will think that it is not necessary for us to travel to heathen countries, to learn how mournfully the human mind may misrepresent the Deity.

The moral argument against Calvinism, of which we have spoken, must seem irresistible to common and unperverted minds, after attending to the brief statement now given. It will be asked with astonishment, How is it possible that men can hold these doctrines, and yet maintain God's goodness and equity? — what principles can be more contradictory? To remove the objection to Calvinism, which is drawn from its repugnance to the Divine perfections, recourse has been had, as before observed, to the distinction between natural and moral inability, and to other like subtleties. But a more common reply, we conceive, has been drawn from the weakness and imperfection of the human mind, and from its incapacity of comprehending God. Calvinists will tell us, that because a doctrine opposes our convictions of rectitude, it is not necessarily false; that apparent are not always real inconsistencies; that God is an infinite and incomprehensible being, and not to be tried by *our* ideas of fitness and morality; that we bring their system to an incompetent tribunal, when we submit it to the decision of human reason and conscience; that we are weak judges of what is right and wrong, good and evil in the Deity; that the happiness of the universe may require an administration of human affairs which is very offensive to limited understandings; that we must follow revelation, not reason or moral feeling, and must consider doctrines which shock us in revelation, as awful mysteries, which are dark through our ignorance, and which time will enlighten. How little, it is added, can man explain or understand God's ways? How inconsistent the miseries of life appear with goodness in the Creator? How prone, too, have men always been to confound good and evil, to call the just unjust? How presumptuous is it in such a being to sit in judgment upon God, and to question the rectitude of the divine administration, because it shocks *his* sense of rectitude? Such we conceive to be a fair statement of the manner in which the Calvinist frequently meets the objection, that his system is at war with God's attributes — such the reasoning by which the voice of conscience and nature is stifled, and men are reconciled to doctrines which, if tried by the established principles of morality, would be rejected with horror. On this reasoning we purpose to offer some remarks; and we shall avail ourselves of the opportunity, to give our views of *the confidence which is due to our rational and moral faculties in religion.*

That God is infinite, and that man often errs, we affirm as strongly as our Calvinistic brethren. We desire to think humbly of ourselves, and reverently of our Creator. In the strong language of Scripture, "We now see through a glass darkly." "We cannot by searching find out God unto perfection. Clouds and darkness are round about him. His judgments are a great deep." God is great and good beyond utterance or thought. We have no disposition to idolize our own powers, or to penetrate the secret counsels of the Deity. But on the other hand, we think it ungrateful to disparage the powers which our Creator has given us, or to question the certainty or importance of the knowledge which he has seen fit to place within our reach. There is an affected humility, we think, as dangerous as pride. We may rate our faculties too meanly, as well as too boastingly. The worst error in religion, after all, is that of the sceptic, who records triumphantly the weaknesses and wanderings of the human intellect, and maintains that no trust is due to the decisions of this erring reason. We by no means conceive, that man's greatest danger springs from pride of understanding, though we may think as badly of this vice as other Christians. The history of the church proves, that men may trust their faculties too little as well as too much, and that the timidity, which shrinks from investigation, has injured the mind, and betrayed the interests of Christianity, as much as an irreverent boldness of thought.

It is an important truth, which, we apprehend, has not been sufficiently developed, that the ultimate reliance of a human being is and must be on his own mind. To confide in God, we must first confide in the faculties by which He is apprehended, and by which the proofs of his existence are weighed. A trust in our ability to distinguish between truth and falsehood, is implied in every act of belief; for to question this ability would of necessity unsettle all belief. We cannot take a step in reasoning or action without a secret reliance on our own minds. Religion, in particular, implies, that we have understandings endowed and qualified for the highest employments of intellect. In affirming the existence and perfections of God, we suppose and affirm the existence in ourselves of faculties which correspond to these sublime objects, and which are fitted to discern them. Religion is a conviction and an act of the human soul; so that in denying confidence to the one, we subvert the truth and claims of the other. Nothing is gained to piety by degrading human nature, for in the competency of this nature to know and judge of God, all piety has its foundation. Our proneness to err instructs us indeed to use our powers with great caution, but not to contemn and neglect them. The occasional abuse of our faculties, be it ever so enormous, does not prove them unfit for their highest end, which is, to form clear and consistent views of God. Because our eyes sometimes fail or deceive us, would a wise man pluck them out, or cover them with a bandage, and choose to walk and work in the dark? — or, because they cannot distinguish distant objects, can they discern nothing clearly in their proper sphere, and is sight to be pronounced a fallacious guide? Men who, to support a creed, would shake our trust in the calm, deliberate, and distinct decisions of our rational and moral powers, endanger religion more than its open foes, and forge the deadliest weapon for the infidel.

It is true that God is an infinite being, and also true, that his powers and perfections, his purposes and operations, his ends and means, being unlimited, are *incomprehensible*. In other words, they cannot be *wholly taken in* or *embraced* by the human mind. In the strong and figurative language of Scripture, we "know nothing" of God's ways; that is, we know *very few* of them. But this is just as true of the most advanced archangel as of man. In comparison with the vastness of God's system, the range of the highest created intellect is narrow; and in this particular man's lot does not differ from that of his elder brethren in heaven. We are both confined in our observation and experience to a little spot in the creation. But are an angel's faculties worthy of no trust, or is his knowledge uncertain, because he learns and reasons from a small part of God's works? or are his judgments respecting the Creator to be charged with presumption, because his views do not spread through the whole extent of the universe? We grant, that our understandings cannot stretch beyond a very narrow sphere. But still, the lessons which we learn within this sphere, are just as sure as if it were indefinitely enlarged. Because much is unexplored, we are not to suspect what we have actually discovered. Knowledge is not the less real, because confined. The man who has never set foot beyond his native village, knows its scenery and inhabitants as undoubtingly, as if he had travelled to the poles. We indeed see very little; but that little is as true, as if everything else were seen; and our future discoveries must agree with and support it. Should the whole order and purposes of the universe be opened to us, it is certain that nothing would be disclosed which would in any degree shake our persuasion, that the earth is inhabited by rational and moral beings, who are authorized to expect from their Creator the most benevolent and equitable government. No extent of observation can unsettle those primary and fundamental principles of moral truth, which we derive from our highest faculties operating in the relations in which God has fixed us. In every region and period of the universe, it will be as true as it is now on the earth, that knowledge and power are the measures of responsibility, and that natural incapacity absolves from guilt. These and other moral verities, which are among our clearest perceptions, would, if possible, be strengthened, in proportion as our powers should be enlarged; because harmony and consistency are the characters of God's administration, and all our researches into the universe only serve to manifest its unity, and to show a wider operation of the laws which we witness and experience on earth.

We grant that God is *incomprehensible,* in the sense already given. But he is not therefore *unintelligible;* and this distinction we conceive to be important. We do not pretend to know the *whole* nature and properties of God, but still we can form some *clear ideas* of him, and can reason from these ideas as justly as from any other. The truth is, that we cannot be said to comprehend any being whatever, not the simplest plant or animal. All have hidden properties. Our knowledge of all is limited. But have we therefore no distinct ideas of the objects around us, and is all our reasoning about them unworthy of trust? Because God is infinite, his name is not therefore a mere sound. It is a representative of some distinct conceptions of our Creator; and these conceptions are as sure, and important, and as proper materials for the reasoning faculty, as they would be if our views were indefinitely enlarged. We cannot indeed trace God's goodness and rectitude through the whole field of his operations; but we know the essential nature of these attributes, and therefore can often judge what accords with and opposes them. God's goodness, because infinite, does not cease to be goodness, or essentially differ from the same attribute in man; nor does justice change its nature, so that it cannot be understood, because it is seated in an unbounded mind. There have indeed been philosophers, "falsely so called," who have argued from the unlimited nature of God, that we cannot ascribe to him justice and other moral attributes, in any proper or definite sense of those words; and the inference is plain, that all religion or worship, wanting an intelligible object, must be a misplaced, wasted offering. This doctrine from the infidel we reject with abhorrence; but something not very different, too often reaches us from the mistaken Christian, who, to save his creed, shrouds the Creator in utter darkness. In opposition to both, we maintain that God's attributes are intelligible, and that we can conceive as truly of his goodness and justice, as of these qualities in men. In fact, these qualities are essentially the same in God and man, though differing in degree, in purity, and in extent of operation. We know not and we cannot conceive of any other justice and goodness, than we learn from our own nature; and if God have not these, he is altogether unknown to us as a moral being; he offers nothing for esteem and love to rest upon; the objection of the infidel is just, that worship is wasted; "we worship we know not what."

It is asked, on what authority we ascribe to God goodness and rectitude, in the sense in which these attributes belong to men, or how we can judge of the nature of attributes in the mind of the Creator? We answer by asking, How is it that we become acquainted with the mind of a fellow-creature? The last is as invisible, as removed from *immediate* inspection, as the first. Still we do not hesitate to speak of the justice and goodness of a neighbour; and how do we gain our knowledge? We answer, by witnessing the effects, operations, and expressions of these attributes. It is a law of our nature to argue from the effect to the cause, from the action to the agent, from the ends proposed and from the means of pursuing them, to the character and disposition of the being in whom we observe them. By these processes, we learn the invisible mind and character of man; and by the same we ascend to the mind of God, whose works, effects, operations, and ends, are as expressive and significant of justice and goodness, as the best and most decisive actions of men. If this reasoning be sound (and all religion rests upon it), then God's justice and goodness are intelligible attributes, agreeing essentially with the same qualities in ourselves. Their operation indeed is infinitely wider, and they are employed in accomplishing not only immediate but remote and unknown ends. Of consequence, we must expect that many parts of the divine administration will be *obscure,* that is, will not produce *immediate* good, and an *immediate* distinction between virtue and vice. But still the unbounded operation of these attributes does not change their nature. They are still the same as if they acted in a narrower sphere. We can still determine in many cases what does not accord with them. We are particularly sure that those essential principles of justice, which enter into and even form our conception of this attribute, must pervade every province and every period of the administration of a just being, and that to suppose the Creator in any instance to forsake them, is to charge him directly with unrighteousness, however loudly the lips may compliment his equity.

"But is it not presumptuous in man," it is continually said, "to sit in judgment on God?" We answer, that "to sit in judgment on God," is an ambiguous and offensive phrase, conveying to common minds the ideas of irreverence, boldness, familiarity. The question would be better stated thus: — Is it not presumptuous in man to judge concerning God, and concerning what agrees or disagrees with his attributes? We answer confidently, No; for in many cases we are competent and even bound to judge. And we plead first in our defence the Scriptures. How continually does God in his Word appeal to the understanding and moral judgment of man? "O inhabitants of Jerusalem and men of Judah, judge, I pray you, between me and my vineyard. What could have been done more to my vineyard, than I have not done in it?" We observe in the next place, that all religion supposes and is built on judgments passed by us on God and on his operations. Is it not, for example, our duty and a leading part of piety, to *praise* God? And what is praising a being, but to adjudge and ascribe to him just and generous deeds and motives? And of what value is praise, except from those who are capable of distinguishing between actions which exalt, and actions which degrade the character? Is it presumption to call God *excellent*? And what is this, but to refer his character to a standard of excellence, to try it by the established principles of rectitude, and to pronounce its conformity to them; that is, to judge of God and his operations?

We are presumptuous, we are told, in judging of our Creator. But he himself has made this our duty, in giving us a moral faculty; and to decline it, is to violate the primary law of our nature. Conscience, the sense of right, the power of perceiving moral distinctions, the power of discerning between justice and injustice, excellence and baseness, is the highest faculty given us by God, the whole foundation of our responsibility, and our sole capacity for religion. Now we are forbidden by this faculty to love a being who wants, or who fails to discover, moral excellence. God, in giving us conscience, has implanted a principle within us, which forbids us to prostrate ourselves before mere power, or to offer praise where we do not discover worth; a principle, which challenges our supreme homage for supreme goodness, and which absolves us from guilt, when we abhor a severe and unjust administration. Our Creator has consequently waived his own claims on our veneration and obedience, any farther than he discovers himself to us in characters of benevolence, equity, and righteousness. He rests his authority on the perfect coincidence of his will and government with those great and fundamental principles of morality written on our souls. He desires no worship, but that which springs from the exercise of our moral faculties upon his character, from our discernment and persuasion of his rectitude and goodness. . . .

[1820]

Nature   RALPH WALDO EMERSON

Ralph Waldo Emerson (1803–82) was born in Boston of an old Puritan family, a member of what Oliver Wendell Holmes called "the Brahmin caste of New England." His father having died when Emerson was eleven, he grew up in genteel poverty and was compelled to work his way through Harvard. In 1826 he was licensed to preach, but six years later he resigned his pastorate because of misgivings about administering the Lord's Supper. His well-known *Essays* were an outgrowth of the lecturing to which he then turned as a means of livelihood, as was the small volume entitled *Nature* (1836), from which the present selection is taken. As a lecturer, poet, essayist, and philosopher, Emerson was widely admired during his lifetime; today, a century later, he remains one of America's great writers.

Nature was the first published expression of Emerson's transcendentalism. Frequently it expresses ideas to which his later work would give fuller expression, such as the call for "an original relation to the universe"; a trust in "the perfection of the creation"; the reality of spirit; the relation of practical and abstract truth; delight in nature; the relations of man to nature, nature to God and man to God. The style, too, is characteristic — the telling image (sometimes exaggerated), the gnomic concision of phrase, the general absence of connectives (Emerson referred to his sentences as "mutually repellent particles"). Such devices, more generally associated with poetry than with prose, suited a man whose approach to truth was less through workaday reason than through feeling, through intuition.

". . . Why should we not also enjoy an original relation to the universe? . . ."

INTRODUCTION

Our age is retrospective. It builds the sepulchres of the fathers. It writes biographies, histories, and criticism. The foregoing generations beheld God and nature face to face; we, through their eyes. Why should not we also enjoy an original relation to the universe? Why should not we have a poetry and philosophy of insight and not of tradition, and a religion by revelation to us, and not the history of theirs? Embosomed for a season in nature, whose floods of life stream around and through us, and invite us, by the powers they supply, to action proportioned to nature, why should we grope among the dry bones of the past, or put the living generation into masquerade out of its faded wardrobe? The sun shines to-day also. There is more wool and flax in the fields. There are new lands, new men, new thoughts. Let us demand our own works and laws and worship.

Undoubtedly we have no questions to ask which are unanswerable. We must trust the perfection of the creation so far, as to believe that whatever curiosity the order of things has awakened in our minds, the order of things can satisfy. Everyman's condition is a solution in hieroglyphic to those inquiries he would put. He acts it as life, before he apprehends it as truth. In like manner, nature is already, in its forms and tendencies, describing its own design. Let us interrogate the great apparition, that shines so peacefully around us. Let us inquire, to what end is nature?

All science has one aim, namely, to find a theory of nature. We have theories of races and of functions, but scarcely yet a remote approximation to an idea of creation. We are now so far from the road to truth, that religious teachers dispute and hate each other, and speculative men are esteemed unsound and frivolous. But to a sound judgment, the most abstract truth is the most practical. Whenever a true theory appears, it will be its own evidence. Its test is, that it will explain all phenomena. Now many are thought not only unexplained but inexplicable; as language, sleep, dreams, beasts, sex.

Philosophically considered, the universe is composed of Nature and the Soul. Strictly speaking, therefore, all that is separate from us, all which Philosophy distinguishes as the NOT ME, that is, both nature and art, all other men and my own body, must be ranked under this name, NATURE. In enumerating the values of nature and casting up their sum, I shall use the word in both senses; — in its common and in its philosophical import. In inquiries so general as our present one, the inaccuracy is not material; no confusion of thought will occur. Nature, in the common sense, refers to essences unchanged by man; space, the air, the river, the leaf. Art is applied to the mixture of his will with the same things, as in a house, a canal, a statue, a picture. But his operations taken together are so insignificant, a little chipping, baking, patching, and washing, that in an impression so grand as that of the world on the human mind, they do not vary the result.

I

To go into solitude, a man needs to retire as much from his chamber as from society. I am not solitary whilst I read and write, though nobody is with me. But if a man would be alone, let him look at the stars. The rays that come from those heavenly worlds, will separate between him and vulgar things. One might think the atmosphere was made transparent with this design, to give man, in the heavenly bodies, the perpetual presence of the sublime. Seen in the streets of cities, how great they are! If the stars should appear one night in a thousand years, how would men believe and adore; and preserve for many generations the remembrance of the city of God which had been shown! But every night come out these preachers of beauty, and light the universe with their admonishing smile.

The stars awaken a certain reverence, because though always present, they are always inaccessible; but all natural objects make a kindred impression, when the mind is open to their influence. Nature never wears a mean appearance. Neither does the wisest man extort all her secret, and lose his curiosity by finding out all her perfection. Nature never became a toy to a wise spirit. The flowers, the animals, the mountains, reflected all the wisdom of his best hour, as much as they had delighted the simplicity of his childhood.

When we speak of nature in this manner, we have a distinct but most poetical sense in the mind. We mean the integrity of impression made by manifold natural objects. It is this which distinguishes the stick of timber of the wood-cutter, from the tree of the poet. The charming landscape which I saw this morning, is indubitably made up of some twenty or thirty farms. Miller owns this field, Locke that, and Manning the woodland beyond. But none of them owns the landscape. There is a property in the horizon which no man has but he whose eye can integrate all the parts, that is, the poet. This is the best part of these men's farms, yet to this their land-deeds give no title.

To speak truly, few adult persons can see nature. Most persons do not see the sun. At least they have a very superficial seeing. The sun illuminates only the eye of the man, but shines into the eye and the heart of the child. The lover of nature is he whose inward and outward senses are still truly adjusted to each other; who has retained the spirit of infancy even into the era of manhood. His intercourse with heaven and earth, becomes part of his daily food. In the presence of nature, a wild delight runs through the man, in spite of real sorrows. Nature says, — he is my creature, and maugre all his impertinent griefs, he shall be glad with me. Not the sun or the summer alone, but every hour and season yields its tribute of delight; for every hour and change corresponds to and authorizes a different state of the mind, from breathless noon to grimmest midnight. Nature is a setting that fits equally well a comic or a mourning piece. In good health, the air is a cordial of incredible virtue. Crossing a bare common, in snow puddles, at twilight, under a clouded sky, without having in my thoughts any occurrence of special good fortune, I have enjoyed a perfect exhilaration. Almost I fear to think how glad I am. In the woods too, a man casts off his years, as the snake his slough, and at what period soever of life, is always a child. In the woods, is perpetual youth. Within these plantations of God, a decorum and sanctity reign, a perennial festival is dressed, and the guest sees not how he should tire of them in a thousand years. In the woods, we return to reason and faith. There I feel that nothing can befall me in life, — no disgrace, no calamity, (leaving me my eyes,) which nature cannot repair. Standing on the bare ground, — my head bathed by the blithe air, and uplifted into infinite space, — all mean egotism vanishes. I become a transparent eyeball. I am nothing. I see all. The currents of the Universal Being circulate through me; I am part or particle of God. The name of the nearest friend sounds then foreign and accidental. To be brothers, to be acquaintances — master or servant, is then a trifle and a disturbance. I am the lover of uncontained and immortal beauty. In the wilderness, I find something more dear and connate than in streets or villages. In the tranquil landscape, and especially in the distant line of the horizon, man beholds somewhat as beautiful as his own nature.

The greatest delight which the fields and woods minister, is the suggestion of an occult relation between man and the vegetable. I am not alone and unacknowledged. They nod to me and I to them. The waving of the boughs in the storm, is new to me and old. It takes me by surprise, and yet is not unknown. Its effect is like that of a higher thought or a better emotion coming over me, when I deemed I was thinking justly or doing right.

Yet it is certain that the power to produce this delight, does not reside in nature, but in man, or in a harmony of both. It is necessary to use these pleasures with great temperance. For, nature is not always tricked in holiday attire, but the same scene which yesterday breathed perfume and glittered as for the frolic of the nymphs, is overspread with melancholy today. Nature always wears the colors of the spirit. To a man laboring under calamity, the heat of his own fire hath sadness in it. Then, there is a kind of contempt of the landscape felt by him who has just lost by death a dear friend. The sky is less grand as it shuts down over less worth in the population.

[1836]

Eight Poems   EMILY DICKINSON

Emily Dickinson (1830–86), greatest of America's women poets, lived most of her life as a spinster recluse in the home of her father, a prominent lawyer of Amherst, Massachusetts. Though a flood of verses came from her pen, only five were published during her lifetime. Living quietly at home, she yet enjoyed the critical company, through letters, of several men whom she referred to as her "tutors." Mostly, however, she wrote for herself alone — some fifteen hundred untitled poems by the time of her death. She was not interested in their publication and left instructions that her manuscripts be destroyed after her death, instructions which her sister Lavinia fortunately ignored. Of the following poems, only the first was published during her lifetime.

Like Emerson, under whose strong influence she wrote, Emily Dickinson delighted in the terse and epigrammatic, cared little for grace and finish of metre or exactness of rhyme — qualities which made her a forerunner of our century's "new poetry." Like Emerson, too, she was not greatly preoccupied with consistency. (How consistent is she, for example, in what she says about God in these poems?) Her principal aim was fresh and penetrating insight into the world about her. It was a limited world in a way, but it was also unlimited — a microcosm which allowed her to say important things about the universal themes of nature, love, life, and death. Emily Dickinson saw, as she said, "New Englandly," but in doing so she saw much else as well.

"... certain am I of the spot. ..."

Some keep the Sabbath going to church;
I keep it staying at home,
With a bobolink for a chorister,
And an orchard for a dome.

Some keep the Sabbath in surplice;
I just wear my wings,
And instead of tolling the bell for church,
Our little sexton sings.

God preaches, — a noted clergyman, —
And the sermon is never long;
So instead of getting to heaven at last,
I'm going all along!

*   *   *

I never saw a moor,
I never saw the sea;
Yet know I how the heather looks,
And what a wave must be.

I never spoke with God,
Nor visited in heaven;
Yet certain am I of the spot
As if the chart were given.

*   *   *

Papa above!
        Regard a Mouse
O'erpowered by the Cat;
Reserve within thy Kingdom
A "mansion" for the Rat!

Snug in seraphic cupboards
To nibble all the day
While unsuspecting cycles
Wheel pompously away.

* * *

Drowning is not so pitiful
As the attempts to rise.
Three times, 'tis said, a sinking man
Comes up to face the skies,
And then declines forever
To that abhorred abode
Where hope and he part company, —
For he is grasped of God.
The Maker's cordial visage,
However good to see,
Is shunned, we must admit it,
Like an adversity.

* * *

I never lost as much but twice
And that was in the sod;
Twice have I stood a beggar
Before the door of God!

Angels, twice descending
Reimbursed my store.
Burglar, banker, father,
I am poor once more!

* * *

Is Heaven a physician?
    They say that He can heal;
But medicine posthumous
    Is unavailable.

Is Heaven an exchequer?
    They speak of what we owe;
But that negotiation
    I'm not a party to.

* * *

I've seen a dying eye
Run round and round a room
In search of something, as it seemed,
Then cloudier become;
And then, obscure with fog,
And then be soldered down,
Without disclosing what it be,
'Twere blessed to have seen.

* * *

Because I could not stop for Death,
He kindly stopped for me;
The carriage held but just ourselves
And Immortality.

We slowly drove, he knew no haste,
And I had put away
My labor, and my leisure too,
For his civility.

We passed the school where children played
At wrestling in a ring;
We passed the fields of gazing grain,
We passed the setting sun.

We paused before a house that seemed
A swelling of the ground;
The roof was scarcely visible,
The cornice but a mound.

Since then 'tis centuries; but each
Feels shorter than the day
I first surmised the horses' heads
Were toward eternity.

Frontier Revival   PETER CARTWRIGHT

Peter Cartwright (1785–1872) was one of the traveling preachers who
brought religion to the American frontier. Camp meetings were a specialty. Converted at sixteen, he was licensed to preach in 1802 and
became famous through Kentucky, Tennessee, Indiana, Ohio, and Illinois
as a powerful captain in the army of the Lord. In the preface to his *Autobiography* (1857), from which "Frontier Revival" is taken, he remarks
that many like him could not "conjugate a verb or parse a sentence, and

murdered the king's English almost every lick. But there was a divine unction attended the word preached, and thousands fell under the mighty power of God, and thus the Methodist Episcopal Church was planted firmly in this Western wilderness, and many glorious signs have followed, and will follow, to the end of time."

Cartwright's *Autobiography* rambles but is at the same time strongly unified in theme. In reading it, we learn much about frontier life in general as well as about frontier religion. Also, we begin to understand Cartwright's popularity and power: his language, while generally dignified, is kept pleasantly unpretentious by an occasional colloquialism; his tone, for a man of obviously strong convictions, is yet one of humor and moderation; the unabashed honesty of his descriptions is that of a man with little or nothing to hide.

"*. . . a new exercise broke out among us, called the* jerks. *. . .*"

Somewhere between 1800 and 1801, in the upper part of Kentucky, at a memorable place called "Cane Ridge," . . . the mighty power of God was displayed in a very extraordinary manner; many were moved to tears, and bitter and loud crying for mercy. The meeting was protracted for weeks. Ministers of almost all denominations flocked in from far and near. The meeting was kept up by night and day. Thousands heard of the mighty work, and came on foot, on horseback, in carriages and wagons. It was supposed that there were in attendance at times during the meeting from twelve to twenty-five thousand people. Hundreds fell prostrate under the mighty power of God, as men slain in battle. Stands were erected in the woods from which preachers of different Churches proclaimed repentance toward God and faith in our Lord Jesus Christ, and it was supposed, by eye and ear witnesses, that between one and two thousand souls were happily and powerfully converted to God during the meeting. It was not unusual for one, two, three, and four to seven preachers to be addressing the listening thousands at the same time from the different stands erected for the purpose. The heavenly fire spread in almost every direction. It was said, by truthful witnesses, that at times more than one thousand persons broke out into loud shouting all at once, and that the shouts could be heard for miles around.

From this camp-meeting, for so it ought to be called, the news spread through all the Churches, and through all the land, and it excited great wonder and surprise; but it kindled a religious flame that spread all over Kentucky and through many other states. And I may here be permitted to say, that this was the first camp-meeting ever held in the United States, and here our camp-meetings took their rise. . . .

The Presbyterians and Methodists in a great measure united in this work, met together, prayed together, and preached together. . . . They would erect their camps with logs or frame them, and cover them with clapboards or shingles. They would also erect a shed, sufficiently large to protect five thousand people from wind and rain, and cover it with boards or shingles; build a large stand, seat the shed, and here they would collect together from forty to fifty miles around, sometimes further than that. Ten, twenty, and sometimes thirty ministers, of different denominations, would come together and preach night and day, four or five days together; and, indeed, I have known these camp-meetings to last three or four weeks, and great good resulted from them. I have seen more than a hundred sinners fall like dead men under one powerful sermon, and I have seen and heard more than five hundred Christians all shouting aloud the high praises of God at once; and I will venture to assert that many happy thousands were awakened and converted to God at these camp-meetings. Some sinners mocked, some of the old dry professors opposed, some of the old starched Presbyterian preachers preached against these exercises, but still the work went on and spread almost in every direction, gathering additional force, until our country seemed all coming home to God.

In this great revival the Methodists kept moderately balanced; for we had excellent preachers to steer the ship or guide the flock. But some of our members ran wild, and indulged in some extravagancies that were hard to control.

The Presbyterian preachers and members, not being accustomed to much noise or shouting, when they yielded to it went into great extremes and downright wildness, to the great injury of the cause of God. Their old preachers licensed a great many young men to preach, contrary to their Confession of Faith. That Confession of Faith required their ministers to believe in unconditional election and reprobation, and the unconditional and final perseverance of the saints. But in this revival they, almost to a man, gave up these points of high Calvinism, and preached a free salvation to all mankind. The Westminster Confession required every man, before he could be licensed to preach, to have a liberal education; but this qualification was dispensed with, and a great many fine men were licensed to preach without this literary qualification or subscribing to those high-toned doctrines of Calvinism.

This state of things produced great dissatisfaction in the Synod of Kentucky, and messenger after messenger was sent to wait on the Presbytery to get them to desist from their erratic course, but without success. Finally they were cited to trial before the constituted authorities of the Church. Some were censured, some were suspended, some retraced their steps, while others surrendered their credentials of ordination, and the rest were cut off from the Church.

While in this amputated condition, they called a general meeting of all their licentiates. They met our presiding elder, J. Page, and a number of Methodist ministers at a quarterly meeting in Logan County, and proposed to join the Methodist Episcopal Church as a body; but our aged ministers declined this offer, and persuaded them to rise up and embody themselves together, and constitute a Church. They reluctantly yielded to this advice, and, in due time and form, constituted what they denominated the "Cumberland Presbyterian Church;" and in their confession of faith split, as they supposed, the difference between the Predestinarians and the Methodists, rejecting a partial atonement or special election and reprobation, but retaining the doctrine of the final unconditional perseverance of the saints.

What an absurdity! While a man remains a sinner he may come, as a free agent, to Christ, if he will, and if he does not come his damnation will be just, because he refused offered mercy; but as soon as he gets converted his free agency is destroyed, the best boon of Heaven is then lost, and although he may backslide, wander away from Christ, yet he shall be brought in. He cannot finally be lost if he has ever been really converted to God.

They make a very sorry show in their attempt to support this left foot of Calvinism. But be it spoken to their credit, they do not often preach this doctrine. They generally preach Methodist doctrine, and have been the means of doing a great deal of good, and would have done much more if they had left this relic of John Calvin behind.

In this revival, usually termed in the West the Cumberland revival, many joined the different Churches, especially the Methodist and Cumberland Presbyterians. The Baptists also came in for a share of the converts, but not to any great extent. Infidelity quailed before the mighty power of God, which was displayed among the people. Universalism was almost driven from the land. The Predestinarians of almost all sorts put forth a mighty effort to stop the work of God.

Just in the midst of our controversies on the subject of the powerful exercises among the people under preaching, a new exercise broke out among us, called the *jerks,* which was overwhelming in its effects upon the bodies and minds of the people. No matter whether they were saints or sinners, they would be taken under a warm song or sermon, and seized with a convulsive jerking all over, which they could not by any possibility avoid, and the more they resisted the more they jerked. If they would not strive against it and pray in good earnest, the jerking would usually abate. I have seen more than five hundred persons jerking at one time in my large congregations. Most usually persons taken with the jerks, to obtain relief, as they said, would rise up and dance. Some would run, but could not get away. Some would resist; on such the jerks were generally very severe.

To see those proud young gentlemen and young ladies, dressed in their silks, jewelry, and prunella, from top to toe, take the *jerks,* would often excite my risibilities. The first jerk or so, you would see their fine bonnets, caps, and combs fly; and so sudden would be the jerking of the head that their long loose hair would crack almost as loud as a wagoner's whip.

At one of my appointments in 1804 there was a very large congregation turned out to hear the Kentucky boy, as they called me. Among the rest there were two very finely-dressed, fashionable young ladies, attended by two brothers with loaded horsewhips. Although the house was large, it was crowded. The two young ladies, coming in late, took their seats near where I stood, and their two brothers stood in the door. I was a little unwell, and I had a phial of peppermint in my pocket. Before I commenced preaching I took out my phial and swallowed a little of the peppermint. While I was preaching, the congregation was melted into tears. The two young gentlemen moved off to the yard fence, and both the young ladies took the jerks, and they were greatly mortified about it. There was a great stir in the congregation. Some wept, some shouted, and before our meeting closed several were converted.

As I dismissed the assembly a man stepped up to me, and warned me to be on my guard, for he had heard the two brothers swear they would horsewhip me when meeting was out, for giving their sisters the jerks. "Well," said I, "I'll see to that."

I went out and said to the young men that I understood they intended to horsewhip me for giving their sisters the jerks. One replied that he did. I undertook to expostulate with him on the absurdity of the charge against me, but he swore I need not deny it; for he had seen me take out a phial, in which I carried some truck that gave his sisters the jerks. As quick as thought it came into my mind how I would get clear of my whipping, and, jerking out the peppermint phial, said I, "Yes; if I gave your sisters the jerks I'll give them to you." In a moment I saw he was scared. I moved toward him, he backed, I advanced, and he wheeled and ran, warning me not to come near him, or he would kill me. It raised the laugh on him, and I escaped my whipping. I had the pleasure, before the year was out, of seeing all four soundly converted to God, and I took them into the Church.

While I am on this subject I will relate a very serious circumstance which I knew to take place with a man who had the jerks at a camp-meeting, on what was called the Ridge, in William Magee's congregation. There was a great work of religion in the encampment. The jerks were very prevalent. There was a company of drunken rowdies who came to interrupt the meeting. These rowdies were headed by a very large drinking man. They came with their bottles of whisky in their pockets. This large man cursed the jerks, and all religion. Shortly afterward he took the jerks, and he started to run, but he jerked so powerfully he could not get away. He halted among some saplings, and, although he was violently agitated, he took out his bottle of whisky, and swore he would drink the damned jerks to death; but he jerked at such a rate he could not get the bottle to his mouth, though he tried hard. At length he fetched a sudden jerk, and the bottle struck a sapling and was broken to pieces, and spilled his whisky on the ground. There was a great crowd gathered round him, and when he lost his whisky he became very much enraged, and cursed and swore very profanely, his jerks still increasing. At length he fetched a very violent jerk, snapped his neck, fell, and soon expired, with his mouth full of cursing and bitterness. . . .

There were many other strange and wild exercises into which the subjects of this revival fell; such, for instance, as what was called the running, jumping, barking exercise. The Methodist preachers generally preached against this extravagant wildness. I did it uniformly in my little ministrations, and sometimes gave great offense; but I feared no consequences when I felt my awful responsibilities to God. From these wild exercises, another great evil arose from the heated and wild imaginations of some. They professed to fall into trances and see visions; they would fall at meetings and sometimes at home, and lay apparently powerless and motionless for days, sometimes for a week at a time, without food or drink; and when they came to, they professed to have seen heaven and hell, to have seen God, angels, the devil and the damned; they would prophesy, and, under the pretense of Divine inspiration, predict the time of the end of the world, and the ushering in of the great millennium.

This was the most troublesome delusion of all; it made such an appeal to the ignorance, superstition, and credulity of the people, even saint as well as·

sinner. I watched this matter with a vigilant eye. If I opposed it, I would have to meet the clamor of the multitude; and if any one opposed it, these very visionists would single him out, and denounce the dreadful judgments of God against him. They would even set the very day that God was to burn the world, like the self-deceived modern Millerites. They would prophesy, that if any one did oppose them, God would send fire down from heaven and consume him, like the blasphemous Shakers. They would proclaim that they could heal all manner of diseases, and raise the dead, just like the diabolical Mormons. They professed to have converse with spirits of the dead in heaven and hell, like the modern spirit rappers. Such a state of things I never saw before, and I hope in God I shall never see again. . . .

We had at this early day no course of study prescribed, as at present; but William M'Kendree, afterward bishop, but then my presiding elder, directed me to a proper course of reading and study. He selected books for me, both literary and theological; and every quarterly visit he made, he examined into my progress, and corrected my errors, if I had fallen into any. He delighted to instruct me in English grammar.

Brother Lakin had charge of the circuit. My business was to preach, meet the classes, visit the society and the sick, and then to my books and study; and I say that I am more indebted to Bishop M'Kendree for my little attainments in literature and divinity, than to any other man on earth. And I believe that if presiding elders would do their duty by young men in this way, it would be more advantageous than all the colleges and Biblical institutes in the land; for they then could learn and practice every day. . . .

The Presbyterians, and other Calvinistic branches of the Protestant Church, used to contend for an educated ministry, for pews, for instrumental music, for a congregational or stated salaried ministry. The Methodists universally opposed these ideas; and the illiterate Methodist preachers actually set the world on fire, (the American world at least), while they were lighting their matches!

Methodist preachers were called by literary gentlemen illiterate, ignorant babblers. I recollect once to have come across one of these Latin and Greek scholars, a regular graduate in theology. In order to bring me into contempt in a public company he addressed me in Greek. In my younger days I had learned considerable of German. I listened to him as if I understood it all, and then replied in Dutch. This he knew nothing about, neither did he understand Hebrew. He concluded that I had answered him in Hebrew, and immediately caved in, and stated to the company that I was the first educated Methodist preacher he ever saw.

I do not wish to undervalue education, but really I have seen so many of these educated preachers who forcibly reminded me of lettuce growing under the shade of a peach-tree, or like a gosling that had got the straddles by wading in the dew, that I turn away sick and faint. . . .

A Methodist preacher in those days, when he felt that God had called him to preach, instead of hunting up a college or Biblical institute, hunted up a hardy pony of a horse, and some traveling apparatus, and with his library always at hand, namely, Bible, Hymn Book, and Discipline, he started, and with a text that never wore out nor grew stale, he cried, "Behold the Lamb of God, that taketh away the sin of the world." In this way he went through storms of wind, hail, snow, and rain; climbed hills and mountains, traversed valleys, plunged through swamps, swam swollen streams, lay out all night, wet, weary, and hungry, held his horse by the bridle all night, or tied him to a limb, slept with his saddle blanket for a bed, his saddle or saddle-bags for his pillow, and his old big coat or blanket, if he had any, for a covering. Often he slept in dirty cabins, on earthen floors, before the fire; ate roasting ears for bread, drank butter-milk for coffee, or sage tea for imperial; took, with a hearty zest, deer or bear meat, or wild turkey, for breakfast, dinner, and supper, if he could get it. His text was always ready, "Behold the Lamb of God," &c. This was old-fashioned Methodist preacher fare and fortune. Under such circumstances, who among us would now say, "Here am I, Lord, send me!"

[1857]

The Skeptical Vein

Young Goodman Brown   NATHANIEL HAWTHORNE

Nathaniel Hawthorne (1804–64) was born at Salem, Massachusetts, of a family which included the famous Judge Hawthorne of the Salem witch trials. After a boyhood of rather somber solitariness, he attended Bowdoin and graduated in 1825. Returning to Salem, he began setting down the tales of early New England for which he is famous. Later he moved to Boston, spent some time at Brook Farm, and married Sophia Peabody, friend and admirer of the transcendental great of Concord, particularly of Emerson. The optimism of this group was not for Hawthorne, who continued his explorations of the dark corners of the New England ancestral mind. His best known longer works are *The Scarlet Letter* (1850) and *The House of Seven Gables* (1851). Today, a century after his death, Hawthorne clearly ranks as one of America's major writers.

Although "Young Goodman Brown" is given a Puritan setting, it is clearly an allegory of human experience that is not limited to a particular place or time. Like the Puritans, Hawthorne is much concerned with the idea of original sin; unlike them, he treated it with marked ambiguity. He never, for example, makes clear whether the meeting in the forest actually took place or occurred in a dream. And he repeatedly suggests more than one interpretation of an event. Hawthorne has been called a skeptic, and certainly there is much skepticism suggested in this powerful tale. His friend Melville wrote of Hawthorne's "power of blackness" and remarked that it "derives its force from its appeals to that Calvinistic sense of Innate Depravity and Original Sin, from whose visitations in some sense or other, no deeply thinking mind is always and wholly free."

". . . Evil is the nature of mankind. Evil must be your only happiness. . . ."

Young Goodman Brown came forth at sunset into the street at Salem village; but put his head back, after crossing the threshold, to exchange a parting kiss with his young wife. And Faith, as the wife was aptly named, thrust her own pretty head into the street, letting the wind play with the pink ribbons of her cap while she called to Goodman Brown.

"Dearest heart," whispered she, softly and rather sadly, when her lips were close to his ear, "prithee put off your journey until sunrise and sleep in your own bed to-night. A lone woman is troubled with such dreams and such thoughts that she's afeard of herself sometimes. Pray tarry with me this night, dear husband, of all nights in the year."

"My love and my Faith," replied young Goodman Brown, "of all nights in the year, this one night must I tarry away from thee. My journey, as thou callest it, forth and back again, must needs be done 'twixt now and sunrise. What, my sweet, pretty wife, dost thou doubt me already, and we but three months married?"

"Then God bless you!" said Faith, with the pink ribbons; "and may you find all well when you come back."

"Amen!" cried Goodman Brown. "Say thy prayers, dear Faith, and go to bed at dusk, and no harm will come to thee."

So they parted; and the young man pursued his way until, being about to turn the corner by the meeting-house, he looked back and saw the head of Faith still peeping after him with a melancholy air, in spite of her pink ribbons.

"Poor little Faith!" thought he, for his heart smote him. "What a wretch am I to leave her on such an errand! She talks of dreams, too. Methought as she spoke there was trouble in her face, as if a dream had warned her what work is to be done to-night. But no, no; 'twould kill her to think it. Well, she's a blessed angel on earth; and after this one night I'll cling to her skirts and follow her to heaven."

With this excellent resolve for the future, Goodman Brown felt himself justified in making more haste on his present evil purpose. He had taken a dreary road, darkened by all the gloomiest trees of the forest, which barely stood aside to let the narrow path creep through, and closed immediately behind. It was all as lonely as could be; and there is this peculiarity in such a solitude, that the traveller knows not who may be concealed by the innumerable trunks and the thick boughs overhead; so that with lonely footsteps he may yet be passing through an unseen multitude.

"There may be a devilish Indian behind every tree," said Goodman Brown to himself; and he glanced fearfully behind him as he added, "What if the devil himself should be at my very elbow!"

His head being turned back, he passed a crook of the road, and, looking forward again, beheld the figure of a man, in grave and decent attire, seated at the foot of an old tree. He arose at Goodman Brown's approach and walked onward side by side with him.

"You are late, Goodman Brown," said he. "The clock of the Old South was striking as I came through Boston, and that is full fifteen minutes agone."

"Faith kept me back a while," replied the young man, with a tremor in his voice, caused by the sudden appearance of his companion, though not wholly unexpected.

It was now deep dusk in the forest, and deepest in that part of it where these two were journeying. As nearly as could be discerned, the second traveller was about fifty years old, apparently in the same rank of life as Goodman Brown, and bearing a considerable resemblance to him, though perhaps more in expression than features. Still they might have been taken for father and son. And yet, though the elder person was as simply clad as the younger, and as simple in manner too, he had an indescribable air of one who knew the world, and who would not have felt abashed at the governor's dinner table or in King William's court, were it possible that his affairs should call him thither. But the only thing about him that could be fixed upon as remarkable was his staff, which bore the likeness of a great black snake, so curiously wrought that it might almost be seen to twist and wriggle itself like a living serpent. This, of course, must have been an ocular deception, assisted by the uncertain light.

"Come, Goodman Brown," cried his fellow-traveller, "this is a dull pace for the beginning of a journey. Take my staff, if you are so soon weary."

"Friend," said the other, exchanging his slow pace for a full stop, "having kept covenant by meeting thee here, it is my purpose now to return whence I came. I have scruples touching the matter thou wot'st of."

"Sayest thou so?" replied he of the serpent, smiling apart. "Let us walk on, nevertheless, reasoning as we go; and if I convince thee not thou shalt turn back. We are but a little way in the forest yet."

"Too far! too far!" exclaimed the goodman, unconsciously resuming his walk. "My father never went into the woods on such an errand, nor his father before him. We have been a race of honest men and good Christians since the days of the martyrs; and shall I be the first of the name of Brown that ever took this path and kept" —

"Such company, thou wouldst say," observed the elder person, interpreting his pause. "Well said, Goodman Brown! I have been as well acquainted with your family as with ever a one among the Puritans; and that's no trifle to say. I helped your grandfather, the constable, when he lashed the Quaker woman so smartly through the streets of Salem; and it was I that brought your father a pitch-pine knot, kindled at my own hearth, to set fire to an Indian village, in King Philip's war. They were my good friends, both; and many a pleasant walk have we had along this path, and returned merrily after midnight. I would fain be friends with you for their sake."

"If it be as thou sayest," replied Goodman Brown, "I marvel they never spoke of these matters, or, verily, I marvel not, seeing that the least rumor of the sort would have driven them from New England. We are a people of prayer, and good works to boot, and abide no such wickedness."

"Wickedness or not," said the traveller with the twisted staff, "I have a very general acquaintance here in New England. The deacons of many a church have drunk the communion wine with me; the selectmen of divers towns make me their chairman; and a majority of the Great and General Court are firm supporters of my interest. The governor and I, too — But these are state secrets."

"Can this be so?" cried Goodman Brown, with a stare of amazement at his undisturbed companion. "Howbeit, I have nothing to do with the governor and council; they have their own ways, and are no rule for a simple husbandman like me. But, were I to go on with thee, how should I meet the eye of that good old man, our minister, at Salem village? Oh, his voice would make me tremble both Sabbath day and lecture day."

Thus far the elder traveller had listened with due gravity; but now burst into a fit of irrepressible mirth, shaking himself so violently that his snake-like staff actually seemed to wriggle in sympathy.

"Ha! ha! ha!" shouted he again and again; then composing himself, "Well, go on, Goodman Brown, go on; but, prithee, don't kill me with laughing."

"Well, then, to end the matter at once," said Goodman Brown, considerably nettled, "there is my wife, Faith. It would break her dear little heart; and I'd rather break my own."

"Nay, if that be the case," answered the other, "e'en go thy ways, Goodman Brown. I would not for twenty old women like the one hobbling before us that Faith should come to any harm."

As he spoke he pointed his staff at a female figure on the path, in whom Goodman Brown recognized a very pious and exemplary dame, who had taught him his catechism in youth, and was still his moral and spiritual adviser, jointly with the minister and Deacon Gookin.

"A marvel, truly, that Goody Cloyse should be so far in the wilderness at nightfall," said he. "But with your leave, friend, I shall take a cut through the woods until we have left this Christian woman behind. Being a stranger to you, she might ask whom I was consorting with and whither I was going."

"Be it so," said his fellow-traveller. "Betake you to the woods, and let me keep the path."

Accordingly the young man turned aside, but took care to watch his companion, who advanced softly along the road until he had come within a staff's length of the old dame. She, meanwhile, was making the best of her way, with singular speed for so aged a woman, and mumbling some indistinct words — a prayer, doubtless — as she went. The traveller put forth his staff and touched her withered neck with what seemed the serpent's tail.

"The devil!" screamed the pious old lady.

"Then Goody Cloyse knows her old friend?" observed the traveller, confronting her and leaning on his writhing stick.

"Ah, forsooth, and is it your worship indeed?" cried the good dame. "Yea, truly is it, and in the very image of my old gossip, Goodman Brown, the grandfather of the silly fellow that now is. But — would your worship believe it? — my broomstick hath strangely disappeared, stolen, as I suspect, by that unhanged witch, Goody Cory, and that, too, when I was all anointed with the juice of smallage, and cinquefoil, and wolf's bane" —

"Mingled with fine wheat and the fat of a new-born babe," said the shape of old Goodman Brown.

"Ah, your worship knows the recipe," cried the old lady, cackling aloud. "So, as I was saying, being all ready for the meeting, and no horse to ride on, I made up my mind to foot it; for they tell me there is a nice young man to be taken into communion to-night. But now your good worship will lend me your arm, and we shall be there in a twinkling."

"That can hardly be," answered her friend. "I may not spare you my arm, Goody Cloyse; but here is my staff, if you will."

So saying, he threw it down at her feet, where, perhaps, it assumed life, being one of the rods which its owner had formerly lent to the Egyptian magi. Of this fact, however, Goodman Brown could not take cognizance. He had cast up his eyes in astonishment, and, looking down again, beheld neither Goody Cloyse nor the serpentine staff, but his fellow-traveller alone, who waited for him as calmly as if nothing had happened.

"That old woman taught me my catechism," said the young man; and there was a world of meaning in this simple comment.

They continued to walk onward, while the elder traveller exhorted his companion to make good speed and persevere in the path, discoursing so aptly that his arguments seemed rather to spring up in the bosom of his auditor than to be suggested by himself. As they went, he plucked a branch of maple to serve for a walking stick, and began to strip it of the twigs and little boughs, which were wet with evening dew. The moment his fingers touched them they became strangely withered and dried up as with a week's sunshine. Thus the pair proceeded, at a good free pace, until suddenly, in a gloomy hollow of the road, Goodman Brown sat himself down on the stump of a tree and refused to go any farther.

"Friend," said he, stubbornly, "my mind is made up. Not another step will I budge on this errand. What if a wretched old woman do choose to go to the devil when I thought she was going to heaven: is that any reason why I should quit my dear Faith and go after her?"

"You will think better of this by and by," said his acquaintance, composedly. "Sit here and rest yourself a while; and when you feel like moving again, there is my staff to help you along."

Without more words, he threw his companion the maple stick, and was as speedily out of sight as if he had vanished into the deepening gloom. The young man sat a few moments by the roadside, applauding himself greatly, and thinking with how clear a conscience he should meet the minister in his morning walk, nor shrink from the eye of good old Deacon Gookin. And what calm sleep would be his that very night, which was to have been spent so wickedly, but so purely and sweetly now, in the arms of Faith! Amidst these pleasant and praiseworthy meditations, Goodman Brown heard the tramp of horses along the road, and deemed it advisable to conceal himself within the verge of the forest, conscious of the guilty purpose that had brought him thither, though now so happily turned from it.

On came the hoof tramps and the voices of the riders, two grave old voices, conversing soberly as they drew near. These mingled sounds appeared to pass along the road, within a few yards of the young man's hiding-place; but, owing doubtless to the depth of the gloom at that particular spot, neither the travellers nor their steeds were visible. Though their figures brushed the small boughs by the wayside, it could not be seen that they intercepted, even for a moment, the faint gleam from the strip of bright sky athwart which they must have passed. Goodman Brown alternately crouched and stood on tiptoe, pulling aside the branches and thrusting forth his head as far as he durst without discerning so much as a shadow. It vexed him the more, because he could have sworn, were such a thing possible, that he recognized the voices of the minister and Deacon Gookin, jogging along quietly, as they were wont to do, when bound to some ordination or ecclesiastical council. While yet within hearing, one of the riders stopped to pluck a switch.

"Of the two, reverend sir," said the voice like the deacon's, "I had rather miss an ordination dinner than to-night's meeting. They tell me that some of our community are to be here from Falmouth and beyond, and others from Connecticut and Rhode Island, besides several of Indian powwows, who, after their fashion, know almost as much deviltry as the best of us. Moreover, there is a goodly young woman to be taken into communion."

"Mighty well, Deacon Gookin!" replied the solemn old tones of the minister. "Spur up, or we shall be late. Nothing can be done you know until I get on the ground."

The hoofs clattered again; and the voices, talking so strangely in the empty air, passed on through the forest, where no church had ever been gathered or solitary Christian prayed. Whither, then, could these holy men be journeying so deep into the heathen wilderness? Young Goodman Brown caught hold of a tree for support, being ready to sink down on the ground, faint and over-burdened with the heavy sickness of his heart. He looked up to the sky, doubting whether there really was a heaven above him. Yet there was the blue arch, and the stars brightening in it.

"With heaven above and Faith below, I will yet stand firm against the devil!" cried Goodman Brown.

While he still gazed upward into the deep arch of the firmament and had lifted his hands to pray, a cloud, though no wind was stirring, hurried across the zenith and hid the brightening stars. The blue sky was still visible, except directly overhead, where this black mass of cloud was sweeping swiftly north-ward. Aloft in the air, as if from the depths of the cloud, came a confused and doubtful sound of voices. Once the listener fancied that he could distinguish the accents of towns-people of his own, men, and women, both pious and ungodly, many of whom he had met at the communion table, and had seen others rioting at the tavern. The next moment, so indistinct were the sounds, he doubted whether he had heard aught but the murmur of the old forest, whispering without a wind. Then came a stronger swell of those familiar tones, heard daily in the sunshine at Salem village, but never until now from a cloud of night. There was one voice of a young woman, uttering lamenta-tions, yet with an uncertain sorrow, and entreating for some favor, which, perhaps, it would grieve her to obtain; and all the unseen multitude, both saints and sinners, seemed to encourage her onward.

"Faith!" shouted Goodman Brown, in a voice of agony and desperation; and the echoes of the forest mocked him, crying, "Faith! Faith!" as if bewil-dered wretches were seeking her all through the wilderness.

The cry of grief, rage, and terror was yet piercing the night, when the unhappy husband held his breath for a response. There was a scream, drowned immediately in a louder murmur of voices, fading into far-off laughter, as the dark cloud swept away, leaving the clear and silent sky above Goodman Brown. But something fluttered lightly down through the air and caught on the branch of a tree. The young man seized it, and beheld a pink ribbon.

"My Faith is gone!" cried he, after one stupefied moment. "There is no good on earth; and sin is but a name. Come, devil; for to thee is this world given."

And, maddened with despair, so that he laughed loud and long, did Goodman Brown grasp his staff and set forth again, at such a rate that he seemed to fly along the forest path rather than to walk or run. The road grew wilder and drearier and more faintly traced, and vanished at length, leaving him in the heart of the dark wilderness, still rushing onward with the instinct that guides mortal man to evil. The whole forest was peopled with frightful sounds — the creaking of the trees, the howling of wild beasts, and the yell of Indians; while sometimes the wind tolled like a distant church bell, and sometimes gave a broad roar around the traveller, as if all Nature were laughing him to scorn. But he was himself the chief horror of the scene, and shrank not from its other horrors.

"Ha! ha! ha!" roared Goodman Brown when the wind laughed at him. "Let us hear which will laugh loudest. Think not to frighten me with your deviltry. Come witch, come wizard, come Indian powwow, come devil himself, and here comes Goodman Brown. You may as well fear him as he fear you."

In truth, all through the haunted forest there could be nothing more frightful than the figure of Goodman Brown. On he flew among the black pines, brandishing his staff with frenzied gestures, now giving vent to an inspiration of horrid blasphemy, and now shouting forth such laughter as set all the echoes of the forest laughing like demons around him. The fiend in his own shape is less hideous than when he rages in the breast of man. Thus sped the demoniac on his course, until, quivering among the trees, he saw a red light before him, as when the felled trunks and branches of a clearing have been set on fire, and throw up their lurid blaze against the sky, at the hour of midnight. He paused, in a lull of the tempest that had driven him onward, and heard the swell of what seemed a hymn, rolling solemnly from a distance with the weight of many voices. He knew the tune; it was a familiar one in the choir of the village meeting-house. The verse died heavily away, and was lengthened by a chorus, not of human voices, but of all the sounds of the benighted wilderness pealing in awful harmony together. Goodman Brown cried out, and his cry was lost to his own ear by its unison with the cry of the desert.

In the interval of silence he stole forward until the light glared full upon his eyes. At one extremity of an open space, hemmed in by the dark wall of the forest, arose a rock, bearing some rude, natural resemblance either to an altar or a pulpit, and surrounded by four blazing pines, their tops aflame, their stems untouched, like candles at an evening meeting. The mass of foliage that had overgrown the summit of the rock was all on fire, blazing high into the night and fitfully illuminating the whole field. Each pendent twig and leafy festoon was in a blaze. As the red light arose and fell, a numerous congregation alternately shone forth, then disappeared in shadow, and again grew, as it were, out of the darkness, peopling the heart of the solitary woods at once.

"A grave and dark-clad company," quoth Goodman Brown.

In truth they were such. Among them, quivering to and fro between gloom and splendor, appeared faces that would be seen next day at the council board of the province, and others which, Sabbath after Sabbath, looked devoutly heavenward, and benignantly over the crowded pews, from the holiest pulpits in the land. Some affirm that the lady of the governor was there. At least there were high dames well known to her, and wives of honored husbands, and widows, a great multitude, and ancient maidens, all of excellent repute, and fair young girls, who trembled lest their mothers should espy them. Either the sudden gleams of light flashing over the obscure field bedazzled Goodman Brown, or he recognized a score of the church members of Salem village famous for their especial sanctity. Good old Deacon Gookin had arrived, and waited at the skirts of that venerable saint, his revered pastor.

But, irreverently consorting with these grave, reputable, and pious people, these elders of the church, these chaste dames and dewy virgins, there were men of dissolute lives and women of spotted fame, wretches given over to all mean and filthy vice, and suspected even of horrid crimes. It was strange to see that the good shrank not from the wicked, nor were the sinners abashed by the saints. Scattered also among their pale-faced enemies were the Indian priests, or powwows, who had often scared their native forest with more hideous incantations than any known to English witchcraft.

"But where is Faith?" thought Goodman Brown; and, as hope came into his heart, he trembled.

Another verse of the hymn arose, a slow and mournful strain, such as the pious love, but joined to words which expressed all that our nature can conceive of sin, and darkly hinted at far more. Unfathomable to mere mortals is the lore of fiends. Verse after verse was sung; and still the chorus of the desert swelled between like the deepest tone of a mighty organ; and with the final peal of that dreadful anthem there came a sound, as if the roaring wind, the rushing streams, the howling beasts, and every other voice of the unconcerted wilderness were mingling and according with the voice of guilty man in homage to the prince of all. The four blazing pines threw up a loftier flame, and obscurely discovered shapes and visages of horror on the smoke wreaths above the impious assembly. At the same moment the fire on the rock shot redly forth and formed a glowing arch above its base, where now appeared a figure. With reverence be it spoken, the figure bore no slight similitude, both in garb and manner, to some grave divine of the New England churches.

"Bring forth the converts!" cried a voice that echoed through the field and rolled into the forest.

At the word, Goodman Brown stepped forth from the shadow of the trees and approached the congregation, with whom he felt a loathful brotherhood by the sympathy of all that was wicked in his heart. He could have well-nigh sworn that the shape of his own dead father beckoned him to advance, looking downward from a smoke wreath, while a woman, with dim features of despair, threw out her hand to warn him back. Was it his mother? But he had no power to retreat one step, nor to resist, even in thought, when the minister and good old Deacon Gookin seized his arms and led him to the blazing rock. Thither came also the slender form of a veiled female, led between Goody Cloyse, that pious teacher of the catechism, and Martha Carrier, who had received the devil's promise to be queen of hell. A rampant hag was she. And there stood the proselytes beneath the canopy of fire.

"Welcome, my children," said the dark figure, "to the communion of your race. Ye have found thus young your nature and your destiny. My children, look behind you!"

They turned; and flashing forth, as it were, in a sheet of flame, the fiend worshippers were seen; the smile of welcome gleamed darkly on every visage.

"There," resumed the sable form, "are all whom ye have reverenced from youth. Ye deemed them holier than yourselves, and shrank from your own sin, contrasting it with their lives of righteousness and prayerful aspirations heavenward. Yet here are they all in my worshipping assembly. This night it shall be granted you to know their secret deeds: how hoary-bearded elders

of the church have whispered wanton words to the young maids of their house-
holds; how many a woman, eager for widows' weeds, has given her husband
a drink at bedtime and let him sleep his last sleep in her bosom; how beardless
youths have made haste to inherit their fathers' wealth; and how fair damsels
— blush not, sweet ones — have dug little graves in the garden, and bidden me,
the sole guest to an infant's funeral. By the sympathy of your human hearts
for sin ye shall scent out all the places — whether in church, bedchamber,
street, field, or forest — where crime has been committed, and shall exult to
behold the whole earth one stain of guilt, one mighty blood spot. Far more
than this. It shall be yours to penetrate, in every bosom, the deep mystery of
sin, the fountain of all wicked arts, and which inexhaustibly supplies more
evil impulses than human power — than my power at its utmost — can make
manifest in deeds. And now, my children, look upon each other."

They did so; and, by the blaze of the hell-kindled torches, the wretched
man beheld his Faith, and the wife her husband, trembling before that un-
hallowed altar.

"Lo, there ye stand, my children," said the figure, in a deep and solemn
tone, almost sad with its despairing awfulness, as if his once angelic nature
could yet mourn for our miserable race. "Depending upon one another's
hearts, ye have still hoped that virtue were not all a dream. Now are ye un-
deceived. Evil is the nature of mankind. Evil must be your only happiness.
Welcome again, my children, to the communion of your race."

"Welcome," repeated the fiend worshippers, in one cry of despair and
triumph.

And there they stood, the only pair, as it seemed, who were yet hesitating
on the verge of wickedness in this dark world. A basin was hollowed, naturally, in the rock. Did it contain water, reddened by the lurid light? or was it
blood? or, perchance, a liquid flame? Herein did the shape of evil dip his
hand and prepare to lay the mark of baptism upon their foreheads, that they
might be partakers of the mystery of sin, more conscious of the secret guilt of
others, both in deed and thought, than they could now be of their own. The
husband cast one look at his pale wife, and Faith at him. What polluted
wretches would the next glance show them to each other, shuddering alike at
what they disclosed and what they saw!

"Faith! Faith!" cried the husband, "look up to heaven, and resist the
wicked one."

Whether Faith obeyed he knew not. Hardly had he spoken when he
found himself amid calm night and solitude, listening to a roar of the wind
which died heavily away through the forest. He staggered against the rock,
and felt it chill and damp; while a hanging twig, that had been all on fire,
besprinkled his cheek with the coldest dew.

The next morning young Goodman Brown came slowly into the street of
Salem village, staring around him like a bewildered man. The good old
minister was taking a walk along the graveyard to get an appetite for breakfast and meditate his sermon, and bestowed a blessing, as he passed, on
Goodman Brown. He shrank from the venerable saint as if to avoid an
anathema. Old Deacon Gookin was at domestic worship, and the holy words
of his prayer were heard through the open window. "What God doth the

wizard pray to?" quoth Goodman Brown. Goody Cloyse, that excellent old Christian, stood in the early sunshine at her own lattice, catechizing a little girl who had brought her a pint of morning's milk. Goodman Brown snatched away the child as from the grasp of the fiend himself. Turning the corner by the meeting-house, he spied the head of Faith, with the pink ribbons, gazing anxiously forth, and bursting into such joy at sight of him that she skipped along the street and almost kissed her husband before the whole village. But Goodman Brown looked sternly and sadly into her face, and passed on without a greeting.

Had Goodman Brown fallen asleep in the forest and only dreamed a wild dream of a witch-meeting?

Be it so if you will; but, alas! it was a dream of evil omen for young Goodman Brown. A stern, a sad, a darkly meditative, a distrustful, if not a desperate man did he become from the night of that fearful dream. On the Sabbath day, when the congregation were singing a holy psalm, he could not listen because an anthem of sin rushed loudly upon his ear and drowned all the blessed strain. When the minister spoke from the pulpit with power and fervid eloquence, and, with his hand on the open Bible, of the sacred truths of our religion, and of saint-like lives and triumphant deaths, and of future bliss or misery unutterable, then did Goodman Brown turn pale, dreading lest the roof should thunder down upon the gray blasphemer and his hearers. Often, waking suddenly at midnight, he shrank from the bosom of Faith; and at morning or eventide, when the family knelt down at prayer, he scowled and muttered to himself, and gazed sternly at his wife, and turned away. And when he had lived long, and was borne to his grave a hoary corpse, followed by Faith, an aged woman, and children and grandchildren, a goodly procession, besides neighbors not a few, they carved no hopeful verse upon his tombstone, for his dying hour was gloom.

[1835]

A Fundamentalist Examined

CLARENCE DARROW
WILLIAM JENNINGS BRYAN

In 1925 John Thomas Scopes, a Tennessee high school teacher, was prosecuted for violating a state law prohibiting the teaching of evolution in the public schools. He was found guilty and was fined a hundred dollars, but not before the trial had attracted international attention. Because of the importance of the principles involved, Clarence Darrow (1857–1938), one of the most celebrated courtroom lawyers of his time, and William Jennings Bryan (1860–1925), three times Democratic candidate for President, offered their respective services to the defense and to the prosecution. Toward the end of the trial, the fundamentalist Bryan took the witness stand to be examined by the skeptical Darrow. On the following day this cross-examination, part of which is printed below, was ordered stricken from the record as being irrelevant.

Probably the most interesting aspect of this remarkable cross-examination is the view it gives us of two eminent men as they confront each other on an issue of basic importance. Even from a brief excerpt it is possible to infer some of the qualities of mind and spirit which distinguish the two antagonists. The transcript has some of the qualities we expect in fiction: plot, character, conflict, theme, and suspense.

". . . I believe what the Bible says. . . ."

Mr. Darrow: Your honor, before you send for the jury, I think it my duty to make this motion. Off to the left of where the jury sits a little bit and about ten feet in front of them is a large sign about ten feet long reading, "Read Your Bible," and a hand pointing to it. The word "Bible" is in large letters. I move that it be removed. . . .

The Court: The issues in this case, as they have been finally determined by this court, is whether or not it is unlawful to teach that man descended from a lower order of animals. I do not understand that that issue involves the Bible. If the Bible is involved, I believe in it and am always on its side, but it is not for me to decide in this case. If the presence of the sign irritates anyone, or if anyone thinks it might influence the jury in any way, I have no purpose except to give both sides a fair trial in this case. Feeling that way about it, I will let the sign come down. (*The sign was removed.*) . . .

Mr. Hays: The defense desires to call Mr. Bryan as a witness, and, of course, since the only question here is whether Mr. Scopes taught what these children said he taught, we recognize what Mr. Bryan says as a witness would not be very valuable. We think there are other questions involved, and we should want to take Mr. Bryan's testimony for the purposes of our record, even if your honor thinks it is not admissible in general, so we wish to call him now. . . .

The Court: Mr. Bryan, you are not objecting to going on the stand?
Mr. Bryan: Not at all.
The Court: Do you want Mr. Bryan sworn?
Mr. Darrow: No.
Mr. Bryan: I can make affirmation; I can say "So help me God, I will tell the truth."
Mr. Darrow: No, I take it you will tell the truth, Mr. Bryan. You have given considerable study to the Bible, haven't you, Mr. Bryan? . . .
Mr. Bryan: Yes, I have; I have studied the Bible for about fifty years, or something more than that, but, of course, I have studied it more as I have become older than when I was but a boy.
Q—Do you claim that everything in the Bible should be literally interpreted?
A—I believe everything in the Bible should be accepted as it is given there; some of the Bible is given illustratively. For instance: "Ye are the salt of the earth." I would not insist that man was actually salt, or that he had flesh of salt, but it is used in the sense of salt as saying God's people.

Mr. Darrow: But when you read that Jonah swallowed the whale — or that the whale swallowed Jonah — excuse me, please — how do you literally interpret that?

Mr. Bryan: When I read that a big fish swallowed Jonah — it does not say whale.

Q — Doesn't it? Are you sure?

A — That is my recollection of it. A big fish, and I believe it, and I believe in a God who can make a whale and can make a man and make both do what He pleases.

Q — Mr. Bryan, doesn't the New Testament say whale?

A — I am not sure. My impression is that it says fish; but it does not make so much difference; I merely called your attention to where it says fish — it does not say whale.

Q — But in the New Testament it says whale, doesn't it?

A — That may be true; I cannot remember in my own mind what I read about it.

Q — Now, you say, the big fish swallowed Jonah, and he there remained how long — three days — and then he spewed him upon the land. You believe that the big fish was made to swallow Jonah?

A — I am not prepared to say that; the Bible merely says it was done.

Q — You don't know whether it was the ordinary run of fish, or made for that purpose?

A — You may guess; you evolutionists guess. . . .

Q — You are not prepared to say whether that fish was made especially to swallow a man or not?

A — The Bible doesn't say, so I am not prepared to say. . . .

Q — Do you consider the story of Jonah and the whale a miracle?

A — I think it is.

Q — Do you believe Joshua made the sun stand still?

A — I believe what the Bible says. I suppose you mean that the earth stood still?

Q — I don't know. I am talking about the Bible now.

A — I accept the Bible absolutely.

Q — The Bible says Joshua commanded the sun to stand still for the purpose of lengthening the day, doesn't it, and you believe it?

A — I do.

Q — Do you believe at that time the sun went around the earth?

A — No, I believe that the earth goes around the sun. . . .

Q — Have you an opinion as to whether — whoever wrote the book, I believe Joshua, the Book of Joshua, thought the sun went around the earth or not? . . .

A — I believe that the Bible is inspired, with an inspired author. Whether one who wrote as he was directed to write understood the things he was writing about, I don't know.

Q — Whoever inspired it? Do you think whoever inspired it believed that the sun went around the earth?

A — I believe it was inspired by the Almighty, and He may have used language that could be understood at that time. . . .

Mr. Darrow: Don't you believe that in order to lengthen the day it would have been construed that the earth stood still?

Mr. Bryan: I would not attempt to say what would have been necessary, but I know this, that I can take a glass of water that would fall to the ground without the strength of my hand and to the extent of the glass of water I can overcome the law of gravitation and lift it up. Whereas without my hand it would fall to the ground. If my puny hand can overcome the law of gravitation, the most universally understood, to that extent, I would not set power to the hand of Almighty God that made the universe.

Q — I read that years ago. Can you answer my question directly? If the day was lengthened by stopping either the earth or the sun, it must have been the earth?

A — Well, I should say so.

Q — Yes? But it was language that was understood at that time, and we now know that the sun stood still as it was with the earth.

A — Well, no —

Q — We know also the sun does not stand still?

A — Well, it is relatively so, as Mr. Einstein would say.

Q — I ask you if it does stand still?

A — You know as well as I know.

Q — Better. You have no doubt about it?

A — No. And the earth moves around.

Q — Yes?

A — But I think there is nothing improper if you will protect the Lord against your criticism.

Q — I suppose He needs it?

A — He was using language at that time the people understood. . . .

Mr. Darrow: You believe the story of the flood to be a literal interpretation?

Mr. Bryan: Yes, sir. . . .

Q — How long ago was the flood, Mr. Bryan?

A — Let me see Usher's calculation about it.

Mr. Darrow: Surely. (*Hands a Bible to the witness.*) . . .

Mr Bryan: It is given here, as 2,348 years B.C.

Q — Well, 2,348 years B.C. You believe that all the living things that were not contained in the ark were destroyed?

A — I think the fish may have lived.

Q — Outside of the fish?

A — I cannot say.

Q — You cannot say?

A — No, except that just as it is, I have no proof to the contrary.

Q — I am asking you whether you believe.

A — I do.

Q — That all living things outside of the fish were destroyed?

A — What I say about the fish is merely a matter of humor. . . .

Q — I am referring to the fish, too.

A — I accept that, as the Bible gives it and I have never found any reason for denying, disputing, or rejecting it.

Mr. Darrow: Let us make it definite, 2,348 years?

Mr. Bryan: I didn't say that. That is the time given there (*indicating a Bible*) but I don't pretend to say that is exact. . . .

Q — Don't you know there are any number of civilizations that are traced back to more than 5,000 years?

A — I know we have people who trace things back according to the number of ciphers they have. But I am not satisfied they are accurate.

Q — You are not satisfied there is any civilization that can be traced back 5,000 years?

A — I would not want to say there is because I have no evidence of it that is satisfactory.

Q — Would you say there is not?

A — Well, so far as I know, but when the scientists differ, from 24,000,000 to 306,000,000 in their opinion, as to how long ago life came here, I want them nearer, to come nearer together before they demand of me to give up my belief in the Bible.

Q — Do you say that you do not believe that there were any civilizations on this earth that reach back beyond 5,000 years?

A — I am not satisfied by any evidence that I have seen. . . .

Q — Don't you know that the ancient civilizations of China are 6,000 or 7,000 years old, at the very least?

A — No; they would not run back beyond the creation, according to the Bible, 6,000 years.

Q — You don't know how old they are, is that right?

A — I don't know how old they are, but probably you do. (*Laughter in the courtyard.*) I think you would give the preference to anybody who opposed the Bible, and I give the preference to the Bible.

Q — I see. Well, you are welcome to your opinion. Have you any idea how old the Egyptian civilization is?

A — No.

Q — Do you know of any record in the world, outside of the story of the Bible, which conforms to any statement that it is 4,200 years ago or thereabouts that all life was wiped off the face of the earth?

A — I think they have found records.

Q — Do you know of any?

A — Records reciting the flood, but I am not an authority on the subject. . . .

Q — Do you know anything about how many people there were in Egypt 3,500 years ago, or how many people there were in China 5,000 years ago?

A — No.

Q — Have you ever tried to find out?

A — No, sir. You are the first man I ever heard of who has been interested in it. (*Laughter.*)

Q — Mr. Bryan, am I the first man you ever heard of who has been interested in the age of human societies and primitive man?

A — You are the first man I ever heard speak of the number of people at those different periods.

Q — Where have you lived all your life?

A — Not near you. (*Laughter and applause.*)

Mr. Darrow: Nor near anybody of learning?

Mr. Bryan: Oh, don't assume you know it all.

Q — Do you know there are thousands of books in our libraries on all those subjects I have been asking you about?

A — I couldn't say, but I will take your word for it.

Q — Did you ever read a book on primitive man? Like Tyler's "Primitive Culture," or Boaz, or any of the great authorities?

A — I don't think I ever read the ones you have mentioned.

Q — Have you read any?

A — Well I have read a little from time to time. But I didn't pursue it, because I didn't know I was to be called as a witness.

Q — You have never in all your life made any attempt to find out about the other peoples of the earth — how old their civilizations are — how long they have existed on the earth, have you?

A — No, sir, I have been so well satisfied with the Christian religion that I have spent no time trying to find arguments against it. . . . I have all the information I want to live by and to die by.

Q — And that's all you are interested in?

A — I am not looking for any more on religion.

Q — You don't care how old the earth is, how old man is and how long the animals have been here?

A — I am not so much interested in that.

Q — You have never made any investigation to find out?

A — No, sir, I have never. . . .

Mr. Darrow: Do you think the earth was made in six days?

Mr. Bryan: Not six days of twenty-four hours.

Q — Doesn't it say so?

A — No, sir.

State Prosecutor: I want to interpose another objection. What is the purpose of this examination?

Mr. Bryan: The purpose is to cast ridicule on everybody who believes in the Bible, and I am perfectly willing that the world shall know that these gentlemen have no other purpose than ridiculing every Christian who believes in the Bible.

Mr. Darrow: We have the purpose of preventing bigots and ignoramuses from controlling the education of the United States and you know it, and that is all. . . .

The Court: Are you about through, Mr. Darrow?

Mr. Darrow: I want to ask a few more questions about the creation. . . .

The Court: Be very brief, Mr. Darrow.

Mr. Darrow: Mr. Bryan, do you believe that the first woman was Eve?

Mr. Bryan: Yes.

Q — Do you believe she was literally made out of Adam's rib?

A — I do.

Q — Did you ever discover where Cain got his wife?

A — No, sir; I leave the agnostics to hunt for her.

Q — You have never found out?

Mr. Bryan: I have never tried to find out.

Mr. Darrow: You have never tried to find out?

A — No.

Q — The Bible says he got one, doesn't it? Were there other people on the earth at that time?

A — I cannot say.

Q — *You* cannot say. Did that ever enter your consideration?

A — Never bothered me.

Q — There were no others recorded, but Cain got a wife.

A — That is what the Bible says.

Q — Where she came from you do not know. All right. Does the statement, "The morning and the evening were the first day," and "The morning and the evening were the second day," mean anything to you?

A — I do not think it necessarily means a twenty-four hour day.

Q — You do not?

A — No.

Q — What do you consider it to be?

A — I have not attempted to explain it. If you will take the second chapter — let me have the book. (*Examines Bible.*) The fourth verse of the second chapter says: "These are the generations of the heavens and of the earth, when they were created in the day that the Lord God made the earth and the heavens." The word "day" there in the very next chapter is used to describe a period. I do not see that there is any necessity for construing the words, "the evening and the morning," as meaning necessarily a twenty-four hour day, "in the day when the Lord made the heaven and the earth."

Q — Then, when the Bible said, for instance, "and God called the firmament heaven. And the evening and the morning were the second day," that does not necessarily mean twenty-four hours?

A — I do not think it necessarily does.

Q — Do you think it does or does not?

A — I know a great many think so.

Q — What do you think?

A — I do not think it does.

Q — You think those were not literal days? . . .

A — No. But I think it would be just as easy for the kind of God we believe in to make the earth in six days as in six years or in 6,000,000 years or in 600,000,000 years. I do not think it important whether we believe one or the other.

Q — Do you think those were literal days?

A — My impression is they were periods, but I would not attempt to argue as against anybody who wanted to believe in literal days.

Q — Have you any idea of the length of the periods?

A — No; I don't.

Q — Do you think the sun was made on the fourth day?

A — Yes.

Q — And they had evening and morning without the sun?

A — I am simply saying it is a period.

Mr. Darrow: They had evening and morning for four periods without the sun, do you think?

Mr. Bryan: I believe in creation as there told, and if I am not able to explain it I will accept it.

Q — Then you can explain it to suit yourself. Mr. Bryan, what I want to know is, do you believe the sun was made on the fourth day?

A — I believe just as it says there.

Q — Do you believe the sun was made on the fourth day?

A — Read it.

Q — I am very sorry; you have read it so many times you would know, but I will read it again: (*Reading.*)

"And God said, let there be lights in the firmament of the heaven, to divide the day from the night; and let them be for signs, and for seasons, and for days, and years. And let them be for lights in the firmament of the heaven, to give light upon the earth; and it was so. And God made two great lights; the greater light to rule the day, and the lesser light to rule the night; He made the stars also. And God set them in the firmament of the heaven, to give light upon the earth, and to rule over the day and over the night, and to divide the light from the darkness; and God saw that it was good. And the evening and the morning were the fourth day."

Do you believe, whether it was a literal day or a period, the sun and the moon were not made until the fourth day?

A — I believe they were made in the order in which they were given there. . . .

Q — And they had the evening and the morning before that time for three days or three periods. All right, that settles it. Now, if you call those periods, they may have been a very long time.

A — They might have been.

Q — The creation might have been going on for a very long time?

A — It might have continued for millions of years.

Q — Yes. All right. Do you believe the story of the temptation of Eve by the serpent?

A — I do.

Q — Do you believe that after Eve ate the apple, or gave it to Adam, which-ever way it was, that God cursed Eve, and at that time decreed that all woman-kind thenceforth and forever should suffer the pains of childbirth in the reproduction of the earth?

A — I believe what it says, and I believe the fact as fully——

Q — That is what it says, doesn't it?

A — Yes.

Q — And for that reason, every woman born of woman, who has to carry on the race, has childbirth pains because Eve tempted Adam in the Garden of Eden?

A — I will believe just what the Bible says. I ask to put that in the lan-guage of the Bible, for I prefer that to your language. Read the Bible and I will answer.

Mr. Darrow: All right, I will do that: (*Reading.*) "And I will put enmity between thee and the woman" — that is referring to the serpent?

Mr. Bryan: The serpent.

Q — (*Reading*): "and between thy seed and her seed; it shall bruise thy head, and thou shalt bruise his heel. Unto the woman he said, I will greatly multiply thy sorrow and thy conception; in sorrow thou shalt bring forth children; and thy desire shall be to thy husband, and he shall rule over thee."

That is right, is it?

A — I accept it as it is.

Q — And you believe that came about because Eve tempted Adam to eat the fruit?

A — Just as it says.

Q — And you believe that is the reason that God made the serpent to go on his belly after he tempted Eve?

A — I believe the Bible as it is, and I do not permit you to put your language in the place of the language of the Almighty. You read that Bible and ask me questions, and I will answer them. I will not answer your questions in your language.

Q — I will read it to you from the Bible: (*Reading.*)

"And the Lord God said unto the serpent, because thou hast done this, thou art cursed above all cattle, and above every beast of the field; upon thy belly shalt thou go and dust shalt thou eat all the days of thy life."

Do you think that is why the serpent is compelled to crawl upon his belly?

A — I believe that.

Q — Have you any idea how the snake went before that time?

A — No, sir.

Q — Do you know whether he walked on his tail or not?

A — No, sir. I have no way to know. (*Laughter in audience.*)

Q — Now, you refer to the cloud that was put in the heaven after the flood as the rainbow. Do you believe in that?

A — Read it.

Q — All right, Mr. Bryan, I will read it for you.

Mr. Bryan: Your honor, I think I can shorten this testimony. The only purpose Mr. Darrow has is to slur at the Bible, but I will answer his question. I will answer it all at once, and I have no objection in the world, I want the world to know that this man, who does not believe in a God, is trying to use a court in Tennessee —

Mr. Darrow: I object to that.

Mr. Bryan (continuing): — to slur at it, and while it will require time, I am willing to take it.

Mr. Darrow: I object to your statement. I am examining you on your fool ideas that no intelligent Christian on earth believes.

(*The court is adjourned.*)

[1925]

The Hollow Men

T. S. ELIOT

Thomas Stearns Eliot (1888–   ), descendant of Massachusetts Puritans, was born in St. Louis and educated at Harvard, the Sorbonne, and Merton College, Oxford. He has lived in Europe since 1914 and became a British citizen in 1927. Pursuing his career as a writer at the same time that he was a teacher, a banker, and an editor, he became perhaps the most influential figure in English and American poetry during the first half of this century. His best known volumes are *Prufrock and Other Observations* (1917), *The Wasteland* (1922), *Ash-Wednesday* (1930), and *Four Quartets* (1944). He has also written important criticism and a number of successful verse plays. In 1948 he was awarded the Nobel Prize for Literature.

"The Hollow Men" voices the despair of a post-war generation for whom everything has become "meaningless as wind in dry grass." Its author later wrote about religious poetry that what we learn from it "is what it *feels* like to believe." Similarly, in "The Hollow Men" we learn what it feels like not to believe. Eliot is not trying to convince us of anything; his aim is rather to communicate a mood. Quite typically, he does this through the use of symbols appropriate to that mood. It is also typical that he juxtaposes the accents of a nursery rhyme with those of the Lord's Prayer. This and other circumstances, including a number of implicit references to Dante's *Inferno*, perhaps point toward that acceptance of the Christian faith which was to be a central theme of Eliot's later work. The first epigraph is a line from Joseph Conrad's *Heart of Darkness* announcing the death of Mr. Kurtz, whose vision of life had been summed up in his final whisper, "the horror!" "A penny for the Old Guy" is a saying by which English children get money for fireworks on Guy Fawkes Day, November 5. Both illuminate Eliot's meaning with regard to "the hollow men."

> "... This is the way the world ends
> Not with a bang but a whimper...."

Mistah Kurtz — he dead.
A penny for the Old Guy

I

We are the hollow men
We are the stuffed men
Leaning together
Headpiece filled with straw. Alas!
Our dried voices, when   5
We whisper together
Are quiet and meaningless

As wind in dry grass
Or rats' feet over broken glass
In our dry cellar   10

Shape without form, shade without color,
Paralyzed force, gesture without motion;

Those who have crossed
With direct eyes, to death's other Kingdom
Remember us — if at all — not as lost   15
Violent souls, but only
As the hollow men
The stuffed men.

II

Eyes I dare not meet in dreams
In death's dream kingdom   20
These do not appear:
There, the eyes are
Sunlight on a broken column
There, is a tree swinging
And voices are   25
In the wind's singing
More distant and more solemn
Than a fading star.

Let me be no nearer
In death's dream kingdom   30
Let me also wear
Such deliberate disguises
Rat's coat, crowskin, crossed staves
In a field
Behaving as the wind behaves   35
No nearer —

Not that final meeting
In the twilight kingdom

III

This is the dead land
This is cactus land   40
Here the stony images
Are raised, here they receive
The supplication of a dead man's hand
Under the twinkle of a fading star.

Is it like this   45
In death's other kingdom

Waking alone
At the hour when we are
Trembling with tenderness
Lips that would kiss   50
Form prayers to broken stone.

IV

The eyes are not here
There are no eyes here
In this valley of dying stars
In this hollow valley   55
This broken jaw of our lost kingdoms

In this last of meeting places
We grope together
And avoid speech
Gathered on this beach of the tumid river   60

Sightless, unless
The eyes reappear
As the perpetual star
Multifoliate rose
Of death's twilight kingdom   65
The hope only
Of empty men

V

Here we go round the prickly pear
Prickly pear prickly pear
Here we go round the prickly pear   70
At five o'clock in the morning.

Between the idea
And the reality
Between the motion
And the act   75
Falls the Shadow
                    For Thine is the Kingdom

Between the conception
And the creation
Between the emotion   80
And the response
Falls the Shadow
                    Life is very long

Between the desire
And the spasm   85

Between the potency
And the existence
Between the essence
And the descent
Falls the Shadow   90
              For Thine is the Kingdom

For Thine is
Life is
For Thine is the

This is the way the world ends   95
This is the way the world ends
This is the way the world ends
Not with a bang but a whimper.

                                                    [1925]

#5   LAWRENCE FERLINGHETTI

In September of 1957, Lawrence Ferlinghetti was arrested for having published and sold a poem called "Howl" by Allen Ginsberg. By the time he was found not guilty of "publishing and selling obscene writings" he and his City Lights bookshop and the San Francisco "beats" in general had become a lively topic of national interest. Ferlinghetti has written several books, but the best known is *A Coney Island of the Mind* (1958), from which "5" is taken.

Speaking for the Beats generally, Ferlinghetti has said that he desires "to get poetry out of the inner esthetic sanctum and out of the classroom into the street." The poem "5," for example, was first delivered before a San Francisco television camera. The word "delivered" is important, for poetry that is primarily intended to be listened to rather than read will tend toward a clarity and simplicity of statement not found in poetry of the "intellectual" tradition, where the emphasis is on complexity of statement and a studied ambiguity. Critics are divided in their judgment of Beat poetry; some find it fresh and stimulating while to others it seems sophomoric and shallow.

"*. . . They stretch him on the Tree to cool. . . .*"

        Sometime during eternity
                                    some guys show up
and one of them

                    who shows up real late
                                        is a kind of carpenter
          from some square-type place
                                like Galilee
            and he starts wailing
                                and claiming he is hep
                to who made heaven
                                and earth
                                            and that the cat
                who really laid it on us
                                    is his Dad

      And moreover
          he adds
                    It's all writ down
                                        on some scroll-type parchments
            which some henchmen
                                leave lying around the Dead Sea somewheres
              a long time ago
                                and which you won't even find
      for a coupla thousand years or so
                                    or at least for
          nineteen hundred and fortyseven
                                        of them
                  to be exact
                            and even then
          nobody really believes them
                                    or me
                                        for that matter

      You're hot
                    they tell him

      And they cool him

      They stretch him on the Tree to cool

      And everybody after that
                                    is always making models
                    of this Tree
                                with Him hung up
        and always crooning His name
                                    and calling Him to come down
                  and sit in
                            on their combo
                as if he is *the* king cat
                                    who's got to blow
              or they can't quite make it

Only he don't come down
                              from His Tree
   Him just hang there
                     on His Tree
                                 looking real Petered out
              and real cool
                           and also
              according to a roundup
                             of late world news
         from the usual unreliable sources
                                      real dead

                                                                    [1958]

The Theology of Jonathan Edwards   PHYLLIS MC GINLEY

Phyllis McGinley (1905–   ) was born in Ontario, Oregon, and attended
schools in Colorado, Utah, and California. Besides being a literary critic,
she has written a number of volumes of highly regarded light verse.
For her writing she has received a number of awards: in 1955, the
Christopher Medal, the Catholic Writers Guild Award, and the Poetry
Society Award; in 1956, the St. Catherine of Sienna Medal.

   Miss McGinley is critical of Jonathan Edwards's theology and of the
psychological basis of the Great Awakening. She is not, however, merely
poking fun. The poem suggests, furthermore, that her critical attitude
does not extend to all religious belief. The essentially serious nature of
what she has to say becomes clear if it is given prose statement. It seems
"funny" and "light" because of its rhythm and, more particularly perhaps,
its feminine rhymes.

                     ". . . God the Holy Terror. . . ."

              Whenever Mr. Edwards spake
                 In church about Damnation,
              The very benches used to quake
                 For awful agitation.

              Good men would pale and roll their eyes   5
                 While sinners rent their garments
              To hear him so anatomize
                 Hell's orgiastic torments

The blood, the flames, the agonies
   In store for frail or flighty   10
New Englanders who did not please
   A whimsical Almighty.

Times were considered out of tune
   When half a dozen nervous
Female parishioners did not swoon   15
   At every Sunday service;

And, if they had been taught aright,
   Small children, carried bedwards,
Would shudder lest they meet that night
   The God of Mr. Edwards,   20

Abraham's God, the Wrathful One,
   Intolerant of error —
Not God the Father or the Son
   But God the Holy Terror.

                                               [1957]

Some Modern Credos

Credo   EDWIN ARLINGTON ROBINSON

Edwin Arlington Robinson (1869–1935) grew up in Gardiner, Maine, and entered Harvard in 1891. Little about formal education interested him, however, and he withdrew after two years. His first book of poems — from which "Credo" is taken — was *The Torrent and the Night Before* (1896), but it was not until twenty years later that *The Man Against the Sky* (1916) established his high position as a poet. He later received three Pulitzer prizes for his work and is today regarded by many as the outstanding American poet of his time.

In both theme and form, "Credo" is typical of Robinson's work. Expressing the "modern" attitude toward life, it is traditional in its Petrarchan sonnet form. Its point of view is ambivalent: the opening statement of despair is apparently contradicted by the last line. Robinson objected to reviewers who called his work unrelievedly somber: "The world is not a 'prison-house,'" he said, "but a kind of spiritual kindergarten where bewildered infants are trying to spell God with the wrong blocks."

". . . I feel the coming glory of the light. . . ."

I cannot find my way: there is no star
In all the shrouded heavens anywhere;
And there is not a whisper in the air
Of any living voice but one so far
That I can hear it only as a bar
Of lost, imperial music, played when fair
And angel fingers wove, and unaware,
Dead leaves to garlands where no roses are.
No, there is not a glimmer, nor a call,
For one that welcomes, welcomes when he fears,
The black and awful chaos of the night;
For through it all — above, beyond it all —
I know the far-sent message of the years,
I feel the coming glory of the Light.

[1896]

Is Life Worth Living?   WILLIAM JAMES

William James (1842–1910) was born in New York City, the son of a
well-known Swedenborgian lecturer and writer, Henry James, Sr. He
and his younger brother, Henry junior, were educated irregularly in
America and Europe. Eventually William entered Harvard and in 1869
took a medical degree. He began teaching at Harvard in 1872 and remained for thirty-five years, teaching first physiology, then psychology,
and finally philosophy. Among his more significant works are *The Principles of Psychology* (1890), *The Will to Believe* (1897), from which
the present selection is taken, *The Varieties of Religious Experience*
(1901–02), and *Pragmatism* (1907).

James is known as a pragmatist — one, that is, who turns away from
abstractions, fixed principles, and absolutes towards "concreteness and
adequacy, towards facts, towards action and towards power." His later
works develop this position and specifically apply it to the problem of
religion, but in "Is Life Worth Living?" there are already evidences of
"pragmatic" attitudes. James is noted for the excellence of his prose style,
and certainly its qualities of ease, grace, and logical clarity are well
exemplified in this essay. In developing his ideas James here uses definition, examples, analysis, contrast, and, most effectively perhaps, analogy.

". . . Be not afraid of life. . . ."

Religion has meant many things in human history; but when from now
onward I use the word I mean to use it in the supernaturalist sense, as de-
claring that the so-called order of nature, which constitutes this world's experience, is only one portion of the total universe, and that there stretches beyond
this visible world an unseen world of which we now know nothing positive,
but in its relation to which the true significance of our present mundane life
consists. A man's religious faith (whatever more special items of doctrine it
may involve) means for me essentially his faith in the existence of an unseen
order of some kind in which the riddles of the natural order may be found
explained. In the more developed religions the natural world has always
been regarded as the mere scaffolding or vestibule of a truer, more eternal
world, and affirmed to be a sphere of education, trial, or redemption. In these
religions, one must in some fashion die to the natural life before one can
enter into life eternal. The notion that this physical world of wind and water,
where the sun rises and the moon sets, is absolutely and ultimately the
divinely aimed-at and established thing, is one which we find only in very
early religions, such as that of the most primitive Jews. It is this natural
religion (primitive still, in spite of the fact that poets and men of science
whose good-will exceeds their perspicacity keep publishing it in new editions
tuned to our contemporary ears) that . . . has suffered definitive bankruptcy
in the opinion of a circle of persons, among whom I must count myself, and
who are growing more numerous every day. For such persons the physical
order of nature, taken simply as science knows it, cannot be held to reveal

any one harmonious spiritual intent. It is mere *weather,* as Chauncey Wright called it, doing and undoing without end.

Now, I wish to make you feel . . . that we have a right to believe the physical order to be only a partial order; that we have a right to supplement it by an unseen spiritual order which we assume on trust, if only thereby life may seem to us better worth living again. But as such a trust will seem to some of you sadly mystical and execrably unscientific, I must first say a word or two to weaken the veto which you may consider that science opposes to our act.

There is included in human nature an ingrained naturalism and materialism of mind which can only admit facts that are actually tangible. Of this sort of mind the entity called "science" is the idol. Fondness for the word "scientist" is one of the notes by which you may know its votaries; and its short way of killing any opinion that it disbelieves in is to call it "unscientific." It must be granted that there is no slight excuse for this. Science has made such glorious leaps in the last three hundred years, and extended our knowledge of nature so enormously both in general and in detail; men of science, moreover, have as a class displayed such admirable virtues, — that it is no wonder if the worshippers of science lose their heads. . . . I have heard more than one teacher say that all the fundamental conceptions of truth have already been found by science, and that the future has only the details of the picture to fill in. But the slightest reflection on the real conditions will suffice to show how barbaric such notions are. They show such a lack of scientific imagination, that it is hard to see how one who is actively advancing any part of science can make a mistake so crude. Think how many absolutely new scientific conceptions have arisen in our own generation, how many new problems have been formulated that were never thought of before, and then cast an eye upon the brevity of science's career. It began with Galileo, not three hundred years ago. Four thinkers since Galileo, each informing his successor of what discoveries his own lifetime had seen achieved, might have passed the torch of science into our hands as we sit here in this room. Indeed, for the matter of that, an audience much smaller than the present one, an audience of some five or six score people, if each person in it could speak for his own generation, would carry us away to the black unknown of the human species, to days without a document or monument to tell their tale. Is it credible that such a mushroom knowledge, such a growth overnight as this, *can* represent more than the minutest glimpse of what the universe will really prove to be when adequately understood? No! our science is a drop, our ignorance a sea. Whatever else be certain, this at least is certain, — that the world of our present natural knowledge *is* enveloped in a larger world of *some* sort of whose residual properties we at present can frame no positive idea.

Agnostic positivism, of course, admits this principle theoretically in the most cordial terms, but insists that we must not turn it to any practical use. We have no right, this doctrine tells us, to dream dreams, or suppose anything about the unseen part of the universe, merely because to do so may be for what we are pleased to call our highest interests. We must always wait for sensible evidence for our beliefs; and where such evidence is inaccessible we must frame no hypotheses whatever. Of course this is a safe enough position *in abstracto*. If a thinker had no stake in the unknown, no vital needs, to live or languish according to what the unseen world contained, a philosophic neutrality and refusal to believe either one way or the other would be his wisest cue. But, unfortunately, neutrality is not only inwardly difficult, it is also outwardly unrealizable, where our relations to an alternative are practical and vital. This is because, as the psychologists tell us, belief and doubt are living attitudes, and involve conduct on our part. Our only way, for example, of doubting or refusing to believe, that a certain thing *is*, is continuing to act as if it were *not*. If, for instance, I refuse to believe that the room is getting cold, I leave the windows open and light no fire just as if it still were warm. If I doubt that you are worthy of my confidence, I keep you uninformed of all my secrets just as if you were *un*worthy of the same. If I doubt the need of insuring my house, I leave it uninsured as much as if I believed there were no need. And so if I must not believe that the world is divine, I can only express that refusal by declining ever to act distinctively as if it were so, which can only mean acting on certain critical occasions as if it were *not* so, or in an irreligious way. There are, you see, inevitable occasions in life when inaction is a kind of action, and must count as action, and when not to be for is to be practically against; and in all such cases strict and consistent neutrality is an unattainable thing.

And, after all, is not this duty of neutrality, where only our inner interests would lead us to believe, the most ridiculous of commands? Is it not sheer dogmatic folly to say that our inner interests can have no real connection with the forces that the hidden world may contain? In other cases divinations based on inner interests have proved prophetic enough. Take science itself! Without an imperious inner demand on our part for ideal logical and mathematical harmonies, we should never have attained to proving that such harmonies lie hidden between all the chinks and interstices of the crude natural world. Hardly a law has been established in science, hardly a fact ascertained, which was not first sought after, often with sweat and blood, to gratify an inner need. Whence such needs come from we do not know: we find them in us, and biological psychology so far only classes them with Darwin's "accidental variations." But the inner need of believing that this world of nature is a sign of something more spiritual and eternal than itself is just as strong and authoritative in those who feel it, as the inner need of uniform laws of causation ever can be in a professionally scientific head. The toil of many generations has proved the latter need prophetic. Why *may* not the former one be prophetic, too? And if needs of ours outrun the visible universe, why *may* not that be a sign that an invisible universe is there? What, in short, has authority to debar us from trusting our religious demands? Science as such assuredly has no authority, for she can only say what is, not what is not; and the agnostic "thou shalt not believe without coercive sensible evidence" is simply an expression (free to any one to make) of private personal appetite for evidence of a certain peculiar kind.

Now, when I speak of trusting our religious demands, just what do I mean by "trusting"? Is the word to carry with it license to define in detail an invisible world, and to anathematize and excommunicate those whose trust is different? Certainly not! Our faculties of belief were not primarily given us to make orthodoxies and heresies withal; they were given us to live by. And to trust our religious demands means first of all to live in the light of them, and to act as if the invisible world which they suggest were real. It is a fact of human nature, that men can live and die by the help of a sort of faith that goes without a single dogma of definition. The bare assurance that this natural order is not ultimate but a mere sign or vision, the eternal staging of a many-storied universe, in which spiritual forces have the last word and are eternal, — this bare assurance is to such men enough to make life seem worth living in spite of every contrary presumption suggested by its circumstances on the natural plane. Destroy this inner assurance, however, vague as it is, and all the light and radiance of existence is extinguished for these persons at a stroke. Often enough the wild-eyed look at life — the suicidal mood — will then set in.

And now the application comes directly home to you and me. Probably to almost everyone of us here the most adverse life would seem well worth living, if we only could be *certain* that our bravery and patience with it were terminating and eventuating and bearing fruit somewhere in an unseen spiritual world. By granting we are not certain, does it then follow that a bare trust in such a world is a fool's paradise and lubberland, or rather that it is a living attitude in which we are free to indulge? Well, we are free to trust at our own risks anything that is not impossible, and that can bring analogies to bear in its behalf. That the world of physics is probably not absolute, all the converging multitude of arguments that make in favor of idealism tend to prove; and that our whole physical life may lie soaking in a spiritual atmosphere, a dimension of being that we at present have no organ for apprehending, is vividly suggested to us by the analogy of our domestic animals. Our dogs, for example, are in our human life but not of it. They witness hourly the outward body of events whose inner meaning cannot, by any possible operation, be revealed to their intelligence, — events in which they themselves often play the cardinal part. My terrier bites a teasing boy, and the father demands damages. The dog may be present at every step of the negotiations, and see the money paid, without an inkling of what it all means, without a suspicion that it has anything to do with *him;* and he never *can* know in his natural dog's life. Or take another case which used greatly to impress me in my medical-student days. Consider a poor dog whom they are vivisecting in a laboratory. He lies strapped on a board and shrieking at his executioners, and to his own dark consciousness is literally in a sort of hell. He cannot see a single redeeming ray in the whole business; and yet all these diabolical-seeming events are often controlled by human intentions with which, if his poor benighted mind could only be made to catch a glimpse of them, all that is heroic in him would religiously acquiesce. Healing truth, relief to future sufferings of beast and man, are to be bought by them. It may be genuinely a process of redemption. Lying on his back on the board there he may be performing a function incalculably higher than any that prosperous canine life admits of; and yet, of the whole performance, this function is the one portion that must remain absolutely beyond his ken.

Now turn from this to the life of man. In the dog's life we see the world invisible to him because we live in both worlds. In human life, although we only see our world, and his within it, yet encompassing both these worlds a still wider world may be there, as unseen by us as our world is by him; and to believe in that world *may* be the most essential function that our lives in this world have to perform. But "*may* be! *may* be!" one now hears the positivist contemptuously exclaim; "what use can a scientific life have for maybes?" Well, I reply, the "scientific" life itself has much to do with maybes, and human life at large has everything to do with them. So far as man stands for anything, and is productive or originative at all, his entire vital function may be said to have to deal with maybes. Not a victory is gained, not a deed of faithfulness or courage is done, except upon a maybe; not a service, not a sally of generosity, nor a scientific exploration or experiment or text-book, that may not be a mistake. It is only by risking our persons from one hour to another that we live at all. And often enough our faith beforehand in an uncertified result *is the only thing that makes the result come true.* Suppose, for instance, that you are climbing a mountain, and have worked yourself into a position from which the only escape is by a terrible leap. Have faith that you can successfully make it, and your feet are nerved to its accomplishment. But mistrust yourself, and think of all the sweet things you have heard the scientists say of *maybes*, and you will hesitate so long that, at last, all unstrung and trembling, and launching yourself in a moment of despair, you roll in the abyss. In such a case (and it belongs to an enormous class), the part of wisdom as well as of courage is to *believe what is in the line of your needs,* for only by such belief is the need fulfilled. Refuse to believe, and you shall indeed be right, for you shall irretrievably perish. But believe, and again you shall be right, for you shall save yourself. You make one or the other of two possible universes true by your trust or mistrust, — both universes having been only *maybes,* in this particular, before you contributed your act.

Now, it appears to me that the question whether life is worth living is subject to conditions logically much like these. It does, indeed, depend on you *the liver.* If you surrender to the nightmare view and crown the evil edifice by your own suicide, you have indeed made a picture totally black. Pessimism, completed by your act, is true beyond a doubt, so far as your world goes. Your mistrust of life has removed whatever worth your own enduring existence might have given to it; and now, throughout the whole sphere of possible influence of that existence, the mistrust has proved itself to have had divining power. But suppose, on the other hand, that instead of giving way to the nightmare view you cling to it that this world is not the *ultimatum.* Suppose you find yourself a very wellspring, as Wordsworth says, of —

> Zeal, and the virtue to exist by faith
> As soldiers live by courage; as, by strength
> Of heart, the sailor fights with roaring seas.

Suppose, however thickly evils crowd upon you, that your unconquerable subjectivity proves to be their match, and that you find a more wonderful joy than any passive pleasure can bring in trusting ever in the larger whole. Have you not now made life worth living on these terms? What sort of a thing would life really be, with your qualities ready for a tussle with it, if it only brought fair weather and gave these higher faculties of yours no scope? Please remember that optimism and pessimism are definitions of the world, and that our own reactions on the world, small as they are in bulk, are integral parts of the whole thing, and necessarily help to determine the definition. They may even be the decisive elements in determining the definition. A large mass can have its unstable equilibrium overturned by the addition of a feather's weight; a long phrase may have its sense reversed by the addition of the three letters *n-o-t*. This life *is* worth living, we can say, *since it is what we make it, from the moral point of view*; and we are determined to make it from that point of view, so far as we have anything to do with it, a success.

Now, in this description of faiths that verify themselves I have assumed that our faith in an invisible order is what inspires those efforts and that patience which make this visible order good for moral men. Our faith in the seen world's goodness (goodness now meaning fitness for successful moral and religious life) has verified itself by leaning on our faith in the unseen world. But will our faith in the unseen world similarly verify itself? Who knows?

Once more it is a case of *maybe*; and once more *maybes* are the essence of the situation. I confess that I do not see why the very existence of an invisible world may not in part depend on the personal response which any one of us may make to the religious appeal. God himself, in short, may draw vital strength and increase of very being from our fidelity. For my own part, I do not know what the sweat and blood and tragedy of this life mean, if they mean anything short of this. If this life be not a real fight, in which something is eternally gained for the universe by success, it is no better than a game of private theatricals from which one may withdraw at will. But it *feels* like a real fight, — as if there were something really wild in the universe which we, with all our idealities and faithfulnesses, are needed to redeem; and first of all to redeem our own hearts from atheisms and fears. For such a half-wild, half-saved universe our nature is adapted. The deepest thing in our nature is this *Binnenleben* (as a German doctor lately has called it), this dumb region of the heart in which we dwell alone with our willingnesses and unwillingnesses, our faiths and fears. As through the cracks and crannies of caverns those waters exude from the earth's bosom which then form the fountain-heads of springs, so in these crepuscular depths of personality the sources of all our outer deeds and decisions take their rise. Here is our deepest organ of communication with the nature of things; and compared with all these concrete movements of our soul all abstract statements and scientific arguments — the veto, for example, which the strict positivist pronounces upon our faith — sound to us like mere chatterings of the teeth. For here possibilities, not finished facts, are the realities with which we have acutely to deal; and to quote my friend William Salter, of the Philadelphia Ethical Society, "as the essence of courage is to stake one's life on a possibility, so the essence of faith is to believe that the possibility exists."

These, then, are my last words to you: Be *not* afraid of life. Believe that life *is* worth living, and your belief will help create the fact. The "scientific proof" that you are right may not be clear before the day of judgment (or some stage of being which that expression may serve to symbolize) is reached. But the faithful fighters of this hour, or the beings that then and there will represent them, may turn to the faint-hearted, who here decline to go on, with words like those with which Henry IV greeted the tardy Crillon after a great victory had been gained: "Hang yourself, brave Crillon! we fought at Arques, and you were not there."

[1897]

New Thoughts Can Remake You   NORMAN VINCENT PEALE

After study at Ohio Wesleyan University and Boston University, Norman Vincent Peale (1898–   ) was ordained a minister in the Methodist Episcopal Church. He now preaches to overflow crowds at the Marble Collegiate Church in New York City and is widely known as a writer on religious topics for newspapers and popular magazines. He has also written several best-selling books in the vein of *The Power of Positive Thinking* (1952), from which the following selection is taken.

In the first paragraph Peale takes as his text a sentence from William James (see the previous selection). It is interesting, therefore, to compare these two pieces in style, tone, and quality of ideas. (Let it be noted that elsewhere James refers to success as a "bitch-goddess.") While the connections are less direct, it is profitable to make similar comparisons between Peale and such other writers in this section as Paine, Cartwright, and Edwards. Differences in "tone" are particularly worth noting.

"*. . . visualize, prayerize, and finally actualize. . . .*"

One of the most important and powerful facts about you is expressed in the following statement by William James, who was one of the very few wisest men America has produced. William James said, "The greatest discovery of my generation *is that human beings can alter their lives by altering their attitudes of mind.*" As you think, so shall you be. So flush out all old, tired, worn-out thoughts. Fill your mind with fresh, new creative thoughts of faith, love, and goodness. By this process you can actually remake your life. . . .

That is the simple fact which is at the basis of an astonishing law of prosperity and success. In three words: Believe and succeed.

I learned this law in a very interesting manner. Some years ago a group of us consisting of Lowell Thomas, Captain Eddie Rickenbacker, Branch Rickey, Raymond Thornburg, and others established an inspirational self-help magazine called *Guideposts*. This magazine has a double function: first, by relating stories of people who through their faith have overcome difficulties, it teaches techniques of victorious living, victory over fear, over circumstances, over obstacles, over resentment. It teaches faith over all manner of negativism.

Second, as a non-profit, non-sectarian, inter-faith publication it teaches the great fact that God is in the stream of history and that this nation was founded on belief in God and His laws.

The magazine reminds its readers that America is the first great nation in history to be established on a definitely religious premise and that unless we keep it so our freedoms will deteriorate.

Mr. Raymond Thornburg as publisher and I as editor in starting the magazine had no financial backing to underwrite it. It was begun on faith. In fact, its first offices were in rooms above a grocery store in the little village of Pawling, New York. There was a borrowed typewriter, a few rickety chairs, and that was all; all except a great idea and great faith. Slowly a subscription list of 25,000 developed. The future seemed promising. Suddenly one night fire broke out, and within an hour the publishing house was destroyed and with it the total list of subscribers. Foolishly no duplicate list had been made.

Lowell Thomas, loyal and efficient patron of *Guideposts* from the very start, mentioned this sad circumstance on his radio broadcast and as a result we soon had 30,000 subscribers, practically all the old ones and many new ones.

The subscription list rose to approximately 40,000, but costs increased even more rapidly. The magazine, which has always been sold for less than cost in order widely to disseminate the message, was more expensive than anticipated and we were faced with difficult financial problems. In fact, at one time it seemed almost impossible to keep it going.

At this juncture we called a meeting, and I'm sure you never attended a more pessimistic, negative, discouraging meeting. It dripped with pessimism. Where were we going to get the money to pay our bills? We figured out ways of robbing Peter to pay Paul. Complete discouragement filled our minds.

A woman had been invited to this meeting whom we all regarded most highly. But one reason she was included in this meeting was because, on a previous occasion, she had contributed $2,000 to help inaugurate *Guideposts* magazine. It was hoped that lightning might strike twice in the same place. But this time she gave us something of more value than money.

As this dismal meeting progressed she remained silent for a long time, but finally said, "I suppose you gentlemen would like me to make another financial contribution. I might as well put you out of your misery. I am not going to give you another cent."

This did not put us out of our misery. On the contrary, it put us deeper into our misery. "But," she continued, "I will give you something far more valuable than money."

This astonished us, for we could not possibly imagine anything of more value than money in the circumstances.

"I am going to give you an idea," she continued, "a creative idea."

"Well," we thought to ourselves unenthusiastically, "how can we pay our bills with an idea?"

Ah, but an idea is just what will help you pay bills. Every achievement in this world was first projected as a creative idea. First the idea, then faith in it, then the means of implementing the idea. That is the way success proceeds.

"Now," she said, "here is the idea. What is your present trouble? It is that you *lack* everything. You *lack* money. You *lack* subscribers. You *lack* equipment. You *lack* ideas. You *lack* courage. Why do you *lack* all these requirements? Simply because you are thinking *lack.* If you think *lack* you create the conditions that produce a state of *lack.* By this constant mental emphasis upon what you *lack* you have frustrated the creative forces that can give impetus to the development of *Guideposts.* You have been working hard from the standpoint of doing many things, but you have failed to do the one all-important thing that will lend power to all your other efforts: you have not employed positive thinking. Instead, you have thought in terms of *lack.*

"To correct that situation — reverse the mental process and begin to think prosperity, achievement, success. This will require practice but it can be done quickly if you will demonstrate faith. The process is to visualize; that is, to see *Guideposts* in terms of successful achievement. Create a mental picture of *Guideposts* as a great magazine, sweeping the country. Visualize large numbers of subscribers, all eagerly reading this inspirational material and profiting thereby. Create a mental image of lives being changed by the philosophy of achievement which *Guideposts* teaches monthly in its issues.

"Do not hold mental pictures of difficulties and failures, but lift your mind above them and visualize powers and achievements. When you elevate your thoughts into the area of visualized attainment you look down on your problems rather than from below up at them and thus you get a much more encouraging view of them. Always come up over your problems. Never approach a problem from below.

"Now let me continue further," she said. "How many subscribers do you need at the moment to keep going?"

We thought quickly and said "100,000." We had 40,000.

"All right," she said confidently, "that is not hard. That is easy. Visualize 100,000 people being creatively helped by this magazine and you will have them. In fact the minute you can see them in your mind, you already have them."

She turned to me and said, "Norman, can you see 100,000 subscribers at this minute? Look out there, look ahead of you. In your mind's eye can you see them?"

I wasn't convinced as yet, and I said rather doubtfully, "Well, maybe so, but they seem pretty dim to me."

She was a little disappointed in me, I thought, as she asked, "Can't you imaginatively visualize 100,000 subscribers?"

I guess my imagination wasn't working very well because all I could see was the insufficient but actual 40,000.

Then she turned to my old friend Raymond Thornburg who has been blessed with a gloriously victorious personality, and she said, calling him by his nickname, "Pinky, can you visualize 100,000 subscribers?"

I rather doubted that Pinky would see them. He is a rubber manufacturer who gives his time freely from his own business to help advance this inspirational, non-profit magazine, and you would not ordinarily think that a rubber manufacturer would respond to this type of thinking. But he has the faculty of creative imagination. I noticed by the fascinated look on his face that she had him. He was gazing straight ahead with rather a look of wonder when she asked, "Do you see the 100,000 subscribers?"

"Yes," he cried with eagerness, "yes, I do see them."

Electrified, I demanded, "Where? Point them out to me."

Then I, too, began to visualize them.

"Now," continued our friend, "let us bow our heads and together thank God for giving us 100,000 subscribers."

Frankly I thought that was pushing the Lord rather hard, but it was justified by a verse in the Scriptures where it says, "And all things, whatsoever ye shall ask in prayer, believing, ye shall receive them." (Matthew 21:22) That means when you pray for something, at the same time visualize what you pray for. Believe that if it is God's will and is worth while, not selfishly sought after, but for human good, that it is at that moment given you.

If you have difficulty in following this reasoning, let me tell you that from that moment until the present writing Guideposts never lacked for anything. It has found wonderful friends and has had fine support. It has been able always to meet its bills, purchase needed equipment, finance itself, and as I write these words Guideposts is nearing the half million mark and more subscriptions are coming in regularly, sometimes as many as three or four thousand per day.

I recite this instance not for the purpose of advertising Guideposts, although I strongly recommend this magazine to all my readers, and if you would like to be a subscriber, write to Guideposts, Pawling, New York, for information. But I tell the story because I was awed by this experience, realizing that I had stumbled upon a law, a tremendous law of personal victory. I decided to apply it thereafter to my own problems and wherever I have done so can report a marvelous result. Wherever I have failed to do so, I have missed great results.

It is as simple as this — put your problem in God's hands. In your thoughts rise above the problem so that you look down upon it, not up at it. Test it according to God's will. That is, do not try to get success from something that is wrong. Be sure it is right morally, spiritually, and ethically. You can never get a right result from an error. If your thinking is wrong, it is wrong and not right and can never be right so long as it is wrong. If it is wrong in the essence it is bound to be wrong in the result.

Therefore be sure it is right, then hold it up in God's name and visualize a great result. Keep the idea of prosperity, of achievement, and of attainment firmly fixed in your mind. Never entertain a failure thought. Should a negative thought of defeat come into your mind, expel it by increasing the positive affirmation. Affirm aloud, "God is now giving me success. He is now giving me attainment." The mental vision which you create and firmly hold in consciousness will be actualized if you continually affirm it in your thoughts and if you work diligently and effectively. This creative process simply stated is: visualize, prayerize, and finally actualize. . . .

Following are seven practical steps for changing your mental attitudes from negative to positive, for releasing creative new thoughts, and for shifting from error patterns to truth patterns. Try them — keep on trying them. They will work.

1. For the next twenty-four hours, deliberately speak hopefully about everything, about your job, about your health, about your future. Go out of your way to talk optimistically about everything. This will be difficult, for possibly it is your habit to talk pessimistically. From this negative habit you must restrain yourself even if it requires an act of will.

2. After speaking hopefully for twenty-four hours, continue the practice for one week, then you can be permitted to be "realistic" for a day or two. You will discover that what you meant by "realistic" a week ago was actually pessimistic, but what you now mean by "realistic" is something entirely different; it is the dawning of the positive outlook. When most people say they are being "realistic" they delude themselves: they are simply being negative.

3. You must feed your mind even as you feed your body, and to make your mind healthy you must feed it nourishing, wholesome thoughts. Therefore, today start to shift your mind from negative to positive thinking. Start at the beginning of the New Testament and underscore every sentence about *Faith*. Continue doing this until you have marked every such passage in the four books, Matthew, Mark, Luke, and John. Particularly note Mark 11, verses 22, 23, 24. They will serve as samples of the verses you are to underscore and fix deeply in your consciousness.

4. Then commit the underscored passages to memory. Commit one each day until you can recite the entire list from memory. This will take time, but remember you have consumed much more time becoming a negative thinker than this will require. Effort and time will be needed to unlearn your negative pattern.

5. Make a list of your friends to determine who is the most positive thinker among them and deliberately cultivate his society. Do not abandon your negative friends, but get closer to those with a positive point of view for a while, until you have absorbed their spirit, then you can go back among your negative friends and give them your newly acquired thought pattern without taking on their negativism.

6. Avoid argument, but whenever a negative attitude is expressed, counter with a positive and optimistic opinion.

7. Pray a great deal and always let your prayer take the form of thanksgiving on the assumption that God is giving you great and wonderful things; for if you think He is, He surely is. God will not give you any greater blessing than you can believe in. He wants to give you great things, but even He cannot make you take anything greater than you are equipped by faith to receive. "According to your faith (that is, in proportion to) be it unto you." (Matthew 9:29)

The secret of a better and more successful life is to cast out those old dead, unhealthy thoughts. Substitute for them new vital, dynamic faith thoughts. You can depend upon it — an inflow of new thoughts will remake you and your life.

[1952]

i thank You God   **E. E. CUMMINGS**

E. E. Cummings (1894–   ), son of a Cambridge professor and minister, graduated from Harvard in 1915. He received an M.A. after another year of study, spent some time in New York, and then enlisted in the same ambulance corp in France as John Dos Passos (see p. 310) and Ernest Hemingway. In 1917 he was unjustly imprisoned for three months on a charge of treason, an experience which resulted in his best known book, *The Enormous Room* (1922), an autobiographical narrative.

Like Robinson's "Credo," Cummings's "i thank You God" is a religious sonnet. Unlike the Robinson poem, it employs some rather unconventional techniques — unusual verbal juxtapositions, disregard of normal grammar, startling images, odd punctuation. Interestingly enough, they are techniques which seem to lend themselves to what Cummings is saying.

". . . i who have died am alive again today . . ."

i thank You God for most this amazing
day:for the leaping greenly spirits of trees
and a blue true dream of sky;and for everything
which is natural which is infinite which is yes

(i who have died am alive again today,
and this is the sun's birthday,this is the birth
day of life and of love and wings:and of the gay
great happening illimitably earth)

how should tasting touching hearing seeing
breathing any — lifted from the no
of all nothing — human merely being
doubt unimaginable You?

(now the ears of my ears awake and
now the eyes of my eyes are opened)

[1948]

West-running Brook

ROBERT FROST

Robert Frost (1874–   ) has lived to see himself recognized, in the words of his fellow poet Randall Jarrell, as "that rare thing, a complete or representative poet." Such recognition did not come easily. Born in San Francisco, he grew up in New England (as had nine generations of his ancestors before him), graduated at the head of his high school class, and entered Dartmouth. College didn't satisfy him and he soon quit (later he tried Harvard, stayed two years, again dropped out). For a few years he tried farming, school teaching, and writing poetry. Finally, at the age of thirty-six, he abandoned the first two of these pursuits (for the time being) and moved with his family to England to devote full time to poetry. There he published *A Boy's Will* (1913) and *North of Boston* (1914), which received critical acclaim, and when Frost returned to America in 1915, he found recognition among his own countrymen. Since that time he has received numerous honors and awards, including four Pulitzer Prizes. Other poems by Frost are on pages 362 and 447.

"West-running Brook" begins as a playful dialogue and quickly becomes something more. We learn, for example, quite a bit about the two speakers and their relation to each other. We have also been given some effective examples of natural description — what Frost elsewhere refers to as truth breaking in "with all her matter of fact." And we learn what the poet thinks it is "in nature we are from." All this in the easy, conversational blank verse of which Frost is so peculiarly a master. "The Strong Are Saying Nothing" is different in form but similar in its search for truth in nature's face. Frost has called himself "a Synecdochist; for I am fond of synecdoche in poetry, that figure of speech in which we use the part for the whole." Both of these poems bear him out.

"... *from this in nature we are from....*"

"Fred, where is north?"

                              "North? North is there, my love.
The brook runs west."

                              "West-running Brook then call it."
(West-running Brook men call it to this day.)
"What does it think it's doing running west
When all the other country brooks flow east
To reach the ocean? It must be the brook
Can trust itself to go by contraries
The way I can with you — and you with me —
Because we're — we're — I don't know what we are.
What are we?"

"Young or new?"

                              "We must be something.   10
We've said we two. Let's change that to we three.
As you and I are married to each other,
We'll both be married to the brook. We'll build
Our bridge across it, and the bridge shall be
Our arm thrown over it asleep beside it.   15
Look, look, it's waving to us with a wave
To let us know it hears me."

                              "Why, my dear,
That wave's been standing off this jut of shore — "
(The black stream, catching on a sunken rock,
Flung backward on itself in one white wave,   20
And the white water rode the black forever,
Not gaining but not losing, like a bird
White feathers from the struggle of whose breast
Flecked the dark stream and flecked the darker pool
Below the point, and were at last driven wrinkled   25
In a white scarf against the far shore alders.)
"That wave's been standing off this jut of shore
Ever since rivers, I was going to say,
Were made in heaven. It wasn't waved to us."

"It wasn't, yet it was. If not to you   30
It was to me — in an annunciation."

"Oh, if you take it off to lady-land,
As't were the country of the Amazons
We men must see you to the confines of
And leave you there, ourselves forbid to enter, —   35
It is your brook! I have no more to say."

"Yes, you have, too. Go on. You thought of something."

"Speaking of contraries, see how the brook
In that white wave runs counter to itself.
It is from that in water we were from   40
Long, long before we were from any creature.
Here we, in our impatience of the steps,
Get back to the beginning of beginnings,
The stream of everything that runs away.
Some say existence like a Pirouot   45
And Pirouette, forever in one place,
Stands still and dances, but it runs away,
It seriously, sadly, runs away
To fill the abyss' void with emptiness.

It flows beside us in this water brook,   50
But it flows over us. It flows between us
To separate us for a panic moment.
It flows between us, over us, and *with* us.
And it is time, strength, tone, light, life and love —
And even substance lapsing unsubstantial;   55
The universal cataract of death
That spends to nothingness — and unresisted,
Save by some strange resistance in itself,
Not just a swerving, but a throwing back,
As if regret were in it and were sacred.   60
It has this throwing backward on itself
So that the fall of most of it is always
Raising a little, sending up a little.
Our life runs down in sending up the clock.
The brook runs down in sending up our life.   65
The sun runs down in sending up the brook.
And there is something sending up the sun.
It is this backward motion toward the source,
Against the stream, that most we see ourselves in,
The tribute of the current to the source.   70
It is from this in nature we are from.
It is most us."

                      "Today will be the day
You said so."

                      "No, today will be the day
You said the brook was called West-running Brook."

"Today will be the day of what we both said."   75

                                                     [1928]

The Strong Are Saying Nothing   ROBERT FROST

"... *There may be little or much beyond the grave* ..."

The soil now gets a rumpling soft and damp,
And small regard to the future of any weed.
The final flat of the hoe's approval stamp
Is reserved for the bed of a few selected seed.

There is seldom more than a man to a harrowed piece.   5
Men work alone, their lots plowed far apart,

One stringing a chain of seed in an open crease,
And another stumbling after a halting cart.

To the fresh and black of the squares of early mould
The leafless bloom of a plum is fresh and white;   10
Though there's more than a doubt if the weather is not too cold
For the bees to come and serve its beauty aright.

Wind goes from farm to farm in wave on wave,
But carries no cry of what is hoped to be.
There may be little or much beyond the grave,   15
But the strong are saying nothing until they see.

[1936]

Of Modern Poetry   WALLACE STEVENS

After attending Harvard University and the New York Law School,
Wallace Stevens (1879–1955) became a practicing lawyer and then an
insurance executive. In the latter capacity he spent the last twenty years
of his life as a vice president of the Hartford Accident and Indemnity
Company. Though he began writing poetry as an undergraduate, it was
not until 1914 that he gained serious attention for his work, receiving in
that year a prize given by *Poetry* magazine. Beginning with *Harmonium*
(1923), Stevens published a number of volumes of poetry, including *The
Man with the Blue Guitar* (1937) and *Notes Toward a Supreme Fiction*
(1942). He was awarded the Bollingen Prize in 1950 and the Pulitzer
Prize in 1955.
    Stevens is known as an "intellectual" poet, and yet his work has also
been called "a triumph of the imagination." "Of Modern Poetry" has
for its theme the function of poetry, but the nature of this function suggests something yet more basic — a concern pointed to by Stevens' statement that poetry is to him "a very important sanction to life." A striking
feature of the poem is its consistent use of a central metaphor.

"*. . . what will suffice. . . .*"

The poem of the mind in the act of finding
What will suffice. It has not always had
To find: the scene was set; it repeated what
Was in the script.
                    Then the theatre was changed
To something else. Its past was a souvenir.   5

It has to be living, to learn the speech of the place.
It has to face the men of the time and to meet
The women of the time. It has to think about war
And it has to find what will suffice. It has
To construct a new stage. It has to be on that stage   10
And, like an insatiable actor, slowly and
With meditation speak words that in the ear,
In the delicatest ear of the mind, repeat,
Exactly, that which it wants to hear, at the sound
Of which, an invisible audience listens,   15
Not to the play, but to itself, expressed
In an emotion as of two people, as of two
Emotions becoming one. The actor is
A metaphysician in the dark, twanging
An instrument, twanging a wiry string that gives   20
Sounds passing through sudden rightnesses, wholly
Containing the mind, below which it cannot descend,
Beyond which it has no will to rise.
                              It must
Be the finding of a satisfaction, and may   25
Be of a man skating, a woman dancing, a woman
Combing. The poem of the act of the mind.

                                        [1942]

The Lost Dimension in Religion   PAUL TILLICH

Paul Tillich (1886–) was born in Prussia and studied and taught
theology in Germany before coming to the United States in 1933. In this
country he has been professor of philosophy and theology at Union Theological Seminary (1933–55) and at Harvard (1955–). Author of
numerous works — e.g., *The Religious Situation* (1948), *The Courage
to Be* (1952), *The Dynamics of Faith* (1957) — he is widely recognized
as one of the leading existentialist thinkers of our time.

    In this essay Tillich follows standard problem-solving procedure: he
defines a problem, specifies causes, and propounds a solution. Thus the
organization is simple and quite clear. Why, then, does the piece remain
hard reading? One reason is that his concepts of "the dimension of depth"
and "the horizontal dimension," though carefully dealt with, are not
finally easy to grasp. The same is true of the idea that modern art, literature, and philosophy "ask the religious question more radically and more
profoundly than most directly religious expressions of our time." And
the reader must also wrestle with Tillich's definition of the two main
schools of present-day philosophical thought, "the analytic and the existentialist." Tillich, in short, makes greater demands on the reader than,

say, Norman Vincent Peale. Fortunately the rewards of understanding him are commensurately increased.

". . . Is there an answer? . . ."

Every observer of our Western civilization is aware of the fact that something has happened to religion. It especially strikes the observer of the American scene. Everywhere he finds symptoms of what one has called religious revival, or more modestly, the revival of interest in religion. He finds them in the churches with their rapidly increasing membership. He finds them in the mushroomlike growth of sects. He finds them on college campuses and in the theological faculties of universities. Most conspicuously, he finds them in the tremendous success of men like Billy Graham and Norman Vincent Peale, who attract masses of people Sunday after Sunday, meeting after meeting. The facts cannot be denied, but how should they be interpreted? It is my intention to show that these facts must be seen as expressions of the predicament of Western man in the second half of the twentieth century. But I would even go a step further. I believe that the predicament of man in our period gives us also an important insight into the predicament of man generally — at all times and in all parts of the earth.

There are many analyses of man and society in our time. Most of them show important traits in the picture, but few of them succeed in giving a general key to our present situation. Although it is not easy to find such a key, I shall attempt it and, in so doing, will make an assertion which may be somewhat mystifying at first hearing. The decisive element in the predicament of Western man in our period is his loss of the dimension of depth. Of course, "dimension of depth" is a metaphor. It is taken from the spatial realm and applied to man's spiritual life. What does it mean?

It means that man has lost an answer to the question: What is the meaning of life? Where do we come from, where do we go to? What shall we do, what should we become in the short stretch between birth and death? Such questions are not answered or even asked if the "dimension of depth" is lost. And this is precisely what has happened to man in our period of history. He has lost the courage to ask such questions with an infinite seriousness — as former generations did — and he has lost the courage to receive answers to these questions, wherever they may come from.

I suggest that we call the dimension of depth the religious dimension in man's nature. Being religious means asking passionately the question of the meaning of our existence and being willing to receive answers, even if the answers hurt. Such an idea of religion makes religion universally human, but it certainly differs from what is usually called religion. It does not describe religion as the belief in the existence of gods or one God, and as a set of activities and institutions for the sake of relating oneself to these beings in thought, devotion and obedience. No one can deny that the religions which have appeared in history are religions in this sense. Nevertheless, religion in its innermost nature is more than religion in this narrower sense. It is the state of being concerned about one's own being and being universally.

There are many people who are ultimately concerned in this way who feel far removed, however, from religion in the narrower sense, and therefore from every historical religion. It often happens that such people take the question of the meaning of their life infinitely seriously and reject any historical religion just for this reason. They feel that the concrete religions fail to express their profound concern adequately. They are religious while rejecting the religions. It is this experience which forces us to distinguish the meaning of religion as living in the dimension of depth from particular expressions of one's ultimate concern in the symbols and institutions of a concrete religion. If we now turn to the concrete analysis of the religious situation of our time, it is obvious that our key must be the basic meaning of religion and not any particular religion, not even Christianity. What does this key disclose about the predicament of man in our period?

If we define religion as the state of being grasped by an infinite concern we must say: Man in our time has lost such infinite concern. And the resurgence of religion is nothing but a desperate and mostly futile attempt to regain what has been lost.

How did the dimension of depth become lost? Like any important event, it has many causes, but certainly not the one which one hears often mentioned from ministers' pulpits and evangelists' platforms, namely that a widespread impiety of modern man is responsible. Modern man is neither more pious nor more impious than man in any other period. The loss of the dimension of depth is caused by the relation of man to his world and to himself in our period, the period in which nature is being subjected scientifically and technically to the control of man. In this period, life in the dimension of depth is replaced by life in the horizontal dimension. The driving forces of the industrial society of which we are a part go ahead horizontally and not vertically. In popular terms this is expressed in phrases like "better and better," "bigger and bigger," "more and more." One should not disparage the feeling which lies behind such speech. Man is right in feeling that he is able to know and transform the world he encounters without a foreseeable limit. He can go ahead in all directions without a definite boundary.

A most expressive symbol of this attitude of going ahead in the horizontal dimension is the breaking through of the space which is controlled by the gravitational power of the earth into the world-space. It is interesting that one calls this world-space simply "space" and speaks, for instance, of space travel, as if every trip were not travel into space. Perhaps one feels that the true nature of space has been discovered only through our entering into indefinite world-space. In any case, the predominance of the horizontal dimension over the dimension of depth has been immensely increased by the opening up of the space beyond the space of the earth.

If we now ask what does man do and seek if he goes ahead in the horizontal dimension, the answer is difficult. Sometimes one is inclined to say that the mere movement ahead without an end, the intoxication with speeding forward without limits, is what satisfies him. But this answer is by no means sufficient. For on his way into space and time man changes the world he encounters. And the changes made by him change himself. He transforms everything he encounters into a tool; and in doing so he himself becomes a tool. But if he asks, a tool for what, there is no answer.

One does not need to look far beyond everyone's daily experience in order to find examples to describe this predicament. Indeed our daily life in office and home, in cars and airplanes, at parties and conferences, while reading magazines and watching television, while looking at advertisements and hearing radio, are in themselves continuous examples of a life which has lost the dimension of depth. It runs ahead, every moment is filled with something which must be done or seen or said or planned. But no one can experience depth without stopping and becoming aware of himself. Only if he has moments in which he does not care about what comes next can he experience the meaning of this moment here and now and ask himself about the meaning of his life. As long as the preliminary, transitory concerns are not silenced, no matter how interesting and valuable and important they may be, the voice of the ultimate concern cannot be heard. This is the deepest root of the loss of the dimension of depth in our period — the loss of religion in its basic and universal meaning.

If the dimension of depth is lost, the symbols in which life in this dimension has expressed itself must also disappear. I am speaking of the great symbols of the historical religions in our Western world, of Judaism and Christianity. The reason that the religious symbols became lost is not primarily scientific criticism, but it is a complete misunderstanding of their meaning; and only because of this misunderstanding was scientific critique able, and even justified, in attacking them. The first step toward the non-religion of the Western world was made by religion itself. When it defended its great symbols, not as symbols, but as literal stories, it had already lost the battle. In doing so the theologians (and today many religious laymen) helped to transfer the powerful expressions of the dimension of depth into objects or happenings on the horizontal plane. There the symbols lose their power and meaning and become an easy prey to physical, biological and historical attack.

If the symbol of creation which points to the divine ground of everything is transferred to the horizontal plane, it becomes a story of events in a removed past for which there is no evidence, but which contradicts every piece of scientific evidence. If the symbol of the Fall of Man, which points to the tragic estrangement of man and his world from their true being is transferred to the horizonal plane, it becomes a story of a human couple a few thousand years ago in what is now present-day Iraq. One of the most profound psychological descriptions of the general human predicament becomes an absurdity on the horizontal plane. If the symbols of the Saviour and the salvation through Him which point to the healing power in history and personal life are transferred to the horizontal plane, they become stories of a half-divine being coming from a heavenly place and returning to it. Obviously, in this form, they have no meaning whatsoever for people whose view of the universe is determined by scientific astronomy.

If the idea of God (and the symbols applied to Him) which expresses man's ultimate concern is transferred to the horizontal plane, God becomes a being among others whose existence or nonexistence is a matter of inquiry. Nothing, perhaps, is more symptomatic of the loss of the dimension of depth than the permanent discussion about the existence or nonexistence of God — a discussion in which both sides are equally wrong, because the discussion itself is wrong and possible only after the loss of the dimension of depth.

When in this way man has deprived himself of the dimension of depth and the symbols expressing it, he then becomes a part of the horizontal plane. He loses his self and becomes a thing among things. He becomes an element in the process of manipulated production and manipulated consumption. This is now a matter of public knowledge. We have become aware of the degree to which everyone in our social structure is managed, even if one knows it and even if one belongs himself to the managing group. The influence of the gang mentality on adolescents, of the corporation's demands on the executives, of the conditioning of everyone by public communication, by propaganda and advertising under the guidance of motivation research, et cetera, have all been described in many books and articles.

Under these pressures, man can hardly escape the fate of becoming a thing among the things he produces, a bundle of conditioned reflexes without a free, deciding and responsible self. The immense mechanism, set up by man to produce objects for his use, transforms man himself into an object used by the same mechanism of production and consumption.

But man has not ceased to be man. He resists this fate anxiously, desperately, courageously. He asks the question, for what? And he realizes that there is no answer. He becomes aware of the emptiness which is covered by the continuous movement ahead and the production of means for ends which become means again without an ultimate end. Without knowing what has happened to him, he feels that he has lost the meaning of life, the dimension of depth.

Out of this awareness the religious question arises and religious answers are received or rejected. Therefore, in order to describe the contemporary attitude toward religion, we must first point to the places where the awareness of the predicament of Western man in our period is most sharply expressed. These places are the great art, literature and, partly at least, the philosophy of our time. It is both the subject matter and the style of these creations which show the passionate and often tragic struggle about the meaning of life in a period in which man has lost the dimension of depth. This art, literature, philosophy is not religious in the narrower sense of the word; but it asks the religious question more radically and more profoundly than most directly religious expressions of our time.

It is the religious question which is asked when the novelist describes a man who tries in vain to reach the only place which could solve the problem of his life, or a man who disintegrates under the memory of a guilt which persecutes him, or a man who never had a real self and is pushed by his fate without resistance to death, or a man who experiences a profound disgust of everything he encounters.

It is the religious question which is asked when the poet opens up the horror and the fascination of the demonic regions of his soul, of if he leads us into the deserts and empty places of our being, or if he shows the physical and moral mud under the surface of life, or if he sings the song of transitoriness, giving words to the ever-present anxiety of our hearts.

It is the religious question which is asked when the playwright shows the illusion of a life in a ridiculous symbol, or if he lets the emptiness of a life's work end in self-destruction, or if he confronts us with the inescapable bondage to mutual hate and guilt, or if he leads us into the dark cellar of lost hopes and slow disintegration.

It is the religious question which is asked when the painter breaks the visible surface into pieces, then reunites them into a great picture which has little similarity with the world at which we normally look, but which expresses our anxiety and our courage to face reality.

It is the religious question which is asked when the architect, in creating office buildings or churches, removes the trimmings taken over from past styles because they cannot be considered an honest expression of our own period. He prefers the seeming poverty of a purpose-determined style to the deceptive richness of imitated styles of the past. He knows that he gives no final answer, but he does give an honest answer.

The philosophy of our time shows the same hiddenly religious traits. It is divided into two main schools of thought, the analytic and the existentialist. The former tries to analyze logical and linguistic forms which are always used and which underlie all scientific research. One may compare them with the painters who dissolve the natural forms of bodies into cubes, planes and lines; or with those architects who want the structural "bones" of their buildings to be conspicuously visible and not hidden by covering features. This self-restriction produces the almost monastic poverty and seriousness of this philosophy. It is religious — without any contact with religion in its method — by exercising the humility of "learned ignorance."

In contrast to this school the existentialist philosophers have much to say about the problems of human existence. They bring into rational concepts what the writers and poets, the painters and architects, are expressing in their particular material. What they express is the human predicament in time and space, in anxiety and guilt and the feeling of meaninglessness. From Pascal in the seventeenth century to Heidegger and Sartre in our time, philosophers have emphasized the contrast between human dignity and human misery. And by doing so, they have raised the religious question. Some have tried to answer the question they have asked. But if they did so, they turned back to past traditions and offered to our time that which does not fit our time. Is it possible for our time to receive answers which are born out of our time?

Answers given today are in danger of strengthening the present situation and with it the questions to which they are supposed to be the answers. This refers to some of the previously mentioned major representatives of the so-called resurgence of religion, as for instance the evangelist Billy Graham and the counseling and healing minister, Norman Vincent Peale. Against the validity of the answers given by the former, one must say that, in spite of his personal integrity, his propagandistic methods and his primitive theological fundamentalism fall short of what is needed to give an answer to the religious question of our period. In spite of all his seriousness, he does not take the radical questions of our period seriously.

The effect that Norman Peale has on large groups of people is rooted in the fact that he confirms the situation which he is supposed to help overcome. He heals people with the purpose of making them fit again for the demands of the competitive and conformist society in which we are living. He helps them to become adapted to the situation which is characterized by the loss of the dimension of depth. Therefore, his advice is valid on this level; but it is the validity of this level that is the true religious question of our time. And this question he neither raises nor answers.

In many cases the increase of church membership and interest in religious activities does not mean much more than the religious consecration of a state of things in which the religious dimension has been lost. It is the desire to participate in activities which are socially strongly approved and give internal and a certain amount of external security. This is not necessarily bad, but it certainly is not an answer to the religious question of our period.

Is there an answer? There is always an answer, but the answer may not be available to us. We may be too deeply steeped in the predicament out of which the question arises to be able to answer it. To acknowledge this is certainly a better way toward a real answer than to bar the way to it by deceptive answers. And it may be that in this attitude the real answer (within available limits) is given. The real answer to the question of how to regain the dimension of depth is not given by increased church membership or church attendance, nor by conversion or healing experiences. But it is given by the awareness that we have lost the decisive dimension of life, the dimension of depth, and that there is no easy way of getting it back. Such awareness is in itself a state of being grasped by that which is symbolized in the term, dimension of depth. He who realizes that he is separated from the ultimate source of meaning shows by this realization that he is not only separated but also reunited. And this is just our situation. What we need above all — and partly have — is the radical realization of our predicament, without trying to cover it up by secular or religious ideologies. The revival of religious interest would be a creative power in our culture if it would develop into a movement of search for the lost dimension of depth.

This does not mean that the traditional religious symbols should be dismissed. They certainly have lost their meaning in the literalistic form into which they have been distorted, thus producing the critical reaction against them. But they have not lost their genuine meaning, namely, of answering the question which is implied in man's very existence in powerful, revealing and saving symbols. If the resurgence of religion would produce a new understanding of the symbols of the past and their relevance for our situation, instead of premature and deceptive answers, it would become a creative factor in our culture and a saving factor for many who live in estrangement, anxiety and despair. The religious answer has always the character of "in spite of." In spite of the loss of dimension of depth, its power is present, and most present in those who are aware of the loss and are striving to regain it with ultimate seriousness.

[1958]

The Pursuit of the Dollar

In F. Scott Fitzgerald's novel *The Great Gatsby*, Nick Carraway speculates on the thoughts of those who saw for the first time the "fresh green breast of the new world." He imagines that "for a transitory enchanted moment man must have held his breath in the presence of this continent . . . face to face for the last time in history with something commensurate to his capacity for wonder." *The Great Gatsby* deals with the loss of that enchantment through the corrupting power of money.

Perhaps Fitzgerald over-simplifies, for surely part of the wonder of the early settlers came from economic opportunities which most of them saw as a blessing rather than as an evil. The Puritans, for instance, strove for outer prosperity as a symbol of inner grace, a rationalization later referred to as the Protestant Ethic. This paradoxical attitude was pointed up by the Puritan preacher John Cotton when he spoke of "diligence in worldly business and deadness to the world" as a combination desirable in "every lively, holy Christian."

By the nineteenth century Americans generally found the issue less complicated. The immense popularity of the "rags to riches" theme suggests that great wealth had come to seem an unquestioned good — not as a means to something better but in and of itself. By the beginning of the twentieth century William James, most sympathetically American of all philosophers, was complaining that the ordinary citizen was dedicated to "the exclusive worship of the bitch-goddess SUCCESS. That — with the squalid cash interpretation put on the word success — is our national disease." The Protestant Ethic had taken on an almost completely secular cast.

Many present-day American writers, like Thoreau and Emerson before them, berate us for our narrow dedication to financial success. As Lionel Trilling has pointed out, "The conflict of capital and labor is at present a contest for the possession of the goods in a single way of life, and not a cultural struggle." Walter Reuther admits this but adds that "At the point where everyone has all the things they need essentially, then the values that get associated with having three Cadillacs are going to go." Whyte describes just such a changing pattern of values, from the Protestant Ethic to what he calls the Social Ethic. Nevertheless, one does not have to look far to see that the Protestant Ethic is still alive and that even in the Social Ethic strong traces of the Puritan paradox yet remain.

The Protestant Ethic

Three Puritans on Prosperity   A. WHITNEY GRISWOLD

A. Whitney Griswold (1906–   ) at the time this article appeared was a young instructor in history at Yale. Since 1950 he has been president of that institution. It is interesting to note that all three of Griswold's subjects in the following article were also associated with American higher education. Like him, Timothy Dwight (1752–1817) (see p. 69) was president of Yale; Cotton Mather (1663–1728), the most eminent divine of his era, long aspired to the presidency of Harvard; Benjamin Franklin (1706–1790) (see p. 398) helped found what later became the University of Pennsylvania.

Griswold's essay is a succinct and readable analysis of what three early Puritan-Americans thought about the relation between piety and riches. In making this analysis he gives us, in effect, a definition of the Protestant Ethic. The essay is also worth considering as a good example of the documented report. It is tightly organized, gracefully phrased, closely reasoned. It uses both primary and secondary sources. It leaves us in no doubt as to its author's thesis, and it supports that thesis convincingly.

" . . . they . . . believed that God desired Americans to be rich. . . ."

I

Since the German economist, Max Weber, first called serious attention to the relationship of Protestantism and capitalism, various scholars have become intrigued with the idea.[1] Some have taken issue with Weber on minor points, but most have accepted his general conclusions. R. H. Tawney, in particular, has elaborated the thesis, and integrated it with the history of the Reformation.[2]

From *The New England Quarterly*. Reprinted by permission of *The New England Quarterly* and the author.

[1] Weber's work first appeared in *Archiv fur Sozialwissenschaft und Sozialpolitik*, 1904–1905. It was published as a book in Germany in 1920 and afterwards translated into English and published as *The Protestant Ethic and the Spirit of Capitalism* (London, 1930).

[2] In *Religion and the Rise of Capitalism* (London, 1929). For an excellent review of both Weber and Tawney, see Georgia Harkness, *John Calvin, the Man and His Ethics* (New York, 1931), 187–191. These, and other critics of Weber, have picked minor flaws in his argument, such as his over-simplification of Calvinism and his neglect of the social and economic origins of capitalism. They point out that before Luther and Calvin, Thomas Aquinas bestowed a rather negative sanction upon the virtue of thrift. But they uphold as sound Weber's main thesis, that since the Reformation, Protestantism has supplied both inspiration and ethical basis for the capitalist economy.

Ernst Troeltsch has shown its development in sectarian ethics.[3] Yet so far, no one has sought to demonstrate the forms in which this relationship has manifested itself in American history.

For three centuries, Americans have been taught to admire material success: the "frontier," perhaps, provided the economic basis for the lesson. The growing sense of nationalism, the democratic levelling of social barriers, immense natural resources have combined to make us a nation of "rugged individualists," intent upon getting rich. In addition, we have been harangued, severally and individually, on the virtue of making money by a race of success-prophets indigenous to our soil. It is with three early members of that race that this paper deals.

It is worth while, by way of orientation, to review, in brief, the essence of Weber's theory. Because no one has done this so concisely as Professor Morison, let us borrow from his *Builders of the Bay Colony:*

> Max Weber, a German economist of the last century, propounded the interesting theory that Calvinism released the business man from the clutches of the priest, and sprinkled holy water on economic success. According to him, John Calvin defended the taking of interest on loans, which the medieval church had condemned under the name of usury. Since God would not justify reprobates by prosperity, so the argument goes, the successful business man was probably one of God's elect; hence the Puritan sought success as evidence of his election to eternal bliss.

This is the theory to which Tawney, Troeltsch, and others have given added currency. Not so Mr. Morison. He rejects it on the grounds that "in none of the scores of funeral sermons which I have read, is it hinted 'Our departed friend was successful, so he must be in Heaven.'" Further, Mr. Morison proceeds to the conclusion of Professor Clive Day that "the economic ideas of the New England Puritans were medieval; and so far as their church had political power, it regulated rather than stimulated business enterprise."[4]

With the economic implications of the criticism of Messrs. Morison and Day, we are not specifically concerned. Yet their suggestion that "the economic ideas of the New England Puritans were medieval"[5] needs considerable qualification. In spite of the evidence offered by Mr. Day in support of this contention,[6] we can not overlook the failure of the collectivist experiment at Plymouth. It is incorrect to deny that at least the seeds of rugged individualism came over on the *Mayflower*. Later they grew so luxuriantly as to shut collectivism completely out of the Puritan sun. In partial proof of this we offer the sermons of our three Puritans.

Mr. Morison's criticism of the rational process suggested by Weber holds more water. Weber would have us believe that the New England farmer

---

[3] In *The Social Teaching of the Christian Churches* (London, 1931). See also Preserved Smith, *The Age of the Reformation* (New York, 1920), and Reinhold Niebuhr, "Puritanism and Prosperity," in the *Atlantic Monthly*, CXXXVII, 721.

[4] S. E. Morison, *Builders of the Bay Colony* (Boston, 1930), 160.

[5] The words are Professor Morison's.

[6] Clive Hart Day, "Capitalistic and Socialistic Tendencies in the Puritan Colonies," *Annual Report of the American Historical Association . . . 1920* (Washington, 1925), 225–235.

of Calvinist persuasion sought to make money not in order to secure the approval of God, but to prove to himself that God already had bestowed His approval, that he was already a member of the elect. The notion is over-subtle. Doubtless it has been entertained by wealthy merchants of the Back Bay and Salem; but, whether through inadvertence or shame, none seems to have committed it to writing. This does not justify the conclusion that Weber is entirely wrong. The fact is that God did "sprinkle holy water on economic success." Only He did it in a much more forthright manner, which the masses could understand, and which neither the Teutonic intellect of Herr Weber nor the sharp wit of Mr. Morison would have missed had they been citizens of that Puritan world. The three Puritans will speak for them-selves. They are far from the old-world seats of learning. They address frontier audiences. They have no use for subtleties. They deal in plain truths for plain men.

II

Cotton Mather dealt most specifically with the relationship of business and religion in *Two Brief Discourses, one Directing a Christian in his General Calling; another Directing him in his Personal Calling,* a document of 1701 published in Boston the same year. Mather has become a much-quoted authority for the Weber thesis. Weber himself hastens over this document. It may profit us to turn its pages more leisurely. As its explicit title implies, the work deals with the relation of a man's business to his religion. There is a "calling" for each. The "general calling" is "to serve the Lord Jesus Christ," the "personal calling" "a certain Particular Employment by which his *Usefulness* in his neighborhood is distinguished."[7] Each is a matter of the utmost seriousness. A godly man must worship the Lord punctiliously. At the same time he should contract to do no business he "cannot comfortably venture to pray over." And he must have a business. Worshipping the Lord in prayer and hymn is not enough. Contemplation of the good means nothing with-out accomplishment of the good. A man must not only be pious; he must be useful.

Now it follows also, that a man must not only be useful but likewise successful. The Lord had made provision for that, too. One should "be care-ful about the point: *What call from God have I to be in this place and at this work? Am I now where my Lord Jesus Christ would have me to be?*". After assuming this propitious attitude, he might safely trust in God "for the *Success* of all our *Business,* all the day long." But if he refused so to do, failure would be his lot, for "At no time of the Day, may we expect that our Business will succeed without *God's Blessing.*"[8]

In Mather's congregation there must have been some logicians, especially among the business men. It was a comfort for them to hear their occupations sanctified. If they were to undertake no business they could not "comfortably venture to pray over," might they not calm uneasy consciences by praying harder? Might not the prayer draw up the business to its own level? We are not surprised to find Puritan merchants mentioning God prominently in their

7 Mather, *Two Brief Discourses,* 37.
8 Mather, *Two Brief Discourses,* 22–23.

invoices — thanking Him for profit gained, or ascribing losses to *His* greater glory.[9] Neither are we at pains to discover one source of a typically American habit. Mention business to a business man, and he pulls a long face and assumes an air of mystery. This is not all pedantry. For business to Americans has been more than a struggle for existence, more than a career: it has been a "calling."

As for success in that calling, we need not depend on logic to be informed of what Mather thought of it. "A Christian, at his *Two Callings*," he elaborated, "is a man in a Boat, Rowing for Heaven; the House which our Heavenly Father hath intended for us. If he mind but one of his *Callings*, be it which it will, he pulls the *oar*, but on one side of the Boat, and will make but a poor dispatch to the Shoar of Eternal Blessedness." Let a man pray with might and main, he can not get to Heaven unless he attends well to his personal calling, "some *Settled Business*, wherein a Christian should for the most part spend most of his time [the words which follow are significant] and this, that so he may glorify God, by doing of *Good* for *others*, and getting of *Good* for *himself*."[10]

The meaning of these words is clear enough. We may have difficulty in reconciling the principles of "doing of *Good* for *others*," and "getting of *Good* for *himself*"; but that is the paradox which pervades the ethics of Protestantism. As we shall find in the pages which follow, it is sometimes hard to determine where the greater emphasis lies: whether upon a man's impersonal social usefulness, or on his own individual economic success. Cotton Mather did not forget the welfare of society. He reminded his listeners that their occupations should not be anti-social, that they should "have a tendency to the Happiness of Mankind."[11] Yet we submit that Cotton Mather was thinking primarily as an individual, and that he was laying the true moral foundations for rugged American individualism.

The further he pursues his subject, the more specific become his rules of conduct.

> Would a man *Rise* by his Business? I say, then let him *Rise* to his Business. It was foretold. Prov. 22.29, *Seest thou a man Diligint* [sic] *in his Business? He shall stand before Kings; He shall come to preferment.* And it was instanced by him who foretold it; 1 Kings 11.28. *Solomon, seeing that the young man was industrious, he made him a Ruler.* I tell you, with *Diligence* a man may do marvallous [sic] things. *Young* man, work hard while you are *Young:* You'l Reap the effects of it when you are *Old.* Yea, How can you Ordinarily enjoy any Rest at *Night,* if you have not been well at work in the *Day?* Let your *Business* engross the most of your time.[12] . . . Let every man have the *Discretion* to be well instructed in, and well acquainted with, all the mysteries of his *Occupation.* Be a master of your trade; count it a disgrace to be no workman.[13]

[9] William B. Weeden, *Economic and Social History of New England, 1620–1789* (Boston and New York, 1890), I, 250.
[10] Mather, *Two Brief Discourses,* 38. The italics are Mather's.
[11] Mather, *Two Brief Discourses,* 49.
[12] Mather, *Two Brief Discourses,* 48.
[13] Mather, *Two Brief Discourses,* 53.

It may well have been that Mather himself thought of individual prosperity as an instrument of social welfare. But he presented it to his congregation first and foremost as both the temporal and spiritual reward for a life spent in industrious enterprise. Individuals should achieve salvation individually. Because industry tended to rally the Christian virtues within a man, industry should be encouraged. Thus the material fruits of industry were blessed in the sight of God.

In Mather's system of the two complementary callings, God had the material success of individuals entirely at his disposal. Piety, therefore, was an instrument in achieving it. Practise the Christian virtues; kneel daily in prayer, and "all your *Business* will go on the better, all the day, for your being thus faithful to God."[14] The individual could be reassured by this. It meant that however he might lack in native ability, piety would repair the deficiency. He had Mather's word for it, for the latter said, "with the *Help of God* never fear, but your Hands will be sufficient for you."[15] To the democratic implications of this system we shall return directly. For the moment we may see in it another manifestation of God's concern for the individual prosperity of Puritan business men.

So far, it may be objected, we have judged Mather by only one sermon. Although of all his writings it is the one which deals most specifically with our subject, let us see if he afterwards changed his mind. Twenty years elapse, and he returns to the old theme in "The Vain Presumption of Living and Thriving in the World; which does too often possess and poison the *Children of* this *World*."[16] A large congregation has assembled to hear him preach. The title gives a clue to the content. In 1720 too many people seem to have been finding economic success possible without piety. They have, as it were, been rowing themselves around in circles with the oar of "personal calling" and consequently are drifting away from the "Shoar of Eternal Blessedness." Mather pleads with them:

> Acknowledge thy *Dependence* on the glorious God, for thy *Thriving* in the World. It is what we are minded of; Deut. VIII.18. *Thou shalt remember the Lord thy God; for it is He that gives thee Power to get wealth.* Be sensible of this; *Riches* not always to them who are sharpest at inventing the most probable Methods of coming at it. Be sensible of this; The way to succeed in our Enterprizes, *O Lord, I know the way of man is not in himself!* Be sensible of this; In our *Occupation* we spread our *Nets*; but it is God who brings unto our *Nets* all that comes into them.[17]

One pictures a worldly congregation, some of which was no doubt thinking about other things than the sermon — of clever ways to outwit English customs-officers. Others, more serious, might have been wondering if God filled even smugglers' nets.

[14] Mather, *Two Brief Discourses*, 67.
[15] Mather, *Two Brief Discourses*, 69.
[16] Cotton Mather, *Sober Sentiments*, funeral sermon, *Produced by the Premature and Much-lamented Death of Mr. Joshua Lamb* (Boston, 1722).
[17] Mather, *Sober Sentiments*, 25.

Mather has changed his emphasis but not his doctrine. God is still vitally interested in man's economic lot. He still desires that to be successful. Moreover, according to the great divine, God had vouchsafed success to the poorest mortals, to men of the humblest parts. For wealth was "not always to them who are sharpest at inventing the most probable methods of coming at it." The social ethics embodied in Mather's preaching were reflected in the exigencies of frontier life — or did the ethics reflect the frontier? It is often asserted that religion generally sanctions the customs of society. What of the Puritanism of Cotton Mather? The most eminent spiritual leader of the Puritans for half a century, he held up to them an ideal of success to be achieved for the glory of God. Conditions on the frontier made collectivism difficult: at Plymouth it was tried and abandoned. Servants were lured away by the opportunity to acquire farms of their own for nothing. Wages, in several colonies, became so exorbitant as to necessitate statutory limits. Most obvious of all, one had to work in the wilderness, or die. Conditions demanded precisely the same moral qualities of industry, perseverance, sobriety, thrift, and prudence, as did Cotton Mather. They stressed, likewise, individual enterprise. Indeed, we might suppose that the frontier would have created a system of social ethics closely resembling Mather's if America had never heard of Luther and Calvin, were it not for one phrase which lingers: Wealth "not always to them who are sharpest at inventing the most probable methods of coming at it." This was the perfervid hope which the Puritanism of Cotton Mather held out to the common man. It meant, in humble ken, that God had made provision for all men to succeed.

As worldliness crept into the Puritan religion, occasioning the desperate effort of Jonathan Edwards to revive the fire and brimstone of primitive Calvinism, the social ethics preached by Mather did not die. American Protestants became divided into hostile sects: Methodists, Baptists, Unitarians. Some called themselves Deists. But as a general rule, their business remained a vital part of their religion, a calling. God continued to fill the nets of individual enterprise. Call it rationalization, hypocrisy, inspiration, or what you will, Puritans clung to the doctrine that God would point the way to individual prosperity, and would be pleased at its achievement.

Cotton Mather did not invent this doctrine: he merely gave it expression. His utterances are of interest to us not so much for the persuasive influence they may have had upon his contemporaries, as because they represent the mind of orthodox Puritanism two centuries ago. They indicate that thinking men were casting about in their minds for a moral sanction for money-making, and that they found that sanction in the ethical system originally propounded by Martin Luther and John Calvin. Thus, in a sense, Cotton Mather deserves recognition as one of the first to teach American business men to serve God by making money.

III

One day in 1724 Cotton Mather received a young caller at his home in Boston. It was a sober youth of eighteen years who presented himself. Benjamin Franklin had returned from Philadelphia for a brief visit to his native town, and had stopped to pay his respects to the great Puritan, whom he much admired. Franklin's later account of the visit indicates that it made some impression on him. Mather

> . . . received me in his library [he wrote] and on my taking leave showed me a shorter way out of the house, through a narrow passage, which was crossed by a beam overhead. We were talking as I withdrew, he accompanying me behind, and I turning partly towards him, when he said hastily, "Stoop, stoop!" I did not understand him till I felt my head hit against the beam. He was a man that never missed any occasion of giving instruction, and upon this he said to me: "You are young, and have the world before you; stoop as you go through it, and you will miss many hard thumps." This advice, thus beat into my head, has frequently been of use to me, and I often think of it when I see pride mortified and misfortunes brought upon people by carrying their heads too high.[18]

Was this all that Mather had to offer his visitor; or was there a real spiritual bond between the two?

The God in which Franklin consistently professed belief was far more genial than Cotton Mather's stern Jehovah. Out of a vast "Chorus of Worlds" He was merely "that particular Wise and good God, who is the author and owner of our System."[19] His greatest gift to man was reason, by which man might discover his true function in the scheme of things. So glaring are the inconsistencies in Franklin's life that we take whatever he said with many grains of salt. We should not, for example, attach too much importance to the "Articles of Faith and Acts of Religion" which he drew up, with solemn precocity at the age of twenty-two. His life proclaims him too palpable a citoyen du monde to warrant much attention to his theology. Yet by virtue of this fact, it is all the more intriguing that he should have subscribed to a system of ethics identical to Cotton Mather's. In his life Franklin was a Deist, if not an out-and-out agnostic; in his writings, he was the soul of Puritanism. Why was this?

To be sure, Franklin had been born a Puritan in Puritan society. In childhood he heard his father admonish him over and over again on the inestimable value of all the Puritan virtues. But neither heredity nor environment can wholly account for Dr. Franklin. Was there some spiritual kinship, then, some intellectual contact with Puritan philosophers? Franklin himself says there was. The books which he precociously read numbered among them Pilgrim's Progress, Plutarch, and the works of Daniel Defoe. But it was from none of these that the spark of Franklin's Puritanism flashed. If we are to take him at his word, we must consider rather a small volume entitled Essays to Do Good by the Reverend Cotton Mather. This, he says in the Autobiography, "perhaps gave me such a turn of thinking that had an influence on some of the principle future events of my life."[20] And in 1784, from the terminus of his great career, he wrote Cotton Mather's son renewing the acknowledgment. The Essays had given him "such a turn of thinking,

18 Benjamin Franklin, Complete Works (New York, 1887), VIII, 484–485.
19 Franklin, Works, I, 308.
20 Franklin, Works, I, 44: this was written in 1771.

as to have an influence on my conduct through life, for I have always set a greater value on the character of a *doer of good,* than on any other kind of reputation; and if I have been, as you seem to think, a useful citizen, the public owes the advantage of it to that book."[21]

Before rejecting Franklin's compliments as insincere, let us see what Mather had to say to him. Let us pause, for a moment, over the strange intellectual kinship of the author of *The Wonders of the Invisible World,* and the man who "discovered" electricity. The central theme of the *Essays to Do Good* is that of the sermons: personal salvation achieved through good works. The two callings receive lengthy treatment; and there is a categorical exposition of methods of doing good. Ministers, school teachers, lawyers, physicians all have their specific functions. But the greatest opportunity awaits persons of wealth. To them Mather has something special to say:

> Sirs, you cannot but acknowledge that it is the sovereign God who has bestowed upon you the riches which distinguish you. A devil himself, when he saw a rich man, could not but make this acknowledgement to the God of heaven: "Thou hast blessed the work of his hands, and his substance is increased in the land."[22]

But the divine esteem enjoyed by the man of property does not diminish his obligations to society. The Lord has made him His "steward." He has charged him with a sacred trust, charity. Moreover, God in His infinite wisdom has made charity an attractive sacrifice, for if we are to believe Cotton Mather, the charitable

> . . . very frequently . . . have been rewarded with remarkable success in their affairs, and increase of their property; and even in this world have seen the fulfillment of those promises: "Cast thy bread upon the waters" — thy grain into the moist ground — and thou shalt find it after many days." "Honor the Lord with thy substance; so shall thy barns be filled with plenty." History has given us many delightful examples of those who have had their *decimations* followed and rewarded by a surprising prosperity of their affairs. Obscure mechanics and husbandmen have risen to estates, of which once they had not the most distant expectation.[23]

So spoke the Reverend Cotton Mather to young Ben Franklin. His words are at once corroborative and prophetic. They are further evidence of his belief in the piety of individual prosperity, and they whisper of the future when thousands of "obscure mechanics and husbandmen" would rise (as millions would aspire) "to estates of which they had not the most distant expectation."

It would be interesting to lay the texts of Mather's *Essays* and Franklin's *Autobiography* side by side, so much is the former reflected in the latter. The purpose in recording his own rise "from the poverty and obscurity in which

[21] Franklin, *Works*, VIII, 484.
[22] Mather, *Essays to Do Good:* American Tract Society (Boston, 1710), 86–87.
[23] Mather, *Essays to Do Good,* 89–90.

I was born and bred, to a state of affluence and some degree of reputation in the world,"[24] Franklin declares, is to allow others to profit by his example. He himself thought it "fit to be imitated" and therefore he would write a book about it. But first he desired "with all humility to acknowledge that I owe the mentioned happiness of my past life to [God's] kind providence, which led me to the means I used and gave them success."[25] How like a Puritan to attribute to the Lord "a state of affluence and some degree of reputation in the world." The *Autobiography* is filled with similar professions of humility and piety. To the uncritical reader, the sermon it preached must have seemed even more convincing than Mather's, for it had received from its author the pragmatic sanction of successful practice. So he declared, at any rate. He had found it helpful as a young printer's apprentice to draw up a chart of the virtues necessary for complete moral perfection, and then to score himself daily on progress made — or not made. Mather himself could not have improved the list. It included temperance, silence, order, resolution, frugality, industry, sincerity, justice, moderation, cleanliness, tranquillity, chastity, and humility. Of these, industry was most important. "Lose no time," he said to himself, "be always employed in something useful; cut off all unnecessary actions."[26]

But it is *Poor Richard* who sings the loudest praise of industry. Luck, says he, is of no account. Americans need only work hard and never trouble themselves about luck, for *"Diligence is the Mother of good luck, and God gives all things to industry."* *Poor Richard* likewise knows all about the calling: *"He that hath a trade hath an estate, and he that hath a calling hath an office of profit and honor."*[27] In fact the way to wealth was, in his own words, "as plain as the way to market" to Benjamin Franklin.

> It depends chiefly on two words, *industry* and *frugality* — that is, waste neither *time* nor *money*, but make the best use of both. Without industry and frugality nothing will do, and with them everything. He that gets all he can and saves all he can . . . will certainly become rich, if that Being who governs the world, to whom all should look for a blessing on their honest endeavors, doth not, in his wise providence, otherwise determine.[28]

Did Franklin learn all this from Cotton Mather? It is authentic Puritanism. Mather had, at times, stooped low enough to commend charity as a profitable business venture. Franklin certainly knew Mather and read his works. Yet the man who paraphrased classic aphorisms for simple Americans feared no Puritan God. The thunderbolt which was the angry voice of Jehovah to Mather trickled harmlessly off a wet kite-string into Franklin's Leyden jar. *Poor Richard's* wisdom is savory with business acumen. Whence, therefore, the piety? Was it an after-thought?

It makes little difference where Franklin got his Puritanism. Very likely

24 Franklin, *Works*, I, 29.
25 Franklin, *Works*, I, 30–31.
26 Franklin, *Works*, I, 176.
27 Franklin, *Works*, I, 444.
28 Franklin, *Works*, II, 120–121.

Mather made substantial contributions. Yet the piety, in all probability, was no after-thought. It was put there with deliberate intent. Let us not forget that Benjamin Franklin was a journalist and publisher by trade. *Poor Richard's Almanac*, like most of his other publications, was distinctly a money-making venture. Its shrewd author knew his trade; and what was more, he knew his public. Any publisher knows that catering to a public's taste is profitable, and that is precisely what Franklin did. He understood Puritanism well enough to realize that it offered assurances of material prosperity to all who followed its code of morals. Piety was inexpensive, and so although he himself was worlds apart from orthodoxy, he preached Puritan ethics as good as Mather's. From an unmoral point of view he perceived that the Puritan virtues had immense utilitarian value. And, skeptic though he was, he doubtless thought it wise to be on the safe side, to propitiate whatever God there might be. However that may be, he knew his public would think so.

The popularity of his writings bears witness to Franklin's shrewdness. The *Autobiography* became a famous American success story. Let its author be accused of hypocrisy in affecting the moral austerity of Puritanism. His public must have been delighted to find that he, a scientist, a patriot, a man who had in actuality risen to "a state of affluence and some degree of reputation in the world" endorsed the same democratic virtues as their ministers. It must have relieved them to have such a man turn thumbs down on chance, as it rejoiced them to hear him re-affirm the sanctity of individual prosperity. Benjamin Franklin not only commended prosperity; he dramatized it.

IV

While Cotton Mather represents the mind of orthodox Puritanism, and Franklin a secularized version of the same, Timothy Dwight is the soul of Puritanism revivalism. Unlike the other two, Dwight was never really a national figure. His fame and his influence are localized in Connecticut, over the spiritual destinies of which he presided as Congregational "Pope." Although a persevering student and a teacher of some accomplishment, Dwight was scarcely a profound thinker. His preaching is of interest to us because it embodies the latter-day Puritanism revived in the outward form of Congregationalism. In a new age, in a new church, Dwight taught the old ethics of his spiritual fathers; and out of them he evolved a primitive social philosophy which became a national religion. The sermons of Timothy Dwight are Puritan documents. As might be expected, they deplored the seven deadly sins; they dealt uncompromisingly with Satan, and they lauded the Christian virtues. In them we find the same doctrine of good works and the calling, the same especial praise for industry. Only Dwight, being somewhat of a scholar, adduced the wisdom of classical antiquity as well as that of the Old Testament to drive home his points. "The diligent hand maketh rich" he balanced with "Diligentia vincit omnia."[29] And speaking for himself, he declared that idleness was "not only a gross vice in itself, but the highway to all the other vices."[30]

[29] Timothy Dwight, *Sermons* (Edinburgh, 1828), I, 308.
[30] *The Charitable Blessed* (New Haven, 1810), 19.

Like Cotton Mather, the man of God, and Benjamin Franklin, the man of the world, Dwight believed that individuals must save their own souls first, the soul of society afterwards. He, too, felt that the Puritan virtues were, and ought to be, individualistic. His exposition of the calling is proof of this. Each man has a soul, he said, and

> . . . the value of that soul is inconceivable. It is infinite. The world, nay the universe, weighed against it is nothing. . . . It claims, therefore, it deserves, all your attention, all your labours, all your prayers. . . . At the same time your earthly concerns are not to be forgotten. They, too, have their importance.

So far, we might be listening to Cotton Mather. But in the words which follow a more specific relationship is established between business and religion than any we have yet observed. It shows that Dwight had begun to look at the whole ethical problem objectively, and was trying to find a rational place for it in American life. Spiritual and earthly concerns, he resumed, are not incompatible.

> Happily for you the attention which they really demand is in no degree inconsistent with the effectual promotion of your eternal welfare. The same sobriety of mind, which is so useful to the advancement of your heavenly interests, is the direct means of your earthly prosperity.[31]

This was a splendid way to popularize "sobriety of mind" among worldly folk, prosperity among the religious.

In a sense, however, Dwight was a child of a new era. A throw-back in his religion, he was a citizen of a new nation. Thus, in addition to commending material prosperity on religious grounds, he did so also on patriotic. If Mather's sermons were at least in part rationalizations of frontier life, Dwight had begun to think in terms of nationalism. The United States was now an independent democracy. Constitutionally it was now easier than ever for "obscure mechanics and husbandmen" to rise "to estates, of which they had not the most distant expectation." Although entirely out of sympathy with those very elements in the rabble of Jefferson's followers, Dwight inconsistently proclaimed the sanctity of industry, and the kindred Puritan virtues which enabled them to rise. He further encouraged them, moreover, in bestowing upon prosperity a patriotic, as well as a religious sanction.

Timothy Dwight was an observer of American society as well as a minister of the gospel. In his extensive travels through New York and New England, he noted with a critical eye the habits of the people in those sections. At Boston, in 1810, he found that "a man, who is not believed to follow some useful business, can scarcely acquire, or retain, even a decent reputation."[32] Proceeding into Vermont, he paid close attention to the social evolution in progress on that frontier. The frontiersman came in for searching analysis in Dwight's note-book, affording him case history by which to substantiate a

---

[31] Dwight, *Sermons*, II, 24–25.
[32] *Travels in New England and New York* (New Haven, 1821), I, 507.

social theory which he now evolved. It was not a new theory. He merely carried the familiar Puritan ethics to their logical conclusion, expressed in terms of American society.

The frontier, to Dwight, was a line of least resistance, the frontiersman a shiftless lover of "this irregular, adventurous, half-working and half-lounging life." He was a painful contrast to the farmer, upon whose "sober industry and prudent economy" rested civilization itself. Dwight painted a dreary picture of his subject. In Vermont, he wrote,

> they are obliged to work, or starve. They accordingly cut down some trees, and girdle others; they furnish themselves with an ill-built log house, and a worse barn; and reduce a part of the forest into fields, half-enclosed, and half-cultivated. The forests furnish browse; and their fields yield a stinted herbage.[33]

A dreary picture, indeed, but an historic picture. For what Dwight saw in Vermont he might have seen at Plymouth in an earlier age, or in Michigan at a later. It was American society in its primitive state. That he should hold it in contempt is indication, among other things, of the progress of civilization in the United States. The frontiersman could send his sons to the college of Timothy Dwight to be educated. But first he had to settle the country.

The great Congregationalist did not, however, despair of frontiersmen. He conceded that they were not entirely lost, for even they could "become sober, industrious citizens, merely by the acquisition of property." This led him immediately to the conclusion that "The love of property to a certain degree seems indispensable to the existence of sound morals."[34] It was, therefore, the duty of those who had the welfare of the state at heart to encourage its individual members to make money.

> The possession of this money removes, perhaps for the first time, the despair of acquiring property; and awakens the hope, and the wish, to acquire more. The secure possession of property demands, every moment, the hedge of law; and reconciles a man, originally lawless, to the restraints of government. Thus situated, he sees that reputation, also, is within his reach. Ambition forces him to aim at it; and compels him to a life of sobriety, and decency. That his children may obtain this benefit, he is obliged to send them to school, and to unite with those around him in supporting a schoolmaster. His neighbours are disposed to build a church, and settle a minister. A regard to his own character, to the character and feelings of his family, and very often to the solicitations of his wife, prompts him to contribute to both these objects; to attend, when they are compassed, upon the public worship of God; and perhaps to become in the end a religious man.[35]

Thus was the common man instructed by Timothy Dwight. Prosperity was the touchstone by which the savage might be civilized, the heathen made Christian.

[33] Dwight, *Travels*, II, 459–460.
[34] Dwight, *Travels*, II, 462.
[35] Dwight, *Travels*, II, 462–463.

V

So spoke three Puritans at various moments in our early history: Cotton Mather from the mysterious universe of Jehovah, Benjamin Franklin from the commercial capital of a new world, Timothy Dwight from the pulpit of revivalism. As their lives overlapped each other, so did their thoughts. And from their several vantage points they came into clear agreement that individual prosperity was a highly desirable thing.

How much influence their teaching may have had it is difficult to say. Possibly it is more than a coincidence that in New England, where business was a calling, and wealth both a sign of heavenly approval and a bulwark of civilization, the Federalists should have their principal strength. When one is told in church that property is sacred, its acquisition a duty, its charitable distribution profitable, it is not strange that he should vote for that same "hedge of law" which Timothy Dwight and Alexander Hamilton thought so essential. Neither is it strange, on the other hand, that a religious gospel promising material success to all who served the Puritans' God should find many adherents among the self-made men who followed Jefferson. One thing is certain, however. Insofar as Cotton Mather, Benjamin Franklin, and Timothy Dwight represent the various facets of American Puritanism, they laid down a code of living the followers of which believed that God desired Americans to be rich.

[1934]

Nineteenth-Century Individualism

Business Habits   HENRY DAVID THOREAU

Refusing to pursue the dollar, scornful of ordinary comfort and security, Henry Thoreau (1817–1862) is one of America's most famous individualists. A key chapter in his life was from July 4, 1845, to September 6, 1847, when he lived in a hut he had built for himself at Walden Pond near Concord. His aim, he said, was "to transact some private business with the fewest obstacles." *Walden* (1854), his report of this experience, has become an American classic. The following selection is from the first chapter, titled "Economy." For other remarks on Thoreau, see page 54.

Using in part the vocabulary of commerce, Thoreau tells of the strictly non-commercial nature of his life. Walden, he maintains with both seriousness and irony, is a good place for "business." Like everything Thoreau wrote, this selection is noteworthy both for its ideas and its style, which is concrete, humorous, epigrammatic and, above all, metaphorical. When Emerson (see p. 152) said of Thoreau that he "gives me in flesh and blood . . . my own ethics," he could have been speaking of his friend's writing as well as of his life.

". . . It is not necessary that a man should earn his living by the sweat of his brow, unless he sweats easier than I do. . . ."

If I should attempt to tell how I have desired to spend my life in years past, it would probably surprise those of my readers who are somewhat acquainted with its actual history; it would certainly astonish those who know nothing about it. I will only hint at some of the enterprises which I have cherished.

In any weather, at any hour of the day or night, I have been anxious to improve the nick of time, and notch it on my stick too; to stand on the meeting of two eternities, the past and future, which is precisely the present moment; to toe that line. You will pardon some obscurities, for there are more secrets in my trade than in most men's, and yet not voluntarily kept, but inseparable from its very nature. I would gladly tell all that I know about it, and never paint "No Admittance" on my gate.

I long ago lost a hound, a bay horse, and a turtle-dove, and am still on their trail. Many are the travellers I have spoken concerning them, describing their tracks and what calls they answered to. I have met one or two who had heard the hound, and the tramp of the horse, and even seen the dove disappear behind a cloud, and they seemed as anxious to recover them as if they had lost them themselves.

To anticipate, not the sunrise and the dawn merely, but, if possible, Nature herself! How many mornings, summer and winter, before yet any neighbor was stirring about his business, have I been about mine! No doubt, many of my townsmen have met me returning from this enterprise, farmers starting for Boston in the twilight, or woodchoppers going to their work. It is true, I never assisted the sun materially in his rising, but, doubt not, it was of the last importance only to be present at it.

So many autumn, ay, and winter days, spent outside the town, trying to hear what was in the wind, to hear and carry it express! I well-nigh sunk all my capital in it, and lost my own breath into the bargain, running in the face of it. If it had concerned either of the political parties, depend upon it, it would have appeared in the Gazette with the earliest intelligence. At other times watching from the observatory of some cliff or tree, to telegraph any new arrival; or waiting at evening on the hill-tops for the sky to fall, that I might catch something, though I never caught much, and that, manna-wise, would dissolve again in the sun.

For a long time I was reporter to a journal, of no very wide circulation, whose editor has never yet seen fit to print the bulk of my contributions, and, as is too common with writers, I got only my labor for my pains. However, in this case my pains were their own reward.

For many years I was self-appointed inspector of snow-storms and rain-storms, and did my duty faithfully; surveyor, if not of highways, then of forest paths and all across-lot routes, keeping them open, and ravines bridged and passable at all seasons, where the public heel had testified to their utility.

I have looked after the wild stock of the town, which give a faithful herdsman of a good deal of trouble by leaping fences; and I have had an eye to the unfrequented nooks and corners of the farm; though I did not always know whether Jonas or Solomon worked in a particular field to-day; that was none of my business. I have watered the red huckleberry, the sand cherry and the nettle-tree, the red pine and the black ash, the white grape and the yellow violet, which might have withered else in dry seasons.

In short, I went on thus for a long time (I may say it without boasting), faithfully minding my business, till it became more and more evident that my townsmen would not after all admit me into the list of town officers, nor make my place a sinecure with a moderate allowance. My accounts, which I can swear to have kept faithfully, I have, indeed, never got audited, still less accepted, still less paid and settled. However, I have not set my heart on that.

Not long since, a strolling Indian went to sell baskets at the house of a well-known lawyer in my neighborhood. "Do you wish to buy any baskets?" he asked. "No, we do not want any," was the reply. "What!" exclaimed the Indian as he went out the gate, "do you mean to starve us?" Having seen his industrious white neighbors so well off, — that the lawyer had only to weave arguments, and, by some magic, wealth and standing followed, — he had said to himself: I will go into business; I will weave baskets; it is a thing which I can do. Thinking that when he made the baskets he would have done his part, and then it would be the white man's to buy them. He had not discovered that it was necessary for him to make it worth the other's while to buy them, or at least make him think that it was so, or to make something else which it would be worth his while to buy. I too had woven a kind of basket of a delicate texture, but I had not made it worth any one's while to buy them. Yet not the less, in my case, did I think it worth my while to weave them, and instead of studying how to make it worth men's while to buy my baskets, I studied rather how to avoid the necessity of selling them. The life which men praise and regard as successful is but one kind. Why should we exaggerate any one kind at the expense of the others?

Finding that my fellow-citizens were not likely to offer me any room in the court house, or any curacy or living anywhere else, but I must shift for myself, I turned my face more exclusively than ever to the woods, where I was better known. I determined to go into business at once, and not wait to acquire the usual capital, using such slender means as I had already got. My purpose in going to Walden Pond was not to live cheaply nor to live dearly there, but to transact some private business with the fewest obstacles; to be hindered from accomplishing which for want of a little common sense, a little enterprise and business talent, appeared not so sad as foolish.

I have always endeavored to acquire strict business habits; they are indispensable to every man. If your trade is with the Celestial Empire, then some small counting house on the coast, in some Salem harbor, will be fixture enough. You will export such articles as the country affords, purely native products, much ice and pine timber and a little granite, always in native bottoms. These will be good ventures. To oversee all the details yourself in person; to be at once pilot and captain, and owner and underwriter; to buy and sell and keep the accounts; to read every letter received, and write or read every letter sent; to superintend the discharge of imports night and day; to be upon many parts of the coast almost at the same time, — often the richest freight will be discharged upon a Jersey shore; — to be your own telegraph, unweariedly sweeping the horizon, speaking all passing vessels bound coastwise; to keep up a steady despatch of commodities, for the supply of such a distant and exorbitant market; to keep yourself informed of the state of the markets, prospects of war and peace everywhere, and anticipate the tendencies of trade and civilization, — taking advantage of the results of all exploring expeditions, using new passages and all improvements in navigation; — charts to be studied, the position of reefs and new lights and buoys to be ascertained, and ever, and ever, the logarithmic tables to be corrected, for by the error of some calculator the vessel often splits upon a rock that should have reached a friendly pier, — there is the untold fate of La Pérouse; — universal science to be kept pace with, studying the lives of all great discoverers and navigators, great adventurers and merchants, from Hanno and the Phœnicians down to our day; in fine, account of stock to be taken from time to time, to know how you stand. It is a labor to task the faculties of a man, — such problems of profit and loss, of interest, of tare and tret, and gauging of all kinds in it, as demand a universal knowledge.

I have thought that Walden Pond would be a good place for business, not solely on account of the railroad and the ice trade; it offers advantages which it may not be good policy to divulge; it is a good port and a good foundation. No Neva marshes to be filled; though you must everywhere build on piles of your own driving. It is said that a flood-tide, with a westerly wind, and ice in the Neva, would sweep St. Petersburg from the face of the earth. . . .

For more than five years I maintained myself . . . solely by the labor of my hands, and I found that, by working about six weeks in a year, I could meet all the expenses of living. The whole of my winters, as well as most of my summers, I had free and clear for study. . . . As I preferred some things to others, and especially valued my freedom, as I could fare hard and yet succeed well, I did not wish to spend my time in earning rich carpets or other fine furniture, or delicate cookery, or a house in the Grecian or the Gothic style just yet. If there are any to whom it is no interruption to acquire these things, and who know how to use them when acquired, I relinquish to them the pursuit. Some are "industrious," and appear to love labor for its own sake, or perhaps because it keeps them out of worse mischief; to such I have at present nothing to say. Those who would not know what to do with more leisure than they now enjoy, I might advise to work twice as hard as they do, — work till they pay for themselves, and get their free papers. For myself I found that the occupation of a day-laborer was the most independent of any, especially as it required only thirty or forty days in a year to support one. The laborer's day ends with the going down of the sun, and he is then free to devote himself to his chosen pursuit, independent of his labor; but his employer, who speculates from month to month, has no respite from one end of the year to the other.

In short, I am convinced, both by faith and experience, that to maintain one's self on this earth is not a hardship but a pastime, if we will live simply and wisely; as the pursuits of the simpler nations are still the sports of the more artificial. It is not necessary that a man should earn his living by the sweat of his brow, unless he sweats easier than I do.

[1854]

Days   RALPH WALDO EMERSON

Ralph Waldo Emerson (1803–1882) was Henry Thoreau's neighbor, friend, and benefactor; for several years in the 1840's Thoreau was a member of the Emerson household. For a note on Emerson, see page 152.

Like *Walden*, Emerson's poem expresses a high-minded philosophy of the main chance; like Thoreau, Emerson is a seeker after riches — of a kind. Both are devoted to the Puritan idea of *carpe diem*; neither would accept the application given it by Griswold's three figures. In Emerson's essay titled "Works and Days" this statement appears: "The days . . . come and go like muffled and veiled figures, sent from a distant friendly party; but they say nothing, and if we do not use the gifts they bring, they carry them as silently away." It is instructive to consider what Emerson has done in converting this prose sentiment into poetry.

" . . . I . . . took a few herbs and apples. . . ."

Daughters of Time, the hypocritic Days,
Muffled and dumb like barefoot dervishes,
And marching single in an endless file,
Bring diadems and fagots in their hands.
To each they offer gifts after his will,
Bread, kingdoms, stars, and sky that holds them all.
I, in my pleached garden, watched the pomp,
Forgot my morning wishes, hastily
Took a few herbs and apples, and the Day
Turned and departed silent. I, too late,
Under her solemn fillet saw the scorn.

[1857]

Squire Hawkins and His Tennessee Land

SAMUEL LANGHORNE CLEMENS

The Gilded Age (1873) was the joint work of Charles Dudley Warner
and his friend Samuel Clemens (1835–1910), who is usually called by
his pen name, Mark Twain. All the chapters of real merit in the book
were written by Twain. Doubtless with such work as this in mind,
William Dean Howells called Mark Twain "the very marrow of Americanism." In *The Gilded Age* he captured the spirit of his time so successfully that this somewhat inaccurate designation has ever since been
applied to the years after the Civil War.

   In this first chapter of *The Gilded Age* Twain presents the greed,
crudity, and unscrupulousness of the period; he also lets us feel its vitality,
courage, and optimism. Squire Hawkins' grandiose schemes never mate-
rialize, nor do those of his friend Colonel Sellers, so that the rather
inconclusive ending of this chapter anticipates the work as a whole. Mark
Twain's individualism is of a somewhat different stamp than that of
Thoreau or Emerson; to understand it, one must consider the author's
rather mixed attitude toward Squire Hawkins. Among the distinctive
characteristics of this selection are Twain's "realistic" method and his
use of humor.

" . . . Oceans of money in it — anybody could see that. . . ."

June 18 — . Squire Hawkins sat upon the pyramid of large blocks, called the
"stile," in front of his house, contemplating the morning.
   The locality was Obedstown, East Tennessee. You would not know that

Obedstown stood on the top of a mountain, for there was nothing about the landscape to indicate it — but it did: a mountain that stretched abroad over whole counties, and rose very gradually. The district was called the "Knobs of East Tennessee," and had a reputation like Nazareth, as far as turning out any good thing was concerned.

The Squire's house was a double log cabin, in a state of decay; two or three gaunt hounds lay asleep about the threshold, and lifted their heads sadly whenever Mrs. Hawkins or the children stepped in and out over their bodies. Rubbish was scattered about the grassless yard; a bench stood near the door with a tin wash basin on it and a pail of water and a gourd; a cat had begun to drink from the pail, but the exertion was overtaxing her energies, and she had stopped to rest. There was an ash-hopper by the fence, and an iron pot, for soft-soap-boiling, near it.

This dwelling constituted one-fifteenth of Obedstown; the other fourteen houses were scattered about among the tall pine trees and among the cornfields in such a way that a man might stand in the midst of the city and not know but that he was in the country if he only depended on his eyes for information.

"Squire" Hawkins got his title from being postmaster of Obedstown — not that the title properly belonged to the office, but because in those regions the chief citizens always must have titles of some sort, and so the usual courtesy had been extended to Hawkins. The mail was monthly, and sometimes amounted to as much as three or four letters at a single delivery. Even a rush like this did not fill up the postmaster's whole month, though, and therefore he "kept store" in the intervals.

The Squire was contemplating the morning. It was balmy and tranquil, the vagrant breezes were laden with the odor of flowers, the murmur of bees was in the air, there was everywhere that suggestion of repose that summer woodlands bring to the senses, and the vague, pleasurable melancholy that such a time and such surroundings inspire.

Presently the United States mail arrived, on horseback. There was but one letter, and it was for the postmaster. The long-legged youth who carried the mail tarried an hour to talk, for there was no hurry; and in a little while the male population of the village had assembled to help. As a general thing, they were dressed in homespun "jeans," blue or yellow — there were no other varieties of it; all wore one suspender and sometimes two — yarn ones knitted at home, — some wore vests, but few wore coats. Such coats and vests as did appear, however, were rather picturesque than otherwise, for they were made of tolerably fanciful patterns of *calico* — a fashion which prevails there to this day among those of the community who have tastes above the common level and are able to afford style. Every individual arrived with his hands in his pockets; a hand came out occasionally for a purpose, but it always went back again after service; and if it was the head that was served, just the cant that the dilapidated straw hat got by being uplifted and rooted under, was retained until the next call altered the inclination; many hats were present, but none were erect and no two were canted just alike. We are speaking impartially of men, youths and boys. And we are also speaking of these three estates when we say that every individual was either chewing natural leaf tobacco prepared on his own premises, or smoking the same in a corn-cob pipe. Few of the men wore whiskers; none wore moustaches; some had a thick jungle of hair under the chin and hiding the throat — the only pattern recognized there as being the correct thing in whiskers; but no part of any individual's face had seen a razor for a week.

These neighbors stood a few moments looking at the mail carrier reflectively while he talked; but fatigue soon began to show itself, and one after another they climbed up and occupied the top rail of the fence, hump-shouldered and grave, like a company of buzzards assembled for supper and listening for the death-rattle. Old Damrell said:

"Tha hain't no news 'bout the jedge, hit ain't likely?"

"Cain't tell for sartin; some thinks he's gwyne to be 'long toreckly, and some thinks 'e hain't. Russ Mosely he tole ole Hanks he mought git to Obeds tomorrer or nex' day he reckoned."

"Well, I wisht I knowed. I got a prime sow and pigs in the cote-house, and I hain't got no place for to put 'em. If the jedge is a gwyne to hold cote, I got to roust 'em out, I reckon. But tomorrer'll do, I 'spect."

The speaker bunched his thick lips together like the stem-end of a tomato and shot a bumble-bee dead that had lit on a weed seven feet away. One after another the several chewers expressed a charge of tobacco juice and delivered it at the deceased with steady aim and faultless accuracy.

"What's a stirrin', down 'bout the Forks?" continued Old Damrell.

"Well, I dunno, skasely. Ole Drake Higgins he's ben down to Shelby las' week. Tuck his crap down; couldn't git shet o' the most uv it; hit warn't no time for to sell, he say, so he fotch it back agin, 'lowin' to wait tell fall. Talks 'bout goin' to Mozouri — lots uv 'ems talkin' that-away down thar, Ole Higgins say. Cain't make a livin' here no mo', sich times as these. Si Higgins he's ben over to Kaintuck n' married a high-toned gal thar, outen the fust families, an' he's come back to the Forks with jist a hell's-mint o' whoop-jamboree notions, folks says. He's tuck an' fixed up the ole house like they does in Kaintuck, he say, an' tha's ben folks come cler from Turpentine for to see it. He's tuck an' gawmed it all over on the inside with plarsterin'."

"What's plarsterin'?"

"I dono. Hit's what he calls it. Ole Mam Higgins, she tole me. She say she warn't gwyne to hang out in no sich a dern hole like a hog. Says it's mud, or sich kind 'o nastness that sticks on n' kivers up everything. Plarsterin', Si calls it."

This marvel was discussed at considerable length; and almost with animation. But presently there was a dog-fight over in the neighborhood of the blacksmith shop, and the visitors slid off their perch like so many turtles and strode to the battle-field with an interest bordering on eagerness. The Squire remained, and read his letter. Then he sighed, and sat long in meditation. At intervals he said:

"Missouri, Missouri. Well, well, well, everything is so uncertain."

At last he said:

"I believe I'll do it. — A man will just rot, here. My house, my yard, everything around me, in fact, shows that I am becoming one of these cattle — and I used to be thrifty in other times."

He was not more than thirty-five, but he had a worn look that made him seem older. He left the stile, entered that part of his house which was the store, traded a quart of thick molasses for a coonskin and a cake of beeswax to an old dame in linsey-woolsey, put his letter away, and went into the kitchen. His wife was there, constructing some dried apple pies; a slovenly urchin of ten was dreaming over a rude weather-vane of his own contriving; his small sister, close upon four years of age, was sopping corn-bread in some gravy left in the bottom of a frying-pan and trying hard not to sop over a finger-mark that divided the pan through the middle — for the other side belonged to the brother, whose musings made him forget his stomach for the moment; a negro woman was busy cooking, at a vast fire-place. Shiftlessness and poverty reigned in the place.

"Nancy, I've made up my mind. The world is done with me, and perhaps I ought to be done with it. But no matter — I can wait. I am going to Missouri. I won't stay in this dead country and decay with it. I've had it on my mind some time. I'm going to sell out here for whatever I can get, and buy a wagon and team and put you and the children in it and start."

"Anywhere that suits you, suits me, Si. And the children can't be any worse off in Missouri than they are here, I reckon."

Motioning his wife to a private conference in their own room, Hawkins said: "No, they'll be better off. I've looked out for *them,* Nancy," and his face lighted. "Do you see these papers? Well, they are evidence that I have taken up Seventy-five Thousand Acres of Land in this county — think what an enormous fortune it will be some day! Why, Nancy, enormous don't express it — the word's too tame! I tell you, Nancy ——"

"For goodness sake, Si ——"

"Wait, Nancy, wait — let me finish — I've been secretly boiling and fuming with this grand inspiration for weeks, and I *must* talk or I'll burst! I haven't whispered to a soul — not a word — have had my *countenance* under lock and key, for fear it might drop something that would tell even these animals here how to discern the gold mine that's glaring under their noses. Now all that is necessary to hold this land and keep it in the family is to pay the trifling taxes on it yearly — five or ten dollars — the whole tract would not sell for over a third of a cent an acre now, but some day people will be glad to get it for twenty dollars, fifty dollars, a hundred dollars an acre! What should you say to" [here he dropped his voice to a whisper and looked anxiously around to see that there were no eavesdroppers,] "*a thousand dollars an acre!*

"Well, you may open your eyes and stare! But it's so. You and I may not see the day, but *they'll* see it. Mind I tell you, they'll see it. Nancy, you've heard of steamboats, and may be you believed in them — of course you did. You've heard these cattle here scoff at them and call them lies and humbugs, — but they're not lies and humbugs, they're a reality and they're going to be a more wonderful thing some day than they are now. They're going to make a revolution in this world's affairs that will make men dizzy to contemplate. I've been watching — I've been watching while some people slept, and I know what's coming.

"Even you and I will see the day that steamboats will come up that little Turkey river to within twenty miles of this land of ours — and in high water they'll come right *to* it! And this is not all, Nancy — it isn't even half! There's a bigger wonder — the railroad! These worms here have never even heard of it — and when they do they'll not believe in it. But it's another fact. Coaches that fly over the ground twenty miles an hour — heavens and earth, think of that, Nancy! Twenty miles an hour. It makes a man's brain whirl. Some day, when you and I are in our graves, there'll be a railroad stretching hundreds of miles — all the way down from the cities of the Northern States to New Orleans — and it's got to run within thirty miles of this land — may be even touch a corner of it. Well, do you know, they've quit burning wood in some places in the Eastern States? And what do you suppose they burn? Coal!" [He bent over and whispered again:] *"There's whole worlds of it on this land!* You know that black stuff that crops out of the bank of the branch? — well, that's it. You've taken it for rocks; so has every body here; and they've built little dams and such things with it. One man was going to build a chimney out of it. Nancy I expect I turned as white as a sheet! Why, it might have caught fire and told everything. I showed him it was too crumbly. Then he was going to build it of copper ore — splendid yellow forty-per-cent ore! There's fortunes upon fortunes of copper ore on our land! It scared me to death, the idea of this fool starting a smelting furnace in his house without knowing it, and getting his dull eyes opened. And then he was going to build it of *iron* ore! There's mountains of iron ore here, Nancy — whole mountains of it. I wouldn't take any chances. I just stuck by him — I haunted him — I never let him alone till he built it of mud and sticks like all the rest of the chimneys in this dismal country. Pine forests, wheat land, corn land, iron, copper, coal — wait till the railroads come, and the steamboats! *We'll* never see the day, Nancy, — never in the world — never, never, child. We've got to drag along, drag along, and eat crusts in toil and poverty, all hopeless and forlorn — but *they'll* ride in coaches, Nancy! They'll live like the princes of the earth; they'll be courted and worshiped; their names will be known from ocean to ocean! Ah, well-a-day! Will they ever come back here, on the railroad and the steamboat, and say 'This one little spot shall not be touched — this hovel shall be sacred — for here our father and our mother suffered for us, thought for us, laid the foundations of our future as solid as the hills!' "

"You are a great, good, noble soul, Si Hawkins, and I am an honored woman to be the wife of such a man" — and the tears stood in her eyes when she said it. "We *will* go to Missouri. You are out of your place, here, among these groping dumb creatures. We will find a higher place, where you can walk with your own kind, and be understood when you speak — not stared at as if you were talking some foreign tongue. I would go anywhere, anywhere in the wide world with you. I would rather my body should starve and die than your mind should hunger and wither away in this lonely land."

"Spoken like yourself, my child! But we'll not starve, Nancy. Far from it. I have a letter from Eschol Sellers — just came this day. A letter that — I'll read you a line from it!"

He flew out of the room. A shadow blurred the sunlight in Nancy's face — there was uneasiness in it, and disappointment. A procession of disturbing thoughts began to troop through her mind. Saying nothing aloud, she sat with her hands in her lap; now and then she clasped them, then unclasped

them, then tapped the ends of the fingers together; sighed, nodded, smiled —
occasionally paused, shook her head. This pantomime was the elocutionary
expression of an unspoken soliloquy which had something of this shape:

"I was afraid of it — was afraid of it. Trying to make our fortune in
Virginia, Eschol Sellers nearly ruined us — and we had to settle in Kentucky
and start over again. Trying to make our fortune here, he brought us clear
down to the ground, nearly. He's an honest soul, and means the very best in
the world, but I'm afraid, I'm afraid he's too flighty. He has splendid ideas,
and he'll divide his chances with his friends with a free hand, the good
generous soul, but something does seem to always interfere and spoil everything. I never did think he was right well balanced. But I don't blame my
husband, for I do think that when that man gets his head full of a new
notion, he can out-talk a machine. He'll make anybody believe in that notion
that'll listen to him ten minutes — why I do believe he would make a deaf
and dumb man believe in it and get beside himself, if you only set him where
he could see his eyes talk and watch his hands explain. What a head he has
got! When he got up that idea there in Virginia of buying up whole loads
of negroes in Delaware and Virginia and Tennessee, very quiet, having papers
drawn to have them delivered at a place in Alabama and take them and pay
for them, away yonder at a certain time, and then in the meantime get a
law made stopping everybody from selling negroes to the south after a certain
day — it was somehow that way — mercy how the man would have made
money! Negroes would have gone up to four prices. But after he'd spent
money and worked hard, and traveled hard, and had heaps of negroes all
contracted for, and everything going along just right, he couldn't get the laws
passed and down the whole thing tumbled. And there in Kentucky, when he
raked up that old numskull that had been inventing away at a perpetual
motion machine for twenty-two years, and Eschol Sellers saw at a glance
where just one more little cog-wheel would settle the business, why I could
see it as plain as day when he came in wild at midnight and hammered us
out of bed and told the whole thing in a whisper with the doors bolted and
the candle in an empty barrel. Oceans of money in it — anybody could see
that. But it did cost a deal to buy the old numskull out — and then when
they put the new cog-wheel in they'd overlooked something somewhere and
it wasn't any use — the troublesome thing wouldn't go. That notion he got
up here did look as handy as anything in the world; and how him and Si
did sit up nights working at it with the curtains down and me watching to
see if any neighbors were about. The man did honestly believe there was a
fortune in that black gummy oil that stews out of the bank Si says is coal;
and he refined it himself till it was like water, nearly, and it *did* burn, there's
no two ways about that; and I reckon he'd have been all right in Cincinnati
with his lamp that he got made, that time he got a house full of rich speculators to see him exhibit only in the middle of his speech it let go and almost
blew the heads off the whole crowd. I haven't got over grieving for the money
that cost, yet. I am sorry enough Eschol Sellers is in Missouri, now, but I
was glad when he went. I wonder what his letter says. But of course it's
cheerful; *he's* never down-hearted — never had any trouble in his life — didn't
know it if he had. It's always sunrise with that man, and fine and blazing,

at that — never gets noon, though — leaves off and rises again. Nobody can help liking the creature, he means so well — but I do dread to come across him again; he's bound to set us all crazy, of course. Well, there goes old widow Hopkins — it always takes her a week to buy a spool of thread and trade a hank of yarn. Maybe Si can come with the letter, now."

And he did:

"Widow Hopkins kept me — I haven't any patience with such tedious people. Now listen, Nancy — just listen at this:

'Come right along to Missouri! Don't wait and worry about a good price but sell out for whatever you can get, and come along, or you might be too late. Throw away your traps, if necessary, and come empty-handed. You'll never regret it. It's the grandest country — the loveliest land — the purest atmosphere — I can't describe it; no pen can do it justice. And it's filling up, every day — people coming from everywhere. I've got the biggest scheme on earth — and I'll take you in; I'll take in every friend I've got that's ever stood by me, for there's enough for all, and to spare. Mum's the word — don't whisper — keep yourself to yourself. You'll see! Come! — rush! — hurry! — don't wait for anything!'

"It's the same old boy, Nancy, just the same old boy — ain't he?"

"Yes, I think there's a little of the old sound about his voice yet. I suppose you — you'll still go, Si?"

"Go! Well, I should think so, Nancy. It's all a chance, of course, and chances haven't been kind to us, I'll admit — but whatever comes, old wife, *they're* provided for. Thank God for that!"

"Amen," came low and earnestly.

And with an activity and a suddenness that bewildered Obedstown and almost took its breath away, the Hawkinses hurried through with their arrangements in four short months and flitted out into the great mysterious blank that lay beyond the Knobs of Tennessee.

[1873]

How I Served My Apprenticeship   ANDREW CARNEGIE

Andrew Carnegie (1835–1919) was born in Scotland and grew up in extreme poverty. As a young immigrant to America, he started at the bottom — as a worker in a cotton mill — but by the age of thirty-three he had an income of fifty thousand a year. His later success in the American steel industry became legendary, as did his preoccupation with distributing the wealth it brought him. In 1889 he caused a great stir with an article titled "The Gospel of Wealth," which developed the idea that a rich man "died disgraced" if he left behind him great sums of money: he should have distributed his wealth for the public good. *Argent oblige.* Rightly conceived, the millionaire was a "trustee" who held his wealth for the benefit of all. Carnegie's own public benefactions amounted to over a third of a billion dollars.

"How I Served My Apprenticeship" focuses on the beginning of Carnegie's spectacularly prosperous career. His simply but forcefully written story exhibits prevalent nineteenth-century attitudes concerning the relation of work, wealth, and well-being. Characteristic of the time also is the strongly affirmative tone of the piece. Still, Carnegie's attitude toward money-making is quite different from that of Squire Hawkins.

". . . I cannot tell you how proud I was. . . ."

It is a great pleasure to tell how I served my apprenticeship as a business man. But there seems to be a question preceding this: Why did I become a business man? I am sure that I should never have selected a business career if I had been permitted to choose.

The eldest son of parents who were themselves poor, I had, fortunately, to begin to perform some useful work in the world while still very young in order to earn an honest livelihood, and was thus shown even in early boyhood that my duty was to assist my parents and, like them, become, as soon as possible, a breadwinner in the family. What I could get to do, not what I desired, was the question.

When I was born my father was a well-to-do master weaver in Dunfermline, Scotland. He owned no less than four damask-looms and employed apprentices. This was before the days of steam-factories for the manufacture of linen. A few large merchants took orders, and employed master weavers, such as my father, to weave the cloth, the mechants supplying the materials.

As the factory system developed hand-loom weaving naturally declined, and my father was one of the sufferers by the change. The first serious lesson of my life came to me one day when he had taken in the last of his work to the merchant, and returned to our little home greatly distressed because there was no more work for him to do. I was then just about ten years of age, but the lesson burned into my heart, and I resolved then that the wolf of poverty should be driven from our door some day, if I could do it.

The question of selling the old looms and starting for the United States came up in the family council, and I heard it discussed from day to day. It was finally resolved to take the plunge and join relatives already in Pittsburg. I well remember that neither father nor mother thought the change would be otherwise than a great sacrifice for them, but that "it would be better for the two boys."

In after life, if you can look back as I do and wonder at the complete surrender of their own desires which parents make for the good of their children, you must reverence their memories with feelings akin to worship.

On arriving in Allegheny City (there were four of us: father, mother, my younger brother, and myself), my father entered a cotton factory. I soon followed, and served as a "bobbin-boy," and this is how I began my preparation for subsequent apprenticeship as a business man. I received one dollar and twenty cents a week, and was then just about twelve years old.

I cannot tell you how proud I was when I received my first week's own earnings. One dollar and twenty cents made by myself and given to me because I had been of some use in the world! No longer entirely dependent upon my parents, but at last admitted to the family partnership as a contributing member and able to help them! I think this makes a man out of a boy sooner than almost anything else, and a real man, too, if there be any germ of true manhood in him. It is everything to feel that you are useful.

I have had to deal with great sums. Many millions of dollars have since passed through my hands. But the genuine satisfaction I had from that one dollar and twenty cents outweighs any subsequent pleasure in money-getting. It was the direct reward of honest, manual labor; it represented a week of very hard work — so hard that, but for the aim and end which sanctified it, slavery might not be much too strong a term to describe it.

For a lad of twelve to rise and breakfast every morning, except the blessed Sunday morning, and go into the streets and find his way to the factory and begin to work while it was still dark outside, and not be released until after darkness came again in the evening, forty minutes' interval only being allowed at noon, was a terrible task.

But I was young and had my dreams, and something within always told me that this would not, could not, should not last — I should some day get into a better position. Besides this, I felt myself no longer a mere boy, but quite a little man, and this made me happy.

A change soon came, for a kind old Scotsman, who knew some of our relatives, made bobbins, and took me into his factory before I was thirteen. But here for a time it was even worse than in the cotton factory, because I was set to fire a boiler in the cellar, and actually to run the small steam-engine which drove the machinery. The firing of the boiler was all right, for fortunately we did not use coal, but the refuse wooden chips; and I always liked to work in wood. But the responsibility of keeping the water right and of running the engine, and the danger of my making a mistake and blowing the whole factory to pieces, caused too great a strain, and I often awoke and found myself sitting up in bed through the night, trying the steam-gages. But I never told them at home that I was having a hard tussle. No, no! everything must be bright to them.

This was a point of honor, for every member of the family was working hard, except, of course, my little brother, who was then a child, and we were telling each other only all the bright things. Besides this, no man would whine and give up — he would die first.

There was no servant in our family, and several dollars per week were earned by my mother by binding shoes after her daily work was done! Father was also hard at work in the factory. And could I complain?

My kind employer, John Hay — peace to his ashes! — soon relieved me of the undue strain, for he needed some one to make out bills and keep his accounts, and finding that I could write a plain schoolboy hand and could "cipher," he made me his only clerk. But still I had to work hard upstairs in the factory, for the clerking took but little time.

You know how people moan about poverty as being a great evil, and it seems to be accepted that if people had only plenty of money and were rich, they would be happy and more useful, and get more out of life.

As a rule, there is more genuine satisfaction, a truer life, and more obtained from life in the humble cottages of the poor than in the palaces of the rich. I always pity the sons and daughters of rich men, who are attended by servants, and have governesses at a later age, but am glad to remember that they do not know what they have missed.

They have kind fathers and mothers, too, and think that they enjoy the sweetness of these blessings to the fullest: but this they cannot do; for the poor boy who has in his father his constant companion, tutor, and model, and in his mother — holy name! — his nurse, teacher, guardian angel, saint, all in one, has a richer, more precious fortune in life than any rich man's son who is not so favored can possibly know, and compared with which all other fortunes count for little.

It is because I know how sweet and happy and pure the home of honest poverty is, how free from perplexing care, from social envies and emulations, how loving and how united its members may be in the common interest of supporting the family, that I sympathize with the rich man's boy and congratulate the poor man's boy; and it is for these reasons that from the ranks of the poor so many strong, eminent, self-reliant men have always sprung and always must spring.

If you will read the list of the immortals who "were not born to die," you will find that most of them have been born to the precious heritage of poverty.

It seems, nowadays, a matter of universal desire that poverty should be abolished. We should be quite willing to abolish luxury, but to abolish honest, industrious, self-denying poverty would be to destroy the soil upon which mankind produces the virtues which enable our race to reach a still higher civilization than it now possesses.

I come now to the third step in my apprenticeship, for I had already taken two, as you see — the cotton factory and then the bobbin factory; and with the third — the third time is the chance, you know — deliverance came. I obtained a situation as messenger boy in the telegraph office of Pittsburg when I was fourteen. Here I entered a new world.

Amid books, newspapers, pencils, pens and ink and writing-pads, and a clean office, bright windows, and literary atmosphere, I was the happiest boy alive.

My only dread was that I should some day be dismissed because I did not know the city; for it is necessary that a messenger boy should know all the firms and addresses of men who are in the habit of receiving telegrams. But I was a stranger in Pittsburg. However, I made up my mind that I would learn to repeat successively each business house in the principal streets, and was soon able to shut my eyes and begin at one side of Wood Street, and call every firm successively to the top, then pass to the other side and call every firm to the bottom. Before long I was able to do this with the business streets generally. My mind was then at rest upon that point.

Of course every ambitious messenger boy wants to become an operator, and before the operators arrive in the early mornings the boys slipped up to the instruments and practised. This I did, and was soon able to talk to the boys in the other offices along the line, who were also practising.

One morning I heard Philadelphia calling Pittsburg, and giving the signal, "death message." Great attention was then paid to "death messages," and I thought I ought to try to take this one. I answered and did so, and went off and delivered it before the operator came. After that the operators sometimes used to ask me to work for them.

Having a sensitive ear for sound, I soon learned to take messages by the ear, which was then very uncommon — I think only two persons in the United States could then do it. Now every operator takes by ear, so easy is it to follow and do what any other boy can — if you only have to. This brought me into notice, and finally I became an operator, and received the, to me, enormous recompense of twenty-five dollars per month — three hundred dollars a year!

This was a fortune — the very sum that I had fixed when I was a factory-worker as the fortune I wished to possess, because the family could live on three hundred dollars a year and be almost or quite independent. Here it was at last! But I was soon to be in receipt of extra compensation for extra work.

The six newspapers of Pittsburg received telegraphic news in common. Six copies of each despatch were made by a gentleman who received six dollars per week for the work, and he offered me a gold dollar every week if I would do it, of which I was very glad indeed, because I always liked to work with news and scribble for newspapers.

The reporters came to a room every evening for the news which I had prepared, and this brought me into most pleasant intercourse with these clever fellows, and besides, I got a dollar a week as pocket-money, for this was not considered family revenue by me.

I think this last step of doing something beyond one's task is fully entitled to be considered "business." The other revenue, you see, was just salary obtained for regular work; but here was a little business operation upon my own account, and I was very proud indeed of my gold dollar every week.

The Pennsylvania Railroad shortly after this was completed to Pittsburg, and that genius, Thomas A. Scott, was its superintendent. He often came to the telegraph office to talk to his chief, the general superintendent, at Altoona, and I became known to him in this way.

When that great railway system put up a wire of its own, he asked me to be his clerk and operator; so I left the telegraph office — in which there is great danger that a young man may be permanently buried, as it were — and became connected with the railways.

The new appointment was accompanied by what was, to me, a tremendous increase of salary. It jumped from twenty-five to thirty-five dollars per month. Mr. Scott was then receiving one hundred and twenty-five dollars per month, and I used to wonder what on earth he could do with so much money.

I remained for thirteen years in the service of the Pennsylvania Railroad Company, and was at last superintendent of the Pittsburg division of the road, successor to Mr. Scott, who had in the meantime risen to the office of vice-president of the company.

One day Mr. Scott, who was the kindest of men, and had taken a great fancy to me, asked if I had or could find five hundred dollars to invest.

Here the business instinct came into play. I felt that as the door was opened for a business investment with my chief, it would be wilful flying in the face of providence if I did not jump at it; so I answered promptly:

"Yes, sir; I think I can."

"Very well," he said, "get it; a man has just died who owns ten shares in the Adams Express Company which I want you to buy. It will cost you fifty dollars per share, and I can help you with a little balance if you cannot raise it all."

Here was a queer position. The available assets of the whole family were not five hundred dollars. But there was one member of the family whose ability, pluck, and resource never failed us, and I felt sure the money could be raised somehow or other by my mother.

Indeed, had Mr. Scott known our position he would have advanced it himself; but the last thing in the world the proud Scot will do is to reveal his poverty and rely upon others. The family had managed by this time to purchase a small house and pay for it in order to save rent. My recollection is that it was worth eight hundred dollars.

The matter was laid before the council of three that night, and the oracle spoke: "Must be done. Mortgage our house. I will take the steamer in the morning for Ohio, and see uncle, and ask him to arrange it. I am sure he can." This was done. Of course her visit was successful — where did she ever fail?

The money was procured, paid over; ten shares of Adams Express Company stock was mine; but no one knew our little home had been mortgaged "to give our boy a start."

Adams Express stock then paid monthly dividends of one per cent, and the first check for five dollars arrived. I can see it now, and I well remember the signature of "J. C. Babcock, Cashier," who wrote a big "John Hancock" hand.

The next day being Sunday, we boys — myself and my ever-constant companions — took our usual Sunday afternoon stroll in the country, and sitting down in the woods, I showed them this check, saying, "Eureka! We have found it."

Here was something new to all of us, for none of us had ever received anything but from toil. A return from capital was something strange and new.

How money could make money, how, without any attention from me, this mysterious golden visitor should come, led to much speculation upon the part of the young fellows, and I was for the first time hailed as a "capitalist."

You see, I was beginning to serve my apprenticeship as a business man in a satisfactory manner.

A very important incident in my life occurred when, one day in a train, a nice, farmer-looking gentleman approached me, saying that the conductor had told him I was connected with the Pennsylvania Railroad, and he would like to show me something. He pulled from a small green bag the model of the first sleeping-car. This was Mr. Woodruff, the inventor.

Its value struck me like a flash. I asked him to come to Altoona the following week, and he did so. Mr. Scott, with his usual quickness, grasped the idea. A contract was made with Mr. Woodruff to put two trial cars on the Pennsylvania Railroad. Before leaving Altoona, Mr. Woodruff came and offered me an interest in the venture, which I promptly accepted. But how I was to make my payments rather troubled me, for the cars were to be paid for in monthly installments after delivery, and my first monthly payment was to be two hundred and seventeen dollars and a half.

I had not the money, and I did not see any way of getting it. But I finally decided to visit the local banker and ask him for a loan, pledging myself to repay at the rate of fifteen dollars per month. He promptly granted it. Never shall I forget his putting his arm over my shoulder, saying, "Oh, yes, Andy; you are all right!"

I then and there signed my first note. Proud day this; and surely now no one will dispute that I was becoming a "business man." I had signed my first note, and, most important of all — for any fellow can sign a note — I had found a banker willing to take it as "good."

My subsequent payments were made by the receipts from the sleeping-cars, and I really made my first considerable sum from this investment in the Woodruff Sleeping-car Company, which was afterward absorbed by Mr. Pullman — a remarkable man whose name is now known over all the world.

Shortly after this I was appointed superintendent of the Pittsburg division, and returned to my dear old home, smoky Pittsburg. Wooden bridges were then used exclusively upon the railways, and the Pennsylvania Railroad was experimenting with a bridge built of cast-iron. I saw that wooden bridges would not do for the future, and organized a company in Pittsburg to build iron bridges.

Here again I had recourse to the bank, because my share of the capital was twelve hundred and fifty dollars, and I had not the money; but the bank lent it to me, and we began the Keystone Bridge Works, which proved a great success. This company built the first great bridge over the Ohio River, three hundred feet span, and has built many of the most important structures since.

This was my beginning in manufacturing; and from that start all our other works have grown, the profits of one building the other. My "apprenticeship" as a business man soon ended, for I resigned my position as an officer of the Pennsylvania Railroad Company to give exclusive attention to business.

I was no longer merely an official working for others upon a salary, but a full-fledged business man working upon my own account.

I never was quite reconciled to working for other people. At the most, the railway officer has to look forward to the enjoyment of a stated salary, and he has a great many people to please; even if he gets to be president, he has sometimes a board of directors who cannot know what is best to be done; and even if this board be satisfied, he has a board of stockholders to criticise him, and as the property is not his own he cannot manage it as he pleases.

I always liked the idea of being my own master, of manufacturing something and giving employment to many men. There is only one thing to think of manufacturing if you are a Pittsburger, for Pittsburg even then had asserted her supremacy as the "Iron City," the leading iron-and-steel-manufacturing city in America.

So my indispensable and clever partners, who had been my boy companions, I am delighted to say — some of the very boys who had met in the grove to wonder at the five-dollar check — began business, and still continue extending it to meet the ever-growing and ever-changing wants of our most progressive country, year after year.

Always we are hoping that we need expand no farther; yet ever we are finding that to stop expanding would be to fall behind; and even to-day the successive improvements and inventions follow each other so rapidly that we see just as much yet to be done as ever.

When the manufacturer of steel ceases to grow he begins to decay, so we must keep on extending. The result of all these developments is that three pounds of finished steel are now bought in Pittsburg for two cents, which is cheaper than anywhere else on the earth, and that our country has become the greatest producer of iron in the world.

And so ends the story of my apprenticeship and graduation as a business man.

[1900]

The Reign of the Bitch-Goddess

My Business Apprenticeship   JACK LONDON

When Jack London (1876–1916) committed suicide at forty he was world famous and earning as much as seventy-five thousand a year from his pen. His climb had been rapid, but life had never been easy. As the illegitimate son of an itinerant astrologer, he early knew the roughness of the workaday world and its monotony. The roughness he did not so much mind; the monotony he escaped through such romantic ventures as a sealing voyage to Japan and a gold-hunting expedition to Alaska. In the following selection from *John Barleycorn* (1913) we see him as a young man determined to make his mark in the best American tradition — that is, by pluck and luck. He has taken a job in the jute mills for a dollar a day with the understanding that he will soon get an increase.

Although London's account of his early effort to mount the ladder of success is clear and direct, an ironic tone may be discerned throughout. The irony is increased if London's apprenticeship is compared with Carnegie's. Both men view their early efforts from the vantage point of later years and thus reveal their attitude toward their younger selves. London was guilty of a good deal of hack work, but at his best he tells a convincing story and his energetic style makes for easy reading.

> "... Any boy ... could, by thrift, energy, and sobriety,
> learn the business and rise. ..."

The jute mills failed of its agreement to increase my pay to a dollar and a quarter a day, and I, a free-born American boy whose direct ancestors had fought in all the wars from the old pre-Revolutionary Indian wars down, exercised my sovereign right of free contract by quitting the job.

I was still resolved to settle down, and I looked about me. One thing was clear. Unskilled labor didn't pay. I must learn a trade, and I decided on electricity. The need for electricians was constantly growing. But how to become an electrician? I hadn't the money to go to a technical school or university; besides, I didn't think much of schools. I was a practical man in a practical world. Also, I still believed in the old myths which were the heritage of the American boy when I was a boy.

A canal boy could become a president. Any boy, who took employment with any firm, could, by thrift, energy, and sobriety, learn the business and rise from position to position until he was taken in as a junior partner. After that the senior partnership was only a matter of time. Very often — so ran the myth — the boy, by reason of his steadiness and application, married his employer's daughter. By this time I had been encouraged to such faith in myself in the matter of girls that I was quite certain I would marry my employer's daughter. There wasn't a doubt of it. All the little boys in the myths did it as soon as they were old enough.

So I bade farewell forever to the adventure-path, and went out to the power-plant of one of our Oakland street-railways. I saw the superintendent himself, in a private office so fine that it almost stunned me. But I talked straight up. I told him I wanted to become a practical electrician, that I was unafraid of work, that I was used to hard work, and that all he had to do was look at me to see I was fit and strong. I told him that I wanted to begin right at the bottom and work up, that I wanted to devote my life to this one occupation and this one employment.

The superintendent beamed as he listened. He told me that I was the right stuff for success, and that he believed in encouraging American youth that wanted to rise. Why, employers were always on the lookout for young fellows like me, and alas, they found them all too rarely. My ambition was fine and worthy, and he would see to it that I got my chance. (And as I listened with swelling heart, I wondered if it was his daughter I was to marry.)

"Before you can go out on the road and learn the more complicated and higher details of the profession," he said, "you will, of course, have to work in the car house with the men who install and repair the motors. (By this time I was sure that it was his daughter, and I was wondering how much stock he might own in the company.)

"But," he said, "as you yourself so plainly see, you couldn't expect to begin as a helper to the car house electricians. That will come when you have worked up to it. You will really begin at the bottom. In the car house your first employment will be sweeping up, washing the windows, keeping things clean. And after you have shown yourself satisfactory at that, then you may become a helper to the car house electricians."

I didn't see how sweeping and scrubbing a building was any preparation for the trade of electrician; but I did know that in the books all the boys started with the most menial tasks and by making good ultimately won to the ownership of the whole concern.

"When shall I come to work?" I asked, eager to launch on this dazzling career.

"But," said the superintendent, "as you and I have already agreed, you must begin at the bottom. Not immediately can you in any capacity enter the car house. Before that you must pass through the engine room as an oiler."

My heart went down slightly and for the moment, as I saw the road lengthen between his daughter and me; then it rose again. I would be a better electrician with knowledge of steam engines. As an oiler in the great engine room I was confident that few things concerning steam would escape me. Heavens! My career shone more dazzling than ever.

"When shall I come to work?" I asked gratefully.

"But," said the superintendent, "you could not expect to enter immediately into the engine room. There must be preparation for that. And through the fire room, of course. Come, you see the matter clearly, I know. And you will see that even the mere handling of coal is a scientific matter and not to be sneezed at. Do you know that we weigh every pound of coal we burn? Thus, we learn the value of the coal we buy; we know to a tee the last penny of cost of every item of production, and we learn which firemen are the most wasteful, which firemen, out of stupidity or carelessness, get the least out of the coal they fire." The superintendent beamed again. "You see how very important the little matter of coal is, and by as much as you learn of this little matter you will become that much better a workman — more valuable to us, more valuable to yourself. Now, are you prepared to begin?"

"Any time," I said valiantly. "The sooner the better."

"Very well," he answered. "You will come to-morrow morning at seven o'clock."

I was taken out and shown my duties. Also, I was told the terms of my employment — a ten-hour day, every day in the month including Sundays and holidays, with one day off each month, with a salary of thirty dollars a month. It wasn't exciting. Years before, at the cannery, I had earned a dollar a day for a ten-hour day. I consoled myself with the thought that the reason my earning capacity had not increased with my years and strength was because I had remained an unskilled laborer. But it was different now. I was beginning to work for skill, for a trade, for career and fortune and the superintendent's daughter.

And I was beginning in the right way — right at the beginning. That was the thing. I was passing coal to the firemen, who shoveled it into the furnaces where its energy was transformed into steam, which, in the engine room, was transformed into the electricity with which the electricians worked. This passing of coal was surely the very beginning . . . unless the superintendent should take it into his head to send me to work in the mines from which the coal came in order to get a completer understanding of the genesis of electricity for street railways.

Work! I, who had worked with men, found that I didn't know the first thing about real work. A ten-hour day! I had to pass coal for the day and night shifts, and, despite working through the noon-hour, I never finished my task before eight at night. I was working a twelve- to thirteen-hour day, and I wasn't being paid overtime as in the cannery.

I might as well give the secret away right here. I was doing the work of two men. Before me, one mature able-bodied laborer had done the day shift and another equally mature able-bodied laborer had done the night shift. They had received forty dollars a month each. The superintendent, bent on an economical administration, had persuaded me to do the work of both men for thirty dollars a month. I thought he was making an electrician of me. In truth and fact, he was saving fifty dollars a month operating expenses to the company.

But I didn't know I was displacing two men. Nobody told me. On the contrary, the superintendent warned everybody not to tell me. How valiantly I went at it that first day. I worked at top speed, filling the iron wheelbarrow with coal, running it on the scales and weighing the load, then trundling it into the fire room and dumping it on the plates before the fires.

Work! I did more than the two men whom I had displaced. They had merely wheeled in the coal and dumped it on the plates. But while I did this for the day coal, the night coal I had to pile against the wall of the fire room. Now the fire room was small. It had been planned for a night coal-passer. So I had to pile the night coal higher and higher, buttressing up the heap with stout planks. Toward the top of the heap I had to handle the coal a second time, tossing it up with a shovel.

I dripped with sweat, but I never ceased from my stride, though I could feel exhaustion coming on. By ten o'clock in the morning, so much of my body's energy had I consumed, I felt hungry and snatched a thick double-slice of bread and butter from my dinner pail. This I devoured, standing, grimed with coal dust, my knees trembling under me. By eleven o'clock, in this fashion, I had consumed my whole lunch. But what of it? I realized that it would enable me to continue working through the noon hour. And I worked all afternoon. Darkness came on, and I worked under the electric lights. The day fireman went off and the night fireman came on. I plugged away.

At half-past eight, famished, tottering, I washed up, changed my clothes, and dragged my weary body to the car. It was three miles to where I lived, and I had received a pass with the stipulation that I could sit down as long as there were no paying passengers in need of a seat. As I sank into a corner outside seat I prayed that no passenger might require my seat. But the car filled up, and, half way in, a woman came on board, and there was no seat for her. I started to get up, and to my astonishment found that I could not. With the chill wind blowing on me, my spent body had stiffened into the seat. It took me the rest of the run in to unkink my complaining joints and muscles and get into a standing position on the lower step. And when the car stopped at my corner I nearly fell to the ground when I stepped off.

I hobbled two blocks to the house and limped into the kitchen. While my mother started to cook I plunged into bread and butter; but before my appetite was appeased, or the steak fried, I was sound asleep. In vain my mother strove to shake me awake enough to eat the meat. Failing in this, with the assistance of my father she managed to get me to my room, where I collapsed dead asleep on the bed. They undressed me and covered me up. In the morning came the agony of being awakened. I was terribly sore, and worst of all my wrists were swelling. But I made up for my lost supper, eating an enormous breakfast, and when I hobbled to catch my car I carried a lunch twice as big as the one the day before.

Work! Let any youth just turned eighteen try to out-shovel two man-grown coal-shovelers. Work! Long before midday I had eaten the last scrap of my huge lunch. But I was resolved to show them what a husky young fellow determined to rise could do. The worst of it was that my wrists were swelling and going back on me. There are few who do not know the pain of walking on a sprained ankle. Then imagine the pain of shoveling coal and trundling a loaded wheelbarrow with two sprained wrists.

Work! More than once I sank down on the coal where no one could see me, and cried with rage, and mortification, and exhaustion, and despair. That second day was my hardest, and all that enabled me to survive it and get in the last of the night coal at the end of thirteen hours was the day fireman, who bound both my wrists with broad leather straps. So tightly were they buckled that they were like slightly flexible plaster casts. They took the stresses and pressures which thitherto had been borne by my wrists, and they were so tight that there was no room for the inflammation to rise in the sprains.

And in this fashion I continued to learn to be an electrician. Night after night I limped home, fell asleep before I could eat my supper, and was helped into bed and undressed. Morning after morning, always with huger lunches in my dinner pail, I limped out of the house on my way to work.

I no longer read my library books. I made no dates with the girls. I was a proper work-beast. I worked, and ate, and slept, while my mind slept all the time. The whole thing was a nightmare. I worked every day, including Sunday, and I looked far ahead to my one day off at the end of a month, resolved to lie abed all that day and just sleep and rest up. . . .

I had often noticed the day fireman staring at me in a curious way. At last, one day, he spoke. He began by swearing me to secrecy. He had been warned by the superintendent not to tell me, and in telling me he was risking his job. He told me of the day coal-passer and the night coal-passer, and of the wages they had received. I was doing for thirty dollars a month what they had received eighty dollars for doing. He would have told me sooner, the fireman said, had he not been so certain that I would break down under the work and quit. As it was, I was killing myself, and all to no good purpose. I was merely cheapening the price of labor, he argued, and keeping two men out of a job.

Being an American boy, and a proud American boy, I did not immediately quit. This was foolish of me, I know; but I resolved to continue the work long enough to prove to the superintendent that I could do it without breaking down. Then I would quit, and he would realize what a fine young fellow he had lost.

All of which I faithfully and foolishly did. I worked on until the time came when I got in the last of the night coal by six o'clock. Then I quit the job of learning electricity by doing more than two men's work for a boy's wages, went home, and proceeded to sleep the clock around.

Fortunately, I had not stayed by the job long enough to injure myself — though I was compelled to wear straps on my wrists for a year afterward. But the effect of this work orgy in which I had indulged was to sicken me with work. I just wouldn't work. The thought of work was repulsive. I didn't care if I never settled down. Learning a trade could go hang. It was a whole lot better to royster and frolic over the world in the way I had previously done. So I headed out on the adventure-path again, starting to tramp East by beating my way on the railroads.

[1913]

Power Superpower   JOHN DOS PASSOS

"Power Superpower" is taken from *The Big Money* (1936), third volume
of a trilogy by John Dos Passos (1896–   ) called *U. S. A.* In these
volumes he intersperses his narrative with such things as "newsreels"
(headlines of the day, popular songs, advertisements), "the Camera Eye"
(stream-of-consciousness passages giving the author's point of view), and
short biographies of Americans, of which the present one about Samuel
Insull is a good example. For further notes on Dos Passos, see p. 310 and
p. 443.

Jack London and John Dos Passos are both writing about the power
industry, but with radically different styles and from different approaches.
Both are rich in irony, however, and they share a critical point of view.
Dos Passos' style has been praised for its vitality and "American tempo"
as well as criticized for its "restless dissatisfaction with conventional rules."

". . . *Electric power turned the ladder into an elevator. . . .*"

In eighteen-eighty when Thomas Edison's agent was hooking up the first telephone in London, he put an ad in the paper for a secretary and stenographer.
The eager young cockney with sprouting muttonchop whiskers who answered
it

had recently lost his job as officeboy. In his spare time he had been learning shorthand and bookkeeping and taking dictation from the editor of the
English *Vanity Fair* at night and jotting down the speeches in Parliament for
the papers. He came of temperance smallshopkeeper stock; already he was
butting his bullethead against the harsh structure of caste that doomed boys
of his class to a life of alpaca jackets, penmanship, subordination. To get a
job with an American firm was to put a foot on the rung of a ladder that led
up into the blue.

He did his best to make himself indispensable; they let him operate the
switchboard for the first halfhour when the telephone service was opened.
Edison noticed his weekly reports on the electrical situation in England
and sent for him to be his personal secretary.

Samuel Insull landed in America on a raw March day in eightyone.
Immediately he was taken out to Menlo Park, shown about the little group
of laboratories, saw the strings of electriclightbulbs shining at intervals across
the snowy lots, all lit from the world's first central electric station. Edison put
him right to work and he wasn't through till midnight. Next morning at six
he was on the job; Edison had no use for any nonsense about hours or vacations. Insull worked from that time on until he was seventy without a break;
no nonsense about hours or vacations. Electric power turned the ladder into
an elevator.

Young Insull made himself indispensable to Edison and took more and more charge of Edison's business deals. He was tireless, ruthless, reliable as the tides, Edison used to say, and fiercely determined to rise.

In ninetytwo he induced Edison to send him to Chicago and put him in as president of the Chicago Edison Company. Now he was on his own. *My engineering,* he said once in a speech, when he was sufficiently czar of Chicago to allow himself the luxury of plain speaking, *has been largely concerned with engineering all I could out of the dollar.*

He was a stiffly arrogant redfaced man with a closecropped mustache; he lived on Lake Shore Drive and was at the office at 7:10 every morning. It took him fifteen years to merge the five electrical companies into the Commonwealth Edison Company. *Very early I discovered that the first essential, as in other public utility business, was that it should be operated as a monopoly.*

When his power was firm in electricity he captured gas, spread out into the surrounding townships in northern Illinois. When politicians got in his way, he bought them, when labor-leaders got in his way he bought them. Incredibly his power grew. He was scornful of bankers, lawyers were his hired men. He put his own lawyer in as corporation counsel and through him ran Chicago. When he found to his amazement that there were men (even a couple of young lawyers, Richberg and Ickes) in Chicago that he couldn't buy, he decided he'd better put on a show for the public;

Big Bill Thompson, the Builder:
punch King George in the nose,
the hunt for the treeclimbing fish,
the Chicago Opera.

It was too easy; the public had money, there was one of them born every minute, with the founding of Middle West Utilities in nineteen twelve Insull began to use the public's money to spread his empire. His companies began to have open stockholders' meetings, to ballyhoo service, the small investor could sit there all day hearing the bigwigs talk. It's fun to be fooled. Companyunions hypnotized his employees; everybody had to buy stock in his companies, employees had to go out and sell stock, officeboys, linemen, trolley-conductors. Even Owen D. Young was afraid of him. *My experience is that the greatest aid in the efficiency of labor is a long line of men waiting at the gate.*

War shut up the progressives (no more nonsense about trustbusting, controlling monopoly, the public good) and raised Samuel Insull to the peak.

He was head of the Illinois State Council of Defense. *Now,* he said delightedly, *I can do anything I like.* With it came the perpetual spotlight, the purple taste of empire. If anybody didn't like what Samuel Insull did he was a traitor. Chicago damn well kept its mouth shut.

The Insull companies spread and merged put competitors out of business until Samuel Insull and his stooge brother Martin controlled through the leverage of holdingcompanies and directorates and blocks of minority stock
light and power, coalmines and tractioncompanies

in Illinois, Michigan, the Dakotas, Nebraska, Arkansas, Oklahoma, Missouri, Maine, Kansas, Wisconsin, Virginia, Ohio, North Carolina, Indiana, New York, New Jersey, Texas, in Canada, in Louisiana, in Georgia, in Florida and Alabama.

(It has been figured out that one dollar in Middle West Utilities controlled seventeen hundred and fifty dollars invested by the public in the subsidiary companies that actually did the work of producing electricity. With the delicate lever of a voting trust controlling the stock of the two top holding-companies he controlled a twelfth of the power output of America).

Samuel Insull began to think he owned all that the way a man owns the roll of bills in his back pocket.

Always he'd been scornful of bankers. He owned quite a few in Chicago. But the New York bankers were laying for him; they felt he was a bounder, whispered that this financial structure was unsound. Fingers itched to grasp the lever that so delicately moved this enormous power over lives,

superpower, Insull liked to call it.

A certain Cyrus S. Eaton of Cleveland, an exBaptist-minister, was the David that brought down this Goliath. Whether it was so or not he made Insull believe that Wall Street was behind him.

He started buying stock in the three Chicago utilities. Insull in a panic for fear he'd lose his control went into the market to buy against him. Finally the Reverend Eaton let himself be bought out, shaking down the old man for a profit of twenty million dollars.

The stockmarket crash.

Paper values were slipping. Insull's companies were intertwined in a tangle that no bookkeeper has ever been able to unravel.

The gas hissed out of the torn balloon. Insull threw away his imperial pride and went on his knees to the bankers.

The bankers had him where they wanted him. To save the face of the tottering czar he was made a receiver of his own concerns. But the old man couldn't get out of his head the illusion that the money was all his. When it was discovered that he was using the stockholders' funds to pay off his brothers' brokerage accounts it was too thick even for a federal judge. Insull was forced to resign.

He held directorates in eightyfive companies, he was chairman of sixtyfive, president of eleven: it took him three hours to sign his resignations.

As a reward for his services to monopoly his companies chipped in on a pension of eighteen thousand a year. But the public was shouting for criminal prosecution. When the handouts stopped newspapers and politicians turned on him. Revolt against the moneymanipulators was in the air. Samuel Insull got the wind up and ran off to Canada with his wife.

Extradition proceedings. He fled to Paris. When the authorities began to close in on him there he slipped away to Italy, took a plane to Tirana, another to Salonika and then the train to Athens. There the old fox went to earth. Money talked as sweetly in Athens as it had in Chicago in the old days.

The American ambassador tried to extradite him. Insull hired a chorus of Hellenic lawyers and politicos and sat drinking coffee in the lobby of the

Grande Bretagne, while they proceeded to tie up the ambassador in a snarl of chicanery as complicated as the bookkeeping of his holdingcompanies. The successors of Demosthenes were delighted. The ancestral itch in many a Hellenic palm was temporarily assuaged. Samuel Insull settled down cozily in Athens, was stirred by the sight of the Parthenon, watched the goats feeding on the Pentelic slopes, visited the Areopagus, admired marble fragments ascribed to Phidias, talked with the local bankers about reorganizing the public utilities of Greece, was said to be promoting Macedonian lignite. He was the toast of the Athenians; Madame Kouryoumdjouglou, the vivacious wife of a Bagdad date-merchant, devoted herself to his comfort. When the first effort at extradition failed, the old gentleman declared in the courtroom, as he struggled out from the embraces of his four lawyers: *Greece is a small but great country.*

The idyll was interrupted when the Roosevelt Administration began to put the heat on the Greek Foreign Office. Government lawyers in Chicago were accumulating truckloads of evidence and chalking up more and more drastic indictments.

Finally after many a postponement (he had hired physicians as well as lawyers, they cried to high heaven that it would kill him to leave the genial climate of the Attic plain),

he was ordered to leave Greece as an undesirable alien, to the great indignation of Balkan society and of Madame Kouryoumdjouglou.

He hired the *Maiotis* a small and grubby Greek freighter and panicked the foreignnews services by slipping off for an unknown destination.

It was rumored that the new Odysseus was bound for Aden, for the islands of the South Seas, that he'd been invited to Persia. After a few days he turned up rather seasick in the Bosporus on his way, it was said, to Rumania where Madame Kouryoumdjouglou had advised him to put himself under the protection of her friend la Lupescu.

At the request of the American ambassador the Turks were delighted to drag him off the Greek freighter and place him in a not at all comfortable jail. Again money had been mysteriously wafted from England, the healing balm began to flow, lawyers were hired, interpreters expostulated, doctors made diagnoses;

but Angora was boss

and Insull was shipped off to Smyrna to be turned over to the assistant federal districtattorney who had come all that way to arrest him.

The Turks wouldn't even let Madame Kouryoumdjouglou, on her way back from making arrangements in Bucharest, go ashore to speak to him. In a scuffle with the officials on the steamboat the poor lady was pushed overboard

and with difficulty fished out of the Bosporus.

Once he was cornered the old man let himself tamely be taken home on the *Exilona,* started writing his memoirs, made himself agreeable to his fellow passengers, was taken off at Sandy Hook and rushed to Chicago to be arraigned.

In Chicago the government spitefully kept him a couple of nights in jail; men he'd never known, so the newspapers said, stepped forward to go on his twohundredandfiftythousand-dollar bail. He was moved to a hospital that he himself had endowed. Solidarity. The leading businessmen in Chicago were photographed visiting him there. Henry Ford paid a call.

The trial was very beautiful. The prosecution got bogged in finance technicalities. The judge was not unfriendly. The Insulls stole the show.

They were folks, they smiled at reporters, they posed for photographers, they went down to the courtroom by bus. Investors might have been ruined but so, they allowed it to be known, were the Insulls; the captain had gone down with the ship.

Old Samuel Insull rambled amiably on the stand, told his lifestory: from officeboy to powermagnate, his struggle to make good, his love for his home and the kiddies. He didn't deny he'd made mistakes; who hadn't, but they were honest errors. Samuel Insull wept. Brother Martin wept. The lawyers wept. With voices choked with emotion headliners of Chicago business told from the witnessstand how much Insull had done for business in Chicago. There wasn't a dry eye in the jury.

Finally driven to the wall by the prosecutingattorney Samuel Insull blurted out that yes, he had made an error of some ten million dollars in accounting but that it had been an honest error.

Verdict: Not Guilty.

Smiling through their tears the happy Insulls went to their towncar amid the cheers of the crowd. Thousands of ruined investors, at least so the newspapers said, who had lost their life savings sat crying over the home editions at the thought of how Mr. Insull had suffered. The bankers were happy, the bankers had moved in on the properties.

In an odor of sanctity the deposed monarch of superpower, the officeboy who made good, enjoys his declining years spending the pension of twenty-one thousand a year that the directors of his old companies dutifully restored to him. *After fifty years of work,* he said, *my job is gone.*

[1936]

Babbitt at Work   SINCLAIR LEWIS

The first American to receive the Nobel Prize for Literature, Sinclair Lewis (1885–1951) won much fame and made numerous enemies by his satiric portraits of men and institutions in "the good old U. S. A." For a further note on Lewis, see p. 368.

In *Babbitt* (1922) Lewis achieved his most memorable characterization and added a word to the language. Here, as elsewhere, Lewis criticized American life without turning into a cynic. Like Mark Twain, he felt a sympathy — even a kind of affection — for the things he spent his life holding up to ridicule. His portrait of Babbitt at work is too much infused with delight to be utterly damning. The reader may debate whether Lewis' picture is caricature or realism, but he is unlikely to deny its force and interest. Lewis' style is without subtlety, but this lack is so happily suited to his subject as to constitute a strength.

". . . I don't mean to say that every ad I write is literally true. . . ."

The most important thing [Babbitt] dictated that morning was the fortnightly form-letter, to be mimeographed and sent out to a thousand "prospects." It was diligently imitative of the best literary models of the day; of heart-to-heart-talk advertisements, "sales-pulling" letters, discourses on the "development of Will-power," and hand-shaking house-organs, as richly poured forth by the new school of Poets of Business. He had painfully written out a first draft, and he intoned it now like a poet delicate and distrait:

SAY, OLD MAN!

I just want to know can I do you a whaleuva favor? Honest! No kidding! I know you're interested in getting a house, not merely a place where you hang up the old bonnet but a love-nest for the wife and kiddies — and maybe for the flivver out beyant (be sure and spell that b-e-y-a-n-t, Miss McGoun) the spud garden. Say, did you ever stop to think that we're here to save you trouble? That's how we make a living — folks don't pay us for our lovely beauty! Now take a look:

Sit right down at the handsome carved mahogany escritoire and shoot us in a line telling us just what you want, and if we can find it we'll come hopping down your lane with the good tidings, and if we can't, we won't bother you. To save your time, just fill out the blank enclosed. On request will also send blank regarding store properties in Floral Heights, Silver Grove, Linton, Bellevue, and all East Side residential districts.

Yours for service,

P.S. — Just a hint of some plums we can pick for you — some genuine bargains that came in to-day:

SILVER GROVE. — Cute four-room California bungalow, a.m.i., garage, dandy shade tree, swell neighborhood, handy car line. $3700, $780 down and balance liberal, Babbitt-Thompson terms, cheaper than rent.

DORCHESTER. — A corker! Artistic two-family house, all oak trim, parquet floors, lovely gas log, big porches, colonial, HEATED ALL-WEATHER GARAGE, a bargain at $11,250. . . .

*   *   *

It was a morning of artistic creation. Fifteen minutes after the purple prose of Babbitt's form-letter, Chester Kirby Laylock, the resident salesman at Glen Oriole, came in to report a sale and submit an advertisement. Babbitt disapproved of Laylock, who sang in choirs and was merry at home over games of Hearts and Old Maid. He had a tenor voice, wavy chestnut hair, and a mustache like a camel's-hair brush. Babbitt considered it excusable in a family-man to growl, "Seen this new picture of the kid — husky little devil, eh?" but Laylock's domestic confidences were as bubbling as a girl's.

"Say, I think I got a peach of an ad for the Glen, Mr. Babbitt. Why don't we try something in poetry? Honest, it'd have wonderful pulling-power. Listen:

> 'Mid pleasures and palaces
> Wherever you may roam,
> You just provide the little bride
> And we'll provide the home.

Do you get it? See — like 'Home Sweet Home.' Don't you — "

"Yes, yes, yes, hell yes, of course I get it. But — Oh, I think we'd better use something more dignified and forceful, like 'We lead, others follow,' or 'Eventually, why not now?' Course I believe in using poetry and humor and all that junk when it turns the trick, but with a high-class restricted development like the Glen we better stick to the more dignified approach, see how I mean? Well, I guess that's all, this morning, Chet."

* * *

By a tragedy familiar to the world of art, the April enthusiasm of Chet Laylock served only to stimulate the talent of the older craftsman, George F. Babbitt. He grumbled to Stanley Graff, "That tan-colored voice of Chet's gets on my nerves," yet he was aroused and in one swoop he wrote:

DO YOU RESPECT YOUR LOVED ONES?

When the last sad rites of bereavement are over, do you know for certain that you have done your best for the Departed? You haven't unless they lie in the Cemetery Beautiful

LINDEN LANE

the only strictly up-to-date burial place in or near Zenith, where exquisitely gardened plots look from daisy-dotted hill-slopes across the smiling fields of Dorchester.

SOLE AGENTS
BABBITT-THOMPSON REALTY COMPANY
REEVES BUILDING

He rejoiced, "I guess that'll show Chan Mott and his weedy old Wildwood Cemetery something about modern merchandising!"

* * *

He sent Mat Penniman to the recorder's office to dig out the names of the owners of houses which were displaying For Rent signs of other brokers; he talked to a man who desired to lease a store-building for a pool-room; he ran over the list of homeleases which were about to expire; he sent Thomas Bywaters, a street-car conductor who played at real estate in spare time, to call on side-street "prospects" who were unworthy the strategies of Stanley Graff. But he had spent his credulous excitement of creation, and these routine details annoyed him. . . .

* * *

His morning was not sharply marked into divisions. Interwoven with correspondence and advertisement-writing were a thousand nervous details: calls from clerks who were incessantly and hopefully seeking five furnished rooms and bath at sixty dollars a month; advice to Mat Penniman on getting money out of tenants who had no money.

Babbitt's virtues as a real-estate broker — as the servant of society in the department of finding homes for families and shops for distributors of food — were steadiness and diligence. He was conventionally honest, he kept his records of buyers and sellers complete, he had experience with leases and titles and an excellent memory for prices. His shoulders were broad enough, his voice deep enough, his relish of hearty humor strong enough, to establish him as one of the ruling caste of Good Fellows. Yet his eventual importance to mankind was perhaps lessened by his large and complacent ignorance of all architecture save the types of houses turned out by speculative builders; all landscape gardening save the use of curving roads, grass, and six ordinary shrubs; and all the commonest axioms of economics. He serenely believed that the one purpose of the real-estate business was to make money for George F. Babbitt. True, it was a good advertisement at Boosters' Club lunches, and all the varieties of Annual Banquets to which Good Fellows were invited, to speak sonorously of Unselfish Public Service, the Broker's Obligation to Keep Inviolate the Trust of His Clients, and a thing called Ethics, whose nature was confusing but if you had it you were a High-class Realtor and if you hadn't you were a shyster, a piker, and a fly-by-night. These virtues awakened Confidence, and enabled you to handle Bigger Propositions. But they didn't imply that you were to be impractical and refuse to take twice the value of a house if a buyer was such an idiot that he didn't jew you down on the asking-price.

Babbitt spoke well — and often — at these orgies of commercial righteousness about the "realtor's function as a seer of the future development of the community, and as a prophetic engineer clearing the pathway for inevitable changes" — which meant that a real-estate broker could make money by guessing which way the town would grow. This guessing he called Vision.

In an address at the Booster's Club he had admitted, "It is at once the duty and the privilege of the realtor to know everything about his own city and its environs. Where a surgeon is a specialist on every vein and mysterious cell of the human body, and the engineer upon electricity in all its phases, or every bolt of some great bridge majestically arching o'er a mighty flood, the realtor must know his city, inch by inch, and all its faults and virtues."

Though he did know the market-price, inch by inch, of certain districts of

Zenith, he did not know whether the police force was too large or too small, or whether it was in alliance with gambling and prostitution. He knew the means of fireproofing buildings and the relation of insurance-rates to fireproofing, but he did not know how many firemen there were in the city, how they were trained and paid, or how complete their apparatus. He sang eloquently the advantages of proximity of school-buildings to rentable homes, but he did not know — he did not know that it was worth while to know — whether the city schoolrooms were properly heated, lighted, ventilated, furnished; he did not know how the teachers were chosen; and though he chanted "One of the boasts of Zenith is that we pay our teachers adequately," that was because he had read the statement in the *Advocate-Times*. Himself, he could not have given the average salary of teachers in Zenith or anywhere else.

He had heard it said that "conditions" in the County Jail and the Zenith City Prison were not very "scientific"; he had, with indignation at the criticism of Zenith, skimmed through a report in which the notorious pessimist Seneca Doane, the radical lawyer, asserted that to throw boys and young girls into a bull-pen crammed with men suffering from syphilis, delirium tremens, and insanity was not the perfect way of educating them. He had controverted the report by growling, "Folks that think a jail ought to be a bloomin' Hotel Thornleigh make me sick. If people don't like a jail, let 'em behave 'emselves and keep out of it. Besides, these reform cranks always exaggerate." That was the beginning and quite completely the end of his investigations into Zenith's charities and corrections; and as to the "vice districts" he brightly expressed it, "Those are things that no decent man monkeys with. Besides, smatter fact, I'll tell you confidentially: it's a protection to our daughters and to decent women to have a district where tough nuts can raise cain. Keeps 'em away from our own homes."

As to industrial conditions, however, Babbitt had thought a great deal, and his opinions may be coördinated as follows:

"A good labor union is of value because it keeps out radical unions, which would destroy property. No one ought to be forced to belong to a union, however. All labor agitators who try to force men to join a union should be hanged. In fact, just between ourselves, there oughtn't to be any unions allowed at all; and as it's the best way of fighting the unions, every business man ought to belong to an employers'-association and to the Chamber of Commerce. In union there is strength. So any selfish hog who doesn't join the Chamber of Commerce ought to be forced to."

In nothing — as the expert on whose advice families moved to new neighborhoods to live there for a generation — was Babbitt more splendidly innocent than in the science of sanitation. He did not know a malaria-bearing mosquito from a bat; he knew nothing about tests of drinking water; and in the matters of plumbing and sewage he was as unlearned as he was voluble. He often referred to the excellence of the bathrooms in the houses he sold. He was fond of explaining why it was that no European ever bathed. Some one had told him, when he was twenty-two, that all cesspools were unhealthy; and he still denounced them. If a client impertinently wanted him to sell a house which had a cesspool, Babbitt always spoke about it — before accepting the house and selling it.

When he laid out the Glen Oriole acreage development, when he ironed woodland and dipping meadow into a glenless, orioleless, sunburnt flat prickly with small boards displaying the names of imaginary streets, he righteously put in a complete sewage-system. It made him feel superior; it enabled him to sneer privily at the Martin Lumsen development, Avonlea, which had a cesspool; and it provided a chorus for the full-page advertisements in which he announced the beauty, convenience, cheapness, and supererogatory health-fulness of Glen Oriole. The only flaw was that the Glen Oriole sewers had insufficient outlet, so that waste remained in them, not very agreeably, while the Avonlea cesspool was a Waring septic tank.

The whole of the Glen Oriole project was a suggestion that Babbitt, though he really did hate men recognized as swindlers, was not too unrea-sonably honest. Operators and buyers prefer that brokers should not be in competition with them as operators and buyers themselves, but attend to their clients' interests only. It was supposed that the Babbitt-Thompson Company were merely agents for Glen Oriole, serving the real owner, Jake Offutt, but the fact was that Babbitt and Thompson owned sixty-two per cent. of the Glen, the president and purchasing agent of the Zenith Street Traction Com-pany owned twenty-eight per cent., and Jake Offut (a gang-politician, a small manufacturer, a tobacco-chewing old farceur who enjoyed dirty politics, busi-ness diplomacy, and cheating at poker) had only ten per cent., which Babbitt and the Traction officials had given to him for "fixing" health inspectors and fire inspectors and a member of the State Transportation Commission.

But Babbitt was virtuous. He advocated, though he did not practise, the prohibition of alcohol; he praised, though he did not obey, the laws against motor-speeding; he paid his debts; he contributed to the church, the Red Cross, and the Y. M. C. A.; he followed the custom of his clan and cheated only as it was sanctified by precedent; and he never descended to trickery — though, as he explained to Paul Riesling:

"Course I don't mean to say that every ad I write is literally true or that I always believe everything I say when I give some buyer a good strong selling-spiel. You see — you see it's like this: In the first place, maybe the owner of the property exaggerated when he put it into my hands, and it certainly isn't my place to go proving my principal a liar! And then most folks are so darn crooked themselves that they expect a fellow to do a little lying, so if I was fool enough to never whoop the ante I'd get the credit for lying anyway! In self-defense I got to toot my own horn, like a lawyer defending a client — his bounden duty, ain't it, to bring out the poor dub's good points? Why, the Judge himself would bawl out a lawyer that didn't, even if they both knew the guy was guilty! But even so, I don't pad out the truth like Cecil Rountree or Thayer or the rest of these realtors. Fact, I think a fellow that's willing to deliberately up and profit by lying ought to be shot!"

Babbitt's value to his clients was rarely better shown than this morning, in the conference at eleven-thirty between himself, Conrad Lyte, and Archibald Purdy.

Conrad Lyte was a real-estate speculator. He was a nervous speculator. Before he gambled he consulted bankers, lawyers, architects, contracting builders, and all of their clerks and stenographers who were willing to be cornered and give him advice. He was a bold entrepreneur, and he desired nothing more than complete safety in his investments, freedom from attention to details, and the thirty or forty per cent. profit which, according to all authorities, a pioneer deserves for his risks and foresight. He was a stubby man with a cap-like mass of short gray curls and clothes which, no matter how well cut, seemed shaggy. Below his eyes were semicircular hollows, as though silver dollars had been pressed against them and had left an imprint.

Particularly and always Lyte consulted Babbitt, and trusted in his slow cautiousness.

Six months ago Babbitt had learned that one Archibald Purdy, a grocer in the indecisive residential district known as Linton, was talking of opening a butcher shop beside his grocery. Looking up the ownership of adjoining parcels of land, Babbitt found that Purdy owned his present shop but did not own the one available lot adjoining. He advised Conrad Lyte to purchase this lot, for eleven thousand dollars, though an appraisal on a basis of rents did not indicate its value as above nine thousand. The rents, declared Babbitt, were too low; and by waiting they could make Purdy come to their price. (This was Vision.) He had to bully Lyte into buying. His first act as agent for Lyte was to increase the rent of the battered store-building on the lot. The tenant said a number of rude things, but he paid.

Now, Purdy seemed ready to buy, and his delay was going to cost him ten thousand extra dollars — the reward paid by the community to Mr. Conrad Lyte for the virtue of employing a broker who had Vision and who understood Talking Points, Strategic Values, Key Situations, Underappraisals, and the Psychology of Salesmanship.

Lyte came to the conference exultantly. He was fond of Babbitt, this morning, and called him "old hoss." Purdy, the grocer, a long-nosed man and solemn, seemed to care less for Babbitt and for Vision, but Babbitt met him at the street door of the office and guided him toward the private room with affectionate little cries of "This way, Brother Purdy!" He took from the correspondence-file the entire box of cigars and forced them on his guests. He pushed their chairs two inches forward and three inches back, which gave an hospitable note, then leaned back in his desk-chair and looked plump and jolly. But he spoke to the weakling grocer with firmness.

"Well, Brother Purdy, we been having some pretty tempting offers from butchers and a slew of other folks for that lot next to your store, but I persuaded Brother Lyte that we ought to give you a shot at the property first. I said to Lyte, 'It'd be a rotten shame,' I said, 'if somebody went and opened a combination grocery and meat market right next door and ruined Purdy's nice little business.' Especially——" Babbitt leaned forward, and his voice was harsh, "— it would be hard luck if one of these cash-and-carry chain-stores got in there and started cutting prices below cost till they got rid of competition and forced you to the wall!"

Purdy snatched his thin hands from his pockets, pulled up his trousers, thrust his hands back into his pockets, tilted in the heavy oak chair, and tried to look amused, as he struggled:

"Yes, they're bad competition. But I guess you don't realize the Pulling Power that Personality has in a neighborhood business."

The great Babbitt smiled. "That's so. Just as you feel, old man. We thought we'd give you first chance. All right then —— "

"Now look here!" Purdy wailed. "I know f'r a fact that a piece of property 'bout same size, right near, sold for less 'n eighty-five hundred, 'twa'n't two years ago, and here you fellows are asking me twenty-four thousand dollars! Why, I'd have to mortgage —— I wouldn't mind so much paying twelve thousand but —— Why good God, Mr. Babbitt, you're asking more 'n twice its value! And threatening to ruin me if I don't take it!"

"Purdy, I don't like your way of talking! I don't like it one little bit! Supposing Lyte and I were stinking enough to want to ruin any fellow human, don't you suppose we know it's to our own selfish interest to have everybody in Zenith prosperous? But all this is beside the point. Tell you what we'll do: We'll come down to twenty-three thousand — five thousand down and the rest on mortgage — and if you want to wreck the old shack and rebuild, I guess I can get Lyte here to loosen up for a building-mortgage on good liberal terms. Heavens, man, we'd be glad to oblige you! We don't like these foreign grocery trusts any better 'n you do! But it isn't reasonable to expect us to sacrifice eleven thousand or more just for neighborliness, is it! How about it, Lyte? You willing to come down?"

By warmly taking Purdy's part, Babbitt persuaded the benevolent Mr. Lyte to reduce his price to twenty-one thousand dollars. At the right moment Babbitt snatched from a drawer the agreement he had had Miss McGoun type out a week ago and thrust it into Purdy's hands. He genially shook his fountain pen to make certain that it was flowing, handed it to Purdy, and approvingly watched him sign.

The work of the world was being done. Lyte had made something over nine thousand dollars, Babbitt had made a four-hundred-and-fifty dollar commission, Purdy had, by the sensitive mechanism of modern finance, been provided with a business-building, and soon the happy inhabitants of Linton would have meat lavished upon them at prices only a little higher than those down-town.

It had been a manly battle, but after it Babbitt drooped. This was the only really amusing contest he had been planning. There was nothing ahead save details of leases, appraisals, mortgages.

He muttered, "Makes me sick to think of Lyte carrying off most of the profit when I did all the work, the old skinflint! And —— What else have I got to do to-day? . . . Like to take a good long vacation. Motor trip. Something."

He sprang up, rekindled by the thought of lunching with Paul Riesling.

[1922]

The Princess and the Tin Box   JAMES THURBER

James Thurber (1894–1961) has been recognized for over three decades as one of America's leading humorists, having first gained attention in 1929 with a book called *Is Sex Necessary?* For most of his professional life he was an important contributor to *The New Yorker,* and many of his stories, essays, and cartoons made their first appearance in that magazine.

Humor arises from incongruities, a number of which — in both content and method — may be noted in "The Princess and the Tin Box." Frequently, also, it has the incongruous aim of making us think as well as laugh; as T. S. Eliot has said of Thurber, his is "a form of humor which is also a way of saying something serious." The apparent casualness with which Thurber displays his humorous gift can be misleading; the fact is that he frequently rewrites a piece as many as ten times before submitting it for publication.

"... it is the most valuable of all the gifts. ..."

Once upon a time, in a far country, there lived a king whose daughter was the prettiest princess in the world. Her eyes were like the cornflower, her hair was sweeter than the hyacinth, and her throat made the swan look dusty.

From the time she was a year old, the princess had been showered with presents. Her nursery looked like Cartier's window. Her toys were all made of gold or platinum or diamonds or emeralds. She was not permitted to have wooden blocks or china dolls or rubber dogs or linen books, because such materials were considered cheap for the daughter of a king.

When she was seven, she was allowed to attend the wedding of her brother and throw real pearls at the bride instead of rice. Only the nightingale, with his lyre of gold, was permitted to sing for the princess. The common blackbird, with his boxwood flute, was kept out of the palace grounds. She walked in silver-and-samite slippers to a sapphire-and-topaz bathroom and slept in an ivory bed inlaid with rubies.

On the day the princess was eighteen, the king sent a royal ambassador to the courts of five neighboring kingdoms to announce that he would give his daughter's hand in marriage to the prince who brought her the gift she liked the most.

The first prince to arrive at the palace rode a swift white stallion and laid at the feet of the princess an enormous apple made of solid gold which he had taken from a dragon who had guarded it for a thousand years. It was placed on a long ebony table set up to hold the gifts of the princess's suitors. The second prince, who came on a gray charger, brought her a nightingale made of a thousand diamonds, and it was placed beside the golden apple. The third prince, riding on a black horse, carried a great jewel box made of platinum and sapphires, and it was placed next to the diamond nightingale. The fourth prince, astride a fiery yellow horse, gave the princess a gigantic heart made of rubies and pierced by an emerald arrow. It was placed next to the platinum-and-sapphire jewel box.

Now the fifth prince was the strongest and handsomest of all the five suitors, but he was the son of a poor king whose realm had been overrun by mice and locusts and wizards and mining engineers so that there was nothing much of value left in it. He came plodding up to the palace of the princess on a plow horse, and he brought her a small tin box filled with mica and feldspar and hornblende which he had picked up on the way.

The other princes roared with disdainful laughter when they saw the tawdry gift the fifth prince had brought to the princess. But she examined it with great interest and squealed with delight, for all her life she had been glutted with precious stones and priceless metals, but she had never seen tin before or mica or feldspar or hornblende. The tin box was placed next to the ruby heart pierced with an emerald arrow.

"Now," the king said to his daughter, "you must select the gift you like best and marry the prince that brought it."

The princess smiled and walked up to the table and picked up the present she liked the most. It was the platinum-and-sapphire jewel box, the gift of the third prince.

"The way I figure it," she said, "is this. It is a very large and expensive box, and when I am married, I will meet many admirers who will give me precious gems with which to fill it to the top. Therefore, it is the most valuable of all the gifts my suitors have brought me and I like it the best."

The princess married the third prince that very day in the midst of great merriment and high revelry. More than a hundred thousand pearls were thrown at her and she loved it.

Moral: All those who thought the princess was going to select the tin box filled with worthless stones instead of one of the other gifts will kindly stay after class and write one hundred times on the blackboard "I would rather have a hunk of aluminum silicate than a diamond necklace."

[1945]

The Emergence of a New Ethic

The Pipe Line WILLIAM H. WHYTE, JR.

William H. Whyte, Jr. (1917–   ) has been a prolific and popular writer
and editor for *Fortune* magazine since 1946. In 1956 he published the
much-discussed *The Organization Man,* from which the present selection
is taken. For other remarks on Whyte, see p. 390.

In "The Pipe Line" Whyte describes the executive-training programs
of two large American corporations and sees in them a shift from the
Protestant Ethic to what he terms the Social Ethic. In the introduction to
the book he says that "By social ethic I mean that contemporary body of
thought which makes morally legitimate the pressures of society against
the individual." The welfare of the group is all-important and the job of
the individual is to become a "good member of the team." As the Protestant Ethic encouraged "rugged individualism," so the Social Ethic encourages conformity. The spirit of "tooth and claw" gives way to something
called "togetherness." College seniors stop dreaming of opportunity and
"the chance to make a killing"; they think instead of security and a modest
but comfortable life in the suburbs. The reader will want to decide
whether, in his experience, the shift Whyte speaks of has taken place in
our society. He might also decide whether Whyte is right in remarking,
just prior to the selection printed here, that perhaps his experience of the
Vick's program made him "unduly garrulous" in writing of it.

> ". . . one must compete — but not too much, and
> certainly not too obviously. . . ."

It was a school — the Vick School of Applied Merchandising, they called it.
The idea, as it was presented to job-hunting seniors at the time, was that those
who were chosen were not going off to a job, but to a postgraduate training institution set up by a farsighted management. In September, some thirty graduates would gather from different colleges to start a year's study in modern
merchandising. There would be a spell of classroom work in New York, a
continuing course in advertising, and, most important, eleven months of field
study under the supervision of veteran students of merchandising and
distribution. . . .

The formal schooling we got was of the briefest character. During our
four weeks in New York, we learned of Richardson's discovery of VapoRub,

spent a day watching the VapoRub being mixed, and went through a battery of tests the company was fooling around with to find the Vick's type. Most of the time we spent in memorizing list prices, sales spiels, counters to objections, and the prices and techniques of Plough, Inc., whose Penetro line was one of Vick's most troublesome competitors. There was no talk about the social responsibilities of business or the broad view that I can remember, and I'm quite sure the phrase *human relations* never came up at all.

What management philosophy we did get was brief and to the point. Shortly before we were to set out from New York, the president, Mr. H. S. Richardson, took us up to the Cloud Club atop the Chrysler Building. The symbolism did not escape us. As we looked from this executive eyrie down on the skyscraper spires below, Golconda stretched out before us. One day, we gathered, some of us would be coming back up again — and not as temporary guests either. Some would not. The race would be to the swiftest.

Over coffee Mr. Richardson drove home to us the kind of philosophy that would get us back up. He posed a hypothetical problem. Suppose, he said, that you are a manufacturer and for years a small firm has been making paper cartons for your product. He has specialized so much to service you, as a matter of fact, that that's all he does make. He is utterly dependent on your business. For years the relationship has continued to be eminently satisfactory to both parties. But then one day another man walks in and says he will make the boxes for you cheaper. What do you do?

He bade each one of us in turn to answer.

But *how much* cheaper? we asked. How much time could we give the old supplier to match the new bid? Mr. Richardson became impatient. There was only one decision. Either you were a businessman or you were not a businessman. The new man, obviously, should get the contract. Mr. Richardson, who had strong views on the necessity of holding to the old American virtues, advised us emphatically against letting sentimentality obscure fundamentals. Business was survival of the fittest, he indicated, and we would soon learn the fact.

He was as good as his word. The Vick curriculum was just that — survival of the fittest. In the newer type of programs, companies will indeed fire incompetents, but a man joins with the idea that the company intends to keep him, and this is the company's wish also. The Vick School, however, was frankly based on the principle of elimination. It wouldn't make any difference how wonderful all of us might turn out to be; of the thirty-eight who sat there in the Cloud Club, the rules of the game dictated that only six or seven of us would be asked to stay with Vick. The rest would graduate to make way for the next batch of students.

Another difference between Vick's approach and that now more characteristic became very evident as soon as we arrived in the field. While the work, as the company said, was educational, it was in no sense make-work. Within a few days of our session at the Cloud Club, we were dispatched to the hinterland — in my case, the hill country of eastern Kentucky. Each of us was given a panel delivery truck, a full supply of signs, a ladder, a stock of samples, and an order pad. After several days under the eye of a senior salesman, we were each assigned a string of counties and left to shift for ourselves.

The merchandising was nothing if not applied. To take a typical day of any one of us, we would rise at 6:00 or 6:30 in some bleak boarding house or run-down hotel and after a greasy breakfast set off to squeeze in some advertising practice before the first call. This consisted of bostitching a quota of large fiber signs on barns and clamping smaller metal ones to telephone poles and trees by hog rings. By eight, we would have arrived at a general store for our exercise in merchandising. Our assignment was to persuade the dealer to take a year's supply all at once, or, preferably, more than a year's supply, so that he would have no money or shelf space left for other brands. After the sale, or no-sale, we would turn to market research and note down the amount sold him by "chiseling" competitors (i.e., competitors; there was no acknowledgment on our report blanks of any other kind).

Next we did some sampling work: "Tilt your head back, Mr. Jones," we would suddenly say to the dealer. For a brief second he would obey and we would quickly shoot a whopping dropperful of Vatronol up his nose. His eyes smarting from the sting, the dealer would smile with simple pleasure. Turning to the loungers by the stove, he would tell them to let the drummer fella give them some of that stuff. After the messy job was done, we plastered the place with cardboard signs, and left. Then, some more signposting in barnyards, and ten or twelve miles of mud road to the next call. So, on through the day, the routine was repeated until at length, long after dark, we would get back to our lodgings in time for dinner — and two hours' work on our report forms.

The acquisition of a proper frame of mind toward all this was a slow process. The faded yellow second sheets of our daily report book tell the story. At first, utter demoralization. Day after day, the number of calls would be a skimpy eight or nine, and the number of sales sometimes zero. But it was never our fault. In the large space left for explanations, we would affect a cheerful humor — the gay adventurer in the provinces — but this pathetic bravado could not mask a recurrent note of despair.[1]

To all these bids for sympathy, the home office was adamantine. The weekly letter written to each trainee would start with some perfunctory remarks that it was too bad about the clutch breaking down, the cut knee, and so on. But this spurious sympathy did not conceal a strong preoccupation with results, and lest we miss the point we were told of comrades who would no longer be with us. We too are sorry about those absent dealers, the office would say. Perhaps if you got up earlier in the morning?

As the office sensed quite correctly from my daily reports, I was growing sorry for myself. I used to read timetables at night, and often in the evening I would somehow find myself by the C & O tracks when the George Wash-

---

[1] I quote some entries from my own daily report forms: "They use 'dry' creek beds for roads in this country. 'Dry!' Ha! Ha! . . . Sorry about making only four calls today, but I had to go over to Ervine to pick up a drop shipment of ¾ tins and my clutch broke down. . . . Everybody's on WPA in this county. Met only one dealer who sold more than a couple dozen VR a year. Ah, well, it's all in the game! . . . Bostitched my left thumb to a barn this morning and couldn't pick up my first call until after lunch. . . . The local brick plant here is shut down and nobody's buying anything. . . . Five, count 'em, *five* absent dealers in a row. . . . Sorry about the $20.85 but the clutch broke down again. . . ."

ington swept by, its steamy windows a reminder of civilization left behind. I was also sorry for many of the storekeepers, most of whom existed on a precarious credit relationship with wholesalers, and as a consequence I sold them very little of anything.

The company sent its head training supervisor to see if anything could be salvaged. After several days with me, this old veteran of the road told me he knew what was the matter. It wasn't so much my routine, wretched as this was. It was my state of mind. "Fella," he told me, "you will never sell anybody anything until you learn one simple thing. The man on the other side of the counter is the *enemy*."

It was a gladiators' school we were in. Selling may be no less competitive now, but in the Vick program, strife was honored far more openly than today's climate would permit. Combat was the ideal — combat with the dealer, combat with the "chiseling competitors," and combat with each other. There was some talk about "the team," but it was highly abstract. Our success depended entirely on beating our fellow students, and while we got along when we met for occasional sales meetings the camaraderie was quite extracurricular.

Slowly, as our sales-to-calls ratios crept up, we gained in rapacity. Somewhere along the line, by accident or skill, each of us finally manipulated a person into doing what we wanted him to do. Innocence was lost, and by the end of six months, with the pack down to about twenty-three men, we were fairly ravening for the home stretch back to the Cloud Club. At this point, the company took us off general store and grocery work and turned us loose in the rich drugstore territory.

The advice of the old salesman now became invaluable. While he had a distaste for any kind of dealer, with druggists he was implacably combative. He was one of the most decent and kindly men I have ever met, but when he gave us pep talks about this enemy ahead of us, he spoke with great intensity. Some druggists were good enough fellows, he told us (i.e., successful ones who bought big deals), but the tough ones were a mean, servile crew; they would insult you, keep you waiting while they pretended to fill prescriptions, lie to you about their inventory, whine at anything less than a 300 per cent markup, and switch their customers to chiseling competitors.

The old salesman would bring us together in batches for several days of demonstration. It was a tremendous experience for us, for though he seemed outwardly a phlegmatic man, we knew him for the artist he was. Outside the store he was jumpy and sometimes perspired, but once inside, he was composed to the point of apparent boredom. He rarely smiled, almost never opened with a joke. His demeanor seemed to say, I am a busy man and you are damned lucky I have stopped by your miserable store. Sometimes, if the druggist was unusually insolent, he would blow cigar smoke at his face. "Can't sell it if you don't have it," he would say contemptuously, and then, rather pleased with himself, glance back at us, loitering in the wings, to see if we had marked that.

Only old pros like himself could get away with that, he told us in the post-mortem sessions, but there were lots of little tricks we could pick up. As we gathered around him, like Fagin's brood, he would demonstrate how to watch for the victim's shoulders to relax before throwing the clincher; how to pick up the one-size jar of a competitive line that had an especially thick glass bottom and chuckle knowingly; how to feign suppressed worry that maybe the deal was too big for "the smaller druggist like yourself" to take; how to disarm the nervous druggist by fumbling and dropping a pencil. No mercy, he would tell us; give the devils no mercy.

We couldn't either. As the acid test of our gall the company now challenged us to see how many drugstores we could desecrate with "flange" signs. By all the standards of the trade this signposting should have been an impossible task. Almost every "chiseling competitor" would give the druggist at least five dollars to let him put up a sign; we could not offer the druggist a nickel. Our signs, furthermore, were not the usual cardboard kind the druggist could throw away after we had left. They were of metal, they were hideous, and they were to be screwed to the druggists' cherished oak cabinets.

The trick was in the timing. When we were in peak form the procedure went like this: Just after the druggist had signed the order, his shoulders would subside, and this would signal a fleeting period of mutual bonhomie. "New fella, aren't you?" the druggist was likely to say, relaxing. This was his mistake. As soon as we judged the good will to be at full flood, we would ask him if he had a ladder. (There was a ladder out in the car, but the fuss of fetching it would have broken the mood.) The druggist's train of thought would not at that moment connect the request with what was to follow, and he would good-naturedly dispatch someone to bring out a ladder. After another moment of chatter, we would make way for the waiting customer who would engage the druggist's attention. Then, forthrightly, we would slap the ladder up against a spot we had previously reconnoitered. "Just going to get this sign up for you," we would say, as if doing him the greatest favor in the world. He would nod absent-mindedly. Then up the ladder we would go; a few quick turns of the awl, place the bracket in position, and then, the automatic screwdriver. Bang! bang! Down went the sign. (If the druggist had been unusually mean, we could break the thread of the screw for good measure.) Then down with the ladder, shift it over to the second spot, and up again.

About this time the druggist would start looking up a little unhappily, but the good will, while ebbing, was still enough to inhibit him from action. *He* felt sorry for us. Imagine that young man thinking those signs are good looking! Just as he would be about to mumble something about one sign being enough, we would hold up the second one. It had a picture on it of a woman squirting nose drops up her nostrils. We would leer fatuously at it. "Just going to lay this blonde on the top of the cabinet for you, Mr. Jones," we would say, winking. We were giants in those days.

I suppose I should be ashamed, but I must confess I'm really not, and to this day when I enter a drugstore I sometimes fancy the sound of the awl biting irretrievably into the druggist's limed oak. I think the reader will understand, of course, that I am not holding up the Vick School of Applied Merchandising as an ideal model, yet I must add, in all fairness to Vick, that most of us were grateful for the experience. When we get together periodically (we have an informal alumni association), we wallow in talk about how they really separated the men from the boys then, etc. It was truly an experience, and if we shudder to recall the things we did, we must admit that as a cram course in reality it was extraordinarily efficient.

The General Electric program to which I now turn was in full force in the thirties and is actually an older one than the Vick's program. Where the latter was a late flowering of a philosophy already in the descendant, however, GE's was a harbinger of things to come. Even today, it is still somewhat ahead of its time; at this moment there are not many corporation training programs which come near General Electric's, either in the size or elaborateness of facilities or, more importantly, in consistency of principles. Yet I believe that as we take up these principal features of the General Electric program, we will be seeing what in a decade or so hence may be the middle of the road.[2]

The most immediately apparent thing about the General Electric program is the fact that it *is* a school. While the plants serve as part of the campus, the company maintains a full-time staff of 250 instructors and an educational plant complete to such details as company-published textbooks, examinations, classrooms, and alumni publications. In direct operating costs alone the company spends over five million dollars annually — a budget larger than many a medium-sized college.

The program is highly centralized. To keep this plant running, GE's corps of recruiters each year delivers between 1,000 and 1,500 college graduates, mostly engineers, to the company's Schenectady headquarters. There the trainees enter what is for them a continuation of college life. Like fraternity brothers, they live together in boarding houses and attend classes in groups. For afterhours recreation, they have the privileges of the Edison Club where, along with other GE employees with college degrees, they can meet after classes to play golf, bridge, and enjoy a planned series of parties and dances. (GE employees who haven't gone to college are eligible to join if they have achieved a supervisory rating.)

The curriculum is arranged in much the same manner as a university's. The trainee enters under one of several courses, such as engineering and accounting. All these courses will have much in common, however, for the trainee's first eighteen months are regarded as the basic part of his training. At the end of this time he will then go on to a "major." If he has been in the manufacturing training course, for example, he can elect as a major factory operations, manufacturing engineering, production and purchasing, or plant engineering.

The work the trainee does during this training is not, like Vick's applied merchandising, considered an end in itself. From time to time the trainee will work at specific jobs, but these jobs, while not mere make-work, are out-

---

[2] Even Vick has moved considerably in this direction. The heroic years are over; now it is "The Vick Executive Development Program," and though there has been no basic shift in underlying philosophy (Mr. Richardson is still at the helm), Vick now offers many of the material features of the GE program. Security is reasonably guaranteed; no longer are trainees "graduated" — of the roughly one hundred seniors taken in each year, all but a handful can remain as permanent employees. They are exposed to many more aspects of management and they don't have to do things like putting up flange signs.

side the regular cost-accounted operations of the company. The company considers them vehicles for training, and it rotates students from one to another on a regular schedule.

The most noteworthy feature of the General Electric approach is the emphasis on the "professional" manager. As in all training programs, the bulk of the instruction is on specifics. Unlike most, however, there is considerable study in subjects that cut across every kind of job. Trainees study personnel philosophy, labor relations, law, and, most important, the managerial viewpoint.[3]

Only a minority of the trainees will ever become managers; in ten years 1,500 to 2,000 executive slots will open up, and this means that most of the thousands of young men trained during this time will never get further than middle management. Nevertheless, it is those future executive slots that the company is thinking of, and it makes its concern plain to the trainee. On the report card form for trainees, there is a space for an evaluation as to whether the trainee is suited "for individual contribution" or whether, instead, he is suited "to manage the work of others." The company tells the trainees that it is perfectly all right for them to aim at "individual contribution," which is to say, a specialty. It would be a dull trainee, however, who did not pause before consigning himself to such a role. In one of GE's textbooks there is a picture of a man looking at two ladders. One leads up to a specialty, the other to general managing. The question before the young man, the textbook states, is: "Will I specialize in a particular field?" — or "Will I become broad-gauge, capable of effort in many fields?"

Who wants to be narrow-gauge? Trainees do not have to read too strenuously between the lines to see that one should aim to manage; as a matter of fact, they are predisposed to read a good bit more between the lines than many of their elders would like them to. Which brings us to an important point. In gauging the impact of the curriculum on the young man, his predispositions are as important as the weighting of the courses. Elders at General Electric can demonstrate that the actual amount of time devoted to the abstract arts of management is far less than the time devoted to specific skills. But the managerial part is what the trainees want to hear — and they want to hear it so much that one hour's exposure to the managerial view can be as four or five hours of something else in proportion to its effect on impressionable minds. Trainees are interested, to be sure, in how turbines are made, in the techniques of the accounting department and such, but they do not want to be *too* interested. It would make them unbalanced.

They regard specific work very much as many educators view "subject matter" courses: narrowing. As trainees play back the lesson, they see a distinction, sometimes a downright antithesis, between the qualities of the broad-

---

[3] Among other things, the trainees take HOBSO. This is the course in How One Business System Operates, originally developed by Du Pont to inoculate blue-collar employees against creeping socialism. Though GE has no reason to fear its trainees are ideologically unsound, it explains that the course will help them "detect any bad guidance they receive from union and political leaders, and even from educational and spiritual leaders."

gauge executive and the qualities that one must have to do a superlative piece of concrete work. Not work itself but the managing of other people's work is the skill that they aspire to. As they describe it, the manager is a man in charge of people getting along together, and his *expertise* is relatively independent of who or what is being managed. Or why.

Not surprisingly, the part of the curriculum for which they have the greatest affinity is the human-relations instruction. They are particularly enthusiastic about the "Effective Presentation" course worked up by the sales-training department. They can hardly be blamed. "YOU CAN ALWAYS GET ANYBODY TO DO WHAT YOU WISH," the textbook proclaims. To this end the students spend four months eagerly studying a battery of communication techniques and psychological principles which General Electric tells them will help them to be good managers. (Sample principle: "Never say anything controversial.")

There is nothing novel about teaching people how to manipulate other people, and GE's scientific psychological techniques bear a strong resemblance to the how-to-be-a-success precepts standard in the U.S. for decades. What is different about them is their justification. They are not presented on the grounds that they will help make people do what you want them to do so that you can make more money. GE trainees see it in much more eleemosynary terms. They do like the part about selling yourself to others so you can get ahead, for they think a lot about this. But they don't abide the thought of enemies on the other side of the counter; they see the manipulative skills as something that in the long run will make other people *happy*. When in years to come the trainees are charged with the destiny of subordinates — a possibility most take remarkably much for granted — they will be able to achieve a stable, well-adjusted work group. They won't drive subordinates, they explain. They will motivate them.

Trainees are also predisposed to emphasis on co-operation rather than competition, and this they get too. The emphasis is built into the structure of the school. For one thing, the student is given a high measure of security from the beginning, and while there may be promotion of the fittest there can be survival for all. There are exceptions, but one must be a very odd ball to be one. For the first two years the trainee is part of a system in which his salary raises will be automatic, and while later on he will be more on his own there will be no planned elimination as there was at Vick, nor an up-or-out policy such as the Navy's.

To get ahead, of course, one must compete — but not too much, and certainly not too obviously. While overt ambition is a bad posture for the ambitious anywhere, the GE system has especial sanctions for the rate-buster. The trainee is, first of all, a member of a group, and the group is entrusted to a surprise degree with the resolution of his future. How well, the company wants to know, does he fit in? His fellow trainees provide the answer, and in the "case study" group discussions the eager beaver or the deviant is quickly exposed. And brought to heel. Trainees speak frequently of the way close fraternity life atmosphere is valuable in ironing out some trainees' aberrant tendencies. It may be tough on him, they concede, but better now than later. In a few years the trainee will be released from this close association and the social character that he has perfected will be a fundamental necessity; he will be moving from one company branch to another, and he must be able to fit into the same kind of integrated social system.

The company officially recognizes the disciplining of the group. In its periodic rating of the man, the company frequently calls on his comrades to participate in the rating. If a man is liked especially well not only by his superiors but by his peers, he may be given the job of guiding about eight or ten of his fellow trainees. He is now a "sign-up," and if he keeps on maturing he may become a "head-of-tests," the seven "sign-ups" reporting to him. Since the opinions of one's peers are so integral to advancement, this system virtually insures that the overzealous or the "knocker" type of man will not get ahead — or, at the very least, that he will successfully remold himself to the managerial image.

The fact that the trainee must spend so much time thinking of what other people think of him does not oppress him. Quite the opposite, the constant surveillance is one of the things the average trainee talks about most enthusiastically. The rating system is highly standardized, he explains; it is the product of *many* people rather than one, and this denominator of judgments frees him from the harshness or caprice that might result from the traditional boss-employee relationship. He is also freed from being ignored; the system insures that other people must be thinking about him quite as much as he is thinking about them, and for this reason he won't get pigeonholed. At General Electric, as one trainee remarked, not only can't you get lost, you can't even hide.

Needless to say, ambition still pulses, and I am not trying to suggest that the General Electric man is any less set on the main chance than my Vick comrades. It is quite obvious, nevertheless, that he must pursue the main chance in a much more delicate fashion. To get ahead, he must co-operate with the others — but co-operate *better* than they do.

[1956]

The Mythological Base

Paul Bunyan and Rip Van Winkle   LOUIS LE FEVRE

Louis LeFevre (1894–   ) lives near the Catskills and wrote "Paul
Bunyan and Rip Van Winkle," he says, as the result of asking himself
"why Rip Van Winkle became a local hero." He is now at work on a
book which will develop the ideas of this essay in greater detail.

LeFevre expresses the American drive for financial success in terms
different from but related to those used by Griswold and Whyte. In fact,
the significance he sees in Paul and Rip illuminates all the arguments
about money-making which the writers in this section have advanced.
And the various individuals, fictional or real, which appear in the section
can be said to be the sons of one folk hero or the other. Elements of humor
appear in LeFevre's article, in considering which it is well to remember
that humor can refer to a characteristic cast of personality as well as to
the quality of being funny. A suggestive and readable book on this topic
is Constance Rourke's *American Humor*.

> "... The conflict between Paul and Rip goes on within the mind
> and emotions of every American. ..."

The favorite heroes and legends of a people tell a great deal about their goals
and the roads by which they seek satisfaction for their desires. Achilles and
Odysseus represent contrasting phases of ancient Greek character; Siegfried
and Hagen are not without value for the understanding of modern Germany;
and the story of the Forty-Seven Ronin sheds light on Japanese ideals and
Japanese methods of warfare. American life may be symbolized as a continuing debate between Paul Bunyan and Rip Van Winkle.

Paul is the epic hero of America, the man who gets things done on a vast
scale. The giant logger, according to the legends, left Puget Sound, the Grand
Canyon, and the Rocky Mountains as memorials of his exploits. Puget Sound
fills the grave which Paul dug for Babe, the Blue Ox, who measured forty-
two ax handles and a plug of chewing tobacco between the horns. The desert
is barren because Paul drove all the trees down under the ground, using one
of the Rocky Mountain peaks as a pile-driver. Paul is only one of a cluster
of heroes, to whom such fabulous deeds are ascribed in popular legend. Tony
Beaver, another logging superman, John Henry, the giant Negro, and Pecos
Bill, the cowboy who rode a cyclone, are avatars of the same tradition.

Like Achilles, Siegfried, and other epic heroes, Paul Bunyan embodies the drive of impotent mankind for power. But Paul is not a warrior, nor does he seek leadership among men through wily tricks like Odysseus or Hagen. His goal is power over nature — forests, mountains, and rivers — not primarily over other men.

Paul represents the American frontier tradition of titanic material achievement. The frontier had its Indian wars, which left such heroes as Daniel Boone; but the Indians were not formidable enough to make the struggle against them the major drama of the American stage. The ordinary American dreamed of exploiting the wealth of a continent more than of the conquest of a human foe. The Germans, whose heroes are Siegfried and Hagen, have followed such martial leaders as Frederick, Bismarck, and Hitler. With Paul Bunyan as a popular hero, America gave birth to lavish oil wells and swarming cars, to John D. Rockefeller and Henry Ford.

While men love power, they hate drudgery. Rip Van Winkle as a folk hero goes back to the legend of the Garden of Eden. The primal curse imposed on Adam was that he must earn his bread through sweat and toil. Adam's children have never welcomed this decree.

Our earliest human ancestors were wandering hunters, who took their food where they found it and, according to their skill and good fortune, feasted or starved. But with the development of agriculture, men learned by harsh experience through thousands of years that somebody must labor long hours in the fields in order to produce an abundant harvest. It was also necessary to save part of the crop for seed and to build up reserves for bad seasons to prevent famine. These necessities bore heavily on mankind. The burden of irksome labor was shifted whenever possible to slaves, or sometimes to the women of the tribe. Men remembered in legends of a Golden Age a happy past when their ancestors had been free from toil; and they dreamed of a future Utopia, where drudgery would no longer be enforced on their children. Philosophers and religious leaders offered similar ideals to their chosen followers. Plato exempted the citizens of his Republic from all physical labor. Jesus of Nazareth commended to his disciples the example of the lilies of the field, who neither toil nor spin, and admonished them to take no thought for the morrow, how they should eat or clothe themselves.

One of the most pervasive, almost universal American folk heroes is Rip Van Winkle. After Irving first told the story, Joseph Jefferson toured the country for forty years in the role of the lovable ne'er-do-well, who wandered with his dog and gun through the Catskill Mountains and slept for twenty years rather than stay at home to work and provide for his family.

Irving portrayed him with luminous clarity: "The great error in Rip's composition was an insuperable aversion to all kinds of profitable labor. It could not be from the want of assiduity or perseverance; for he would sit on a wet rock, with a rod as long and heavy as a Tartar's lance, and fish all day without a murmur, even though he should not be encouraged by a single nibble. He would carry a fowling-piece on his shoulder for hours together, trudging through woods and swamps, and up hill and down dale, to shoot a few squirrels or wild pigeons. He would never refuse to assist a neighbor even in the roughest toil, and was a foremost man at all country frolics for husking Indian corn, or building stone fences; the women of the village, too, used to employ him to run their errands, and to do such little odd jobs as their less obliging husbands would not do for them. In a word, Rip was ready to attend to anybody's business but his own; but as to doing family duty, and keeping his farm in order, he found it impossible."

Essentially the same character appears through every generation in American plays, songs, stories, on the radio and in the movies. This character is often presented as engaging and sympathetic, while the descendants of Dame Van Winkle, who tried vainly to nag her husband into compliance with the orthodox economic virtues, are the villains of the tale.

The economic virtues, nevertheless, were so vitally imperative that they almost completely established their supremacy. In the theories of Adam Smith and his successors, they were accepted as the mainspring of society. The settlement and tremendous growth of America, a virgin continent with a fabulous wealth of natural resources, opened an arena of incomparable magnitude. Here the spirit of Paul Bunyan found abundant fulfilment.

For the development of a continent, however, even under the most favorable conditions, many generations strove through lives of hard work and self-denial. Steady labor and thrift inevitably require a great deal of frustration and repression of normal human impulses. These repressions present areas for study, perhaps as important as those explored by Freud in his investigation of sexual repression. It is no more natural for man to toil long hours at disagreeable tasks, or to deny himself beefsteaks and pleasure driving, than it is for him to suppress his sexual impulses. The Rip Van Winkle complex may mean as much as the Oedipus complex in the modern American world.

The conflict between Paul and Rip can be traced through manifold phases of American literature and American life. It appears vividly in Tom Sawyer and Huckleberry Finn. Tom's bold spirit and inventive mind mark a true scion of the Paul Bunyan tradition. He is so eager to achieve adventures that when no real difficulties arise in setting Jim, the fugitive slave, free, he creates his own difficulties with fantastic ingenuity. In the whitewashing episode, he combines the triumphs of Paul and Rip; he gets the job done, while the other boys do the work. But Huck is the authentic heir of Rip. Drifting down the Mississippi on his raft with Jim, he escapes the well-meant efforts of the Widow Douglas to civilize him. "Other places do seem so cramped up and smothery," says Huck, "but a raft don't. You feel mighty free and easy and comfortable on a raft." There is nothing to do, he goes on, but fish and swim and sleep and drift with the current. And all the respectably trained boys envied Huck's freedom.

The tradition of Paul represents the conscious ambition of Americans to do great deeds, exaggerated to fantasy. It is expressed today in the Superman comics with all their swarm of imitators. American boys brag about their dreams of emulating such legendary heroes. In the world of reality, the spirit of Paul has filled American roads with cars in time of peace and the skies of the whole world with planes in time of war. The atomic bomb is the latest in a long series of triumphs.

Not many Americans, perhaps, would consciously admit a desire to follow in Rip's footsteps. But if the popular arts enable us to give vicarious satisfaction to our repressed desires, the protean descendants of Rip clearly manifest a powerful American rebellion against the orthodox virtues of sober thrift and hard work. Frank Bacon and Will Rogers as lightnin' Bill Jones, the Sycamore family in *You Can't Take It with You*, the Tussies in Jesse Stuart's yarn, Elwood P. Dowd in *Harvey*, John, the witch boy, in *Dark of the Moon*, are legitimate children of Rip.

A movie, *Tom, Dick and Harry*, some years ago illustrated with unusual clarity Rip's perennial appeal. In this film, Ginger Rogers, as a telephone operator, received proposals from three suitors. Tom was a hard-working, ambitious salesman; Dick a rich man, apparently the perfect answer to a working girl's fondest hopes; and Harry a happy-go-lucky irresponsible boy, who, in Ginger's dream about him, welcomed the loss of his job, because it would give him more time to go fishing. At the end of the picture, Ginger refused the other two wooers to ride away on Harry's motor-cycle, today's equivalent of Huckleberry Finn's raft or Rip's magic flagon. A significant point is that three endings were made for this movie and were tried out on various audiences in pre-view showings. The choice of Harry represented a decisive popular verdict.

Illustrations might be multiplied. The desire of men for ease and leisure attains the same vicarious satisfaction in two categories of books immensely popular in America. A hundred years ago, Herman Melville returned from the South Seas to write *Typee*. Since then, Stevenson, Frederick O'Brien, Nordhoff and Hall have repeatedly demonstrated the enthusiasm of our reading public for stories of South Sea Island life. The relative freedom of the islanders from the curse of Adam has perhaps contributed as much to their popularity as the unveiled charms of island girls. The unending series of best-sellers about Southern plantation life also testifies to the perpetual attraction for the American mind of a leisure class who transferred the necessity for labor to their slaves.

The conflict between Paul and Rip goes on within the mind and emotions of every American. All men have some degree of ambition for achievement and some measure of desire for ease. This conflict can never find a final solution; like other struggles which involve the individual libido, it will be resolved most effectively when it is exposed to the full light of consciousness. Unconscious frustration and repression of emotional drives are the banes that irreparably poison our lives.

Like Paul Bunyan's ambitious dreams, Rip's rebellion against drudgery has directly affected the realities of American life. In the days of unrestricted immigration, native-born white Americans showed a decided tendency to avoid physical labor and to turn it over to Negroes and newcomers. Judge Cary of the United States Steel Corporation argued forcibly that the steel industry could not find the necessary workers without a constant flow of fresh immigration. Our emphasis on labor-saving as a goal still surprises foreign visitors. Automatic furnaces and electric kitchens are as American as corn on the cob. The automobile, which by its almost universal use most conspicuously distinguishes American life, gives satisfaction to the aspirations of both Paul and Rip. We generally drive our own cars; the driver enjoys the thrill of power under his command, while at the same time he escapes the physical labor of walking. Thus the ambivalent aspects of the American spirit are reconciled.

Henry Ford, as much as any living American, embodies the spirit of Paul Bunyan. His achievements in mass production are legendary marvels over the whole world. Ford tells in his autobiography that his father wanted him to stay on the farm; but his earliest recollection was that "there was too much hard hand labor" in farming and he still felt that way. He was willing to work night and day on his machines. "I cannot say that it was hard work. No work with interest is ever hard." Ford, like other men, in short, loved power and hated drudgery.

In our vast war industry, the exploits of such men as Henry Kaiser and Andrew Jackson Higgins exemplify the same combination of motives, with the mammoth plans of Paul accomplished by the minimum possible employment of manual labor. The Japanese built their airfields by the toil of countless coolies. We built ours with myriads of cats and bulldozers.

Our industrial civilization has profoundly changed the environment in which Paul Bunyan and Rip Van Winkle must seek to attain their goals. Paul has been a hero of American business men, the archetype of free enterprise. American capitalism has exploited the continent with bold imagination and abounding vigor. It has also supplied immensely powerful motives to counterbalance Rip's normal human weaknesses. It exerted the most vigorous pressure on each individual to work, to save, and to provide the good things of life for his family. This intellectual and emotional climate has perhaps contributed as much as our huge natural resources to the mechanical and industrial leadership of America. The growth of giant industry, however, itself limits the opportunities for individuals to fulfil Paul's dreams. When some private enterprises number their workers by the hundred thousand, clearly not every boy can run a business of his own. But today our great enterprises are, of course, not all private enterprises, as witness the Panama Canal, Grand Coulee Dam, and the prolific activities of the T.V.A. which were government projects undertaken mainly for the public good rather than personal profit. The Russian Five-Year Plans have added more evidence that it is quite possible to make vast strides and to divorce the spirit of Paul from an exclusive devotion to personal financial profit.

The Industrial Revolution has also created a new world for Rip. It offers, for the first time, the possibility of freedom from the immemorial bondage of drudgery and scarcity; but it has multiplied a proletariat for whom the conditions of labor are sometimes more monotonous and irksome than before. Strong currents in modern life limit Paul's dream of individual power and exasperate Rip's rebellion against drudgery.

The appeal of Communist theory to idealists in all countries derives primarily from its ultimate promise of a free classless society in which all men will be liberated from the ancient lot of the masses, long hours of labor poorly paid. We no longer need throngs of hewers of wood and drawers of water. Wood stoves can be replaced by automatic furnaces; water can be brought a hundred miles from Rip's Catskills to the kitchens and baths of New York. The work that remains necessary can be divided so that everyone does his share, with no idle leisure class living on the toil of men reduced to abject poverty.

Communism is based, however, not only on a golden promise for the future but on bitterness for the present and the past. The doctrines of the class war and the dictatorship of the proletariat offer to labor a chance to avenge the frustrations imposed by the factory system. These doctrines express emotional drives like those which stirred Dame Van Winkle to natural indignation at the sight of her idle husband. The dancing grasshopper has always exasperated the ant. The Marxist theory of the class war is formulated in objective, scientific terminology; it looks towards a Utopian future of prosperity for all mankind; but it derives its fighting spirit from the frustrations of workers embittered by the knowledge that other men are not obliged to labor.

Class conflict is sharpened by the chasm between Paul and Rip, between men to whom work is a means to power and men to whom work is drudgery. Wherever Americans identify themselves with Paul Bunyan in their dreams, Marxist slogans fall on stony ground. Business executives, engineers, landowning farmers, and highly skilled craftsmen, for example, are seldom zealots of the class struggle. But workers on factory assembly lines will never look at their labor with the spirit of Paul. They have no individual choice as to how they shall do their work, little variety and no escape during working hours from the tedious routine of their jobs. They must find satisfaction elsewhere for their impulses and desires. When their lives do not yield an essential minimum of satisfaction, their frustration is often expressed in revolt against the conditions of their work. Outlaw strikes for trivial grievances may arise primarily from the age-old rebellion of Rip's children against the compulsion to irksome labor.

Frustration in any field, as Dr. John Dollard and his associates have shown, is easily transformed into aggression against others. The sex impulse may be sublimated in art or diverted into fierce advocacy of puritanical restraints for other people. The desires of men for ease and leisure may likewise be sublimated in stories of Rip Van Winkle or Huckleberry Finn, or in prophetic visions of Utopias; but when these desires are too harshly repressed, they provide fertile soil for the growth of racial and class hatreds. Men who live harsh lives often gain a sadistic satisfaction from the reduction of others to a still lower level. Many Southern poor whites hate the Negroes for the evils they themselves endure; and many middle-class Germans, ruined by inflation and the great economic collapse, listened eagerly to Hitler's tirades against Jews and foreigners.

Every newspaper shows that today's world is filled and overflowing with frustration for multitudes of men. But in a democracy, our leaders, to hold power, must convince the voters that the necessities of labor and self-denial are allotted according to principles of justice. These necessities can be ameliorated with advancing economic progress. In the world of the future, every man may have a measure of opportunity to realize his ambitions and of leisure to express his dreams.

In this country, the time is past when Paul Bunyan could go into the wilderness and carve out his individual empire in virgin country. The world which he seeks to develop is populated by other men. If he ignores the nature of human beings and confines his attention to mastery of material resources, he may destroy a people with atomic bombs or conquer them and rule by force. But democratic peoples are controlled by men skilled in the arts of persuasion; in short, they are governed by politicians.

A successful politician must understand the people whom he wishes to govern. He cannot act as if they were perfect citizens, moved only by disinterested reason; he must take them as they are. The alchemists, who tried to use chemical substances in accordance with preconceived theories as to how they ought to behave, did not accomplish very much. The politician deals with substances more complex and variegated than chemical elements; but this does not absolve him from the necessity of understanding the materials with which he works. In modern America, he must understand both Paul Bunyan and Rip Van Winkle.

No people could long survive the storms of harsh reality who accepted Rip's guidance as sole pilot. The South Sea islanders yielded before the white man. Owners of vast Southern plantations saw their culture uprooted and laid waste. Escape from all obligation to labor would mean destruction at the hands of more aggressive peoples.

Toil and hardship for their own sake, however, are dubious values in a machine age. The Germans preferred guns to butter; and the Japanese also looked with scorn on the softness and ease of American life. Our enemies found too late that we could outbuild the rest of the world in planes, precisely because mass production was prepared to give almost every American family a car.

There is no virtue certainly in labor and privation delegated to others. It does not harden our own children if other men's children work in sweatshops or live in slums. Sweatshops and slums everywhere in the world breed disease, cut-throat competition, unemployment, and war. Mass unemployment is the deadliest of all threats to the adventurous, constructive spirit of Paul Bunyan. Praise of traditional American values will strike deaf ears if ten million men can find no work and no income except a scanty dole.

The fatal doom of ruling classes and dominant nations through all history has been to seek Rip's goal of ease and leisure for their own children, while drudgery and poverty were imposed on men who could not escape their inferior lot. But frustrations imposed on subjects breed rebellions which eventually destroy the rulers. Rich men's sons are not often actuated by the fierce driving energy which impels those who fight their way up from poverty. Thus the attainment of wealth and power may sterilize the motives by which they were won. Paul Bunyan's children follow Rip's way of life until they are conquered by ambitious newcomers.

Neither Paul nor Rip can ever completely attain his goal in any human society. But the American tradition offers abundant opportunities for struggle towards both greater power and greater leisure for all mankind. In America, power over material things has far surpassed that attained in other lands. Power over other men rests on a fundamental basis of popular consent. And in America the struggle for freedom from drudgery has also won its greatest victories. With all our faults and failures, our economic injustice and racial discrimination, we try with increasing success to impose the harshest burdens of labor, not on slaves or women, servants or permanently depressed classes, but on our machines. Both Paul and Rip may still take hope in American life.

[1946]

Patriotism of the Early Republic

In Civil Strife

To Save the World for Democracy: Retrospect

Search for National Meaning

New Sovereignties

The Sense of Nationality

American patriotism is distinguished by the fact that it attaches less to a land than to a set of principles and institutions. The German's sense of "father-land" is profound, as is the Russian's feeling toward "mother Russia" and the Frenchman's for "la belle France." The American, however, particularly in times of national peril, has tended to ally himself less with a place than an ideal, less with a country than a cause. In each of our great wars the issue has been, in an important sense, less national than ideological. In each — the American Revolution, the Civil War, the two World Wars — men have marched under the banner of *freedom*. America has no monopoly on that banner, of course, but she has been more than usually prone to employ it. Lincoln's insistence that the major issue of the Civil War was national unity had a much narrower appeal than "The Battle-Hymn of the Republic," whose central idea was, as its author said, "the sacredness of human liberty." Franklin Roosevelt's suggestion that the Second World War be termed the War for Survival found little support; the American people preferred Dwight Eisen-hower's idea that we were engaged in a Crusade in Europe.

In the eighteenth and nineteenth centuries, the Americans' pride in "the good old U. S. A." was intense, but it was a pride conditioned by the fact that there were, after all, other more powerful nations in the world. Then sud-denly, in the years after World War I, we found ourselves second to none, at least in power, so that by 1941 *Life* magazine could speak of "The American Century." It was time, wrote its publisher, Henry Luce, "to accept whole-heartedly our duty and our opportunity as the most powerful and vital nation in the world and in consequence to exert upon the world the full impact of our influence, for such purposes as we see fit and by such means as we see fit."

Thus in 1941. Today, only two decades later, the world has been trans-formed by the atomic and hydrogen bombs, by the continuing tensions of the Cold War, and, hopefully, by the United Nations as an international force. Still, though our confidence is somewhat shaken, our sense of national identity remains strong. Recently, when a British statesman remarked that a Russian triumph would be preferable to the universal extinction of a nuclear war, Eleanor Roosevelt replied that, in her opinion, "most people in the United States . . . would say: 'If we have to be dominated by the Soviet Union, we would rather be wiped out.'"

Patriotism of the Early Republic

Speech in the Virginia Convention of Delegates   PATRICK HENRY

Patrick Henry (1736–1799) actively participated in the American Revolution as a member of the first and second Continental Congresses, as a soldier, and as a Governor of Virginia; he is chiefly remembered, however, for his address to the Virginia Convention of Delegates in Richmond on March 23, 1775. No actual copy of the speech remains, and it may, in fact, never have been written out; the version we have is a reconstruction, believed to be quite accurate, by Henry's biographer, William Wirt. There is perhaps no more widely known American patriotic utterance than that contained in the final sentences of this speech. Henry spoke, wrote Wirt, with "his arms extended aloft, his brows knit, every feature marked with the resolute purpose of his soul, and his voice swelled to its boldest note of exclamation."

Though Henry's basic appeal is emotional throughout, he doesn't put logic entirely aside until the final paragraph. Playing on the themes of hopes-disappointed and dangers-at-hand, appealing to his audience of Virginia gentlemen in terms they cherish and understand, he swiftly and with a sense of inevitability moves toward an appeal to arms. Much of Henry's phrasing is general and abstract, but there is effective use of the specific instance and concrete image as well. Unlike the typical public speaker of today, his posture is heroic, his style "grand."

". . . If we wish to be free . . . we must fight! . . ."

No man thinks more highly than I do of the patriotism, as well as abilities, of the very worthy gentlemen who have just addressed the house. But different men often see the same subjects in different lights; and, therefore, I hope it will not be thought disrespectful to those gentlemen, if, entertaining as I do, opinions of a character very opposite to theirs, I shall speak forth my sentiments freely, and without reserve. This is no time for ceremony. The question before the house is one of awful moment to this country. For my own part, I consider it as nothing less than a question of freedom or slavery. And in proportion to the magnitude of the subject, ought to be the freedom of the debate. It is only in this way that we can hope to arrive at truth, and fulfil the great responsibility which we hold to God and our country. Should I keep back my opinions at such a time, through fear of giving offence, I should consider myself as guilty of treason towards my country, and of an act of disloyalty toward the majesty of Heaven, which I revere above all earthly kings.

Mr. President, it is natural to man to indulge in the illusions of hope. We are apt to shut our eyes against a painful truth and listen to the song of that syren, till she transforms us into beasts. Is this the part of wise men, engaged in a great and arduous struggle for liberty? Are we disposed to be of the number of those, who having eyes, see not, and having ears, hear not, the things which so nearly concern their temporal salvation? For my part, whatever anguish of spirit it may cost, I am willing to know the whole truth; to know the worst, and to provide for it.

I have but one lamp by which my feet are guided; and that is the lamp of experience. I know of no way of judging of the future but by the past. And judging by the past, I wish to know what there has been in the conduct of the British ministry for the last ten years, to justify those hopes with which gentlemen have been pleased to solace themselves and the house? Is it that insidious smile with which our petition has been lately received? Trust it not, sir; it will prove a snare to your feet. Suffer not yourselves to be betrayed with a kiss. Ask yourselves how this gracious reception of our petition comports with those warlike preparations which cover our waters and darken our land. Are fleets and armies necessary to a work of love and reconciliation? Have we shown ourselves so unwilling to be reconciled, that force must be called in to win back our love? Let us not deceive ourselves, sir. These are the implements of war and subjugation, the last arguments to which kings resort.

I ask, gentlemen, sir, what means this martial array, if its purpose be not to force us to submission? Can gentlemen assign any other possible motive for it? Has Great Britain any enemy in this quarter of the world, to call for all this accumulation of navies and armies? No, sir, she has none. They are meant for us; they can be meant for no other. They are sent over to bind and rivet upon us those chains, which the British ministry have been so long forging. And what have we to oppose to them? Shall we try argument? Sir, we have been trying that for the last ten years. Have we any thing new to offer upon the subject? Nothing. We have held the subject up in every light of which it is capable; but it has been all in vain. Shall we resort to entreaty and humble supplication? What terms shall we find, which have not been already exhausted? Let us not, I beseech you, sir, deceive ourselves longer. Sir, we have done every thing that could be done, to avert the storm which is now coming on. We have petitioned, we have remonstrated, we have supplicated, we have prostrated ourselves before the throne, and have implored its interposition to arrest the tyrannical hands of the ministry and parliament. Our petitions have been slighted; our remonstrances have produced additional violence and insult; our supplications have been disregarded; and we have been spurned, with contempt, from the foot of the throne. In vain, after these things, may we indulge the fond hope of peace and reconciliation. There is no longer any room for hope. If we wish to be free, if we mean to preserve inviolate those inestimable privileges for which we have been so long contending, if we mean not basely to abandon the noble struggle in which we have been so long engaged, and which we have pledged ourselves never to abandon, until the glorious object of our contest shall be obtained, we must fight! — I repeat it, sir, we must fight!! An appeal to arms and to the God of Hosts is all that is left us!

They tell us, sir, that we are weak, unable to cope with so formidable an adversary. But when shall we be stronger? Will it be the next week or the next year? Will it be when we are totally disarmed, and when a British guard shall be stationed in every house? Shall we gather strength by irresolution and inaction? Shall we acquire the means of effectual resistance by lying supinely on our backs, and hugging the delusive phantom of hope, until our enemies shall have bound us hand and foot? Sir, we are not weak, if we make a proper use of those means which the God of nature hath placed in our power. Three millions of people, armed in the holy cause of liberty, and in such a country as that which we possess, are invincible by any force which our enemy can send against us. Besides, sir, we shall not fight our battles alone. There is a just God who presides over the destinies of nations, and who will raise up friends to fight our battles for us. The battle, sir, is not to the strong alone; it is to the vigilant, the active, the brave. Besides, sir, we have no election. If we were base enough to desire it, it is now too late to retire from the contest. There is no retreat, but in submission and slavery! Our chains are forged. Their clanking may be heard on the plains of Boston! The war is inevitable — and let it come!! I repeat it, sir, let it come!!!

It is in vain, sir, to extenuate the matter. Gentlemen may cry, peace, peace — but there is no peace. The war is actually begun! The next gale that sweeps from the north will bring to our ears the clash of resounding arms! Our brethren are already in the field! Why stand we here idle? What is it that gentlemen wish? What would they have? Is life so dear, or peace so sweet, as to be purchased at the price of chains and slavery? Forbid it, Almighty God! I know not what course others may take; but as for me, give me liberty or give me death!

[1775]

A Declaration of Independency   JOHN ADAMS

John Adams (1735–1826) served as American envoy to several European capitals and was the first Vice President and second President of the United States. As the present selection shows, he was also active in the first Continental Congress, where he served on the committee which drew up the Declaration of Independence. Adams is writing to his wife Abigail. Since the declaration was passed, as the letter shows, on July 2, that and not July 4 is the actual anniversary date of American independence.

The tone of Adams' letter, despite his "enthusiasm," is quite different from that of Henry's oration, his purpose being not to persuade, but to inform, to share his joy, and also to take sober stock of the present situation. Adams reveals his heritage of New England Calvinism through certain attitudes which were notably absent in the thinking of his lifelong associate, the equalitarian Thomas Jefferson.

". . . I can see the rays of ravishing light and glory. . . ."

Philadelphia, 3 July, 1776.

Yesterday, the greatest question was decided, which ever was debated in America, and a greater, perhaps, never was nor will be decided among men. A resolution was passed without one dissenting colony, "that these United Colonies are, and of right ought to be, free and independent States, and as such they have, and of right ought to have, full power to make war, conclude peace, establish commerce, and to do all other acts and things which other States may rightfully do." You will see in a few days a Declaration setting forth the causes which have impelled us to this mighty revolution, and the reasons which will justify it in the sight of God and man. A plan of confederation will be taken up in a few days.

When I look back to the year 1761, and recollect the argument concerning writs of assistance in the superior court, which I have hitherto considered as the commencement of this controversy between Great Britain and America, and run through the whole period, from that time to this, and recollect the series of political events, the chain of causes and effects, I am surprised at the suddenness as well as greatness of this revolution. Britain has been filled with folly, and America with wisdom. At least, this is my judgment. Time must determine. It is the will of Heaven that the two countries should be sundered forever. It may be the will of Heaven that America shall suffer calamities still more wasting, and distresses yet more dreadful. If this is to be the case, it will have this good effect at least. It will inspire us with many virtues, which we have not, and correct many errors, follies and vices which threaten to disturb, dishonor, and destroy us. The furnace of affliction produces refinement, in States as well as individuals. And the new governments we are assuming in every part will require a purification from our vices, and an augmentation of our virtues, or they will be no blessings. The people will have unbounded power, and the people are extremely addicted to corruption and venality, as well as the great. But I must submit all my hopes and fears to an overruling Providence, in which, unfashionable as the faith may be, I firmly believe.

Had a Declaration of Independency been made seven months ago, it would have been attended with many great and glorious effects. We might, before this hour, have formed alliances with foreign states. We should have mastered Quebec, and been in possession of Canada. You will perhaps wonder how such a declaration would have influenced our affairs in Canada, but if I could write with freedom, I could easily convince you that it would, and explain to you the manner how. Many gentlemen in high stations and of great influence have been duped by the ministerial bubble of commissioners to treat. And in real, sincere expectation of this event, which they so fondly wished, they have been slow and languid in promoting measures for the reduction of that province. Others there are in the colonies who really wished that our enterprise in Canada would be defeated, that the colonies might be brought into danger and distress between two fires, and be thus induced to submit. Others really wished to defeat the expedition to Canada, lest the conquest of it should elevate the minds of the people too much to hearken to those terms of reconciliation, which, they believed, would be offered us. These jarring views, wishes, and designs, occasioned an opposition to many salutary measures, which were proposed for the support of that expedition, and caused obstructions, embarrassments, and studied delays, which have finally lost us the province.

All these causes, however, in conjunction, would not have disappointed us, if it had not been for a misfortune which could not be foreseen, and, perhaps, could not have been prevented — I mean the prevalence of the small-pox among our troops. This fatal pestilence completed our destruction. It is a frown of Providence upon us, which we ought to lay to heart.

But on the other hand, the delay of this Declaration to this time has many great advantages attending it. The hopes of reconciliation which were fondly entertained by multitudes of honest and well-meaning though weak and mis-taken people, have been gradually and at last totally extinguished. Time has been given for the whole people maturely to consider the great question of Independence, and to ripen their judgment, dissipate their fears, and allure their hopes, by discussing it in newspapers and pamphlets, by debating it in assemblies, conventions, committees of safety and inspection, in town and county meetings, as well as in private conversations, so that the whole people, in every colony of the thirteen, have now adopted it as their own act. This will cement the union, and avoid those heats, and perhaps convulsions, which might have been occasioned by such a Declaration six months ago.

But the day is past. The second day of July, 1776, will be the most memorable epocha in the history of America. I am apt to believe that it will be celebrated by succeeding generations as the great anniversary festival. It ought to be commemorated as the day of deliverance, by solemn acts of devo-tion to God Almighty. It ought to be solemnized with pomp and parade, with shows, games, sports, guns, bells, bonfires, and illuminations, from one end of this continent to the other, from this time forward forevermore.

You will think me transported with enthusiasm, but I am not. I am well aware of the toil and blood and treasure it will cost us to maintain this Declaration and support and defend these States. Yet, through all the gloom, I can see the rays of ravishing light and glory. I can see that the end is more than worth all the means. And that posterity will triumph in this day's trans-action, even though we should rue it, which I trust in God we shall not.

To the Memory of the Brave Americans   PHILIP FRENEAU

The first American after Edward Taylor (see p. 128) to possess an impor-tant poetic talent was Philip Freneau (1752–1832), (see p. 141), sea captain, newspaper editor, and democratic partisan. He graduated from Princeton in 1771 with classmates Aaron Burr, James Madison, and Hugh Henry Brackenridge, with the last of whom he wrote a commence-ment poem titled "The Rising Glory of America." During the Revolution he wrote a number of verses in support of the American cause, served as a blockade runner, and was captured by the British. After the war he became editor of the Jeffersonian *The National Gazette* and wrote such violent anti-Federalist diatribes that Washington spoke of him as "that rascal Freneau." The last years of his life Freneau spent in poverty and obscurity, finally dying of exposure in a blizzard at the age of eighty. Such things, however, lay far in the future when the young patriot-poet wrote his tribute "to the memory of the brave Americans, under General Greene, in South Carolina, who fell in the action of September 8, 1781." Greene's troops had forced a British retreat, but they suffered over five hundred casualties when the enemy rallied.

Freneau's poem is typical of much eighteenth-century verse. The gentle melancholy — so different from the tone of either Patrick Henry or John Adams — the personification, the regularity of metre and rhyme, the concern with death, the classical allusions, the "poetic diction," all mark the poem as "neo-classical." The honesty and depth of Freneau's patriotic feeling, however, makes the poem more than a conventional literary exercise.

"*. . . None griev'd, in such a cause, to die. . . .*"

At Eutaw springs the valiant died:
Their limbs with dust are cover'd o'er —
Weep on, ye springs, your tearful tide;
How many heroes are no more!

If in this wreck of ruin, they   5
Can yet be thought to claim a tear,
O smite thy gentle breast, and say
The friends of freedom slumber here!

Thou, who shalt trace this bloody plain,
If goodness rules thy generous breast,   10
Sigh for the wasted rural reign;
Sigh for the shepherds, sunk to rest!

Stranger, their humble graves adorn;
You too may fall, and ask a tear:
'Tis not the beauty of the morn   15
That proves the evening shall be clear —

They saw their injur'd country's woe;
The flaming town, the wasted field;
Then rush'd to meet the insulting foe;
They took the spear — but left the shield,   20

Led by thy conquering genius, GREENE,
The Britons they compell'd to fly:

None distant view'd the fatal plain,
None griev'd, in such a cause, to die —

But, like the Parthian, fam'd of old,   25
Who, flying, still their arrows threw;
These routed Britons, full as bold,
Retreated, and retreating slew.

Now rest in peace, our patriot band;
Though far from Nature's limits thrown,   30
We trust, they find a happier land,
A brighter sun-shine of their own.

                                                        [1781]

Pre-Sumter Symbolism of the Democratic Faith   RALPH GABRIEL

When he retired in 1958, Ralph Henry Gabriel (1890–   ) had been
associated with Yale University for almost fifty years, first as a student and
then as a teacher of history. "The Pre-Sumter Symbolism of the Democratic Faith" is taken from chapter eight of *The Course of American
Democratic Thought* (1940), a well-known and widely respected work.
It is one of the few in the field of American historical literature which, in
the words of Henry Steele Commager, "attempt interpretation on the
grand scale."
    In clearly ordered paragraphs and unpretentious style, Gabriel here
analyzes some of the symbols by which pre-Civil War America expressed
its fervent patriotism. It is worth comparing the nature of these symbols
to patriotic symbols in our own day, a time when, as Gabriel remarks,
they have become "instruments of power often consciously manipulated
by individuals, organizations, or governments to further definite ends."

"... The Fourth of July ... was both a gala day and a national sabbath. ..."

A nation is an in-group whose members cooperate to achieve certain ends.
Yet the citizens compete with one another for the prizes of life. The need
to cooperate is a frustrating factor in their lives. It leads inevitably to aggres-
sions which tend to disrupt the group. Patriotism, national consciousness,
group feeling (all are synonyms) is a force operating mostly at the level of
the emotions to counteract the disruptive tendencies which, if unchecked,
sometimes destroy group cohesion. The democratic faith appeared in American culture as one of the principal forces making for what Whitman used to

call adhesiveness. The ultimate appeal of the formula was to the feelings. If it were to have utility in the culture, it must be able to evoke an emotional response. To stir the sentiments of the people the faith must express itself in symbols. . . .

One of the more extraordinary political events of the eighteenth century was the coalescing of thirteen rebelling provinces into a stable political unit. The nation in 1783, when distances are measured in time, was larger than the United States of the twentieth century. Each state represented an in-group with particular traditions which, in some cases, included antagonism to other states. The war emergency compelled these former colonies to cooperate, and the events of the struggle for independence gave, to all, common experiences and memories. The conflict, moreover, gave them in the rebel general, Washington, a living personification of the idea of unity. Where Washington established his headquarters, there was the heart of the Revolution.

Washington's generation gave to him the title of "Father of His Country." It is difficult to overestimate his significance in the founding of the nation. He was a product of the culture of his age and he exemplified so well qualities which his generation admired that his person became the rallying point of the rebellion. He combined devotion to the cause, personal integrity, physical courage, a sound judgment of men, and considerable military ability. During the conflict the stature of Congress declined, while that of the general-in-chief increased. After Yorktown, Washington's prestige was greater than that of the government of the United States. The general increased it still further by three acts: he refused the crown suggested by a group who wished to establish a strong State; he persuaded his discontented officers at Newburgh not to use the sword to compel an impotent Congress to give them their pay; and after the signing of the peace treaty he resigned his commission, in a conspicuous ceremony, and returned to private life. The advocates of reform who finally succeeded in bringing about the Constitutional Convention took pains to secure the support of Washington at the outset of their movement, for they well knew that without the support of his prestige their effort would be futile. Even after the Philadelphia instrument was ratified, Americans called upon him to take the lead in organizing the new government.

In a country in which James Madison said that he knew as little of the affairs of Georgia as he did of Kamchatka, the surprising thing is that, after the menace of the common enemy had been removed, two or three nations did not come into being. One of the most important of the factors which prevented such an outcome was the existence of a leader who not only personified national unity but in his behavior conformed to the ideals for which the rebellion had been fought. The importance of this personification is suggested by the reference to Washington, still living but no longer president, in the first of the patriotic songs of the new United States. Robert Treat Paine published in 1798 "Adams and Liberty" which was sung to the old tune which Francis Scott Key later used for the "Star-Spangled Banner":

> Should the tempest of war overshadow our land
> Its bolts could ne'er rend Freedom's temple asunder;

For, unmoved, at its portal would Washington stand
And repulse with his breast the assaults of his thunder.

Eighteenth-century American republicans, establishing a new nation, first turned for their symbolism to the greatest republic they knew, Rome. They called the upper house of Congress a Senate. Led by the imaginative Jefferson they used Roman architectural forms in the building of their first national Capitol and of the White House. These Classical Revival buildings were acceptable because they were not far removed from the Georgian structures with which Americans were familiar. The domed Capitol with its Roman columns expressed so well the dignity of the new nation that the type has become virtually indigenous to the United States. When classicism was carried beyond architecture, it failed. The goddess of liberty which appeared on the coins had no emotional value for Americans and persisted only because there was nothing available with which to replace the figure. Classicism degenerated into absurdity in the giant seated statue of the first President done by Horatio Greenough and placed in 1843 before the Capitol building at Washington. The patriotic sculptor stripped the toga-clad Washington to the waist and seated him in a Roman chair. The figure became the joke of the city of hotels and boarding houses sprawling beside the Potomac. Greenough's carving suggests an almost wistful groping after national symbols on the part of the Americans of the Middle Period.

As a result of the poverty in symbolism, the flag became the chief representation of the nation. During the War of 1812, Key's verses began their rise to the ultimate status of national anthem. It is no accident that the two great patriotic songs of the English-speaking peoples, "God Save the King" and "The Star-Spangled Banner," refer to a living symbolic person and to a material symbolic object. The peculiar importance of the national banner in American political symbolism was a result of the rejection of monarchy. The American President who replaced the king was so important a political officer that his value as a symbol was negligible.

A material object can never express an idea or an emotion so effectively as can an individual who in some manner has come to personify it. The worship of the saints in the Catholic Church suggests the importance of associating certain virtues or attitudes with definite personalities. The life of the saint becomes a vehicle for the instruction of the people in what would otherwise be abstract ideas. A flag can never escape abstractness. Americans of the Middle Period, lacking a living symbol, turned for the personification of the idea of the nation and of the principles upon which it was founded to the leader of the Revolution. Greenough's Washington suggested that the apotheosis of a dead hero had been already long in process of development.

Parson Weems in his best-selling biography referred to the father of his country as early as 1800 as a "Demigod." Reverence for the memory of Washington early became a standard American attitude, although it was impaired somewhat during the period of the Virginia dynasty by memories of the first President's Federalist leanings. As the slavery issue became a growing threat to the Union, citizens in both North and South sought to strengthen the symbols of nationality by making the memory of a great name a living force. In 1848, amid impressive ceremonies, the cornerstone of the great obelisk on the bank of the Potomac was laid. Slowly, during the succeeding years, the tiers of stones, contributed for the most part by popular subscription, grew higher. Then Anna Pamela Cunningham of Charleston, South Carolina, sent out her first call in 1853 to the women of the South to rescue Mount Vernon, which had long been falling into dilapidation, from threatened commercial exploitation. "A descendant of Virginia," she wrote, "and now a daughter of South Carolina, moved by feelings of reverence for departed greatness and goodness, — by patriotism and a sense of national and, above all, of Southern honor, — ventures to appeal to you in behalf of the home and grave of Washington!" Five years later the triumphant Charleston lady, who during the entire period of her crusade had been aided by Edward Everett in the North, received the keys of Washington's house, and Mount Vernon became the property of the American people. Equally significant of the same trend were the lines of Oliver Wendell Holmes's "Ode to Washington," written in 1856 when both North and South were roused to anger by bloodshed in Kansas:

> Vain is Empire's mad temptation!
>   Not for him an earthly crown!
> He whose sword hath freed a nation
>   Strikes the offered sceptre down.
> See the throneless conqueror seated,
>   Ruler by a people's choice;
> See the Patriot's task completed;
>   Hear the Father's dying voice;
> "By the name that you inherit
>   By the suffering you recall,
> Cherish the fraternal spirit;
>   Love your country first of all!
> Listen not to idle questions
>   If its bands may be untied;
> Doubt the patriot whose suggestions
>   Strive a nation to divide!"

Before 1861, Washington had come to occupy in American civilization a place similar to that of the culture hero in simpler societies. Like the culture hero his memory was associated with those institutions and customs upon which the people put the highest value. He personified more than the idea of nationality. His biography, as suggested in Holmes's stanzas, seemed to mid-nineteenth-century Americans to dramatize one after another the articles of the democratic faith. He had led to success the people's army in the war for liberty. Instead of taking advantage of his personal power, he had championed the cause of constitutionalism, the philosophy of a government of laws. He was a figure to whom Americans could point and say: This is the type of leader democracy can produce.

The apotheosis of a departed hero did not, however, meet fully the American need for national symbols. This demand was supplied most adequately by the recurring ceremonies on the anniversary of independence. The Fourth of July, in the Middle Period, was both a gala day and a national sabbath. The celebration of "the Glorious Fourth" manifested in some aspects the boisterous extravagances of the camp meetings of evangelical Protestantism and in others the austere dignity of a Calvinist service of worship. Alexis de Tocqueville, stopping at Albany, New York, on July 4, 1831, listened to the public reading of the Declaration of Independence and pronounced it one of the more thrilling experiences of his life. . . .

The Declaration of Independence was for ceremonial purposes vastly more important than the Constitution. There was no celebration of a Constitution Day. A few liberals were, in fact, beginning to complain that the younger generation was growing up without adequate knowledge of that great docu-ment because its text was to be found in few school books. As a result, enter-prising publishers began, with appropriate sales propaganda, to make this "palladium of our liberties" available to the youth of the land. Another diffi-culty that impaired the value of the Constitution as a ceremonial document was the disagreement as to its interpretation between the school of Webster and that of Calhoun. Was the Constitution a palladium of liberty because it was the supreme law of a nation or because it was a compact among sovereign states? Cogent arguments supported either position. Until this question was settled, the Constitution could not become an effective symbol. The Declara-tion, on the contrary, created no problems and roused no controversies. The Declaration was not law but rather rhetoric, brilliant rhetoric. For decades the famous phrases that all men are created equal and are endowed by nature with the right to life, liberty, and the pursuit of happiness provided the text for patriotic homilies. When, however, it became possible in the 1850's to charge Americans who took their stand upon the Declaration with proposing equality and even intermarriage between the races, all national symbolism was failing and crisis was near.

A description of a "Fourth" in the Middle Period helps to suggest the mood of American national ritual in the Middle Period. The citizens of Charleston, South Carolina, were awakened at dawn on July 4, 1843, by the pealing of the bells of St. Michael's, a handsome Georgian church built by eighteenth-century wealth. In its pews on Sundays sat the aristocracy of that ante-bellum heyday of the Cotton Kingdom. On this holiday morning, however, the bells of St. Michael's called to worship not only its own con-gregation, but all citizens in the little city between the Ashley and the Cooper Rivers. Families stirred in houses of brick and stucco huddled together in the friendly gregariousness of a European town. As the clangor of the bells died away, cannon on the battery boomed a salute across the sleepy harbor. Gradually the sidewalks filled with spectators. Men, women, and children walked across gardens still wet with dew and passed through iron gates, often beautifully wrought, to flag-bedecked streets. The Charleston Light Dragoons paraded down the avenues toward the waterfront; the Sixteenth and the Seventeenth Regiments of infantry and the battalion of artillery followed. Near the reviewing stand at the Battery were assembled a crowd of men in tall hats and of ladies in hoop skirts. When the last marching four had passed and the military units were drawn up at attention on the edge of the harbor, the United States cutter *Van Buren*, riding at anchor not far from Fort Sumter, fired a salute. The artillery battalion replied impressively from the shore. The infantry regiments raised their muskets to conclude this part of the day's long ritual with a *feu de joie*.

Back home from the ceremonies on the Battery, Charlestonians sat on their porches to enjoy the coolness which followed the breaking of a heat wave and to read with approval the editorial of the *Courier*. "Year after year rolls on," wrote the editor, "and finds us unabated in our devotion to the principles of the revolution; determined to keep burning for ever the vestal fire of liberty, kindled by our fathers in the temple of union, and rejoicing in the success of our glorious experiment of popular self-government. We have had our reverses and our trials; but, under the blessings of Providence, not only has nothing transpired to shake our confidence in the stability and permanence of our systems, but on the contrary, the experience of the past only brightens the hope of the future, that our career will continue to realize its full promise of individual happiness and national glory."

Already new processions were forming in the city. The Society of the Cincinnati and the Association of 1776 moved together slowly, as befitted old men who remembered the days when Washington commanded the armies of the United States. In the First Baptist Church the marchers listened to a prayer and then to an oration delivered by a member of the '76. Meanwhile the Washington Society had marched in procession to St. Mary's where the ritual consisted of prayer, the reading of the Declaration, and an address. Note the similarity to the normal Protestant service — prayer, scripture reading, and sermon. . . .

The symbols and rituals of the Middle Period were not limited to the idea of nationalism. Some gave concrete expression to the abstract doctrines of the American democratic faith. The national symbolism was new because the nation was young. Beside it in American civilization were two older symbols, brought by tradition from the Old World.

When a traveler in the days of President Pierce entered any of the hundreds of county towns in the United States, the objects which first drew his eye were the churches and the courthouse. The architecture of a people frequently reflects its hierarchy of values. There were points of similarity between the churches and the courthouses. Both stood, often on little greens, apart from the jostling intimacy of the stores, the banks, and the blacksmith's shops on Main Street. Both displayed evidence of builder's desire to achieve dignity. This was usually accomplished in the Middle Period by the plain porticoes and the white columns of the Greek Revival style. The churches and the courthouses which dominated the county towns of mid-nineteenth-century America were material symbols of the fundamental law. Associated with them and giving them meaning were certain stereotyped behavior patterns which amounted to social rituals.

On the Sabbath, villagers put aside their work-day attire and passed down the aisles of the meeting-house to their pews. The flame of religious zeal burned with significant brightness only in the hearts of a minority; Americans were a practical people, preoccupied with the problems of making a living and little given to mysticism. But by inheritance from their Puritan ancestors they were uncompromising Sabbatarians. The practices of respite from work on Sunday, of church attendance, and of church support were deeply imbedded in the American mores of the village and rural communities. And these communities before 1861 contained a very large proportion of the American population. Behind the Sabbath customs was the almost universal conviction that religion maintained the morals of society, and that, if America were to be suddenly bereft of its churches, moral collapse would result. The old war between good and evil stood clearly revealed in every village community. At opposite ends of the American Main Street, the saloon and the church faced each other. The most elementary American symbols were those of the steeple, pointing heavenward, and of the swinging door, concealing iniquity within. The man who stood for respectability went to church, because, no matter how small a part Christianity might play in his personal life, in his heart he believed that morals and good order rest upon religion. Was not the Church dedicated to the task of reminding sinners that they are rebels against the law of God, and that punishment awaits those who refuse to repent? The church building, the services within it, and all the self-denying Sabbath customs were symbolic expressions of a folk belief in an eternal and changeless moral order upon which society rests. Of all the symbolisms in mid-nineteenth-century America these were the most powerful.

Along Illinois roads in the days of President Pierce a lawyer named Abraham Lincoln rode sometimes. Making the circuit with him were other attorneys and the judge. When stopping at an inn in the county town, they spent the evening swapping stories in the friendly intimacy of democratic equals. Next day in the court the scene was different. Court week was a time of unusual stir in the community. The central figures in the cases were personally known to many people; the public seats were normally filled with curious or anxious spectators. The jury of the defendant's peers took their places; farmers and villagers, called from their routine tasks, enjoyed for the moment the conspicuous responsibility of a citizen's duty. Lawyers and court attendants busied themselves with last-minute preparations. The judge entered. At command all persons in the courtroom rose and stood until he took his seat behind the bench. The lawyers, who perhaps the night before had called him by his first name, now addressed him as "Your Honor." The dignity of the Greek columns before the courthouse door was duplicated by the formalized courtesy within. One after another the cases were tried according to the rules of an elaborately ritualistic procedure. The purpose of the procedural rules was not to embarrass unskilled attorneys, as some unsuccessful litigants suspected, but rather to make the accomplishment of justice more certain. From the beginning of the proceedings to the sentencing of the convicted criminal, the behavior of all who had to do with the case was governed by purposeful ritual. The courthouse was the center of the most elaborate symbolic behavior known to American culture. This ritual was not a sudden creation but was the growth of centuries. Its long history suggests its important uses in civilization. One of the greatest was its symbolic representation of the American folk belief in the certainty of the law and of that allied belief that, in the words of Hicks, "the destruction of certitude as a mass attitude toward law would result in the destruction of law itself."

The churches emphasized the moral law; the courts the secular law. But Chancellor Kent had pointed out that the two were, in reality, one. "The law as a science," he had said, "is only a collection of general principles founded on the moral law, and in the common sense of mankind." This union was also expressed in the almost universal American concept of God as a just judge before whose great assize every individual must come on the Last Day.

Americans of the Middle Period, while they groped for symbols to express ideas and to evoke emotions, had little understanding of the importance of symbolism in a culture. Such knowledge is the fruit of modern anthropological and psychological research. In the twentieth century symbols have become instruments of power often consciously manipulated by individuals, organizations, or governments to further definite ends. Early American symbolism was a folk product. As such it is of prime importance in any investigation of popular thought. The symbols which had meaning for the people reveal, as nothing else does, the ideas and attitudes of the inarticulate masses. The symbolism of the Middle Period suggests the hold upon the common man of that pattern of social beliefs which made up the American democratic faith.

[1940]

In Civil Strife

Battle-Hymn of the Republic   JULIA WARD HOWE

Julia Ward Howe (1819–1910) was best known during her lifetime as
promoter of social reform, particularly abolition and women's rights. Today she is remembered primarily as the author of the "Battle-Hymn of
the Republic," written after she visited General McClellan's troops in
December 1861 and heard them singing "John Brown's Body." Her
"more ennobling" set of verses first appeared in the *Atlantic Monthly* for
February 1862.

The "Battle-Hymn" soon became widely popular, and it remains so
today. Part of its popularity is doubtless due to the marching rhythm
of the tune to which it is set; more important is its successful fusion of
religious, social, and patriotic motifs. The familiar images of both Old
and New Testament are wonderfully suited to the triumph-in-tragedy of
the Civil War. Its crusading zeal is of the sort Americans welcome when
called upon to fight. We yearn to march under banners of righteousness.

". . . let us die to make men free. . . ."

Mine eyes have seen the glory of the coming of the Lord:
He is trampling out the vintage where the grapes of wrath are stored;
He hath loosed the fateful lightning of his terrible swift sword:
    His truth is marching on.

I have seen him in the watch-fires of a hundred circling camps;   5
They have builded him an altar in the evening dews and damps;
I can read his righteous sentence by the dim and flaring lamps:
    His day is marching on.

I have read a fiery gospel, writ in burnished rows of steel:
"As ye deal with my contemners, so with you my grave shall deal;   10
Let the Hero, born of woman, crush the serpent with his heel,
    Since God is marching on."

He has sounded forth the trumpet that shall never call retreat;
He is sifting out the hearts of men before his judgment-seat:
O, be swift, my soul, to answer him! be jubilant, my feet!   15
    Our God is marching on.

In the beauty of the lilies Christ was born across the sea,
With a glory in his bosom that transfigures you and me;
As he died to make men holy, let us die to make men free,
  While God is marching on.   20

He is coming like the glory of the morning on the wave,
He is wisdom to the mighty, he is honor to the brave,
So the world shall be his footstool, the soul of wrong his slave,
  Our God is marching on!

                                                        [1862]

The Gettysburg Address   ABRAHAM LINCOLN

In 1862 Abraham Lincoln (1809–1865) wrote Horace Greeley that "My paramount object in this struggle is to save the Union, and it is not either to save or to destroy slavery. If I could save the Union without freeing any slave, I would do it; and if I could save it by freeing all the slaves, I would do it; and if I could save it by freeing some and leaving others alone, I would also do that." This devotion to the national idea, tempered by an abiding awareness of the terrible cost of war in human lives, pervades the following two selections.

"The Gettysburg Address" is deceptively simple. Its noble rhythm, its high dignity, its perfect clarity are quite obvious; not so obvious is its structure of related progressions which narrow the spatial focus while extending the view of time and growth. Edward Everett, who preceded Lincoln and, as main speaker, held forth for two hours, later wrote to Lincoln that he hoped he had come "as near to the central idea of the occasion in two hours as you did in two minutes."

"... We are met on a great battlefield. ..."

Four score and seven years ago our fathers brought forth on this continent a new nation, conceived in liberty, and dedicated to the proposition that all men are created equal.

Now we are engaged in a great civil war, testing whether that nation, or any nation so conceived and so dedicated, can long endure. We are met on a great battlefield of that war. We have come to dedicate a portion of that field as a final resting-place for those who here gave their lives that that nation might live. It is altogether fitting and proper that we should do this.

But in a larger sense we cannot dedicate, we cannot consecrate, we cannot hallow this ground. The brave men, living and dead, who struggled here have consecrated it, far above our poor power to add or detract. The world will little note, nor long remember what we say here, but it can never forget what they did here. It is for us, the living, rather, to be dedicated here to the unfinished work which they who fought here have thus far so nobly advanced. It is rather for us to be here dedicated to the great task remaining before us, — that from these honored dead we take increased devotion to that cause for which they gave the last full measure of devotion; that we here highly resolve that these dead shall not have died in vain; that this nation, under God, shall have a new birth of freedom; and that government of the people, by the people, and for the people, shall not perish from the earth.

[1863]

Letter to Mrs. Bixby   ABRAHAM LINCOLN

It would seem that there is not much to be said about something so simple as Lincoln's letter to Mrs. Bixby — it just *is*. Yet we must ask how it can be that this has been termed "the most impressive" of all Lincoln's letters and a masterpiece of its kind. How can so much sadness, dignity, and dedication be conveyed in so few lines? Part of the answer is of course in what the letter explicitly states. A more important part, however, is in what it leaves unsaid, in what it need not say because of the character of the occasion and the known character of the writer. Lincoln was wise enough not to say the unnecessary. The power which attaches to the result is of the same kind which we feel in the statement: Jesus wept.

". . . the solemn pride that must be yours. . . ."

Executive Mansion
Washington, Nov. 21, 1864

To Mrs. Bixby, Boston, Mass.

Dear Madam. I have been shown in the files of the War Department a statement of the Adjutant-General of Massachusetts that you are the mother of five sons who have died gloriously on the field of battle. I feel how weak and fruitless must be any word of mine which should attempt to beguile you from the grief of a loss so overwhelming. But I cannot refrain from tendering you the consolation that may be found in the thanks of the republic they died to save. I pray that our Heavenly Father may assuage the anguish of your bereavement, and leave you only the cherished memory of the loved and lost, and the solemn pride that must be yours to have laid so costly a sacrifice upon the altar of freedom.

Yours very sincerely and respectfully,

A. Lincoln

War Is Kind   STEPHEN CRANE

Both the life and writings of Stephen Crane (1871–1900) testify to his reaction against the conventional values of his time. Son of a Methodist minister, he wrote that "God lay dead in heaven; / Angels sang the hymn of the end." As a college student he announced that Tennyson's poetry was "swill." As a newspaper reporter he submitted impressionistic stories of events rather than factual statements. In *Maggie: A Girl of the Streets* (1893), he wrote what many consider America's first naturalistic novel. His view of the world, expressed throughout his fiction and poetry, is contained in these lines:

> A man said to the universe:
> "Sir, I exist!"
> "However," replied the universe,
> "The fact has not created in me
> "A sense of obligation."

As the obvious irony of the following poem suggests, Crane's attitude toward patriotism was likewise unconventional. The dimensions of this irony — and also its ambiguity — is in the contrast between the "unexplained glory" of a symbol and "a field where a thousand corpses lie." Nothing is said about noble causes.

". . . Make plain to them the excellence of killing. . . ."

Do not weep, maiden, for war is kind.
Because your lover threw wild hands toward the sky
And the affrighted steed ran on alone,
Do not weep.
War is kind.   5

Hoarse, booming drums of the regiment,
Little souls who thirst for fight,
These men were born to drill and die.
The unexplained glory flies above them,
Great is the battle-god, great, and his kingdom —   10
A field where a thousand corpses lie.

Do not weep, babe, for war is kind.
Because your father tumbled in the yellow trenches,
Raged at his breast, gulped and died
Do not weep.   15
War is kind.

Swift blazing flag of the regiment,
Eagle with crest of red and gold,

These men were born to drill and die.
Point for them the virtue of slaughter,   20
Make plain to them the excellence of killing
And a field where a thousand corpses lie.

Mother whose heart hung humble as a button
On the bright splendid shroud of your son,
Do not weep.   25
War is kind.

[1899]

The Death of Jim Conklin   STEPHEN CRANE

The chapter here reprinted from *The Red Badge of Courage* (1895),
though similar in point of view to "War Is Kind," is less blatant. Ostensibly about the Civil War, *The Red Badge* says nothing about the specific
issues of that struggle. Crane is concerned rather with giving a psycho-
logically authentic portrayal of men in battle. When he wrote the book
he had never seen a battle; after his experiences as a journalist in Cuba
during the Spanish-American War and later in Greece, he was able to
say: "*The Red Badge* is all right." Crane's complete point of view, and
the total impact of this significant American novel, can be gained only by
reading the entire book; but this key chapter by focusing on the death of
a soldier makes a strong, albeit implicit, comment on patriotic death.
Crane has been called a realist, a naturalist, and an impressionist; he is
also noted for his use of symbols, two of the most famous being in "Death
of Jim Conklin": "the red badge" and the sun described in the last line.
As this chapter opens, "the youth," having earlier fled from the battlefield,
has fallen in with a column of wounded soldiers moving to the rear. One
of them, "a tattered soldier," has just made a friendly inquiry about the
youth's wound.

". . . He wished that he, too, had a wound, a red badge of courage. . . ."

The youth fell back in the procession until the tattered soldier was not in
sight. Then he started to walk on with the others.

But he was amid wounds. The mob of men was bleeding. Because of the
tattered soldier's question he now felt that his shame could be viewed. He
was continually casting sidelong glances to see if the men were contemplating
the letters of guilt he felt burned into his brow.

At times he regarded the wounded soldiers in an envious way. He conceived persons with torn bodies to be peculiarly happy. He wished that he,
too, had a wound, a red badge of courage.

The spectral soldier was at his side like a stalking reproach. The man's eyes were still fixed in a stare into the unknown. His gray, appalling face had attracted attention in the crowd, and men, slowing to his dreary pace, were walking with him. They were discussing his plight, questioning him and giving him advice. In a dogged way he repelled them, signing to them to go on and leave him alone. The shadows of his face were deepening and his tight lips seemed holding in check the moan of great despair. There could be seen a certain stiffness in the movements of his body, as if he were taking infinite care not to arouse the passion of his wounds. As he went on, he seemed always looking for a place, like one who goes to choose a grave.

Something in the gesture of the man as he waved the bloody and pitying soldiers away made the youth start as if bitten. He yelled in horror. Tottering forward he laid a quivering hand upon the man's arm. As the latter slowly turned his waxlike features toward him, the youth screamed:

"Gawd! Jim Conklin!"

The tall soldier made a little commonplace smile. "Hello, Henry," he said.

The youth swayed on his legs and glared strangely. He stuttered and stammered. "Oh, Jim — oh, Jim — oh, Jim ——"

The tall soldier held out his gory hand. There was a curious red and black combination of new blood and old blood upon it. "Where yeh been, Henry?" he asked. He continued in a monotonous voice, "I thought mebbe ye got keeled over. There's been thunder t' pay t'-day. I was worryin' about it a good deal."

The youth still lamented. "Oh, Jim — oh, Jim — oh, Jim ——"

"Yeh know," said the tall soldier, "I was out there." He made a careful gesture. "An', Lord, what a circus! An, b'jiminey, I got shot." He reiterated this fact in a bewildered way, as if he did not know how it came about.

The youth put forth anxious arms to assist him, but the tall soldier went firmly on as if propelled. Since the youth's arrival as a guardian for his friend, the other wounded men had ceased to display much interest. They occupied themselves again in dragging their own tragedies toward the rear.

Suddenly, as the two friends marched on, the tall soldier seemed to be overcome by a terror. His face turned to a semblance of gray paste. He clutched the youth's arm and looked all about him, as if dreading to be over-heard. Then he began to speak in a shaking whisper:

"I tell yeh what I'm 'fraid of, Henry — I'll tell yeh what I'm 'fraid of. I'm 'fraid I'll fall down — an' then yeh know — them damned artillery wagons they like as not'll run over me. That's what I'm 'fraid of ——

The youth cried out to him hysterically: "I'll take care of yeh, Jim! I'll take care of yeh! I swear t' Gawd I will!"

"Sure — will yeh, Henry?" the tall soldier beseeched.

"Yes — yes — I tell yeh — I'll take care of yeh, Jim!" protested the youth. He could not speak accurately because of the gulpings in his throat.

But the tall soldier continued to beg in a lowly way. He now hung babe-like to the youth's arm. His eyes rolled in the wildness of his terror. "I was allus a good friend t' yeh, wa'n't I, Henry? I've allus been a pretty good feller, ain't I? An' it ain't much t' ask, is it? Jest t' pull me along outer th' road? I'd do it fer you, wouldn't I, Henry?"

He paused in piteous anxiety to await his friend's reply.

The youth had reached an anguish where the sobs scorched him. He strove to express his loyalty, but he could only make fantastic gestures.

However, the tall soldier seemed suddenly to forget all those fears. He became again the grim, stalking specter of a soldier. He went stonily forward. The youth wished his friend to lean upon him, but the other always shook his head and strangely protested. "No — no — no — leave me be — leave me be ——"

His look was fixed again upon the unknown. He moved with mysterious purpose, and all of the youth's offers he brushed aside. "No — no — leave me be — leave me be ——"

The youth had to follow.

Presently the latter heard a voice talking softly near his shoulders. Turning he saw that it belonged to the tattered soldier. "Ye'd better take 'im outa th' road, pardner. There's a batt'ry comin' helity-whoop down th' road an' he'll git runned over. He's a goner anyhow in about five minutes — yeh kin see that. Ye'd better take 'im outa th' road. Where th' blazes does he git his stren'th from?"

"Lord knows!" cried the youth. He was shaking his hands helplessly.

He ran forward presently and grasped the tall soldier by the arm. "Jim! Jim!" he coaxed, "come with me."

The tall soldier weakly tried to wrench himself free. "Huh," he said vacantly. He stared at the youth for a moment. At last he spoke as if dimly comprehending. "Oh! Inteh th' fields? Oh!"

He started blindly through the grass.

The youth turned once to look at the lashing riders and jouncing guns of the battery. He was startled from this view by a shrill outcry from the tattered man.

"Gawd! He's runnin'!"

Turning his head swiftly, the youth saw his friend running in a staggering and stumbling way toward a little clump of bushes. His heart seemed to wrench itself almost free from his body at this sight. He made a noise of pain. He and the tattered man began a pursuit. There was a singular race.

When he overtook the tall soldier he began to plead with all the words he could find. "Jim — Jim — what are you doing — what makes you do this way — you'll hurt yerself."

The same purpose was in the tall soldier's face. He protested in a dulled way, keeping his eyes fastened on the mystic place of his intentions. "No — no — don't tech me — leave me be — leave me be ——"

The youth, aghast and filled with wonder at the tall soldier, began quaveringly to question him. "Where yeh goin', Jim? What you thinking about? Where you going? Tell me, won't you, Jim?"

The tall soldier faced about as upon relentless pursuers. In his eyes there was a great appeal. "Leave me be, can't yeh? Leave me be fer a minnit."

The youth recoiled. "Why, Jim," he said, in a dazed way, "what's the matter with you?"

The tall soldier turned and, lurching dangerously, went on. The youth and the tattered soldier followed, sneaking as if whipped, feeling unable to face the stricken man if he should again confront them. They began to have thoughts of a solemn ceremony. There was something rite-like in these movements of the doomed soldier. And there was a resemblance in him to a devotee of a mad religion, blood-sucking, muscle-wrenching, bone-crushing. They were awed and afraid. They hung back lest he have at command a dreadful weapon.

At last, they saw him stop and stand motionless. Hastening up, they perceived that his face wore an expression telling that he had at last found the place for which he had struggled. His spare figure was erect; his bloody hands were quietly at his side. He was waiting with patience for something that he had come to meet. He was at the rendezvous. They paused and stood, expectant.

There was a silence.

Finally, the chest of the doomed soldier began to heave with a strained motion. It increased in violence until it was as if an animal was within and was kicking and tumbling furiously to be free.

This spectacle of gradual strangulation made the youth writhe, and once as his friend rolled his eyes, he saw something in them that made him sink wailing to the ground. He raised his voice in a last supreme call.

"Jim — Jim — Jim ——"

The tall soldier opened his lips and spoke. He made a gesture. "Leave me be — don't tech me — leave me be ——"

There was another silence while he waited.

Suddenly, his form stiffened and straightened. Then it was shaken by a prolonged ague. He stared into space. To the two watchers there was a curious and profound dignity in the firm lines of his awful face.

He was invaded by a creeping strangeness that slowly enveloped him. For a moment the tremor of his legs caused him to dance a sort of hideous hornpipe. His arms beat wildly about his head in expression of implike enthusiasm.

His tall figure stretched itself to its full height. There was a slight rending sound. Then it began to swing forward, slow and straight, in the manner of a falling tree. A swift muscular contortion made the left shoulder strike the ground first.

The body seemed to bounce a little way from the earth. "God!" said the tattered soldier.

The youth had watched, spellbound, this ceremony at the place of meeting. His face had been twisted into an expression of every agony he had imagined for his friend.

He now sprang to his feet and, going closer, gazed upon the pastelike face. The mouth was open and the teeth showed in a laugh.

As the flap of the blue jacket fell away from the body, he could see that the side looked as if it had been chewed by wolves.

The youth turned, with sudden, livid rage, toward the battlefield. He shook his fist. He seemed about to deliver a philippic.

"Hell ——"

The red sun was pasted in the sky like a wafer.

[1895]

To Save the World for Democracy:
Retrospect

The Unknown Soldier   KIRKE L. SIMPSON

Kirke L. Simpson (1880–) was born in San Francisco and began his journalistic career in that city. He became a feature writer for the Associated Press and in that capacity wrote the following account of the Unknown Soldier's burial. It won a Pulitzer Prize for 1921.

"The Unknown Soldier" was Simpson's effort to give expression to a new national symbol. Momentarily he seemed to have succeeded, for so many requests came in for reprints that the piece was issued in the form of a special pamphlet for national distribution. Today, however, it has lost much of its force, both because of writing weaknesses (e.g., the quality of its phrasing and its images) and because events of the last forty years have subtracted from the meaning of the occasion it describes. Perhaps the account is most interesting now as a symbol in itself of a national attitude which was characteristic two generations ago.

". . . A loyal comrade was being laid to his last, long rest. . . ."

Washington, Nov. 11, 1921. – (By the Associated Press) – Under the wide and starry skies of his own home-land America's unknown dead from France sleeps tonight, a soldier home from the wars.

Alone, he lies in the narrow cell of stone that guards his body; but his soul has entered into the spirit that is America. Wherever liberty is held close in men's hearts, the honor and the glory and the pledge of high endeavor poured out over this nameless one of fame, will be told and sung by Americans for all time.

Scrolled across the marble arch of the memorial raised to American soldier and sailor dead, everywhere, which stands like a monument behind his tomb, runs this legend: "We here highly resolve that these dead shall not have died in vain."

The words were spoken by the martyred Lincoln over the dead at Gettysburg. And today, with voice strong with determination and ringing with deep emotion, another President echoed that high resolve over the coffin of the soldier who died for the flag in France.

Great men in the world's affairs heard that high purpose reiterated by the man who stands at the head of the American people. Tomorrow they will gather in the city that stands almost in the shadow of the new American shrine of liberty dedicated today. They will talk of peace; of the curbing of the havoc of war.

They will speak of the war in France, that robbed this soldier of life and name and brought death to comrades of all nations by the hundreds of thousands. And in their ears when they meet must ring President Harding's declaration today beside the flag-wrapped, honor-laden bier:

"There must be, there shall be, the commanding voice of a conscious civilization against armed warfare."

Far across the seas, other unknown dead, hallowed in memory by their countrymen, as this American soldier is enshrined in the heart of America, sleep their last. He, in whose veins ran the blood of British forebears, lies beneath a great stone in ancient Westminster Abbey; he of France, beneath the Arc de Triomphe, and he of Italy under the altar of the Fatherland in Rome.

And it seemed today that they, too, must be here among the Potomac hills to greet an American comrade come to join their glorious company, to testify their approval of the high words of hope spoken by America's President. All day long the nation poured out its heart in pride and glory for the nameless American. Before the first crash of the minute gun roared its knell for the dead from the shadow of Washington Monument, the people who claim him as their own were trooping out to do him honor. They lined the long road from the Capitol to the hillside where he sleeps tonight; they flowed like a tide over the slopes about his burial place; they choked the bridges that lead across the river to the fields of the brave, in which he is the last comer.

As he was carried past through the banks of humanity that lined Pennsylvania Avenue a solemn, reverent hush held the living walls. Yet there was not so much of sorrow as of high pride in it all, a pride beyond the reach of shouting and the clamor that marks less sacred moments in life.

Out there in the broad avenue was a simple soldier, dead for honor of the flag. He was nameless. No man knew what part in the great life of the nation he had filled when last he passed over his home soil. But in France he had died as Americans always have been ready to die, for the flag and what it means. They read the message of the pageant clear, these silent thousands along the way. They stood in almost holy awe to take their own part in what was theirs, the glory of the American people, honored here in the honors showered on America's nameless son from France.

Soldiers, sailors and marines — all played their part in the thrilling spectacle as the cortege rolled along. And just behind the casket, with its faded French flowers on the draped flag, walked the President, the chosen leader of a hundred million, in whose name he was chief mourner at his bier. Beside him strode the man under whom the fallen hero had lived and died in France, General Pershing, wearing only the single medal of Victory that every American soldier might wear as his only decoration.

Then, row on row, came the men who lead the nation today or have guided its destinies before. They were all there, walking proudly with age and frailties of the flesh forgotten. Judges, Senators, Representatives, highest officers of every military arm of government and a trudging little group of the nation's most valorous sons, the Medal of Honor men. Some were gray and bent and drooping with old wounds; some trim and erect as the day they won their way to fame. All walked gladly in this nameless comrade's last parade.

Behind these came the carriage in which rode Woodrow Wilson, also stricken down by infirmities as he served in the highest place of the nation, just as the humble private riding in such state ahead had gone down before a shell or bullet. For the dead man's sake, the former President had put aside his dread of seeming to parade his physical weakness and risked health, perhaps life, to appear among the mourners for the fallen.

There was handclapping and a cheer here and there for the man in the carriage, a tribute to the spirit that brought him to honor the nation's name-less hero, whose commander-in-chief he had been.

After President Harding and most of the high dignitaries of the Government had turned aside at the White House, the procession, headed by its solid blocks of soldiery and the battalions of sailor comrades, moved on with Pershing, now flanked by Secretaries Weeks and Denby, for the long road to the tomb. It marched on, always between the human borders of the way of victory the nation had made for itself of the great avenue; on over the old bridge that spans the Potomac, on up the long hill to Fort Myer, and at last to the great cemetery beyond, where soldier and sailor folk sleep by the thousands. There the lumbering guns of the artillery swung aside, the cavalry drew their horses out of the long line and left to the foot soldiers and the sailors and marines the last stage of the journey.

Ahead, the white marble of the amphitheater gleamed through the trees. It stands crowning the slope of the hills that sweep upward from the river and just across was Washington, its clustered buildings and monuments to great dead who have gone before, a moving picture in the autumn breeze.

People in thousands were moving about the great circle of the amphi-theater. The great ones to whom places had been given in the sacred inclosure and the plain folk who trudged the long way just to glimpse the pageant from afar were finding their places. Everywhere within the pillared inclosure bright uniforms of foreign soldiers appeared. They were laden with the jeweled order of rank to honor an American private soldier, great in the majesty of his sacrifices, in the tribute his honors paid to all Americans who died.

Down below the platform placed for the casket, in a stone vault, lay wreaths and garlands brought from England's King and guarded by British soldiers. To them came the British Ambassador in the full uniform of his rank to bid them keep these tributes from overseas safe against that hour.

Above the platform gathered men whose names ring through history — Briand, Foch, Beatty, Balfour, Jacques, Diaz and others — in a brilliant array of place and power. They were followed by others, Baron Kato from Japan, the Italian statesmen and officers, by the notables from all countries gathered here for tomorrow's conference and by some of the older figures in American life too old to walk beside the approaching funeral train.

Down around the circling pillars the marbled box filled with distinguished men and women, with a cluster of shattered men from army hospitals accompanied by uniformed nurses. A surpliced choir took its place to wait the dead.

Faint and distant, the silvery strains of a military band stole into the big white bowl of the amphitheater. The slow cadences and mourning notes of a funeral march grew clearer amid the roll and mutter of the muffled drums.

At the arch where the choir waited the heroic dead, comrades lifted his casket down and, followed by the Generals and the Admirals, who had walked beside him from the Capitol, he was carried to the place of honor. Ahead moved the white-robed singers, chanting solemnly. Carefully, the casket was placed above the banked flowers and the Marine Band played sacred melodies until the moment the President and Mrs. Harding stepped to their places beside the casket; then the crashing, triumphant chords of "The Star-Spangled Banner" swept the gathering to its feet again.

A prayer, carried out over the crowd by amplifiers so that no word was missed, took a moment or two, then the sharp, clear call of the bugle rang "Attention!" and for two minutes the nation stood at pause for the dead, just at high noon. No sound broke the quiet as all stood with bowed heads. It was much as though a mighty hand had checked the world in full course. Then the band sounded and in a mighty chorus rolled up the words of "America" from the hosts within and without the great open hall of valor.

President Harding stepped forward beside the coffin to say for America the thing that today was nearest to the nation's heart, that sacrifices such as this nameless man, fallen in battle, might perhaps be made unnecessary down through the coming years. Every word that President Harding spoke reached every person through the amplifiers and reached other thousands upon thousands in New York and San Francisco.

Mr. Harding showed strong emotion as his lips formed the last words of the address. He paused, then with raised hand and head bowed, went on in the measured, rolling period of the Lord's Prayer. The response that came back to him from the thousands he faced, from the other thousands out over the slopes beyond, perhaps from still other thousands away near the Pacific, or close packed in the heart of the nation's greatest city, arose like a chant. The marble arches hummed with the solemn sound.

Then the foreign officers who stand highest among the soldiers or sailors of their flags came one by one to the bier to place gold and jeweled emblems for the brave above the breast of the sleeper. Already, as the great prayer ended, the President had set the American seal of admiration for the valiant, the nation's love for brave deeds and the courage that defies death, upon the casket.

Side by side he laid the Medal of Honor and the Distinguished Service Cross. And below, set in place with reverent hands, grew the long line of foreign honors, the Victoria Cross, never before laid on the breast of any but those who had served the British flag; all the highest honors of France and Belgium and Italy and Rumania and Czecho-Slovakia and Poland.

To General Jacques of Belgium it remained to add his own touch to these honors. He tore from the breast of his own tunic the Medal of Valor pinned there by the Belgian King, tore it with a sweeping gesture, and tenderly bestowed it on the unknown American warrior.

Through the religious services that followed, and prayers, the swelling crowd sat motionless until it rose to join in the old, consoling "Rock of Ages," and the last rite for the dead was at hand. Lifted by his hero bearers from the stage, the Unknown was carried in his flag-wrapped, simple coffin out to the wide sweep of the terrace. The bearers laid the sleeper down above the crypt on which had been placed a little of the soil of France. The dust his blood helped redeem from alien hands will mingle with his dust as time marches by.

The simple words of the burial ritual were said by Bishop Brent, flowers from war mothers of America and England were laid in place.

For the Indians of America, Chief Plenty Coos came to call upon the Great Spirit of the Red Men, with gesture and chant and tribal tongue that the dead should not have died in vain, that war might end, peace be purchased by such blood as this. Upon the casket he laid the coup stick of his tribal office and the feathered war bonnet from his own head. Then the casket, with its weight of honors, was lowered into the crypt.

A rocking blast of gunfire rang from the woods. The glittering circle of bayonets stiffened to a salute to the dead. Again the guns shouted their message of honor and farewell. Again they boomed out; a loyal comrade was being laid to his last, long rest.

High and clear and true in the echoes of the guns, a bugle lifted the old, old notes of taps, the lullaby for the living soldier, in death his requiem. Long ago some forgotten soldier poet caught its meaning clear and set it down that soldiers everywhere might know its message as they sing to rest:

> *Fades the light;*
> *And afar*
> *Goeth day, cometh night;*
> *And a star,*
> *Leadeth all, speedeth all,*
> *To their rest.*

The guns roared out again in the national salute. He was home, The Unknown, to sleep forever among his own.

[1921]

The Body of an American   JOHN DOS PASSOS

John Dos Passos (1896–   ) is best known for his *U. S. A.* trilogy, from the second volume of which, titled *1919* (1932), "The Body of an American" is taken. Like the piece on Samuel Insull (see p. 252), it is an example of the brief biographies which Dos Passos intersperses in his

From *U. S. A.* by John Dos Passos, published by Houghton Mifflin Co. Copyright by John Dos Passos.

narrative. It is also an example of the bitterness and disillusionment which became characteristic of Dos Passos' generation. After graduating from Harvard in 1916, he himself had served in the French ambulance service and, after America's entry into the war, in the U. S. medical corps.

The savage irony in almost every line of "The Body of an American" is successfully emphasized by unconventional typography, punctuation, images, grammar, and diction. More important is Dos Passos' cynical anger toward that which convention regarded with solemn respect. In some respects "The Body of an American" seems dated, but if the reader considers the reasons for Dos Passos' attitude, he will find something more than the reactions of the 1930's to World War I; he will find what Dos Passos thinks might be the basis for a truer patriotism.

". . . how beautiful sad . . . it was to have the bugler play. . . ."

Whereasthe Congressoftheunitedstates byaconcurrentresolutionadoptedon the-4thdayofmarch lastauthorizedthe Secretaryofwar to cause to be brought to theunitedstatesthe body of an American whowasamemberoftheamericanexpe-ditionaryforceineuropewholosthislifeduringtheworldwarandwhoseidentityhas notbeenestablished for burial inthememorialamphitheatreofthenationalceme-teryatarlingtonvirginia

---

In the tarpaper morgue at Châlons-sur-Marne in the reek of chloride of lime and the dead, they picked out the pine box that held all that was left of
enie menie minie moe plenty other pine boxes stacked up there containing what they'd scraped up of Richard Roe
and other person or persons unknown. Only one can go. How did they pick John Doe?
Make sure he ain't a dinge, boys,
make sure he ain't a guinea or a kike,
how can you tell a guy's a hunredpercent when all you've got's a gunny-sack full of bones, bronze buttons stamped with the screaming eagle and a pair of roll puttees?
. . . and the gagging chloride and the puky dirtstench of the yearold dead . . .

The day withal was too meaningful and tragic for applause. Silence, tears, songs and prayer, muffled drums and soft music were the instru-mentalities today of national approbation.

John Doe was born (thudding din of blood in love into the shuddering soar of a man and a woman alone indeed together lurching into
and ninemonths sick drowse waking into scared agony and the pain and blood and mess of birth). John Doe was born
and raised in Brooklyn, in Memphis, near the lakefront in Cleveland, Ohio, in the stench of the stockyards in Chi, on Beacon Hill, in an old brick

house in Alexandria, Virginia, on Telegraph Hill, in a halftimbered Tudor
cottage in Portland, the city of roses,
in the Lying-In Hospital old Morgan endowed on Stuyvesant Square,
across the railroad tracks, out near the country club, in a shack cabin
tenement apartmenthouse exclusive residential suburb;
scion of one of the best families in the social register, won first prize in
the baby parade at Coronado Beach, was marbles champion of the Little Rock
grammarschools, crack basketballplayer at the Booneville High, quarterback
at the State Reformatory, having saved the sheriff's kid from drowning in
the Little Missouri River was invited to Washington to be photographed
shaking hands with the President on the White House steps; —

> though this was a time of mourning, such an assemblage necessarily
> has about it a touch of color. In the boxes are seen the court uniforms of
> foreign diplomats, the gold braid of our own and foreign fleets and armies,
> the black of the conventional morning dress of American statesmen, the
> varicolored furs and outdoor wrapping garments of mothers and sisters
> come to mourn, the drab and blue of soldiers and sailors, the glitter of
> musical instruments and the white and black of a vested choir

— busboy harveststiff hogcaller boyscout champeen cornshucker of Western Kansas bellhop at the United States Hotel at Saratoga Springs officeboy
callboy fruiter telephone-lineman longshoreman lumberjack plumber's helper,
worked for an exterminating company in Union City, filled pipes in an
opium joint in Trenton, New Jersey.
Y.M.C.A. secretary, express agent, truckdriver, fordmechanic, sold books
in Denver, Colorado: Madam would you be willing to help a young man
work his way through college?

> President Harding, with a reverence seemingly more significant be-
> cause of his high temporal station, concluded his speech:
>
> *We are met today to pay the impersonal tribute;*
> *the name of him whose body lies before us took flight with his*   *im-*
> *perishable soul . . .*
> *as a typical soldier of this representative democracy he fought and died*
> *believing in the indisputable justice of his country's cause. . .*
> by raising his right hand and asking the thousands within the sound
> of his voice to join in the prayer:
> *Our Father which art in heaven hallowed be thy name . . .*

Naked he went into the army;
they weighed you, measured you, looked for flat feet, squeezed your penis
to see if you had clap, looked up your anus to see if you had piles, counted
your teeth, made you cough, listened to your heart and lungs, made you read
the letters on the card, charted your urine and your intelligence,
gave you a service record for a future (imperishable soul)
and an identification tag stamped with your serial number to hang around
your neck, issued O.D. regulation equipment, a condiment can and a copy of
the articles of war.

Atten'SHUN suck in your gut you c——r wipe that smile off your face eyes right wattja tink dis is a choirch-social? For-war-D'ARCH.

John Doe
and Richard Roe and other person or persons unknown
drilled, hiked, manual of arms, ate slum, learned to salute, to soldier, to loaf in the latrines, forbidden to smoke on deck, overseas guard duty, forty men and eight horses, shortarm inspection and the ping of shrapnel and the shrill bullets combining the air and the sorehead woodpeckers the machineguns mud cooties gasmasks and the itch.

Say feller tell me how I can get back to my outfit.

John Doe had a head.
for twentyodd years intensely the nerves of the eyes the ears the palate the tongue the fingers the toes the armpits, the nerves warmfeeling under the skin charged the coiled brain with hurt sweet warm cold mine must don't sayings print headlines:
Thou shalt not the multiplication table long division, Now is the time for all good men knocks but once at a young man's door, It's a great life if Ish gebibbel, The first five years'll be the Safety First, Suppose a Hun tried to rape your my country right or wrong, Catch 'em young What he don't know won't treat 'em rough, Tell 'em nothin', He got what was coming to him he got his, This is a white man's country, Kick the bucket, Gone west, If you don't like it you can croaked him.
Say buddy can't you tell me how I can get back to my outfit?

Can't help jumpin' when them things go off, give me the trots them things do. I lost my identification tag swimmin' in the Marne, roughhousin' with a guy while we was waitin' to be deloused, in bed with a girl named Jeanne (Love moving picture wet French postcard dream began with saltpeter in the coffee and ended at the propho station); —
Say soldier for chrissake can't you tell me how I can get back to my outfit?

John Doe
heart pumped blood:
alive thudding silence of blood in your ears
down in the clearing in the Oregon forest where the punkins were punkincolor pouring into the blood through the eyes and the fallcolored trees and the bronze hoopers were hopping through the dry grass, where tiny striped snails hung on the underside of the blades and the flies hummed, wasps droned, bumblebees buzzed, and the woods smelt of wine and mushrooms and apples, homey smell of fall pouring into the blood,
and I dropped the tin hat and the sweaty pack and lay flat with the dogday sun licking my throat and adamsapple and the tight skin over the breastbone.

The shell had his number on it.

The blood ran into the ground.

The service record dropped out of the filing cabinet when the quarter-master sergeant got blotto that time they had to pack up and leave the billets in a hurry.
The identification tag was in the bottom of the Marne.

The blood ran into the ground, the brains oozed out of the cracked skull and were licked up by the trenchrats, the belly swelled and raised a genera-tion of bluebottle flies,
and the incorruptible skeleton,
and the scraps of dried viscera and skin bundled in khaki

they took to Châlons-sur-Marne
and laid it out neat in a pine coffin
and took it home to God's Country on a battleship
and buried it in a sarcophagus in the Memorial Amphitheater in the Arlington National Cemetery
and draped the Old Glory over it
and the bugler played taps
and Mr. Harding prayed to God and the diplomats and the generals and the admirals and the brasshats and the politicians and the handsomely dressed ladies out of the society column of the *Washington Post* stood up solemn
and thought how beautiful sad Old Glory God's Country it was to have the bugler play taps and the three volleys made their ears ring.

Where his chest ought to have been they pinned
the Congressional Medal, the D.S.C., the Médaille Militaire, the Belgian Croix de Guerre, the Italian gold medal, the Vitutea Militara sent by Queen Marie of Rumania, the Czechoslovak War Cross, the Virtuti Militari of the Poles, a wreath sent by Hamilton Fish, Jr., of New York, and a little wampum presented by a deputation of Arizona redskins in warpaint and feathers. All the Washingtonians brought flowers.

Woodrow Wilson brought a bouquet of poppies.

[1932]

Threes   CARL SANDBURG

Although Carl Sandburg (1878–   ) decided very early to be a writer, he served a long apprenticeship as a hobo, a laborer at various trades, and as a soldier during the Spanish-American War, when he spent several months in Puerto Rico. He expresses his strong democratic faith in colloquial language and relaxed free-verse rhythms that make his poetry relatively easy to appreciate.

Sandburg here raises some large historical and personal questions about patriotic death. Though his own belief as to what is worth dying for is not made altogether clear, there is yet a progression of attitude through the four stanzas to an apparent conclusion.

> "*. . . I asked*
> *why men die for words. . . .*"

I was a boy when I heard three red words
a thousand Frenchmen died in the streets
for: Liberty, Equality, Fraternity — I asked
why men die for words.

I was older; men with mustaches, sideburns,   5
lilacs, told me the high golden words are:
Mother, Home, and Heaven — other older men with
face decorations said: God, Duty, Immortality
— they sang these threes slow from deep lungs.

Years ticked off their say-so on the great clocks   10
of doom and damnation, soup and nuts: meteors flashed
their say-so: and out of great Russia came three
dusky syllables workmen took guns and went out to die
for: Bread, Peace, Land.

And I met a marine of the U.S.A., a leatherneck with   15
a girl on his knee for a memory in ports circling the
earth and he said: Tell me how to say three things
and I always get by — gimme a plate of ham and eggs —
how much? — and — do you love me, kid?

[1920]

Next to of course god   E. E. CUMMINGS

For a biographical note on Cummings see page 202.

Using a traditional poetic form to state a conventional theme, Cummings yet writes a highly unconventional poem. Far from being devices •

used for their own unconventional sake, the unusual typography and syntactical juxtapositions turn out to be instruments of Cummings' central intent.

". . . by jingo by gee by gosh by gum . . ."

"next to of course god america i
love you land of the pilgrims' and so forth oh
say can you see by the dawn's early my
country 'tis of centuries come and go
and are no more what of it we should worry
in every language even deafanddumb
thy sons acclaim your glorious name by gorry
by jingo by gee by gosh by gum
why talk of beauty what could be more beautiful than these heroic happy dead
who rushed like lions to the roaring slaughter
they did not stop to think they died instead
then shall the voice of liberty be mute?"

He spoke.   And drank rapidly a glass of water.

[1926]

Search for National Meaning

Patriotism—But How?   HOWARD MUMFORD JONES

Howard Mumford Jones (1892–   ) was born in Saginaw, Michigan, and attended the universities of Wisconsin and Chicago before beginning his teaching career as a teacher of English at the University of Texas in 1916. He has also taught at the universities of Montana, North Carolina, and Michigan, and since 1936 he has been at Harvard. The author of a number of scholarly works, he has also translated and written poetry. The breadth of his interests is suggested by the nature of "Patriotism — But How?"

In this well organized essay Jones is more concerned with posing a problem than providing all the answers, as is seen in the ending of the piece and in its title. He involves the reader in this problem by his many specific allusions to poorly remembered details of the American past. In this and other respects the essay retains its interest; in others it is slightly dated, having been written in 1938.

". . . We debunked too much. . . ."

While discussion clubs incline a serious ear to speeches on "Can Democracy Survive?" and our better correspondents smuggle dispatches out of Europe showing that the dictator countries are committing economic suicide, few people seem to inquire why, if the fascist and communistic nations are economically insane, they constitute so serious a menace to political democracy. At this distance it looks as if they had something democracy does not possess, or rather something American democracy has lost during the dolorous twentieth century. That something is not state regulation of business, nor holidays for workingmen, nor concentration camps, nor a well-oiled bureaucracy, nor even the capacity to make trains run on time. We can show American precedents for all these. What the dictator countries have succeeded in doing is to make patriotism glamorous. Among higher liberal circles in the United States patriotism seems nowadays to be regarded as the last refuge of a scoundrel.

Glamour has turned the trick. The technical name for this sort of trick is propaganda, but it is not ideational propaganda I am talking about. What I refer to is the prompt and efficient creation by the dictators of glamorous mythological images. These images please their downtrodden subjects, make

Reprinted from *The Atlantic Monthly* by permission of the author.

them feel swell, and send them off to the army or a labor camp singing mis-
taken patriotic songs. We used to have Glamour in this country, but during
the rush of intellection to the head in the twenties we rubbed it all off.

It is, of course, commonplace that Mussolini is a semi-divine Duce and
Hitler a sacrosanct Führer. It is also commonplace that you can't turn around
in Berlin or Rome or Moscow without seeing a swastika, the Roman fasces,
or a sickle and hammer. Everybody knows about the parades, the "spontane-
ous" cheering, the farcical elections, the uniforms, and the perpetual celebra-
tions. Naziism has its martyrs, — the "Horst Wessel" song commemorates one
of them, — fascism its saints, and communism its heroes. It is true that the
official history of these countries, which obedient citizens are required to
swallow, would not delude even a weak-minded freshman in the United
States, but that is not the point: the point is that the official history is full
of heroism, chivalry, romance. It takes the form of the rescuing of the helpless maiden Germania or Italia or Russia by knights-errant against overwhelming odds. It is a modern version of the King Arthur story, the American Revolution, and freeing the slaves, all in one. The result is that the
communist or fascist citizen, at least in his public moments, has an exhilarat-
ing sense of living in a vast grand opera.

Why is there no American grand opera to correspond? Why has American democracy mislaid its mythology and lost its glamour? The answer is in
part that we had our own grand opera until, under the combined attacks of
"progressive" educators, the debunking biographer, and social historians, we
grew shamefaced about it. Take, for example, the matter of the musical score.
"The Star-Spangled Banner," though unsingable, is just as vigorous a tune as
"Giovinezza," but we don't know the words. "Columbia, the Gem of the
Ocean" tingles with vitality, but try to get it sung at a ball park! "The Battle
Hymn of the Republic" (peace to the South!) is a superb song — we can sing
the chorus, some of us chanting "Glory, glory, hallelujah" and others "John
Brown's body lies a-mouldering in the grave." I do not care for "America,"
with its mouldy flavor of commencement programmes, but "Yankee Doodle"
is a good fighting song, which we can't even burble. Everybody shouts when
the band plays "Dixie," but will some kind Rotarian recite the verses? The
sorrowful fact that well-intentioned citizens mistake Sousa's "Stars and Stripes
Forever" for the national anthem is not the sort of error that Mussolini or
Hitler or Stalin permits.

Grand opera, however, is more than a musical score; it supposes characters and a plot. Let us have an examination in the plot of the American story.
Can any little boy or girl earn a dime by telling me the anecdote which gave
birth to each of the following sentences? "Damn the torpedoes — full speed
ahead!" "You may fire when ready, Gridley." "We have met the enemy and
they are ours." "Don't cheer, boys — the poor devils are dying." "Don't give
up the ship." "Millions for defence, but not one cent for tribute." "I would
rather be right than be President" (No, Sammy, this does *not* refer to George
M. Cohan). "I only regret that I have but one life to lose for my country."
"Our Federal Union: it must be preserved."

The class will next recite from memory, thus rivaling good communists,
(1) Patrick Henry's oration; (2) the Declaration of Independence as far as

the bill of particulars; (3) the peroration of Webster's "Reply to Hayne"; (4) Senator Thurston on Cuban affairs; (5) Lincoln's Second Inaugural Address. Next, the boys and girls will tell teacher the facts in the case of (a) Molly Pitcher; (b) Johnny Appleseed; (c) Kit Carson; (d) Davy Crockett; (e) R. P. Hobson; (f) Stephen Decatur; (g) Marcus Whitman; and (h) General Stark. The examination will conclude by having the scholars identify the author and name the poem in which each of the following phrases occurs: "When Freedom from her mountain height"; "Ay, tear her tattered ensign down"; "The Turk lay dreaming of the hour"; "All quiet along the Potomac"; "Out of the focal and foremost fire"; "By the flow of the inland river Whence the fleets of iron have fled"; "John P. Robinson, he sez he wunt vote fer Guvener B."; "When faith is lost, when honor dies, The man is dead"; "Blindness we may forgive, but baseness we will smite." (Southern children will be placed under a slight handicap concerning one of these items.)

If this is too hard, the C students may identify any five of the following: (1) Old Fuss and Feathers; (2) the Swamp Fox; (3) the Mill Boy of the Slashes; (4) The Pathfinder (not Natty Bumppo); (5) the Rock of Chickamauga; (6) The American Farmer; (7) Me Too Platt; (8) Hosea Biglow; (9) Old Rough-and-Ready; (10) Tippecanoe and Tyler too. No fair looking in a reference book. A grade of fifty will be considered passing.

I realize, of course, that a number of these items have a regrettable military flavor, which World Peaceways, Inc., would not approve. I can only say that the heroic moments of history seem to be commonly associated with the danger of death. In fact, I shall dare the scorn of advanced intellectuals by citing a quotation guaranteed to make the ghost of Hart Crane wince: —

> And how can man die better
> Than facing fearful odds,
> For the ashes of his fathers
> And the temples of his gods?

No, this is not an American poem, and it is banned from our better school readers because its author has passed out of fashion. Its sentiment, however, seems to be powerful in an important Mediterranean kingdom, somewhat to the present embarrassment of the nation which produced the poet.

I likewise freely admit that under the searchlight of historical science some of the sentences I have quoted have been proved apocryphal, and some of the heroes whose sobriquets are given above have been conclusively shown up by modern writers. I also know that Washington did not pray at Valley Forge, that the Boston Massacre was not a massacre, that John Hancock made a good thing out of violating the revenue laws, that Sheridan's ride never occurred, and that the charge on San Juan Hill was, from every sensible point of view, an hilarious absurdity. I have, however, one advantage over the rising generation: I knew my American mythology before I knew its historical corrective; and inasmuch as the vaunted conflict among ideologies threatens to be won by the nation with the greatest belief in its own mythology, I wonder, now that scientific historians have destroyed most of the American myth, what it is that American democrats are to believe in during the coming struggle. To

quote from another frayed classic, also scorned in intellectual circles, Harvard
men who died in the Civil War were men who, in Lowell's opinion,

> . . . followed [Truth] and found her
> Where all may hope to find,
> Not in the ashes of the burnt-out mind,
> But beautiful, with danger's sweetness round her.

If democracy should have to fight, will it be emotionally inspired by the
sound historic fact that the Lincoln administration is supposed to have favored
the high-tariff crowd?

II

In the nineteenth century, Americans were simple-minded enough to have
a mythology. The facts of American history were widely known. Rising
generations learned them in school. On Friday afternoon classes were adjourned while perspiring victims declaimed fragments of nationally known
orations, patriotic poetry, and sound rhetorical pieces describing a blind
preacher, narrating a thrilling climb up the Natural Bridge, or excoriating
Benedict Arnold. No child of the Iodine State who toiled through William
Gilmore Simms's history of South Carolina, written for schools, could be
ignorant of the exploits of Francis Marion or General Nathanael Greene.
No schoolboy put through *Appleton's Fifth Reader* failed to discover that
Daniel Webster was the greatest man who ever lived. No boy who learned
both text and gestures from the immortal McGuffey but was thoroughly
grounded in the dramatic moments of the history of freedom: —

> "Make way for liberty," he cried,
> Made way for liberty, and died.

> Breathes there the man with soul so dead
> Who never to himself hath said,
> This is my own, my native land!

> The boy stood on the burning deck,
> Whence all but him had fled.

The fact that a perverse and adulterate generation continues this last quotation by an apocryphal reference to goobers is simply a tribute to the thoroughness with which the nation was once taught to admire Mrs. Hemans's
hero. But if you did not care for the immortal youth you could hang out the
old flag with Barbara Frietchie or ride twenty miles with Phil Sheridan and
Thomas Buchanan Read.

The patriotic reader met an immense and genuine demand. Throughout
most of the nineteenth century every American knew that this nation was
the greatest thing that had ever happened in the history of the human race.
Every Fourth of July some rising young lawyer read aloud the Declaration
on the village green. At every county fair an itinerant Congressman pulled
the lion's tail and made the eagle scream. All good Americans abhorred the

effete monarchies of Europe. All good Americans understood that the immediate purpose of any British duke was to place his heel on the neck of free-
born republicans. The image of Washington or Jackson or Lincoln or Lee
held precisely the same place in the esteem of the people as Mussolini or
Hitler or Stalin wants to hold in the esteem of his own nation. In those times
we made the welkin ring, painted the firmament red, white, and blue, and
announced to an amused universe that Columbia was bounded on the north
by the Aurora Borealis, on the east by the Garden of Eden, on the west by
the Fortunate Isles, and on the south by the Day of Judgment. We made
ourselves supremely ridiculous and supremely happy. Observers like Dickens,
Mrs. Trollope, Miss Martineau, and others satirized our effervescence and
envied our simplicity. We had our mythology, and we believed in it.

To-day Washington is a figure on a postage stamp, we are not quite sure
whether Andy or Stonewall Jackson beat the British at New Orleans, and
purple passages about the American eagle are no longer heard, even in Congress. We are all for social justice or the Townsend plan, but neither programme has yet produced its demigod. When economic analysis comes in at
the door, patriotic figures of speech fly out at the window. It is impossible to
twist the lion's tail with one hand and make a graph of the wages of coal
miners with the other. In all the argument over minimum-wage laws, nobody
has referred to the full dinner pail, the pauper millions of Europe, or pressing
a crown of thorns upon the brow of labor. Statistics are valuable, but a little
old-fashioned Fourth-of-July oratory is the tonic we really need.

The fervor has gone out of our sublime and ridiculous enthusiasm in the
twentieth century for a variety of reasons — economic determinism, sociological analysis, the radio (which killed off the string-tie orator), realism on the
stage and in fiction, which forbids romantic gestures and heroic thought. One
cause worth discussing is professional enthusiasm for a new sort of education
supposed to develop the free personality of the child.

The fact that the child was to develop in the United States of America
and not in a gray abstraction called the modern world has not troubled educators who look down on Jean Jacques Rousseau as an unscientific generalizer.
The child is to remain a child as long as possible, and consequently he is not
to be given adult stuff to read until the latest possible moment. The child is
supposed to be brought up to love his fellow man, and therefore stories like
the fight of the *Serapis* and the *Bonhomme Richard* have been quietly dropped
from school. Instead, he learns to love the kindly Indians, who built tepees.
The child is nevertheless supposed to develop into a little voter, and in place
of learning to hate Benedict Arnold he is instructed in the mysteries of the
local waterworks. It is not yet clear, after a quarter of a century of advanced
education, that the results, as shown in municipal politics, have justified the
erasure of romantic drama from the American school.

Think of the comment of sturdy Mr. McGuffey upon the book from
which a friend of mine, aged six, is learning to read. I quote from the incredible preface: —

The purpose of *Our Animal Books* is to motivate in the growing citizen,
from his pre-school days to junior high school, an intelligent regard for his

own pets and for the animals of his city, state, and country. He, however, rather than the animal, is the chief factor [sic] in the book. . . .

The primer, *Fuzzy Tail,* is devoted to the kitten, telling in story form just how a kitten should be fed, handled, and properly played with [!].

I have no doubt that school superintendents who adopt this series look down on Maria Edgeworth (if they have ever heard of her) as a didactic old woman bent on ruining the lives of children, though the precise difference between this sort of pedagogy and eighteenth-century didacticism is not evident. But let us return to *Our Animal Books.* After *Fuzzy Tail,* we rise through *Sniff,* which "gives youthful owners similar instruction in the feeding, housing, exercising, and general upbringing of a puppy, again through story medium" (why medium?), to *Paths to Conservation,* which "points toward participation in the protection and conservation of the vanishing bird and mammal life of our country." (As the little boy said, mammals are apparently not as extinct as they used to be.) I read likewise that "all information pertaining to the care and treatment of animals has been checked carefully by respective [sic] authorities."

Let us not make fun of McGuffey's rhetoric. McGuffey never dreamed that a child had to be "motivated" as a "factor," knew not the word "correlation," more blessed than the waters of Abana and Pharpar, and failed to consult "respective" authorities. Nevertheless, I ever and again meet aging Americans who can with honest pride recite piece after piece from McGuffey or Appleton, but in the course of teaching several thousand undergraduates over a period of years I do not find that they can recite anything at all, and their ignorance of American history is so immense that Harvard University has just instituted a system of competitive prizes to get them to read some of it.

The history books have gone the way of the school readers. I admire Professor Charles A. Beard, like all who have to do with American history; but, from the point of view of keeping alive a necessary patriotic glow in the juvenile breast, he has had an unfortunate influence. The school of social historians has substituted movements for personalities, conflicts of economic interest for dramatic events, sociology for the romance of personal endeavor, and "citizenship" for hairbreadth escapes by sea and land. Some stories, it is true, have been spared. General Lee still rides sadly through the Confederate Army on Traveller, and Lincoln is still assassinated by the cowardly Booth. I have no doubt the school histories are sounder, better, and more intelligent books than Simms's parochial *History of South Carolina* or Ridpath's *History of the World.* I do not deny that to learn how the Puritans grew corn or what early railways were like is exciting. But I cannot picture a younger generation going into Armageddon, should that be tragically necessary, inspired by memories of railroad grants or aglow with accounts of the rise of sectionalism in the Deep South.

We debunked too much. During the iconoclastic twenties spirited biographers laid about them with a mighty modern hand. They told us that Lincoln was a small-town politician, Washington a land grabber, Grant a stubborn and conceited mule, and Bryan an amusing idiot. We learned that there was something to be said for Aaron Burr, but not very much for Sam Adams,

Longfellow, or Harriet Beecher Stowe. In place of being American vikings, the pioneers turned out to be neurotic, dissatisfied fellows unpopular in their home towns, and Columbia, the gem of the ocean, was described as a sort of kept woman in the pay of millionaires. Apparently the only Americans who ever died to make the world safe for democracy died in 1917–1918, and made a mistake in doing so. I do not deny either the truth or the necessity of many of these modern biographies. I am no more comfortable than the next man in a room full of plaster saints. But, when the biographers got through, all the heroes had disappeared.

Meanwhile in Germany, Italy, and Russia the manufacture of heroes has gone steadily forward. There is no use in saying they are fake heroes. The only way to conquer an alien mythology is to have a better mythology of your own.

III

What we need is a patriotic renaissance, but we need not shut our eyes to the dangerous fact that a patriotic renaissance is exactly what a number of interested pressure groups are playing for. Advanced liberals are perfectly right in assuming that every patriot is guilty until he is proved innocent. Too many selfish interests have adopted the star-spangled manner. In fact, one of the difficulties of rehabilitating our mythology is that all the stirring phrases have been appropriated by organizations of the right or organizations of the left. The Liberty League, the American Legion, the Constitution Society, the American Minute Men, the Daughters of the American Revolution, the International League for Peace and Freedom, the United Daughters of the Confederacy, the Colonial Dames — the trouble is that most of these bodies have an axe to grind. They want to call somebody else un-American.

Patriotism may not always be the last refuge of a scoundrel, but it is too often a convenient disguise for a one-hundred-per-center who wants somebody else to go back home. Nor are radicals without guile. If the La Follette committee has turned the spotlight on reactionaries whose favorite reading matter is the Constitution whenever they import plug-uglies to break a strike, I have noted a wonderful interest in the Bill of Rights among communists in danger of arrest and deportation. The devil can cite Scripture for his purpose. There is scarcely a pressure group in the country that cannot cite Jefferson or Lincoln, Washington or Wilson, in support of a quiet little programme of its own.

It is not thus that a patriotic renaissance is to come about. Because the dictator countries have cleverly manipulated a patriotic mythology for sinister ends it does not follow, because we are not yet a dictator country, that patriotic mythology cannot be manipulated for sinister ends in the United States. We regard ourselves as a free and enlightened people, but so do patriotic Italians, Germans, and Russians regard themselves. If we think they are deceived, they have a right to retort the argument on us. I do not wish to be so deceived. I do not want any scientifically manipulated propaganda. I regret that Americans cannot sing their own national anthem, but if it comes to a choice between singing it under compulsion or remaining silent in a concentration camp I trust I shall not be too old to go to the concentration camp. If, as the overzealous believe, there is a red network over the land, God forbid that we should now create a red-white-and-blue network. I have no desire to echo Madame Roland's pathetic cry: "O Liberty! Liberty! how many crimes are committed in thy name!"

Neither do we want any unhistorical history. Official persons who suppress school texts in the interests of "Americanism" because some honest historian has tried to tell the truth as he sees it are not only thoroughly un-American, but doing in a small way precisely what Messrs. Mussolini, Hitler, and Stalin are doing on a larger scale. If the "Aryan" version of history is funny, or would be if it were not so deplorable, an "American" version of history would be just as comic and just as disastrous. We want no legends marked: "Approved by the Bureau of Propaganda, Washington, D. C." I do not propose that on a given date all good Americans shall devoutly believe that Washington cut down the cherry tree, cheerfully remarking, "Father, I cannot tell a lie." But what seems to have happened is that in our enthusiasm for social forces we have omitted most of the thrilling anecdotes. We have modernized American history so thoroughly that it is everywhere up to date, and as a result John Smith, Thomas Jefferson, and Buffalo Bill are made to behave as if they were members of the Kiwanis Club looking for better business sites.

It would be idle to deny the economic motive which sent adventurers to the New World, but it seems to me equal folly to omit for that reason the tale of the lonely and heroic exploits which they wrought. I have no doubt that the Massachusetts Bay Colony was intended as a profitable commercial enterprise, but the Pilgrims and the Puritans both wanted to worship God in their own way. General Oglethorpe was really a noble soul, and Roger Williams is still a great man. The debtor classes and hardboiled merchants undoubtedly egged on the American Revolution; nevertheless Tom Paine was not writing nonsense when he exclaimed: "These are the times that try men's souls!" Does the fact that Vergennes wanted to increase French prestige lessen the romantic gallantry of Lafayette? Washington did not cross the Delaware in the fatuous manner of the celebrated painting; nevertheless he crossed it, and it was full of floating ice. I may add that he and his ragged Continentals were likewise extremely uncomfortable at Valley Forge.

A whole regiment of researchers looking for sectionalism cannot rob the little American navy of glorious episodes during the Tripolitan campaign or the War of 1812. Such, however, is our zeal for sociology and economic determinism that Mr. Stephen Vincent Benét seems to be the only American to realize that Daniel Webster was a great and thrilling man. If it was wrong for Jared Sparks to correct the erratic spelling of the Father of his Country, what shall we say of historical works which dismiss the Lewis and Clark expedition in a single phrase, send the Mormons to Utah in a sentence, and mention Custer's Last Stand in a footnote? We have a picturesque and romantic past, which we seem bent on making as dull and modern as we can.

IV

If we really want to believe that political democracy is worth fighting for, we need to be told over and over again what pain and suffering it has cost.

Wiser than we, the nineteenth century kept its eye on that issue. Scientific historians we have in abundance; what we lack is a Macaulay, sure that the Whigs were right and the Tories wrong, and heartily concerned less political liberty might suffer. We need to be told about Magna Charta and Arnold von Winkelried and John Huss and Savonarola and Pym and Hampden and the Gray Champion and Sergeant Moultrie and the burning zeal of Calhoun and the fervid faith of William Lloyd Garrison and the quiet heroism of Grant's last years and the career of Fighting Bob La Follette. We need to know about the Watauga settlement and Boonesboro and Fort Bridger and the Oregon trail. We need to know these things, not as the products of economic forces, but as human drama. Men are but children of a larger growth. They will listen to a tale of D'Artagnan and Richelieu when a dissertation on the economic policy of Colbert leaves them cold.

Mr. Bernard DeVoto is a novelist and critic for whom I have a vast respect. Recently he argued that the historical novel came to its full flower in the works of Mr. James Boyd, the theory being that Mr. Boyd is the first person to picture adequately the experiences and emotions of an average, inarticulate man participating in great events. This is what may be called the realistic theory of historical fiction, and there is a great deal to be said for it. But there is also a great deal to be said on the other side of the argument. There is such a thing as historical romance. Any practising novelist can write rings around Thomas Nelson Page and George W. Cable, but the practical result of the romantic school of Southern historical novelists was to make Southern history a living tradition in that region. What I should like to see is a school of writers and dramatists trying to make the history of liberty a living tradition.

Such a literature will fail, however, if it confines its interests to the Colonial Society of Massachusetts and the F. F. V.'s. "Old Americans" (hateful phrase!) tend to take the point of view that American history is their private possession because they were here first. Aside from the fact that the only persons entitled to the benefit of this silly argument are the Indians, the assumption is not even true. In New England the French Canadians have a better claim, or at least as good a one; and as for the South, your proud first families will have to mingle with the Mexican descendants of Spaniards who pushed their frontier up into North Carolina if they are consistent.

It is unfortunate that neither the *Mayflower* nor Captain Smith's little fleet carried anybody by the name of Shimultowski, Cohen, Paladopolous, Tokanyan, Lauria, McGillicuddy, Swenson, or Schimmelpfennig on their rolls, because it is precisely the children and grandchildren of the millions who "came over" some centuries after these earlier immigrations who need to have their imaginations kindled by American mythology. The gulf between the Boston Brahmins and the Boston Irish, old Detroiters and the swarming thousands of automobile workers, the first families of Cleveland and the Poles, the Armenians, the Czechs, the Ruthenians, and other racial groups, is not, however, going to be bridged by a bright recital of the French and Indian Wars.

No race or religion or group or nationality can be permitted to assume that it has a monopoly of American history, and no race or religion or group or nationality can be permitted to feel it is excluded, if political democracy is to survive. The founding fathers did not, unfortunately, include race-ism among the elements to be combated in the Bill of Rights; for in the eighteenth century men were men, not herds of stock for breeding purposes. Consequently, if democracy is to revive its living legend, it cannot confine that legend to the exploits of a favored few. We shall somehow have to include the drama of human liberty in our renaissance, no less than the drama of American democracy.

As the letter paper of the National Rededication Movement remarks: "America in unbelievably undersold to its own citizens." True, but who are the Americans? How shall we revive patriotism without chauvinism, economic self-interest, or racial snobbery? And if we do not revive the history of liberty as a living faith, how shall we combat an alien mythology of race, militarism, and an uncomfortable version of the heroic in history?

[1938]

What the War Is About   ARTHUR MILLER

Arthur Miller (1915–   ) is recognized as one of our leading contemporary playwrights. His *Death of a Salesman* (1949) won him a Pulitzer Prize, and *The Crucible* (1953), based on the Salem witch trials, has been highly praised. In 1944 Miller visited army camps throughout the country in preparation for writing a movie called *G. I. Joe;* out of this trip came a book called *Situation Normal,* from which the present selection is taken.

Miller raises the question of what the American soldier in World War II thinks he is fighting for. Taking advantage of the roving reporter's role, he hopes to build a convincing basis for his final conclusions through an inductive examination of cases. It is interesting to compare what Miller has to say in wartime with what Howard Mumford Jones said a few years earlier.

". . . the kind of thing we fight for is a very old thing. . . ."

What part if any do the ideas of our time play in the heavily loaded brain of the American soldier? Some people say he has no ideas which cannot be summed up in three words: beer, women, and going home. Others more charitable claim that he is a devout Democrat and still others seem to feel that all soldiers want to go into business when they return, whereupon they will mostly be Republicans. But all sides seemed then, and still seem to be agreed that he is a kind of mentally helpless puppy, a literal dogface stoically suffering the buffetings of a fate he does not understand, a kind of good schlemiel destined throughout history to take the rap and still give away his candy rations to kids in some newly captured foreign town. I started out with a mixture of these preconceptions. But . . . I had to get rid of them because they do not conform to the truth, and I had an opportunity to see the truth. . . .

I knew a soldier who before the war was a congenial kind of man with petty racketeering ambitions. He was a ruthless character driving a cab; if you were standing on the south side of the street and waved a cab, he would swing over from the north side and get there first and if the other cabby who rightfully deserved your fare, being closer, should utter protest, my friend would drag him out of his cab and bat him over the head. My friend was utterly egocentric. He rolled drunks at night, he was always coming home with more money than a cabby had a right to earn. He dressed like a diplomat and was very handsome. He stopped living with his wife because she got sick. He was a nice, pleasant louse. Everything was a racket and anybody who uttered an ideal was strictly off his nut. I liked the guy. He knew how to handle himself and was too naïve to be dishonest about admitting his methods. In his heart he knew that everybody in the world was out for number one. He just had to work a little harder at it.

Well, the Army called him. He was sore as hell. He had always had some pains in his back. Here big war money was to be made at last and he has to go in the Army. His back pains start getting worse as induction day approaches. He goes to the induction center prepared with a story only he could act out convincingly. He gets to the doctor who examines bones, backs, and muscles, and right away informs him that he has a bad back. He even stands in line holding his back. The pain is terrible. It happens that there is a kid one place ahead of him in the line who has a slight club foot. The kid, about eighteen, comes up in turn and the doctor immediately starts rejecting him. The kid pleads in sweat that he can do anything anybody else can do. The doctor tells him to rise up on his toes. The club foot doesn't rise quite as high as the good one. The doctor tells him to turn his ankles out. The kid does, but the club won't turn out all the way. He taps the doctor's shoulder and says, watch how I walk. He walks without a limp, but not with ease. He makes the doctor watch him run. He is in a stew of supplication. He shows how he kicks a football. He swears he can kick it "two sewers." The doctor finally tells him to wait on the side for reconsideration, and then turns to the remaining men and says, "Didn't somebody say something about a back?" Nobody answers. My friend has already left off supporting his back with his hand. He doesn't answer the doctor. The doctor asks again, impatiently. My friend keeps shut. They inducted him.

As a civilian one of my friend's deepest pleasures was getting dressed. He could play the ambassador from Argentina in any man's movie; only when he opens his mouth does the cab come out. He bought only the finest, including silk underwear. And fine taste. No sharp stuff on him. Well, what happened? In the Army you wear the same every day. He is not in three months before he changes that. *He* has a private's uniform made by a fine tailor. Nobody can tell the difference, but he can and it satisfies. At night he goes to his barracks, and if nobody much is around he puts on a white civilian shirt and tie and looks at himself in the mirror from the waist up. Something is happening to him. He comes home on leave and he doesn't gripe at all. He claims he is in the best outfit in the Army. They are making him a sergeant. He don't like for nobody to say nutn about da Commander an' Chief. He is suddenly a citizen. Of course he is winning all the crap games in camp and I don't doubt he still has his methods, but a light has dawned. He has found the country. All his life his country was as big as his footprints, now it is growing. He wants very much to go overseas. He wants to see how his outfit makes out. His regiment is put on the alert for shipment. A most astonishing wire comes from him. His wife is to sell his meticulously packed clothes or give them away.

I would never have believed that one neuron in that man's mind could ever had been made ready for sacrifice. I know the pride in his outfit has helped, and the realization — he always was a realist — that he couldn't beat this rap also pushed him toward sending that wire. But as he was before the Army got him there was nothing. I say nothing in this world that could have brought him to the point of accepting death or its possibility especially if it carried the load of sacrifice with it. When he penned that wire he was diving headlong into the end of his life. It was like a doctor wiring back to sell his instruments. And there is belief in that. If you don't like that word change it, but it is belief anyway. Belief that at rock bottom the war is necessary and morally right. And if you don't like those words change them too but morality is in it and citizenship is in it and the flag of the United States. The trouble is, those goddam words have been mauled and mocked and used dishonestly, but what they meant originally is still in operation in the hearts of this Army's men. . . .

There are hundreds of things a man does in the Army that he would certainly do in school for the reward of a sweater with a block letter on it. But there are also actions — sometimes more important ones — which he will *not* do for that kind of reward. And yet, it may not necessarily be the Belief which is required to make him do these harder things. I am beginning to feel the evidence of the existence of two kinds of men. Those who require a clear faith, and those who never pierce through to the need for any faith at all. The first may be demoralized by this country's nonstatement of political and moral beliefs. The second never heard of them and will probably go into hell for a furlough. I suppose what I am fighting against is the wide-spread, wise-guy notion that Belief is unnecessary because we have no men in the Army who are affected either way by such factors. But we must have a sizable mass of men who need the Belief because the French had such a mass and that mass did not fight well for lack of the Belief. The Russians and to lesser degree the British seem to have that Belief and they are fighting quite well. It does not seem possible that because we are Americans our minds operate under totally different laws than other nations do. I am sure there is French and Russian in us all. The question is, how much of either in this Army? And what real difference will these percentages make? I hope we find out before another twenty years go by. It certainly would help the picture if I could find out now.

Now what do I mean by my "Believer," my man who is definitely affected by what he thinks the war is about? Unfortunately my best example was not born or raised here. The officers introduced me to him after the calisthenics. He is a Czech, thirty-one years old, who was a 2nd lieutenant in the Czech army. After the sellout at Munich he got to Italy, then to Tangiers, then to the U. S. He is training to be an officer with our army. His father, mother and sister are in the old country and there has been no word from them in two years. There was a hardness of will, and yet a sophisticated good humor that held me when he spoke. "I like best about this country the friendliness. I am a lawyer, but for a while in Hartford I worked in a fruit store for my keep. In two days the owner was calling me Ernst. In my country I would have to be there thirty years before I could be so human to the boss as to be called Ernst.

"The American soldier is much more intelligent than any in Europe. In all European armies the private must salute the Pfc., the Pfc. salutes the corporal and so on. It would be unheard of for an enlisted man to approach an officer and say, 'Excuse me sir, I would like to talk to you,' as they do here.

"I am fighting for my country, yes. But now this is my country, I am a citizen here now. And so I have two countries and I feel like fighting twice as hard."

He laughed. When he said the army was going to use him to interrogate German prisoners there was a fiendish glint in his eye. Oh, that would be wonderful. How do you feel now, Fritz? Now regarding the master race, Herr Fritz. . . . And this question of Prague and the massacre of the students there. . . .

There can be in barracks this single-minded, yet humorous Czech, waiting studiously and methodically for his day. Learning every detail, drinking up this marvelous training . . . all for that day.

But then there is Bodine. Bodine is an old man of twenty-three. Five years ago he was hunting in his home state of Michigan. For a while he tried going to college but the depression finished that. He hopped a freight and went west. On the coast he was a stevedore until he made friends with a man who turned out to be an Army recruiting sergeant on his day off. He was sold on the adventure of the Philippines. There he hunted women and caribou and fish. He is a great hunter. After the war he wants to study to be a chiropractor and enter his cousin's practice. In season he will run a little hunting lodge in northern Wisconsin. For a while he made his living in Wisconsin as a hunting guide.

His speech is very considered, almost judicial. Like a man who has had enemies. "I can tell a hunter a long way off. Especially when we're out in the woods and they pop those targets at us from out behind the trees. A hunter will fire before he even thinks. These others turn, study the thing a minute, then fire. Or if they spring those noises on us: suddenly, you'll hear a click as you're walking along. A man who's no hunter will turn to listen for the click to come again. He's dead in battle. A hunter will swing and fire. He knows where that click is coming from before it stops clicking.

"I hate war, but I like fighting. I'm a fighter. I taught all my men every piece of dirty fighting I ever learned. (He was a sergeant before being chosen for officer training.) American kids are funny. You tell a man to kick a guy in the balls and he looks at you. I taught them how to do it. I haven't fought a clean fight since I was in high school. I hate to have to fight, but when I'm in it I love it. The Finns up home taught me how to use a knife. I can nick you or cut your cheek off with the same thrust. There's ways. War's dirty. Any guy who goes across who doesn't believe and like this war because it's dirty is not going to come back, or if he does he'll do it with a blank stare the rest of his life. I got my men so tough they were hoping somebody'd come up and spit in their eyes. I got cuts on me I could show you. All over."

Later, we were standing in the company street beside the barracks. He told me about his wife. By this time I had found out from his officers that he had a 148 IQ, and an excellent service record. He had been brought back from Tulagi thirty-five days before Pearl Harbor. He was married. His wife awaits him somewhere in Michigan.

"The first night we were married we got in about one in the morning and we got to bed right away, naturally. I'd been in the army about three years then. About quarter to six in the morning I open my eyes. I see daylight. I jump up and grab a broom and start sweeping under the bed. She looks at me like something turned around in my head. Then I really woke up and remembered where I was. Yeh, the army does it to you. The Army does it."

The sun was hot. He was wearing rimless, strangely wrong glasses for his tight face and practically shaven head. He stared down the company street as I asked him how he actually felt about going across. "I tell ya. I've shot and killed a lot of different kinds of animals. Big animals. All big animals are beautiful. A pity to kill them. It's a small heartbreak when you walk over and see them dying, and that's why we hunt. I keep wondering how it'll be to kill a man. I can't get it out of my head. It keeps coming back just when I'm falling off to sleep . . . how it'll be to draw a bead on a living man and take his life away. I really can't wait to get over."

Bodine does not want to stay on in the Army after the war. He wants peace, chiropractic, a hunting lodge and his woman. But don't say he's "fighting for" those things. If he wants to fight at all it is for reasons of caliber and trajectory. . . .

The Negro was a lawyer from Nebraska. There were two others of his people in the barracks. I was surprised that they bunked with the whites and did everything the whites did without discrimination. He was a kindly man, thirty-two or three, and had a good practice up home, he said. His two brothers and his father are lawyers. He has two children. He volunteered because he felt that he must do something personally to help win the war. "Because if this country loses, my people are going to fall back five decades. There's hardly anybody in this country who stands to lose more than we do if this war isn't won." Literally. He had a way of saying ideas that was natural and not speechlike. "My father was born and raised in South Carolina. I traveled the south myself. People are mean, yes, but only when they don't understand." We talked for half an hour while [other officer] Candidates studied, moved, talked around us. Nobody treated him or the two other

Negroes with any special attitude. I asked him how the southern boys in the barracks felt about him sleeping among them. He pointed to the bed next to his. "I don't suppose this boy . . . the boy who sleeps here . . . ever dreamed he'd be sleeping next to one of my kind, but he does it and if he feels upset about it I never caught any of that feeling in him. I haven't felt embarrassed in that way since I came to Fort Benning. It's a wonderful time of my life." I asked him about the Negro troops at the replacement center. Before I tell his answer, let me say that I had asked my Negro chauffeur there what the boys felt about the Army. After some heavy prompting he said that he didn't know any who wanted to be in the Army. This lawyer at Benning, however, summed it up like this: "Most white people don't know it, but there have been a great many outrages against colored soldiers since war was declared. Hardly a month passes without something bad happening. At the replacement center I was a private like everybody else, and I got their feeling correctly, I think. It changes every day. When some Negro soldier is unjustly treated anywhere, they will discuss it and become soured on the Army. But that passes. Deep down in them is the instinctive knowledge that whatever is done to them and whatever they feel they must do in return they must show themselves as good soldiers, first, last and all the time. That is one thing they will not let anyone deprive them of. They have an intense, burning wish to be regarded as good troops. However much they may be alienated from the stream of life in America and in the rest of the Army they will never allow themselves to become anti-Americans. This country is their only hope, but it must be a victorious country, an independent country. All they want is the continuing right to belong to America. The uniform itself says they do and that's why they feel hope when they wear it. At the same time, though, the uniform highlights all the irony of our position; we are asked to die for a country that literally doesn't always let us live. In short I think you could get a wave of patriotic selflessness out of all Negroes if you just gave them a chance to give themselves wholeheartedly. They want to do this, they feel cheated when they are forced to feel like suckers.". . .

From the first day of this war we should have understood that the kind of thing we fight for is a very old thing. We fought for it in 1776 and in 1865, and we found the words for it then, and they are perfectly good words, easy to understand, and not at all old-fashioned. They are good words because they recur more times in our ordinary conversation and in the historic conversations of our long tradition than any other words. They represent a concept which, to the vast majority of Americans, must not be offended. The words are not "free enterprise," as the well known ads of our big industries maintain. Nor are the words, "Keep America the Same," as a certain automobile company insists nearly every week in the national magazines. Neither the people of America nor those of any other nation ever fought a war in order to keep everything the same, and certainly never for free enterprise or jobs. No man in his right mind would risk his life to get a job. But we did fight two wars for our Belief. And that Belief says, simply, that we believe all men are equal. We really believe it, most of us, and because a powerful force has arisen in the world dedicated to making the people of the world —

us included — unequal, we have therefore decided to fight. We insist upon a state of affairs in which all men will be regarded as equal. There is no nonsense about it. We believe that everything will rot and decline and go backwards if we are forced to live under laws that hold certain nations and peoples to be inferior and without rights. We are thinking primarily of ourselves and our own rights, naturally, but that is perfectly all right, for once our right to be equal is assured we will want nothing better than to see every nation on our level. I believe the majority of Americans agree to this.

[1944]

New Sovereignties

The Study of Something New in History   EUGENE KINKEAD

Eugene Kinkead (1906–   ), a staff writer for *The New Yorker,* found himself in the midst of a heated controversy when, in the October 26, 1957, issue, he published a report on the patriotism of the American soldier in Korea, (from which this reading is selected). Undeterred by the angry criticism it aroused, Kinkead expanded his article into an equally controversial book entitled *In Every War but One* (1959).

With the apparent approval of the military authorities, Kinkead strongly impugns the patriotism of American soldiers in the Korean conflict. His critics have pointed out that he did not interview the soldiers themselves, that he uses only War Department information, that he does not place the blame where it belongs, namely on the generals. While such criticism may weaken, it would hardly seem to invalidate Kinkead's main point: traditional patriotism was to a large extent lacking among American prisoners of war in Korea. As to his method of dealing with his material, Kinkead has said: "I felt that presenting the mass of technical material in orthodox expository form would merely bury the statistics under their own weight and beget a handful of dry generalities. Accordingly, I decided to assemble the data in an interview pattern which would, I hoped, maintain the quality of human poignancy and lend cumulative narrative strength."

". . . many of the men appeared to lose all sense of allegiance. . . ."

In every war but one that the United States has fought, the conduct of those of its service men who were held in enemy prison camps presented no unforeseen problems to the armed forces and gave rise to no particular concern in the country as a whole. In some of those camps – among them British camps during the Revolution, both Union and Confederate camps during the Civil War, and Japanese camps during the Second World War – our men were grievously treated, and fell victim to starvation and disease, yet there was no wholesale breakdown of morale or wholesale collaboration with the captors. Moreover, whatever the rigors of the camps, in every war but that one a respectable number of prisoners managed, through ingenuity, daring, and plain good luck, to escape. The exception was the Korean War. As everybody knows, twenty-one of the Americans captured as members of the United Nations forces decided to remain with the enemy — the only time in history that American captives have chosen not to return home because they preferred the enemy's form of government to our own. What was even more shocking — for, after all, the twenty-one men could be regarded as ideological cranks — was the fact that roughly one out of every three American prisoners in Korea was guilty of some sort of collaboration with the enemy, ranging from such serious offenses as writing anti-American propaganda and informing on comrades to the relatively innocuous one of broadcasting Christmas greetings home, and thereby putting the Communists in a favorable light, because such broadcasts had to include a report of good treatment at their hands. Then, when the war ended and the prisoners began to return, it became clear that some of them had behaved brutally to their fellow-prisoners, and for a time the newspapers carried reports of grisly incidents in the prison camps, including the murder of Americans by other Americans. (The most notorious offender, perhaps was Sergeant James C. Gallagher, who was convicted by a court-martial of killing two seriously ill fellow-prisoners by throwing them out into the snow.) Furthermore, during the entire Korean conflict not one of our men escaped from a prison camp. And, finally, to mention another calamity that might not, on the face of it, seem to point to any moral or disciplinary weakness among the prisoners, thirty-eight per cent of them — 2,730 out of a total of 7,190 — died in captivity. This was a higher prisoner death rate than that in any of our previous wars, including the Revolution, in which it is estimated to have been about thirty-three per cent.

All in all, regrettable things happened in the prison camps of North Korea, and the public has been inclined to attribute them solely to the cruelty of the Communists and, in particular, to the mysterious technique known as brainwashing. The officials involved, however — in the Defense Department and especially in the Army, which, because of the nature of the operations in Korea, supplied more than ninety per cent of the American service men who fought there — could not accept an explanation as simple as that. For one thing, there was evidence that the high death rate was due primarily not to Communist maltreatment but to the ignorance or the callousness of the prisoners themselves. For another, the prisoners, as far as Army psychiatrists have been able to discover, were not subjected to anything that could properly be called brainwashing. Indeed, the Communist treatment of prisoners, while it came nowhere near fulfilling the requirements of the Geneva Convention, rarely involved outright cruelty, being instead a highly novel blend of leniency and pressure. If our prisoners had behaved strangely, then, the explanation was bound to be a complex one.

That some of them were behaving strangely had become evident surprisingly early in the hostilities — at 11:55 A.M., Greenwich time, on July 9, 1950, to be precise, or only four days after our ground forces first engaged the enemy in Korea — when an American Army officer, taken prisoner some forty-eight hours before, made a nine-hundred-word broadcast in the enemy's behalf over the Seoul radio. Purportedly speaking for all American soldiers, this man said, among other things, "We did not know at all the cause of the war and the real state of affairs, and were compelled to fight against the people of Korea. It was really most generous of the Democratic People's Republic of Korea to forgive us and give kind consideration for our health, for food, clothing, and habitation." Service authorities were dumfounded — parts of the statement, of course, were actually treasonable — but a tape recording had been made of the broadcast and there was no mistaking the officer's voice. Within a few weeks, many statements of this sort were picked up by American listening posts in the Far East, and the Army immediately began collecting data for a formal study of the behavior of our Korean prisoners of war in all its aspects — medical, psychological, propagandistic, and legal. The study turned out to be a massive one — it was not completed until July 29, 1955, two years and two days after the signing of the armistice at Panmunjom — and as it went along, its findings produced a serious dispute within the armed services concerning the degree to which a captive might collaborate without being ultimately answerable to his government. In May, 1955, to resolve the dispute, the Defense Department set up an Advisory Committee on Prisoners of War, composed of five civilians and five retired generals and admirals, which thereupon conducted an intensive three-month survey of all the prisoner-of-war problems that had arisen in Korea. On August 17, 1955, shortly after the committee had turned in its report, President Eisenhower issued the following six-point Code of Conduct for members of the armed forces in combat and captivity:

I am an American fighting man. I serve in the forces which guard my country and our way of life. I am prepared to give my life in their defense.

I will never surrender of my own free will. If in command I will never surrender my men while they have the means to resist.

If I am captured I will continue to resist by all means available. I will make every effort to escape and aid others to escape. I will accept neither parole nor special favors from the enemy.

If I become a prisoner of war I will keep faith with my fellow prisoners. I will give no information or take part in any action which might be harmful to my comrades. If I am senior, I will take command. If not I will obey the lawful orders of those appointed over me and will back them up in every way.

When questioned, should I become a prisoner of war, I am bound to give only name, rank, service number, and date of birth. I will evade answering further questions to the utmost of my ability. I will make no oral or written statements disloyal to my country and its allies or harmful to their cause.

I will never forget that I am an American fighting man, responsible for my actions, and dedicated to the principles which made my country free. I will trust in my God and in the United States of America.

Like the events in Korea that inspired it, the Code of Conduct was unprecedented — the principles of conduct prescribed for our soldiers had always been covered in regular training manuals, and no other President had found it necessary to restate or clarify them — and it has led, in each of the services, to unprecedented courses of training designed to teach our service men how to survive captivity and not buckle under it. . . .

By this time, I was eager to learn about the Communist methods of indoctrination and interrogation, and for this I went to Colonel Willis A. Perry, then G-2's Deputy Assistant Chief of Staff for Zone of the Interior Operations, which is the section charged with security matters; he is now a brigadier-general, serving in California. . . .

As a result of its study, Perry continued, the Army believes that Communist indoctrination in the prison camps had three aims: propaganda, the control of prisoners with a minimum of difficulty, and, finally, the conversion of these prisoners to Communism — or, at least, to acquiescence in the possible rightness of the Communist position. The program appears to have achieved its first two aims. In the case of the third, its success may reasonably be doubted, though it will take some time to determine precisely how much it accomplished. "In any event," the Colonel said, "the great lesson we learned is that the enemy program was by no means irresistible. Its success depended absolutely on our men's compliance. Perhaps half a dozen times during the war, there were instances of organized mass resistance on the part of our prisoners. In one camp, they refused in a body to march carrying Communist flags. Each time, the prisoners won, and were not even punished. It had to be so. There is no way of compelling a group, by any sort of mass psychological pressure, to do something it says firmly it won't do. Under such circumstances, mass resistance always wins."

The Turks, Colonel Perry said, provided a spectacular example of mass resistance to psychological pressure, and of other kinds of resistance as well. Two hundred and twenty-nine Turkish soldiers were captured during the war, and they withstood indoctrination almost a hundred per cent. The secret of this achievement was discipline and organization, the Colonel declared. In prison, the Turks maintained their chain of command unbroken, and were able to present a completely united front to all pressure. To illustrate this, the Colonel read to me part of a Turkish officer's account of his prison experience, given to one of our interrogators. "I told the Chinese commander of the camp that I was in charge of my group," the Turkish officer said. "If he wanted anything done, he was to come to me, and I would see that it was done. If he removed me, the responsibility would fall not on him but on the man next below me, and after that on the man below him. And so on, down through the ranks, until there were only two privates left. Then the senior private would be in charge. They could kill us, I told him, but they couldn't make us do what we didn't want to do. Discipline was our salvation, and we all knew it. If a Turk had questioned an order from his superior to share his food or lift a litter, the way I understand some of your men did, he would literally have had his teeth knocked in. Not by his superior, either, but by the Turk nearest to him. The Communists made attempts to indoctrinate the Turks, acting through a Turkish-speaking Chinese, but they failed almost completely, and eventually gave up."

Turkish discipline led to another magnificent achievement, the Colonel went on. Though almost half of the two hundred and twenty-nine Turkish prisoners were wounded when they were captured, not one died in prison. "It is a remarkable record," Colonel Perry said, "and all the more so by comparison with our own. At Death Valley, one of the temporary prison camps established by the North Korean Communists in the early days of the war, where the sick and wounded poured in for weeks in a ghastly stream, the Turks lost not a single man out of a hundred and ten, while we lost four hundred to eight hundred out of fifteen hundred to eighteen hundred. When a Turk got sick, the rest nursed him back to health. If a sick Turk was ordered to the hospital, two well Turks went along. They ministered to him hand and foot while he was there, and when he was discharged, they carried him back to the compound. The Turks all shared their clothing and their food equally. When the Communists did the cooking for the camp, two Turks were dispatched to bring back food for the group, and it was divided in equal portions down to the last morsel. There was no hogging, no rule of dog eat dog.". . .

Next I called on the doctor — Major Clarence L. Anderson, a tall, dark-haired thirty-two-year-old man, who was then on temporary duty in the Pentagon. (He is currently attached to the Letterman Army Hospital, in San Francisco.) Anderson himself was captured by the Chinese on November 3, 1950, at Unsan. After his repatriation, nearly three years later, he was awarded the Distinguished Service Cross for his heroism in rounding up the wounded there and administering first aid to them, and for his refusal to leave them when the unwounded members of his battalion pulled out in retreat. In the weeks that followed his capture, he was marched along Korean roads with columns of other prisoners, pausing at temporary holding camps on the way. Then, in January, 1951, he was assigned to the first permanent prison camp, situated in an evacuated portion of the Yalu River town of Pytok-tong. Later known as Camp No. 5, this camp eventually became the headquarters of the whole Chinese prison system, and it was notorious as a center of highly intensive indoctrination. During the first months of his captivity, Major Anderson was allowed by the Communists to move freely among the camp compounds and give medical attention to prisoners. Consequently, his knowledge of conditions among the prisoners was much wider than that of most captives, who knew only the men in their own squads.

The death rate among American prisoners, I knew, was highest in the early days of the war — of the 2,634 Army captives who died, ninety-nine and two-thirds per cent died in the first year — and I had, of course, heard that the Army felt the deaths to be the result less of Communist maltreatment than of the shortcomings of our own men. After capture, many of the men appeared to lose all sense of allegiance not only to their country but to their fellow-prisoners — a lapse that psychologists have accounted for, in part, by the fact that all prisoners are initially in a state of shock. "While this may be an explanation, it is not an excuse, and the Army does not consider it one," I had been told.

Now Major Anderson bore out what I had heard. "It is a sad fact, but it is a fact, that the men who were captured in large groups early in the war often became unmanageable," he said. "They refused to obey orders, and they cursed and sometimes struck officers who tried to enforce orders. Naturally, the chaos was encouraged by the Communists who told the captives immediately after they were taken that rank no longer existed among them — that they were all equal as simple prisoners of war released from capitalist bondage. At first, the badly wounded suffered most. On the marches back from the line to the temporary holding camps, casualties on litters were often callously abandoned beside the road. Able-bodied prisoners refused to carry them, even when their officers commanded them to do so. If a Communist guard ordered a litter shouldered, our men obeyed; otherwise the wounded were left to die. On the march, in the temporary camps, and in the permanent ones, the strong regularly took food from the weak. There was no discipline to prevent it. Many men were sick, and these men, instead of being helped and nursed by the others, were ignored, or worse. Dysentery was common, and it made some men too weak to walk. On winter nights, helpless men with dysentery were rolled outside the huts by their comrades, and left to die in the cold."

What struck Major Anderson most forcibly was the almost universal inability of the prisoners to adjust to a primitive situation. "They lacked the old Yankee resourcefulness," he said. "This was partly — but *only* partly, I believe — the result of the psychic shock of being captured. It was also, I think, the result of some new failure in the childhood and adolescent training of our young men — a new softness." For a matter of months — until about April of 1951 Anderson said — most prisoners displayed signs of shock, remaining within little shells they had created to protect them from reality. There was practically no communication among the men, and most of them withdrew into a life of inactivity. In fact, very few seemed to be interested even in providing themselves with the basic necessities of food, warmth, and shelter. The Chinese sometimes gave prisoners a chance to go up into the nearby hills and bring down firewood, but the men were too lethargic to do it. The whole routine of Army life collapsed. One prisoner could not challenge another to act like a soldier, because too often the other man would say he wasn't a soldier any more. As Anderson and another doctor made their daily rounds, the one way they could even begin to arouse a sense of responsibility in the men was by urging them to act not like soldiers but like human beings — to wash once in a while, to keep their clothes and their quarters moderately clean, and to lend each other a hand sometimes. This very weak plea, Anderson said, was the only one to which there was any response at all.

The prisoners' attitude was not "What can I do to help myself?" but "What can be done to help me?" The doctors saw it in practically every hut they visited. Although the Communists had segregated the officers, each compound still had a senior noncommissioned officer, who, if he had exercised control, could have improved the lot of the entire group. "Let me show you what I mean by a healthy prisoner organization," the Major said. "If things had been done right, the men in a squad or a platoon would have got up at a specified time in the morning at an order from their senior member, washed, and lined up for chow. They would have eaten indoors or out, depending on the temperature, and then cleaned up the area, gathered wood, and got water. Each man would have seen to keeping his body and his clothing free of lice by squeezing the insects between two fingernails — an important and time-consuming task. In a properly run unit, men would have been detailed to look after the sick — wash their clothes, give them water, prevent them from lying in one position too long and getting bedsores, and scrounge better food for them. In the Korean prison camps, a man's thigh muscles, apparently because of poor diet, would often contract so the knee was bent, and he sometimes could not rise after a night's sleep. A little massage would have corrected this, and it could have been done by the other men in the hut. It usually wasn't. Anything that keeps prisoners occupied, gets their minds off themselves, is good for them, so the leader of a well-run outfit would have organized calisthenics and sports, and got the men to make chess and checker sets. If this sort of disciplined program had been carried out, our prisoners would have maintained their identities as loyal American soldiers and would have functioned as such. Captivity is a miserable situation under the best of conditions, but in Korea it could have been much easier than it was. If we had had proper organization, many of those who returned would not be haunted, as they are, by nightmares of guilt. And, of course, more of us would have returned."

Major Anderson told me that the Army's daily combat ration is thirty-five hundred calories, and that early in the war the prisoners, by his estimate, were getting twelve hundred. This is an inadequate diet, he said, but not a starvation one. In the main, the North Koreans gave the prisoners corn or millet, which was boiled in the usual Korean manner — in an iron pot hung over a fire — and these cereals contained very few proteins, minerals, and vitamins. The lack was sometimes aggravated, as it happened, by the prisoners themselves. "During the worst early days," the Major said, "the enemy gave us a few soybeans. They contained more protein than anything else we had, but the men disliked them, and thought they caused diarrhea. When they did, it was only because they had been insufficiently cooked, as some of the more intelligent men tried to make plain. Nobody believed them, and the men complained so much about the beans that the Chinese stopped giving them to us. This left a big gap in our nutriment. If our organization had been better, we would have had regular cooks among the prisoners. The cooks we had were volunteers, and they made no effort to prepare the beans properly. If the men complained, those cooks just quit." Anderson said that in his opinion most of the deaths from malnutrition — and malnutrition ranked right after pneumonia and dysentery as the chief cause of death — were the result of a deficiency of proteins, minerals, or vitamins, rather than a calorie deficiency, and that almost all cases of malnutrition were aggravated, if not actually caused, by the prisoners' disinclination to eat unfamiliar foods. Not long after the Chinese put the system of permanent camps into operation, the food improved in both quality and quantity, eventually reaching a level of twenty-four hundred calories, which was pretty well maintained until the end of the war.

I asked Anderson about housing conditions in the camps, and about clothing. He said that since most of the camps had formerly been villages, the prisoners were housed in thatched huts. These had mud walls and were usually divided into two rooms. Some of the windows had glass, and some did not. The rooms were small, and prisoners slept on the floor — sometimes in a space per man half as wide as an upper berth in a Pullman. A single electric-light bulb in one of the rooms was the only illumination, and heat came from a stove in the cellar that sent hot air through flues beneath the floor — a simple version of the radiant heat now fashionable with our architects, though in Korea it sometimes had the disadvantage of making the floor too hot to lie on. That wasn't a common complaint in winter, though, particularly when the temperature fell to thirty or forty degrees below zero. At Camp No. 5, the huts were in a valley that in winter got only three hours of sunshine a day. The summers, however, were pleasant — rather like summers in the Adirondacks, Anderson said — and prisoners were then allowed to swim in the Yalu. Clothing, on the whole, was adequate, and the prisoners probably suffered less from lack of it than from any other cause. There was an issue of clothing two or three times a year, and generally the total issue for the year consisted of three shirts, three pairs of shorts, three pairs of socks, one quilted winter uniform, and two cotton summer uniforms. Other winter clothes, issued somewhat irregularly, were quilted overcoats, fur-lined leather-and-canvas boots, and hair-lined caps. In cold weather, summer uniforms were often worn under the quilted clothing for greater warmth. Socks wore out first, and until new ones were issued the prisoners improvised foot wrappings from any cloth they had.

One of the worst problems in the camps, Anderson told me, was an illness known, at least in Camp No. 5, as "give-up-itis." "You could follow its progress all too easily," he said. "First, the sufferer became despondent; then he lay down and covered his head with a blanket; then he wanted ice water to drink with his food; next, no food, only water; and eventually, if he was not got to and helped, he would die. You could actually predict how long it would take. If you didn't get to him within three weeks, he was a goner; if you got to him sooner, he could usually be saved. But in a camp of three thousand men, which was what we had at the start, and with only a few doctors, it was hard to locate all these cases." I asked Anderson whether it was the younger or the older men who tended to succumb to give-up-itis, and he said that as a rule it was the younger. The treatment was to force-feed the man and then drag him upright and compel him to move his limbs. Sometimes a man was choked till he consented to take food. If he spat it out, it was scooped up and put back in his mouth. Only if he agreed to sit up and eat something would the doctor take his hands off him. Thereafter, he was carefully watched, and if he continued to eat and to move about a little, he was usually all right in ten days. "One of the best ways to get a man on his feet to begin with," the Major said, "was to make him so mad by goading him, or even hitting him, that he tried to get up and beat you. If this happened, the man invariably got well."

Major Anderson said that after repatriation he and four other Army physicians who had been prisoners were called in to advise the Surgeon General's Office on methods by which Army personnel could in the future be better prepared to face internment in a Communist prison camp. The doctors all agreed that by far the greatest error of our troop-training program had been to teach the men that Americans are "the best-cared-for soldiers on the globe." "An American soldier goes into the field with comforts that the majority of the world's population doesn't have even at home," said Anderson. "What he was not told in the Korean War was that if he was captured the comforts would vanish into thin air. Why, during those early marches in Korea I saw sick prisoners lying down at the side of the road and waiting to be picked up by an ambulance. They thought that just because our Army had ambulances for picking up straggling prisoners, the Communists would have them, too. Well, they didn't. When you're a Communist prisoner, such comforts do not exist. It should be explained emphatically to our soldiers that people have always got sick, and through the centuries most of them subsequently got well without elaborate care or extensive medication." One of the first things that all five doctors noted in the camps was the reaction of the average prisoner to the lack of ordinary field and hospital comforts. He seemed lost without a bottle of pills and a toilet that flushed. In order to survive under prison conditions, a man must often consume things that would normally be repellent, such as wormy indigenous foods and dirty water; he needs to realize that he will die a lot sooner from starvation than he will from ailments that he might possibly get as a result of eating unpleasant things. "The prisoner in a camp has to be ready to live like an animal," Anderson said. "Plenty of people, including our enemies, live that way. If it means the difference between life and death for our men, the policy of teaching them to live like animals should be adopted without hesitation or apology." In essence, the doctors felt that the Army should maintain the high standard of living of its soldiers in the field but at the same time should make its trainees understand that upon capture their comforts may abruptly disappear, and teach them how to make do with practical, if disagreeable, substitutes. . . .

The fantastic amount of fraternizing with the enemy in the Korean prison camps was in strong contrast to the hatred that American prisoners had felt toward the Japanese in the Second World War. The Japanese, who wanted no Americans in their Greater East Asia Co-Prosperity Sphere, treated captives with physical harshness, thus solidly banding the men together against them. The Chinese, on the other hand, subtly controlled the prisoners' resentment, transferring it from themselves to other objects. Often, in fact, a prisoner's resentment was ultimately turned against himself. Most returned prisoners expressed sincere gratitude for the way the Chinese treated them, although the conditions they had lived under were far worse than anything they had previously known. When they talked about politics, they often used the word "Socialism" rather than "Communism," thus showing a significant emotional identification with the enemy's point of view, and many of them said that while Socialism might not work in the United States, where the people are for the most part well off to begin with, it was a good thing for China and other less advanced nations. As further evidence of the success of the Communist techniques, [an Army psychiatrist, Major] Segal told me that most of the repatriates came home thinking of themselves not as part of a group, bound by common loyalties, but as isolated individuals. This emerged in their response to questions about what their service outfit had been. Where the Turks, for example, said proudly, "Third Company, First Regiment, Turkish Volunteer Brigade," or whatever it may have been, the Americans were likely to respond with the number of their prison camp and the company or platoon they had belonged to there. . . .

A number of measures have been taken as a result of the prisoner-of-war study. Perhaps the most important are based on the President's six-point code, and deal with the education of the whole Army in the proper conduct of troops after capture. "Many of the men who collaborated in Korean camps pleaded innocent of misconduct on the ground that they had acted on orders from their superiors," said Milton[, the Assistant Secretary of the Army]. "One of the hardest things to make clear, both legally and logically, is that a man has a loyalty to discipline but also an independent loyalty to his country. The two should be reconciled, and they must be reconciled if our men are to cope with a devious enemy like the Communists, who, naturally, try to see to it that orders favorable to their own ends will be issued by weak officers and that weak men will obey them. With our new program, the Army feels that this reconciliation between the two kinds of loyalty can be accomplished." In connection with this program, the Army has issued a basic pamphlet explaining Communist indoctrination and interrogation methods in detail and suggesting simple ways to render them ineffective, and has also prepared several training circulars and films presenting techniques that will help men trapped behind enemy lines to evade capture or, if they are captured, to escape. Tackling the problem from another direction, the Army has instituted a group replacement policy, known as Operation Gyroscope, whereby units, instead of individuals, are rotated in assignments at home and abroad. This, it is believed, enables a soldier to identify himself more strongly with his unit, and thus greatly increases his loyalty to it; the unit should consequently be more effective in combat, and also, if any of its members are captured, they should be more able to resist pressure in a prison camp.

The Army has decided to adhere to its policy of authorizing prisoners to give the enemy nothing more than their name, rank, serial number, and date of birth. This decision was reached after months of investigation and soul-searching as to the best course to follow, both practically and ethically. "You can argue about such things till doomsday, but the Communist challenge has got to be met," said Milton. "And it's got to be met in an American way — no compromise with evil. If this means that our troops must withstand emotional pressure and psychological pain, then, for the good of the country, these must be borne. If the Communists alter their methods to include physical torture, that, too, must be endured."

The Army, Milton went on, wants as many people as possible to think about these matters. "Overcoming Communism is not simply an Army problem," he said. "It's a truly national problem. And don't forget — the battle against Communism is waged largely at the level of the individual, and the earlier the preparation the better. The Army would like to see every American parent, teacher, and clergyman work to instill in every one of our children a specific understanding of the differences between our way of life and the Communist way of life, and, even more important, give every child, in the blunt, old-fashioned spirit, a firm regard for right and an abiding distaste for wrong. The Army's period of training is too brief to make changes in the habits of a lifetime. By the time a young man enters the Army, he should possess a set of sound moral values and the strength of character to live by them. Then, with Army training, he may become something very close to military perfection — the ideal citizen soldier."

[1957]

Ode for the American Dead in Korea   THOMAS MC GRATH

Thomas McGrath (1918–   ) received the Swallow poetry book award for *Figures from a Double World* (1955), in which appeared "Ode for the American Dead in Korea."

McGrath is a poet much concerned with political issues. As a result, according to one critic, the ideas in McGrath's weaker poems "are still present as arguments, when they should have been transformed into the unarguable images of poetry." It is interesting to consider the application of this judgment to "Ode for the American Dead in Korea."

> "... *All your false flags were*
> *Of bravery and ignorance.* ..."

1

God love you now, if no one else will ever,
Corpse in the paddy, or dead on a high hill
In the fine and ruinous summer of a war
You never wanted. All your false flags were
Of bravery and ignorance, like grade school maps: 5
Colors of countries you would never see —
Until that weekend in eternity
When, laughing, well armed, perfectly ready to kill
The world and your brother, the safe commanders sent
You into your future. Oh, dead on a hill,   10
Dead in a paddy, leeched and tumbled to
A tomb of footnotes. We mourn a changeling: you:
Handselled to poverty and drummed to war
By distinguished masters whom you never knew.

2

The bee that spins his metal from the sun,   15
The shy mole drifting like a miner ghost
Through midnight earth — all happy creatures run

As strict as trains on rails the circuits of
Blind instinct. Happy in your summer follies,
You mined a culture that was mined for war: 20
The state to mold you, church to bless, and always
The elders to confirm you in your ignorance.
No scholar put your thinking cap on nor
Warned that in dead seas fishes died in schools
Before inventing legs to walk the land.   25
The rulers stuck a tennis racket in your hand,
An Ark against the flood. In time of change
Courage is not enough: the blind mole dies
And you on your hill, who did not know the rules.

3

Wet in the windy counties of the dawn   30
The lone crow skirls his draggled passage home:
And God (whose sparrows fall aslant his gaze,
Like grace or confetti) blinks and he is gone,
And you are gone. Your scarecrow valor grows
And rusts like early lilac while the rose   35
Blooms in Dakota and the stock exchange
Flowers. Roses, rents, all things conspire
To crown your death with wreaths of living fire.
And the public mourners come: the politic tear
Is cast in the Forum. But, in another year,   40
We will mourn you, whose fossil courage fills
The limestone histories: brave: ignorant: amazed:
Dead in the rice paddies, dead on the nameless hills.

[1955]

The Inflatable Globe   THEODORE SPENCER

Theodore Spencer (1902–1949) was educated in this country (Princeton
and Harvard) and abroad (the University of Cambridge). From 1928
until his death he taught English at Harvard, assuming the famous chair
of Boylston Professor of Rhetoric and Oratory in 1946. Besides being a
poet, Spencer was an Elizabethan scholar and an authority on contemporary fiction and poetry. "The Inflatable Globe" was first printed in *The
Paradox in the Circle* (1941).
    Written just before America's entry into World War II, "The In-

flatable Globe" is yet not tied to any particular national situation in the
manner of the three previous selections. The "allegorical man" seems, in
fact, to question the whole concept of nationality with his "stupid trick."
The quiet, almost flat tone of understatement is reinforced through repetition, rhyme scheme, and the attitude of "us all."

". . . With a blow of my breath I inflate this ball. . . ."

> When the allegorical man came calling,
> He told us all he would show us a trick,
> And he showed us a flat but inflatable ball.
> 'Look at this ball,' he told us all;
> 'Look at the lines marked out on this ball.'   5
> We looked at the ball and the lines on the ball:
> England was red, and France was blue;
> Germany orange and Russia brown:
> 'Look at this ball,' he told us all,
> 'With a blow of my breath I inflate this ball.'   10
> He blew, and it bounced, and bouncing, falling,
> He bounced it against the wall with a kick.
> 'But without my breath it will flatten and fall,'
> Said the allegorical man; and down
> Flat came his hand and squashed the ball,   15
> And it fell on the floor with no life at all
> Once his breath had gone out of the ball . . .
> It seemed to us all a stupid trick.

[1941]

The Portable Phonograph   WALTER VAN TILBURG CLARK

Walter Van Tilburg Clark (1909–   ) was born in Maine but grew up
in Reno, Nevada, where his father was president of the University of
Nevada. Now a professor of English at San Francisco State College, Clark
is author of *The Ox-bow Incident* (1940), *The City of Trembling Leaves*
(1945), and *The Track of the Cat* (1949). All of these works have
Western settings.

"The Portable Phonograph" may be located in the American West
but, if so, at a time when both region and country have lost their meaning.
The issue of nationality is not explicit in this story, but Clark strongly
suggests such an issue both by his description of a ruined world and his
portrayal of the survivors. There is little plot in "The Portable Phono-

graph" and little individual characterization; but these elements are perhaps not necessary for the effect Clark wishes to achieve.

". . . We are the doddering remnant of a race of mechanical fools. . . ."

The red sunset, with narrow, black cloud strips like threats across it, lay on
the curved horizon of the prairie. The air was still and cold, and in it settled
the mute darkness and greater cold of night. High in the air there was wind,
for through the veil of the dusk the clouds could be seen gliding rapidly south
and changing shapes. A sensation of torment, of two-sided, unpredictable
nature, arose from the stillness of the earth air beneath the violence of the
upper air. Out of the sunset, through the dead, matted grass and isolated
weed stalks of the prairie, crept the narrow and deeply rutted remains of a
road. In the road, in places, there were crusts of shallow, brittle ice. There
were little islands of an old oiled pavement in the road too, but most of it was
mud, now frozen rigid. The frozen mud still bore the toothed impress of
great tanks, and a wanderer on the neighboring undulations might have
stumbled, in this light, into large, partially filled-in and weed-grown cavities,
their banks channeled and beginning to spread into badlands. These pits
were such as might have been made by falling meteors, but they were not.
They were the scars of gigantic bombs, their rawness already made a little
natural by rain, seed and time. Along the road there were rakish remnants of
fence. There was also, just visible, one portion of tangled and multiple barbed
wire still erect, behind which was a shelving ditch with small caves, now very
quiet and empty, at intervals in its back wall. Otherwise there was no structure or remnant of a structure visible over the dome of the darkling earth,
but only, in sheltered hollows, the darker shadows of young trees trying again.
    Under the wuthering arch of the high wind a V of wild geese fled south.
The rush of their pinions sounded briefly, and the faint, plaintive notes of
their expeditionary talk. Then they left a still greater vacancy. There was
the smell and expectation of snow, as there is likely to be when the wild geese
fly south. From the remote distance, toward the red sky, came faintly the
protracted howl and quick yap-yap of a prairie wolf.
    North of the road, perhaps a hundred yards, lay the parallel and deeply
intrenched course of a small creek, lined with leafless alders and willows. The
creek was already silent under ice. Into the bank above it was dug a sort of
cell, with a single opening, like the mouth of a mine tunnel. Within the cell
there was a little red of fire, which showed dully through the opening, like
a reflection or a deception of the imagination. The light came from the chary
burning of four blocks of poorly aged peat, which gave off a petty warmth
and much acrid smoke. But the precious remnants of wood, old fence posts
and timbers from the long-deserted dugouts, had to be saved for the real
cold, for the time when a man's breath blew white, the moisture in his nostrils
stiffened at once when he stepped out, and the expansive blizzards paraded
for days over the vast open, swirling and settling and thickening, till the dawn
of the cleared day when the sky was a thin blue-green and the terrible cold,

in which a man could not live for three hours unwarmed, lay over the uniformly drifted swell of the plain.

Around the smoldering peat four men were seated cross-legged. Behind them, traversed by their shadows, was the earth bench, with two old and dirty army blankets, where the owner of the cell slept. In a niche in the opposite wall were a few tin utensils which caught the glint of the coals. The host was rewrapping in a piece of daubed burlap, four fine, leather-bound books. He worked slowly and very carefully, and at last tied the bundle securely with a piece of grass-woven cord. The other three looked intently upon the process, as if a great significance lay in it. As the host tied the cord, he spoke. He was an old man, his long, matted beard and hair gray to nearly white. The shadows made his brows and cheekbones appear gnarled, his eyes and cheeks deeply sunken. His big hands, rough with frost and swollen by rheumatism, were awkward but gentle at their task. He was like a prehistoric priest performing a fateful ceremonial rite. Also his voice had in it a suitable quality of deep, reverent despair, yet perhaps, at the moment, a sharpness of selfish satisfaction.

"When I perceived what was happening," he said, "I told myself, 'It is the end. I cannot take much; I will take these.'

"Perhaps I was impractical," he continued. "But for myself, I do not regret, and what do we know of those who will come after us? We are the doddering remnant of a race of mechanical fools. I have saved what I love; the soul of what was good in us here; perhaps the new ones will make a strong enough beginning not to fall behind when they become clever."

He rose with slow pain and placed the wrapped volumes in the niche with his utensils. The others watched him with the same ritualistic gaze.

"Shakespeare, the Bible, *Moby Dick, The Divine Comedy*," one of them said softly. "You might have done worse; much worse."

"You will have a little soul left until you die," said another harshly. "That is more than is true of us. My brain becomes thick, like my hands." He held the big, battered hands, with their black nails, in the glow to be seen.

"I want paper to write on," he said. "And there is none."

The fourth man said nothing. He sat in the shadow farthest from the fire, and sometimes his body jerked in its rags from the cold. Although he was still young, he was sick, and coughed often. Writing implied a greater future than he now felt able to consider.

The old man seated himself laboriously, and reached out, groaning at the movement, to put another block of peat on the fire. With bowed heads and averted eyes, his three guests acknowledged his magnanimity.

"We thank you, Doctor Jenkins, for the reading," said the man who had named the books.

They seemed then to be waiting for something. Doctor Jenkins understood, but was loath to comply. In an ordinary moment he would have said nothing. But the words of *The Tempest*, which he had been reading and the religious attention of the three, made this an unusual occasion.

"You wish to hear the phonograph," he said grudgingly.

The two middle-aged men stared into the fire, unable to formulate and expose the enormity of their desire.

The young man, however, said anxiously, between suppressed coughs, "Oh, please," like an excited child.

The old man rose again in his difficult way, and went to the back of the cell. He returned and placed tenderly upon the packed floor, where the firelight might fall upon it, an old, portable phonograph in a black case. He smoothed the top with his hand, and then opened it. The lovely green-felt-covered disk became visible.

"I have been using thorns as needles," he said. "But tonight, because we have a musician among us" — he bent his head to the young man, almost invisible in the shadow — "I will use a steel needle. There are only three left."

The two middle-aged men stared at him in speechless adoration. The one with the big hands, who wanted to write, moved his lips, but the whisper was not audible.

"Oh, don't," cried the young man, as if he were hurt. "The thorns will do beautifully."

"No," the old man said. "I have become accustomed to the thorns, but they are not really good. For you, my young friend, we will have good music tonight.

"After all," he added generously, and beginning to wind the phonograph, which creaked, "they can't last forever."

"No, nor we," the man who needed to write said harshly. "The needle, by all means."

"Oh, thanks," said the young man. "Thanks," he said again, in a low, excited voice, and then stifled his coughing with a bowed head.

"The records, though," said the old man when he had finished winding, "are a different matter. Already they are very worn. I do not play them more than once a week. One, once a week, that is what I allow myself.

"More than a week I cannot stand it; not to hear them," he apologized.

"No, how could you?" cried the young man. "And with them here like this."

"A man can stand anything," said the man who wanted to write, in his harsh, antagonistic voice.

"Please, the music," said the young man.

"Only the one," said the old man. "In the long run we will remember more that way."

He had a dozen records with luxuriant gold and red seals. Even in that light the others could see that the threads of the records were becoming worn. Slowly he read out the titles, and the tremendous, dead names of the composers and the artists and the orchestras. The three worked upon the names in their minds, carefully. It was difficult to select from such a wealth what they would at once most like to remember. Finally the man who wanted to write named Gershwin's "New York."

"Oh, no," cried the sick young man, and then could say nothing more because he had to cough. The others understood him, and the harsh man withdrew his selection and waited for the musician to choose.

The musician begged Doctor Jenkins to read the titles again, very slowly, so that he could remember the sounds. While they were read, he lay back against the wall, his eyes closed, his thin, horny hand pulling at his light beard, and listened to the voices and the orchestras and the single instruments in his mind.

When the reading was done he spoke despairingly. "I have forgotten," he complained. "I cannot hear them clearly."

"There are things missing," he explained.

"I know," said Doctor Jenkins. "I thought that I knew all of Shelley by heart. I should have brought Shelley."

"That's more soul than we can use," said the harsh man. "*Moby Dick* is better."

"By God, we can understand that," he emphasized.

The doctor nodded.

"Still," said the man who had admired the books, "we need the absolute if we are to keep a grasp on anything."

"Anything but these sticks and peat clods and rabbit snares," he said bitterly.

"Shelley desired an ultimate absolute," said the harsh man. "It's too much," he said. "It's no good; no earthly good."

The musician selected a Debussy nocturne. The others considered and approved. They rose to their knees to watch the doctor prepare for the playing, so that they appeared to be actually in an attitude of worship. The peat glow showed the thinness of their bearded faces, and the deep lines in them, and revealed the condition of their garments. The other two continued to kneel as the old man carefully lowered the needle onto the spinning disk, but the musician suddenly drew back against the wall again, with his knees up, and buried his face in his hands.

At the first notes of the piano the listeners were startled. They stared at each other. Even the musician lifted his head in amazement, but then quickly bowed it again, strainingly, as if he were suffering from a pain he might not be able to endure. They were all listening deeply, without movement. The wet, blue-green notes tinkled forth from the old machine, and were individual, delectable presences in the cell. The individual, delectable presences swept into a sudden tide of unbearably beautiful dissonance, and then continued fully the swelling and ebbing of that tide, the dissonant inpourings, and the resolutions, and the diminishments, and the little, quiet wavelets of interlude lapping between. Every sound was piercing and singularly sweet. In all the men except the musician, there occurred rapid sequences of tragically heightened recollection. He heard nothing but what was there. At the final, whispering disappearance, but moving quietly, so that the others would not hear him and look at him, he let his head fall back in agony, as if it were drawn there by the hair, and clenched the fingers of one hand over his teeth. He sat that way while the others were silent, and until they began to breathe again normally. His drawn-up legs were trembling violently.

Quickly Doctor Jenkins lifted the needle off, to save it, and not to spoil the recollection with scraping. When he had stopped the whirling of the sacred disk, he courteously left the phonograph open and by the fire, in sight.

The others, however, understood. The musician rose last, but then abruptly, and went quickly out at the door without saying anything. The others stopped at the door and gave their thanks in low voices. The doctor nodded magnificently.

"Come again," he invited, "in a week. We will have the 'New York.'"

When the two had gone together, out toward the rimed road, he stood in the entrance, peering and listening. At first there was only the resonant boom of the wind overhead, and then, far over the dome of the dead, dark plain, the wolf cry lamenting. In the rifts of clouds the doctor saw four stars flying. It impressed the doctor that one of them had just been obscured by the beginning of a flying cloud at the very moment he heard what he had been listening for, a sound of suppressed coughing. It was not near by, however. He believed that down against the pale alders he could see the moving shadow.

With nervous hands he lowered the piece of canvas which served as his door, and pegged it at the bottom. Then quickly and quietly, looking at the piece of canvas frequently, he slipped the records into the case, snapped the lid shut, and carried the phonograph to his couch. There, pausing often to stare at the canvas and listen, he dug earth from the wall and disclosed a piece of board. Behind this there was a deep hole in the wall, into which he put the phonograph. After a moment's consideration, he went over and reached down his bundle of books and inserted it also. Then, guardedly, he once more sealed up the hole with the board and the earth. He also changed his blankets, and the grass-stuffed sack which served as a pillow, so that he could lie facing the entrance. After carefully placing two more blocks of peat on the fire, he stood for a long time watching the stretched canvas, but it seemed to billow naturally with the first gusts of a lowering wind. At last he prayed, and got in under his blankets, and closed his smoke-smarting eyes. On the inside of the bed, next the wall, he could feel with his hand, the comfortable piece of lead pipe.

[1941]

Country

The Chosen People   JEFFERSON
The Husbandman   MENCKEN
The Making of Paths   STEGNER
The Death of the Hired Man   FROST

Town

Gopher Prairie   LEWIS
Knoxville: Summer of 1915   AGEE

City

The Magnet Attracting: A Waif Amid Forces   DREISER
The Rock   WOLFE
Death in the City   WOLFE

Suburbia

The Transients   WHYTE

Town and Country

The contest between town and country is as old as civilized man and as recent as the latest election returns. Continued domination of both state and national legislatures by rural interests is defended and attacked in terms that the citizens of Greece and Rome would find familiar, namely that "God made the country and man made the town" and, contrariwise, that a nation without great cities must be poor not only in commerce but in culture as well. These two points of view have had dramatic representation at every stage of America's development, from the earliest years of the Republic when Jefferson extolled the virtues of the agrarian way and Hamilton called for more "manufactures" to the present-day struggle over legislative reapportionment. The Civil War, the great watershed of our national life, was primarily a contest between the Southern agrarian and Northern industrial ways of life. The American Westward movement left the cities of the East behind, and those who participated in it tended to look back with a mixture of resentment and distrust. If the South was in bondage to the North, the West felt itself in bondage to the East — as the farmer was in bondage to the banker.

The American city has won. Its suburbs are swallowing up the countryside, and the Carrie Meebers and George Webbers of America continue to feel the pull of the metropolis, refusing not only to stay "down on the farm" once they have learned of Chicago and New York, but refusing to stay in Gopher Prairie as well. ("If God made the country and man made the town, then the devil made the country-town.") More than this, rural America has been industrialized and the country town has become a metropolitan adjunct. The one-time distinction between town and country dweller has tended to disappear. Willy-nilly, we are almost all of us now attached to megalopolis.

Despite the American's contribution to the triumph of the city, however, he retains a sense of divided allegiance. A refugee from the countryside, he becomes a refugee from the city as well. If he is able, he flees, first to the suburb, and ultimately to a home in the country, returning to his daily stint in the city with conscript stoicism. The comforts of metropolitan existence redeem it only to the extent of making it, in the words of one city dweller, a "fur-lined purgatory." The America of "The Old Swimmin'-Hole" and proud, independent farmers ("That brow without a stain, that fearless eye . . .") constitute a golden image of the national past by which we continue to dream if not to live.

Country

The Chosen People   THOMAS JEFFERSON

Thomas Jefferson (1743–1826) is principally known as the author of the Declaration of Independence and as the third president of the United States. But politics was only one of his fields of interest and achievement. Another was agriculture, both as a profession and a way of life. The life of the farmer seemed to him far superior to that of men in great cities. Long experience in both Europe and America told him this was true. So did the writings of the Physiocrats, a group of French thinkers who argued that a nation's only true wealth was the land and its products. The first of the following paragraphs stating Jefferson's position on this subject comes from a letter to John Jay (1785), the second and third from Jefferson's *Notes on the State of Virginia* (1784), and the fourth from a letter to James Madison (1787).

In black and white terms Jefferson sharply contrasts the "mobs of the great cities" with the "cultivators." Although Jefferson's assertions have an authoritative ring, for the most part he is stating a credo rather than building a case.

". . . Those who labor in the earth are the chosen people of God. . . ."

Cultivators of the earth are the most valuable citizens. They are the most vigorous, the most independent, the most virtuous, and they are tied to their country, and wedded to its liberty and interests, by the most lasting bonds. As long, therefore, as they can find employment in this line, I would not convert them into mariners, artisans, or anything else. But our citizens will find employment in this line, till their numbers, and of course their productions, become too great for the demand, both internal and foreign. This is not the case as yet, and probably will not be for a considerable time. As soon as it is, the surplus of hands must be turned to something else. I should then, perhaps, wish to turn them to the sea in preference to manufactures; because, comparing the characters of the two classes, I find the former the most valuable citizens. I consider the class of artificers as the panders of vice, and the instruments by which the liberties of a country are generally overturned. . . .

*   *   *

Those who labor in the earth are the chosen people of God, if ever He had a chosen people, whose breasts He has made His peculiar deposit for substantial and genuine virtue. It is the focus in which he keeps alive that sacred fire, which otherwise might escape from the face of the earth. Corruption of morals in the mass of cultivators is a phenomenon of which no age nor nation has furnished an example. It is the mark set on those, who, not looking up to heaven, to their own soil and industry, as does the husbandman, for their subsistence, depend for it on casualties and caprice of customers. Dependence begets subservience and venality, suffocates the germ of virtue, and prepares fit tools for the designs of ambition. . . .

*　*　*

Generally speaking, the proportion which the aggregate of the other classes of citizens bears in any State to that of its husbandmen, is the proportion of its unsound to its healthy parts, and is a good enough barometer whereby to measure its degree of corruption. While we have land to labor then, let us never wish to see our citizens occupied at a work-bench, or twirling a distaff. Carpenters, masons, smiths, are wanting in husbandry; but, for the general operations of manufacture, let our workshops remain in Europe. It is better to carry provisions and materials to workmen there, than bring them to the provisions and materials, and with them their manners and principles. The loss by the transportation of commodities across the Atlantic will be made up in happiness and permanence of government. The mobs of great cities add just so much to the support of pure government, as sores do to the strength of the human body. . . .

*　*　*

When we get piled upon one another in large cities, as in Europe, we shall become corrupt as in Europe, and go to eating one another as they do there.

The Husbandman

H. L. MENCKEN

One does not have to read far in H. L. Mencken (1880–1956) to understand why in his heyday he was cordially hated by many of his fellow countrymen and enthusiastically applauded by others, principally such as considered themselves members of "the civilized minority." What Mencken saw as the stodginess, provincialism, and stupidity in American life provided him with endless material for laughter and scorn. Nothing was sacred. College professors, Rotarians, residents of the "Bible Belt," politicians, the great mass of Americans (the "booboisie"), all felt the jab of his tireless pen. The more respectable the person or institution, the sharper his attack, although he did admire some things, such as good food and drink, the ideas of Nietzsche, the music of Wagner, and the honesty of writers like Lewis and Dreiser. Born in Baltimore of German parents,

Mencken did not attend college but became a newspaper reporter instead, a profession in which he soon became famous. Though best remembered for his assaults on contemporary mores which he put into six books of *Prejudices* (1919–1927), Mencken is also important for his lively but painstaking study, *The American Language* (1919). Supplements to this work in 1945 and 1948 added to the stature of this scholarly achievement.

Apparently outraged, Mencken in "The Husbandman" launches an assault on the American farmer which is in direct contradiction to Jefferson's praise. He is liberal in his wrath, however, and it is not only the farmer who gets the critical axe. What makes Mencken so readable is the savage humor which colors every paragraph — the slashing epithets, the piling up of extravagant phrases, the recondite allusions. It is a humor which appeals not only to the artist in his reader but also to the sadist and the snob. But Mencken is not just being "readable." If we cut through the invective, we can discover the reasons — substantial or otherwise — for his scorn.

> "... we are asked to venerate this prehensile moron as . . . the foundation stone of the state! . . ."

A reader for years of the *Congressional Record,* I have encountered in its dense and pregnant columns denunciations of almost every human act or idea that is imaginable to political pathology, from adultery to Zionism, and of all classes of men whose crimes the legislative mind can grasp, from atheists to Zoroastrians, but never once, so far as I can recall, has that great journal shown the slightest insolence, direct or indirect, to the humble husbandman, the lonely companion of *Bos taurus,* the sweating and persecuted farmer. He is, on the contrary, the pet above all other pets, the enchantment and delight, the saint and archangel of all the unearthly Sganarelles and Scaramouches who roar in the two houses of Congress. He is more to them, day in and day out, than whole herds of Honest Workingmen, Gallant Jack Tars and Heroic Miners; he is more, even, than a platoon of Unknown Soldiers. There are days when one or another of these totems of the statesman is bathed with such devotion that it would make the Gracchi blush, but there is never a day that the farmer, too, doesn't get his share, and there is many a day when he gets ten times his share — when, indeed, he is completely submerged in rhetorical vaseline, so that it is hard to tell which end of him is made in the image of God and which is mere hoof. . . .

The farmer is praised by all who mention him at all, from archbishops to zoölogists, day in and day out. He is praised for his industry, his frugality, his patriotism, his altruistic passion. He is praised for staying on the farm, for laboriously wringing our bread and meat from the reluctant soil, for renouncing Babylon to guard the horned cattle on the hills. He is praised for his patient fidelity to the oldest of learned professions, and the most honorable, and the most necessary to all of us. He takes on, in political speeches and newspaper editorials, a sort of mystical character. He is no longer a mundane laborer, scratching for the dollar, full of staphylococci, smelling heavily of sweat and dung; he is a high priest in a rustic temple, pouring out his heart's blood upon the altar of Ceres. The farmer, thus depicted, grows heroic, lyrical, pathetic, affecting. To murmur against him becomes a sort of sacrilege, like murmuring against the Constitution, Human Freedom, the Cause of Democracy. . . . Nevertheless, being already doomed, I herewith and hereby presume to do it. More, my murmur is scored in the manner of Berlioz, for ten thousand trombones *fortissimo*, with harsh, cacophonous chords for bombardons and ophicleides in the bass clef. Let the farmer, so far as I am concerned, be damned forevermore! To hell with him, and bad luck to him! He is, unless I err, no hero at all, and no priest, and no altruist, but simply a tedious fraud and ignoramus, a cheap rogue and hypocrite, the eternal Jack of the human pack. He deserves all that he suffers under our economic system, and more. Any city man, not insane, who sheds tears for him is shedding tears of the crocodile.

No more grasping, selfish and dishonest mammal, indeed, is known to students of the Anthropoidea. When the going is good for him he robs the rest of us up to the extreme limit of our endurance; when the going is bad he comes bawling for help out of the public till. Has anyone ever heard of a farmer making any sacrifice of his own interests, however slight, to the common good? Has anyone ever heard of a farmer practising or advocating any political idea that was not absolutely self-seeking — that was not, in fact, deliberately designed to loot the rest of us to his gain? Greenbackism, free silver, government guarantee of prices, all the complex fiscal imbecilities of the cow State John Baptists — these are the contributions of the virtuous husbandmen to American political theory. There has never been a time, in good seasons or bad, when his hands were not itching for more; there has never been a time when he was not ready to support any charlatan, however grotesque, who promised to get it for him. Why, indeed, are politicians so polite to him — before election, so romantically amorous? For the plain and simple reason that only one issue ever interests or fetches him, and that is the issue of his own profit. He must be promised something definite and valuable, to be paid to him alone, or he is off after some other mountebank. He simply cannot imagine himself as a citizen of a commonwealth, in duty bound to give as well as take; he can imagine himself only as getting all and giving nothing.

Yet we are asked to venerate this prehensile moron as the *Ur*-burgher, the citizen *par excellence*, the foundation-stone of the state! And why? Because he produces something that all of us must have — that we must get somehow on penalty of death. And how do we get it from him? By submitting helplessly to his unconscionable blackmailing — by paying him, not under any rule of reason, but in proportion to his roguery and incompetence, and hence to the direness of our need. . . . They are all willing and eager to pillage us by starving us, but they can't do it because they can't resist attempts to swindle each other. Recall, for example, the case of the cotton-growers in the South. They agreed among themselves to cut down the cotton acreage in order to inflate the price — and instantly every party to the agreement began planting *more* cotton in order to profit by the abstinence of his neighbors. That abstinence being wholly imaginary, the price of cotton fell instead of going up — and then the entire pack of scoundrels began demanding assistance from the national treasury — in brief, began demanding that the rest of us indemnify them for the failure of their plot to blackmail us!

The same demand is made almost annually by the wheat farmers of the Middle West. It is the theory of the zanies who perform at Washington that a grower of wheat devotes himself to that banal art in a philanthropic and patriotic spirit — that he plants and harvests his crop in order that the folks of the cities may not go without bread. It is the plain fact that he raises wheat because it takes less labor than any other crop — because it enables him, after working sixty days a year, to loaf the rest of the twelve months. If wheat-raising could be taken out of the hands of such lazy *fellahin* and organized as the production of iron or cement is organized, the price might be reduced by a half, and still leave a large profit for *entrepreneurs*. It vacillates dangerously to-day, not because speculators manipulate it, but because the crop is irregular and undependable — that is to say, because those who make it are incompetent. The worst speculators, as everyone knows, are the farmers themselves. They hold their wheat as long as they can, borrowing our money from the country banks and hoping prayerfully for a rise. If it goes up, then we pay them an extra and unearned profit. If it goes down, then they demand legislation to prevent it going down next time. Sixty days a year they work; the rest of the time they gamble with our bellies. . . .

Well, these are the sweet-smelling and altruistic agronomists whose sorrows are the *leit-motif* of our politics, whose votes keep us supplied with Bryans and Bleases, whose welfare is alleged to be the chief end of democratic statecraft, whose patriotism is the so-called bulwark of this so-called Republic!

[1924]

The Making of Paths   WALLACE STEGNER

Wallace Stegner (1909–   ) was born on a farm in Iowa and lived as a boy in several far western states and in Saskatchewan. After earning the Ph.D. at the University of Iowa, Stegner taught at several universities before coming to Stanford in 1945 as Professor of English and Director of the Creative Writing Center. He is the author of a much admired novel, *The Big Rock Candy Mountain* (1943), and of a number of prize-winning short stories.

Of his life in Saskatchewan between 1914 and 1919, Stegner has written: "I think those five years . . . are more important to me than any five years of my life. And living in the country has given me an apparently permanent distaste for cities and city ways." "The Making of Paths"

"The Making of Paths" by Wallace Stegner. First published in *The New Yorker*. Copyright © 1958 by *The New Yorker* Magazine, Inc. Reprinted by permission of Brandt & Brandt.

both derives from this sentiment and explains it. In a sense, nothing much happens in this brief reminiscence — a cyclone that just missed is the nearest thing to suspense; yet Stegner orders the various parts so effectively and sketches the various scenes so vividly that the reader is adequately prepared for the poignant final paragraph. If nothing much happens, much is nevertheless said of man's place both on the Saskatchewan prairie and in the world.

". . . I . . . loved the trails and paths we made. . . ."

On the Saskatchewan homestead that we located in 1915 there was at first absolutely nothing. I remember it as it originally was, for my brother and I, aged eight and six, accompanied my father when he went out to make the first "improvements." Our land lay exactly on the international border; the four-foot iron post jutting from the prairie just where our wagon track met the section-line trail to Hydro, Montana, marked not only the otherwise invisible distinction between Canada and the United States but the division between our land and all other, anywhere.

There were few other marks to show which three hundred and twenty acres of that empty plain were ours. The land spread as flat as if it had been graded, except where, halfway to our western line, a shallow, nearly imperceptible coulee began, feeling its way, turning and turning again, baffled and blocked, a watercourse so nearly a slough that the spring runoff had hardly any flow at all, its water not so much flowing as pushed by the thaw behind it and having to go somewhere, until it passed our land and turned south, and near the line found another lost coulee, which carried in most seasons some water — not enough to run but enough to seep, and with holes that gave sanctuary to a few minnows and suckers. That was Coteau Creek, a part of the Milk-Missouri watershed. In good seasons we sometimes got a swim of sorts in its holes; in dry years we hauled water from it in barrels, stealing from the minnows to serve ourselves and our stock. Between it and our house we wore, during the four or five summers we spent vainly trying to make a wheat farm there, one of our private wagon tracks.

Coteau Creek was a landmark and sometimes a hazard. Once my father, gunning our old Model T across one of its fords, hit something and broke an axle. Next day he walked forty miles into Chinook, Montana, leaving me with a homesteader family, and the day after that he brought back the axle on his back and installed it himself after the homesteader's team had hauled the Ford out of the creek bed. I remember that square, high car, with its yellow spoke wheels and its brass bracing rods from windshield to mudguards and its four-eared brass radiator cap. It stuck up black and foreign, a wanderer from another planet, on the flats by Coteau Creek, while my father, red-faced and sweating, crawled in and out under the jacked-up rear end and I squatted in the car's shade and played what games I could with pebbles and a blue robin's egg. We sat there on the plain, something the earth refused to swallow, right in the middle of everything and with the prairie as empty as nightmare clear to the line where hot earth met hot sky. I saw the sun flash off brass, a heliograph winking off a message into space, calling attention to us, saying "Look, look!"

Because that was the essential feeling of the country for me — the sense of being foreign and noticeable, of sticking out — I did not at first feel even safe, much less that I was taking charge of and making my own a parcel of the world. I moped for the town on the Whitemud River, forty miles north, where we lived in winter, where all my friends were, where my mother was waiting until we got a shelter built on the homestead. Out here we did not belong to the earth as the prairie dogs and burrowing owls and picket-pin gophers and weasels and badgers and coyotes did, or to the sky as the hawks did, or to any combination as meadow larks and robins and sparrows did. Our shack, covered with tar paper, was an ugly rectangle on the face of the prairie, and not even the low roof, rounded like the roof of a railroad car to give the wind less grip on it, could bind it into the horizontal world.

Before we got the shack built, we lived in a tent, which the night wind constantly threatened to blow away, flapping the canvas and straining the ropes and pulling the pegs from the gravel. And when, just as we were un-loading the lumber for the shack, a funnel-shaped cloud appeared in the south, moving against a background of gray-black shot with lightning-forks, and even while the sun still shone on us, the air grew tense and metallic to breathe, and a light like a reflection from brass glowed around us, and high above, pure and untroubled, the zenith was blue — then indeed exposure was like paralysis or panic, and we looked at the strangely still tent, bronzed in the yellow air, and felt the air shiver and saw a dart of wind move like a lizard across the dust and vanish again. My father rushed us to the three shallow square holes, arranged in a triangle, with the iron section stake at their apex, that marked the corner of our land, and with ropes he lashed us to the stake and made us cower down in the holes. They were no more than a foot deep; they could in no sense be called shelter. Over their edge our eyes, level with the plain, looked southward and saw nothing between us and the ominous funnel except gopher mounds, the still unshaken grass. Across the coulee a gopher sat up, erect as the picket pin from which he took his name.

Then the grass stirred; it was as if gooseflesh prickled suddenly on the prairie's skin. The gopher disappeared as if some friend below had reached up and yanked him into his burrow. Even while we were realizing it, the yellow air darkened, and then all the brown and yellow went out of it and it was blue-black. The wind began to pluck at the shirts on our backs, the hair on our heads was wrenched, the air was full of dust. From the third hole my father, glaring over the shallow rim, yelled to my brother and to me to keep down, and with a fierce rush rain trampled our backs, and the curly buffalo grass at the level of my squinted eyes was strained out straight and whistling. I popped my head into my arms and fitted my body to the earth. To give the wind more than my flat back, I felt, would be sure destruction, for that was a wind, and that was a country, that hated a foreign and vertical thing.

The cyclone missed us; we got only its lashing edge. We came up cau-tiously from our muddy burrows and saw the clearing world and smelled the air, washed and rinsed of all its sultry oppressiveness. I for one felt better about being who I was, but for a good many weeks I watched the sky with suspicion; exposed as we were, it could jump on us like a leopard from a tree. And I know I was disappointed in the shack my father swiftly put together on our arid flat. A soddy that poked its low brow no higher than the tailings of a gopher's burrow would have suited me better. The bond with the earth that all the footed and winged creatures felt in that country was quite as valid for me.

And that was why I so loved the trails and paths we made; they were ceremonial, an insistence not only that we had a right to be in sight on those prairies but that we owned a piece of them and controlled it. In a country practically without landmarks, as that part of Saskatchewan was, it might have been assumed that any road would comfort the soul. But I don't recall feeling anything special about the graded road that led us three-quarters of the forty miles of our annual June pilgrimage from town to homestead, or for the wiggling tracks that turned off it to the homesteads of others. It was our own trail, lightly worn, its ruts a slightly fresher green where old cured grass had been rubbed away, that lifted my heart; it took off across the prairie like an extension of myself. Our own wheels had made it; broad, iron-shod wagon wheels first, then narrow democrat wheels that cut through the mat of grass and scored the earth until it blew and washed and started a rut, then finally the wheels of the Ford.

By the time we turned off it, the road we had followed from town had itself dwindled to a pair of ruts, but it never quite disappeared; it simply divided into branches like ours. I do not know why the last miles, across buffalo grass and burnouts, past a shack or two abandoned by the homesteaders who had built them, across Coteau Creek, and on westward until the ruts passed through our gate in our fence and stopped before our house, should always have excited me so, unless it was that the trail was a thing we had exclusively created and that it led to a place we had exclusively built. Those tracks demonstrated our existence as triumphantly as an Indian is demonstrated by his handprint painted in ochre on a cliff wall. Not so idiotically as the stranded Ford, this trail and the shack and chicken house and privy at its end said, "See? We are here." Thus, in a sense, was "located" a homestead.

More satisfying than the wagon trail, even, because more intimately and privately made, were the paths that our daily living wore in the prairie. I loved the horses for poking along the pasture fence looking for a way out, because that habit very soon wore a plain path all around inside the barbed wire. Whenever I had to go and catch them for something, I went out of my way to walk in it, partly because the path was easier on my bare feet but more because I wanted to contribute my feet to the wearing process. I scuffed and kicked at clods and persistent grass clumps, and twisted my weight on incipient weeds and flowers, willing that the trail around the inside of our pasture should be beaten dusty and plain, a worn border to our inheritance.

It was the same with the path to the woodpile and the privy. In June, when we reached the homestead, that would be nearly overgrown, the faintest sort of radius line within the fireguard. But our feet quickly wore it anew, though there were only the four of us, and though other members of the

family, less addicted to paths than I, often frustrated and irritated me by
cutting across from the wrong corner of the house, or detouring past the fence-
post pile to get a handful of cedar bark for kindling, and so neglecting their
plain duty to the highway. It was an unspeakable satisfaction to me when
after a few weeks I could rise in the flat morning light that came across the
prairie in one thrust, like a train rushing down a track, and see the beaten
footpath, leading gray and dusty between grass and cactus and the little orange
flowers of the false mallow that we called wild geranium, until it ended, its
purpose served, at the hooked privy door.

Wearing any such path in the earth's rind is an intimate act, an act like
love, and it is denied to the dweller in cities. He lacks the proper mana for
it, he is out of touch. Once, on Fifty-eighth Street in New York, I saw an
apartment dweller walking his captive deer on a leash. They had not the
pleasure of leaving a single footprint, and the sound of the thin little hoofs
on concrete seemed as melancholy to me as, at the moment, the sound of
my own.

[1958]

The Death of the Hired Man   ROBERT FROST

For a note on Frost, see p. 203.
Here, in deceptively relaxed and idiomatic blank verse, Frost not only
tells a story but gives us the characters of several persons and describes a
way of life. The title points directly to the central event of the poem; but
its relation to the poem as a whole is less distinct. "The Death of the
Hired Man" should be measured against Frost's statement that a poem
"begins with a lump in the throat; a homesickness or a lovesickness. It is
a reaching-out toward expression; an effort to find fulfillment. A complete
poem is one where an emotion has found its thought and the thought has
found the words."

". . . It all depends on what you mean by home. . . ."

Mary sat musing on the lamp-flame at the table
Waiting for Warren. When she heard his step,
She ran on tip-toe down the darkened passage
To meet him in the doorway with the news
And put him on his guard. 'Silas is back.'   5
She pushed him outward with her through the door

And shut it after her. 'Be kind,' she said.
She took the market things from Warren's arms
And set them on the porch, then drew him down
To sit beside her on the wooden steps.   10

'When was I ever anything but kind to him?
But I'll not have the fellow back,' he said.
'I told him so last haying, didn't I?
If he left then, I said, that ended it.
What good is he? Who else will harbour him   15
At his age for the little he can do?
What help he is there's no depending on.
Off he goes always when I need him most.
He thinks he ought to earn a little pay,
Enough at least to buy tobacco with,   20
So he won't have to beg and be beholden.
"All right," I say, "I can't afford to pay
Any fixed wages, though I wish I could."
"Someone else can." "Then someone else will have to."
I shouldn't mind his bettering himself   25
If that was what it was. You can be certain,
When he begins like that, there's someone at him
Trying to coax him off with pocket-money, —
In haying time, when any help is scarce.
In winter he comes back to us, I'm done.'   30

'Sh! not so loud: he'll hear you,' Mary said.

'I want him to: he'll have to soon or late.'

'He's worn out. He's asleep beside the stove.
When I came up from Rowe's I found him here,
Huddled against the barn-door fast asleep,   35
A miserable sight, and frightening, too —
You needn't smile — I didn't recognize him —
I wasn't looking for him — and he's changed.
Wait till you see.'

                'Where did you say he'd been?'

'He didn't say. I dragged him to the house,   40
And gave him tea and tried to make him smoke.
I tried to make him talk about his travels.
Nothing would do: he just kept nodding off.'

'What did he say? Did he say anything?'

'But little.'

'Anything? Mary, confess   45
He said he'd come to ditch the meadow for me.'

'Warren!'

'But did he? I just want to know.'

'Of course he did. What would you have him say?
Surely you wouldn't grudge the poor old man
Some humble way to save his self-respect.   50
He added, if you really care to know,
He meant to clear the upper pasture, too.
That sounds like something you have heard before?
Warren, I wish you could have heard the way
He jumbled everything. I stopped to look   55
Two or three times — he made me feel so queer —
To see if he was talking in his sleep.
He ran on Harold Wilson — you remember —
The boy you had in haying four years since.
He's finished school, and teaching in his college.   60
Silas declares you'll have to get him back.
He says they two will make a team for work:
Between them they will lay this farm as smooth!
The way he mixed that in with other things.
He thinks young Wilson a likely lad, though daft   65
On education — you know how they fought
All through July under the blazing sun,
Silas up on the cart to build the load,
Harold along beside to pitch it on.'

'Yes, I took care to keep well out of earshot.'   70

'Well, those days trouble Silas like a dream.
You wouldn't think they would. How some things linger!
Harold's young college boy's assurance piqued him.
After so many years he still keeps finding
Good arguments he sees he might have used.   75
I sympathize. I know just how it feels
To think of the right thing to say too late.
Harold's associated in his mind with Latin.
He asked me what I thought of Harold's saying
He studied Latin like the violin   80
Because he liked it — that an argument!
He said he couldn't make the boy believe
He could find water with a hazel prong —
Which showed how much good school had ever done him.
He wanted to go over that. But most of all   85
He thinks if he could have another chance

To teach him how to build a load of hay —'

'I know, that's Silas' one accomplishment.
He bundles every forkful in its place,
And tags and numbers it for future reference,   90
So he can find and easily dislodge it
In the unloading. Silas does that well.
He takes it out in bunches like big birds' nests.
You never see him standing on the hay
He's trying to lift, straining to lift himself.'   95

'He thinks if he could teach him that, he'd be
Some good perhaps to someone in the world.
He hates to see a boy the fool of books.
Poor Silas, so concerned for other folk,
And nothing to look backward to with pride,   100
And nothing to look forward to with hope,
So now and never any different.'

Part of a moon was falling down the west,
Dragging the whole sky with it to the hills.
Its light poured softly in her lap. She saw it   105
And spread her apron to it. She put out her hand
Among the harp-like morning-glory strings,
Taut with the dew from garden bed to eaves,
As if she played unheard some tenderness
That wrought on him beside her in the night.   110
'Warren,' she said, 'he has come home to die:
You needn't be afraid he'll leave you this time.'

'Home,' he mocked gently.

                          'Yes, what else but home?
It all depends on what you mean by home.
Of course he's nothing to us, any more   115
Than was the hound that came a stranger to us
Out of the woods, worn out upon the trail.'

'Home is the place where, when you have to go there,
They have to take you in.'

                          'I should have called it
Something you somehow haven't to deserve.'   120

Warren leaned out and took a step or two,
Picked up a little stick, and brought it back
And broke it in his hand and tossed it by.
'Silas has better claim on us you think

Than on his brother? Thirteen little miles   125
As the road winds would bring him to his door.
Silas has walked that far no doubt to-day.
Why didn't he go there? His brother's rich,
A somebody — director in the bank.'

'He never told us that.'

                    'We know it though.'   130

'I think his brother ought to help, of course.
I'll see to that if there is need. He ought of right
To take him in, and might be willing to —
He may be better than appearances.
But have some pity on Silas. Do you think   135
If he had any pride in claiming kin
Or anything he looked for from his brother,
He'd keep so still about him all this time?'

'I wonder what's between them.'

                       'I can tell you.
Silas is what he is — we wouldn't mind him —   140
But just the kind that kinsfolk can't abide.
He never did a thing so very bad.
He don't know why he isn't quite as good
As anybody. Worthless though he is,
He won't be made ashamed to please his brother.'   145

'I can't think Si ever hurt anyone.'

'No, but he hurt my heart the way he lay
And rolled his old head on that sharp-edged chair-back.
He wouldn't let me put him on the lounge.
You must go in and see what you can do.   150
I made the bed up for him there to-night.
You'll be surprised at him — how much he's broken.
His working days are done; I'm sure of it.'

'I'd not be in a hurry to say that.'

'I haven't been. Go, look, see for yourself.   155
But, Warren, please remember how it is:
He's come to help you ditch the meadow.
He has a plan. You mustn't laugh at him.
He may not speak of it, and then he may.
I'll sit and see if that small sailing cloud   160
Will hit or miss the moon.'

It hit the moon.
Then there were three there, making a dim row,
The moon, the little silver cloud, and she.

Warren returned — too soon, it seemed to her,
Slipped to her side, caught up her hand and waited.   165

'Warren?' she questioned.

'Dead,' was all he answered.

[1914]

Town

Gopher Prairie   SINCLAIR LEWIS

Sinclair Lewis (1885–1951) was born in Sauk Center, Minnesota, a town which later became the Gopher Prairie of *Main Street*. After graduating from Yale in 1907, he made several trips abroad and traveled throughout the United States, supporting himself by a variety of jobs including that of ghost-writing plots for Jack London. He had published several novels before he had his first big success with *Main Street* (1920). This was followed by several other important novels satirizing the American scene: *Babbitt* (1922) (see p. 256), *Arrowsmith* (1925), *Elmer Gantry* (1927), and *Dodsworth* (1929). He continued writing until the time of his death, but his later work fell short of that done in the 1920's.

Lewis has been called "violently American," though the ambivalence of his feeling about American life is not easily apparent in the present selection. In this "thirty-two minute" tour of Gopher Prairie, Lewis makes the town seem appallingly real through the use of selected detail.

". . . like the town? . . ."

When Carol had walked for thirty-two minutes she had completely covered the town, east and west, north and south; and she stood at the corner of Main Street and Washington Avenue and despaired.

Main Street with its two-story brick shops, its story-and-a-half wooden residences, its muddy expanse from concrete walk to wall, its huddle of Fords and lumber-wagons, was too small to absorb her. The broad, straight, unenticing gashes of the streets let in the grasping prairie on every side. She realized the vastness and the emptiness of the land. The skeleton iron windmill on the farm a few blocks away, at the north end of Main Street, was like the ribs of a dead cow. She thought of the coming of the Northern winter, when the unprotected houses would crouch together in terror of storms galloping out of that wild waste. They were so small and weak, the little brown houses. They were shelters for sparrows, not homes for warm laughing people.

She told herself that down the street the leaves were a splendor. The maples were orange; the oaks a solid tint of raspberry. And the lawns had been nursed with love. But the thought would not hold. At best the trees resembled a thinned woodlot. There was no park to rest the eyes. And since not Gopher Prairie but Wakamin was the county-seat, there was no court-house with its grounds.

She glanced through the fly-specked windows of the most pretentious building in sight, the one place which welcomed strangers and determined their opinion of the charm and luxury of Gopher Prairie — the Minniemashie House. It was a tall lean shabby structure, three stories of yellow-streaked wood, the corners covered with sanded pine slabs purporting to symbolize stone. In the hotel office she could see a stretch of bare unclean floor, a line of rickety chairs with brass cuspidors between a writing-desk with advertise-ments in mother-of-pearl letters upon the glass-covered back. The dining-room beyond was a jungle of stained table-cloths and catsup bottles.

She looked no more at the Minniemashie House.

A man in cuffless shirt-sleeves with pink arm-garters, wearing a linen collar but no tie, yawned his way from Dyer's Drug Store across to the hotel. He leaned against the wall, scratched a while, sighed, and in a bored way gos-siped with a man tilted back in a chair. A lumber-wagon, its long green box filled with large spools of barbed-wire fencing, creaked down the block. A Ford, in reverse, sounded as though it were shaking to pieces, then recovered and rattled away. In the Greek candy-store was the whine of a peanut-roaster, and the oily smell of nuts.

There was no other sound nor sign of life.

She wanted to run, fleeing from the encroaching prairie, demanding the security of a great city. Her dreams of creating a beautiful town were ludi-crous. Oozing out from every drab wall, she felt a forbidding spirit which she could never conquer.

She trailed down the street on one side, back on the other, glancing into the cross streets. It was a private Seeing Main Street tour. She was within ten minutes beholding not only the heart of a place called Gopher Prairie, but ten thousand towns from Albany to San Diego:

Dyer's Drug Store, a corner building of regular and unreal blocks of artificial stone. Inside the store, a greasy marble soda-fountain with an electric lamp of red and green and curdled-yellow mosaic shade. Pawed-over heaps of toothbrushes and combs and packages of shaving-soap. Shelves of soap-cartons, teething-rings, garden-seeds, and patent medicines in yellow packages — nostrums for consumption, for "women's diseases" — notorious mixtures of opium and alcohol, in the very shop to which her husband sent patients for the filling of prescriptions.

From a second-story window the sign "W. P. Kennicott, Phys. & Surgeon," gilt on black sand.

A small wooden motion-picture theater called "The Rosebud Movie Palace." Lithographs announcing a film called "Fatty in Love."

Howland & Gould's Grocery. In the display window, black, overripe bananas and lettuce on which a cat was sleeping. Shelves lined with red crêpe paper which was now faded and torn and concentrically spotted. Flat against the wall of the second story the signs of lodges — the Knights of Pythias, the Maccabees, the Woodmen, the Masons.

Dahl & Oleson's Meat Market — a reek of blood.

A jewelry shop with tinny-looking wrist-watches for women. In front of it, at the curb, a huge wooden clock which did not go.

A fly-buzzing saloon with a brilliant gold and enamel whisky sign across the front. Other saloons down the block. From them a stink of stale beer, and thick voices bellowing pidgin German or trolling out dirty songs — vice gone feeble and unenterprising and dull — the delicacy of a mining-camp minus its vigor. In front of the saloons, farmwives sitting on the seats of wagons, waiting for their husbands to become drunk and ready to start home.

A tobacco shop called "The Smoke House," filled with young men shaking dice for cigarettes. Racks of magazines, and pictures of coy fat prostitutes in striped bathing-suits.

A clothing store with a display of "ox-blood-shade Oxfords with bull-dog toes." Suits which looked worn and glossless while they were still new, flabbily draped on dummies like corpses with painted cheeks.

The Bon Ton Store — Haydock & Simons' — the largest shop in town. The first-story front of clear glass, the plates cleverly bound at the edges with brass. The second story of pleasant tapestry brick. One window of excellent clothes for men, interspersed with collars of floral piqué which showed mauve daisies on a saffron ground. Newness and an obvious notion of neatness and service. Haydock & Simons. Haydock. She had met a Haydock at the station; Harry Haydock; an active person of thirty-five. He seemed great to her, now, and very like a saint. His shop was clean!

Axel Egge's General Store, frequented by Scandinavian farmers. In the shallow dark window-space heaps of sleazy sateens, badly woven galateas, canvas shoes designed for women with bulging ankles, steel and red glass buttons upon cards with broken edges, a cottony blanket, a granite-ware frying-pan reposing on a sun-faded crêpe blouse.

Sam Clark's Hardware Store. An air of frankly metallic enterprise. Guns and churns and barrels of nails and beautiful shiny butcher knives.

Chester Dashaway's House Furnishing Emporium. A vista of heavy oak rockers with leather seats, asleep in a dismal row.

Billy's Lunch. Thick handleless cups on the wet oilcloth-covered counter. An odor of onions and the smoke of hot lard. In the doorway a young man audibly sucking a toothpick.

The warehouse of the buyer of cream and potatoes. The sour smell of a dairy.

The Ford Garage and the Buick Garage, competent one-story brick and cement buildings opposite each other. Old and new cars on grease-blackened concrete floors. Tire advertisements. The roaring of a tested motor; a racket which beat at the nerves. Surly young men in khaki union-overalls. The most energetic and vital places in town.

A large warehouse for agricultural implements. An impressive barricade of green and gold wheels, of shafts and sulky seats, belonging to machinery of which Carol knew nothing — potato-planters, manure-spreaders, silage-cutters, disk-harrows, breaking-plows.

A feed store, its windows opaque with the dust of bran, a patent medicine advertisement painted on its roof.

Ye Art Shoppe, Prop. Mrs. Mary Ellen Wilks, Christian Science Library open daily free. A touching fumble at beauty. A one-room shanty of boards recently covered with rough stucco. A show-window delicately rich in error: vases starting out to imitate tree-trunks but running off into blobs of gilt — an aluminum ash-tray labeled "Greetings from Gopher Prairie" — a Christian Science magazine — a stamped sofa-cushion portraying a large ribbon tied to a small poppy, the correct skeins of embroidery-silk lying on the pillow. Inside the shop, a glimpse of bad carbon prints of bad and famous pictures, shelves of phonograph records and camera films, wooden toys, and in the midst an anxious small woman sitting in a padded rocking chair.

A barber shop and pool room. A man in shirt sleeves, presumably Del Snafflin the proprietor, shaving a man who had a large Adam's apple.

Nat Hicks's Tailor Shop, on a side street off Main. A one-story building. A fashion-plate showing human pitchforks in garments which looked as hard as steel plate.

On another side street a raw red-brick Catholic Church with a varnished yellow door.

The post-office — merely a partition of glass and brass shutting off the rear of a mildewed room which must once have been a shop. A tilted writing-shelf against a wall rubbed black and scattered with official notices and army recruiting-posters.

The damp, yellow-brick schoolbuilding in its cindery grounds.

The State Bank, stucco masking wood.

The Farmers' National Bank. An Ionic temple of marble. Pure, exquisite, solitary. A brass plate with "Ezra Stowbody, Pres't."

A score of similar shops and establishments.

Behind them and mixed with them, the houses, meek cottages or large, comfortable, soundly uninteresting symbols of prosperity.

In all the town not one building save the Ionic bank which gave pleasure to Carol's eyes; not a dozen buildings which suggested that, in the fifty years of Gopher Prairie's existence, the citizens had realized that it was either desirable or possible to make this, their common home, amusing or attractive.

It was not only the unsparing unapologetic ugliness and the rigid straightness which overwhelmed her. It was the planlessness, the flimsy temporariness of the buildings, their faded unpleasant colors. The street was cluttered with electric-light poles, telephone poles, gasoline pumps for motor cars, boxes of goods. Each man had built with the most valiant disregard of all the others. Between a large new "block" of two-story brick shops on one side, and the fire-brick Overland garage on the other side, was a one-story cottage turned into a millinery shop. The white temple of the Farmers' Bank was elbowed back by a grocery of glaring yellow brick. One store-building had a patchy galvanized iron cornice; the building beside it was crowned with battlements and pyramids of brick capped with blocks of red sandstone.

She escaped from Main Street, fled home.

She wouldn't have cared, she insisted, if the people had been comely. She had noted a young man loafing before a shop, one unwashed hand holding the cord of an awning; a middle-aged man who had a way of staring at women as though he had been married too long and too prosaically; an old farmer, solid, wholesome, but not clean — his face like a potato fresh from the earth. None of them had shaved for three days.

"If they can't build shrines, out here on the prairie, surely there's nothing to prevent their buying safety-razors!" she raged.

She fought herself: "I must be wrong. People do live here. It *can't* be as ugly as — as I know it is! I must be wrong. But I can't do it. I can't go through with it."

She came home too seriously worried for hysteria; and when she found Kennicott waiting for her, and exulting, "Have a walk? Well, like the town? Great lawns and trees, eh?" she was able to say, with a self-protective maturity new to her, "It's very interesting."

[1920]

Knoxville: Summer of 1915   JAMES AGEE

James Agee (1909–1955) was born in Knoxville and later moved with his family to Maine. In 1932 he graduated from Harvard, where he had won the Poetry Prize and edited the *Advocate*. Poet and novelist, script writer and movie critic, Agee performed with distinction in each of these capacities. "Knoxville: Summer of 1915" was first published in *Partisan Review* in 1938 and later became part of *A Death in the Family,* a posthumous novel which won the Pulitzer Prize in 1958.

Agee's qualities as a poet are clearly apparent in this prose evocation of the quality of a summer evening in the Knoxville of his boyhood. A notable characteristic of the passage is its rich and varied imagery. It is instructive to compare the small boy's apprehension of the life about him with that of Carol Kennicott in the preceding selection — and to account for the difference.

". . . I lived . . . disguised to myself as a child. . . ."

We are talking now of summer evenings in Knoxville Tennessee in the time that I lived there so successfully disguised to myself as a child. It was a little bit mixed sort of block, fairly solidly lower middle class, with one or two juts apiece on either side of that. The houses corresponded: middle-sized gracefully fretted wood houses built in the late nineties and early nineteen hundred, with small front and side and more spacious back yards, and trees in the yards, and porches. These were soft-wooded trees, poplars, tulip trees, cottonwoods. There were fences around one or two of the houses, but mainly the yards ran into each other with only now and then a low hedge that wasn't

Reprinted by permission of *Partisan Review* and Mrs. Agee.

doing very well. There were few good friends among the grown people, and they were not poor enough for the other sort of intimate acquaintance, but everyone nodded and spoke, and even might talk short times, trivially, and at the two extremes of the general or the particular, and ordinarily nextdoor neighbors talked quite a bit when they happened to run into each other, and never paid calls. The men were mostly small businessmen, one or two very modestly executives, one or two worked with their hands, most of them clerical, and most of them between thirty and forty-five.

But it is of these evenings, I speak.

Supper was at six and was over by half past. There was still daylight, shining softly and with a tarnish, like the lining of a shell; and the carbon lamps lifted at the corners were on in the light, and the locusts were started, and the fireflies were out, and a few frogs were flopping in the dewy grass, by the time the fathers and the children came out. The children ran out first hell bent and yelling those names by which they were known; then the fathers sank out leisurely in crossed suspenders, their collars removed and their necks looking tall and shy. The mothers stayed back in the kitchen washing and drying, putting things away, recrossing their traceless footsteps like the lifetime journeys of bees, measuring out the dry cocoa for breakfast. When they came out they had taken off their aprons and their skirts were dampened and they sat in rockers on their porches quietly.

It is not of the games children play in the evening that I want to speak now, it is of a contemporaneous atmosphere that has little to do with them: that of the fathers of families, each in his space of lawn, his shirt fishlike pale in the unnatural light and his face nearly anonymous, hosing his lawn. The hoses were attached at spigots that stood out of the brick foundations of the houses. The nozzles were variously set but usually so there was a long sweet stream of spray, the nozzle wet in the hand, the water trickling the right forearm and the peeled-back cuff, and the water whishing out a long loose and low-curved cone, and so gentle a sound. First an insane noise of violence in the nozzle, then the still irregular sound of adjustment, then the smoothing into steadiness and a pitch as accurately tuned to the size and style of stream as any violin. So many qualities of sound out of one hose: so many choral differences out of those several hoses that were in earshot. Out of any one hose, the almost dead silence of the release, and the short still arch of the separate big drops, silent as a held breath, and the only noise the flattering noise on leaves and the slapped grass at the fall of each big drop. That, and the intense hiss with the intense stream; that, and that same intensity not growing less but growing more quiet and delicate with the turn of the nozzle, up to that extreme tender whisper when the water was just a wide bell of film. Chiefly, though, the hoses were set much alike, in a compromise between distance and tenderness of spray (and quite surely a sense of art behind this compromise, and a quiet, deep joy, too real to recognize itself) and the sounds therefore were pitched much alike; pointed by the snorting start of a new hose; decorated by some man playful with the nozzle; left empty, like God by the sparrow's fall, when any single one of them desists: and all, though near alike, of various pitch; and in this unison. These sweet pale streamings in the light lift out their pallors and their voices all together, mothers hushing their children, the hushing unnaturally prolonged, the men gentle and silent and each snail-like withdrawn into the quietude of what he singly is doing, the urination of huge children stood loosely military against an invisible wall, and gently happy and peaceful, tasting the mean goodness of their living like the last of their suppers in their mouths; while the locusts carry on this noise of hoses on their much higher and sharper key. The noise of the locust is dry, and it seems not to be rasped or vibrated but urged from him as if through a small orifice by a breath that can never give out. Also there is never one locust but an illusion of at least a thousand. The noise of each locust is pitched in some classic locust range out of which none of them varies more than two full tones: and yet you seem to hear each locust discrete from all the rest, and there is a long, slow, pulse in their noise, like the scarcely defined arch of a long and high set bridge. They are all around in every tree, so that the noise seems to come from nowhere and everywhere at once, from the whole shell of heaven, shivering in your flesh and teasing your eardrums, the boldest of all the sounds of night. And yet it is habitual to summer nights, and is of the great order of noises, like the noises of the sea and of the blood her precocious grandchild, which you realize you are hearing only when you catch yourself listening. Meantime from low in the dark, just outside the swaying horizons of the hoses, conveying always grass in the damp of dew and its strong green-black smear of smell, the regular yet spaced noises of the crickets, each a sweet cold silver noise three-noted, like the slipping each time of three matched links of a small chain.

But the men by now, one by one, have silenced their hoses and drained and coiled them. Now only two, and now only one, is left, and you see only ghostlike shirt with the sleeve garters, and sober mystery of his mild face like the lifted face of large cattle enquiring of your presence in a pitchdark pool of meadow; and now he too is gone; and it has become that time of evening when people sit on their porches, rocking gently and talking gently and watching the street and the standing up into their sphere of possession of the trees, of birds' hung havens, hangars. People go by; things go by. A horse, drawing a buggy, breaking his hollow iron music on the asphalt: a loud auto: a quiet auto: people in pairs, not in a hurry, scuffling, switching their weight of aestival body, talking casually, the taste hovering over them of vanilla, strawberry, pasteboard, and starched milk, the image upon them of lovers and horsemen, squared with clowns in hueless amber. A streetcar raising its iron moan; stopping; belling and starting, stertorous; rousing and raising again its iron increasing moan and swimming its gold windows and straw seats on past and past and past, the bleak spark crackling and cursing above it like a small malignant spirit set to dog its tracks; the iron whine rises on rising speed; still risen, faints; halts; the faint stinging bell; rises again, still fainter; fainting, lifting, lifts, faints foregone: forgotten. Now is the night one blue dew.

Now is the night one blue dew, my father has drained, he has coiled the hose.
Low on the length of lawns, a frailing of fire who breathes.
Content, silver, like peeps of light, each cricket makes his comment over and
over in the drowned grass.

A cold toad thumpily flounders.

Within the edges of damp shadows of side yards are hovering children nearly
    sick with joy of fear, who watch the unguarding of a telephone pole.

Around white carbon corner lamps bugs of all sizes are lifted elliptic, solar
    systems. Big hardshells bruise themselves, assailant: he is fallen on his
    back, legs squiggling.

Parents on porches: rock and rock. From damp strings morning glories hang
    their ancient faces.

The dry and exalted noise of the locusts from all the air at once enchants my
    eardrums.

On the rough wet grass of the back yard my father and mother have
spread quilts. We all lie there, my mother, my father, my uncle, my aunt, and
I too am lying there. First we were sitting up, then one of us lay down, and
then we all lay down, on our stomachs, or on our sides, or on our backs, and
they have kept on talking. They are not talking much, and the talk is quiet,
of nothing in particular, of nothing at all in particular, of nothing at all.
The stars are wide and alive, they seem each like a smile of great sweetness,
and they seem very clear. All my people are larger bodies than mine, quiet,
with voices gentle and meaningless like the voices of sleeping birds. One is
an artist, he is living at home. One is a musician, she is living at home. One
is my mother who is good to me. One is my father who is good to me. By
some chance, here they are, all on this earth; and who shall ever tell the
sorrow of being on this earth, lying, on quilts, on the grass, in a summer
evening, among the sounds of the night. May God bless my people, my
uncle, my aunt, my mother, my good father, oh, remember them kindly in
their time of trouble; and in the hour of their taking away.

After a little I am taken in and put to bed. Sleep, soft smiling, draws me
unto her: and those receive me, who quietly treat me, as one familiar and
well-beloved in that home: but will not, oh, will not, not now, not ever; but
will not ever tell me who I am.

[1938]

City

The Magnet Attracting: A Waif Amid Forces   THEODORE DREISER

Theodore Dreiser (1871–1945) was born in Terre Haute, Indiana, the twelfth of thirteen children in a poverty-stricken family. Like most of his brothers and sisters he left home early (partly in search of money and partly in flight from the religious fanaticism of his father), arriving in Chicago at the age of sixteen. He worked at a variety of jobs, managed a year at the University of Indiana, and at the age of twenty-one began a period of newspaper work in Chicago, St. Louis, Cleveland, and Pittsburgh. In 1894 he went to New York where he wrote for magazines and became a successful editor. Then *Sister Carrie* (1900) was accepted for publication on the enthusiastic recommendation of Frank Norris (see p. 404), but the publisher's wife was shocked at Dreiser's frankness in describing Carrie's life in the big city and insisted that the book be withdrawn. Next year it was published in London, and in 1907 it was finally reissued in this country. Other important novels by Dreiser include *Jennie Gerhardt* (1911), *The "Genius"* (1915), and *An American Tragedy* (1925). Though his writing is often clumsy, Dreiser is a major literary figure with a reputation as "the father of American naturalism." As one critic has remarked, we are inclined to overlook Dreiser's defects because they are "like a warrior's wounds . . . eloquent of struggle."

The title of this first chapter of *Sister Carrie* emphasizes Drieser's naturalistic point of view, as do some of the ideas presented in the text. This selection, however, is not so important for representing a school of literature as for its descriptive power. The differences between the city and the small town are not presented directly. Rather they are suggested in characterization which dramatizes the underlying theme skillfully, despite the charge of one critic that Dreiser's characters are "as vulgar as his diction."

" . . . she was . . . a lone figure in a tossing, thoughtless sea. . . ."

When Caroline Meeber boarded the afternoon train for Chicago, her total outfit consisted of a small trunk, a cheap imitation alligator-skin satchel, a small lunch in a paper box, and a yellow leather snap purse, containing her ticket, a scrap of paper with her sister's address in Van Buren Street, and four dollars in money. It was in August, 1889. She was eighteen years of age, bright, timid, and full of the illusions of ignorance and youth. Whatever touch of regret at parting characterised her thoughts, it was certainly not for advantages now being given up. A gush of tears at her mother's farewell kiss, a touch in her throat when the cars clacked by the flour mill where her father worked by the day, a pathetic sigh as the familiar green environs of the village passed in review, and the threads which bound her so lightly to girlhood and home were irretrievably broken.

To be sure there was always the next station, where one might descend and return. There was the great city, bound more closely by these very trains which came up daily. Columbia City was not so very far away, even once she was in Chicago. What, pray, is a few hours — a few hundred miles? She looked at the little slip bearing her sister's address and wondered. She gazed at the green landscape, now passing in swift review, until her swifter thoughts replaced its impression with vague conjectures of what Chicago might be.

When a girl leaves her home at eighteen, she does one of two things. Either she falls into saving hands and becomes better, or she rapidly assumes the cosmopolitan standard of virtue and becomes worse. Of an intermediate balance, under the circumstances, there is no possibility. The city has its cunning wiles, no less than the infinitely smaller and more human tempter. There are large forces which allure with all the soulfulness of expression possible in the most cultured human. The gleam of a thousand lights is often as effective as the persuasive light in a wooing and fascinating eye. Half the undoing of the unsophisticated and natural mind is accomplished by forces wholly superhuman. A blare of sound, a roar of life, a vast array of human hives, appeal to the astonished senses in equivocal terms. Without a counsellor at hand to whisper cautious interpretations, what falsehoods may not these things breathe into the unguarded ear? Unrecognised for what they are, their beauty, like music, too often relaxes, then weakens, then perverts the simpler human perceptions.

Caroline, or Sister Carrie, as she had been half affectionately termed by the family, was possessed of a mind rudimentary in its power of observation and analysis. Self-interest with her was high, but not strong. It was, nevertheless, her guiding characteristic. Warm with the fancies of youth, pretty with the insipid prettiness of the formative period, possessed of a figure promising eventual shapeliness and an eye alight with certain native intelligence, she was a fair example of the middle American class — two generations removed from the emigrant. Books were beyond her interest — knowledge a sealed book. In the intuitive graces she was still crude. She could scarcely toss her head gracefully. Her hands were almost ineffectual. The feet, though small, were set flatly. And yet she was interested in her charms, quick to understand the keener pleasures of life, ambitious to gain in material things. A half-equipped little knight she was, venturing to reconnoitre the mysterious city and dreaming wild dreams of some vague, far-off supremacy, which should make it prey and subject — the proper penitent, grovelling at a woman's slipper.

"That," said a voice in her ear, "is one of the prettiest little resorts in Wisconsin."

"Is it?" she answered nervously.

The train was just pulling out of Waukesha. For some time she had been conscious of a man behind. She felt him observing her mass of hair. He had been fidgetting, and with natural intuition she felt a certain interest growing in that quarter. Her maidenly reserve, and a certain sense of what was conventional under the circumstances, called her to forestall and deny this familiarity, but the daring and magnetism of the individual, born of past experiences and triumphs, prevailed. She answered.

He leaned forward to put his elbows upon the back of her seat and proceeded to make himself volubly agreeable.

"Yes, that is a great resort for Chicago people. The hotels are swell. You are not familiar with this part of the country, are you?"

"Oh, yes, I am," answered Carrie. "That is, I live at Columbia City. I have never been through here, though."

"And so this is your first visit to Chicago," he observed.

All the time she was conscious of certain features out of the side of her eye. Flush, colourful cheeks, a light moustache, a grey fedora hat. She now turned and looked upon him in full, the instincts of self-protection and coquetry mingling confusedly in her brain.

"I didn't say that," she said.

"Oh," he answered, in a very pleasing way and with an assumed air of mistake, "I thought you did."

Here was a type of the travelling canvasser for a manufacturing house — a class which at that time was first being dubbed by the slang of the day "drummers." He came within the meaning of a still newer term, which had sprung into general use among Americans in 1880, and which concisely expressed the thought of one whose dress or manners are calculated to elicit the admiration of susceptible young women — a "masher." His suit was of a striped and crossed pattern of brown wool, new at that time, but since become familiar as a business suit. The low crotch of the vest revealed a stiff shirt bosom of white and pink stripes. From his coat sleeves protruded a pair of linen cuffs of the same pattern, fastened with large, gold plate buttons, set with the common yellow agates known as "cat's-eyes." His fingers bore several rings — one, the ever-enduring heavy seal — and from his vest dangled a neat gold watch chain, from which was suspended the secret insignia of the Order of Elks. The whole suit was rather tight-fitting, and was finished off with heavy-soled tan shoes, highly polished, and the grey fedora hat. He was, for the order of intellect represented, attractive, and whatever he had to recommend him, you may be sure was not lost upon Carrie, in this, her first glance.

Lest this order of individual should permanently pass, let me put down some of the most striking characteristics of his most successful manner and method. Good clothes, of course, were the first essential, the things without which he was nothing. A strong physical nature, actuated by a keen desire for the feminine, was the next. A mind free of any consideration of the problems or forces of the world and actuated not by greed, but an insatiable love of variable pleasure. His method was always simple. Its principal element was daring, backed, of course, by an intense desire and admiration for the sex. Let him meet with a young woman once and he would approach her with an air of kindly familiarity, not unmixed with pleading, which would result in most cases in a tolerant acceptance. If she showed any tendency to coquetry he would be apt to straighten her tie, or if she "took up" with him at all, to call her by her first name. If he visited a department store it was to lounge familiarly over the counter and ask some leading questions. In more exclusive circles, on the train or in waiting stations, he went slower. If some seemingly vulnerable object appeared he was all attention — to pass the compliments of the day, to lead the way to the parlor car, carrying her grip, or, failing that, to take a seat next her with the hope of being able to court her to her destination. Pillows, books, a footstool, the shade lowered; all these figured in the things which he could do. If, when she reached her destination he did not alight and attend her baggage for her, it was because, in his own estimation, he had signally failed.

A woman should some day write the complete philosophy of clothes. No matter how young, it is one of the things she wholly comprehends. There is an indescribably faint line in the matter of a man's apparel which somehow divides for her those who are worth glancing at and those who are not. Once an individual has passed this faint line on the way downward he will get no glance from her. There is another line at which the dress of a man will cause her to study her own. This line the individual at her elbow now marked for Carrie. She became conscious of an inequality. Her own plain blue dress, with its black cotton tape trimmings, now seemed to her shabby. She felt the worn state of her shoes.

"Let's see," he went on, "I know quite a number of people in your town. Morgenroth the clothier and Gibson the dry goods man."

"Oh, do you?" she interrupted, aroused by memories of longings their show windows had cost her.

At last he had a clew to her interest, and followed it deftly. In a few minutes he had come about into her seat. He talked of sales of clothing, his travels, Chicago, and the amusements of that city.

"If you are going there, you will enjoy it immensely. Have you relatives?"

"I am going to visit my sister," she explained.

"You want to see Lincoln Park," he said, "and Michigan Boulevard. They are putting up great buildings there. It's a second New York — great. So much to see — theatres, crowds, fine houses — oh, you'll like that."

There was a little ache in her fancy of all he described. Her insignificance in the presence of so much magnificence faintly affected her. She realised that hers was not to be a round of pleasure, and yet there was something promising in all the material prospect he set forth. There was something satisfactory in the attention of this individual with his good clothes. She could not help smiling as he told her of some popular actress of whom she reminded him. She was not silly, and yet attention of this sort had its weight.

"You will be in Chicago some little time, won't you?" he observed at one turn of the now easy conversation.

"I don't know," said Carrie vaguely — a flash vision of the possibility of her not securing employment rising in her mind.

"Several weeks, anyhow," he said, looking steadily into her eyes.

There was much more passing now than the mere words indicated. He recognised the indescribable thing that made up for fascination and beauty in her. She realised that she was of interest to him from the one standpoint which a woman both delights in and fears. Her manner was simple, though for the very reason that she had not yet learned the many little affectations with which women conceal their true feelings. Some things she did appeared bold. A clever companion — had she ever had one — would have warned her never to look a man in the eyes so steadily.

"Why do you ask?" she said.

"Well, I'm going to be there several weeks. I'm going to study stock at our place and get new samples. I might show you 'round."

"I don't know whether you can or not. I mean I don't know whether I can. I shall be living with my sister, and——"

"Well, if she minds, we'll fix that." He took out his pencil and a little pocket note-book as if it were all settled. "What is your address there?"

She fumbled her purse which contained the address slip.

He reached down in his hip pocket and took out a fat purse. It was filled with slips of paper, some mileage books, a roll of greenbacks. It impressed her deeply. Such a purse had never been carried by any one attentive to her. Indeed, an experienced traveller, a brisk man of the world, had never come within such close range before. The purse, the shiny tan shoes, the smart new suit, and the *air* with which he did things, built up for her a dim world of fortune, of which he was the centre. It disposed her pleasantly toward all he might do.

He took out a neat business card, on which was engraved Bartlett, Caryoe & Company, and down in the left-hand corner, Chas. H. Drouet.

"That's me," he said, putting the card in her hand and touching his name. "It's pronounced Drew-eh. Our family was French, on my father's side."

She looked at it while he put up his purse. Then he got out a letter from a bunch in his coat pocket. "This is the house I travel for," he went on, pointing to a picture on it, "corner of State and Lake." There was pride in his voice. He felt that it was something to be connected with such a place, and he made her feel that way.

"What is your address?" he began again, fixing his pencil to write.

She looked at his hand.

"Carrie Meeber," she said slowly. "Three hundred and fifty-four West Van Buren Street, care S. C. Hanson."

He wrote it carefully down and got out the purse again. "You'll be at home if I come around Monday night?" he said.

"I think so," she answered.

How true it is that words are but the vague shadows of the volumes we mean. Little audible links, they are, chaining together great inaudible feelings and purposes. Here were these two, bandying little phrases, drawing purses, looking at cards, and both unconscious of how inarticulate all their real feelings were. Neither was wise enough to be sure of the working of the mind of the other. He could not tell how his luring succeeded. She could not realise that she was drifting, until he secured her address. Now she felt that she had yielded something — he, that he had gained a victory. Already they felt that they were somehow associated. Already he took control in directing the conversation. His words were easy. Her manner was relaxed.

They were nearing Chicago. Signs were everywhere numerous. Trains flashed by them. Across wide stretches of flat, open prairie they could see lines of telegraph poles stalking across the fields toward the great city. Far away were indications of suburban towns, some big smoke-stacks towering high in the air.

Frequently there were two-story frame houses standing out in the open fields, without fence or trees, lone outposts of the approaching army of homes.

To the child, the genius with imagination, or the wholly untravelled, the approach to a great city for the first time is a wonderful thing. Particularly if it be evening — that mystic period between the glare and gloom of the world when life is changing from one sphere or condition to another. Ah, the promise of the night. What does it not hold for the weary! What old illusion of hope is not here forever repeated! Says the soul of the toiler to itself, "I shall soon be free. I shall be in the ways and the hosts of the merry. The streets, the lamps, the lighted chamber set for dining, are for me. The theatre, the halls, the parties, the ways of rest and the paths of song — these are mine in the night." Though all humanity be still enclosed in the shops, the thrill runs abroad. It is in the air. The dullest feel something which they may not always express or describe. It is the lifting of the burden of toil.

Sister Carrie gazed out of the window. Her companion, affected by her wonder, so contagious are all things, felt anew some interest in the city and pointed out its marvels.

"This is Northwest Chicago," said Drouet. "This is the Chicago River," and he pointed to a little muddy creek, crowded with the huge masted wanderers from far-off waters nosing the black-posted banks. With a puff, a clang, and a clatter of rails it was gone. "Chicago is getting to be a great town," he went on. "It's a wonder. You'll find lots to see here."

She did not hear this very well. Her heart was troubled by a kind of terror. The fact that she was alone, away from home, rushing into a great sea of life and endeavour, began to tell. She could not help but feel a little choked for breath — a little sick as her heart beat so fast. She half closed her eyes and tried to think it was nothing, that Columbia City was only a little way off.

"Chicago! Chicago!" called the brakeman, slamming open the door. They were rushing into a more crowded yard, alive with the clatter and clang of life. She began to gather up her poor little grip and closed her hand firmly upon her purse. Drouet arose, kicked his legs to straighten his trousers, and seized his clean yellow grip.

"I suppose your people will be here to meet you?" he said. "Let me carry your grip."

"Oh, no," she said. "I'd rather you wouldn't. I'd rather you wouldn't be with me when I meet my sister."

"All right," he said in all kindness. "I'll be near, though, in case she isn't here, and take you out there safely."

"You're so kind," said Carrie, feeling the goodness of such attention in her strange situation.

"Chicago!" called the brakeman, drawing the word out long. They were under a great shadowy train shed, where the lamps were already beginning to shine out, with passenger cars all about and the train moving at a snail's pace. The people in the car were all up and crowding about the door.

"Well, here we are," said Drouet, leading the way to the door. "Good-bye, till I see you Monday."

"Good-bye," she answered, taking his proffered hand.

"Remember, I'll be looking till you find your sister."

She smiled into his eyes.

They filed out, and he affected to take no notice of her. A lean-faced, rather commonplace woman recognized Carrie on the platform and hurried forward.

"Why, Sister Carrie!" she began, and there was a perfunctory embrace of welcome.

Carrie realised the change of affectional atmosphere at once. Amid all the maze, uproar, and novelty she felt cold reality taking her by the hand. No world of light and merriment. No round of amusement. Her sister carried with her most of the grimness of shift and toil.

"Why, how are all the folks at home?" she began; "how is father, and mother?"

Carrie answered, but was looking away. Down the aisle, toward the gate leading into the waiting-room and the street, stood Drouet. He was looking back. When he saw that she saw him and was safe with her sister he turned to go, sending back the shadow of a smile. Only Carrie saw it. She felt something lost to her when he moved away. When he disappeared she felt his absence thoroughly. With her sister she was much alone, a lone figure in a tossing, thoughtless sea.

[1900]

The Rock   THOMAS WOLFE

Thomas Wolfe (1900–1938) is often compared with Walt Whitman. Like Whitman he was a romantic genius who took all experience for his province and attempted to speak to and of all America. In the opinion of no less a writer than William Faulkner, the magnitude of Wolfe's attempt makes him, in a sense, the best American novelist of his time. Wolfe was born in Asheville, N.C., attended the state university, and later earned an M.A. at Harvard. He taught for a time, but his primary aim was to be a writer. His first book, *Look Homeward, Angel* (1929), established his reputation and gave him sufficient income to devote himself to the prodigious outpouring of words which occupied the remainder of his life. Other principal works are *Of Time and the River* (1935), the posthumous *The Web and the Rock* (1939), from which this selection is taken, and *You Can't Go Home Again* (1940).

Reading almost any passage by Wolfe, one is uneasily aware of emotional excess and rhetorical posturing; but one is at least equally aware of

romantic gusto and power. George Webber, some thirty years after
Dreiser's Carrie Meeber (see the previous selection), is coming to a big
city for the first time, and he shares some of her reactions to it. But their
different temperaments, like those of their creators, lead to sharply distinguished experiences.

> *". . . there was a terrific explosion.*
> *It was New York. . . ."*

Some fifteen or more years ago (as men measure, by those diurnal instruments which their ingenuity has created, the immeasurable universe of time),
at the end of a fine, warm, hot, fair, fresh, fragrant, lazy, furnacelike day of
sweltering heat across the body, bones, sinews, tissues, juices, rivers, mountains, plains, streams, lakes, coastal regions, and compacted corporosity of the
American continent, a train might have been observed by one of the lone
watchers of the Jersey Flats approaching that enfabled rock, that ship of life,
that swarming, million-footed, tower-masted, and sky-soaring citadel that bears
the magic name of the Island of Manhattan, at terrific speed.

At this moment, indeed, one of the lone crayfishers, who ply their curious
trade at this season of the year throughout the melancholy length and breadth
of those swamplike moors which are characteristic of this section of the Jersey
coast, lifted his seamed and weather-beaten face from some nets which he
had been mending in preparation for the evening's catch, and, after gazing
for a moment at the projectile fury of the Limited as it thundered past, turned
and, speaking to the brown-faced lad beside him, said quietly:

"It is the Limited."

And the boy, returning his father's look with eyes as sea-far and as lonely
as the old man's own, and in a voice as quiet, said:

"On time, father?"

The old man did not answer for a moment. Instead, he thrust one gnarled
and weather-beaten hand into the pocket of his pea-jacket, fumbled a moment,
and then pulled forth an enormous silver watch with compass dials, an heir-
loom of three generations of crayfishing folk. He regarded it a moment with
a steady, reflective gaze.

"Aye, lad," he said simply, "on time — or thereabouts. She will not miss
it much tonight, I reckon."

But already the great train was gone in a hurricane of sound and speed.
The sound receded into silence, leaving the quiet moors as they had always
been, leaving them to silence, the creaking of the gulls, the low droning of
the giant mosquitoes, the melancholy and funereal pyres of burning trash
here and there, and to the lonely fisher of the moors and his young son. For
a moment, the old man and the lad regarded the receding projectile of the
train with quiet eyes. Then, silently, they resumed their work upon their
nets again. Evening was coming, and with it the full tide, and, with the
coming of the tide, the cray. So all was now as it had always been. The
train had come and gone and vanished, and over the face of the flats brooded
as it had always done the imperturbable visage of eternity.

Within the train, however, there was a different scene, a kind of wakening of hope and of anticipation. Upon the faces of the passengers there might have been observed now all the expressions and emotions which the end of a long journey usually evokes, whether of alert readiness, eager constraint, or apprehensive dread. And on the face of one, a youth in his early twenties, there might have been observed all of the hope, fear, longing, exultancy, faith, belief, expectancy, and incredible realization that every youth on earth has always felt on his approach for the first time to the enchanted city. Although the other people in the coach were already restless, stirring, busy with their preparations for the journey's end, the boy sat there by a window like one rapt in dreams, his vision tranced and glued against the glass at the rushing landscape of the lonely moors. No detail of the scene escaped the ravenous voracity of his attention.

The train rushed past a glue factory. With the expression of one drunk with wonder the young man drank the pageant in. He saw with joy the great stacks, the glazed glass windows, the mighty furnaces of the enormous works; the pungent fragrance of the molten glue came to him and he breathed it in with rapturous appeasement.

The train swept on across a sinuous stream, itself an estuary of the infinite and all-taking sea, itself as motionless as time, scummed richly with a moveless green; the sheer beauty of the thing went home into his mind and heart forever.

He raised his eyes as men against the West once raised their eyes against the shining ramparts of the mountains. And there before him, at the edges of the marsh, rose the proud heights of Jersey City — the heights of Jersey City blazing forever to the traveler the smoldering welcome of their garbage dumps — the heights of Jersey City, raised proudly against the desolation of those lonely marshes as a token of man's fortitude, a symbol of his power, a sign of his indomitable spirit that flames forever like a great torch in the wilderness, that lifts against the darkness and the desolation of blind nature the story of its progress — the heights of Jersey, lighted for an eternal feast.

The train swept on and underneath the crests of yon proud, battlemented hill. The hill closed in around the train, the train roared in beneath the hill, into the tunnel. And suddenly darkness was upon them. The train plunged in beneath the mighty bed of the unceasing river, and dumbness smote the youth's proud, listening ears.

He turned and looked upon his fellow passengers. He saw wonder on their faces and something in their hearts that none could divine; and even as he sat there, dumb with wonder, he heard two voices, two quiet voices out of life, the voices of two nameless ciphers out of life, a woman's and a man's.

"Jeez, but I'll be glad to get back home again," the man said quietly.

For a moment the woman did not answer, then, in the same quiet tone, but with a meaning, a depth of feeling, that the boy would never after that forget, she answered simply, "You said it."

Just that, and nothing more. But, simple as those words were, they sank home into his heart, in their brief eloquence of time and of the bitter briefness of man's days, the whole compacted history of his tragic destiny.

And now, even as he paused there, rapt in wonder at this nameless eloquence, he heard another voice, close to his ears, a voice soft, low, and urgent,
sweet as honey dew, and suddenly, with a start of recognition and surprise,
he realized the words were meant for him, for him alone.

"Is you comin', boss?" the soft voice said. "We'se gettin' in. Shall I bresh
you off?"

The boy turned slowly and surveyed his dark interrogator. In a moment
he inclined his head in a slight gesture of assent and quietly replied:

"I am ready. Yes, you may."

But even now the train was slowing to a halt. Grey twilight filtered
through the windows once again. The train had reached the tunnel's mouth.
On both sides now were ancient walls of masonry, old storied buildings, dark
as time and ancient as man's memory. The boy peered through the window,
up as far as eyes could reach, at all those tiers of life, those countless cells of
life, the windows, rooms, and faces of the everlasting and eternal city. They
leaned above him in their ancient silence. They returned his look. He looked
into their faces and said nothing, no word was spoken. The people of the
city leaned upon the sills of evening and they looked at him. They looked
at him from their old walls of ancient, battlemented brick. They looked at
him through the silent yet attentive curtains of all their ancient and historic
laundries. They looked at him through pendant sheets, through hanging
underwear, through fabrics of a priceless and unknown tapestry, and he knew
that all was now as it had always been, as it would be tomorrow and forever.

But now the train was slowing to a halt. Long tongues of cement now
appeared, and faces, swarming figures, running forms beside the train. And
all these faces, forms, and figures slowed to instancy, were held there in the
alertness of expectant movement. There was a grinding screech of brakes, a
slight jolt, and, for a moment, utter silence.

At this moment there was a terrific explosion.

It was New York.

There is no truer legend in the world than the one about the country boy,
the provincial innocent, in his first contact with the city. Hackneyed by repetition, parodied and burlesqued by the devices of cheap fiction and the slapstick of vaudeville humor, it is nevertheless one of the most tremendous and
vital experiences in the life of a man, and in the life of the nation. It has
found inspired and glorious tongues in Tolstoy and in Goethe, in Balzac and
in Dickens, in Fielding and Mark Twain. It has found splendid examples in
every artery of life, as well in Shakespeare as in the young Napoleon. And
day after day the great cities of the world are being fed, enriched, and replenished ceaselessly with the life-blood of the nation, with all the passion,
aspiration, eagerness, faith, and high imagining that youth can know, or that
the tenement of life can hold.

For one like George Webber, born to the obscure village and brought
up within the narrow geography of provincial ways, the city experience is
such as no city man himself can ever know. It is conceived in absence and
in silence and in youth; it is built up to the cloud-capped pinnacles of a boy's

imagining; it is written like a golden legend in the heart of youth with a plume plucked out of an angel's wing; it lives and flames there in his heart and spirit with all the timeless faery of the magic land.

When such a man, therefore, comes first to the great city — but how can we speak of such a man coming first to the great city, when really the great city is within him, encysted in his heart, built up in all the flaming images of his brain: a symbol of his hope, the image of his high desire, the final crown, the citadel of all that he has ever dreamed of or longed for or imagined that life could bring to him? For such a man as this, there really is no coming to the city. He brings the city with him everywhere he goes, and when that final moment comes when he at last breathes in the city's air, feels his foot upon the city street, looks around him at the city's pinnacles, into the dark, unceasing tide of city faces, grips his sinews, feels his flesh, pinches himself to make sure he is really there — for such a man as this, and for such a moment, it will always be a question to be considered in its bewildering ramifications by the subtle soul psychologists to know which city is the real one, which city he has found and seen, which city for this man is really there.

For the city has a million faces, and just as it is said that no two men can really know what each is thinking of, what either sees when he speaks of "red" or "blue," so can no man ever know just what another means when he tells about the city that he sees. For the city that he sees is just the city that he brings with him, that he has within his heart; and even at that immeasurable moment of first perception, when for the first time he sees the city with his naked eye, at that tremendous moment of final apprehension when the great city smites at last upon his living sense, still no man can be certain he has seen the city as it is, because in the hairbreadth of that instant recognition a whole new city is composed, made out of sense but shaped and colored and unalterable from all that he has felt and thought and dreamed about before.

And more than this! There are so many other instant, swift, and accidental things that happen in a moment, that are gone forever, and that shape the city in the heart of youth. It may be a light that comes and goes, a grey day, or a leaf upon a bough; it may be the first image of a city face, a woman's smile, an oath, a half-heard word; it may be sunset, morning, or the crowded traffics of the street, the furious pinnacle of dusty noon; or it may be April, April, and the songs they sang that year. No one can say, except it may be something chance and swift and fleeting, as are all of these, together with the accidents of pine and clay, the weather of one's youth, the place, the structure, and the life from which one came, and all conditioned so, so memoried, built up into the vision of the city that a man first brings there in his heart. . . .

[1939]

Death in the City   THOMAS WOLFE

This is a carefully structured, tightly unified, and intensely dramatic
sketch from Wolfe's short story "Death the Proud Brother." In a sense its
theme contradicts that of "The Rock" (see preceding selection); in
another sense it extends it. It is instructive to contrast the method, language, and statement of this sketch with Frost's "The Death of the Hired
Man" (see p. 362).

". . . Sure! I seen it! I seen it! Dat's what I'm tellin' yuh! . . ."

I was coming along one of the dingy cross-streets in the upper east-side district — a street still filled with the harsh and angular fronts of old brown-
stone houses, which once no doubt had been the homes of prosperous people
but were now black with the rust and grime of many years. These streets
were seething with the violent and disorderly life of dark-faced, dark-eyed,
strange-tongued people, who surged back and forth, innumerably, namelessly,
with the tidal, liquid, and swarming fluency that all dark bloods and races
have, so that the lean precision, the isolation, and the severe design characteristic of the lives of northern peoples — like something lonely, small, pitifully
yet grandly itself — are fractured instantly by this tidal darkness. The numberless and ageless man-swarm of the earth is instantly revealed in all its
fathomless horror, and will haunt one later in dreams, even if one sees only a
half-dozen of these dark faces in a street.

Upon the corner of this swarming street, where it joined one of the great
grimy streets that go up and down the city, and that are darkened forever by
the savage violence and noise of the elevated structure, so that not only the
light which swarms through the rusty iron webbing, but all the life and
movement underneath it seems harsh, driven, beaten, violent, bewildered,
and confused — on such a corner the man was killed. He was a little middle-
aged Italian who had a kind of flimsy cart which was stationed at the curb,
and in which he had a shabby and miscellaneous stock of cigarettes, cheap
candies, bottled drinks, a big greasy-looking bottle of orange juice turned neck
downward into a battered cylinder of white enamelled tin, and a small oil
stove on which several pots of food — sausages and spaghetti — were always
cooking.

The accident occurred just as I reached the corner opposite the man's
stand. The traffic was roaring north and south beneath the elevated structure.
At this moment an enormous covered van — of the kind so powerful and
cumbersome that it seems to be as big as a locomotive and to engulf the
smaller machines around it, to fill up the street so completely that one wonders
at the skill and precision of the driver who can manipulate it — came roaring

through beneath the elevated structure. It curved over and around, in an attempt to get ahead of a much smaller truck, and as it did so, swiped the little truck a glancing blow that wrecked it instantly, and sent it crashing across the curb into the vendor's wagon with such terrific force that the cart was smashed to splinters, and the truck turned over it completely and lay beyond it in a stove-in wreckage of shattered glass and twisted steel.

The driver of the truck, by the miracle of chance, was uninjured, but the little Italian vendor was mangled beyond recognition. As the truck smashed over him the bright blood burst out of his head in an instant fountain so that it was incredible so small a man could have such fountains of bright blood in him; and he died there on the sidewalk within a few minutes, and before the ambulance could reach him. A great crowd of shouting, dark-faced people gathered around the dying man at once, police appeared instantly in astonishing numbers, and began to thrust and drive in brutally among the excited people, cursing and mauling them, menacing them with their clubs, and shouting savagely:

"Break it up, deh! Break it up! On your way, now!". . . "Where yuh goin'?" one snarled suddenly, grabbing a man by the slack of his coat, lifting him and hurling him back into the crowd as if he were a piece of excrement. "Break it up, deh! Break it up! G'wan, youse guys — yuh gotta move!"

Meanwhile the police had carried the dying man across the curb, laid him down on the sidewalk, and made a circle around him from the thrusting mob. Then the ambulance arrived with its furious and dreadful clangor of bells, but by this time the man was dead. The body was taken away, the police drove and lashed the crowds before them, whipping and mauling them along, as if they were surly and stupid animals, until at length the whole space around the wreck was clear of people.

Then two policemen, clearing the street again for its unceasing traffic, half pushed, half carried the twisted wreckage of the vendor's cart to the curb, and began to pick up his strewn stock, boxes, broken cups and saucers, fragments of broken glass, cheap knives and forks, and finally his tin spaghetti pots, and to throw them into the heap of wreckage. The spaghetti, pieces of brain, and fragments of the skull were mixed together on the pavement in a horrible bloody welter. One of the policemen looked at it for a moment, pushed the thick toe of his boot tentatively into it, and then turned away with a grimace of his brutal red face, as he said, "Jesus!"

At this moment, a little gray-faced Jew, with a big nose, screwy and greasy-looking hair that reached backward from his painful and reptilian brow, rushed from the door of a dismal little tailor shop across the sidewalk, breathing stertorously with excitement, and carrying a bucket full of water in his hand. The Jew ran swiftly out into the street, with a funny bandy-legged movement, dashed the water down upon the bloody welter and then ran back into the shop as fast as he had come. Then a man came out of another shop with a bucket full of sawdust in his hand which he began to strew upon the bloody street until the stain was covered over. Finally, nothing was left except the wreckage of the truck and the vendor's cart, two policemen who conferred quietly together with notebooks in their hands, some people staring with dull fascinated eyes upon the blood-stain on the pavement, and little groups of people on the corners talking to one another in low, excited tones, saying:

"Sure! I seen it! I seen it! Dat's what I'm tellin' yuh! I was talkin' to 'm myself not two minutes before it happened! I saw duh whole t'ing happen! I was standin' not ten feet away from 'im when it hit him!" — as they revived the bloody moment, going over it again and again with an insatiate and feeding hunger.

Such was the first death that I saw in the city. Later, the thing I would remember most vividly, after the horror of the blood and brains and the hideous mutilation of man's living flesh were almost forgotten, was the memory of the bloody and battered tins and pots in which the vendor had cooked his spaghetti, as they lay strewn on the pavement, and as the policeman picked them up to fling them back into the pile of wreckage. For later it seemed these dingy and lifeless objects were able to evoke, with a huge pathos, the whole story of the man's life, his kindly warmth and smiling friendliness — for I had seen him many times — and his pitiful small enterprise, to eke out shabbily, but with constant hope and as best he could, beneath an alien sky, in the heart of the huge indifferent city, some little reward for all his bitter toil and patient steadfastness — some modest but shining goal of security, freedom, escape, and repose, for which all men on this earth have worked and suffered.

And the huge indifference with which the vast and terrible city had in an instant blotted out this little life, soaking the shining air and all the glory of the day with blood, the huge and casual irony of its stroke — for the great van which had wrecked the truck and killed the man, had thundered ahead and vanished, perhaps without its driver even knowing what had happened — was evoked unforgettably, with all its pity, pathos, and immense indifference, by the memory of a few battered pots and pans. This, then, was the first time I saw death in the city.

[1933]

Suburbia

The Transients   WILLIAM H. WHYTE, JR.

For the series of articles from which this selection was taken, William H. Whyte, Jr. (1918–) was given the Benjamin Franklin Magazine Award for "The Best Writing Depicting Life, Culture, or Institutions in the United States" to appear in magazines of general circulation during 1953. For other remarks on Whyte, see p. 266.

Whyte here discusses the phenomenon of the "interchangeable" man who populates the "Levittown-like suburbs" and speculates that it will have a profound effect on American life. But he does not indicate clearly what his own attitude is toward what is taking place. The reasons for Whyte's success as a "quality" magazine writer may be deduced from both the subject and method of this piece. Whyte's style and tone are right for a national audience of amateur sociologists: he is free of specialized jargon; he bears his authority lightly; he deals in human specifics. Along with the clarity of individual sentences, the organizational clarity of each paragraph and of the piece as a whole is evident even from the portions printed here.

". . . Underneath the television aerials lies a revolution. . . ."

For a quick twinge of superiority there is nothing quite like driving past one of the new Levittown-like suburbs. To visitors from older communities, the sight of rank after rank of little boxes stretching off to infinity, one hardly distinguishable from the other, is weird, and if they drive along the streets at dusk, when the little blue lights of the television sets begin to shine out of the picture windows, they can speculate that if they were to blink their eyes in proper rhythm the scene flashing by would freeze into one motionless picture. Appalling! If this is progress, God help us . . . 1984. But, onlookers are also likely to conclude, one must be sympathetic too; after all, it is a step up in life for the people who live there, and one should not begrudge them the opiate of TV; here, obviously, is a group of anonymous beings submerged in a system they do not understand.

The onlooker had better wipe the sympathy off his face. Underneath the television aerials lies a revolution. What he has seen is not the home of little cogs and drones. What he has seen is the dormitory of the next managerial class.

The most important single group in these communities is what has been variously called business bureaucrats, industrial civil servants, technicians of society — the junior executives, research workers, young corporation lawyers, engineers, salesmen. The bond they share is that they are (1) between twenty-five and thirty-five, (2) organization men, (3) and all on the move. It is significant enough that there are now so many of them that whole towns have to be built to hold them; more significant, it is these unostentatious, salaried nomads who will be running our business society twenty years from now.

Many future managers, of course, do not live in such places; and many work for companies that don't require them to move. Nevertheless, it may be the new suburban communities that provide the sharpest picture of tomorrow's management. Not only are managerial transients concentrated here, they are concentrated almost totally free of the pressures of older traditions and older people that would affect them elsewhere. In such propinquity, they bring out in each other — perhaps at times caricature — tendencies latent elsewhere, and one sees in bold relief what might be almost invisible in more conventional environments. To an older eye, perhaps the picture is abnormal, but what may be abnormal today is very likely to be normal tomorrow. . . .

After the war, one thing looked sure. Americans had had their bellyful of moving; now, everybody agreed, they were going to settle down and stop this damned traipsing around. Here is the way things worked out:

Americans are moving more than ever before: Never have long-distance movers had it so good; according to figures provided by the five leading firms, moving is now at a rate even higher than in wartime. And compared with prewar, the five firms are all moving at least three times as many families, and one is moving ten times as many. Furthermore, not only are more families moving, those who move, move more frequently; one out of every seven of its customers, Allied Van Lines reports, will *within a year* pick up stakes and move again to a new state, and seven out of ten will be "repeaters" within the next five years.

This is not just a matter of moving from one part of town to another; in 1951, 7 per cent of all male adults moved away from their county, and of these roughly half moved out of the state entirely. Concentrate on the twenty-five to thirty-five-year-old group and the figure goes up sharply; in 1951 roughly 12 per cent of men twenty-five to thirty-five years old moved outside of their county, and 6 per cent moved to a new state.

The more education, the more mobility: If a man goes to college now, the chances are almost even that he won't work in his home state. Recent census figures and *Time* Magazine's study, "They Went to College," indicate that the educational level is higher among migrants than among non-migrants, and the higher the educational level, the more intensive the migration. In the twenty-five to thirty-five-year-old group, to extrapolate from census figures, about sixteen out of every hundred men who have a high-school education have been interstate migrants, versus 29 per cent of those who have had at least one year of college. Of men who complete college, 46 per cent move. Of those who worked their way through in a college outside their home state, about 70 per cent don't go back. And for all college men, incidentally, the higher the grades, the more likely they are to go to work elsewhere than in their home states.

Organization people move the most: To judge from studies by direct-mail experts of *Time, Life, Fortune,* and McGraw-Hill, the greatest amount of address changing occurs among managerial people. Similarly, records of long-distance movers show that the greatest single group among their customers, upwards of 40 per cent, consists of corporation people being transferred from one post to another (with the employer usually footing the bill). If to this group are added government, Army, and Navy people, and men joining new companies, over 70 per cent of all moves are accounted for by members of large institutions.

The impact of this transiency on United States society is incalculable. The small town, for example, has long exported some of its youth; but what was once a stream has become a flood. It is no longer a case of the special boy who had to get out of town to cross the tracks or find an outlet for his energies; now as many as three-quarters of the town's young college men may be in the same position. Where are they to go after college? Back home? Lawyers and doctors can, and the majority do; they are in the happy position of being able to go home, to keep professionally alert, and to make a good bit of money at the same time. But for the others, opportunity seems to be elsewhere — not just for the delivery boy who became an Air Force lieutenant, but for the young man on the Hill who's gone off to join du Pont.

In terms of status it is difficult to say whether the migrants have gone up or down. But they have moved more than geographically; what is taking place is a horizontal movement in which the transients have come together in a new kind of group that fits none of the old social categories.

And they will never come back. Once the cord is broken, a return carries overtones of failure. "I'm fed up with New York," says one executive, "but if I went to Taylorston I know damned well they'd think my tail was between my legs." The point is that he probably would think so too; one of the great tacit bonds the transients share is a feeling, justifiable or not, that by moving they acquire an intellectual sophistication that will forever widen the gap between them and their home towns. "Dave and I thought often about going back to East Wells," a successful young executive's wife explains. "It is a beautiful old New England town and we both had such happy times there. But all the people who had anything on the ball seem to have left. There are a few who took over their fathers' businesses, but the rest — well, I hate to sound so snobbish, but dammit, I *do* feel superior to them."

It is curious how much the transients think about the home town. A majority of the people interviewed by *Fortune* spontaneously brought it up, and the phrase, "No, I'll never go back" was repeated almost verbatim scores of times. Many transients left a lot behind them or at least in retrospect it seems so to them; most came from reasonably prosperous families and when they look back they recall the kinfolk and friends about, and the reassuring feeling that they were in that fortunate group who counted. But local prestige, they now well know, is not for export. "This is quite a conflict today," says anthropologist Lloyd Warner. "John Marquand shows this very well. Why does Charles Gray in *Point of No Return* go back to visit Newburyport? Why does John, for that matter? That's something all of us want to do, to keep the old image of our position."

Even, if by chance the company sends the transients back, they can never really go home. As one puts it, "Because of this last transfer I'm back here, almost by accident, where I was born. It ought to be a setup; frankly, my family is as old guard around here as they come. Well, it's a lot of crap, sure, but I must say I get a good bit of pleasure knowing that I can join the City Club and my boss can't. But it's damned privately I think about it. If I am going to go ahead in this organization, the people I've got to get along with are the office crowd, and don't think I wouldn't get the business if they started reading about me in the social columns." Says another, "It's odd. Here I've got a social position a lot of people would give a fortune to get, but the minute I joined the corporation I had to turn my back on it. We're sort of declassed, and as far as Amy and I are concerned, it is as if we weren't born here at all."

But the most important reason they can't go home is that they won't find it there if they do. In the rapid growth of the metropolitan areas, once self-contained market towns have been transformed into suburbs, and more important yet, the plant expansion of American industry has turned others into industrial towns. In many towns, as a result, the migration of the young people has been offset by such an influx of newcomers that those who have stayed put are in the position of being abroad at home. . . .

In the wake of this shift to the big organization is the moving van. Certainly the recruit does not join up because he *wants* to move a lot, and it is often in spite of it. But moving, he knows, has become part of the bargain, and unsettling as transfer might be, even more unsettling are the implications of not being asked to transfer. "We never plan to transfer," as one company president explains, a bit dryly, "and we never make a man move. Of course, he kills his career if he doesn't. But we never *make* him do it." The fact is well understood; it is with a smile that the recruit moves — and keeps on moving, year after year; until, perhaps, that distant day when he is summoned back to Rome.

It is not just more moves per man. Even companies reporting no increase in the number of times each individual moves report an increase in the sheer number of men being moved. General Electric has compared a cross section of its forty-five-year-old executives with one of its thirty-five-year-olds; in the ten years after they were twenty-five, 42 per cent of the older group had moved at least once; during the same age period, 58 per cent of the younger had moved.

Corporations never planned it quite that way. Decentralization and expansion, rather than deliberate personnel policy, have determined the pattern. Companies have systematized it, to be sure; moves are settling into more of a rhythm, almost invariably they are sweetened with a raise, and in some companies, sweetened by special departments that handle all the housekeeping fuss of the trip. By and large, however, the question of the man's personal development — however emphasized when the boss breaks the news to him —

has been secondary to the day-to-day necessity of filling vacancies out in the empire.

That is, up until now. Periodic transfer, some companies are coming to believe, is a positive good in itself; and even where no immediate functional reason exists, it might often be important to move the man anyway. What better way, they ask, to produce the well-rounded executive?

Instead of leaving transfer to be determined haphazardly by different departments, some companies, like General Electric, have made such decisions part of a systematic managerial program. By thus making a man's "permanent" assignment (i.e., one lasting at least three years) part of a deliberate rotation policy, the man is given "more choices in life to make," and the company, as a result, is given a pool of seasoned talent. Other companies agree; by deliberately exposing a man to a succession of environments, they best obtain that necessity of the large organization — the man who can fit in anywhere. "The 'training,'" as an I.B.M. executive succinctly puts it, "makes our men interchangeable." . . .

What has already happened to the salaried transient suggests that if mobility continues to increase it may produce a rootlessness that can have far-reaching consequences. What, in the years to come, will be the effect on the younger members of management, on their children — and on the organizations some will one day head — of a way of life so much more nomadic than that of their elders? The development of new values in the transients' suburban villages indicates that the effect will be profound. . . .

[1953]

Men and Machines

A discussion of men and machines logically accompanies a discussion of town and country; in many respects the two themes are one. Jefferson's fear of the city was a fear of what machines — which is to say the industrial-metropolitan way of life — must do to the hearts and minds of free men. His espousal of agrarianism derives from the same kind of commitment as that of the writers in the present section who, like Loren Eiseley, declare their belief in "life . . . not machines."

But just as the city has won, so has the machine. However much we may yearn for an agrarian idyll at some point in our nation's past ("Blessings on thee, barefoot boy!"), the fact remains that ours is irretrievably and increasingly a world of pavement and production lines. In the darkest view, we seem to be like the sorcerer's apprentice, irresponsibly creating mechanical monsters which serve us, alas, only too well. Among the telling symbols of our technological well-being are mammoth road-building machines which construct super-highways at an ever-increasing rate so that ever-more-numerous automobiles can ricochet across the nation, as Keats puts it, in a kind of fantastic parody of Brownian movement. Yet we are assured that this movement means prosperity and that for it to cease would be a national disaster. Instead of men owning the machines, in short, machines would seem to own the men. "Things," said Emerson in 1846, "are in the saddle and ride mankind." In the 1960's he might wish to change his metaphor but hardly his opinion.

Although there is doubtless much truth in the pessimistic view, it is not the whole truth, obviously. The machine has released man from the kind of drudgery which had been his lot through the ages. Furthermore, as Roger Burlingame argues, machines were probably indispensable to America's growth as a free nation. A democracy of men, he says, finds its essential expression in a "democracy of things."

Lewis Mumford shrewdly points to the invention of the clock — the time-machine — as the beginning of modern man, and certainly it is true that if the clock had never been invented, present-day life would be much different. But it has been invented, as have the production line, the automobile and the dynamo — and there is little we can do about it. Hundreds of years ago machines began changing the life of man; today, the hermitic life aside, man no longer has the option to choose or reject them. What he does have is the responsibility, and the opportunity, of learning to live with them and yet remain man.

A New Turn to Human Affairs

The Second Aerial Voyage by Man BENJAMIN FRANKLIN

Throughout a long life devoted to public affairs, Benjamin Franklin (1706–1790) maintained an equal or greater interest in science. His experiments with electricity are famous, and his practical inventions included the Franklin stove, bifocal spectacles, a new kind of clock, and the lightning rod. His curiosity was endless. Once, riding with friends, he saw a whirlwind. "The rest of the company stood looking after it," writes Franklin, "but my curiosity being stronger, I followed it." True to the spirit of the Enlightenment, he looked to the future with enthusiasm: "It is impossible to imagine the height to which may be carried in a thousand years, the power of man over matter. We may perhaps learn to deprive large masses of their gravity, and give them absolute levity, for the sake of easy transport. Agriculture may diminish its labour and double its produce. . . ." His only regret was that he had been born "too soon."

Franklin's letters here describing man's "aerial voyage" contains abundant evidence of his curiosity, practicality, and vision, not to mention his easy and unpretentious command of language. It is characteristic of Franklin that having observed "the philosophical experiment," he immediately turned his mind to the problems and possibilities involved in it. In this respect his attitude toward the new "machine" is modern. Less so is his freedom from trepidation as to what it might eventually mean in human affairs.

"... It appears ... to be a discovery of great importance, and what may possibly give a new turn to human affairs. . . ."

TO SIR JOSEPH BANKS

Passy, Dec. 1, 1783.

Dear Sir. — In mine of yesterday I promised to give you an account of Messrs. Charles & Robert's experiment, which was to have been made this day, and at which I intended to be present. Being a little indisposed, and the air cool, and the ground damp, I declined going into the garden of the Tuileries, where the balloon was placed, not knowing how long I might be obliged to wait there before it was ready to depart, and chose to stay in my carriage near the statue of Louis XV., from whence I could well see it rise, and have an extensive view of the region of air through which, as the wind sat, it was likely to pass. The morning was foggy, but about one o'clock the air became tolerably clear, to the great satisfaction of the spectators, who were infinite, notice having been given of the intended experiment several days before in the papers, so

398

that all Paris was out, either about the Tuileries, on the quays and bridges, in the fields, the streets, at the windows, or on the tops of houses, besides the inhabitants of all the towns and villages of the environs. Never before was a philosophical experiment so magnificently attended. Some guns were fired to give notice that the departure of the balloon was near, and a small one was discharged, which went to an amazing height, there being but little wind to make it deviate from its perpendicular course, and at length the sight of it was lost. Means were used, I am told, to prevent the great balloon's rising so high as might endanger its bursting. Several bags of sand were taken on board before the cord that held it down was cut, and the whole weight being then too much to be lifted, such a quantity was discharged as to permit its rising slowly. Thus it would sooner arrive at that region where it would be in equilibrio with the surrounding air, and by discharging more sand afterwards, it might go higher if desired. Between one and two o'clock, all eyes were gratified with seeing it rise majestically from among the trees, and ascend gradually above the buildings, a most beautiful spectacle. When it was about two hundred feet high, the brave adventurers held out and waved a little white pennant, on both sides of their car, to salute the spectators, who returned loud claps of applause. The wind was very little, so that the object though moving to the northward, continued long in view; and it was a great while before the admiring people began to disperse. The persons embarked were Mr. Charles, professor of experimental philosophy, and a zealous promoter of that science; and one of the Messieurs Robert, the very ingenious constructors of the machine. When it arrived at its height, which I suppose might be three or four hundred toises, it appeared to have only horizontal motion. I had a pocketglass, with which I followed it, till I lost sight first of the men, then of the car, and when I last saw the balloon, it appeared no bigger than a walnut. I write this at seven in the evening. What became of them is not yet known here. I hope they descended by daylight, so as to see and avoid falling among trees or on houses, and that the experiment was completed without any mischievous accident, which the novelty of it and the want of experience might well occasion. I am the more anxious for the event, because I am not well informed of the means provided for letting themselves down, and the loss of these very ingenious men would not only be a discouragement to the progress of the art, but be a sensible loss to science and society.

I shall inclose one of the tickets of admission, on which the globe was represented, as originally intended, but is altered by the pen to show its real state when it went off. When the tickets were engraved the car was to have been hung to the neck of the globe, as represented by a little drawing I have made in the corner.

I suppose it may have been an apprehension of danger in straining too much the balloon or tearing the silk, that induced the constructors to throw a net over it, fixed to a hoop which went round its middle, and to hang the car to that hoop.

Tuesday morning, December 2d. — I am relieved from my anxiety by hearing that the adventurers descended well near L'Isle Adam before sunset. This place is near seven leagues from Paris. Had the wind blown fresh they might have gone much farther.

If I receive any further particulars of importance, I shall communicate them hereafter.

With great esteem, I am, dear sir, your most obedient and most humble servant,

                                                                    B. Franklin.

P.S. *Tuesday evening.* — Since writing the above I have received the printed paper and the manuscript containing some particulars of the experiment, which I enclose. I hear further that the travellers had perfect command of their carriage, descending as they pleased by letting some of the inflammable air escape, and rising again by discharging some sand; that they descended over a field so low as to talk with the labourers in passing, and mounted again to pass a hill. The little balloon falling at Vincennes shows that mounting higher it met with a current of air in a contrary direction, an observation that may be of use to future aerial voyagers.

TO JAN INGENHOUSZ

Passy, Jan. 16, 1784.

Dear Friend, — I have this day received your favor of the 2d inst. Every information in my power, respecting the balloons, I sent you just before Christmas, contained in copies of my letters to Sir Joseph Banks. There is no secret in the affair, and I make no doubt that a person coming from you would easily obtain a sight of the different ballons of Montgolfier and Charles, with all the instructions wanted; and, if you undertake to make one, I think it extremely proper and necessary to send an ingenious man here for that purpose: otherwise, for want of attention to some particular circumstance, or of not being acquainted with it, the experiment might miscarry, which, in an affair of so much public expectation, would have bad consequences, draw upon you a great deal of censure, and affect your reputation. It is a serious thing to draw out from their affairs all the inhabitants of a great city and its environs, and a disappointment makes them angry. At Bordeaux lately a person who pretended to send up a balloon, and had received money from many people, not being able to make it rise, the populace were so exasperated that they pulled down his house, and had like to have killed him.

It appears, as you observe, to be a discovery of great importance, and what may possibly give a new turn to human affairs. Convincing sovereigns of the folly of wars may perhaps be one effect of it; since it will be impracticable for the most potent of them to guard his dominions. Five thousand balloons, capable of raising two men each, could not cost more than five ships of the line; and where is the prince who can afford so to cover his country with troops for its defence, as that ten thousand men descending from the clouds might not in many places do an infinite deal of mischief, before a force could be brought together to repel them? It is a pity that any national jealousy should, as you imagine it may, have prevented the English from prosecuting the experiment, since they are such ingenious mechanicians, that in their hands it might have made a more rapid progress towards perfection, and all the utility it is capable of affording.

The balloon of Messrs. Charles and Robert was really filled with inflammable air. The quantity being great, it was expensive, and tedious filling, requiring two or three days and nights constant labour. It had a *soupape,* [or valve,] near the top, which they could open by pulling a string and thereby let out some air when they had a mind to descend; and they discharged some of their ballast of sand when they would rise again. A great deal of air must have been let out when they landed, so that the loose part might envelope one of them: yet, the car being lightened by that one getting out of it, there was enough left to carry up the other rapidly. They had no fire with them. That is only used in M. Montgolfier's globe, which is open at bottom, and straw constantly burnt to keep it up. This kind is sooner and cheaper filled; but must be much bigger to carry up the same weight; since air rarified by heat is only twice as light as common air, and inflammable air is ten times lighter. M. de Morveau, a famous chemist at Dijon, has found an inflammable air that will cost only a 25th part of the price of what is made by oil of vitriol poured on iron filings. They say it is made from sea coal. Its comparative weight is not mentioned.

Yours most affectionately,

B. Franklin.

The March of the Machines

I Like to See It Lap the Miles   EMILY DICKINSON

Emily Dickinson (1830–1886) had personal occasion to salute the arrival
of the locomotive in the Amherst countryside, for her father was a sponsor
of the Amherst and Belcherton Railway. The poem that she wrote, however, suggests that her concern is disinterestedly poetic. For a biographical
note on Emily Dickinson, see p. 155.

Dickinson's poem animates the locomotive with startlingly appropriate
adjectives and verbs, building to the Boanerges figure in the last stanza.
With her mixture of strange and familiar imagery and language, and with
her distant viewpoint toward the subject, the poet suggests the peculiar
impact of the railroad on a sensitive nature. Conventionality of stanza
pattern contrasts with an unusual scheme of partial rhymes, fresh diction,
and bold use of sound patterns especially suited to the subject.

"... *In horrid, hooting stanza.* ..."

I like to see it lap the miles,
And lick the valleys up,
And stop to feed itself at tanks;
And then, prodigious, step

Around a pile of mountains,   5
And, supercilious, peer
In shanties by the sides of roads;
And then a quarry pare

To fit its sides, and crawl between,
Complaining all the while   10
In horrid, hooting stanza;
Then chase itself down hill

And neigh like Boanerges;
Then, punctual as a star,
Stop — docile and omnipotent —   15
At its own stable door.

                                        [1891]

To a Locomotive in Winter
WALT WHITMAN

Walt Whitman (1819–1892) first published this poem in 1876 and later incorporated it in the seventh edition of *Leaves of Grass* (1881–1882). For a biographical note on Whitman, see p. 61.

Viewing the locomotive close at hand, Whitman chants a free-verse catalog of admiring images (primarily visual) to suggest not only the power of the "fierce-throated beauty" but the "pulse of the continent" as well.

> "... *Type of the modern* ...
> *For once come serve the Muse. ...*"

Thee for my recitative,
Thee in the driving storm even as now, the snow, the winter-day declining,
Thee in thy panoply, thy measur'd dual throbbing and thy beat convulsive,
The black cylindric body, golden brass and silvery steel,
Thy ponderous side-bars, parallel and connecting rods, gyrating, shuttling
    at thy sides,   5
Thy metrical, now swelling pant and roar, now tapering in the distance,
Thy great protruding head-light fix'd in front,
Thy long, pale, floating vapor-pennants, tinged with delicate purple,
The dense and murky clouds out-belching from thy smokestack,
Thy knitted frame, thy springs and valves, the tremulous twinkle of thy
    wheels,   10
Thy train of cars, behind, obedient, merrily following,
Through gale or calm, now swift, now slack, yet steadily careering;
Type of the modern — emblem of motion and power — pulse of the con-
    tinent,
For once come serve the Muse and merge in verse, even as here I see thee,
With storm and buffeting gusts of wind and falling snow,   15
By day thy warning ringing bell to sound its notes,
By night thy silent signal lamps to swing.

Fierce-throated beauty!
Roll through my chant with all thy lawless music, thy swinging lamps at
    night,
Thy madly-whistled laughter, echoing, rumbling like an earthquake, rous-
    ing all,   20
Law of thyself complete, thine own track firmly holding,
(No sweetness debonair of tearful harp or glib piano thine,)
Thy trills of shrieks by rock and hills return'd,
Launch'd o'er the prairies wide, across the lakes,
To the free skies unpent and glad and strong.   25

[1876]

The Colossus   FRANK NORRIS

(Benjamin) Frank(lin) Norris (1870–1902), along with his contemporaries Theodore Dreiser (see p. 376), Stephen Crane (see p. 302), and Jack London (see p. 247), was an important early figure in American literary naturalism. His *McTeague*, begun in the early 1890's and published in 1899, is a landmark in the movement. When he died at thirty-two, Norris was at work on a monumental trilogy, an "Epic of the Wheat." *The Octopus* (1901) is a story of the growing and harvesting of the wheat; *The Pit* (1903) deals with speculation on the Chicago Board of Trade; *The Wolf* had been planned around the problem of Old-World famine.

In the following passage from the first chapter of *The Octopus*, Presley, a poet, becomes aware of the great fecundity of the California earth and of its possible perversion by the monopolistic Pacific and Southwestern Railroad. This theme, which is central to the book, is nowhere more vividly symbolized than here. Even in this short passage Norris's strengths and weaknesses as a writer are evident.

" . . . Presley saw again, in his imagination, the galloping monster, the terror of steel and steam. . . ."

As from a pinnacle, Presley, from where he now stood, dominated the entire country. The sun had begun to set, everything in the range of his vision was overlaid with a sheen of gold. . . . Beyond the fine line of the horizons, over the curve of the globe, the shoulder of the earth, were other ranches, equally vast, and beyond these, others, and beyond these, still others, the immensities multiplying, lengthening out vaster and vaster. The whole gigantic sweep of the San Joaquin expanded. Titanic, before the eye of the mind, flagellated with heat, quivering and shimmering under the sun's red eye. At long intervals, a faint breath of wind out of the south passed slowly over the levels of the baked and empty earth, accentuating the silence, marking off the stillness. It seemed to exhale from the land itself, a prolonged sigh as of deep fatigue. It was the season after the harvest, and the great earth, the mother, after its period of reproduction, its pains of labour, delivered of the fruit of its loins, slept the sleep of exhaustion, the infinite repose of the colossus, benignant, eternal, strong, the nourisher of nations, the feeder of an entire world.

Ha! there it was, his epic, his inspiration, his West, his thundering progression of hexameters. A sudden uplift, a sense of exhilaration, of physical exaltation appeared abruptly to sweep Presley from his feet. As from a point high above the world, he seemed to dominate a universe, a whole order of things. He was dizzied, stunned, stupefied, his morbid supersensitive mind reeling, drunk with the intoxication of mere immensity. Stupendous ideas for which there were no names drove headlong through his brain. Terrible, formless shapes, vague figures, gigantic, monstrous, distorted, whirled at a gallop through his imagination.

He started homeward, still in his dream, descending from the hill, emerging from the cañon, and took the short cut straight across the Quien Sabe ranch, leaving Guadalajara far to his left. He tramped steadily on through the wheat stubble, walking fast, his head in a whirl.

Never had he so nearly grasped his inspiration as at that moment on the hill-top. Even now, though the sunset was fading, though the wide reach of valley was shut from sight, it still kept him company. Now the details came thronging back — the component parts of his poem, the signs and symbols of the West. . . . the sunsets behind the altar-like mesas, the baking desolation of the deserts; the strenuous, fierce life of forgotten towns, down there, far off, lost below the horizons of the southwest; the sonorous music of unfamiliar names — Quijotoa, Uintah, Sonora, Laredo, Uncompaghre. It was in the Mission, with its cracked bells, its decaying walls, its venerable sun dial, its fountain and old garden, and in the Mission Fathers themselves, the priests, the padres, planting the first wheat and oil and wine to produce the elements of the Sacrament — a trinity of great industries, taking their rise in a religious rite.

Abruptly, as if in confirmation, Presley heard the sound of a bell from the direction of the Mission itself. It was the *de Profundis,* a note of the Old World; of the ancient régime, an echo from the hillsides of mediæval Europe, sounding there in this new land, unfamiliar and strange at this end-of-the-century time.

By now, however, it was dark. Presley hurried forward. He came to the line fence of the Quien Sabe ranch. Everything was very still. The stars were all out. There was not a sound other than the *de Profundis,* still sounding from very far away. At long intervals the great earth sighed dreamily in its sleep. All about, the feeling of absolute peace and quiet and security and untroubled happiness and content seemed descending from the stars like a benediction. The beauty of his poem, its idyl, came to him like a caress; that alone had been lacking. It was that, perhaps, which had left it hitherto incomplete. At last he was to grasp his song in all its entity.

But suddenly there was an interruption. Presley had climbed the fence at the limit of the Quien Sabe ranch. Beyond was Los Muertos, but between the two ran the railroad. He had only time to jump back upon the embankment when, with a quivering of all the earth, a locomotive, single, unattached, shot by him with a roar, filling the air with the reek of hot oil, vomiting smoke and sparks; its enormous eye, Cyclopean, red, throwing a glare far in advance, shooting by in a sudden crash of confused thunder; filling the night with the terrific clamour of its iron hoofs.

Abruptly Presley remembered. This must be the crack passenger engine of which Dyke had told him, the one delayed by the accident on the Bakersfield division and for whose passage the track had been opened all the way to Fresno.

Before Presley could recover from the shock of the irruption, while the earth was still vibrating, the rails still humming, the engine was far away, flinging the echo of its frantic gallop over all the valley. For a brief instant it roared with a hollow diapason on the Long Trestle over Broderson Creek, then plunged into a cutting farther on, the quivering glare of its fires losing itself in the night, its thunder abruptly diminishing to a subdued and distant humming. All at once this ceased. The engine was gone.

But the moment the noise of the engine lapsed, Presley — about to start forward again — was conscious of a confusion of lamentable sounds that rose into the night from out the engine's wake. Prolonged cries of agony, sobbing wails of infinite pain, heart-rending, pitiful.

The noises came from a little distance. He ran down the track, crossing the culvert, over the irrigating ditch, and at the head of the long reach of track — between the culvert and the Long Trestle — paused abruptly, held immovable at the sight of the ground and rails all about him.

In some way, the herd of sheep — Vanamee's herd — had found a breach in the wire fence by the right of way and had wandered out upon the tracks. A band had been crossing just at the moment of the engine's passage. The pathos of it was beyond expression. It was a slaughter, a massacre of innocents. The iron monster had charged full into the midst, merciless, inexorable. To the right and left, all the width of the right of way, the little bodies had been flung; backs were snapped against the fence posts; brains knocked out. Caught in the barbs of the wire, wedged in, the bodies hung suspended. Under foot it was terrible. The black blood, winking in the starlight, seeped down into the clinkers between the ties with a prolonged sucking murmur.

Presley turned away, horror-struck, sick at heart, overwhelmed with a quick burst of irresistible compassion for this brute agony he could not relieve. The sweetness was gone from the evening, the sense of peace, of security, and placid contentment was stricken from the landscape. The hideous ruin in the engine's path drove all thought of his poem from his mind. The inspiration vanished like a mist. The *de Profundis* had ceased to ring.

He hurried on across the Los Muertos ranch, almost running, even putting his hands over his ears till he was out of hearing distance of that all but human distress. Not until he was beyond earshot did he pause, looking back, listening. The night had shut down again. For a moment the silence was profound, unbroken.

Then, faint and prolonged, across the levels of the ranch, he heard the engine whistling for Bonneville. Again and again, at rapid intervals in its flying course, it whistled for road crossings, for sharp curves, for trestles; ominous notes, hoarse, bellowing, ringing with the accents of menace and defiance; and abruptly Presley saw again, in his imagination, the galloping monster, the terror of steel and steam, with its single eye, Cyclopean, red, shooting from horizon to horizon; but saw it now as the symbol of a vast power, huge, terrible, flinging the echo of its thunder over all the reaches of the valley, leaving blood and destruction in its path; the leviathan, with tentacles of steel clutching into the soil, the soulless Force, the iron-hearted Power, the monster, the Colossus, the Octopus.

[1901]

The Dynamo and the Virgin   HENRY ADAMS

Toward the end of his life, Henry Adams (1838–1918) undertook to
assess what he had learned in his careers as writer, historian, teacher,
traveler, amateur philosopher-scientist. The result was a classic of American cultural and intellectual history, *The Education of Henry Adams*
(1907). Looking back to the time of his birth, Adams wrote that "Probably no child, born in the year, held better cards than he." Grandson and
great-grandson of American Presidents, Adams had both a superior mind
and whatever social and cultural advantages America could offer. Yet the
Education describes a failure, not so much in terms of Adams personally
as of Adams representing the forces of his time. "The historian's business
is to follow the track of the energy"; he wrote, "to find where it comes
from and where it went. . . ." That is his concern in this chapter — central
in the book — titled "The Dynamo and the Virgin."

Adams here gives his reactions to the Paris Exposition of 1900, where
the scientist Langley instructed him in "the forces" of a new age. He
comes to see the Virgin as a force and symbol of thirteenth-century unity
and the dynamo as a force and symbol of twentieth-century multiplicity.
As these concepts suggest, Adams is no easy writer; tracing his many
allusions constitutes an education in itself. Still, the progression of his
thought in this chapter is clear enough, as he tries to organize the past
and present through these symbols.

*". . . he began to feel the forty-foot dynamo as a moral force,
much as the early Christians felt the Cross. . . ."*

Until the Great Exposition of 1900 closed its doors in November, Adams
haunted it, aching to absorb knowledge, and helpless to find it. He would have
liked to know how much of it could have been grasped by the best-informed
man in the world. While he was thus meditating chaos, Langley came by,
and showed it to him. At Langley's behest, the Exhibition dropped its super-
fluous rags and stripped itself to the skin, for Langley knew what to study,
and why, and how; while Adams might as well have stood outside in the night,
staring at the Milky Way. Yet Langley said nothing new, and taught nothing
that one might not have learned from Lord Bacon, three hundred years before;
but though one should have known the "Advancement of Science" as well as
one knew the "Comedy of Errors," the literary knowledge counted for nothing
until some teacher should show how to apply it. Bacon took a vast deal of
trouble in teaching King James I and his subjects, American or other, towards
the year 1620, that true science was the development or economy of forces;
yet an elderly American in 1900 knew neither the formula nor the forces; or
even so much as to say to himself that his historical business in the Exposition
concerned only the economies or developments of force since 1893, when he
began the study at Chicago.

Nothing in education is so astonishing as the amount of ignorance it accumulates in the form of inert facts. Adams had looked at most of the accumulations of art in the storehouses called Art Museums; yet he did not know how to look at the art exhibits of 1900. He had studied Karl Marx and his doctrines of history with profound attention, yet he could not apply them at Paris. Langley, with the ease of a great master of experiment, threw out of the field every exhibit that did not reveal a new application of force, and naturally threw out, to begin with, almost the whole art exhibit. Equally, he ignored almost the whole industrial exhibit. He led his pupil directly to the forces. His chief interest was in new motors to make his airship feasible, and he taught Adams the astonishing complexities of the new Daimler motor, and of the automobile, which, since 1893, had become a nightmare at a hundred kilometres an hour, almost as destructive as the electric tram which was only ten years older; and threatening to become as terrible as the locomotive steam-engine itself, which was almost exactly Adams's own age.

Then he showed his scholar the great hall of dynamos, and explained how little he knew about electricity or force of any kind, even of his own special sun, which spouted heat in inconceivable volume, but which, as far as he knew, might spout less or more, at any time, for all the certainty he felt in it. To him, the dynamo itself was but an ingenious channel for conveying somewhere the heat latent in a few tons of poor coal hidden in a dirty engine-house carefully kept out of sight; but to Adams the dynamo became a symbol of infinity. As he grew accustomed to the great gallery of machines, he began to feel the forty-foot dynamos as a moral force, much as the early Christians felt the Cross. The planet itself seemed less impressive, in its old-fashioned, deliberate, annual or daily revolution, than this huge wheel, revolving within arm's-length at some vertiginous speed, and barely murmuring—scarcely humming an audible warning to stand a hair's-breadth further for respect of power —while it would not wake the baby lying close against its frame. Before the end, one began to pray to it; inherited instinct taught the natural expression of man before silent and infinite force. Among the thousand symbols of ultimate energy, the dynamo was not so human as some, but it was the most expressive.

Yet the dynamo, next to the steam-engine, was the most familiar of exhibits. For Adams's objects its value lay chiefly in its occult mechanism. Between the dynamo in the gallery of machines and the engine-house outside, the break of continuity amounted to abysmal fracture for a historian's objects. No more relation could he discover between the steam and the electric current than between the Cross and the cathedral. The forces were interchangeable if not reversible, but he could see only an absolute *fiat* in electricity as in faith. Langley could not help him. Indeed, Langley seemed to be worried by the same trouble, for he constantly repeated that the new forces were anarchical, and specially that he was not responsible for the new rays, that were little short of parricidal in their wicked spirit towards science. His own rays, with which he had doubled the solar spectrum, were altogether harmless and beneficent; but Radium denied its God—or, what was to Langley the same thing, denied the truths of his Science. The force was wholly new.

A historian who asked only to learn enough to be as futile as Langley or

Kelvin, made rapid progress under this teaching, and mixed himself up in
the tangle of ideas until he achieved a sort of Paradise of ignorance vastly
consoling to his fatigued senses. He wrapped himself in vibrations and rays
which were new, and he would have hugged Marconi and Branly had he met
them, as he hugged the dynamo; while he lost his arithmetic in trying to
figure out the equation between the discoveries and the economies of force.
The economies, like the discoveries, were absolute, supersensual, occult; incapable of expression in horse-power. What mathematical equivalent could
he suggest as the value of a Branly coherer? Frozen air, or the electric furnace,
had some scale of measurement, no doubt, if somebody could invent a ther-
mometer adequate to the purpose; but X-rays had played no part whatever in
man's consciousness, and the atom itself had figured only as a fiction of
thought. In these seven years man had translated himself into a new universe
which had no common scale of measurement with the old. He had entered a
supersensual world, in which he could measure nothing except by chance
collisions of movements imperceptible to his senses, perhaps even imperceptible to his instruments, but perceptible to each other, and so to some known
ray at the end of the scale. Langley seemed prepared for anything, even for
an indeterminable number of universes interfused — physics stark mad in
metaphysics.

Historians undertake to arrange sequences, — called stories, or histories —
assuming in silence a relation of cause and effect. These assumptions, hidden
in the depths of dusty libraries, have been astounding, but commonly unconscious and childlike; so much so, that if any captious critic were to drag them
to light, historians would probably reply, with one voice, that they had never
supposed themselves required to know what they were talking about. Adams,
for one, had toiled in vain to find out what he meant. He had even published
a dozen volumes of American history for no other purpose than to satisfy
himself whether, by the severest process of stating, with the least possible
comment, such facts as seemed sure, in such order as seemed rigorously con-
sequent, he could fix for a familiar moment a necessary sequence of human
movement. The result had satisfied him as little as at Harvard College.
Where he saw sequence, other men saw something quite different, and no
one saw the same unit of measure. He cared little about his experiments and
less about his statesmen, who seemed to him quite as ignorant as himself and,
as a rule, no more honest; but he insisted on a relation of sequence, and if he
could not reach it by one method, he would try as many methods as science
knew. Satisfied that the sequence of men led to nothing and that the sequence
of their society could lead no further, while the mere sequence of time was
artificial, and the sequence of thought was chaos, he turned at last to the
sequence of force; and thus it happened that, after ten years' pursuit, he found
himself lying in the Gallery of Machines at the Great Exposition of 1900, his
historical neck broken by the sudden irruption of forces totally new.

Since no one else showed much concern, an elderly person without other
cares had no need to betray alarm. The year 1900 was not the first to upset
schoolmasters. Copernicus and Galileo had broken many professorial necks
about 1600; Columbus had stood the world on its head towards 1500; but the
nearest approach to the revolution of 1900 was that of 310, when Constantine

set up the Cross. The rays that Langley disowned, as well as those which he fathered, were occult, supersensual, irrational; they were what, in terms of medieval science, were called immediate modes of the divine substance.

The historian was thus reduced to his last resources. Clearly if he was bound to reduce all these forces to a common value, this common value could have no measure but that of their attraction on his own mind. He must treat them as they had been felt; as convertible, reversible, interchangeable attractions on thought. He made up his mind to venture it; he would risk translating rays into faith. Such a reversible process would vastly amuse a chemist, but the chemist could not deny that he, or some of his fellow physicists, could feel the force of both. When Adams was a boy in Boston, the best chemist in the place had probably never heard of Venus except by way of scandal, or of the Virgin except as idolatry; neither had he heard of dynamos or automobiles or radium; yet his mind was ready to feel the force of all, though the rays were unborn and the women were dead.

Here opened another totally new education, which promised to be by far the most hazardous of all. The knife-edge along which he must crawl, like Sir Lancelot in the twelfth century, divided two kingdoms of force which had nothing in common but attraction. They were as different as a magnet is from gravitation, supposing one knew what a magnet was, or gravitation, or love. The force of the Virgin was still felt at Lourdes, and seemed to be as potent as X-rays but in America neither Venus nor Virgin ever had value as a force — at most as sentiment. No American had ever truly been afraid of either.

This problem in dynamics gravely perplexed an American historian. The Woman had once been supreme; in France she still seemed potent, not merely as a sentiment, but as a force. Why was she unknown in America? For evidently America was ashamed of her, and she was ashamed of herself, otherwise they would not have strewn fig-leaves so profusely all over her. When she was a true force, she was ignorant of fig-leaves, but the monthly-magazine-made American female had not a feature that would have been recognized by Adam. The trait was notorious, and often humorous, but any one brought up among Puritans knew that sex was a sin. In any previous age, sex was strength. Neither art nor beauty was needed. Every one, even among Puritans, knew that neither Diana of the Ephesians nor any of the Oriental goddesses was worshipped for her beauty. She was goddess because of her force; she was the animated dynamo; she was reproduction — the greatest and most mysterious of all energies; all she needed was to be fecund. Singularly enough, not one of Adams's many schools of education had ever drawn his attention to the opening lines of Lucretius, though they were perhaps the finest in all Latin literature, where the poet invoked Venus exactly as Dante invoked the Virgin: —

"Quae quoniam rerum naturam *sola* gubernas."[1]

The Venus of Epicurean philosophy survived in the Virgin of the Schools: —

---

[1] "Since thou art, then, sole mistress of the nature of things."

"Donna, sei tanto grande, e tanto vali,
Che qual vuol grazia, e a te non ricorre,
Sua disianza vuol volar senz' ali."[2]

All this was to American thought as though it had never existed. The true American knew something of the facts, but nothing of the feelings; he read the letter, but he never felt the law. Before this historical chasm, a mind like that of Adams felt itself helpless; he turned from the Virgin to the Dynamo as though he were a Branly coherer. On one side, at the Louvre and at Chartres, as he knew by the record of work actually done and still before his eyes, was the highest energy ever known to man, the creator of four-fifths of his noblest art, exercising vastly more attraction over the human mind than all the steam-engines and dynamos ever dreamed of; and yet this energy was unknown to the American mind. An American Virgin would never dare command; an American Venus would never dare exist.

The question, which to any plain American of the nineteenth century seemed as remote as it did to Adams, drew him almost violently to study, once it was posed; and on this point Langleys were as useless as though they were Herbert Spencers or dynamos. The idea survived only as art. There one turned as naturally as though the artist were himself a woman. Adams began to ponder, asking himself whether he knew of any American artist who had ever insisted on the power of sex, as every classic had always done; but he could think only of Walt Whitman; Bret Harte, as far as the magazines would let him venture; and one or two painters, for the flesh-tones. All the rest had used sex for sentiment, never for force; to them, Eve was a tender flower, and Herodias an unfeminine horror. American art, like the American language and American education, was as far as possible sexless. Society regarded this victory over sex as its greatest triumph, and the historian readily admitted it, since the moral issue, for the moment, did not concern one who was studying the relations of unmoral force. He cared nothing for the sex of the dynamo until he could measure its energy.

Vaguely seeking a clue, he wandered through the art exhibit, and, in his stroll, stopped almost every day before St. Gaudens's General Sherman, which had been given the central post of honor. St. Gaudens himself was in Paris, putting on the work his usual interminable last touches, and listening to the usual contradictory suggestions of brother sculptors. Of all the American artists who gave to American art whatever life it breathed in the seventies, St. Gaudens was perhaps the most sympathetic, but certainly the most inarticulate. General Grant or Don Cameron had scarcely less instinct of rhetoric than he. All the others — the Hunts, Richardson, John La Farge, Stanford White — were exuberant; only St. Gaudens could never discuss or dilate on an emotion, or suggest artistic arguments for giving to his work the forms that he felt. He never laid down the law, or affected the despot, or became brutalized like Whistler by the brutalities of his world. He required no incense; he was no egoist; his simplicity of thought was excessive; he could not imitate, or give

[2] Lady, thou are so great, and so prevailing,
That he who wishes grace, nor runs to thee,
His aspirations without wings would fly.

any form but his own to the creations of his hand. No one felt more strongly than he the strength of other men, but the idea that they could affect him never stirred an image in his mind.

This summer his health was poor and his spirits were low. For such a temper, Adams was not the best companion, since his own gaiety was not *folle;* but he risked going now and then to the studio on Mont Parnasse to draw him out for a stroll in the Bois de Boulogne, or dinner as pleased his moods, and in return St. Gaudens sometimes let Adams go about in his company.

Once St. Gaudens took him down to Amiens, with a party of Frenchmen, to see the cathedral. Not until they found themselves actually studying the sculpture of the western portal, did it dawn on Adams's mind that, for his purposes, St. Gaudens on that spot had more interest to him than the cathedral itself. Great men before great monuments express great truths, provided they are not taken too solemnly. Adams never tired of quoting the supreme phrase of his idol Gibbon, before the Gothic cathedrals: "I darted a contemptuous look on the stately monuments of superstition." Even in the footnotes of his history, Gibbon had never inserted a bit of humor more human than this, and one would have paid largely for a photograph of the fat little historian, on the background of Notre Dame of Amiens, trying to persuade his readers — perhaps himself — that he was darting a contemptuous look on the stately monument, for which he felt in fact the respect which every man of his vast study and active mind always feels before objects worthy of it; but besides the humor, one felt also the relation. Gibbon ignored the Virgin, because in 1789 religious monuments were out of fashion. In 1900 his remark sounded fresh and simple as the green fields to ears that had heard a hundred years of other remarks, mostly no more fresh and certainly less simple. Without malice, one might find it more instructive than a whole lecture of Ruskin. One sees what one brings, and at that moment Gibbon brought the French Revolution. Ruskin brought reaction against the Revolution. St. Gaudens had passed beyond all. He liked the stately monuments much more than he liked Gibbon or Ruskin; he loved their dignity; their unity; their scale; their lines; their lights and shadows; their decorative sculpture; but he was even less conscious than they of the force that created it all — the Virgin, the Woman — by whose genius "the stately monuments of superstition" were built, through which she was expressed. He would have seen more meaning in Isis with the cow's horns, at Edfoo, who expressed the same thought. The art remained, but the energy was lost even upon the artist.

Yet in mind and person St. Gaudens was a survival of the 1500; he bore the stamp of the Renaissance, and should have carried an image of the Virgin round his neck, or stuck in his hat, like Louis XI. In mere time he was a lost soul that had strayed by chance into the twentieth century, and forgotten where it came from. He writhed and cursed at his ignorance, much as Adams did at his own, but in the opposite sense. St. Gaudens was a child of Benvenuto Cellini, smothered in an American cradle. Adams was a quintessence of Boston, devoured by curiosity to think like Benvenuto. St. Gaudens's art was starved from birth, and Adams's instinct was blighted from babyhood. Each had but half of a nature, and when they came together before the Virgin of Amiens they ought both to have felt in her the force that made them one;

but it was not so. To Adams she became more than ever a channel of force; to St. Gaudens she remained as before a channel of taste.

For a symbol of power, St. Gaudens instinctively preferred the horse, as was plain in his horse and Victory of the Sherman monument. Doubtless Sherman also felt it so. The attitude was so American that, for at least forty years, Adams had never realized that any other could be in sound taste. How many years had he taken to admit a notion of what Michael Angelo and Rubens were driving at? He could not say; but he knew that only since 1895 had he begun to feel the Virgin or Venus as force, and not everywhere even so. At Chartres — perhaps at Lourdes — possibly at Cnidos if one could still find there the divinely naked Aphrodite of Praxiteles — but otherwise one must look for force to the goddesses of Indian mythology. The idea died out long ago in the German and English stock. St. Gaudens at Amiens was hardly less sensitive to the force of the female energy than Matthew Arnold at the Grande Chartreuse. Neither of them felt goddesses as power — only as reflected emotion, human expression, beauty, purity, taste, scarcely even as sympathy. They felt a railway train as power; yet they, and all other artists, constantly complained that the power embodied in a railway train could never be embodied in art. All the steam in the world could not, like the Virgin, build Chartres.

Yet in mechanics, whatever the mechanicians might think, both energies acted as interchangeable forces on man, and by action on man all known force may be measured. Indeed, few men of science measured force in any other way. After once admitting that a straight line was the shortest distance between two points, no serious mathematician cared to deny anything that suited his convenience, and rejected no symbol, unproved or unproveable, that helped him to accomplish work. The symbol was force, as a compass-needle or a triangle was force, as the mechanist might prove by losing it, and nothing could be gained by ignoring their value. Symbol or energy, the Virgin had acted as the greatest force the Western world ever felt, and had drawn man's activities to herself more strongly than any other power, natural or supernatural, had ever done; the historian's business was to follow the track of the energy; to find where it came from and where it went to; its complex source and shifting channels; its values, equivalents, conversions. It could scarcely be more complex than radium; it could hardly be deflected, diverted, polarized, absorbed more perplexingly than other radiant matter. Adams knew nothing about any of them, but as a mathematical problem of influence on human progress, though all were occult, all reacted on his mind, and he rather inclined to think the Virgin easiest to handle.

The pursuit turned out to be long and tortuous, leading at last into the vast forests of scholastic science. From Zeno to Descartes, hand in hand with Thomas Aquinas, Montaigne, and Pascal, one stumbled as stupidly as though one were still a German student of 1860. Only with the instinct of despair could one force one's self into this old thicket of ignorance after having been repulsed at a score of entrances more promising and more popular. Thus far, no path had led anywhere, unless perhaps to an exceedingly modest living. Forty-five years of study had proved to be quite futile for the pursuit of power; one controlled no more force in 1900 than in 1850, although the amount of force controlled by society had enormously increased. The secret of education still hid itself somewhere behind ignorance, and one fumbled over it as feebly as ever. In such labyrinths, the staff is a force almost more necessary than the legs; the pen becomes a sort of blind-man's dog, to keep him from falling into the gutters. The pen works for itself, and acts like a hand, modelling the plastic material over and over again to the form that suits it best. The form is never arbitrary, but is a sort of growth like crystallization, as any artist knows too well; for often the pencil or pen runs into side-paths and shapelessness, loses its relations, stops or is bogged. Then it has to return on its trail, and recover, if it can, its line of force. The result of a year's work depends more on what is struck out than on what is left in; on the sequence of the main lines of thought, than on their play or variety. Compelled once more to lean heavily on this support, Adams covered more thousands of pages with figures as formal as though they were algebra, laboriously striking out, altering, burning, experimenting, until the year had expired, the Exposition had long been closed, and winter drawing to its end before he sailed from Cherbourg, on January 19, 1901 for home.

[1907]

Life in the Machine Age

The Tractors   JOHN STEINBECK

When *The Grapes of Wrath* by John Steinbeck (1902–   ) was published in 1939, it was immediately hailed as one of the most significant books of the decade, and was awarded the Pulitzer Prize for 1940. The title echoes a phrase from "The Battle-Hymn of the Republic" (see p. 298); and like the poem, the novel is a call to battle. Steinbeck's wrath over social injustice, his appreciation of the worth of the dispossessed individuals comprising the great mass of the "unsuccessful" is one of the principal qualities of this work: it has been called the "Uncle Tom's Cabin" of the twentieth century. On the narrative level, the book tells us the story of the Joads — "Oakies" driven from their dust bowl farms by drouth, by the depression and by machines — who migrate to the promised land of California. For another note on Steinbeck, see p. 83.

The following passages are chapters five and eleven, typical of the essays interspersed among the narrative sections of the book to illuminate and extend the experience of the Joads. They are saved from being merely sociological commentary by the strongly personal note in the first passage, in which the issue is dramatized rather than described, and by poetic language in the second, the rhythms of which are frequently Biblical. In both passages the sense of conflict, the carefully evoked atmosphere, the characterizations — stereotypic though they are — and the strong thematic note produce a short-story quality. Here, as elsewhere, Steinbeck's writing is a mixture of realism and romanticism.

"... The man sitting in the iron seat did not look like a man; ...
he was part of the monster, a robot. ..."

The owners of the land came onto the land, or more often a spokesman for the owners came. They came in closed cars, and they felt the dry earth with their fingers, and sometimes they drove big earth augers into the ground for soil tests. The tenants, from their sun-beaten dooryards, watched uneasily when the closed cars drove along the fields. And at last the owner men drove into the dooryards and sat in their cars to talk out of the windows. The tenant men stood beside the cars for a while, and then squatted on their hams and found sticks with which to mark the dust.

In the open doors the women stood looking out, and behind them the children — corn-headed children, with wide eyes, one bare foot on top of the other bare foot, and the toes working. The women and the children watched their men talking to the owner men. They were silent.

Some of the owner men were kind because they hated what they had to do, and some of them were angry because they hated to be cruel, and some of them were cold because they had long ago found that one could not be an owner unless one were cold. And all of them were caught in something larger than themselves. Some of them hated the mathematics that drove them, and some were afraid, and some worshiped the mathematics because it provided a refuge from thought and from feeling. If a bank or a finance company owned the land, the owner man said, The Bank — or the Company — needs — wants — insists — must have — as though the Bank or the Company were a monster, with thought and feeling, which had ensnared them. These last would take no responsibility for the banks or the companies because they were men and slaves, while the banks were machines and masters all at the same time. Some of the owner men were a little proud to be slaves to such cold and powerful masters. The owner men sat in the cars and explained. You know the land is poor. You've scrabbled at it long enough, God knows.

The squatting tenant men nodded and wondered and drew figures in the dust, and yes, they knew, God knows. If the dust only wouldn't fly. If the top would only stay on the soil, it might not be so bad.

The owner men went on leading to their point: You know the land's getting poorer. You know what cotton does to the land; robs it, sucks all the blood out of it.

The squatters nodded — they knew, God knew. If they could only rotate the crops they might pump blood back into the land.

Well, it's too late. And the owner men explained the workings and the thinkings of the monster that was stronger than they were. A man can hold land if he can just eat and pay taxes; he can do that.

Yes, he can do that until his crops fail one day and he has to borrow money from the bank.

But — you see, a bank or a company can't do that, because those creatures don't breathe air, don't eat side-meat. They breathe profits; they eat the interest on money. If they don't get it, they die the way you die without air, without side-meat. It is a sad thing, but it is so. It is just so.

The squatting men raised their eyes to understand. Can't we just hang on? Maybe the next year will be a good year. God knows how much cotton next year. And with all the wars — God knows what price cotton will bring. Don't they make explosives out of cotton? And uniforms? Get enough wars and cotton'll hit the ceiling. Next year, maybe. They looked up questioningly.

We can't depend on it. The Bank — the monster has to have profits all the time. It can't wait. It'll die. No, taxes go on. When the monster stops growing, it dies. It can't stay one size.

Soft fingers began to tap the sill of the car window, and hard fingers tightened on the restless drawing sticks. In the doorways of the sun-beaten tenant houses, women sighed and then shifted feet so that the one that had been down was now on top, and the toes working. Dogs came sniffing near the owner cars and wetted on all four tires one after another. And chickens

lay in the sunny dust and fluffed their feathers to get the cleansing dust down
to the skin. In the little sties the pigs grunted inquiringly over the muddy
remnants of the slops.

The squatting men looked down again. What do you want us to do? We
can't take less share of the crop — we're half starved now. The kids are hungry
all the time. We got no clothes, torn an' ragged. If all the neighbors weren't
the same, we'd be ashamed to go to meeting.

And at last the owner men came to the point. The tenant system won't
work any more. One man on a tractor can take the place of twelve or fourteen
families. Pay him a wage and take all the crop. We have to do it. We don't
like to do it. But the monster's sick. Something's happened to the monster.

But you'll kill the land with cotton.

We know. We've got to take cotton quick before the land dies. Then
we'll sell the land. Lots of families in the East would like to own a piece of
land.

The tenant men looked up alarmed. But what'll happen to us? How'll
we eat?

You'll have to get off the land. The plows'll go through the dooryard.

And now the squatting men stood up angrily. Grampa took up the land,
and he had to kill the Indians and drive them away. And Pa was born here,
and he killed weeds and snakes. Then a bad year came and he had to borrow
a little money. An' we was born here. There in the door — our children born
here. And Pa had to borrow money. The bank owned the land then, but we
stayed and we got a little bit of what we raised.

We know that — all that. It's not us, it's the bank. A bank isn't like a man.
Or an owner with fifty thousand acres, he isn't like a man either. That's the
monster.

Sure, cried the tenant men, but it's our land. We measured it and broke
it up. We were born on it, and we got killed on it, died on it. Even if it's
no good, it's still ours. That's what makes it ours — being born on it, working
it, dying on it. That makes ownership, not a paper with numbers on it.

We're sorry. It's not us. It's the monster. The bank isn't like a man.

Yes, but the bank is only made of men.

No, you're wrong there — quite wrong there. The bank is something
else than men. It happens that every man in a bank hates what the bank
does, and yet the bank does it. The bank is something more than men, I tell
you. It's the monster. Men made it, but they can't control it.

The tenants cried. Grampa killed Indians, Pa killed snakes for the land.
Maybe we can kill banks — they're worse than Indians and snakes. Maybe
we got to fight to keep our land, like Pa and Grampa did.

And now the owner men grew angry. You'll have to go.

But it's ours, the tenant men cried. We——

No. The bank, the monster owns it. You'll have to go.

We'll get our guns, like Grampa when the Indians came. What then?

Well — first the sheriff, and then the troops. You'll be stealing if you try
to stay, you'll be murderers if you kill to stay. The monster isn't men, but it
can make men do what it wants.

But if we go, where'll we go? How'll we go. We got no money.

We're sorry, said the owner men. The bank, the fifty-thousand-acre owner can't be responsible. You're on land that isn't yours. Once over the line maybe you can pick cotton in the fall. Maybe you can go on relief. Why don't you go on west to California? There's work there, and it never gets cold. Why, you can reach out anywhere and pick an orange. Why, there's always some kind of crop to work in. Why don't you go there? And the owner men started their cars and rolled away.

The tenant men squatted down on their hams again to mark the dust with a stick, to figure, to wonder. Their sunburned faces were dark, and their sun-whipped eyes were light. The women moved cautiously out of the door-ways toward their men, and the children crept behind the women, cautiously, ready to run. The bigger boys squatted beside their fathers, because that made them men. After a time the women asked, What did he want?

And the men looked up for a second, and the smolder of pain was in their eyes. We got to get off. A tractor and a superintendent. Like factories.

Where'll we go? the women asked.

We don't know. We don't know.

And the women went quickly, quietly back into the houses and herded the children ahead of them. They knew that a man so hurt and so perplexed may turn in anger, even on people he loves. They left the men alone to figure and to wonder in the dust.

After a time perhaps the tenant man looked about — at the pump put in ten years ago, with a goose-neck handle and iron flowers on the spout, at the chopping block where a thousand chickens had been killed, at the hand plow lying in the shed, and the patent crib hanging in the rafters over it.

The children crowded about the women in the houses. What we going to do, Ma? Where we going to go?

The women said, We don't know, yet. Go out and play. But don't go near your father. He might whale you if you go near him. And the women went on with the work, but all the time they watched the men squatting in the dust — perplexed and figuring.

The tractors came over the roads and into the fields, great crawlers moving like insects, having the incredible strength of insects. They crawled over the ground, laying the track and rolling on it and picking it up. Diesel tractors, puttering while they stood idle; they thundered when they moved, and then settled down to a droning roar. Snubnosed monsters, raising the dust and sticking their snouts into it, straight down the country, across the country, through fences, through dooryards, in and out of gullies in straight lines. They did not run on the ground, but on their own roadbeds. They ignored hills and gulches, water courses, fences, houses.

The man sitting in the iron seat did not look like a man; gloved, goggled, rubber dust mask over nose and mouth, he was a part of the monster, a robot in the seat. The thunder of the cylinders sounded through the country, be-came one with the air and the earth, so that earth and air muttered in sym-pathetic vibration. The driver could not control it — straight across country it went, cutting through a dozen farms and straight back. A twitch at the controls could swerve the cat', but the driver's hands could not twitch because the monster that built the tractors, the monster that sent the tractor out, had somehow got into the driver's hands, into his brain and muscle, had goggled him and muzzled him — goggled his mind, muzzled his speech, goggled his perception, muzzled his protest. He could not see the land as it was, he could not smell the land as it smelled; his feet did not stamp the clods or feel the warmth and power of the earth. He sat in an iron seat and stepped on iron pedals. He could not cheer or beat or curse or encourage the extension of his power, and because of this he could not cheer or whip or curse or encourage himself. He did not know or own or trust or beseech the land. If a seed dropped did not germinate, it was nothing. If the young thrusting plant withered in drought or drowned in a flood of rain, it was no more to the driver than to the tractor.

He loved the land no more than the bank loved the land. He could admire the tractor — its machined surfaces, its surge of power, the roar of its detonating cylinders; but it was not his tractor. Behind the tractor rolled the shining disks, cutting the earth with blades — not plowing but surgery, pushing the cut earth to the right where the second row of disks cut it and pushed it to the left; slicing blades shining, polished by the cut earth. And pulled behind the disks, the harrows combing with iron teeth so that the little clods broke up and the earth lay smooth. Behind the harrows, the long seeders — twelve curved iron penes erected in the foundry, orgasms set by gears, raping methodically, raping without passion. The driver sat in his iron seat and he was proud of the straight lines he did not will, proud of the tractor he did not own or love, proud of the power he could not control. And when that crop grew, and was harvested, no man had crumbled a hot clod in his fingers and let the earth sift past his fingertips. No man had touched the seed, or lusted for the growth. Men ate what they had not raised, had no connection with the bread. The land bore under iron, and under iron gradually died; for it was not loved or hated, it had no prayers or curses.

At noon the tractor driver stopped sometimes near a tenant house and opened his lunch: sandwiches wrapped in waxed paper, white bread, pickle, cheese, Spam, a piece of pie branded like an engine part. He ate without relish. And tenants not yet moved away came out to see him, looked curiously while the goggles were taken off, and the rubber dust mask, leaving white circles around the eyes and a large white circle around nose and mouth. The exhaust of the tractor puttered on, for fuel is so cheap it is more efficient to leave the engine running than to heat the Diesel nose for a new start. Curious children crowded close, ragged children who ate their fried dough as they watched. They watched hungrily the unwrapping of the sandwiches, and their hunger-sharpened noses smelled the pickle, cheese, and Spam. They didn't speak to the driver. They watched his hand as it carried food to his mouth. They did not watch him chewing; their eyes followed the hand that held the sandwich. After a while the tenant who could not leave the place came out and squatted in the shade beside the tractor.

"Why, you're Joe Davis's boy!"

"Sure," the driver said.

"Well, what you doing this kind of work for — against your own people?"

"Three dollars a day. I got damn sick of creeping for my dinner — and not getting it. I got a wife and kids. We got to eat. Three dollars a day, and it comes every day."

"That's right," the tenant said. "But for your three dollars a day fifteen or twenty families can't eat at all. Nearly a hundred people have to go out and wander on the roads for your three dollars a day. Is that right?"

And the driver said, "Can't think of that. Got to think of my own kids. Three dollars a day, and it comes every day. Times are changing, mister, don't you know? Can't make a living on the land unless you've got two, five, ten thousand acres and a tractor. Crop land isn't for little guys like us any more. You don't kick up a howl because you can't make Fords, or because you're not the telephone company. Well, crops are like that now. Nothing to do about it. You try to get three dollars a day someplace. That's the only way."

The tenant pondered. "Funny thing how it is. If a man owns a little property, that property is him, it's part of him, and it's like him. If he owns property only so he can walk on it and handle it and be sad when it isn't doing well, and feel fine when the rain falls on it, that property is him, and some way he's bigger because he owns it. Even if he isn't successful he's big with his property. That is so."

And the tenant pondered more. "But let a man get property he doesn't see, or can't take time to get his fingers in, or can't be there to walk on it — why, then the property is the man. He can't do what he wants, he can't think what he wants. The property is the man, stronger than he is. And he is small, not big. Only his possessions are big — and he's the servant of his property. That is so, too."

The driver munched the branded pie and threw the crust away. "Times are changed, don't you know? Thinking about stuff like that don't feed the kids. Get your three dollars a day, feed your kids. You got no call to worry about anybody's kids but your own. You get a reputation for talking like that, and you'll never get three dollars a day. Big shots won't give you three dollars a day if you worry about anything but your three dollars a day."

"Nearly a hundred people on the road for your three dollars. Where will we go?"

"And that reminds me," the driver said, "you better get out soon. I'm going through the dooryard after dinner."

"You filled in the well this morning."

"I know. Had to keep the line straight. But I'm going through the dooryard after dinner. Got to keep the lines straight. And — well, you know Joe Davis, my old man, so I'll tell you this. I got orders wherever there's a family not moved out — if I have an accident — you know, get too close and cave the house in a little — well, I might get a couple of dollars. And my youngest kid never had no shoes yet."

"I built it with my hands. Straightened old nails to put the sheating on. Rafters are wired to the stringers with baling wire. It's mine. I built it. You bump it down — I'll be in the window with a rifle. You even come too close and I'll pot you like a rabbit."

"It's not me. There's nothing I can do. I'll lose my job if I don't do it. And look — suppose you kill me? They'll just hang you, but long before you're hung there'll be another guy on the tractor, and he'll bump the house down. You're not killing the right guy."

"That's so," the tenant said. "Who gave you orders? I'll go after him. He's the one to kill."

"You're wrong. He got his orders from the bank. The bank told him, 'Clear those people out or it's your job.'"

"Well, there's a president of the bank. There's a board of directors. I'll fill up the magazine of the rifle and go into the bank."

The driver said, "Fellow was telling me the bank gets orders from the East. The orders were, 'Make the land show profit or we'll close you up.'"

"But where does it stop? Who can we shoot? I don't aim to starve to death before I kill the man that's starving me."

"I don't know. Maybe there's nobody to shoot. Maybe the thing isn't men at all. Maybe like you said, the property's doing it. Anyway I told you my orders."

"I got to figure," the tenant said. "We all got to figure. There's some way to stop this. It's not like lightning or earthquakes. We've got a bad thing made by men, and by God that's something we can change." The tenant sat in his doorway, and the driver thundered his engine and started off, tracks falling and curving, harrows combing, and the phalli of the seeder slipping into the ground. Across the dooryard the tractor cut, and the hard, foot-beaten ground was seeded field, and the tractor cut through again; the uncut space was ten feet wide. And back he came. The iron guard bit into the house-corner, crumbled the wall, and wrenched the little house from its foundation so that it fell sideways, crushed like a bug. And the driver was goggled and a rubber mask covered his nose and mouth. The tractor cut a straight line on, and the air and the ground vibrated with its thunder. The tenant man stared after it, his rifle in his hand. His wife was beside him, and the quiet children behind. And all of them stared after the tractor.

* * *

The houses were left vacant on the land, and the land was vacant because of this. Only the tractor sheds of corrugated iron, silver and gleaming, were alive; and they were alive with metal and gasoline and oil, the disks of the plows shining. The tractors had light shining, for there is no day and night for a tractor and the disks turn the earth in the darkness and they glitter in the daylight. And when a horse stops work and goes into the barn there is a life and a vitality left, there is a breathing and a warmth, and the feet shift on the straw, and the jaws clamp on the hay, and the ears and the eyes are alive. There is a warmth of life in the barn, and the heat and smell of life. But when the motor of a tractor stops, it is as dead as the ore it came from. The heat goes out of it like the living heat that leaves a corpse. Then the corrugated iron doors are closed and the tractor man drives home to town, perhaps twenty miles away, and he need not come back for weeks or months, for the tractor is dead. And this is easy and efficient. So easy that the wonder goes out of work, so efficient that the wonder goes out of land and the working of it, and with the wonder the deep understanding and the relation. And in the tractor man there grows the contempt that comes only to a stranger who has little understanding and no relation. For nitrates are not the land, nor phosphates; and the length of fiber in the cotton is not the land. Carbon is not a man, nor salt nor water nor calcium. He is all these, but he is much more, much more; and the land is so much more than its analysis. The man who is more than his chemistry, walking on the earth, turning his plow point for a stone, dropping his handles to slide over an outcropping, kneeling in the earth to eat his lunch; that man who is more than his elements knows the land that is more than its analysis. But the machine man, driving a dead tractor on land he does not know and love, understands only chemistry; and he is contemptuous of the land and of himself. When the corrugated iron doors are shut, he goes home, and his home is not the land.

The doors of the empty houses swung open, and drifted back and forth in the wind. Bands of little boys came out from the towns to break the windows and to pick over the debris, looking for treasures. And here's a knife with half the blade gone. That's a good thing. And — smells like a rat died here. And look what Whitey wrote on the wall. He wrote that in the toilet in school, too, an' teacher made 'im wash it off.

When the folks first left, and the evening of the first day came, the hunting cats slouched in from the fields and mewed on the porch. And when no one came out, the cats crept through the open doors and walked mewing through the empty rooms. And then they went back to the fields and were wild cats from then on, hunting gophers and field mice, and sleeping in ditches in the daytime. When the night came, the bats, which had stopped at the doors for fear of light, swooped into the houses and sailed through the empty rooms, and in a little while they stayed in dark room corners during the day, folded their wings high, and hung head-down among the rafters, and the smell of their droppings was in the empty houses.

And the mice moved in and stored weed seeds in corners, in boxes, in the backs of drawers in the kitchens. And weasels came in to hunt the mice, and the brown owls flew shrieking in and out again.

Now there came a little shower. The weeds sprang up in front of the doorstep, where they had not been allowed, and grass grew up through the porch boards. The houses were vacant, and a vacant house falls quickly apart. Splits started up the sheathing from the rusted nails. A dust settled on the floors, and only mouse and weasel and cat tracks disturbed it.

On a night the wind loosened a shingle and flipped it to the ground. The next wind pried into the hole where the shingle had been, lifted off three, and the next, a dozen. The midday sun burned through the hole and threw a glaring spot on the floor. The wild cats crept in from the fields at night, but they did not mew at the doorstep any more. They moved like shadows of a cloud across the room, into the rooms to hunt the mice. And on windy nights the doors banged, and the ragged curtains fluttered in the broken windows.

[1939]

The Pushbutton Cornucopia   TIME MAGAZINE

This selection is from the March 9, 1959, cover story of *Time*, whose typical style here seems particularly suited to the subject. One nostalgic reader wrote to the *Time* editor that this was "the most depressing thing I have ever read."

". . . In the last 20 years, farming has changed more radically than in the previous two centuries. . . ."

At 5:30 one frosty Indiana morning last week, Farmer Warren North, 45, rolled out of bed to get at his chores. After a hearty breakfast (orange juice, cereal, bacon and eggs), he left his twelve-room white frame and fieldstone house, walked briskly to the barnyard. In the early morning mist the low-lying white barn, surmounted by five giant blue-black silos, rode the frozen prairie like an ocean liner. Like a rumble of surf came the hungry bellowing of 400 white-faced Herefords and the grunting of 500 Hampshire hogs, waiting at row on row of troughs to be fed. In the barn, North stepped up to an instrument panel as intricate as a ship's, began pushing buttons and pulling switches. All around, the barn came to vibrant life. From one silo dropped ground corn, from another silage, from a third shelled corn.

By pushing other buttons, Farmer North shot in supplementary vitamins, mineral and hormone nutrients. Then he cut in the big noisemaker. In a channel in front of the silos a snakelike auger began to turn. As it writhed, it propelled the feed up a steep incline and sent it tumbling out through a conduit that passed directly over 330 feet of feed troughs. At regular intervals, trap doors automatically distributed the individual animal's feed. When all the animals on one side of a trough had been fed, the traps changed position, shunted feed to the animals waiting on the other side.

Ten minutes later, Farmer North was through with a job that would have taken five men half a day working with buckets and pitchforks. He was ready to indulge his hobby. He returned to his farmhouse and poured himself another cup of coffee. While it cooled, he read a story on the "farm problem" in the *Wall Street Journal*. Carrying his cup and a cigarette, he walked into his living room, 40 feet long and beige-carpeted wall to wall. It was dominated at the far end by a two-story pipe organ flanked by two electronic organs and a grand piano. Farmer North sat down at the console, and after running through a few warm-up chords and arpeggios, began to play Johann Sebastian Bach's chorale, *Jesu, Joy of Man's Desiring*.

Farmer North is a symbol — and a prime example — of the profound changes that have been wrought in U.S. agriculture by mechanization and automation, plus the new use of fertilizers. In the last 20 years, farming has changed more radically than in the previous two centuries. Once farmers used to dole out fertilizer thinking only of how much it cost them. Now they pour it on by the carload, confident of getting back bigger profits at harvest time. Farm use of fertilizer has risen in 20 years from 1,500,000 tons to 6,200,000 tons. To handle the huge increase in crops, farmers have had to mechanize almost every farm job. From 1938 to 1958, farmers more than trebled their ownership of tractors, to 4,700,000 (an average 1½ per commercial farm). Since 1945, they have increased their number of newer work-saving machinery by 1,200% — mostly with machines that had not even been invented in 1938. Farmers have invested $17.5 billion in 1,040,000 combines, 745,000 cornpickers, 590,000 pickup hay balers, 255,000 field forage harvesters and other machinery. They spend $1.5 billion for gasoline and oil each year just to keep the equipment going.

Now farmers are taking the big step from mechanization to automation in the raising of animals and fowl; they are copying the assembly-line techniques of industry and bringing animals indoors. Once man felt he could not provide an environment for animals as good as nature's. Now he knows he can do a whole lot better. Behind him, giving him confidence, are ever-new discoveries in antibiotics, hormones, climate control, nutrition and plant and animal genetics. . . .

For Farmer North, the revolution in farming came at precisely the right time. Twenty years ago Warren North could not afford a pair of new work shoes; he did his chores in an overshoe and a boot. Today, by taking full advantage of all the scientific advances, plus an amount of hard work that would have broken a weaker man, North is comfortably a millionaire. But he remembers every struggling step of the way up. Born in 1913 on the farm he now owns, near Brookston (pop. 1,100), in northwest Indiana, North started in field work at the age of seven, the year after his mother died. His father bolted a box to a harrow, and North, riding in the box, drove the team. His father followed, driving another team pulling a corn planter.

At nine, North was experienced enough to work in the fields alone. Life around Brookston was grim for all farmers in those days after the collapse of prices following the World War I boom, and it was harsh at the North farm. Dale North, the father, was not satisfied unless everybody got up at 3:30 to milk, eat and harness up, so they could get into the fields by 5:30. The cheerless life in Widower North's house still troubles Warren North: "We never even had a Christmas tree." By 1930 the father saw the way clear to let Warren's twin sister Wanda go off to teachers college. Warren himself was ready to go away in three months, study the organ for a term, then enter engineering school the following fall.

All this changed when Dale North had a heart attack. Before he died, he told Warren: "Get an education. Don't be a farmer. I wish I hadn't been." The death left Warren North alone at 17 with an $8,500 mortgage on the 180 acres, $1,500 in funeral and other personal debts. He could go away, let the farm go in a forced sale to satisfy the debt. Or he could stay and try to salvage something. He decided to stay: "I was young and strong," he says now with a slow smile. "And I already had done the spring plowing."

Of the next four years, Warren North remembers little except being bone-weary at all times. His father had got up at 3:30. He got up at 1:30 to milk and set the cans out on the road for the creamery that paid him 2¢ a quart. He had to cut his luxuries to 10¢ a week for old Buffalo roll-your-own tobacco. On his rare dates, he limited the evening to a dime — "for two Cokes." Such ruthless self-denial paid off financially. Warren not only kept Wanda in school but paid off the $1,500 of his father's personal debts to close the estate so he and Wanda could legally inherit the 180 acres.

The years left scars. Withdrawn to begin with, Warren became more so. He married three times. He and his third wife separated six years ago. He found consolation in music, the farm and religion; a Baptist, he has long been organist for the Federated Church. The more unlucky he was in love the more his daring touch with farming coined gold. He was one of the first in Indiana to use fertilizer on wheat, pioneered with hybrid corn in 1937. His yield rose from 50 bu. to 65 bu. and ultimately 100 bu. per acre. He made up his own mind. When the experts said Russian hard wheat would not grow in his area, he planted Russian hard wheat. His yield went from 30 bu. to 42 bu. per acre.

He developed a passion for the latest in machinery. He bought his first tractor in 1933 for $550. Gradually he went in for bigger and more expensive models. By 1950 he was paying $3,000 for a tractor. Later he paid $4,800 apiece for three more. In 1952 he bought a $5,500 combine, decided he had made a good deal when the price rose to $8,000. He early realized that to make costly equipment pay he had to have more land to operate it more of the time. He bought Wanda's 90 acres, partly to save the land from going to another buyer, inherited 25 acres from his grandmother. The rest he picked up at steadily rising market prices from other farmers. Year by year he mortgaged and paid off, mortgaged and paid off. Gradually his property line stretched out to enclose 300 acres, then 500, then two years ago 1,000 acres of the finest land in northern Indiana — worth $500 an acre. When his land got ahead of his equipment, he switched from four-blade to six-blade plows to cut plowing time by one third.

By 1957 Warren North had all the land he wanted. The question was how he could best use it. He was selling grain and feeding hogs and some cattle. He decided that raising grain did not pay enough and that he had to go in for mass production of livestock, use all his grain for his own animals. Through the years North had kept a tight rein on his wage outlay. He employed only two year-round hired hands, plus two part-time men in summer. But the going wage in his area had gone up from $100 to $180 a month, plus a house, utilities, etc. "I figured even if I could get more men they would not be any account."

For the same reason that inspired many an industrialist faced with similar cost-price squeeze, North decided to automate his livestock feeding, bought glass-lined steel Harvestore silos, developed by the A. O. Smith Corp. of Milwaukee, Wis., for $55,000. Hermetically sealed to prevent decay, the silos permitted him to store corn and silage as soon as cut, thereby giving it all the feed value of green produce. Since the corn did not have to be dried to bone hardness as in ordinary storage, it would also be easily digestible. (Around Warren North, in a more primitive cycle, many farmers still followed the traditional and inefficient practice of feeding dried corn to cattle, running in hogs to pick out undigested kernels from the manure, then letting chickens clean up.)

North spent another $75,000 on equipment to go with the silos. The result is that he can swiftly raise his livestock feeding output without more capital. By turning his animals over three times a year, he is already running at the rate of 1,200 head of cattle, 1,500 hogs a year. Depending on the market outlook, he can increase this to 1,800 cattle and 4,000 hogs with no additional labor. . . .

What Warren North has done is also being done by many another:

Russell Case, 36, who 20 years ago helped his father and grandfather operate a scrubby 100-acre place, now has two farms totaling 2,500 acres near West Mansfield, Ohio. It takes eight mobile radios to keep the two dozen trucks, 19 tractors, six combines and assorted other mechanical gear shuttling back and forth to harvest crops worth $150,000.

C. E. Benzel cultivates a 180-acre irrigated farm outside Alliance, Neb. which last year produced 625 tons of beet sugar. Using the latest in mechanical planters, thinners and harvesters, Benzel and six helpers do the work of 30 migratory workers.

Bill Farr has just installed an automated $200,000 feed mill, 100 ft. high and 60 ft. long, to prepare food for the 10,000 cattle he fattens on his feed lots near Greeley, Colo. Truckloads of corn, barley, dry beet pulp, dehydrated alfalfa, protein mix, etc. are ground and mixed into eight different types of feed to give the maximum weight gain to cattle at different age levels. In addition to antibiotics and minerals, Farr also adds tranquilizers to make the animals eat more, avoid threshing around and bruising their flesh en route to the slaughterhouse. . . .

Where all this is leading to is obvious to farm experts. The number of farmers will steadily drop as more mechanization and automation increase the investment needed to farm. Economists of the Department of Agriculture estimate that the 3,100,000 commercial farms of 1954 may well be 2,000,000 by 1975. But they see rising prices for land and even used equipment making it easy for farmers to sell out at good prices. Those who stay in will have bigger markets. In 1940 each U.S. farmer fed himself and ten others. He now feeds 20 others. In 1975 experts expect it will be about 42. Increasing agricultural efficiency will make the job easier and more profitable.

[1959]

The Years of Our Ford

JOHN KEATS

John Keats (1920–   ) is an ex-newspaper man who has turned to writing exposés of American life. *The Crack in the Picture Window* (1957) dealt with corruption in development housing. *Schools Without Scholars* (1958) exposed current practices in the public schools. *The Insolent Chariots* (1958), from which "The Years of Our Ford" is taken, indicts the Detroit automobile industry.

Starting with an elaborately developed metaphor, Keats describes the impact of the automobile on our culture. His aim in this first chapter of his book, it should be said, is not to deal authoritatively or exhaustively with his subject but to interest his reader in it and raise some questions. This he succeeds in doing, partly through a style suited to what he calls a "slapstick tragedy."

". . . Quickly the automobile became the nagging wife. . . ."

Once upon a time, the American met the automobile and fell in love. Unfortunately, this led him into matrimony, and so he did not live happily ever after. Cooler heads could have told him the affair was doomed from the start, for in the beginning, the American was poorly prepared to make judgments in such matters. He was merely a rustic Merry Andrew with a cowlick and an adolescent tightening in the groin. In his libidinous innocence, he saw the automobile only as curious, exciting — and obviously willing. Wherefore, he joyfully leaped upon her, and she responded to his caresses by bolting about the landscape in what can only be called a succession of bumps and grinds.

This Arcadian idyll did not persist, of course. Had he loved her and left her, all would have been well. Had he restrained himself, and viewed her as a possible hired woman to be trained for work about the farm and otherwise left strictly alone, all would have been better. But he was innocent; she handed him a likely story and led him to the preacher. Then, before they were fairly out of the churchyard, she began to demonstrate less enchanting aspects of her character. The American, it seems, was trapped by a schemer.

Quickly the automobile became the nagging wife, demanding rubbings and shinings and gifts. She put eyebrows over her windshield in the 1920s, plucked them out in the late 1930s, put them on again in the middle 1940s, and took them off once more in the 1950s. She nagged him for bits of chrome and cursed him for his extravagance when he brought them home. She lifted her face — expensively — from year to year; incessantly demanded new gauds and different colors, developed ever more costly eating habits, threatened to break the family budget and often succeeded, and the American, — poor dolt, not only catered to her whims but decked her out in door-edge guards and silvery Kleenex dispensers.

Since woman from the dawn of time has regarded man as she regards an old house — that is, as something to make over — it is not surprising to note that the automobile wrought dramatic changes in her spouse. Nevertheless, the speed and thoroughness of the transformation is a little awe-inspiring, bespeaking either a weakness on the American's part or a fantastic singleness of purpose on the part of the automobile, or both. For example, in fifty-eight short years the automobile not only became our nation's greatest single topic of conversation, but also unquestionably central to our economy. The automobile became demonstrably more important to us than our human wives, children, jobs and even our food — and I intend to demonstrate this in proper place with fact and figure. The automobile changed our dress, manners, social customs, vacation habits, the shape of our cities, consumer purchasing patterns, common tastes and positions in intercourse.

As the frightful marriage wore on, the automobile's original appeal shrank in inverse proportion to the growth of her demands. She grew sow-fat while demanding bigger, wider, smoother roads. The bigger and better the road, the fatter she became, and the fatter she grew, the greater her demands for even bigger roads. Then, with all the subtlety of a madam affecting a lorgnette, she put tail fins on her overblown bustle and sprouted wavering antennae from each fin. And, of course, her every whim was more costly than the last.

In view of these metamorphoses, it is understandable that the American began to stray. In the mid-1950s, he eyed the European car, and found her good. She was petite, she was new, she was gay, she was inexpensive, she bumped and she ground, and like all mistresses, she promised prestige. Maintaining a mistress when one is married to a Harpy is, however, an intolerable situation, and so we can say that the American's marriage to the American automobile is now at an end, and it is only a matter of minutes to the final pistol shot, although who pulls the trigger has yet to be determined.

While it must be borne in mind that the story of our nation's relationship with the American automobile is essentially the story of a love affair, it may serve our purpose equally well to put matters in less emotional terms. For instance, we can look at the thing historically, scientifically, philosophically or geographically, but no matter how objectively we view it, a quality of slapstick tragedy is always apparent.

For example, let's take the historical view. Since 1900 American automobiles have grown longer, lower, wider, faster, jazzier, more complicated and more, much more expensive — but far less efficient and no safer.

Meanwhile, as all the world knows, General Motors is spending millions on automotive research, and this fact has inspired the press to pose scientific questions. For instance, The New York Times asked Mr. Edward T. Ragsdale, GM's general manager of the Buick Division, what Buick was doing in 1958 toward achieving fuel economy. "Oh," Mr. Ragsdale said lightly, "we're helping the gas companies, the same as our competitors."

Similarly, we can find nourishment for the mind in the philosophical realm. It is now possible for you to walk across Manhattan Island at rush hour in far less time than you could possibly drive. Twenty years ago, this claim could not have been made. A philosophical question therefore becomes: Will the automobile put man back on his feet?

Equally provocative is the geographical view. In 1900, there was hardly enough paved surface in North America to fill a tooth; today there exists enough to cover New England. In other words, 40,000 square miles of our New World is now under pavement. Our new roads, with their ancillaries, the motels, filling stations and restaurants advertising Eats, have made it possible for you to drive from Brooklyn to Los Angeles without a change of diet, scenery or culture, and this, too, is a gift of Detroit. Thus, if we assume human progress to be the steady reduction of life's mad chaos into a semblance of order, it is undeniable that the automobile has helped to make such progress by reducing to an easily recognized standard brand that which had once been a frightful confusion of differing peoples, landscapes, and geographical products. Moreover, in our newest cars, it is possible to make the entire trip at a uniform temperature, and so we note that order has been established in the chaos that was once our national climate.

Assuming that America's marriage to its automobile will somehow endure — that the pistol shot will be definitely delayed — we can make an objective synthesis of the historical, scientific, philosophical and geographical viewpoints and arrive at accurate predictions. For instance, assuming the marriage to continue in the same course it has followed these last fifty-eight years, simple arithmetic can easily determine the precise moment in time when the last square inch of our continent becomes paved; at what pregnant moment everything is one huge, smooth surface from Hudson's Bay to the Gulf of Mexico.

Then, perhaps, on this vast ballroom floor, everyone will scurry around in a kind of Brownian movement, each couple in its own huge car, going 500 miles an hour, here and there, round and round, up and down, day and night, everyone drinking Coca-Cola and watching color television and listening to the national news broadcast while necking; radar doing the driving and guarding against collision. From time to time the cars will, perhaps, come fleetingly to rest, or — maybe — tremble like humming-birds beside floodlit tinsel filling stations built beside swimming-pooled motels, where car-hopping drum majorettes dressed in boots and tassels dance among the bright bodies of the cars, selling souvenirs and serving electronically-cooked, pre-digested frozen TV suppers on dispensable trays. In all this, only the drum majorettes will not be real. They will be clever illusions wrought by cunning lights to disguise the fact the suppers arrive on conveyor belts out of mechanical kitchens. At any rate, these phantom maidens will summon up Detroit's image of love and beauty, for painful research conducted behind the scenes at national automobile conventions reveals that when an automobile manufacturer dreams of Hebe, he envisions a nubile adolescent who chews gum.

The proof of this Nesselrode will be in the eating, of course, so let us prepare to dine. Let us examine, from the disinterested aspect of eternity, some facts of our life, past and present, and start asking questions.

What, let us wonder, would America have become if the American had not married the automobile? Since such a marriage has taken place, what is the real effect of the automobile on our landscape and on the nature of our society? What are Detroit's real reasons for building what it builds? Why do we really buy the machines we buy? What contribution has Detroit really made to our business community? Is the automobile as essential to us as we might suspect? Just where, pray tell, is Man in the automotive age?

Fortunately for our purposes, Man is pretty easy to find. Here comes one now. We see him in the family shape of Edgar Striver, his wife Sue Ella, and their children Donna and Ralph. Together with their dog, Fred, they are part of a slowly moving line of traffic inching through New England on the hottest July day in fifty years. They have started and stopped eighty-seven times in the last three hundred yards on Rhode Island's Route 30. It is late afternoon, they're trying to get to Providence, but there's an accident up ahead and the Strivers are still two miles south of Nooseneck. Fred is carsick. Donna and Ralph are fighting and dripping fried clams onto the new seat covers. Edgar and the radiator are approaching the boiling point, Sue Ella's hair is uncoiling on the nape of her neck and her face is livid with fatigue and the radio is blaring away. The announcer is telling them that for that extra go, for that power the jet jockeys know, for the gasoline that keeps your motor clean, see your Powerblast dealer today. Here is a typical family group in these years of our Ford. Here are four free American pilgrims off to visit Plymouth Rock to have their faith in our institutions renewed. They are on vacation, driving their car, masters of their fates, captains of their souls. They are the idealized family version of Prometheus Unbound.

Man in the automotive age? He is everywhere. Here comes another, Richard Masters by name, encapsulated in chromium, ruler of three hundred and fifty horses which are now drawing him at sixteen miles an hour through downtown Washington, D.C. — for sixteen miles an hour is Washington's top average downtown speed, our traffic scientists say. Masters has entered the world of no U turn, no left turn, no right turn, right turn only, stop, go, one way, slow, no parking from 8:30 A.M. to 6 P.M. and no standing. He is looking for a place to park, along with 350,000 other people.

Man is everywhere in this age, and often his wildest dreams are fulfilled, just as even the worst of marriages boasts random moments of ecstasy. Here is one other we might consider — Howard Blatant. Howard is whizzing down the Pennsylvania Turnpike's northeast extension at 82.7 miles an hour true ground speed. He rests on cushions, rides on air, soothed by music. He is completely and deeply content as he hurtles along in a two-ton Thunderbolt with a momentum of 487,200 pounds per foot per second. Protected from wind, sound, and jolt, Howard idly watches the scenery glide past. It seems to move slowly, for the road is straight, wide and apparently endless. Howard stares ahead, lost in an ineffable trance, but he will not fall asleep . . . will not fall asleep . . . will not fall asl . . . will not fall . . . will not fa . . . will not . . . Mr. Blatant has two seconds left.

Man in the automotive age? He is everywhere; it is an easy question to answer. It may be a little more difficult to answer why he is there, and if he knows where he is. . . .

[1958]

Auto Wreck

KARL SHAPIRO

Karl Shapiro (1913–   ) has published numerous volumes of poetry, including *V-Letter,* which won a Pulitzer Prize for 1945. He was editor of *Poetry: A Magazine of Verse* from 1950 to 1956 when he became a professor of English and editor of *Prairie Schooner* at the University of Nebraska.

It has been said of Shapiro that his "interest in his immediate surroundings, together with his verbal facility, set him apart from those of his fellows who stand in the street damning a disjointed world, and apart, too, from those spinning word-webs in an ivory corner of a prefabricated tower." The opening images of "Auto Wreck" are evidence of the unique "exactness" of poetry, a precision at variance with newspaper exactness in reporting a similar incident. The last lines of the poem, less concerned with sense of fact, raise a question of "richest horror," aftermath of this spattering of "all we know of dénouement."

". . . this invites the occult mind. . . ."

Its quick soft silver bell beating, beating,
And down the dark one ruby flare
Pulsing out red light like an artery,
The ambulance at top speed floating down
Past beacons and illuminated clocks   5
Wings in a heavy curve, dips down,
And brakes speed, entering the crowd.
The doors leap open, emptying light;
Stretchers are laid out, the mangled lifted
And stowed into the little hospital.   10
Then the bell, breaking the hush, tolls once,
And the ambulance with its terrible cargo
Rocking, slightly rocking, moves away,
As the doors, an afterthought, are closed.

We are deranged, walking among the cops   15
Who sweep glass and are large and composed.
One is still making notes under the light.
One with a bucket douches ponds of blood
Into the street and gutter.
One hangs lanterns on the wrecks that cling,   20
Empty husks of locusts, to iron poles.

Our throats were tight as tourniquets,
Our feet were bound with splints, but now,

Like convalescents intimate and gauche,
We speak through sickly smiles and warn   25
With the stubborn saw of common sense,
The grim joke and the banal resolution.
The traffic moves around with care,
But we remain, touching a wound
That opens to our richest horror.   30
Already old, the question Who shall die?
Becomes unspoken Who is innocent?
For death in war is done by hands;
Suicide has cause and stillbirth, logic;
And cancer, simple as a flower, blooms.   35
But this invites the occult mind,
Cancels our physics with a sneer,
And spatters all we know of dénouement
Across the expedient and wicked stones.

                                                          [1941]

The Democracy of Things   ROGER BURLINGAME

Roger Burlingame (1889–   ) was a publisher's book editor when, in
1926, he decided to devote himself to free-lance writing. Since that time
he has published a number of books on a wide variety of subjects. This
selection is from the first chapter of his *Machines That Built America*
(1953).

  Using cause-and-effect analysis, Burlingame supports the thesis that
machinery "was an absolute necessity" for America's development. Ironically enough, the manufactures which Jefferson feared as the enemy of
democracy (see the previous section) here appear as the indispensable
friend of equality and the preserver of national integrity. In setting forth
these ideas, Burlingame is less the artist than the craftsman. His sentences
and paragraphs move competently and uncomplicatedly from statement
to support. This is the prose of utility.

        ". . . we seem to see a great assembly line moving from the
                    Atlantic to the Pacific. . . ."

A trip abroad is, to observant Americans, an extremely valuable experience.
At home we are likely to take the extraordinary mechanical marvels which
ease our existence for granted. A boy or girl born, say, in the late 1930's or
early '40's has never known any other way of life. Even his parents may not
remember a time when there was no car in the family; his grandfather must

tell what it was like to have no electricity or telephone in his home. We seem to have come into a world which was ready-made for us, which functions perfectly in every detail and requires no effort on our part. The lights spring up at the flick of a switch, an exact temperature is maintained by the setting of a thermostat, the food we need today or shall need months from now is on the shelves in cans or below zero in the home freezer. To press a button releases the power of a hundred and sixty horses to transport us a hundred or a thousand miles without the need of any muscular activity beyond the light touch of the hand on steering wheel or gear shift or the foot on the brake. But in other countries we see all round us the great physical exertion which was demanded of our ancestors to secure the bare necessities of life.

We need the sharp visual contrast we find abroad or in some remote rural part of the United States, such as the Cumberland or Ozark mountains, to wake us to the immense gap between the common life of today and that of a century ago. Immediately our minds are flooded with questions. First: How was this development possible over the huge area of our country which, when the republic started, was mostly wilderness? Second: Why have all these things which are luxuries abroad become commonplaces in the United States, owned by people at almost every level of income? Many other questions follow on these two, once we begin to look into history, and some of the easy answers that first suggest themselves are no longer good enough when we discover the facts of our national growth.

The commonest answer is phrased in the two words: Yankee ingenuity. There is a widespread belief that, from the beginning, Americans were born mechanical geniuses. According to this theory even in colonial times every other boy was an inventor from the age of ten up and became absorbed in scientific study as soon as he could read. This idea seems to have resulted from thinking backward. Because in 1953, American boys are handy with tools, are effective trouble-shooters with all sorts of machines and are often apt pupils in mathematics, physics and chemistry, it is assumed that this was always true.

History, however, shows the exact opposite. While there were, as we shall see, certain highly intelligent and inventive American minds, they were extremely few and so far between that communication was impossible among them. When the republic began there were *even fewer* active inventors than there had been when the states were colonies. The reason for this was that as soon as the independence of the United States was achieved, everyone who could moved west to settle the wild lands and become a farmer. Among the first to go were the mechanics, the men skilled in the use of tools, carpenters, metal workers and blacksmiths. One reason for this was that these people were better able to buy land. In any case they went: they moved away from the coastal cities in droves and when they had reached the frontiers they became wholly absorbed in the work of clearing, plowing and planting and in the resulting prosperity.

The result was that throughout the young United States there was an almost complete dearth of skilled artisans of all kinds. In the letters and diaries of the few great inventors like Eli Whitney we keep coming across references to "the low state of the mechanick arts." Whitney had to abandon his important invention, the cotton gin, because he could not find enough skilled workers to build this simple machine in sufficient quantity to make it profitable. In every branch of technics, America was far behind England. No American could design or construct the kind of machine, for instance, that was bringing tremendous wealth to British capitalists through spinning, weaving and other textile operations. More than forty years after Watt invented the steam engine, Robert Fulton had to buy a British engine to supply power to his *Claremont* because Americans had never properly learned the art of engine building. Almost all steel and most iron were imported. Coal which had been one of the factors of the English industrial revolution was unknown here. Tools came from England, Sweden and Germany. We had no canals, practically no roads. The power for our grist-mills, saw-mills, rolling and slitting mills, our forges and foundries was all water power.

The few American inventors of that period — from 1790, say, to 1810 — could find no one interested enough in new mechanical ideas to back them. John Fitch, the true inventor of the steamboat, died in poverty and despair because neither capitalists nor the government would take any interest in his invention. Oliver Evans, one of the greatest of them all, had to fight against ignorance, superstition and blind prejudice to induce millers to adopt his revolutionary flour-milling machinery. With his steam engines and his "road carriage" — a steam automobile — he had even less success. When Charles Newbold patented an iron plow in 1797, farmers refused to use it because they were convinced that the iron would "poison the soil."

It was from this beginning, then, not from the springboard of "Yankee ingenuity" that the United States took off on a career which brought the nation to world leadership in industry. The start, we see, was far behind scratch. We had first to catch up with the rest of civilization in our understanding of technics before we could begin to compete.

Along with this handicap, however, there were other things which aided us. One, oddly enough, was that very westward push which had robbed us of our mechanics and skilled artisans. The migration into the wilderness was on such a vast scale that the needs of these pioneer people out in the empty land suddenly became great. For the first work of clearing forests, "breaking up" and plowing prairie land and building crude temporary log cabins, only axes, mattocks, augers and hand saws, and a few farm implements were needed. But once farmers were fairly started, the work of planting and harvesting the tremendous crops they were able to raise on the virgin soil and of marketing them, left little time for hunting, tanning, cobbling, spinning and weaving which, in their first years on the frontier, the pioneer families had done. It was then, when they were settled and producing, when the first prosperity had come from their crop sales to eastern markets, that the westerners began to want every kind of manufactured goods: cloth, shoes, hardware, glass, flour, clocks, and a hundred other things for the refinement of life in an established community.

At first, when the Revolutionary War was over, it looked as if Americans would continue to import many of those things from abroad as they had done in colonial days. In that time England had done her best to prevent manufacturing in the colonies lest it cut into her own trade. The whole colonial idea, according to English thinking, was for the colonies to grow food, tobacco and such raw materials of manufacture as cotton, indigo and iron for the mother country and to buy from her all their manufactured goods. The laws passed by the English Parliament to enforce this procedure were among the causes of discontent which ended in the fight for independence. But then, even after the Americans had won their liberty, England still tried to prevent factories from starting in the United States. One way of doing this was to flood the country with English goods at far lower prices than the inexperienced Americans could make them. So, for a time, ship after ship unloaded in American ports bales and boxes and barrels of fancy cotton, linen, silk and woolen cloth, leather goods, hardware, clothing, hats — all the things the expanding country needed at such tempting prices and with such easy credit that it was difficult even for the disapproving American patriots to resist buying.

It looked, then, as if the birth of American industry might be indefinitely delayed. In the first place, most of the people did not want factories. Horrible stories of conditions in the "dark Satanic mills," as the great English textile factories were called, had crossed the Atlantic. Long hours, child labor in hot, ill-ventilated buildings, starvation wages and other reputed privations were things to which Americans were unaccustomed. The outdoor hardships of the frontier were far more to their liking. The freedom of the wild lands, teeming with game; the excitement of life in the woods with its challenge of Indians and wild animals, and the pleasures of farming in rich soil were far more appealing than confined labor in spinning and weaving establishments, furnaces and forges. Yet at the same time, to wise and patriotic men whose thoughts were often far in the future, the notion of continued dependence on Britain was intolerable. Alexander Hamilton was such a patriot; so were Franklin and Tench Coxe and others in New England, New York, Pennsylvania and Delaware of whom we shall presently hear.

The infant nation, in those days perilously learning its first steps and making many painful mistakes in the process, was finally saved by events abroad. By 1800, most of Europe had been plunged into war. The French Revolution had been followed by the sweeping conquests of Napoleon. British and French trade with America had come to an end. The United States was then truly thrown on its own. Its only hope was to produce — as much and as fast as possible. It must make every sort of thing it had previously imported. It must make its own cloth — not merely with the spinning wheels and hand looms at home, but on a big enough scale to supply the wants of people who had acquired tastes in foreign factory-made cottons and woolens. It must make shoes, axes, plows, farm implements, guns, buttons, nails, shovels, chisels, pottery, paper, rope, wagons and carriages, pots and kettles, stoves, pewter and silverware, gloves, printing presses, hats and stockings on an increasingly large scale as the civilization of the east moved west.

It was soon obvious that these things could not be made by the few, inefficient artisans and mechanics who were left behind after the first tremendous westward rush. *Some substitute must be found for the missing men.* It was then that it occurred to the handful of great mechanical geniuses that were scattered through the coastal states to replace hand labor with machines.

Machines must be invented each of which would take the place of ten or fifty or a hundred of the missing men. Somehow a man's skill in carving, cutting, forging, bending, shaping, drilling — a hundred other operations which had been painfully performed by a hand-held chisel or knife or gimlet — must be put into a machine which would run along more or less automatically and turn out the things in great quantity while a boy stood by to watch and occasionally fix something which went wrong.

Soon this business of inventing machines began to spread — especially in New England. As the demand grew for every kind of manufactured thing, men began to compete in ingenuity. Gradually more and more people became absorbed in machine production and fewer in farming. Factories, springing up along the rivers in the East, using the power of the moving water to turn the water-wheels which turned the machines, attracted many men and boys who might otherwise have been swallowed by the frontier farms. Finally, when steam came, factories sprang up in the West, too, behind the frontiers, where it was easier to supply the settlers who were making their little rural communities into thriving towns and busy cities. In time, those towns were all tied together by the network of railroads, and manufacturing was carried on everywhere.

It is important to remember, therefore, that machine production began in the United States, not because there were so many mechanically skilled people but because there were so few. Machinery was an absolute necessity in America. For this reason machine production was quite different in the United States from what it had been in England where there was too much, not too little, labor. It had come to England first because there was such a high level of scientific knowledge and education and so many inventors who were not diverted by agriculture, and second because it was cheaper than hand labor and therefore made large fortunes for its owners. For a time, therefore, machinery caused hardship, unemployment and poverty in England because skilled workers lost their jobs when machines could be tended by children. (Many of them, incidentally, migrated to the United States where there was work for all of them.) The designers of English machines also worked more with quality than quantity in mind; American inventors concentrated mainly on the largest possible production and, above all, the greatest possible speed. From the very beginning of the republic the impulse of speed dominated every other. We know now that this speed was necessary if the nation was to hold together; in the early days it seems to have been an unconscious driving force.

There was another reason why what we know as mass production originated in America and only in America. That reason is contained in the Declaration of Independence. The framers of that remarkable document believed it to be a "self-evident" truth "that all men are created equal." That brings us back to the beginning of this chapter where we found a foreign visitor amazed that, in America, luxuries were commonplace. Throughout our history each American has believed that, in some sense, he is the equal of every other American. He may be less intelligent or, as he is likely to put it, less "smart" than his neighbor. He certainly may be less rich, less lucky or less healthy. But he has rarely believed — as many in other lands still believe — that he has not the *right* to the best of everything. Wealth, power, social importance and high office have always been part of the dream of the individual American. As soon as they can understand words, boys are told that they may one day be President of the United States and all of them believe it.

In the days of the great migrations, the pioneers — though they might have had the humblest origins — dreamed of prosperity ahead. "There's gold," they used to say, "in them thar hills" — and there was. When the first fine machines found their way west, every farmer dreamed of owning a reaper or a thresher, a harvester and, finally, a tractor. When sewing machines came, there was not an American woman in the loneliest farmhouse who did not know that her desire for this luxury could, somehow, be fulfilled. Her granddaughters felt the same way about their refrigerators and toasters and dishwashers.

And when machine production got fairly started, the manufacturers invented new devices to meet those unlimited American desires. One of those which most surprised Europeans was the installment plan, instituted by Cyrus McCormick and Isaac Singer, by which only a small "down payment" plus a promise was necessary to have farm machinery or a sewing machine delivered to your home. In Europe, the opposite method was in vogue; something was subscribed for in advance and did not become the property of the subscriber until every penny had been paid. Foreigners simply could not understand this trusting of "lower class" strangers.

As soon as manufacturers realized the size of their markets they built faster and more productive machines until, finally, with their enormous sales, they were able to produce much cheaper things. It was this background which made it possible for Henry Ford to install an assembly line which would turn out a finished car every twenty seconds and, after eighteen years of that kind of production, to sell his cars for $300 apiece.

Another important factor in American mass production was the newspaper. In Europe the press existed mainly for the benefit of educated folk able to discuss with intelligence and understanding the affairs of the day. In America, everyone felt entitled to news and politics, so when the penny newspaper was produced it instantly acquired an enormous circulation. The papers not only told of new inventions but they advertised the new products of the factories and every reader felt that he could find a way to buy these things.

Without machines, without the constant new invention and building of machines, without the extraordinary quantity of things they were able to produce, the settlement of our three million square miles of territory would have taken many hundreds of years. Surely, in that time, our nation would have split into many nations with separate customs and hostility among them. This happened in the slow growth of European civilization and, again, in South America to which machines came late. Different groups of migrants would have become widely separated and the national integrity would have been lost. But, as it was, whenever there was a slowing up of the progress, some new invention came along to give it speed: the rapid machine manufacture of axes to cut the forest, fleets of steamboats to carry goods and people up the rivers and across the lakes, machines to cut and process the grain to make it available to everyone, flour mills to grind the wheat in ever-increasing quantity, packing houses for meat, steel for rails for the railroad, locomotives able to move with speed over quick-laid track up steep grades and round sharp curves, the telegraph for constant liaison and, finally, the organization and transmission of electric power.

As we follow the progress across the continent, it is like finding the pieces of a picture puzzle and fitting them together. Usually, pieces on the frontier are hard to fit until we have completed some part of the picture in the rear. Thus the territory acquired in the Mexican War cannot be fitted in until we have pieces representing the gun factories in Hartford, New Haven and Springfield: the great wheat regions of Minnesota and the Dakotas seem to wait for a piece that will show the McCormick reaper plant in Chicago. The discovery of gold deposits in California and Nevada began the demand for the Pittsburgh iron and steel that went into the transcontinental railroads.

As we look back on it the whole process seems continuous, like mass production itself: we seem to see a great assembly line moving from the Atlantic to the Pacific with all the sub-assemblies coming into it at the right places just as, in an automobile plant, the conveyors bearing the engines and the bodies always meet the chassis as it moves along the main line, precisely when they are needed.

It was not, of course, as simple or as smooth as that. There were desperate moments in the building of America when it seemed as if the whole beautiful structure would collapse. Even now, we cannot always feel the security we should like. Yet somehow our ingenuity has usually got us over the crises. It was not an ingenuity we began with; not the famous, legendary "Yankee ingenuity" but an inventiveness we have acquired slowly and under the pressures of terrible necessity.

[1953]

What Hath Man Wrought?

The Monastery and the Clock   LEWIS MUMFORD

Lewis Mumford (1895–   ) attended several institutions of higher learning but holds no degrees. He has spent most of his life in New York City, writing and serving on various magazines and editorial projects. In 1932 he spent four months in Europe gathering material for *Technics and Civilization* (1934), from which "The Monastery and the Clock" is taken. The author of more than twenty books, Mumford has taught at a number of colleges and universities and since 1957 has been a visiting professor at the Massachusetts Institute of Technology.

Because it has brought about a gradually increasing awareness of "mechanical time," Mumford sees the clock as the basis of modern civilization. Mumford's title suitably identifies his basic informative purpose, but it also suggests that his subject will raise a paradox and lead into some provocative generalizations.

> "... The clock, not the steam-engine, is the key-machine of the modern industrial age...."

Where did the machine first take form in modern civilization? There was plainly more than one point of origin. Our mechanical civilization represents the convergence of numerous habits, ideas, and modes of living, as well as technical instruments; and some of these were, in the beginning, directly opposed to the civilization they helped to create. But the first manifestation of the new order took place in the general picture of the world: during the first seven centuries of the machine's existence the categories of time and space underwent an extraordinary change, and no aspect of life was left untouched by this transformation. The application of quantitative methods of thought to the study of nature had its first manifestation in the regular measurement of time; and the new mechanical conception of time arose in part out of the routine of the monastery. Alfred Whitehead has emphasized the importance of the scholastic belief in a universe ordered by God as one of the foundations of modern physics: but behind that belief was the presence of order in the institutions of the Church itself.

The technics of the ancient world were still carried on from Constantinople and Baghdad to Sicily and Cordova: hence the early lead taken by

Salerno in the scientific and medical advances of the Middle Age. It was, however, in the monasteries of the West that the desire for order and power, other than that expressed in the military domination of weaker men, first manifested itself after the long uncertainty and bloody confusion that attended the breakdown of the Roman Empire. Within the walls of the monastery was sanctuary: under the rule of the order surprise and doubt and caprice and irregularity were put at bay. Opposed to the erratic fluctuations and pulsations of the worldly life was the iron discipline of the rule. Benedict added a seventh period to the devotions of the day, and in the seventh century, by a bull of Pope Sabinianus, it was decreed that the bells of the monastery be rung seven times in the twenty-four hours. These punctuation marks in the day were known as the canonical hours, and some means of keeping count of them and ensuring their regular repetition became necessary.

According to a now discredited legend, the first modern mechanical clock, worked by falling weights, was invented by the monk named Gerbert who afterwards became Pope Sylvester II near the close of the tenth century. This clock was probably only a water clock, one of those bequests of the ancient world either left over directly from the days of the Romans, like the water-wheel itself, or coming back again into the West through the Arabs. But the legend, as so often happens, is accurate in its implications if not in its facts. The monastery was the seat of a regular life, and an instrument for striking the hours at intervals or for reminding the bell-ringer that it was time to strike the bells, was an almost inevitable product of this life. If the mechanical clock did not appear until the cities of the thirteenth century demanded an orderly routine, the habit of order itself and the earnest regulation of time-sequences had become almost second nature in the monastery. Coulton agrees with Sombart in looking upon the Benedictines, the great working order, as perhaps the original founders of modern capitalism: their rule certainly took the curse off work and their vigorous engineering enterprises may even have robbed warfare of some of its glamor. So one is not straining the facts when one suggests that the monasteries — at one time there were 40,000 under the Benedictine rule — helped to give human enterprise the regular collective beat and rhythm of the machine; for the clock is not merely a means of keeping track of the hours, but of synchronizing the actions of men.

Was it by reason of the collective Christian desire to provide for the welfare of souls in eternity by regular prayers and devotions that time-keeping and the habits of temporal order took hold of men's minds: habits that capitalist civilization presently turned to good account? One must perhaps accept the irony of this paradox. At all events, by the thirteenth century there are definite records of mechanical clocks, and by 1370 a well-designed "modern" clock had been built by Heinrich von Wyck at Paris. Meanwhile, bell towers had come into existence, and the new clocks, if they did not have, till the fourteenth century, a dial and a hand that translated the movement of time into a movement through space, at all events struck the hours. The clouds that could paralyze the sundial, the freezing that could stop the water clock on a winter night, were no longer obstacles to time-keeping: summer or winter, day or night, one was aware of the measured clank of the clock. The instrument presently spread outside the monastery; and the regular striking of the bells brought a new regularity into the life of the workman and the merchant. The bells of the clock tower almost defined urban existence. Time-keeping passed into time-serving and time-accounting and time-rationing. As this took place, Eternity ceased gradually to serve as the measure and focus of human actions.

The clock, not the steam-engine, is the key-machine of the modern industrial age. For every phase of its development the clock is both the outstanding fact and the typical symbol of the machine: even today no other machine is so ubiquitous. Here, at the very beginning of modern technics, appeared prophetically the accurate automatic machine which, only after centuries of further effort, was also to prove the final consummation of this technics in every department of industrial activity. There had been power-machines, such as the water-mill, before the clock; and there had also been various kinds of automata, to awaken the wonder of the populace in the temple, or to please the idle fancy of some Moslem caliph: machines one finds illustrated in Hero and Al-Jazari. But here was a new kind of power-machine, in which the source of power and the transmission were of such a nature as to ensure the even flow of energy throughout the works and to make possible regular production and a standardized product. In its relationship to determinable quantities of energy, to standardization, to automatic action, and finally to its own special product, accurate timing, the clock has been the foremost machine in modern technics: and at each period it has remained in the lead: it marks a perfection toward which other machines aspire. The clock, moreover, served as a model for many other kinds of mechanical works, and the analysis of motion that accompanied the perfection of the clock, with the various types of gearing and transmission that were elaborated, contributed to the success of quite different kinds of machine. Smiths could have hammered thousands of suits of armor or thousands of iron cannon, wheelwrights could have shaped thousands of great water-wheels or crude gears, without inventing any of the special types of movement developed in clockwork, and without any of the accuracy of measurement and fineness of articulation that finally produced the accurate eighteenth century chronometer.

The clock, moreover, is a piece of power-machinery whose "product" is seconds and minutes: by its essential nature it dissociated time from human events and helped create the belief in an independent world of mathematically measurable sequences: the special world of science. There is relatively little foundation for this belief in common human experience: throughout the year the days are of uneven duration, and not merely does the relation between day and night steadily change, but a slight journey from East to West alters astronomical time by a certain number of minutes. In terms of the human organism itself, mechanical time is even more foreign: while human life has regularities of its own, the beat of the pulse, the breathing of the lungs, these change from hour to hour with mood and action, and in the longer span of days, time is measured not by the calendar but by the events that occupy it. The shepherd measures from the time the ewes lambed; the farmer measures back to the day of sowing or forward to the harvest: if growth has its own duration and regularities, behind it are not simply matter and motion but the facts of development: in short, history. And while mechanical time is strung out in a succession of mathematically isolated instants, organic time — what Bergson calls duration — is cumulative in its effects. Though mechanical time can, in a sense, be speeded up or run backward, like the hands of a clock or the images of a moving picture, organic time moves in only one direction — through the cycle of birth, growth, development, decay, and death — and the past that is already dead remains present in the future that has still to be born.

Around 1345, according to Thorndike, the division of hours into sixty minutes and of minutes into sixty seconds became common: it was this abstract framework of divided time that became more and more the point of reference for both action and thought, and in the effort to arrive at accuracy in this department, the astronomical exploration of the sky focussed attention further upon the regular, implacable movements of the heavenly bodies through space. Early in the sixteenth century a young Nuremberg mechanic, Peter Henlein, is supposed to have created "many-wheeled watches out of small bits of iron" and by the end of the century the small domestic clock had been introduced in England and Holland. As with the motor car and the airplane, the richer classes first took over the new mechanism and popularized it: partly because they alone could afford it, partly because the new bourgeoisie were the first to discover that, as Franklin later put it, "time is money." To become "as regular as clockwork" was the bourgeois ideal, and to own a watch was for long a definite symbol of success. The increasing tempo of civilization led to a demand for greater power: and in turn power quickened the tempo.

Now, the orderly punctual life that first took shape in the monasteries is not native to mankind, although by now Western peoples are so thoroughly regimented by the clock that it is "second nature" and they look upon its observance as a fact of nature. Many Eastern civilizations have flourished on a loose basis in time: the Hindus have in fact been so indifferent to time that they lack even an authentic chronology of the years. Only yesterday, in the midst of the industrializations of Soviet Russia, did a society come into existence to further the carrying of watches there and to propagandize the benefits of punctuality. The popularization of time-keeping, which followed the production of the cheap standardized watch, first in Geneva, then in America around the middle of the last century, was essential to a well-articulated system of transportation and production.

To keep time was once a peculiar attribute of music: it gave industrial value to the workshop song or the tattoo or the chantey of the sailors tugging at a rope. But the effect of the mechanical clock is more pervasive and strict: it presides over the day from the hour of rising to the hour of rest. When one thinks of the day as an abstract span of time, one does not go to bed with the chickens on a winter's night: one invents wicks, chimneys, lamps, gaslights, electric lamps, so as to use all the hours belonging to the day. When one thinks of time, not as a sequence of experiences, but as a collection of hours, minutes, and seconds, the habits of adding time and saving time come into existence. Time took on the character of an enclosed space: it could be divided, it could be filled up, it could even be expanded by the invention of labor-saving instruments.

Abstract time became the new medium of existence. Organic functions themselves were regulated by it: one ate, not upon feeling hungry, but when prompted by the clock: one slept, not when one was tired, but when the clock sanctioned it. A generalized time-consciousness accompanied the wider use of clocks: dissociating time from organic sequences, it became easier for the men of the Renascence to indulge the fantasy of reviving the classic past or of reliving the splendors of antique Roman civilization: the cult of history, appearing first in daily ritual, finally abstracted itself as a special discipline. In the seventeenth century journalism and periodic literature made their appearance: even in dress, following the lead of Venice as fashion-center, people altered styles every year rather than every generation.

The gain in mechanical efficiency through co-ordination and through the closer articulation of the day's events cannot be overestimated: while this increase cannot be measured in mere horsepower, one has only to imagine its absence today to foresee the speedy disruption and eventual collapse of our entire society. The modern industrial regime could do without coal and iron and steam easier than it could do without the clock.

[1934]

The American Plan   JOHN DOS PASSOS

"The American Plan" is taken from *The Big Money* (1936), the third volume in Dos Passos' trilogy titled *U.S.A.* For biographical and other notes on Dos Passos, see p. 252 and p. 311.

Dos Passos here dramatizes the modern attitude toward time described by Mumford in the preceding selection, seeing it in terms epitomized by Frederick Winslow Taylor. The unconventionality of his biographical sketch can be made clear by contrasting it with those found in standard reference works. By his unusual procedures he manages to get at what Whitman called "the real me." It is at once ironic and appropriate that Taylor should have been fired by those who had found him so useful.

"... He was dead with his watch in his hand. ..."

Frederick Winslow Taylor (they called him Speedy Taylor in the shop) was born in Germantown, Pennsylvania, the year of Buchanan's election. His father was a lawyer, his mother came from a family of New Bedford whalers; she was a great reader of Emerson, belonged to the Unitarian Church and the Browning Society. She was a fervent abolitionist and believed in democratic manners; she was a housekeeper of the old school, kept everybody busy from dawn till dark. She laid down the rules of conduct:

selfrespect, selfreliance, selfcontrol

and a cold long head for figures.

But she wanted her children to appreciate the finer things, so she took them abroad for three years on the Continent, showed them cathedrals, grand opera, Roman pediments, the old masters under their brown varnish in their great frames of tarnished guilt.

Later Fred Taylor was impatient of these wasted years, stamped out of the room when people talked about the finer things; he was a testy young-ster, fond of practical jokes, and a great hand at rigging up contraptions and devices.

At Exeter he was head of his class and captain of the ball-team, the first man to pitch overhand. (When umpires complained that overhand pitching wasn't in the rules of the game, he answered that it got results.)

As a boy he had nightmares; going to bed was horrible for him; he thought they came from sleeping on his back. He made himself a leather harness with wooden pegs that stuck into his flesh when he turned over. When he was grown he slept in a chair or in bed in a sitting position propped up with pillows. All his life he suffered from sleeplessness.

He was a crackerjack tennisplayer. In 1881, with his friend Clark, he won the National Doubles Championship. (He used a spoonshaped racket of his own design.)

At school he broke down from overwork, his eyes went back on him. The doctor suggested manual labor. So instead of going to Harvard he went into the machineshop of a small pump-manufacturing concern, owned by a friend of the family's, to learn the trade of patternmaker and machinist. He learned to handle a lathe and to dress and cuss like a workingman.

Fred Taylor never smoked tobacco or drank liquor or used tea or coffee; he couldn't understand why his fellow-mechanics wanted to go on sprees and get drunk and raise cain Saturday nights. He lived at home; when he wasn't reading technical books he'd play parts in amateur theatricals or step up to the piano in the evening and sing a good tenor in *A Warrior Bold* or *A Spanish Cavalier*.

He served his first year's apprenticeship in the machineshop without pay; the next two years he made a dollar and a half a week, the last year two dollars.

Pennsylvania was getting rich off iron and coal. When he was twenty-two, Fred Taylor went to work at the Midvale Iron Works. At first he had to take a clerical job, but he hated that and went to work with a shovel. At last he got them to put him on a lathe. He was a good machinist, he worked ten hours a day and in the evenings followed an engineering course at Stevens. In six years he rose from machinist's helper to keeper of toolcribs to gangboss to foreman to mastermechanic in charge of repairs to chief drafts-man and director of research to chief engineer of the Midvale Plant.

The early years he was a machinist with the other machinists in the shop, cussed and joked and worked with the rest of them, soldiered on the job when they did. Mustn't give the boss more than his money's worth. But when he got to be foreman, he was on the management's side of the fence, *gathering in on the part of those on the management's side all the great mass of traditional knowledge which in the past has been in the heads of the workmen and in the physical skill and knack of the workman.* He couldn't stand to see an idle lathe or an idle man.

Production went to his head and thrilled his sleepless nerves like liquor or women on a Saturday night. He never loafed and he'd be damned if anybody else would. Production was an itch under his skin.

He lost his friends in the shop; they called him niggerdriver. He was a stockily built man with a temper and a short tongue.

I was a young man in years, but I give you my word I was a great deal older than I am now, what with the worry, meanness, and contemptibleness of the whole damn thing. It's a horrid life for any man to live, not being able to look any workman in the face without seeing hostility there, and a feeling that every man around you is your virtual enemy.

That was the beginning of the Taylor System of Scientific Management.

He was impatient of explanations, he didn't care whose hide he took off in enforcing the laws he believed inherent in the industrial process.

When starting an experiment in any field, question everything, question the very foundations upon which the art rests, question the simplest, the most selfevident, the most universally accepted facts; prove everything,

except the dominant Quaker Yankee (the New Bedford skippers were the greatest niggerdrivers on the whaling seas) rules of conduct. He boasted he'd never ask a workman to do anything he couldn't do.

He devised an improved steamhammer; he standardized tools and equipment, he filled the shop with college students with stopwatches and diagrams, tabulating, standardizing. *There's the right way of doing a thing and the wrong way of doing it; the right way means increased production, lower costs, higher wages, bigger profits:* the American plan.

He broke up the foreman's job into separate functions, speedbosses, gangbosses, timestudy men, order-of-work men.

The skilled mechanics were too stubborn for him; what he wanted was a plain handyman who'd do what he was told. If he was a firstclass man and did firstclass work, Taylor was willing to let him have firstclass pay; that's where he began to get into trouble with the owners.

At thirtyfour he married and left Midvale and took a flyer for the big money in connection with a pulpmill started in Maine by some admirals and political friends of Grover Cleveland's;

the panic of '93 made hash of that enterprise,

so Taylor invented for himself the job of Consulting Engineer in Management and began to build up a fortune by careful investments.

The first paper he read before the American Society of Mechanical Engineers was anything but a success; they said he was crazy. *I have found,* he wrote in 1909, *that any improvement is not only opposed but aggressively and bitterly opposed by the majority of men.*

He was called in by Bethlehem Steel. It was in Bethlehem he made his famous experiments with handling pigiron; he taught a Dutchman named Schmidt to handle fortyseven tons instead of twelve and a half tons of pigiron a day and got Schmidt to admit he was as good as ever at the end of the day.

He was a crank about shovels, every job had to have a shovel of the right weight and size for that job alone; every job had to have a man of the right weight and size for that job alone; but when he began to pay his men in proportion to the increased efficiency of their work,

the owners, who were a lot of greedy smalleyed Dutchmen, began to raise Hail Columbia; when Schwab bought Bethlehem Steel in 1901

Fred Taylor

inventor of efficiency

who had doubled the production of the stampingmill by speeding up the main lines of shafting from ninetysix to twohundred and twentyfive revolutions a minute

was unceremoniously fired.

After that Fred Taylor always said he couldn't afford to work for money.

He took to playing golf (using golfclubs of his own design), doping out methods for transplanting huge boxtrees into the garden of his home.

At Boxly in Germantown he kept open house for engineers, factorymanagers, industrialists;

he wrote papers,

lectured in colleges,

appeared before a congressional committee,

everywhere preached the virtues of scientific management and the Barth slide rule, the cutting-down of waste and idleness, the substitution for skilled mechanics of the plain handyman (like Schmidt the pigiron handler) who'd move as he was told

and work by the piece:

production;

more steel rails more bicycles more spools of thread more armorplate for battleships more bedpans more barbedwire more needles more lightningrods more ballbearings more dollarbills;

(the old Quaker families of Germantown were growing rich, the Pennsylvania millionaires were breeding billionaires out of iron and coal)

production would make every firstclass American rich who was willing to work at piecework and not drink or raise cain or think or stand mooning at his lathe.

Thrifty Schmidt the pigiron handler can invest his money and get to be an owner like Schwab and the rest of the greedy smalleyed Dutchmen and cultivate a taste for Bach and have hundredyearold boxtrees in his garden at Bethlehem or Germantown or Chestnut Hill,

and lay down the rules of conduct;

the American plan
But Fred Taylor never saw the working of the American plan;
in 1915 he went to the hospital in Philadelphia suffering from a breakdown.
Pneumonia developed; the nightnurse heard him winding his watch;
on the morning of his fiftyninth birthday, when the nurse went into his
room to look at him at fourthirty,
he was dead with his watch in his hand.

[1936]

A Lone Striker   ROBERT FROST

For a biographical note on Robert Frost, see p. 203.
    Frost here describes "a lone striker" — a man not antagonistic to the
machine but who nevertheless keeps his own time. Contrasts which form
an integral part of this serio-comic poem include God and man, the human
and the mechanical, nature and the factory, thought and action, the individual and the mass. In sixty lines Frost succeeds in capturing much
that is both typical and untypical of modern industrial life.

"*. . . He knew a path that wanted walking. . . .*"

The swinging mill bell changed its rate
To tolling like the count of fate,
And though at that the tardy ran,
One failed to make the closing gate.
There was a law of God or man   5
That on the one who came too late,
The gate for half an hour be locked,
His time be lost, his pittance docked.
He stood rebuked and unemployed.
The straining mill began to shake.   10
The mill, though many, many eyed,
Had eyes inscrutably opaque;
So that he couldn't look inside
To see if some forlorn machine
Was standing idle for his sake.   15
(He couldn't hope its heart would break.)

And yet he thought he saw the scene:

The air was full of dust and wool.
A thousand yarns were under pull,
But pull so slow, with such a twist,   20
All day from spool to lesser spool,
It seldom overtaxed their strength;
They safely grew in slender length.
And if one broke by any chance,
The spinner saw it at a glance.   25
The spinner still was there to spin.
That's where the human still came in.
Her deft hand showed with finger rings
Among the harp-like spread of strings.
She caught the pieces end to end   30
And, with a touch that never missed,
Not so much tied as made them blend.
Man's ingenuity was good.
He saw it plainly where he stood,
Yet found it easy to resist.   35

He knew another place, a wood,
And in it, tall as trees, were cliffs;
And if he stood on one of these,
'Twould be among the tops of trees,
Their upper branches round him wreathing,   40
Their breathing mingled with his breathing.
If — if he stood! Enough of ifs!
He knew a path that wanted walking;
He knew a spring that wanted drinking;
A thought that wanted further thinking;   45
A love that wanted re-renewing.
Nor was this just a way of talking
To save him the expense of doing.
With him it boded action, deed.

The factory was very fine;   50
He wished it all the modern speed.
Yet, after all, 'twas not divine,
That is to say, 'twas not a church.
He never would assume that he'd
Be any institution's need.   55
But he said then and still would say
If there should ever come a day
When industry seemed like to die
Because he left it in a lurch,
Or even merely seemed to pine   60
For want of his approval, why
Come get him — they knew where to search.

                                                        [1936]

The Unknown Citizen   W. H. AUDEN

W. H. Auden (1907–   ) was born in England and educated at Christ's
Church College, Oxford. After a short period of teaching he devoted
himself to poetry and political activity, serving in 1937, for example, as
an ambulance driver for the Loyalists in Spain. In 1939 he came to live
in the United States and is now an American citizen.

    Auden's portrait of the assembly-line man, filing cabinet digit, is not
necessarily a satiric thrust at American society; its target is rather society
as it has appeared everywhere under machine demands. The "unknown
citizen" he describes could, in principal respects, be a Russian, a German,
or an Englishman. That Auden probably thought of him as an American,
however, is suggested by a statement he made shortly after coming to live
in this country: "The attractiveness of America to the writer is its open-
ness and lack of tradition. . . . You are forced to live here as everyone
else will be forced to live. There is no past, no tradition. No roots — that
is, in the European sense. . . ."

"*. . . Was he free? Was he happy? The question is absurd. . . .*"

[To JS/07/M/378 This Marble Monument Is Erected by the State]

He was found by the Bureau of Statistics to be
One against whom there was no official complaint,
And all the reports on his conduct agree
That, in the modern sense of an old-fashioned word, he was a saint,
For in everything he did he served the Greater Community.   5
Except for the War till the day he retired
He worked in a factory and never got fired,
But satisfied his employers, Fudge Motors Inc.
Yet he wasn't a scab or odd in his views,
For his Union reports that he paid his dues,   10
(Our report on his Union shows it was sound)
And our Social Psychology workers found
That he was popular with his mates and liked a drink.
The Press are convinced that he bought a paper every day
And that his reactions to advertisements were normal in every way.   15
Policies taken out in his name prove that he was fully insured,
And his Health-card shows he was once in hospital but left it cured.
Both Producers Research and High-Grade Living declare
He was fully sensible to the advantages of the Installment Plan
And had everything necessary to the Modern Man,   20
A phonograph, a radio, a car and a frigidaire.
Our researchers into Public Opinion are content

That he held the proper opinions for the time of year;
When there was peace, he was for peace; when there was war, he went.
He was married and added five children to the population,   25
Which our Eugenist says was the right number for a parent of his
    generation,
And our teachers report that he never interfered with their education.
Was he free? Was he happy? The question is absurd:
Had anything been wrong, we should certainly have heard.

[1940]

The Bird and the Machine   LOREN C. EISELEY

Loren C. Eiseley (1907–   ) was born in Lincoln, Nebraska, and educated at the universities of Nebraska and Pennsylvania, receiving his
Ph.D. from the latter institution in 1937. As a young scientist he was a
member of several paleontological expeditions investigating areas in the
Southwest (1931–33) and northern Colorado (1935), expeditions to
which he refers in the following essay. He has been head of the Depart-
men of Anthropology and is now Provost at the University of Pennsylvania.

"The Bird and the Machine" expresses Eiseley's faith in life as opposed to faith in machines. Writing more as a poet than as a scientist,
he deals with this faith in terms of personal experience and metaphor
rather than textbook exposition and argument. The wandering organization in much of the essay is appropriate to a writer with Eiseley's "fine
indeterminate sense of wonder."

". . . It's life I believe in, not machines. . . ."

I suppose their bones have years ago been lost among the stones and winds
of those high glacial pastures. I suppose their feathers blew eventually into
the piles of tumbleweed beneath the straggling cattle fences and rotted there in
the mountain snows, along with dead steers and all the other things that drift
to an end in the corners of the wire. I do not quite know why I should be
thinking of birds over the *New York Times* at breakfast, nor particularly of
the birds of my youth half a continent away. It is a funny thing what the
brain will do with memories and how it will treasure them and finally bring
them into odd juxtapositions with other things, as though it wanted to make
a design, or get some meaning out of them, whether you want it or not, or
even see it.

It used to seem marvelous to me, but I read now that there are machines that can do these things in a small way, machines that can crawl about like animals, and that it may not be long now until they do more things — maybe even make themselves — I saw that piece in the *Times* just now — and then they will, maybe — well, who knows — but you read about it more and more with no one making any protest, and already they can add better than we and reach up and hear things through the dark and finger the guns over the night sky.

This is the new world that I read about at breakfast. This is the world that confronts me in my biological books and journals, until there are times when I sit quietly in my chair and try to hear the little purr of the cogs in my head and the tubes flaring and dying as the messages go through them and the circuits snap shut or open. This is the great age, make no mistake about it; the robot has been born somewhat appropriately along with the atom bomb, and the brain they say now is just another type of more complicated feedback system. The engineers have its basic principles worked out; it's mechanical, you know; nothing to get superstitious about; and man can always improve on nature once he gets the idea. Well, he's got it all right and that's why, I guess, that I sit here in my chair, with the article crunched in my hand, remembering those two birds and that blue mountain sunlight. There is another magazine title on my desk that reads, "Machines Are Getting Smarter Every Day." I don't deny it, but I'll stick with the birds. It's life I believe in, not machines.

Maybe you don't believe there is any difference. A skeleton is all joints and pulleys, I'll admit. And when man was in his simpler stages of machine building in the eighteenth century, he quickly saw the resemblances. "What," wrote Hobbes, "is the heart but a spring, and the nerves but so many strings, and the joints but so many wheels, giving motion to the whole body?" Tinkering about in their shops it was inevitable in the end that men would see the world as a huge machine "subdivided into an infinite number of lesser machines."

The idea took on with a vengeance. Little automatons toured the country — dolls controlled by clockwork. Clocks described as little worlds were taken on tours by their designers. They were made up of moving figures, shifting scenes, and other remarkable devices. The life of the cell was unknown. Man, whether he was conceived as possessing a soul or not, moved and jerked about like these tiny puppets. A human being thought of himself in terms of his own tools and implements. He had been fashioned like the puppets he produced and was only a more clever model made by a greater designer.

Then in the nineteenth century, the cell was discovered, and the single machine in its turn was found to be the product of millions of infinitesimal machines — the cells. Now, finally, the cell itself dissolves away into an abstract chemical machine — and that into some intangible, inexpressible flow of energy. The secret seems to lurk all about, the wheels get smaller and smaller, and they turn more rapidly, but when you try to seize it the life is gone — and so, it is popular to say, the life was never there in the first place. The wheels and the cogs are the secret and we can make them better in time — machines that will run faster and more accurately than real mice to cheese.

I have no doubt it can be done, though a mouse harvesting seeds on an autumn thistle is to me a fine sight and more complicated, I think, in his multiform activity, than a machine "mouse" running a maze. Also, I like to think of the possible shape of the future brooding in mice, just as it brooded once in a rather ordinary mousy insectivore who became a man. It leaves a nice fine indeterminate sense of wonder that even an electronic brain hasn't got, because you know perfectly well that if the electronic brain changes it will be because of something man has done to it. But what man will do to himself he doesn't really know. A certain scale of time and a ghostly intangible thing called change are ticking in him. Powers and potentialities like the oak in the seed, or a red and awful ruin. Either way, it's impressive; and the mouse has it, too — or those birds, I'll never forget those birds, though I learned the lesson of time first of all. I was young then and left alone in a great desert — part of an expedition that had scattered its men over several hundred miles in order to carry on research more effectively. I learned there that time is a series of planes existing superficially in the same universe. The tempo is a human illusion, a subjective clock ticking in our own kind of protoplasm.

A CANYON BETWEEN WORLDS

As the long months passed, I began to live on the slower planes and to observe more readily what passed for life there. I sauntered, I passed more and more slowly up and down the canyons in the dry baking heat of midsummer. I slumbered for long hours in the shade of huge brown boulders that had gathered in tilted companies out on the flats. I had forgotten the world of men and the world had forgotten me. Now and then I found a skull in the canyons and these justified my remaining there. I took a serene cold interest in these discoveries. I had come, like many a naturalist before me, to view life with a wary and subdued attention. I had grown to take pleasure in the divested bone.

I sat once on a high ridge that fell away before me into a waste of sand dunes. I sat through hours of a long afternoon. Finally glancing by my boot an indistinct configuration caught my eye. It was a coiled rattlesnake, a big one. How long he had sat with me I do not know. I had not frightened him. We were both locked in the sleep-walking tempo of the earlier world, baking in the same high air and sunshine. Perhaps he had been there when I came. He slept on as I left, his coils, so ill discerned by me, dissolving once more among the stones and gravel from which I had barely made him out.

Another time, I got on a higher ridge, among some tough little wind-warped pines half covered over with sand in a basin-like depression that caught everything carried by the air up to those heights. There were a few thin bones of birds, some cracked shells of indeterminable age, and the knotty fingers of pine roots bulged out of shape from their long and agonizing grasp upon the crevices of the rock. I lay under the pines in the sparse shade and went to sleep once more.

It grew cold finally, for autumn was in the air by then, and the few things that lived thereabouts were sinking down into an even chillier scale of time. In the moments between sleeping and waking I saw the roots about

me and slowly, slowly, a foot in what seemed many centuries, I moved my
sleep-stiffened hands over the scaling bark and lifted my numbed face after
the vanishing sun. I was a great awkward thing of knots and aching limbs,
trapped up there in some long patient endurance that involved the necessity
of putting living fingers into rock and by slow, aching expansion bursting
those rocks asunder. I suppose, so thin and slow was the time of my pulse
by then, that I might have stayed on to drift still deeper into the lower
cadences of the frost, or the crystalline life that glisters pebbles or shines in
a snow flake, or dreams in the meteoric iron between the worlds.

It was a dim descent but time was present in it. Somewhere far down
in that scale the notion struck me that one might come the other way. Not
many months thereafter, I joined some colleagues heading higher into a remote
windy tableland where huge bones were reputed to protrude like boulders
from the turf. I had drowsed with reptiles and moved with the century-long
pulse of trees; now, lethargically, I was climbing back up some invisible
ladder of quickening hours. There had been talk of birds in connection
with my duties. Birds are intense, fast-living creatures — reptiles — I suppose
one might say — that have escaped out of the heavy sleep of time, transformed
fairy creatures dancing over sunlit meadows. It is a youthful fancy, no doubt,
but because of something that happened up there among the escarpments of
that range, it remains with me a life-long impression. I can never bear to see
a bird imprisoned.

We came into that valley through the trailing mists of a spring night. It
was a place that looked as though it might never have known the foot of
man, but our scouts had been ahead of us and we knew all about the abandoned cabin of stone that lay far up on one hillside. It had been built in the
land rush of the last century and then lost to the cattlemen again as the
marginal soils failed to take to the plow.

There were spots like this all over that country. Lost graves marked by
unlettered stones and old corroding rim-fire cartridge cases lying where somebody had made a stand among the boulders that rimmed the valley. They
are all that remain of the range wars; the men are under the stones now. I
could see our cavalcade winding in and out through the mist below us:
torches, and lights reflected on collecting tins, and the far-off bumping of a
loose dinosaur thigh bone in the bottom of a trailer. I stood on a rock a
moment looking down and thinking what it cost in money and equipment
to capture the past.

We had, in addition, instructions to lay hands on the present. The word
had come through to get them alive, birds, reptiles, anything. A zoo somewhere abroad needed restocking. It was one of those reciprocal matters in
which science involves itself. Maybe our museum needed a stray ostrich egg
and this was the payoff. Anyhow, my job was to help capture some birds
and that was why I was there before the trucks.

The cabin had not been occupied for years. We intended to clean it out
and live in it, but there were holes in the roof and the birds had come in and
were roosting in the rafters. You could depend on it in a place like this
where everything blew away and even a bird needed some place out of the
weather and away from coyotes. A cabin going back to nature in a wild

place draws them till they come in, listening at the eves, I imagine, pecking softly among the shingles till they find a hole and then suddenly the place is theirs and man is forgotten.

Sometimes of late years I find myself thinking the most beautiful sight in the world might be the birds taking over New York after the last man has run away to the hills. I will never live to see it, of course, but I know just how it will sound because I've lived up high and I know the sort of watch birds keep on us. I've listened to sparrows tapping tentatively on the tin of the air conditioners when they thought no one was listening, and I know how other birds test the vibrations that come up to them through the television aerials.

"Is he gone?" they ask, and the vibrations come up from below, "not yet, not yet."

Well, to come back, I got the door open softly and I had the spotlight all ready to turn on and blind whatever birds were there so they couldn't see to get out through the roof. I had a short piece of ladder to put against the far wall where there was a shelf on which I expected to make the biggest haul. I had all the information I needed just like any skilled assassin. I pushed the door open with the hinges only squeaking a little after the oil was put on them. A bird or so stirred — I could hear them — but nothing flew and there was a faint starshine through the holes in the roof.

I padded across the floor, got the ladder up, and the light ready, and slithered up the ladder till my head and arms were over the shelf. Everything was dark as pitch except for the starlight at a little place back of the shelf near the eaves. With the light to blind them, they'd never make it. I had them. I reached my arm carefully over in order to be ready to seize whatever was there and I put the flash on the edge of the shelf where it would stand by itself when I turned it on. That way I'd be able to use both hands.

Everything worked perfectly except for one detail — I didn't know what kind of birds were there. I never thought about it at all and it wouldn't have mattered if I had. My orders were to get something interesting. I snapped on the flash and sure enough there was a great beating and feathers flying, but instead of my having them, they, or rather he, had me. He had my hand, that is, and for a small hawk not much bigger than my fist he was doing all right. I heard him give one short metallic cry when the light went on and my hand descended on the bird beside him; after that he was busy with his claws and his beak was sunk in my thumb. In the struggle I knocked the lamp over on the shelf and his mate got her sight back and whisked neatly through the hole in the roof, and off among the stars outside. It all happened in fifteen seconds and you might think I would have fallen down the ladder, but no, I had a professional assassin's reputation to keep up and the bird, of course, made the mistake of thinking the hand was the enemy and not the eyes behind it. He chewed my thumb up pretty effectively and lacerated my hand with his claws, but in the end I got him, having two hands to work with.

He was a sparrow hawk and a fine young male in the prime of life. I was sorry not to catch the pair of them, but as I dripped blood and folded his wings carefully, holding him by the back so he couldn't strike again, I had to admit the two of them might have been a little more than I could have handled under the circumstances. The little fellow had saved his mate by diverting me, and that was that. He was born to it, and made no outcry now, resting in my hand hopelessly, but peering toward me in the shadows behind the lamp with a fierce, almost indifferent glance. He neither gave nor expected mercy and something out of the high air passed from him to me, stirring a faint embarrassment.

I quit looking into that eye and managed to get my huge carcass with its fist full of prey back down the ladder. I put the bird in a box too small to allow him to injure himself by struggle and walked out to welcome the arriving trucks. It had been a long day and camp still to make in the darkness. In the morning that bird would be just another episode. He would go back with the bones in the truck to a small cage in a city where he would spend the rest of his life. And a good thing, too. I sucked my aching thumb and spat out some blood. An assassin has to get used to these things. I had a professional reputation to keep up.

THE CRY OF THE HAWK

In the morning with the change that comes on suddenly in that high country, the mist that had hovered below us in the valley was gone. The sky was a deep blue and one could see for miles over the high outcroppings of stone. I was up early and brought the box to which the little hawk was imprisoned out onto the grass where I was building a cage. A wind as cool as a mountain spring ran over the grass and stirred my hair. It was a fine day to be alive. I looked up and all around and at the hole in the cabin roof out of which the other little hawk had fled. There was no sign of her anywhere that I could see.

"Probably in the next county by now," I thought cynically, but before beginning work I decided I'd have a look at my last night's capture.

Secretively, I looked again all around the camp and up and down and opened the box. I got him right out in my hand with his wings folded properly and I was careful not to startle him. He lay limp in my grasp and I could feel his heart pound under the feathers but he only looked beyond me and up.

I saw him look that last look away beyond me into a sky so full of light that I could not follow his gaze. The little breeze blew over me again, and nearby a mountain aspen shook all its tiny leaves. I suppose I must have had an idea about then of what I was going to do, but I never let it come up into consciousness. I just reached over and laid the hawk on the grass.

He lay there a long minute without hope, unmoving, his eyes still fixed on that blue vault above him. It must have been that he already was so far away in heart that he never felt the release from my hand. He never even stood. He just lay with his breast against the grass and my eye upon him.

In the next second after that long minute he was gone. Like a flicker of light, he had vanished with my eyes full on him, but without actually seeing even a premonitory wing beat. He was gone straight into that towering emptiness of light and crystal that my eyes could scarcely bear to penetrate. For another long moment there was silence, I could not see him. The light was too intense. Then from far up somewhere a cry came ringing down.

I was young then and had seen little of the world, but when I heard that cry my heart turned over. It was not the cry of the hawk I had captured; for, by shifting my position against the sun, I was now seeing further up. Straight out of the sun's eye, where she must have been soaring restlessly above us for untold hours, hurtled his mate. And from far up, ringing from peak to peak of the summits over us, came a cry of such unutterable and ecstatic joy that it sounds down across the years and tingles among the cups on my quiet breakfast table.

I saw them both now. He was rising fast to meet her. They met in a great soaring gyre — that turned to a whirling circle and a dance of wings. Once more, just once, their two voices, joined in a harsh wild medley of question and response, struck and echoed against the pinnacles of the valley. Then they were gone forever somewhere into those upper regions beyond the eyes of man.

I am older now, and sleep less, and have seen most of what there is to see and am not very impressed any more, I suppose, by anything. "What Next in the Attributes of Machines?" my morning headline runs. "It Might be the Power to Reproduce Themselves."

I lay the paper down and across my mind a phrase floats insinuatingly: "It does not seem that there is anything in the construction, constituents, or behavior of the human being which it is essentially impossible for science to duplicate and synthesize. On the other hand . . ."

All over the city the cogs in the hard, bright mechanism have begun to turn. Figures move through computers, names are spelled out, a thoughtful machine selects the fingerprints of a wanted criminal from an array of thousands. In the laboratory an electronic mouse runs swiftly through a maze toward the cheese it can neither taste nor enjoy. On the second run it does better than a living mouse.

"On the other hand . . ." Ah, my mind takes up, on the other hand the machine does not bleed, ache, hang for hours in the empty sky in a torment of hope to learn the fate of another machine, nor does it cry out with joy nor dance in the air with the fierce passion of a bird. Far off, over a distance greater than space, that remote cry from the heart of heaven makes a faint buzzing among my breakfast dishes and passes on and away.

[1955]

AUTHOR INDEX

Author Index